SAGA

of the

ITALIAN

PENINSULA

People and Places

SAGA

of the

ITALIAN

PENINSULA

People and Places

Monica Nahm

Pentland Press, Inc.
England • USA • Scotland

All photographs, unless otherwise noted, appear courtesy of the author.

The photograph on page 4 appears courtesy of Norman F. Carver, Jr. from <u>Italian Hilltowns</u>.

The photograph on page 172 appears courtesy of George T. Beech.

The photograph on page 206 appears courtesy of Charlotte A. Masiello-Riome.

The photograph on page 249 appears courtesy of Elizabeth Omar.

The photograph on page 323 is taken from Caroline Murat by Joan Baer, William Collins & Co., Ltd., London. Acknowledgment is given to Prince Louis Murat and Ets. J. E. Bulloz.

All maps were designed by Woodstock Design and Illustration in Kalamazoo, Michigan.

PUBLISHED BY PENTLAND PRESS, INC.
5122 Bur Oak Circle, Raleigh, North Carolina 27612
United States of America
919-782-0281

ISBN 1-57197-171-8
Library of Congress Catalog Card Number 99-070435

Printed in the United States of America

Dedicated to the memory of my husband, Andrew C. Nahm

CONTENTS

Part Two: The Medieval World

FOREWORD

Beyond all debate, Italy is the greatest peninsula on earth—huge in size, profound in its impact on the past and present. In attaching it to Europe while extending it into the very center of the Mediterranean, Geography alone decreed that it would become the capital of the ancient world and transmitter of its culture, the crossroads of Medieval life, the cradle of the Renaissance, and a cockpit of competing national and international interests in the centuries since.

But hardly ever do we find a book that tells Italy's *entire* story, which is usually fragmented into the Etruscan era, Magna Graecia, Republican and Imperial Rome, Italy of the Middle Ages, Renaissance Italy, and the like. The whole extraordinary panorama seems lost in a segmented focus on its parts. Or where a whole extraordinary panorama seems lost in a segmented focus on its parts. Or where a whole history of Italy *is* attempted by multiple authors, specialists in its different eras offer differing approaches and styles in their contributions, resulting in a disjointed anthology.

In these pages, however, there is remarkable continuity from one pen. Monica Nahm offers a truly comprehensive view of Italy in all her seasons of life, a peninsula pulsating with unique personalities, places, and events extending from its distant past to its final unification in the modern world.

A cavalcade of colorful characters animate this book (as they did Italy itself): the famous and the infamous, geniuses and scoundrels, lovers and victims, the exploiters and the oppressed—all saints and sinners from any land or era, to be sure, but somehow augmented to sublime or grotesque proportions in the case of Italy. Commanders, consuls, senators, slaves, emperors and empresses, popes and antipopes, kings and queens, lords and their ladies, patrons, poets, musicians, and dictators all jostle for position in these pages, and it is a tribute to the author that their distinctive roles never become confused.

Cleverly, Monica Nahm uses these very personalities as guides for her journey into the past, each of the major players reporting on how he or she shaped the course of events at a particular time in the annals of Italy. The result is history with a human face that cannot but delight the general reader even as it intrigues the serious scholar.

With a theme of these epic proportions, *of course* this book had to be a long one. Such a length could have caused disaster in the hands of a lesser historian, for whom the adage "Big Book, big trouble!" was coined. In happy contrast, Monica Nahm is not only an excellent scholar but a *superb* writer who proved more than equal to the very ambitious task she had set for herself. Her prose is lively, engaging, interest-sustaining, and, above all, graceful. Again and again, the reader will be delighted with the *bons mots,* sparkling phrases, scintillating insights, and ingenious twists that illuminate these pages.

Saga of the Italian Peninsula reflects not only the love the author has for Italy but also her expertise. To sustain interest and make the material user-friendly, she uses a fictional or anecdotal style, but takes no license whatever with historical fact. This book is the fruit of years of research on the part of a gifted teacher and interpreter of Italian, who also lived in Italy for some years. She took the photographs of the monuments, the sculpture, and other works of art that enliven the chapters, all of which complement the maps and genealogies that serve the reader very well indeed.

This book should appeal to a wide range of readers: from history buffs and students of all ages to travelers for business or pleasure, and, above all, to the millions who claim Italian heritage and are anxious to learn more about the land of their ancestors. These pages will delight and inform the reader while unveiling a glorious past as prologue to the vistas of the present.

Paul L. Maier

The Russel H. Seibert
Professor of Ancient History
Western Michigan University

I wish to acknowledge with thanks the help of the following faculty of Western Michigan University: Dr. Paul L. Maier for critical reading of the first drafts of the manuscript and his encouragement, Dr. George T. Beech and Dr. Edward T. Callan for reading portions of the manuscript and providing valuable comment. My special thanks to Ami Proni for technical and editorial assistance in preparing the final draft. I also wish to acknowledge the contributions of many writers and historians, too many to enumerate, whose scholarly research has provided secondary sources and insights into the various periods covered.

Monica Nahm
August 1999

PART ONE

Pre-History and Roman Times

CHAPTER ONE

Early Times

The Italy of Myths

The astronauts of today can look down on the Mediterranean, which in ancient times was the uncharted seas sailed by the Greek Argonauts. Beyond these unexplored shores were mysteries that gave birth to some of the marvelously rich Greek myths. Trailblazers of their day, those heroes sailed in ships and braved the vagaries of the vast expanses of the seas, landing on distant shores far from their homeland and returning with fantastic accounts of their adventures. The watery and then unknown world of the Mediterranean, later to become Mare Nostrum to the Romans, was the outer space of prehistory.

Set in the blue sea, the Italian peninsula—and perhaps even more so the island of Sicily—would later represent coveted jewels to the more advanced cultures that flourished on the coasts of North Africa to the south and Greece and Asia Minor to the east. These people would spill out across the sea to places where the earth had much to offer and the native inhabitants were primitive by comparison and vulnerable to attack. First came the Greeks, establishing significant colonies and leaving behind the undeniable mark of their culture. The Carthaginians, just a leap from their own promontory that is now Tunisia, set their sights on the shores of Sicily and later constituted a major threat to Roman expansion.

For the Greeks in particular, the Italian shores must have held a great fascination in early times for these areas were regarded as "the outer limits of the earth." The Mediterranean was conceived of as a sea fringed by lands guarded by not always hospitable occupants. Indeed, many scenes of Greek mythology are set in these areas. This was the world imagined by Homer in the ninth century B.C. and told in the adventures of Ulysses of *The Odyssey*. There were the temptations of the sirens, and somewhere near what is now Naples was the entrance to the underworld. The cyclops lived on the site of Etna, forge of the god of fire, Hephaestus. These legends would be taken up again in the first century B.C. by the Roman poet Virgil in the *Aeneid*. The god of fire would be known as Vulcan, and his name lives on in our word *volcano*.

Forbidding mythology notwithstanding, the Greeks were exploring and colonizing these parts, bringing their own civilization and language to this new world, confronting unknown interiors and what were perceived as inhospitable natives, much the same as later European adventurers and colonists would do when they reached the shores of the Americas.

Early Inhabitants

As early as the eighth century B.C. the Greeks had established a number of colonies in southern Italy and Sicily. These were city-states fashioned after those in Greece, and the whole collection of dispersed settlements were known as Magna Graecia.

The Greek colonists were not, of course, the first to arrive on the peninsula or in Sicily, which was already a meeting place of races. They certainly encountered people more real than the sirens and cyclops of legend. However, the Greeks remained coastal dwellers, leaving the heart of the peninsula to the various tribes, each with its own language and customs.

Believed to be among some of the first to arrive were two groups from the north. The Ligurians came into the northwest coastal region and also occupied what is now southern France and the Iberian peninsula. These people had fair hair and blue eyes. The other group, consisting of several tribes collectively referred to as the Italics, settled in the central regions of Umbria and Latium and it was from these people that the Latins were to evolve and eventually gain preponderance.

The Italic group is classified by languages as Indo-European. Among these tribes were the Sicani, occupying the center of Sicily; the Itali, in what is now Calabria to the south and from which tribe came the name *Italy;* the Umbrians, who occupied the east-central region that still bears their name; the Veneti, after whom Venice is named, and many others whose names today are less well known, including the Picentes, the Samnites, the Campanians, and the Sabines. Something of the past history of the latter tribe is recorded in a beautiful statue, which may be seen in the Piazza della Signoria in Florence, depicting the rape of the Sabine women by the Romans. Further south was another important tribe called the Oscans whose language, though extinct, still survives as graffiti dating from A.D. 79 and found on the walls of houses excavated in Pompeii. Finally, to become the most significant of the Italic groups were the Latins, occupying an area around Rome and wedged between the Greek settlements to the south and the Etruscans to the north. The peninsula and Sicily together must have been a virtual tower of Babel in about the fourth century B.C. if, as is estimated by certain scholars, some forty different languages were spoken there. To understand how so many tribes, some of which were obviously quite small in terms of numbers, could have occupied the area in question one need only become acquainted with the physical terrain that is Italy's backbone.

Away from the major cities and coastal regions—in the Po valley, which stretches across the northern part of the peninsula—Italy occupies much rugged terrain. Craggy outcrops are frequent sites of villages or small communities. Dwellings seem to be scrunched together and often appear to barely get a foothold, hanging onto the rocks and balanced at the edge of precipices. From north to south, the hill towns are characteristic of Italy's interior landscape. Even today, there are people living in the more isolated areas whose world begins and ends within a radius of a few kilometers. It is believed that many of these sites were inhabited as far back as the second millennium B.C. It is easy to understand how diversity within the interior could have developed or been maintained by groups arriving from the outside through new waves of migrations. The hill towns present a face that often seems anything but hospitable, but at nightfall or in time of danger everyone returned to these safe havens, their natural fortresses.

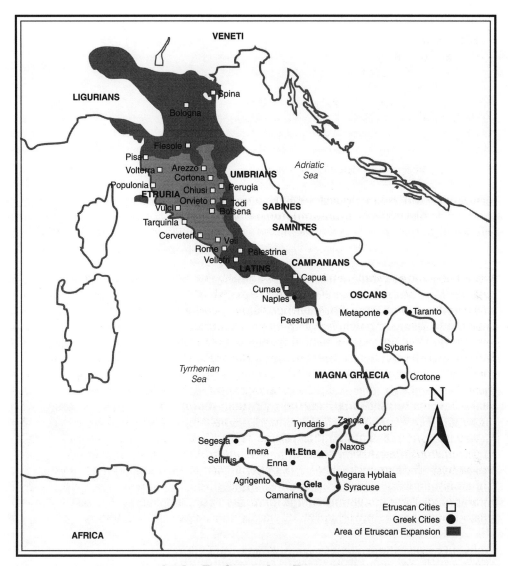

Italy Before the Romans

The Etruscans

By far the most important early inhabitants of the Italian peninsula were the Etruscans. They were not a tribe, but an organized and distinct civilization that occupied a large area between Rome and Florence and points as far south as Cumae, just north of Naples, and north to Piacenza. Their dominion was not limited to the coastal regions, like the Greeks, but stretched back into the rugged interior. In spite of the significance of these people in terms both of their numbers and advanced civilization, where they came from and what happened to them remains a mystery. They disappeared, along with their language.

The dominion of the Etruscans extended into the rugged interior where villages
cling to the craggy outcrops of Italy's backbone.

In any event, by the seventh and sixth centuries B.C. the Etruscans controlled a vast area known as Etruria, comprising some twelve city-states, including the present-day sites of Perugia, Tarquinia, Cerveteri, Volterra, Siena, and Rome itself. Speaking a language not thought to be Indo-European, their origin is the more perplexing; they were quite distinct from, and much more advanced than, the other tribes that occupied the peninsula. For this reason, some scholars believe that they were not native to the land, but came from Asia Minor, bringing with them their unique civilization.

Different and distinct from their Greek neighbors to the south as well, the Etruscans nevertheless exhibited some Greek influence in art and sculpture, and they used a Greek alphabet to write their language (which has not been fully deciphered even today). A major event occurred as late as 1964 with the discovery of three golden tablets found at the Italian port of Cerveteri. Two were inscribed in Etruscan and the other in Phoenician, the language of Carthage, an ally and trading partner. Through these tablets scholars have been able to decipher several Etruscan words.

Before the Romans (who no doubt learned many of their skills from them) the Etruscans were both engineers and architects, building roads and cities. Indeed, much of what is known of the Etruscans is gathered from the remains of buildings. Their towns were built on elevations with walls of huge stones and showed a great sense of planning. Nearby were their burial grounds, where many secrets of their civilization have been revealed to modern-day researchers. Fortunately, the Etruscans were excellent artisans and artists, and today we are able to appreciate some magnificent examples of paintings still in a remarkable state of preservation that have been found in tombs. These paintings portrayed for the dead the pleasures of life with scenes of banquets, music and dancing, hunting, and so on, and offer us a glimpse into what may have been their world. Both men and women adorned themselves with gold ornaments of extraordinary beauty and workmanship. They worked with iron, silver, and copper, and also excelled in producing black earthenware with figures in relief.

Just to the east of what is now Cerveteri stood the ancient Etruscan maritime center of Caere, believed to have been founded in the eighth century B.C. On this site was the necropolis, the most interesting vestige of the vanished city. Caere was undoubtedly a center of refined culture, albeit with a strange mixture of savagery and refinement. In religion they shared the gods with the Greeks, but are believed to have practiced human sacrifice.

As archaeologists constantly go back down the long road of history, the earth grudgingly reveals its secrets, while scholars piece together the vast jigsaw puzzle of which we see only a tantalizing fraction here and there. The lack of written documents forces the historian to rely on interpreting what remnants can be found in stone and metal as well as the marvelous tombs to the dead, some 6,000 of which have come to light around Tarquinia alone.

By the fourth century B.C. Etruria began to decline rapidly and was eventually conquered by the rising power of Rome. The Etruscans and their culture vanished forever, not only from the peninsula but also from the world. Their like has not been found anywhere else, and their language for the most part still remains a closed book.

To follow the decline of the Etruscans and their eventual passage into oblivion one must go back and trace the incredible rise to power of the Romans whose beginnings were so intricately mingled with their neighbors. From its very position,

Rome seems to have emerged right from the belly of Etruria, which she eventually set out to destroy.

The Legend of the She-Wolf

With a large part of the peninsula occupied by the Etruscans, the southern coastal regions controlled by the Greek colonists, and the interior inhabited by some other major groups that would mean trouble for the Latin-speaking tribe occupying the hills above the Tiber River, the birth of a city was about to be recorded.

Rome, by virtue of its location wedged between two major civilizations, would be influenced by or benefit from both. From the Etruscans came the metallurgical and building skills that would give material structure to the empire, while artistic and religious influences would come from the Greeks. The language—a dialect of Latin— was unique to a relatively small group of people.

According to the well-known legend, the city was founded by twin brothers, Romulus and Remus, raised from infancy by a she-wolf. The legend tells that King Numitor, a descendant of Aeneas the Trojan, the offspring of a mortal woman and a Greek god, was deposed by his brother Amulius. Numitor's daughter, Rhea Silvia, was made a vestal virgin so that there would be no young contenders to power. Rhea subsequently gave birth to twin boys, claiming that their father was none other than the god Mars. The babes were to be cast into the river to perish and thereby end the threat to power, but the cruel order was not carried out. They were mercifully left in a cave close by, where they were suckled by a she-wolf. Later on, they were discovered by a herdsman and his wife who took them home and raised them as their own. The boys grew and became members of an adventurous band of youths. Later on they killed Amulius, reinstated their father, and founded the city of Rome. The date generally attributed to the historic event is 753 B.C. Each young man vied for power, and Romulus eventually slayed Remus, an act reminiscent of the biblical Cain and Abel story. After a long and prosperous rule during which Rome grew in power, Romulus disappeared in a storm. The circumstances of his birth and death form some striking parallels with the story of Moses.

The she-wolf and the twins have come to symbolize the foundation of Rome. The most significant monument to the city's birth legend is a magnificent bronze sculpture of a she-wolf, kept in the Palazzo dei Conservatori in Rome, dating from somewhere around 500 B.C. It is now generally accepted that this was the work of Etruscan craftsmen and depicted one of the wild animals then native to the hills in the region. It has since been established that the twin figures, which form part of the statue, were not added until the Renaissance, hundreds of years later.

The Tarquin Kings of Rome

While the Etruscans were busy expanding their sphere of influence and bringing within their orbit areas as far north as Piacenza in the Po valley and south to Pompeii and beyond, Rome was experiencing growing pains. In spite of Etruscan expansion, the Latin-speaking people in their midst retained their language and their cultural identity, although Rome's beginnings were inextricably linked with the Etruscans. These first difficult years are known as the Period of the Kings. Seven kings have actually been identified in the period following Romulus, although kingship was not

Though extinct in the Roman hills, wolves still abound in the city and outside in a variety of forms. This realistic and protective she-wolf appears on the base of an equestrian statue to King Carlo Alberto, seen in the public gardens across from the Quirinal Palace.

hereditary. There is also evidence that boundaries between one tribe or city-state and another were not clearly defined, or alliances were made with neighbors out of need for survival. Romulus supposedly shared his power with the king of the Sabines in some way. An Italic tribe that inhabited the mountainous region east of the Tiber, occupying hilltop villages and towns around Rieti, the Sabines had close relations with early Rome. Romulus's men raided Sabine territory and carried off their women, forcing them to become their wives. Out of this act has come the legendary story of the rape of the Sabine women, which for centuries has provided a subject for writers, artists, and sculptors. In fact, these unfortunate women and their Roman captors were immortalized in a beautiful marble statue in Florence's Piazza della Signoria, the work of Giovanni da Bologna, dating from 1583. Not surprisingly, the next king to be elected by the Romans, Numa Pompilius, was a Sabine.

Then came a warrior-king who bore the appropriate name of Tullus Hostilius. He destroyed the most ancient Latin city of Alba Longa on Lake Albano, thereby increasing the power of Rome. Expansion continued under the fourth king, Ancus Marcius, who established the colony of Ostia where the Tiber River flows into the Mediterranean Sea. Rome was no longer confined to the seven hills. The fifth king, Lucius Tarquinius Priscus, was different from his predecessors in bloodline. He had an Etruscan mother but his father was a Greek. This king was at odds with both the Sabines and the other Latin tribes. His successor, Servius Tullius, was a Roman whose accomplishments included the building of a wall around Rome and the organization of his subjects into classes according to wealth and their ability to provide weapons.

The seventh and last Tarquin king, Tarquinius Superbus, came from the house of the fifth king. To his credit are significant public works, including the main sewer which drained the Forum, Rome's marketplace that occupied the valley between the Capitoline and Palatine hills. Disliked and feared as a cruel tyrant, he was considered a "foreigner." For this reason, it was probably not difficult to gain support of the Romans to bring him down and rid themselves once and for all of Etruscan blood. A Roman called Brutus (meaning "the stupid") led the revolt; it is perhaps a strange coincidence that some 500 years later another Brutus would end the life of Julius Caesar whose power, like that of the Tarquin kings, had also become too great.

The year 509 B.C. was historic as it marked the beginning of the Roman Republic, a fledgling that was getting ready to leave its nest and set about the business of not just survival but the most incredible growth that the world had ever witnessed.

Something different and very important had occurred at this juncture and it was the concept of people power expressed in the phrase "Senatus Populusque Romanus" (Senate and Roman People). Some 2,500 years later, the initials SPQR are still stamped on public property in Rome. From these beginnings, magic, mystique, or military might would propel Rome on a course in history that could only be described as awesome and would be the foundation of many aspects of our own Western civilization as we know it today.

CHAPTER TWO

The Roman Republic's Rise in Power

The Young Republic and Her Heroes

The period of the kings had lasted for two and a half centuries, but the Roman Republic which came into being in the year 509 B.C., would flourish for five centuries. How it survived is amazing and how it became the power that it did is even more incredible.

The system of government was as yet untried and the creators of the Republic gave much thought to its composition. The government was to include all members of the society, though not with equal participation, and the power of individuals would be limited. A single ruler would no longer hold the highest office—there would be two. In the beginning they were called *praetors,* meaning "to show the way," but because they had to consult each other and reach agreement before taking action they were later called *consuls.* These consuls, who were elected for a term of office limited to one year, were also military chiefs in charge of the army, which meant that they were soldiers and generals.

The first two consuls were the now-celebrated Brutus and the obscure figure of Collatinus. Their first task was to defend the fledgling Republic against the Etruscan Tarquins, whose return to power was favored by many in the mixed-tribe Rome. A conspiracy to achieve this was discovered; one can only imagine Brutus's grief when he found out that his own two sons were part of the plot. As consul, the father was faced with the heart-wrenching task of sitting in judgment over his own children and choosing between them and the Republic. Brutus sacrificed his rebel sons for the life of the Republic and by doing so set the standard of dedication to its ideals. Brutus himself later made the supreme sacrifice, dying in combat against a Tarquin son.

The next threat to Rome came from the Etruscans under their general, Porsenna. Rome was protected by her walls, built by Servius Tullius. We have one of the first legendary heroes of the Republic in Publius Horatius Cocles, who single-handedly kept the Etruscans at bay while the bridge over the Tiber River, the only access to the city, was destroyed. The expression "Horatius at the bridge," meaning one man fighting against overwhelming odds, dates back to this time. Unable to enter the city, the Etruscans lay siege but finally left without achieving their goal.

The Tarquins then came up with a better idea for crushing the Romans. In 496 B.C. they joined forces with some Latin cities, members of the Latin League that had been formed during the Period of the Kings as a block against both Etruscans and Greeks. Jealous of Rome's power, they were persuaded to fight against her. The legend goes that the deposed old king, Tarquinius Superbus, accompanied by his sons, rode out at the head of the Latin army and met the Romans at the battle of Lake Regillus. They were soundly defeated by the Romans, the sons met their death, and the old man escaped south to Cumae, where he disappeared from legend.

The lack of cohesion within the bloc prevented the League from posing any significant threat to the Etruscans and the Greeks. However, in spite of their differences, the Romans and the Latin tribes had to form a united front as a matter of survival to face the threat from the hill people. In 493 B.C. they renegotiated a treaty, which was known as the Cassian Treaty. The Oscan-speaking Volscians were instrumental in strengthening the League because they presented the greatest threat. The squabbles between the Latins and the Romans, on the one hand, and the struggles against the Oscan-speaking tribes, on the other, constitute an important page in the history of Rome and the future of the Latin-speaking people.

The period is replete with legends; one of the best-known figures of ancient Rome involves *Coriolanus,* a Roman turned traitor. The less praiseworthy part of his life was dramatized in Shakespeare's play Coriolanus, based on the account of the Greek historian Plutarch. Born Gaius Marcius of a noble Roman family, Coriolanus lost his father when young and was raised by his mother, whom he dearly loved. He became a brave warrior at an early age, revered by the Romans and feared by the enemy, and he fought in many wars with the surrounding tribes as well as against troops of the deposed king, Tarquinius Superbus. As a result of the struggle against the Volscians, however, he would be honored with the name by which he is known, for he led the Romans to the gates of their most important city, Corioli, and eventually captured it after great feats of courage.

In the battles that had brought Coriolanus great honor he knew his enemy and how to fight. There was no armor or sword with which he could defend himself against the enemies within, however, when he later found himself enmeshed in the political intrigues and social turmoil that plagued the early days of the Roman Republic, setting "Patricians" (persons of noble birth) against "Plebeians" (the common people). Victim of these early growing pains and his stubborn inflexibility, he was sent into exile. A bitter man after all the honors that had been showered on him, he sought refuge in the camp of his former and most implacable enemy, Tullus, the leader of the Volscians whose towns he had plundered. The two former enemies came to an understanding, and Coriolanus was even given command of Volscian troops. Eventually, he resolved to return and punish the ungrateful Romans, still in a state of domestic turmoil.

Coriolanus led the Volscian troops to the gates of Rome and laid siege as Senate and citizens alike made sacrifices to the gods and prayed for peace. Rome seemed about to be destroyed by one of her own sons. However, Coriolanus had left in Rome his beloved mother, his wife, and his children. These women set out for the enemy camp when all other entreaties had failed. Through their pleading, Coriolanus was persuaded to negotiate peace and was able to win the support of the Volscians for his actions. However, Tullus had grown jealous of Coriolanus's popularity with the troops and, fearing his power, had him murdered. The last lines of Shakespeare's play, from the mouth of a Volscian conspirator, may serve as his epitaph: "Yet he shall have a noble memory." Tullus eventually met his own death at the hands of the Romans, and the Volscians became subjects of Rome. As for the family of Coriolanus, the Romans considered them saviors of the city and a temple was erected in gratitude, dedicated To The Fortune of Women.

Meanwhile, as the Etruscans and the Greeks fought for control of the rich Campania, the Romans were engaged in battles with the hill people of Aequi. In 458 B.C. another hero appeared on the scene in the person of a citizen-warrior named Lucius Quinctius Cincinnatus. After rescuing the besieged consular army and "in one day" defeating the Aequi, he made a triumphal entry into Rome, then returned to work the fields of his small farm. His name did not fall into obscurity, however, for over twenty centuries later in America, he became the hero-model and inspiration of the Society of the Cincinnati established in 1783, a patriotic organization of officers of the American Revolutionary army. Their insignia bore a gold eagle and the figure of Cincinnatus, ready to leave his plow and defend his republic. It was after this patriotic society that the city of Cincinnati, Ohio, got its name.

By the end of the century, the wars with the hill tribes came to an end, and Rome could turn her attention to another sphere, the Etruscan city of Veii, just twenty miles north. One of the disputes involved control of a route crossing the Tiber River. After a siege that is said to have lasted ten long years, this rich city was finally attacked and conquered by the Romans, who looted its treasures and brought it under its control in 396 B.C. The Faliscans, politically and culturally affiliated with the Etruscans, were later obliged to make a truce of submission to Rome. Rebellious activities, real or suspected, led to Rome's invasion of one of their cities a few years later, and Rome's response was to slaughter some 15,000 Faliscans and literally wipe their city from the face of the earth. Such was the power of Rome!

✳ ✳ ✳

The Romans had become masters of a vast territory, but a devastating humiliation was in store for them. Around 400 B.C. the Gauls, a Celtic people, had crossed the Alps and displaced the Etruscans from the Po valley, occupying an area called Cisalpine Gaul. By 390 B.C. these invaders had moved down and defeated the Romans not far from Rome. They entered the city, looting and burning, and laid siege to the Capitol, which had remained the only stronghold. One colorful story survives that may or may not contain a grain of truth. Apparently, the Gauls had decided to surprise the Roman defenders at night while they slept and, having found a shortcut, quietly made their way up the hill under cover of darkness. This did not escape the vigil of the sacred geese of Juno, which set off the alarm and awoke the Romans who, led by Marcus Manlius, was able to alert his men and save Rome. For his role he earned the name Capitolinus after the Roman hill he had saved. Honors given in this way were like medals that the Romans proudly added to their own names. The Gauls had been stopped, but they placed the city under a siege that lasted some seven months. Legend again obscures the facts. Did the Romans pay tribute in gold, as some say, or were the Gauls defeated by a man called Camillus, just returning from exile at an opportune time?

One of the tragedies of the Gallic invasion was that it resulted in the destruction of records; much of what remains of some three centuries of history is only legend. Roman historians could later write their history to suit their own purposes, but one which they could take no pride in writing concerns the legendary savior of Rome, Marcus Manlius Capitolinus. A good man with a kind heart, Marcus had saved some poor men from the debtors' prison by paying their debts with his own money. The patricians accused him of currying favor with the plebeians for his own ends. He was put on trial, found guilty, and pitilessly executed for his kind actions. The fate of the hero Capitolinus again illustrates the problems that beset the Republic and the climate of political intrigue that was attacking the system from within like a deadly cancer.

The honorific names bestowed on Rome's early heroes were no safeguard against the wrath of their adversaries in a semitribal society experimenting with democracy. Yet it is by these names that such men as Coriolanus and Capitolinus have been immortalized.

Conquests and the Samnite Wars

In Rome's quest for control of the peninsula, among her most formidable foes were the Samnites, a collection of Oscan-speaking tribes occupying the mountainous center of the southern half of the peninsula. They had formed a confederation and were a threat not only to Rome and her allies but also to other tribes on the periphery. It was the call for help from Capua, a city not far north of Naples, that brought Rome to the rescue in 343 B.C., marking the beginning of the First Samnite War. The Samnites were driven out of Capua, and peace was agreed upon. About ten years later, in 334 B.C., another threat to the Republic was removed when the Gauls made peace with Rome and agreed to withdraw to the Po Valley.

No longer under threat from the Samnites and the Gauls, Rome proceeded to consolidate her gains; the former Latin allies, who had revolted against Rome while she had her hands full in Campania, were simply annexed as Roman territory. No longer fighting among themselves, these cities prospered, and people who went to live in Rome could even become Roman citizens. They had been let into the club, so to speak.

The next major event occurred in 332 B.C. and takes us to the heel of Italy where Tarentum (Taranto), the leading Greek colony of Magna Graecia, was under attack by native Italian tribes from the hills. Tarentum appealed to Alexander of Epirus (not Alexander the Great), who sent his army to fight the hill people. The Samnites joined forces with these tribes while Rome allied herself with Alexander against the Samnites. In this complicated war involving Romans, Samnites, Greeks, and hill tribes, Alexander was eventually defeated and met his death in the retreat that followed, and the ungrateful Tarentines had received enough help from their neighbor to save themselves.

The peace between Rome and the Samnites had been broken, and the two were soon at war again. The Second Samnite War, which began in 326 B.C., was for control of the fertile plain of Campania. The alliances had changed as this time the Samnites joined the Greeks to the south. Separating the two allies were the hill tribes of Apulia and Lucania, former allies of the Samnites now aligned with Rome. In 321 B.C. a major showdown in this conflict occurred when the Roman army in Campania was drawn into a trap. After receiving a false report that a city in Apulia was being harassed by the Samnites, the Romans made a beeline to help their ally, taking a shortcut across the mountains and straight through Samnite territory by way of a narrow valley called the Caudine Forks. There was one way into the valley and one way out. When the Romans reached this exit they found their path completely blocked with rocks and felled trees. The deadly mountain trap was sprung as the Samnite troops came up behind the Romans, preventing escape. Rather than slaughter their prey, the Samnites chose to let them starve, risking none of their own men. With their rations used up, the outnumbered and desperate Romans were forced to negotiate a truce.

The price asked by their captors was the return of Samnium territory previously lost. The Roman generals accepted and were allowed to return home with their army, leaving behind 600 hostages. Half-naked and weaponless, the Romans made their way to Capua. As the historian Livy wrote:

"When they came out of the pass they seemed like men brought back from the dead, seeing the light for the first time; yet the real light that showed them their ranks so disgraced was grimmer than any death."

These men returned to Rome like beaten prisoners and took refuge with their families, while the fate of the hostages left behind were in the balance. The Samnites had selected some of Rome's finest cavalrymen to be held as guarantee that the Senate would ratify the agreement of the generals; failing that, they would be killed. The great sacrifices that were made in the name of the Republic were again demonstrated in the action of the Senate, for although most of its members had a relative among those doomed 600 men, who were flowers of the Roman aristocracy, they refused to ratify such a shameful agreement.

The negotiations between the Romans and the Samnites that followed were without resolution, and the war resumed. Then, in an incredible reversal of fate, the Romans were able to make gains and overcome the Samnite garrison in the city of Luceria, where the 600 cavalrymen were being held. Fortunately, the Samnites had not yet carried out their threat of execution, and the hostages were freed. The

Benevento—The Ponte Leproso, built by the Samnites and restored by Appius Claudius and subsequent emperors, spans the River Sabato giving access to the city from the Appian Way which was extended to link Rome with the Adriatic port of Brindisi.

humiliating defeat and shame at the Caudine Forks was to some degree erased. The Samnites soon found themselves confined to the mountainous interior of the peninsula as Rome expanded her frontiers.

* * *

The Roman army had become an institution and a force for conquest, instituted as a standing and trained body of men who were paid for their services instead of being rewarded with land and loot in times of war. As a strike force the army needed to move quickly, and the formidable combination of legions and roads occurred now with the building of the celebrated Appian Way, starting at the Tiber in the heart of Rome and running like a ribbon of stone through the green fields and marshland of Campania to link Rome with the city of Capua 130 miles to the south. Appius Claudius Caecus, a man of Sabine stock, in 312 B.C. gathered together soldiers and peasants alike and built the famous road, which was named after him. It was a fitting memorial to one who was in his time consul, poet, writer, and censor, preceding the Renaissance men of Italy by many centuries. Interestingly, one of the items of the early Roman Code, called the Twelve Tables, provided for maintenance of roads, but nothing like the Appian Way had existed before.

With the building of the Appian Way the Romans could move their armies with great speed and the quarter of a century that followed was one of conquest as they battled Gauls, Etruscans, and Samnites. The Third Samnite War came to an end in 290 B.C., ending half a century of hostilities. An alliance was made that left the Samnites with self-government, but they could only fight under Roman generals. What an astute way of gaining an army of good fighting men!

The Romans had been sharpening their skills in the business of taking over the world.

The Conquest of Magna Graecia

The Romans, who just a hundred years earlier had been clinging to a foothold on Rome's Capitoline hill, now posed an awesome threat to the cities of Magna Graecia. Those few sharp-eared geese may well have been responsible for changing the whole course of history after all. Rome now controlled the central part of Italy, from the Adriatic to the Tyrrhenian Seas. There was no way for small cities that had lived peacefully to defend themselves against the Romans, so it seemed better to join them. The Greek colony of Neapolis (Naples) was one that did just that and wisely chose the route of survival.

Not all cities bowed to Rome's power. Thurii, a Greek colony opposite the proud city of Tarentum on the other side of the Gulf of Taranto, had been occupied by the Romans in 282 B.C. after unwisely calling on them for help against Lucanian hill tribes. Too close for comfort, the Tarentines then sent a force to Thurii, drove out the Roman garrisons, and sunk their little ships, killing their admiral—if one could give him such a title, as Rome did not yet boast a navy.

Swallowing their pride, the Romans wanted to play for time. They sent envoys to Tarentum to negotiate a truce and recover Thurii. The Latin-speaking Romans and the Greek-speaking Tarentines met in Tarentum. The Romans were unsuccessful, but to make matters worse they were thoroughly humiliated and taunted about the way they spoke Greek. The greatest humiliation came by chance, however, when they were on their way out of this foreign city. A man from the crowd urinated on the toga of one of the Roman envoys, to the great delight of the crowd. With the parting threat that the stain would be washed out with Greek blood, the envoys returned to Rome with the soiled toga, which they presented to the Senate as evidence of the insult. So it was that in 281 B.C. the outraged Senate declared war on Tarentum. Now the joke was on the Greeks.

With a soiled toga as a starting flag, the Greek games were about to begin in earnest and Romans and Greeks would have a chance to prove their mettle in yet another arena.

Tarentum was now faced with a declaration of war from the powerful Rome and had to look around for help. Magna Graecia had been reduced to a few survivors of Rome's voracious appetite for territory, which was not about to be satisfied. The Tarentines needed help quickly because the Roman armies could now move fast.

The Greek cities of Sicily were rich and prosperous, but the Tarentines, as they had in the past, looked to nearby Epirus, separated from the heel of Italy by the Adriatic Sea, where it narrows to a mere fifty miles. When a call went out to the restless and ambitious King Pyrrhus in 280 B.C., he lost no time in setting sail immediately with 25,000 men. His army was no collection of peasants with pitchforks, but a trained military force of experienced soldiers. He also had another weapon up his sleeve — the elephants that his men had fought against in the east were now part of their own arsenal, and Pyrrhus brought twenty of them with him. He knew that the Romans would be no match for these huge animals which could thunder into the enemy ranks like tanks, putting the terrorized soldiers to flight or trampling them under foot.

Perhaps Pyrrhus's first challenge came from the Tarentines themselves, accustomed as they were to the comfortable life of a trading city and reluctant to take up arms on their own behalf. Pyrrhus immediately met with resistance when he turned the city into a military camp, training citizens to be soldiers. The sound of music and dancing from theaters and places of entertainment were soon replaced by the shouts of the drill masters. There were protesters to be sure, but the most troublesome ones were simply shipped off to Epirus. Pyrrhus lost no time and engaged the Romans right away in 280 B.C. at Heraclea, midway between Tarentum and Thurii. Named after the Greek hero Heracles (Hercules), it had been established by the Tarentines as a colony when the Greek cities of Thurii and Tarentum had been in conflict as far back as 433 B.C., a fact that indicates the lack of cohesion among the Greek colonies, which eventually brought about their downfall. Pyrrhus won a great victory over the Romans at Heraclea in this first encounter. However, he was smart enough to realize that he was dealing with true fighters when he inspected the battlefield and saw with his own eyes that the fatal wounds of the dead Romans were in front — they had died fighting.

At this juncture, Pyrrhus tried to persuade the Romans to make peace on a live-and-let-live basis, but the counsel of the old censor and builder of the Appian Way, Appius Claudius Caecus, now a blind and feeble man, was that there should be no peace with Pyrrhus until his soldiers were chased out of the peninsula. Pyrrhus took up the challenge and proceeded northwest through Campania as cities fell, the inhabitants dumbstruck by the appearance of the great elephants bearing down like a tidal wave. He brought his army to within just twenty-four miles of the gates of

Rome, but the Latin cities proved their loyalty to Rome and he was stopped in his tracks.

With the approach of winter, Pyrrhus returned to Tarentum. During the lull in fighting, the Romans sent Gaius Fabricius to Tarentum to negotiate the return of Roman prisoners in exchange for ransom. Pyrrhus, on his part, tried to exact a promise of peace by offering Fabricius bribes, which the honorable Roman refused. The story goes that Pyrrhus tried to shake this Roman's resolve by having an elephant brought up behind him and sounding his trumpet. This was like a sword being held at his neck, but Fabricius did not flinch. The astounded Pyrrhus released the Roman prisoners in an act of chivalry.

There was no peace, however, and another battle was fought at Ausculum (Ascoli Satriano), not far from Aquilonia. Again, Pyrrhus won the battle with his trained men and elephants, but it was a costly one—he had lost many of his best and most seasoned veterans. It was because of this battle that the expression "Pyrrhic victory" found its way into our language and our dictionaries, meaning a victory costing more to the victor than to the vanquished.

Meanwhile, Pyrrhus had lost confidence in the Tarentines, who were relying on him to fight their battles, and he realized the futility of continuing a war against the Romans. Besides, armed bands of Gauls were now threatening Macedon, Greece, and Pyrrhus's own Kingdom of Epirus. However, instead of returning home he chose to go to Sicily, where the Greek colonies were engaged in a struggle with Carthage, the North African city that had been an enemy of Greece and controlled part of Sicily. Carthage was an ally of Rome, so Pyrrhus would still be at war with the Romans and not lose face. He set sail for Sicily in 278 B.C. and pushed the Carthaginians back into the western corner of the island.

The Tarentines regretted the departure of Pyrrhus and were glad to welcome him back in 276 B.C. The following year, the third battle with the Romans took place. The site this time was Beneventum in the Apennines. Legend has it that the city, situated on a ridge between the Calore River and its tributary the Sabato, was founded by Diomedes of the Trojan horse and companion of Ulysses.

The Romans, after two unsuccessful battles with Pyrrhus, had learned some lessons; this time they were ready for him with their own version of a Trojan horse. They attacked in a hilly region, which was a serious impediment to Pyrrhus's battle formation, but the real surprise came when the Roman soldiers showered the charging elephants with burning arrows. The terrified beasts stampeded back through Pyrrhus's own ranks, crushing his men and creating panic. That was the last battle for the unfortunate king, who retreated to Tarentum and then made his way home to Epirus and more wars fought to protect his kingdom.

Not long after, Tarentum fell to the Romans, who took the city in 272 B.C. All the efforts of Pyrrhus had been in vain, and one must feel some sympathy for this unfortunate king whose ambitions had been thwarted and whose colorful life was destined to meet an inglorious end. In that same year in the Greek city of Argos, the very city that worshipped Diomedes as their hero, Pyrrhus died during a night skirmish, not by the sword but by a roof tile thrown down by a woman.

Rhegium (Reggio in Calabria) in the toe of Italy, founded by the Greeks in 720 B.C., was the last remaining city of Magna Graecia on the mainland. It fell to the Romans in 270 B.C. and though remaining essentially a Greek city was always loyal to Rome, even during the Empire.

In the five years that followed, the Romans subdued the remaining Etruscan cities, the last one being taken in 265 B.C. All the lands south of the Rubicon River, which was the border with Cisalpine Gaul, were now virtually under the control of Rome.

CHAPTER THREE

The Making of Italy

Sicily: The Coveted Jewel of the Mediterranean

Rome was now ready to turn her attention to Sicily, separated from the mainland by the Strait of Messina — which at its narrowest point is a mere two miles wide — much feared by the sailors of antiquity for the treacherous rocks and whirlpools. It was here that the monsters of Greek mythology — Scylla on the mainland side and Charybdis on the Sicilian — challenged the courage of Ulysses in his wanderings. Sicily, a beautiful triangle set in the Mediterranean Sea, lying between the promontory of North Africa to the southwest and the toe of Italy to the northeast, was a jewel that beckoned to Greeks and Carthaginians alike, both of whom played such a vital role in shaping its history.

The Greeks began to colonize Sicily as early as the eighth century B.C. Their most important cities were on the eastern coast; Messana (Messina), Naxos (Taormina), Catana (Catania), and the fortified city of Syracuse. In fact, Syracuse boasted a population of something like half a million people around 300 B.C. — quite impressive compared with Rome's estimated 150,000 at that time. The Greek cities in Sicily were often ruled by tyrants. One of the strong rulers of the fourth century B.C., Dionysius I, controlled two thirds of Sicily and the toe of Italy.

Not even Dionysius, however, could dislodge the Carthaginians from Sicily. They had staked their claims even before the arrival of the Greeks, but had been pushed back to the western tip of the island. One of their most important cities was Panormus (Palermo), and the impregnable Lilybaeum (Marsala) became the chief city of the Carthaginians in Sicily and their last stronghold.

Who the Carthaginians were and how they got to Sicily is an interesting story in itself. Carthage's mystical beginnings go far back in time, but it was a city founded by the Phoenicians, one of a series of colonial settlements much the same as the Greek. Carthage cannot be found on a map because it no longer exists, but it was located not too far from what is now Tunis. Around 600 B.C. Nebuchadrezzar of Babylon destroyed the power of Phoenicia, leaving the colonies like orphans around Carthage. She was to become a major power in the Mediterranean with an empire that extended along the coast of North Africa and reached over the Mediterranean waters to Sardinia, Corsica, and parts of Spain, as well as Sicily.

As maritime and trading powers, both the Carthaginians and the Greeks hugged the coasts, leaving the central and mountain areas to the native tribes of the Sicani and the Siculi; from the latter the name of Sicily was derived. There was yet another group of people that would play an important role in the next act. The Mamertines, who had been brought to Sicily from mainland Italy as mercenaries by a Greek general a century earlier, had become a thorn in the side of the Greeks. Pyrrhus had also fought against them during his campaign in Sicily and had pushed them back into Messina, but in 270 B.C. they were again causing trouble, and this time it was General Hiero who put them back in their place. For his victory he was made king of Syracuse. During that same year, Rome took the city of Rhegium (Reggio di Calabria), the last foothold of Magna Graecia on the peninsula.

This was the scenario in 265 B.C. when King Hiero, in an uncharacteristic move, entered into an alliance with Carthage for the express purpose of wiping out the troublesome Mamertines once and for all. The Mamertines were helpless against the combined power of Syracuse and Carthage and, being from the Italian peninsula, they were more closely related to the Romans, to whom they sent a call for help. The Romans had been on friendly terms with the Carthaginians for two and a half centuries, but were nevertheless willing to step in and give assistance as "protector" of the Mamertines. Under the command of Appius Claudius Caudex, son of the celebrated builder of the Appian Way, the Roman army left the mainland for the first time and crossed the waters to Sicily. In 263 B.C. the Greeks of Syracuse were defeated and King Hiero, seeing the writing on the wall, signed a peace treaty with Rome, becoming a loyal ally until his death in 215 B.C. It was a time of peace and prosperity for this Greek colony, which for close to half a century flourished in the shadow of the two major opponents, Rome and Carthage.

Ruins of the once magnificent Greek theater at Naxos (Taormina). The site affords a splendid view of Mount Etna, considered by the ancients to be the forge of Vulcan, the god of fire.

The First Punic War and the Struggle for Sicily

The wars between Carthage and Rome are known as the Punic Wars; the word *punic* is derived from the Latin word *punicus*, meaning "Phoenician." The conflict between these two rivals represents one of the most significant contests in the ancient world by reason of the final outcome and because it lasted for over a hundred years.

The state of war that began in 264 B.C. marked the beginning of the First Punic War, which dragged on for twenty-three years. The Romans quickly made gains and scored a major victory over the Carthaginians at Agrigentum on the southern coast of Sicily in 262 B.C., but this first war was predominantly naval. Whereas Carthage was already a sea power, the Romans had to set about the task of not only becoming sailors but also building a fleet of ships to rival that of their opponents. Lacking the knowledge themselves, they are said to have copied from a Carthaginian vessel that had come to grief in a storm off the treacherous coast of the toe of Italy. With the help of their Greek allies, they built the ships and trained their men. In 260 B.C. they were ready to put to sea.

The first real sea battle took place not far from Messana (Messina). The Romans encountered the Carthaginians head-on, taking them by surprise. Using grappling hooks designed by Gaius Duilius Nepos, who was the commander of their fleet, the ingenious Romans attached themselves to the enemy ships. They quickly boarded the enemy vessels and then carried on the fight on the ships' decks. The Carthaginians were completely unprepared for these novel tactics, and their ships were either destroyed or captured.

With this victory at sea, the Romans felt confident enough to take the battle to Carthage itself. Just four years after their encouraging success, in 256 B.C., a fleet of 330 ships under Marcus Atilus Regulus set sail for Carthage. A large Carthaginian fleet was sent out to encounter the Romans, and a sea battle involving close to 1,000 ships raged off the southern coast of Sicily. The victorious Romans made for the undefended city of Carthage and seized control of the area. However, they were eventually defeated by the Carthaginian cavalry and elephants, and their commander was taken prisoner.

On getting the news, the Roman Senate sent reinforcements, which broke through the blockade protecting the African mainland, but then the tide turned against the Romans. They failed to heed the warnings of an approaching storm, and their fleet was destroyed. The Roman army that had come to fight on African soil ended up at the bottom of the sea.

The theater of operations was once more shifted to Sicily, where the Carthaginians had sent troops and elephants, but the persistent Romans scraped together another fleet. In a matter of a few months, they dispatched it to Sicily, where they succeeded in taking Panormus (Palermo). As if to celebrate their victory, they put out to sea and cruised along the African coast, making forays here and there before returning home, but their outing ended in disaster. The sea god was not pleased and once more whipped up a storm that all but destroyed Rome's fleet and took the lives of so many precious sons.

Sicily remained the arena for the war games that dragged on. In 250 B.C., Carthage decided to seek a peaceful settlement and sent a mission to Rome for this purpose. The mission failed, and a year later the Romans were ready with yet another fleet. This time the target was the so-far-unbeaten and impregnable stronghold of Lilybaeum (Marsala) at the extreme western tip of the island. This force was led by

Publius Claudius Pulcher, a brother of Appius Claudius who was anxious to make a name for himself. He decided to attack the Carthaginian fleet a few miles north of the city, even though the omens were against him.

It must be mentioned that sacred chickens were always kept on board ships, and their behavior was interpreted before any action was taken. The birds had refused to eat, which was a bad omen. The impatient Claudius was reputed to have exclaimed angrily, "If they will not eat, let them drink," whereupon he cast them overboard to meet a watery death. Claudius may not have been superstitious himself, but he failed to realize the effect that such a sacrilegious act might have on his men, who became fearful and dispirited. The Romans lost the battle, and many suffered the same fate as the poor chickens as their ships were destroyed. Claudius did not go down with his ship; somehow he managed to survive the battle. Once back in Rome he was put on trial and heavily fined. He committed suicide shortly thereafter, an act that was to become an honorable end for disgraced Romans.

These were dark days for Rome, whose Mare Nostrum of later years had become a watery graveyard of her youth while the city took on the black garb of mourning mothers and widows. By this time Carthage had found her leader in the person of Hamilcar Barca, destined to become one of the great names in history. Appointed leader of the Sicilian armies of Carthage in 248 B.C., Hamilcar gave the Romans a real run for their money. He recaptured Panormus and continued raids in Sicily as he constantly outwitted his opponents. The tenacity of the Romans in their quest for control of Sicily in spite of the setbacks and losses was nothing short of incredible. They bounced back again in 242 B.C. by destroying the Carthaginian fleet that was bringing reinforcements to Hamilcar.

A truce was signed with Rome in 241 B.C.; the long struggle with Carthage had ended in a Roman victory as the First Punic War was finally over. After a presence that had lasted more than 600 years, the Carthaginians were now dislodged from Sicily. Syracuse had remained the faithful ally of Rome all this time and continued to rule in the eastern part of the island. But the rest of Sicily, a melting pot of Carthaginians, Greeks, and native tribes, was to become Rome's first *provincia.*

Italy Complete

For the next twenty years, the two contestants, Rome and Carthage, went about their own business in their respective spheres of influence in the Mediterranean, each growing stronger in its own camp. For the immediate future, however, the problems visited on Carthage as a result of its drawn-out war worked in favor of Rome.

Back in North Africa, the mercenaries, survivors of bloody combat whose loyalties were only as good as the payment and spoils of war they received for their services, presented a threat to Carthage itself. These soldiers of fortune, now abandoned, dispossessed, and desperate, turned on the Carthaginians. Hamilcar Barca was soon called on to deal with the unruly elements that roamed around pillaging and plundering. Alarmed by Hamilcar's ruthless measures in Carthage, the mercenaries in Sardinia, which was still under Carthage, appealed to Rome for protection. In a flagrant breach of the peace treaty so recently signed with Carthage in 241 B.C., the Romans obliged with an occupying force, threatening another war if Carthage did not agree to relinquish its claim on Sardinia, an island it had occupied since the eighth or ninth century B.C.

Carthage was in no position to fight another war and agreed to give up not only Sardinia but also Corsica. Although this annexation took place in 238 B.C., it was no easy task for the Romans to pacify the proud tribes of the beautiful, wild, and mountainous island of Sardinia, and for ten years these people vigorously resisted Roman occupation. However, Sardinia eventually became the second Roman province in 227 B.C.

Rome, meanwhile, turned her attention in another direction. Always good at answering calls for help, this time the call came from the Greeks for protection from the neighboring Illyria, whose piracy had been a constant threat. Now a strong sea power, the Romans took care of the problem with threats and seized the island of Corcyra (Corfu), which had been an Illyrian possession for some fifty years. The Greeks were grateful for Roman protection, and the Romans had gained their respect as well as a foothold right at their back door.

Meanwhile, there was trouble in Cisalpine Gaul, with new invasions southward in 225 B.C. Battles followed, but by 222 B.C. the Romans controlled Cisalpine Gaul and had established colonies in some of the cities, including Cremona and Piacenza. The victorious general, Gaius Flaminius, wanted to consolidate the victory and in 220 B.C., in order to give the army a way to move quickly in case of revolt on the part of these newly conquered people, he began building a road running from Rome across the rugged backbone of the Apennines to the Adriatic coast. The road was called the Flaminian Way in his honor.

A map of the Roman world at this time, except for the islands of Corsica (now French territory), and Corcyra (now the Greek Corfu), coincides with the territory that we today know as ITALY.

Hannibal and the Second Punic War

The next chapter of Italian history had its heroes, but one man took the spotlight as the chief protagonist, and he personified Rome's wars against Carthage. His name was Hannibal. The Second Punic War was unlike any other war before it. Perhaps it was not even a war in the traditional sense, but rather a series of battles, followed by the presence of Hannibal, who got right into the belly of his enemy. For seventeen years, he would remain there like a thorn in their side.

Hannibal was the product of military tradition, schooled in the art of warfare by his famous father, Hamlicar Barca. A formidable enemy and a charismatic leader with superior intelligence, he had sworn eternal enmity to Rome, against which his whole life was dedicated. In 221 B.C., at just twenty-six years of age, he became commander-in-chief of the Carthaginian forces in Spain and proceeded to consolidate power in the region.

The next chapter of Italian history actually begins in Spain when in the spring of 219 B.C. Hannibal attacked the independent Greek town of Saguntum (Sagunto). The citizens called on Rome to intervene, but when the warnings were ignored and the ambassadors were greeted with scorn, the seeds were sown for another war with Carthage. A force was dispatched to Spain under the command of Publius Cornelius Scipio, whose father had put down the last resistance in Sardinia. By the time Scipio got to Spain, however, he found that Hannibal had beaten a rather hasty retreat northward, outflanking the Roman army.

In the historic event with which he is now largely associated, Hannibal led a formidable army of infantry, cavalry, and elephants through hostile Gallic tribes and across the Alps, already snow-covered in the cold months of late autumn. At what geographical point Hannibal made the crossing is not exactly known, but all the passes were narrow and treacherous. Many of the men, horses, and elephants fell to their death from the slippery footholds. By the time he descended into Italy some five months later, he had lost about two thirds of his men and many of his elephants, but he still had a considerable force at his disposal.

In the meantime, the outwitted Scipio had returned to Italy and was ready to meet the invaders at the Po River. In the ensuing battle, the Romans were outmaneuvered and miserably defeated. Among the survivors was General Scipio who, it is claimed, was miraculously rescued by his nineteen-year-old son, also called Publius Cornelius Scipio and destined to become a famous general himself. The Romans failed to stop Hannibal's advance as he made his way across Italy and through territory not yet "pacified" by the Romans. One can only begin to imagine the fear created in the villages and settlements that found themselves in the path of this army on the move—men of different racial origins with animals that they had never before set eyes on.

The second major encounter came in the spring of 217 B.C. at Lake Trasimene. Although the Romans had a much larger force, they suffered an even greater defeat than the first time. Roman forces were all but wiped out, and their general, Flaminius, met his end here. Ironically, the road that Flaminius built that bears his name could now also serve Hannibal's purpose, since it led to the heart of Rome. However, Hannibal chose to bypass Rome and move southward.

The next encounter with the Romans took place at Cannae in Apulia on the fateful second of August, 216 B.C. This time the Roman army was under two generals who were also consuls, and they shared the command on the battlefield as they did in government. Perhaps one of their problems was agreeing on strategy—they were different in temperament, and they apparently took command on alternate days. The army under their command was even larger than the previous one, but Hannibal, grossly outnumbered as he was, still outmaneuvered his opponents and led them into a trap in the rugged terrain of Apulia. The Romans were literally slaughtered by the thousands, with no chance to flee. One general (Paulus) was killed; the other (Varro), unwilling to return to Rome in disgrace, where he would probably have lost his head anyway, was said to have committed suicide.

The disaster of all disasters that occurred at Cannae would never be erased from Roman memory. It was the third devastating defeat the Romans had suffered since the fearful Hannibal had appeared on Italian soil. It seemed that all was lost. Although many of the allies and cities remained loyal to Rome, others decided to join the winning side. Capua and Tarentum were two of the major cities that opened their gates to Hannibal, but were later retaken by Rome with dire consequences. The year that Cannae fell, the Romans also lost their faithful ally of Syracuse with the death of the loyal King Hiero. His successor, believing that Rome was doomed, naturally thought it expedient to switch allegiances now or suffer later.

Surrounded by enemies and having lost many of her finest young men, Rome seemed to gain strength through adversity. The war continued, but instead of fighting Hannibal in Italy she decided to take the battle overseas, to Spain and Carthage. Thus occupied in Spain, the Carthaginians were unable or unwilling to send reinforcements to Hannibal. For the next five years he roamed around the countryside seeking enemies to fight. In the year 211 B.C., Hannibal finally appeared

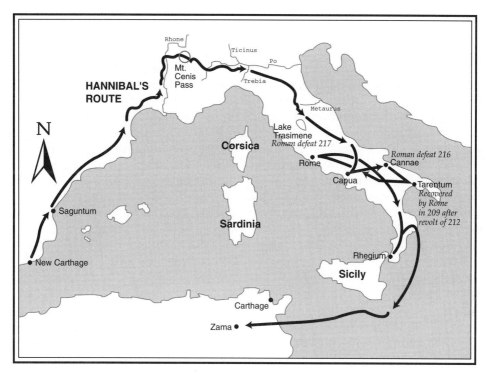

The Second Punic War 218-201 B.C.

outside Rome, and the terrified citizens prepared for a long siege. He never entered the city, however, but just seemed to fade away.

In Italy, the Romans followed the movements of their enemy very carefully and gave him plenty of space, avoiding direct contact. This strategy was favored by the general Quintus Fabius Maximus Rullianus, a grandson and namesake of the man who defeated the Gauls almost eighty years earlier. Fabius lives on in our language in the military term *Fabian strategy,* which means delaying tactics. For years Hannibal roamed the countryside, seemingly abandoned by his own country and not welcomed by another. He must have been a sorry figure with his ragged army, a motley collection of mercenaries who, now trapped in a country which they came to conquer, stayed with the general whom they loved and respected, in spite of the hardships they must have endured.

The help Hannibal needed from Carthage never came. Some ten years after his arrival in Italy, his last chance was his brother, Hasdrubal Barca, who finally brought an army from Spain with the purpose of joining forces with him. Hasdrubal was met by Romans at the Metaurus River, and his army was destroyed. It is said that the head of the dead Hasdrubal was tossed inside Hannibal's camp as he waited for news. One can only imagine the effect that this personal loss and military setback had on Hannibal, who now retreated to the toe of Italy, where he remained for four more years.

Meanwhile things had been happening in North Africa where the Romans, great with making deals, had teamed up with the Numidians. Publius Cornelius Scipio, just over thirty years old, had set sail for Africa in 204 B.C. There he scored victories and found chinks in the alliances. The first to crumble was Numidia (now Algeria). Faced with the threat in Africa, Carthage now sent for Hannibal.

The final chapter in this unfortunate and costly war was played out in North Africa between Hannibal and the young Scipio. On October 19, 202 B.C., a great battle took place at Zama, about 100 miles from Carthage. This time it was Hannibal's army that was destroyed. Carthage had to surrender, and a peace treaty was signed in 201 B.C. as the Second Punic War finally came to an end. Numidia now became Rome's ally, and Carthage had to give up Spain, her fleet, and her elephants as her domain was reduced to that part of Africa around Carthage, now known as Tunisia.

Hannibal had managed to survive. For a time he became head of the government in Carthage, but he was later accused of plotting against Rome in defiance of the peace treaty. He was forced to flee to a kingdom in the east and we shall meet him again later. His opponent, the victorious Scipio, returned to Rome and was given the title of "Africanus," and he is known in the history books as Publius Cornelius Scipio Africanus the elder.

The consequences of the Second Punic War were far reaching. Rome's dominion now extended to North Africa, with Numidia as a loyal ally. She had brought the southern part of Spain into her orbit in 197 B.C. creating two new provinces—one in the east and one in the west—and the province of Sicily now included the entire island. In the peninsula, Latin colonists settled in the north, absorbing the Gallic population, and colonists also moved south, where the Greek cities became increasingly Roman in character. Protected and maintained by a well-disciplined army and strong central rule, a mighty empire was taking shape.

CHAPTER FOUR

Roman Conquests and Trouble at Home

The Aegean Arena

The war with Carthage was over, but Rome had much to do at home to consolidate power in the peninsula. The Romans had weathered a great storm that all but capsized the Republic, but it was built with solid timbers, and the men at the helm were strong in spirit.

The Romans would soon be involved overseas once more, drawn into the Aegean arena where the prizes were still greater. Boasting a well-disciplined army and a navy to be reckoned with, they quickly made gains as peacemakers.

The Greeks, loosely organized into kingdoms and leagues, always seemed to be at odds with each other. There were two major leagues, the Aetolian in the north and the Achaean in the south, and there was the Hellenistic kingdom of Macedonia, ruled by Philip V, a powerful king who had illusions of being the successor to Alexander the Great. When the ambitious Philip, who had sided with Hannibal during the Second Punic War, attacked the Greek island of Rhodes, Rome came to her rescue. This was the beginning of the Second Macedonian War (200–196 B.C.). The victorious Rome stripped Philip of his fleet and forced him to pay a hefty fine, but allowed him to rule his kingdom with the promise of good behavior.

Rome was not just flexing her military muscle, but protecting vital interests in the Aegean. The Romans had come to admire the Greeks for their culture and superior learning and had even adopted their gods with some name changes. Noble families acknowledged the advantage of sending their children to Greece to be schooled in the language, literature, history, and sciences of the Hellenes. (Tragically in 212 B.C. the incredible genius Archimedes had been slain in Syracuse by some overzealous Roman soldiers as he made circles in the dust.)

The Seleucid empire was the next to be taught a lesson by Rome. In 192 B.C. Antiochus III led an army to Greece, egged on by none other than Rome's old enemy, Hannibal. The Romans were ready. They chased him from Greece and across the Aegean to the very shores of Asia Minor. A fierce battle was fought in 190 B.C. at Magnesia in Pergamum (now part of Turkey). Leading the Roman army was Lucius Cornelius Scipio, pitted against the same foe that his brother Scipio Africanus had fought at Carthage. Rome won the battle, and part of the agreement required that Antiochus hand over Hannibal. But this was against his code of honor, and he allowed Hannibal to escape to another kingdom.

An old man now, Hannibal continued to elude the Romans as they chased him around the shores of the Mediterranean. We find him next in Bithynia, a Hellenistic kingdom north of Pergamum that stretched out along the southern shores of the Black

Sea. The squabble between Bithynia and Pergamum came to the attention of Rome. Hannibal had assisted Bithynia in scoring a victory at sea against Rome's ally, Pergamum. It did not take the Romans long to appear on the scene, and the king of Bithynia was forced to hand over their old enemy. Hannibal did not get away this time. Surrounded by Roman soldiers, he realized that this was the end. He took the poison that he apparently always carried with him. By his own hand he escaped forever the Roman grasp. With him went Rome's greatest enemy and one who might well have changed the way the world looks today.

By strange coincidence, Hannibal's archenemy, Scipio Africanus, died in the same year, 183 B.C., and, if it could have been any consolation to Hannibal, he did not exactly die with honor. Scipio's enemy came in the person of Cato, another great Roman from a rival family, who had accused the Scipio brothers of wrongdoing and discredited their name for Rome was not free from political intrigue or deadly family feuds.

By the time the two rivals were dead, Rome had control of all the lands around the Mediterranean or was at least allied with them. The Greeks were still free to govern themselves and might have remained so if all had been quiet on the eastern front. They had lost their colonies, of course, but these had been far-off entities that did not much affect their daily lives. But the incorrigible Macedonia was busy fueling the seeds of discontent and mistrust of the Romans among the Greeks. The Third Macedonian War began in 172 B.C. when Pergamum sounded the alarm, and the Romans came sailing back to settle matters by force. Macedonia did not get the support of the Greek union she had counted on, and, even with the greatest armies since Alexander the Great, she was no match for the seasoned Romans under the

The world of the Eastern Mediterranean around 200 B.C.

command of Lucius Aemilus Paulus, whose father died fighting against Hannibal at Cannae some forty-four years earlier. The major battle took place at Pydna, Macedonia, in 168 B.C. With the Roman victory the Macedonian king, Perseus, was carried off as a prisoner to die in Rome, while his kingdom was divided into four small republics. The Roman general, Paulus, got himself the title of "Macedonicus," thereby salvaging the family honor.

Partly as a result of this conflict the Greeks fell from grace with the Romans. They tried to take a neutral stand and proved to be divided in their feelings so that they could not be trusted. As punishment for their half-hearted efforts, the Romans took some 1,000 hostages back with them. Fortunately for posterity, one of the hostages was none other than the great Greek historian Polybius, to whom we owe much of our knowledge of the period included in these chapters on the Roman Republic. As mentioned, the Romans had come to admire the Greeks, and Paulus Macedonicus took this Greek hostage, a man of great learning and intelligence, to be tutor to his own sons. Through this extraordinary association, Polybius entered the Roman world of the great Scipio family, and his knowledge enriched the lives of his captors. An insight into Roman life and civilization would later be given to us by Polybius in his collection of *Histories,* a window through which we can peek into the events of his day. Fortunately, he lived to be over eighty years of age.

Of course, not all Romans admired the Greeks. One of those who did not was Marcus Porcius Cato, called the Censor, who vigorously blocked any move to have the hostages freed. They were doomed to spend the next seventeen years with their captors. Largely through the diplomatic efforts of the Scipios, staunch opponents of the harsh Cato, the Greeks were eventually freed.

The Third Punic War: Destruction of Carthage

While petty disputes were occurring in Rome, attention had been drawn to Carthage, which had complained to Rome about the raids and incursions of their Numidian neighbor. By treaty Carthage was not allowed to act on her own, but Rome did not respond to the call for help. So in 150 B.C. Carthage finally took up arms against the aggressors, giving Rome an excuse to declare a state of war. Carthage sent missions to Rome and even had her generals put to death to no avail.

The Third Punic War began in 149 B.C. when an army was dispatched to North Africa to deal with Carthage, most wrongfully accused of being the instigators of the trouble. Old Cato, now in his eighties and whose constant refrain had been "Carthage must be destroyed," lived long enough to see the terrible wheels of destruction set in motion. The Carthaginians pleaded with Rome and even gave up their weapons and "promised to do anything." But when the Romans made the unreasonable demand that they abandon the city and rebuild it inland they quite understandably refused to comply. For two years the Carthaginians held out with whatever means they could muster.

Looming on the horizon was yet another Scipio — Scipio the Younger — whose very name must have put mortal fear in the hearts of the Carthaginians. (He was actually the younger son of the general Paulus Macedonicus, adopted by the Scipio family.) In 146 B.C., a date that would be remembered as one of the most infamous in the history of Rome, the Romans took the city of Carthage and burned it to the ground. Of the estimated population of a quarter of a million, only some 50,000 remained at the time of surrender. Some perished in the flames or were massacred by

Roman soldiers, and the survivors were carried off as slaves to Rome. Nothing remained; a city and its culture were completely wiped from the face of the earth. The Romans ordered that nothing be built there and, ironically, dedicated the site to the god of fire. The territory became the province of Africa, and Scipio was given the honorific title of "Africanus Minor" for this heartless act of cruelty.

Polybius, Scipio's old friend and tutor, had witnessed the destruction of Carthage. Polybius was an admirer of the Romans for their uprightness and fairness in battle, their playing according to the rules of the game without tricks and ruses, and their ability to make allies of their defeated enemies. How could he justify such an act? As he wrote of it, *"They had received a voluntary surrender from a people who had given them the right to do what they chose, and when this people had refused to obey their commands, they had applied force to them."*

The Third Punic War had come to an end with a clear victory for Rome, but it was one that brought her dishonor. A page had been added to history with an obituary for the death of Carthage.

Conquests East and West

To follow the history of the period, one is constantly moving from place to place, becoming entangled with events occurring far from Rome, where decisions were being made and destinies forged. Even as the Romans were settling the Carthaginian affair, there was trouble in the Greek world where Andriscus, a man taken prisoner to Rome following the Third Macedonian War, emerged to declare himself king of Macedonia and stir up trouble in the Greek kingdoms. In 148 B.C., tired of dealing with the same naughty child again, the Romans sent an army to crush the Macedonians once and for all, in what was known as the Fourth Macedonian War. Macedonia now became a Roman province.

The Achaean League had not come to the aid of the Macedonians, but were nonetheless guilty of defiance to Rome. Unfortunately for the Greeks, a sympathetic Roman general was replaced with the rough and uneducated Lucius Mummius, who showed no mercy. The terrified Corinth, capital city of the League, surrendered without a fight, but Mummius had the city ruthlessly sacked all the same. There was killing and looting, and many of the inhabitants were taken to be sold as slaves. Priceless works of art were seized to be carried off to Rome, and the stupid Mummius is said to have remarked to one of the soldiers handling some paintings, "Don't let these be damaged or you will have to replace them."

On the other side of the Mediterranean, there was trouble in Spain, which had come under Rome's control following the Second Punic War in 241 B.C., some ninety years earlier. For the past decade, unpacified native tribes had been waging a guerrilla war against the Roman governors under the leadership of a shepherd from Lusitania (now Portugal). Finally, in 133 B.C., the butcher of Carthage, Scipio the Younger, was sent to take care of the indomitable Lusitanians. Scipio went on to subdue the seat of resistance in northern Spain, and that territory was brought under Roman control. All of the Iberian peninsula was now Roman territory, except for the extreme northwest corner.

In 133 B.C., Rome's star was rising in the eastern Mediterranean when a plum literally fell into the lap of the Romans with the acquisition of the Kingdom of Pergamum. A longtime loyal ally of Rome, her king, Attalus III, bequeathed his kingdom to Rome because he had no heirs and did not want to risk it being torn to pieces on his death. Pergamum, in the beautiful Aegean region of present-day Turkey, became the Asian province of Rome.

Soon thereafter, this time on the northern shores of the Mediterranean, another plum was ripe for the picking. The Greek colony of Massilia, established around 600 B.C. and longtime trading center, came under attack from the Gauls. Massilia had been a close ally of Rome and now called on her to help against the aggressors. Roman soldiers were soon on the scene, and the Gauls were repulsed, but instead of departing the Romans, to better "protect" their ally, established a military outpost at what is now Aix-en-Provence. Protection became permanent when in 121 B.C. the region was made a *provincia*. It kept its name, for it is still known today as Provence, a paradise stretching along the southern coast of France and caressed by the waters of the Mediterranean. For the Romans of the time, it was a practical land bridge to Spain and destinations well beyond.

Problems at Home: Of Slaves and Reformers

It may seem that the history of Italy had been taking place away from the peninsula. This is only partially true. A tremendous upheaval was occurring at home as a direct result of what was happening in these wars of conquest which for about 100 years had been almost a Roman way of life.

By this time, Rome in particular, which was the center of it all, was having her own problems as internal struggles were becoming more ruthless. The influx of thousands of slaves destabilized the general order of things and sorely tested the ability of the captors to deal with problems. Although some of the slaves, such as the educated Greeks, were usually well treated, there were those whose condition was so deplorable that death would have been preferable.

One event that has historic significance and that demonstrates the legacy that conquest brought involved the slaves of Sicily. Taken there in large numbers to work on the plantations, they included people of conquered nations and even some Italian soldiers who had been defeated in battle or were deserters. These people were often subjected to particularly cruel treatment at the hands of their masters. In 135 B.C. a Syrian slave called Eunus, claiming to be of the royal Seleucid family, organized a revolt, and other slaves rallied around him. Angered and brutalized by the treatment they had received, they ran amok and committed terrible atrocities against their masters—but the retribution meted out by the Romans was even worse. This revolt, which lasted for three bloody years, is known in the history books as the First Servile War, or slave war.

There were some Romans who saw the danger to the Republic in social unrest, not just in the ranks of the slaves, but among the common people. They took it on themselves to implement reforms that would benefit the growing ranks of the proletariat. The group associated most directly with this movement was the Gracchus family, whose members were referred to as the Gracchi. The story revolves around two brothers, Tiberius and Gaius. Their mother, Cornelia, was the daughter of the renowned Scipio Africanus. Cornelia's husband had fought in Spain and died in 151 B.C. Unlike most widows at the time (and there were many of them), she did not remarry, but devoted herself to her sons and educated them in the Greek tradition. Tiberius had fought bravely under Scipio the Younger at Carthage and in Spain. He was saddened by the social ills and suffering of the poor, and on becoming tribune in the year 134 B.C. he had worked toward land reform to prevent the growth of large estates and to give the peasants back their land. He met with strong opposition; during the events and disturbances that followed he was killed by his enemies and his body was thrown into the Tiber. Tragically, the leader of the gang that killed Tiberius was a member of the Scipio family, and the lenient punishment he received was to be exiled to Spain, where he remained for the rest of his life. Within this family web, Sempronia, sister of the slain Tiberius, was married to Scipio the Younger. It seems that Scipio shed no tears over the death of his brother-in-law, whom he considered a threat to the powerful families of Rome. To make matters worse, Gaius, the surviving Gracchi brother, was at the time serving under Scipio in Spain.

The year after Tiberius's assassination, Gaius returned to Rome and took up his dead brother's cause. But as he tried to push for reforms he, too, became unpopular with the leading families, and there were riots and disorder as interest groups took sides. Gaius was killed in 121 B.C., the very year that Massilia was taken into the Roman fold as a *provincia.*

The tragic heroine in this real life drama was the Gracchi's mother, Cornelia. The sons that had been her life had died as a result of their zeal to improve the lot of Rome's less fortunate citizens and right the wrongs that they saw as a threat to the Republic. This daughter of Scipio Africanus died in seclusion at a villa not far from Naples, but far from the treachery of Rome. On her tomb were inscribed these words: "Cornelia, mother of the Gracchi." Through her life and death the history of an increasingly complex and often corrupt society comes to us also as a poignant personal drama with a distinctly human face.

The First "Italia," Feuding Generals, and Civil War

The Gracchi reformers were gone, but in Rome the voices of protest grew louder, and trouble was always brewing in the wings. No one outside of Rome had any say in what was going on, and the power had gradually been usurped by a few powerful families. The Latin cities, the first to become "allies" of the Republic, still had no vote, that right having remained through the centuries the sole prerogative of the inhabitants of Rome.

The visionary Gracchi brothers had (among other reforms) also favored citizenship for the Latin cities. These Italians had been waiting for this privilege two centuries. When yet another reformer came on the scene in 91 B.C. to champion their cause—only to suffer the same fate as the Gracchi—they could wait no longer. In a bold, breakaway move, the cities formed a separate republic called Italia, and even established a capital at Corfinium (Corfinio) less than 100 miles east of Rome in what was Samnite territory. Rome was caught by surprise as these Italian cities were prepared to fight for their rights.

The task of quelling the "rebels" was in the hands of the Roman army under General Gaius Marius, who was sympathetic with the cause, but he was soon replaced by a political opponent, the ruthless Lucius Cornelius Sulla. Although many of the cities accepted a belated promise of Roman citizenship, others chose to hold out for independence. By the time the war ended three years later, the last elements of resistance, predominantly Samnites, were all but annihilated. Lost also was their Oscan language, which died with them. This was a tragic end to the first embryonic Italia, which had started life away from the protected nest of Rome.

✳ ✳ ✳

While the Romans were occupied with troubles at home, Mithradates VI, the king of Pontus, had occupied the rich and beautiful Pergamum, now Rome's province of Asia. In the reign of terror he carried out, some 80,000 Italian residents of Asia were said to have perished. Most of the Greek cities chose to abandon Rome and ally themselves with the terrible strongman.

The Roman Senate was faced with a serious dilemma because the two generals who held the power and controlled the legions did not get along. Sulla was eventually the man chosen to lead the legions against Mithradates. Gaius Marius was furious and appealed to the tribunes, whose ranks now included the new Italian citizens that had been brought into the voting process. They naturally voted for Marius to take command rather than the cruel Sulla, who had meted out such harsh punishment.

The seeds of civil war had been sown, and the events that followed are some of the most dramatic in Roman history. Two rival generals were pitted against each other like gladiators in the arena, dragging their respective armies with them. Sulla left the city, ostensibly to join the army assigned to him, but instead of proceeding to Greece he marched his army to Rome to confront Marius and his followers. Marius, unable to defend and hold the city, fled southward and eventually reached safety on a small island off the African coast.

The victorious Sulla now had sole control of the legions and quickly made his way east. For her treachery, the ancient city of Athens was ruthlessly sacked. Roman troops routed Mithradates, who conceded defeat, and a quick peace was made in 84 B.C. Although he was allowed to return to his kingdom along the Black Sea, he was stripped of his navy and forced to pay Rome a hefty indemnity.

Having completed his mission, Sulla hastened back to Rome, where a deadly political battle was raging. During his absence, Marius had been called from exile by supporters and had recaptured Rome. The holocaust that followed was terrible. The embittered seventy-year-old Marius took revenge on those who had rejected him in favor of Sulla; among the countless victims were many senators. Marius became a consul, along with Cinna, who had been one of the most instrumental in bringing about his return to power. But his new glory was short-lived—within one month he was dead. Cinna was on his own now and prepared to advance against Sulla, but he was killed in a mutiny at Ancona.

The bloody civil war visited on the Romans by power-hungry men dragged on for two years, ending in 82 B.C. Sulla became dictator of Rome and proceeded to order the execution of his enemies in the popular party, which again included some senators. In 79 B.C. at the age of sixty, Sulla quite unexpectedly stepped down and returned the reins to the Senate. As if his mission in life had been completed, he died the following year.

The two great rivals, Sulla and Marius, were now dead, but they had between them truly bled the Roman wolf. The Republic had survived, but things were never again quite the same for the Senate, henceforth at the mercy of the generals. Among those who narrowly escaped execution on Sulla's orders was an aristocrat named Gaius Julius Caesar. We will meet him a little later, but for now we might repeat the words of Sulla, who allowed this man to live: "Watch out for him."

A Slave Named Spartacus

Meanwhile, the century before the birth of Jesus proceeded with one disaster after another. In 103 B.C. there had been a slave revolt in Sicily, known as the Second Servile War, but a calamity that had been fermenting for some time involved the slaves in the peninsula. It was estimated that there were as many as two million slaves in Italy at that time, accounting for close to a third of the total population. Brought in from the various defeated lands, they were at the mercy of their masters, who had control of life and death. Some of these slaves met death in the arenas in combat with each other or with wild beasts long before it became the practice to throw the Christians to the lions.

For a long time, the Romans had trained their soldiers in the art of hand-to-hand combat, but as time passed these fights became a spectacle with the use of slaves who were trained in gladiatorial schools and then pitted against each other in a death struggle for the pure entertainment of the spectators. By this time, the Romans were hardly squeamish about blood and gore, of which they had seen plenty in their own ranks, and most cared little about the faceless slaves who were being used for this degrading and cruel sport. It should be said, of course, that not all Romans approved of these games, but the populace at large eventually came to expect such entertainment along with their daily bread.

From these times there emerged a slave named Spartacus, a name that would live on as a memorial to the gladiators and the infamy of Roman entertainment. Spartacus was from Thrace, east of Macedon. Being big and strong, he was the perfect candidate for the gladiatorial school at Capua, north of Naples. There he conceived a plan to make a break for freedom. In 73 B.C. he and seventy other slaves made their escape, initially taking refuge on Mount Vesuvius. Spartacus proved to be a capable leader and for the next two years he was able to build up an army of followers, consisting of Gauls, Germans, Italian deserters, and the like. It is believed that at one time he had an army of some 90,000 people, which, operating in the southern part of Italy, confounded the Roman armies sent to crush him. Spartacus wanted to fight his way north and to freedom across the Alps, but his men did not want to follow his plan—they believed they could continue to resist the Roman legions.

In the meantime, Rome had found the man to do the job in Marcus Licinius Crassus. No stranger to atrocities, he had lost both his father and brother at the hands of Marius and Cinna during the civil war and under Sulla had taken his revenge on innocent victims. Spartacus was fortunate to have met his death, along with thousands of others, fighting for his freedom. Many of those who managed to escape were eventually rounded up, and the fate meted out to these survivors of battle was hideous. It is said that some 6,000 of them were crucified on crosses that lined the Appian Way between Rome and Capua.

Thus, what came to be known as the Third Servile War ended in 71 B.C. after a two-year struggle. It was the last slave war as this ignoble act of Crassus and his soldiers discouraged any further uprisings. It remains indelibly written in the pages of history as one of the darker deeds of the Romans who, in the following century, would have to their credit another crucifixion of astounding impact on Western civilization.

CHAPTER FIVE

The Triumvirs

The Triumvirate—A Rule of Three

A landmark date for the Roman Republic was the year 60 B.C., when an unconstitutional three-man rule, known as a triumvirate, was established. The three protagonists who would now occupy center sage were Crassus, Pompey, and Julius Caesar.

We have already met Crassus, who distinguished himself in putting down the slave revolt. Many stories have been told about this incredibly rich man who was referred to as "Crassus Dives" (Crassus the rich), a man without scruples where money was concerned. In 70 B.C., riding the wave of popularity with the Senate, Crassus combined forces with Pompey (real name Gnaeus Pompeius), and together these protégés of the dictator Sulla became consuls.

Pompey's military success had been impressive. In 81–80 B.C. he had recovered Africa and Sicily, earning the title of Magnus (great), and a few years later he suppressed an uprising in Italy. At that time he was responsible for the execution of the father of a man named Brutus, later to take his place in history as the assassin of Julius Caesar. Pompey continued to distinguish himself after joining forces with Crassus, and in 64 B.C. he won victories against the kingdoms of Pontus, Cilicia, and Syria, which were made Roman provinces. Pompey, taking advantage of turmoil in Judea, the Jewish kingdom established by the Maccabees a century earlier, laid siege to Jerusalem. After three months, it fell to the Romans, who committed the sacrilegious act of entering the Holy Temple. Judea and the Jewish people now became vassals of Rome. The victorious Pompey finally returned home in 61 B.C. to a triumphant welcome.

The life and short career of the third man, Julius Caesar, would change the course of the history of the Greco-Roman world. His incredible life and tragic death are known to us more intimately through Shakespeare's play, based on the accounts of the Greek historian Plutarch. Born of an aristocratic family as Gaius Julius Caesar in 100 B.C., at sixteen years of age he was married to Cornelia, the daughter of Cinna, the associate of Marius, whom he greatly admired. This put him in the camp of the radicals. Sulla ordered him to divorce Cornelia, but he refused, barely escaping with his life. He left Italy to do military service in the province of Asia, returning after Sulla's death in 78 B.C. Caesar had his eye on a political career, and he went to Rhodes to study oratory—a must for politicians then as now—but he was captured by pirates and held for ransom. Caesar not only raised the ransom but also a naval force that captured the pirates, who were then crucified. Five years later he was elected *quaestore*, the first rung on the political ladder. In 61 B.C. Caesar was given the governorship of Further Spain, where as soldier and governor he carried out successful military campaigns on the northwest frontier.

Now in the historic year of 60 B.C., as a member of the newly formed triumvirate, Caesar took command of the legions in Gaul, the southern part of which was already a Roman province. Caesar completed the conquest of Gaul. Being a writer and orator of merit, Caesar himself wrote the account of his campaigns in *De Bello Gallico* [Of the War in Gaul], a unique record that not only documents his military actions but also gives some unique insights into the beliefs and ways of the tribes against whom he fought. Much of what we know about these Celtic people and their Druid priests comes through Caesar's writings, for the Gauls had no written history or literature of their own.

Caesar had been away from Rome for eight years on the campaigns in Gaul. During that time he had twice crossed the English Channel to the white cliffs, which beckoned on the other side, just twenty-two miles away. One day, that unexplored and seemingly worthless land would become part of the great Roman Empire. Back in Rome, the political strife had continued, but Caesar had secured his alliance with Pompey, to whom he had given in marriage his only daughter, the lovely Julia, but that tie was broken in 54 B.C. by her untimely death at just thirty years of age. To make matters worse, Pompey then married into a Roman family whose members were enemies of Caesar.

Pompey and Caesar became a rule of two when in 53 B.C. the triumvir Crassus was killed in battle against the Parthians in an area that is now part of Iran. Seeking new glory, Crassus had led his troops across the sands to engage in desert warfare, but the Romans were no match for the formidable forces of the Parthians with their thousands of horse archers and Arabian camels, at home in the hot and waterless desert. Crassus and his Romans met with defeat near Carrhae, now just a small village on the map of Syria. Rome lost an army of seven legions at Carrhae, where many wounded men were left to die a miserable death in an inhospitable region as others tried to flee. The end of Crassus was a tragic one, but quite in character with the savagery of the times. It is said that the Parthians had delivered to the camp of Crassus the head of his son, who had been fighting with him. Crassus himself was later killed as he attempted a truce settlement with the Parthians; one story has it that to show their contempt of this Roman general they had his head filled with molten gold, an act reminiscent of the fate of Midas. True or not, this story served as a reminder that greed has its price, and Crassus was the worst side of Rome personified.

Four years later, in 49 B.C., as the victorious Caesar made his way back to Rome, the Senate became nervous that the strongman would take over. Caesar was therefore told to disband his army before entering Rome, as Pompey had done before him, and the line was the Rubicon River, then the southern border of Cisalpine Gaul. To disobey this order amounted to a declaration of war. Caesar did cross the Rubicon with his army. The term that has come down to us — "to cross the Rubicon" — is an expression meaning to take decisive action with no turning back. It is in the dictionary as a part of our language.

Pompey had meanwhile turned against Caesar and was now the sole defender of Rome, but he had no army. He promptly left for the East, where his popularity lay, taking many senators and young aristocrats with him to be leaders, and he quickly formed an army. Caesar, meanwhile, consolidated his position in Italy, winning partisans in Rome and elsewhere. Joining Caesar in this Second Civil War that was fought at home and abroad was a survivor of the Roman political struggles, Marcus Antonius, the Mark Antony whose name would soon be associated with Cleopatra.

Events moved quickly as Caesar took off after Pompey, catching up with him in Greece and defeating him at Pharsalus, north of Athens, in June of 48 B.C. The fleeing Pompey took a ship and sailed for Egypt, still independent although her rulers were virtually puppets of Rome. Like a predator tracking down its prey, Caesar followed his rival there with a small force and was greeted by the Egyptians. Wishing to show their loyalty to Rome — or to the victor to save their own skins — they presented Caesar with the head of his enemy. Pompey had been murdered on his arrival, stabbed to death under the eyes of his wife and son, who had accompanied him there.

Caesar was nevertheless saddened by the death of this great Roman, murdered through the trickery of the Egyptians. Pompey had, after all, been the husband of Caesar's beloved daughter, Julia. Caesar was now the only man left of the Triumvirate. He could have returned to Italy at this point, but it was his destiny to meet the Egyptian queen, CLEOPATRA.

Julius Caesar

Glimpses into the incredible lives of the major players in this period have been afforded to us through music, art, and drama, but the characters have been romanticized, and the context of their existence is often nebulous. Even those of us who know little or nothing of the history of Italy are nevertheless acquainted with the names of Julius Caesar, Cleopatra, and Mark Antony. To take any one of these and follow the course of their amazing lives is to better understand the times in which they lived and the roles that destiny had assigned them.

Egypt, where the fleeing Pompey met his death and where we now follow Caesar, was ruled jointly by a thirteen-year-old king and his twenty-one-year-old sister, Cleopatra, who succeeded to the throne on the death of their father, Ptolemy XII, of a Macedonian dynasty that had ruled Egypt for 300 years. However, the real power was in the hands of a courtier who had fallen out with the headstrong Cleopatra. At the time of Caesar's arrival, she was in Syria attempting to raise an army to move against the courtier and her younger brother. With Caesar now in Alexandria, the Egyptian capital, she decided to set sail for home with the idea of winning him over to her cause. The story goes that she managed to get an audience with the great Caesar not by arriving on a magic carpet, but rolled up inside one that she had ordered to be delivered to him. Whether or not the first meeting actually took place in this way will never be known, but Cleopatra did win Caesar's heart and his support, for he was taken by her courage and intelligence.

The next few months must have been full of adventure as Caesar waited for reinforcements, managing to stay alive in a country that, previously a faithful ally, was now engaged in a bitter civil war for the succession. Cleopatra's enemies were eventually defeated, and her young brother, King Ptolemy XIII, drowned in the Nile River when the barge on which he was escaping sank. Cleopatra was placed on the throne of Egypt along with her ten-year-old younger surviving brother, Ptolemy XIV.

Mark Antony was not the first to be conquered by the charms of Cleopatra — Caesar dallied in Egypt and took her as his mistress while his wife, Calpurnia, waited back in Rome. Such conquests seem to have been as common place as winning battles, for his reputation had been well established in the many regions of his campaigns and were the subject of popular and ribald ballads of the time. Here is one recorded during the triumph in Gaul:

> Home we bring our bald whoremonger;
> Romans lock your wives away!
> All the bags of gold you lent him
> Went his Gallic tarts to pay.

(*The Twelve Caesars,* by Suetonius; trans. Robert Graves)

Caesar's love affair with the Egyptian queen was a little more serious than his normal escapades, for Cleopatra gave birth to a son known affectionately as Caesarion (Little Caesar). Caesar claimed paternity, and it seems that Cleopatra spent some time in Rome, where a villa had been set aside for her.

Caesar's stay in Rome was short, however, for in 47 B.C. he marched back into Asia Minor, where the son of Mithradates had tried to regain the lost dominions of Pontus. The campaign was so swift that Caesar reported back to Rome with the famous words: "Veni, vidi, vici" [I came, I saw, I conquered]. Following that quick victory, he was off again to deal with problems in Africa and Spain, and during his absence Mark Antony was left in charge of matters in Rome.

Having won his laurels on the battlefield, Caesar's first task was to secure the provinces. Of Caesar as a soldier the following quotes from Suetonius are revealing:

> Caesar was a most skillful swordsman and horseman, and showed surprising powers of endurance. He always led his army, more often on foot than in the saddle. . . .

> If the fight were a hard-fought one he used to send the chargers away – his own among the first – as a warning that those who feared to stand their ground need not hope to escape on horseback.

> This charger of his, an extraordinary animal with feet that looked almost human – each of its hoofs was cloven in five parts, resembling human toes – had been foaled on his private estate. When the soothsayers pronounced that its master would one day rule the world, Caesar carefully reared, and was the first to ride, the beast; nor would it allow anyone else to do so.

There was an unmistakable aura of mystique around Julius Caesar, who in October of 45 B.C. became master of the world – the Roman world – as he was made dictator for life. He was the man of the hour who proved to be more than just a lover and a soldier, but a capable administrator. Through his knowledge of the various, far-flung corners of the realm he realized that a government designed for a city was inadequate. He made it more equally representative by bringing in men from the various provinces and increasing the Senate to 900 members. Roman citizenship was granted to all the people of the peninsula, which included Cisalpine Gaul, and many beyond the borders as well, especially in Spain and Gaul.

Caesar's plans for rebuilding were grandiose, and he initiated the reconstruction of Carthage in Africa and Corinth in Greece, both of which had been destroyed by the Romans. He studied and improved the much-abused welfare system and issuing of free grain. He considered the family an important unit of society. He complained that there were far too many bachelors running around and encouraged marriage by giving tax relief to fathers. Stressing the importance of knowledge, he opened Rome's first public library.

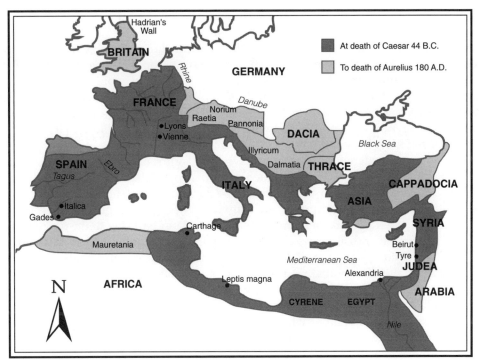

The Roman Empire

One of Caesar's most enduring innovations was introduction on January 1, 45 B.C., of a new calendar, replacing the old lunar calendar that had been followed up to that time. Caesar had observed a better system while in Egypt, and he lost no time in getting an Egyptian astronomer, Sosigenes, to devise a similar one for Rome. This became the Julian calendar, which was Caesar's gift to the world and is named in his honor. "Quintilis," the Roman month in which he was born, was renamed "Julius" to become our July.

By the new calendar, Julius Caesar was born on July 12 in the year 100 B.C. In his mid-fifties, with so many accomplishments to his credit, it seemed that he held the world in the palm of his hand. Unfortunately, his enemies were already plotting against him. On the fateful day of March 15, 44 B.C., the conspirators set upon him as he arrived at the Senate, and they cut him down like a dog. He had not heeded the warnings of a soothsayer to "beware the Ides of March" or the entreaties of his wife, Calpurnia, whose fears came through dreams of disaster. Caesar kept his date with destiny, and his end was in accordance with a wish he is quoted as having said the night before his murder: "Let it come swiftly and unexpectedly."

Among those men who shared in the assassination of Caesar was Marcus Brutus, one whose presence appears to have most surprised him as he fell under their daggers, for he was one that had been most favored and loved. This was the Marcus Brutus who had fought with Pompey in Greece at the battle of Pharsalus, was taken prisoner there, then pardoned and liberated by Caesar, who later appointed him to high office in Rome. Brutus was not alone in the assassination plot, but he has come down in history as the Judas in breach of Caesar's trust. Indeed, Caesar's last incredulous words, uttered on seeing Brutus among the assassins, were said to have been, "You, too, Brutus?"

Shock waves rippled through Rome; the political climate being what it was and conniving and treachery being the order of the day, a bloodbath was expected. Fear mounted as troops moved into Rome under Marcus Aemilius Lepidus, a general who had been loyal to Caesar. The conspirators, realizing the public sympathy for the dead Caesar, did their best to make the assassination look like a brave act to save Rome from a tyrant who, not content with the title of dictator for life, had intended to make himself king. It had been hundreds of years since the last king of Rome, Tarquin the Great, was murdered by another one who, by an uncanny coincidence, was also called Brutus, ushering in the Republic which had prevailed since then. Perhaps it was no accident that another Brutus should be their scapegoat, for it seems he had to be persuaded to join the conspiracy as a duty to Rome. At all events, the conspirators had to move carefully to save their own skins. It was in part due to the quick action of Mark Antony that disaster was averted. As a friend of Caesar, he had the courage to make a speech designed to defuse tensions and negotiate with Lepidus on behalf of the conspirators in an attempt to avoid another civil war. It was agreed that the conspirators be allowed to get out of town with all speed, and the Senate had them assigned to the provinces.

Public grief was apparent when Caesar's friends raised a funeral pyre near the tomb of his daughter, Julia. Suetonius described the funeral:

> Since a procession of mourners laying funeral gifts would have taken more than a day to file past the pyre, everyone was invited to come there by whatever route he pleased, regardless of precedence. . . . Public grief was enhanced by crowds of foreigners lamenting in their own fashion, especially Jews, who came flocking to the Forum for several nights in succession.

It was Mark Antony's turn to be the man of the hour and he was on top of the world, having gotten possession of Caesar's will, which the Senate accepted as valid. There was one point in this will that most certainly changed the course of history, and it concerned the boy who would not only become emperor but also was destined to usher in the longest period of peace in history — the PAX ROMANA. His name was Gaius Octavius, a grandson of Caesar's sister, who was also named Julia. Caesar had fathered many children, but had no legitimate living heirs following the death of his only daughter.

Octavius was a puny individual just nineteen years old and studying in Greece when he got the news. He was hardly the Roman ideal of manhood, but he had a good head and he lost no time returning to Rome, where he had the support of those loyal to Caesar. The power struggle that followed involved Mark Antony, Lepidus the general, Octavius, and the conspirators, who had everything to lose. What ensued in the year following Caesar's death was the Third Civil War where once again, backed by their respective armies, Roman general fought Roman general. General Lepidus was credited with getting Mark Antony and Octavius together in Bologna, where the three decided to join forces against the others. In November of 43 B.C. these three men formed the Second Triumvirate. The following year, the remaining conspirators were wiped out; Brutus, to avoid capture, died bravely by his own hand.

The "triumvirs," as they were called, did not rule as a threesome this time, but thought it best to rule separately and divide the territory into three parts. Lepidus got the west, Mark Antony got the east, and the sickly, twenty-year-old Octavius got the middle part with Rome. He took the illustrious-sounding name Gaius Julius Caesar Octavianus, later to be known as Augustus, the first emperor of Rome.

Antony and Cleopatra

We must leave Rome again and follow Antony to his realm in the East, where he feared the loyalty of Egypt was in question, for her bond with Rome had been broken with Caesar's death. Cleopatra's young brother had died, and she now ruled as queen with her son, Caesarion, the fruit of her liaison with Caesar.

Antony's intentions were anything but romantic when he ordered Cleopatra to meet him at Tarsus (a city in southern Turkey and the birthplace of Saint Paul) after a whole succession of letters to her produced no results. Cleopatra was now a mature woman of twenty-eight and even more wise to the ways of the world and the arrogance of Rome. It had been seven years since she had met Caesar for the first time and brought him over to her side. Now she had to deal with yet another Roman and would again have to use her superior intelligence and proverbial womanly charms as her weapons. Writing some 100 years later, here is how the Greek historian Plutarch so eloquently and romantically described the meeting between the famous lovers:

> She treated him with such disdain that when she appeared it was as if in mockery of his orders. She came sailing up the river Cyndus in a barge with a poop of gold, its purple sails billowing in the winds, while her rowers caressed the water with oars of silver which dipped in time to the music of the flute, accompanied by pipes and lutes. Cleopatra herself reclined beneath a canopy of gold cloth, dressed in the character of Venus . . . while on either side to complete the picture stood boys dressed as cupids, who cooled her with their fans. (Plutarch, *Makers of Rome*)

The description continues in fictional style and must be at least partly treated as such. But it is on this account that many centuries later Shakespeare based his play *Antony and Cleopatra*, which has immortalized the two as the greatest lovers of all time.

Suffice it to say that Mark Antony must have been dazzled in that autumn of 41 B.C., and he later follow her to the Egyptian capital of Alexandria. It was a haven for those escaping the wars and power disputes occurring elsewhere, but he was one of the leaders of the great Roman Republic, and his dallying in the court of this foreign queen gave his enemies in Rome a pretext for discrediting him in the eyes of the Roman people.

Trouble was already brewing back in Rome where Antony's wife, Fulvia, saw Octavius becoming too powerful. She even went as far as to raise a rebel force, but this was put down before Antony could come to her aid. Fulvia fled to Greece, where she died soon thereafter. However, Octavius decided to take some precautions. In the autumn of 40 B.C. he arranged for his lovely half-sister, Octavia, also recently widowed, to be married off to Mark Antony, thus creating a family alliance between the two triumvirs.

Antony spent some time in Rome, and Octavia bore two daughters, but there was trouble in the East and battles to be fought in Parthia. Antony was soon off again to defend his eastern realm, but the legions Octavius had promised did not arrive. Antony's forces, consisting of soldiers of every race and tongue, suffered terrible hardships and staggering losses through sickness and disease as well as combat.

During this fateful period Mark Antony seems to have renewed his relationship with Cleopatra, and the two met at Antioch, Syria, in 37 B.C. He had not seen Cleopatra since she had given birth to twins, Alexander Helios and Cleopatra Selene. The events that followed clearly indicated that Antony, caught between two women, had chosen Cleopatra, and he returned with her to Egypt. Octavia had been rejected and insulted, and this gave Octavius the excuse he needed to go after Mark Antony as a danger to be eliminated.

The Fourth Civil War to rock the boat of the Republic was fought at sea. Octavius got his fleet together and engaged the combined forces of Mark Antony and Cleopatra in a naval battle in the Ionian Sea, just off the southern coast of Epirus near a promontory called Actium, from which the historic and disastrous battle got its name. The combined fleets of Antony and Cleopatra were outmaneuvered by Octavius's general, Agrippa. Cleopatra and her fleet took off in a panic, leaving Mark Antony and his ships at the scene of battle. Mark Antony, so the story goes, abandoned his own loyal followers and in a small vessel took after the fleeing queen as she sailed toward Alexandria. Without their leader, many of Mark Antony's men simply went over to the other side, and the battle was lost almost before it had begun on that September day of 31 B.C. Cleopatra retreated to the temporary safety of her kingdom with her lover in hot pursuit.

Young Octavius had not given up, however, and the following year his fleets approached Egypt from two directions, entering Alexandria on the fateful day of August 1, 30 B.C. The desperate Mark Antony did the only thing possible and committed suicide. The dying man was carried to Cleopatra, who now had to look to her own survival. The days that followed were agonizing ones for Cleopatra as she buried her lover and, alone again, had to meet her own inevitable destiny. In despair, she retreated to her monument, but she needed to use that charm and persuasive powers once more for the sake of her children's safety. She was to meet yet another great Roman in the person of Octavius. The two met, but Cleopatra must have known that this soft-spoken Roman could not be charmed or trusted. She had come between Antony and this man's sister, the beautiful Octavia, and she could not be forgiven for that. Octavius would surely take her back to Rome, but not as a queen. She would be his captive and victory prize to be paraded through the streets of Rome, perhaps in chains. Cleopatra, now thirty-nine years of age, saw no other way of escape and embraced death bravely. The bite of the asp was quick and painless.

It was all over now. Caesarion, Cleopatra's son by Julius Caesar, was put to death, and so was Antyllus, Antony's oldest son by Fulvia—even the boy's tutor was crucified. Antony's widow, Octavia, mercifully took all of his remaining children from both Fulvia and Cleopatra into her household and brought them up with her own.

Egypt lost status as an independent kingdom and became another province of Rome. Most significant was the fact that in 30 B.C., with Lepidus long out of the way, the thirty-three-year-old Octavius had become the absolute ruler of all the vast Roman world. The Republic, through 500 long years of wars, conquests, and alliances, had united the lands around the Mediterranean under the control of Rome and created a vast empire. The Mediterranean had become Mare Nostrum, and in the center of it all was Rome.

CHAPTER SIX

Emperors of the Julian House

The First Emperor

Gaius Julius Caesar Octavius would be known to the world as Augustus, and the period of peace characterized by the first and second centuries of the Roman Empire was the Golden Age. It followed a century of wars, territorial expansion, and civil strife that tore Rome apart and brought about the end of the Roman Republic.

No great military man himself, Augustus had noble plans for the lands he had inherited, and he seems to have believed in the portents and omens that gave signs he had a destiny to fulfill. His contribution in terms of Western civilization cannot be disputed, and his importance as the emperor ruling at the time of Jesus's birth gives him a special place in the context of Christian civilization. This frail young man ruled for forty-five long and prosperous years and lived to be almost seventy-six years old.

To begin with, it must be said that in addition to the mystique of the name Caesar, Augustus had the support of the faithful legions he had inherited from his great uncle Julius Caesar, and he treated the soldiers well, adequately compensating them for their loyalty. He ordered some twenty-eight new farming towns to be established in Italy for veterans. The countryside, no longer plundered and neglected as it had been previously, flourished as marshes were drained and the hillsides planted with vine and olive and fig trees.

In addition to the loyalty of his army, Augustus knew that to survive in office he needed the support of the Senate, and the question of his title became a delicate issue. He took the title of *princeps,* meaning "first man," thus avoiding the odious king label. In theory, the Senate retained the power it had held during the Republic. He reduced the number of senators, which Caesar had previously increased, and helped worthy men get elected in an endeavor to eradicate corruption and graft.

The title of "Augustus" was not conferred on Octavius until 27 B.C. It is the name by which he is usually known in history and to which are credited the accomplishments of his rule, which were considerable. He spent much time organizing the vast domains, stabilizing the Empire, and putting a sound administrative structure into place. At this point the Roman world was divided into new territories and of significance to senatorial Italy was its division into eleven regions. These included Sicily, but Sardinia and Corsica were considered imperial provinces. After conquering lands up to the Rhine and Danube rivers, he desired to make no further conquests, but rather to stabilize the frontiers of existing territories. Three legions had been lost in Germany, and the line dividing the Teutonic tribes from the Roman Empire was pulled back to the Rhine. The border established then corresponds largely to the frontier between France and Germany to this day. This was

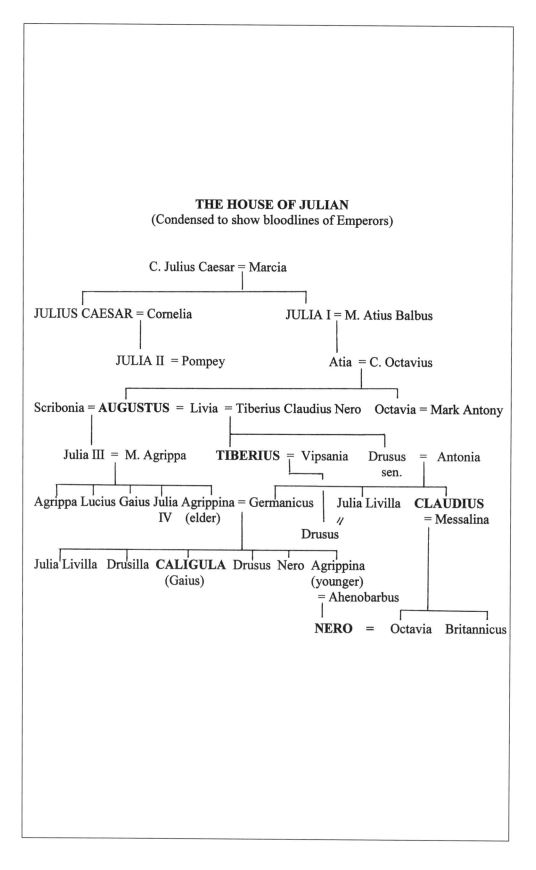

THE HOUSE OF JULIAN
(Condensed to show bloodlines of Emperors)

C. Julius Caesar = Marcia

JULIUS CAESAR = Cornelia   JULIA I = M. Atius Balbus

JULIA II = Pompey   Atia = C. Octavius

Scribonia = **AUGUSTUS** = Livia = Tiberius Claudius Nero   Octavia = Mark Antony

Julia III = M. Agrippa   **TIBERIUS** = Vipsania   Drusus = Antonia
                                                                          sen.

Agrippa Lucius Gaius Julia Agrippina = Germanicus   Julia Livilla   **CLAUDIUS**
                    IV   (elder)   //   = Messalina
                                                           Drusus

Julia Livilla Drusilla **CALIGULA** Drusus Nero Agrippina
                       (Gaius)   (younger)
                                               = Ahenobarbus

                              NERO = Octavia   Britannicus

the limit of Latin influence in Europe, and the spread of Roman culture and language stopped there.

Augustus spent nearly three years in both Spain and France, and these provinces benefited enormously from the building of roads, aqueducts, and other structures. Veterans' colonies served as centers for the process of Romanization and would later become important cities. At these places, extensive building was undertaken; some of the most remarkable feats of Roman engineering (with the help of Greek architects) are found in southern France. The Roman city of Nimes still boasts a well-preserved arena and theater, and the Pont du Gard, over the deep valley of the Gard River, is nothing short of a miracle that 2,000 years have not diminished.

In Rome, too, major building projects were undertaken now that the government was no longer preoccupied with conquest and war. Slums were cleared, and housing for the poor was built. The Tiber was dredged and cleaned of debris; aqueducts were repaired and improved; streets were widened and road building continued; and public baths were built and made free for all to enjoy. New buildings went up that were more in keeping with the tone of an imperial city as glistening white marble from Tuscany replaced or covered the dull brick and concrete of the days of the Republic. Augustus had certainly been inspired by the splendor of Alexandria, where he had seen colored marbles, fine cloth, and exotic produce from the Nile valley.

Augustus knew well the danger of a restless and idle army, and he reduced the number of legions from sixty to twenty-six, using the remaining forces for public works, maintaining the frontiers, and keeping the peace. Local inhabitants were incorporated into these forces, and the process of Romanization was further advanced as many soldiers married local women. Governors were more carefully chosen. No longer allowed to plunder or accept graft, they were paid fixed salaries and held responsible for keeping records and reporting taxes.

One of the initiatives by which Augustus wished to be remembered was the census. During his rule, a census was ordered three times, in 28 B.C., 8 B.C., and again in A.D. 14. These dates are recorded on his mausoleum, and the census that took place in Judea, a client-kingdom ruled by King Herod, was most likely in compliance with the order of 8 B.C. The record of this is found in Luke 2:1–5:

> In those days an order went out from Caesar Augustus that a census should be taken of the whole world. This registration first occurred while Quirinius was governor of Syria.
>
> They all went to be registered, each to his own city, and Joseph, too, went up from Galilee out of the city of Nazareth to Judea, to the city of David called Bethlehem, because he was of the house and family of David, to be registered with Mary, his betrothed wife, whose pregnancy was advanced.

By the issue of this decree, Augustus played a role in the first act of the Christmas story, whereas his successor would be present in the last and more tragic one.

Augustus had the good fortune throughout his rule to have at his side a strong and intelligent woman in the person of his third wife, Livia Drusilla. This union was much criticized at the time by his associate Mark Antony, as Augustus had "dragged" Livia from her husband while she was pregnant with a second child. Her firstborn, Tiberius, was eventually legally adopted and became emperor. Livia was nineteen and Augustus twenty-five years old when they married, and their union lasted for fifty-two years, ending only at Augustus's death, for he loved Livia and was a devoted husband.

It must be said, however, that Augustus was less successful in his private than in his public life. To begin with, there was no offspring from his marriage with Livia. His only child was Julia, born from a previous and short-lived marriage to Scribonia. Julia was married to the loyal and capable general Agrippa, and there were five children born from this union. The two sons who would have been the natural heirs both died in their youth. Here is what the historian Tacitus had to say about these untimely deaths:

> "After Agrippa had died, first Lucius Caesar and then Gaius Caesar met premature natural deaths — unless their stepmother Livia had a secret hand in them. Lucius died on his way to the armies in Spain, Gaius while returning from Armenia incapacitated by a wound."

The possibility that these two grandsons of Augustus did not die natural deaths cannot be discounted in view of the rivalry that must have existed in the household. It included Augustus's sister, Octavia, with her own children, not to mention the brood of orphans already mentioned that she had taken under her wing. In addition, Augustus took in as hostages the children of defeated leaders of other realms to be brought up and educated along with the rest. It was a way of ensuring good behavior on the part of defeated rulers and also of Romanizing the conquered peoples.

Augustus died in A.D. 14 in the Roman month called Sextilis, renamed Augustus in his honor. The people mourned him as a father and feared that his passing would throw the world into chaos. But the succession was assured in Augustus's chosen heir, his stepson Tiberius.

The Emperor Tiberius

Tiberius was quite unlike his stepfather in whose shadow he had walked from an early age. Standing some six feet, four inches tall, he must have dwarfed the Emperor, whom he often accompanied in the early years. Tiberius was essentially a military man, and it was in his campaigns that he distinguished himself. He had fought the Parthians in the east and was credited with having installed a pro-Roman king in Armenia. In 16 B.C. he was governor of Gaul, and in 8 B.C. he took command in Germany, where his only brother, Drusus, had died the year before. As already mentioned, Augustus did not extend the frontiers of the Roman Empire, but the business of subduing the Teutonic tribes was viewed as a triumph for Tiberius. It is said that he took as many as 40,000 prisoners and settled them in Gaul. Nevertheless, he was not entirely new to politics when he became emperor — he had previously held high offices, even under the legal age, as *quaestor*, *praetor*, and consul.

Tiberius was certainly helped along in his career by the machinations of his mother, Livia, but he was also used by his stepfather, Augustus, who forced him to divorce the wife he loved and marry Augustus's daughter, Julia, widowed with five children on the death of Agrippa in 11 B.C. Tiberius had no love for Julia, and he pined for his previous wife, whom he was forbidden even to see. Such an unhappy union was no doubt the cause of Julia's adultery, for which she was later banished by her unforgiving father.

In 7 B.C., Augustus offered Tiberius a command in the East with the power of tribune, but he had fallen out with the Emperor, who was now both stepfather and father-in-law. He chose instead to retire to the island of Rhodes, where he remained for the next seven years. He temporarily escaped the politics of Rome involving his public life and family intrigues. Tiberius enjoyed Greek literature, spoke the Greek language fluently, and kept out of sight. He might well have slipped away into obscurity, but tragedy in the Emperor's family with the death of his two grandsons, Lucius in A.D. 2 and Gaius just two years later, saw him catapulted back into the limelight. In A.D. 4 Tiberius was legally adopted by Augustus as his son and heir, the only surviving grandson and child of Julia, Agrippa Posthumus, having been disowned along with his mother. When Augustus died on August 19, A.D. 14 Tiberius, who had already been administering the provinces as an equal with the aging Emperor, took over the reins as his successor.

Although the Roman Empire remained intact during the twenty-three years that Tiberius was Emperor, a glimpse into this man's private life and the environment of his time fully demonstrate the decay that was eating away at Roman society. The persecution of family members is beyond comprehension in its savagery as one after another was eliminated. By the time Tiberius was finished with the purge, only a handful remained of the large Julian House.

Augustus's surviving grandson and possible rival, Agrippa Posthumus, was promptly executed in A.D. 14. Germanicus, a nephew of Tiberius and child of his only brother, the deceased Drusus, died in Syria in A.D. 19, apparently poisoned, and the death was popularly attributed to the intrigues of Tiberius. Of the dying Germanicus, the historian Tacitus wrote:

> Turning to his wife, Germanicus begged her – by memories of himself and by their children – to forget her pride, submit to cruel fortune, and, back in Rome, to avoid provoking those stronger than herself by competing for their power. That was his public utterance. Privately he said more – warning her of danger (so it was said) from Tiberius.

Germanicus's body was exposed in the square at Antioch, and after the cremation the grieving Agrippina took his ashes back to Rome, where she made no secret of her suspicions.

In A.D. 23 Tiberius's own son died, and this was followed by more killings and persecution of Augustus's family. In A.D. 29 Agrippina and her son Nero (not the infamous one) were arrested, and Nero was executed the following year. Meanwhile, Drusus junior, another son of Agrippina, had been put in prison, where he died. Agrippina ended her life in A.D. 33 by starving herself to death. A man called Sejanus, prefect of the Praetorian guard, was the purported instigator of these acts and was put to death, although the killings did not end there. Many prominent Romans were executed between A.D. 36 and 37 in a whole series of executions.

In A.D. 26 Tiberius left Rome to again find seclusion on an island. This time his place of retreat was the lovely island of Capri in the Bay of Naples from which he ruled the vast Empire and issued his instructions. He built himself a palace on a high promontory with a sheer drop to the sea below. The site is reached by a steep, winding path and remains of the palace's foundations may still be seen today. In the sea below are underwater walls which, according to local legend, contained the bodies of prisoners who were hurled from the high point to certain death among the moray eels, frightening creatures that still lurk in the waters of the Mediterranean.

While Tiberius ruled the Empire from his high cliff, an event took place in Judea that would one day make Rome the center of a different kind of capital. Roman-

Jewish relations had degenerated, and now came a threat to the Emperor in the person of a messiah who it was reported claimed to be King of the Jews. The Roman prefect of Judea, Pontius Pilate, was the one who passed the death sentence on Jesus in A.D. 33, but according to the gospel of Matthew (27:19 and 26) he did this unwillingly and perhaps fearing the wrath of Tiberius if he did not maintain order.

> *While he was seated on the tribunal, his wife sent him a message that said, "Have nothing to do with that innocent man, for I suffered a great deal today in a dream because of Him."*

> *When Pilate saw that he was accomplishing nothing, but that instead a riot was brewing, he took water and washed his hands before the crowd, saying, "I am innocent of the blood of this man; you yourselves see to it."*

Pilate was later called to Rome to defend himself on another matter, and it is thought that he committed suicide in A.D. 37. Suicide had become an honorable end for many of those who feared execution, and there seemed no end to the reign of terror. Here is how one prominent Roman put it prophetically before opening his own veins:

> *"Certainly I might survive the few days until Tiberius dies. But in that case, how can I avoid the young emperor ahead? If Tiberius, in spite of all his experience, has been transformed and deranged by absolute power, will Gaius do better? Almost a boy, wholly ignorant, with a criminal upbringing. . . . I foresee even grimmer slavery ahead. So from evils past, and evils to come, I am escaping." He then opened his veins. (Quoted from Tacitus)*

The feared and hated Tiberius lived to be an old man—he was in his seventy-eighth year when he died on March 16, A.D. 37. It is said that the people in Rome jumped for joy, shouting, "To the Tiber with Tiberius!" However, the joy expressed on his death was mitigated by the fear with which many citizens approached the advent of the new emperor.

With these public forebodings the young Gaius—handsome, intelligent, and well-educated—became emperor at the age of twenty-five. Named Gaius Caesar Germanicus, he is known as Caligula, a nickname meaning "little boot" which he was given by the soldiers of his father, Germanicus. He was one of the unfortunate Agrippina's six children and the only male to survive. Caligula was devoted to his sisters, to whom he must have clung like a frightened little boy in a terrifying world. His particular attachment to Drusilla was thought to have been incestuous, and when she died in A.D. 38 he made her a goddess.

There is little to distinguish Caligula as an emperor, and he has come down through history as an unnatural monster, capable of excessive cruelty and feared by those around him lest his whim should target them for some untimely fate. He was no doubt mentally deranged and suffered from paranoia, a condition that worsened following a serious illness shortly after he became emperor. This troubled young man's end came on January 24, A.D. 41, when he was murdered at the Palatine games by a tribune of his own guards as the result of a conspiracy.

During Caligula's mere four years as emperor, the Roman Empire had not gained or lost anything. Now it was the turn of yet another to emerge from the deadly web of the Julian House. Uncle Claudius, the stutterer, who had limped his way through the mire as a silent and astute observer, was now dragged on stage to play the leading role in the act that followed.

Claudius: The Stuttering Emperor

Claudius was a survivor, and the fact the he became the most powerful man in the known world was nothing short of a miracle. He was fifty-one years old when, in A.D. 41, almost by accident, the terrible burden of power was forced on him to replace his youthful predecessor. Claudius had grown up in a family where he was scorned even by his own grandmother. Born in Lugdunum, now the French town of Lyons, his paternity was in doubt. In addition he was sickly and dull-witted. His mother called him "a monster: a man whom Nature had not finished but had merely begun," and he was the subject of numerous letters written by grandmother Livia to Emperor Augustus discussing what to do about him because he was considered unfit for public life. Imagine the surprise of Livia when she received a letter from Augustus on the subject of Claudius in the following terms:

> *My dear Livia,*
>
> *I'll be damned if your grandson Tiberius Claudius hasn't given me a very pleasant surprise! How on earth anyone who talks so confusedly can nevertheless speak in public with such clearness, saying all that needs to be said, I simply do not understand.* (Suetonius, *The Twelve Caesars*)

Claudius's private adult life was no less tempestuous and unsatisfactory than his early years. The story of the four women he married reads more like fiction than reality, and it is easy to lose sight of the man himself and even more so the emperor. He divorced the first two wives, but the last two were powerful and scheming, backed by their own supporters and favorites. Messalina, his third wife, gave him two children, but was later executed on his orders. His last wife, his niece Agrippina, was most likely his own murderer. The Claudius of the imperial "closet" became the husband of choice for power seekers once he had been elevated to the position of "first man."

The dramatic intrigues involving women form a backdrop to Claudius's public life and, some believe, account for many of his most brutal and seemingly uncharacteristic actions against individuals, including members of his own family, if indeed he was responsible for them.

Against all expectations, Claudius turned out to be a forceful leader and competent administrator, unlike a puppet that the Senate had expected. He was able to institute changes and take actions that not only made a difference in his own time but also altered the course of history.

Many problems had to be dealt with involving the various groupings of society and government. The disparity between rich and poor was enormous and growing worse. The urban poor—the Roman mob—in particular always constituted a factor to be reckoned with, and filling stomachs was a matter to be taken very seriously as food shortages could result in riots and bring a man down. Rome had developed the grain-growing areas of Egypt and North Africa, neglecting the Italian farmers who, it was said, could have provided all the needs of Rome and Italy. However, drought and earthquakes had created shortages at this particular time, and reliance had to be placed on shipments from abroad. The merchants were encouraged by insurances to take risks and brave the rough and unpredictable waters of the vast Mediterranean to ensure Rome's supply of grain, which arrived at the port of Ostia, just fifteen miles southwest of the capital. Out of this concern grew one of Claudius's main projects—the building of the harbor at Ostia, in which he took a particular and personal interest.

Today, excavations reveal a civilization there that boasted a sophisticated sanitation system, shops, club houses, and Roman baths, testifying to the importance of this city, which is said to have had a population of something like 100,000.

In addition to being fed, the people also had to be entertained, and this was done on a grandiose scale during this period and included, of course, gladiatorial contests and chariot races that had become an essential part of Roman life. Claudius also added the attraction of sea battles staged on artificial lakes. Slaves and prisoners took part in these events, and there was considerable loss of life, but the spectacle of death had long since come to be regarded as a form of entertainment in Rome, if not in Italy as a whole. If the accounts of Suetonius are to be given credence, Claudius himself took unnatural delight in closely observing the agonies of tortured and dying men.

One problem that Claudius had been called on to address was that of litigation. With so many adversary parties, the advocates stood to gain handsomely. As the historian Tacitus states, "The most readily purchasable commodity on the market was an advocate's treachery." Augustus had revived a law dating back to 204 B.C. called the Cincian law, which forbade the acceptance of money or even gifts for legal advice and services, and senators now asked that it be enforced. After a prominent and respected individual had taken his life as a result of treachery, one orator is quoted as saying, *"If no one paid a fee for lawsuits, there would be less of them! As it is, feuds, charges, malevolence, and slander are encouraged, for just as physical illness brings revenue to doctors, so a diseased legal system enriches advocate. . . ."* (Tacitus, *The Annals of Imperial Rome*). The senator then went on to praise the great orators whose only reward had been fame. After discussion, Claudius decided to establish a maximum fee; those exceeding this maximum would be guilty of extortion.

Part of Claudius's legacy in the field of administration was the introduction of ministries. He created departments of law, finance, records, and justice. As a kind of balance of power, he nominated as heads of these departments educated freedmen who may be compared to permanent undersecretaries. This did not sit well with the Roman aristocracy, among whom he had already made enemies.

Another serious problem involved the composition of the Senate. Claudius fought for representation from the provinces, and for the first time men from Gaul were appointed to the Senate as equals with Roman citizens of Italy. The emperor had made an eloquent speech to the Senate whose members had opposed the move, one of whom is quoted as saying: *"Do we have to import foreigners in hordes, like groups of prisoners, and leave no careers for our surviving aristocracy?"* and, *"Italy is not so decayed that it cannot provide her own capital with a Senate."*

To this Claudius replied, *"What proved fatal to Sparta and Athens, for all their military strength was the segregation of conquered subjects and aliens. . . ."* (Tacitus). The Senate approved his speech and the first Gauls joined its ranks.

The legions, however, were still an important peacekeeping force whose energies had to be used. In Germany, where the fluid frontiers were now west of the Rhine River, the twenty-three-mile Meuse-Rhine canal was dug. Something had to be done with the four legions Caligula had raised to go into Britain, the one conquest that might have been to his credit if he had lived longer. Claudius decided to use these legions for their intended purpose.

The invasion of Britain began in A.D. 43 and had far-reaching consequences on Western civilization. In Gaul, the Greco-Roman culture had met the Celtic-Druid one, eventually creating a new blend, and this was also the case in Britain. The

Romanization that had occurred in Gaul had to some degree spread on the other side of the channel, which made the conquest of southern Britain somewhat easier. No great battles were fought. Claudius was there at the capture of the city of Camulodunum (Colchester), which later became the capital.

Rome's presence in Britain lasted for four centuries. During that time the land was transformed from a collection of savage tribes to an organized province with roads, cities, and palatial dwellings with works of art, the remnants of which are still extant. Today, still more are being unearthed all over Britain.

Such were the accomplishments of Claudius, but there was another legacy that the world remembers with horror. This was a person and his name was Nero, a product of the viper's nest that was the Julian House. How did this come about?

If bloodline had become one of the criteria for being "the first man," then Claudius should have chosen his own son, Britannicus, the fruit of his marriage with Messalina. But the young Messalina—whose relationship with her slobbering, handicapped husband must have been tedious at best—had a series of lovers. She even committed the ultimate crime of brazenly going through a marriage ceremony with one of them while Claudius was busy with a project at the port of Ostia. Messalina, still just a young girl of twenty-six, was promptly executed. Octavia and Britannicus, her two children by Claudius, were soon to be introduced to a stepmother when Claudius married his brother's daughter. Such a union was incestuous and illegal, but the law was quickly changed and in A.D. 49 Claudius married his niece, Agrippina the Younger.

Agrippina was a survivor of many horrors and was not new to the world of killings and intrigues, some of which she had a hand in herself. She was even accused of poisoning her second husband. Claudius was no match for her scheming, and she persuaded him to choose Nero as his successor over his own son, Britannicus. Could the observant Claudius have been so shortsighted or so lacking in paternal instinct that he rejected his own blood? Here is a passage from Suetonius's *The Twelve Caesars* that might suggest the contrary:

> In his last years Claudius made it pretty plain that he repented of having married Agrippina and adopted Nero. For example, when his freedmen congratulated him on having found a certain woman guilty of adultery, he remarked that he himself seemed fated to marry wives who "were unchaste and remained unchastened"; and presently, meeting Britannicus, embraced him with deep affection. "Grow up quickly, my boy," he said, "and I will then explain what my policy has been." With that he quoted in Greek from the tale of Telephus and Achilles: THE HAND THAT WOUNDED YOU SHALL ALSO HEAL, and declared his intention of letting Britannicus come of age because although immature, he was tall enough to wear the toga of manhood; adding "which will at last provide Rome with a true-born Caesar."

The ambitious Agrippina put an end to Claudius by poisoning him with some mushrooms at a banquet. He died in his sixty-fourth year on October 13, A.D. 54 after a reign of thirteen years. He was not followed by a true-born Caesar, but by the terrible teenager NERO.

Nero: The Last of the Julian House

Of all the Roman emperors, Nero is the one that has lived on in history as perhaps the most infamous and has been represented as the perpetrator of the most monstrous and unnatural acts. Three things are associated with his rule in the popular mind: the murder of his mother, the ruthless persecution of the Christians, and the burning of Rome, although most historians conclude that he was not guilty of the latter.

Nero was just a boy of seventeen when he suddenly succeeded his stepfather as "first man" in A.D. 54, propped up by his ambitious mother, a host of supporters, and his counselors, Burrus and Seneca. His mother had taken steps to prepare her son for the role he was to play for she had previously recalled Seneca, the renowned orator, from exile, and he became Nero's tutor. Here was a man who wrote a famous treatise on clemency and whose influence on the young mind should have been considerable. Ironically, clemency seems to have been one of the qualities that Nero lacked most.

At first, however, Nero was apparently not a bloodthirsty man. It is said that he disliked having to sign death sentences. He did not enjoy blood sports, but preferred music and poetry, even fancying himself an actor. In the beginning, the young emperor was hardly burdened with the cares of government. These were taken care of by his mother and his counselors, Burrus, and Seneca, who virtually held the reins while he played around.

There was one matter to be settled right away, however, and this was the threat posed by Britannicus, the true heir of Claudius by bloodline. Nero had no qualms about getting rid of his rival, a mere boy of fifteen and just three years his junior, for there was no love between the two. In A.D. 55, the year after he became emperor, he arranged for poor Britannicus to be poisoned at a banquet before his very eyes.

The meddling mother, Agrippina, was soon forced into retirement along with her lover, with whom she was thought to be scheming against her own son. For a while, just the counselors ran the government, but as their influence waned and Nero became more independent, his behavior deteriorated. He used his power simply to gratify his worst desires and vices. Nero was married at age sixteen to the young and beautiful Octavia, the sister of Britannicus, a marriage designed to strengthen his position as heir, but he came under the influence of a lady named Poppaea, another man's wife, and his mother's interference in his personal life caused Nero to take care of her permanently by having her murdered.

He used his old tutor, Seneca, to justify the dreadful act of matricide that occurred in A.D. 59 by having mother Agrippina declared a traitor. The graffiti that appeared on the walls of Rome bespeak Nero's reputation and public image. Here are some examples that were recorded by the ancient historian Suetonius:

> *Alcamaeon, Orestes, and Nero are brothers,*
> *Why? Because all of them murdered their mothers.*

> *Aeneas the Trojan hero*
> *Carried off his aged father;*
> *His remote descendant Nero*
> *Likewise carried off his mother.*

Seneca, having failed miserably to influence his pupil, retired in A.D. 62. Now, with no one left to tell him what to do, Nero proceeded to divorce the childless Octavia to marry the scheming Poppaea. Not satisfied with banishment, Poppaea demanded Octavia's death. Nero called on a certain fleet commander called Anicetus and "reminded him of his previous job" on the mother. This time, however, he merely had to "confess" to adultery with Octavia, which he did on threat of death. The helpless Octavia was ordered to take her own life, but the word spread that she had been forcibly bound and all her veins opened. Nero had rid himself of all of his family. No one was safe from the monster.

The great event of Nero's time and one with which he is now most often associated is the burning of Rome in A.D. 64. This devastating disaster was described by Tacitus (a boy of seven or eight years at the time) in his *Annals*. He also points out that the fire started on July 19, the anniversary of the burning and capture of the city by the Gauls in 390 B.C. Since then, 418 years, 418 months, and 418 days had passed. Tacitus's historical account and vivid description in his *Annals* reads in part as follows:

> *"Whether it was accidental or caused by a criminal act on the part of the emperor is uncertain — both versions have supporters. Now started the most terrible and destructive fire which Rome had ever experienced. It began in the Circus, where it adjoins the Palatine and Caelian hills. Breaking out in shops selling inflammable goods, and fanned by the wind, the conflagration instantly grew and swept the whole length of the Circus. There were no walled mansions or temples, or any other obstructions, which could arrest it. First, the fire swept violently over the level spaces, then it climbed the hills — but returned to ravage the lower ground again. . . . The ancient city's narrow winding streets and irregular blocks encouraged its progress.*
>
> *Nobody dared to fight the flames. Attempts to do so were prevented by menacing gangs. Torches, too, were openly thrown in, by men crying that they acted under orders. Perhaps they had received orders. Or they may just have wanted to plunder unhampered."*

Nero was banqueting at Antium, outside of Rome, when the fire started, but rushed back to the city to observe and then battle the inferno. As an artist reacting to this devastating scene, he may well have played his lyre as the legend goes while he watched the progress of the flames that finally engulfed even his own palace.

Whatever the cause of the fire, Rome had been virtually destroyed. Only four districts out of the fourteen remained unharmed; the rest were largely leveled or reduced to ruins. Nero proceeded to provide food and shelter for the survivors, but the end result was taxation imposed on the provinces, so all were victims in some way.

By this time, Nero had fallen too low in public esteem for any act of charity to be of help. He was blamed for the fire, and he looked around for a scapegoat. The Rome that had tolerated all kinds of religions and allowed everyone to worship as he or she pleased, the Rome which boasted a pantheon of gods of her own, was now threatened by a "sect" that was following the teachings of Jesus and Paul. These followers recognized only one god to the exclusion of all others. The threat to the Roman Empire that had begun in Judea had spread like a disease to the very heart of the Empire. Nero seized on the Christians to take the blame, and so began the persecution of these people that would continue into the next two centuries.

Rome, however, would eventually rise from the ashes like a phoenix, more glorious than before. A beautiful city would take shape in accordance with a plan that called for broad streets and solid buildings, their heights restricted and the fronts protected by colonnades. The water supply would be increased, fire-fighting equipment would be provided, and the walls of houses would be of massive, untimbered stone. Work proceeded fast, and bonuses were promised to those who completed building before a given date. A planned city emerged, thanks to Nero and his vision, but the most luxurious of all was being undertaken in the building of the

Golden Palace and its extensive grounds for himself. Once again, Tacitus has provided us with a record of the graffiti:

> *Though Nero may pluck the chords of a lyre,*
> *And the Parthian King the string of a bow,*
> *He who chants to the lyre with heavenly fire*
> *Is Apollo as much as his far-darting foe.*
>
> *The palace is spreading and swallowing Rome.*
> *Let us flee to Veii and make it our home.*
> *Yet the palace is growing so damnably fast*
> *That it threatens to gobble up Veii at last.*

[Veii was the former Etruscan city twenty miles outside Rome]

The bad deeds of the man outweighed the accomplishments of the emperor. A previous attempt to remove him had failed miserably and many senators, along with the man they had championed as their leader, Gaius Calpurnius Piso, had been put to death or committed suicide. The conspirators turned on each other to save their own skins, and in the bloodbath that followed one of the victims was Nero's former tutor and counselor, Seneca.

But enough was enough and now it was time to stop this man. Help came from the provinces in the form of a revolt, and with the backing of legions the Senate moved to support Galba, a man that Nero had appointed governor of Nearer Spain and who had the support of his legions. Nero fled to a villa outside Rome and with the help of a slave he died an infamous death on the ninth day of June, A.D. 68. Was it by some strange coincidence that, according to Suetonius, it was the anniversary of the death of his wife, Octavia?

Nero was only thirty-one when he died, but during his short life he succeeded in leaving his mark on the pages of history as a monster, his accomplishments long since forgotten.

With the death of Nero, the Julian House, which had ruled a great empire for ninety-eight years, had finally come to an end.

CHAPTER SEVEN

Great Emperors and Expansion of the Empire

The Flavian Dynasty

The year following Nero's death is known as "The year of the Four Emperors." The sequence of events brought into sharp focus the problems of succession, and the Roman Empire seemed doomed to disintegrate as her generals vied for the seat of "first man."

First on the scene was the seventy-year-old Galba, who had the support of the legions and the blessing of the Senate. His rule was short, for he was soon slain by the praetorian guards, at the instigation of the ambitious Otho, who briefly claimed the first seat. He in turn was challenged when the legions of the Rhine claimed their commander, Vitellius, as emperor. In April, the opposing legions clashed at Cremona, the defeated Otho committed suicide, and the victorious Vitellius entered Rome in July.

There was yet another man waiting in the wings. Vespasian was holding the trump card inasmuch as he was in control of the Egyptian grain on which Rome depended. He had favored a bloodless takeover by withholding grain supplies and depriving the Roman belly of bread. However, his legions had taken matters into their own hands and, on acclaiming him emperor in July, were soon joined by those from Judea and the region of the Danube. They swept into Rome as victors at the end of December and went in search of Vitellius, who was found hiding in the palace. His end was worse than Otho's—he was dragged half-naked through the streets of Rome to the Forum, then tortured, brutally killed, and his dead body thrown into the Tiber River. The game of the legions was finally over, and Vespasian was proclaimed Emperor by the Senate.

The Empire was saved because the reins had been snatched from the decadent aristocracy and placed in the hands of a man of more humble origin, the bourgeoisie of rural Italy. Born in Reate (Rieti), where valleys meet at the geographical center of Italy, Vespasian (Titus Flavius Vespasianus) was the son of a tax collector assigned to Asia, a man whose honesty was beyond reproach. With the background of a strong moral upbringing, Vespasian would bring back the old ways of modesty and simplicity that had been Roman pride and strength.

Vespasian was the man for the times, for he was acquainted with the far-flung reaches of the Empire as well as the diversity of its people. He had distinguished himself in Claudius's invasion of Britain in A.D. 43, he had been proconsul in Africa in A.D. 63, and three years later Nero had assigned him as special commander to put down the revolt in Judea. Unlike his predecessors, whose many wives created political havoc, Vespasian came to power as a widower with three children, and he never remarried.

Vespasian brought back stability and order at home and protected the frontiers of the Empire, but he also engaged in extensive building programs. One of his most visible legacies is the Colosseum, designed to accommodate the enormous crowds that had come to expect entertainment as their right. Massive and imposing, it still stands as a landmark in place and time. It bespeaks the glory of Rome as well as the darker side of its society and is most readily associated with persecution of the Christians, which began in Nero's time. Built between A.D. 72 and 80 on a site that was the lake in the grounds of Nero's luxurious Golden Palace, it stands 813 feet high on six acres of land. An enormous jewel in its day consisting of concrete, travertine, and precious marble, it could accommodate some 50,000 spectators and be cleared within minutes by its eighty entrances. Known as the Flavian Amphitheater, the Colosseum was actually inaugurated in A.D. 80 by Vespasian's son, Titus. A poem addressed to Titus by Marcus Valerius Martialis (Martial), a poet and epigrammist of the time, seems to give the Colosseum the symbolic value of centerpiece of the Empire. It reads:

> What nation is so remote, Emperor, or so barbarous that someone hasn't come from it to watch the games in your city? There are farmers from the Balkans here, natives from southern Russia bred on horse's blood, people who drink the Nile's waters, and even those from far away Britain. Arabs, people from the shores of the Red Sea, as well as those from southern Turkey, have hurried here and German tribesmen and Ethiopians each with their own peculiar hairstyles.

Known as the Flavian amphitheatre, construction of the Colosseum was initiated in 72 A.D. by Vespasian. It was inaugurated in 80 A.D. by his son, Titus.

A young tourist gives perspective to the massive walls towering behind her as she peers down at the dark passages that ran below the stage.

Through the words of this poet we begin to understand the diversity of races, backgrounds, styles, and of course language that made up the Roman Empire.

Close by the Colosseum and like a sentinel stands the arch of Titus, commemorating his success in putting down the revolt in Judea, a task that his father had left him to complete when he was called to become emperor. In a sense it is ironic that these two massive monuments, so close in time and space, in different ways symbolize actions that were carried out against two religions, Judaism and Christianity, both of which were a threat to Rome inasmuch as they were monotheistic and therefore did not recognize the official religion of Rome, still less the divinity of the Emperor.

Vespasian ruled for only a decade, and during this time he proved to be a very capable administrator. When he died on June 23, A.D. 79, the transfer of power to his son, Titus, was a matter of course.

Titus (Titus Flavius Vespasianus) had been a close colleague of his father, groomed by him for the succession. He was considered a kind-hearted man, and he certainly had ample occasion to show this side of his character during his short rule, which was plagued by a series of natural catastrophes. There had been another fire in Rome, and it had lasted for three days and nights. Titus had done his best to help the victims by using money from his own purse. Then there was a deadly outbreak of the plague. Titus made every attempt to check its spread by searching for medical remedies, as well as sacrifices to the gods. His edicts at the time attest to his caring nature, and the historian Suetonius said of him that "it resembled the deep love of father for his children."

By far the greatest disaster that Titus had to confront, however, occurred just two months after he became emperor—the devastating and sudden eruption of Mount Vesuvius, which entombed the cities of Pompeii and Herculaneum. The site of Pompeii had been inhabited by the Oscans in ancient times, but had later come under the influence of the Greeks, and by the first century B.C. was a Roman colony. Because of its scenic location overlooking the Bay of Naples and the mild climate of southern Italy, it had become a favorite resort for rich Romans. Pompeii was built on a promontory created by a lava flow from Vesuvius, but the volcano had long since been considered dormant. There had been earthquakes in A.D. 62, causing considerable damage and destroying buildings, but reconstruction was rapid in this favorite place and it was more beautiful than ever. Disaster struck on August 24, A.D. 79, when the mountain exploded with a force that sent ash and pumice miles up into the summer sky to rain down on the cities below. In darkness, Pompeii was entombed under debris that solidified to form a crust of volcanic ash. The lost city was forgotten, and life resumed around the base of the killer volcano whose shape had been changed by the explosion. Sixteen hundred years passed before Pompeii was rediscovered. It was by accident that an architect named Fontana made the discovery when he broke through the crust of volcanic ash while making a road. Preserved from the time of the Flavians, what emerged was a sealed tomb of the whole city.

The significance of this terrible disaster was that it provided evidence of an ancient way of life, as residents of the whole city were stopped in their tracks in the middle of their daily activities of living. We can now walk the streets of the excavated city and even admire frescoes on the walls of once sumptuous villas that have been brought to light after eighteen centuries of darkness.

Titus had seen some of the worst disasters ever to strike the Italian peninsula. He died at the age of forty-one on September 13, A.D. 81, after a rule that had lasted just two years, two months, and twenty days. It is said that on his death the entire population went into mourning.

Titus was followed by his brother, Domitian, eleven years his junior, who had walked in his shadow. Now at just thirty-one years of age he was "the first man." Domitian ruled for fifteen years and held the Empire together with his legions, by whom he was admired and respected. He was considered a competent administrator, becoming involved in government at a variety of levels. He also went to great trouble and expense to restock the burned-out libraries, though it is said he did not read much himself. As for his writing and correspondence, this was left to the scribes, but Suetonius records that he wrote a manual entitled *Care of the Hair*, dedicated to a friend who was bald like himself, and with these words: "Cannot you see that I, too, have a tall and beautiful person?"

Unfortunately, Domitian's later years were characterized by acts of terror perpetrated against any who displeased him or seemed to present a threat. He has also come down in history as a lustful man who, according to Suetonius, considered sexual activities as a sport. He even seduced his niece, the only surviving child of his brother, Titus; when she became pregnant, he forced her to have an abortion, which killed her.

Domitian was eventually assassinated in his bed by a group of conspirators thought to have included his own wife. He was mourned by the troops to whom he had been good, but the senators rejoiced. His body was taken away by public undertakers, as though he were a pauper, and cremated in the gardens of his old nurse, who took his ashes to the family temple.

Domitian had no children and with his death on September 18, A.D. 96, the dynasty came to an end.

A Century of Giants

A new century was approaching, and it seemed that the Empire had finally come of age as new men were brought from the provinces and given the purple robe of emperor. Not men of Rome, they would nevertheless leave their mark in the city in timeless monuments of stone, constant reminders to all who pass by, whether about their daily activities or as summer visitors, of the glory that the Empire enjoyed.

On the death of Domitian, M. Cocceius Nerva, an elderly jurist and senator, was proclaimed emperor. Order and tranquillity was restored, and Nerva turned his attention to Italy, taking measures to help the poor farmers, relieve poverty, and increase the birth rate. Having no children of his own, he chose as his heir a man from Spain called Marcus Ulpius Traianus (Trajan) who became co-regent. This was a significant departure from tradition because it introduced the principle of adoption in place of dynastic succession, thus making way for selection of the best man that the great empire as a whole could produce, unhampered by the restrictions of birthright and the risk of unsuitable progeny.

Nerva died in his bed in January A.D. 98 after just two and a half years as emperor. He was a good man, and he also proved to be a good judge of other men.

Trajan: A Man from Spain

Trajan was born at a place appropriately called Italica, near Seville, of a Spanish family most likely of Italian descent. He had held a command in the dangerous Rhine-

Above: Façade of the Celsus Library at Ephesus (Turkey). Ephesus became the capital city of the Roman province of Asia under Emperor Augustus. The library dates from the time of Emperor Trajan.

Left: Dominating the ruins of Trajan's Forum in Rome is the impressive 98 feet high column, depicting scenes from the Dacian campaigns. The bas reliefs show intricate details which are remarkably well preserved.

Danube region for some months before taking his place in Rome, and he enjoyed the respect he had earned from the army. He won the confidence of the Senate through the solemn oath he took never to have any senator executed, and he won the love and respect of the people for his humanity.

Though a child of Spain, Trajan paid particular attention to what was happening in the Italian peninsula and took steps to improve the lot of its people. He reclaimed wastelands and built roads, aqueducts, and new harbors at Ostia, Civitavecchia, and Ancona. Of major significance were the public buildings to his credit and the extensive markets consisting of arcades and a double tier of offices and shops, some examples of which can still be seen at Trajan's Forum in Rome. He continued his predecessors' plans to improve the lot of the hitherto neglected rural poor of Italy and instituted a kind of welfare program for poor children. This reflected a greater social awareness, unlike the policy of "bread and circus" to please and placate the Roman mob, for these recipients of charity were passive victims of a system gone wrong. Senators were also instructed to invest one third of their capital in Italian land instead of taking their wealth abroad.

The Empire was a vast economic unit whose frontiers had remained roughly the same since the reign of Claudius, although the eastern frontiers were always more fluid. In contrast, the northern frontier followed the natural features provided by the waterways of the Rhine and the great Danube, which cuts a course from the Black Forest region of Germany and winds its way some 1,725 watery miles eastward to empty in the Black Sea. It was a vast defense line stretching from the English Channel, protected by colonies, roads, camps, and garrisons, along with fleets patrolling the rivers.

The powerful kingdom of Dacia, north of the Danube and occupying an area that is now part of Rumania, had been a troublesome neighbor in the past and had sided with others against Rome, although Domitian had arranged peace terms and it had been quiet on that frontier. For whatever reason, Trajan decided that Dacia would serve as a wedge between the Empire and the barbarian northern tribes that posed a constant threat. So it was that the Dacian Wars occurred. After two campaigns (A.D. 101–102 and 105–106) Dacia was annexed as an imperial province and its capital made a colony to be occupied by Romans. As many as ten legions now held the Rhine-Danube frontier, with the new province forming a bubble-like appendage to the original line, a bubble—it must be said—that was rich in minerals, silver, and especially gold. The story of these campaigns and Rome's conquest is dramatically recorded in stone in the friezes of Trajan's Column in the Forum. Rome's influence in this region was extensive, and the Rumanian language that developed is classified as a Romance language along with Spanish, Portuguese, and French.

Toward the end of his rule, Trajan turned his attention to the eastern frontiers and conquered the Parthians, thus advancing Rome's eastern boundaries to their greatest extent. During these campaigns he became ill and was forced to return home. He never reached Rome, but died on his way back in Cilicia, part of present-day Turkey, in August of A.D. 117. On his deathbed he adopted Hadrian to succeed him as "the best man" of the Empire.

Hadrian: The Man for an Empire

The reins of the Empire would be held for the next twenty years by yet another man from Spain, Publius Aelius Hadrianus (Hadrian), a distant relative of Trajan who hailed from the same town of Italica.

Hadrian was actually in Syria when he heard of Trajan's death, and there were outstanding problems in the eastern part of the Empire that he had to take care of before returning to Rome. Trajan had made some costly gains of territory beyond the Euphrates River, but Hadrian decided to abandon these and withdrew the Roman troops to the Euphrates, making a peace settlement with the Parthians.

Once Hadrian had established his legitimacy — for some considered the deathbed adoption by Trajan as suspect — his first moves were to gain popularity by a variety of measures, which included the cancellation of debts of Roman citizens to the treasury and continued assistance to the poor. Having straightened matters out at home and secured his position, he soon set out on the many travels around the vast Empire, which would be a unique feature of his reign.

From the eastern limits of the Empire, Hadrian turned his attention to the most northerly reaches, where the unconquered tribes in northern Britain remained a constant threat to the Romans. He decided to draw a line separating the unpacified northern tribes from the rest of Britain, and the famous Hadrian's Wall came into being. Taking advantage of the marvelous natural ridges and elevations where possible, a stone wall was built that snaked its way for seventy-three miles from the Tyne River in the east to the Solway River on the opposite coast, like a chain around the neck of the island of Great Britain, separating north from south at the narrowest point. It marked the most northerly frontier of the Roman Empire, where summer days stretch into long twilight and the nights are short, while the winters are long, damp, and dark.

The northern frontier of the Empire must have been a gloomy place for veterans and new recruits alike. Inscriptions in memory of soldiers both young and old who died there remind one of the personal dramas and the human toll that the Empire exacted. The wall and its forts provide a valuable source of information about Roman defenses and garrison life, and ongoing excavations have yielded such personal items as leather sandals, cloth, and even writing tablets. The Roman Army Museum, created at the site of a fort, takes the visitor back in time. A gentle invitation on one travel folder suggests: "The Romans paid us a visit, why don't you?" It was indeed quite a visit that lasted around 400 years.

Hadrian spent some twelve years of the twenty that he was emperor traveling through the Empire, acquainting himself with its diverse characteristics and problems and seeking solutions, creating and building wherever he went. On the other side of the Roman world was Egypt, where Jewish rebellions had left such desolation that Hadrian took measures to repopulate these lands.

It was in Egypt in A.D. 130 that Hadrian suffered a tragic bereavement that brought his personal life into focus. It happened when his favorite boy, a young man from Bythnia called Antinous, drowned in the waters of the Nile. Of exceptional beauty, Antinous had been the object of Hadrian's homosexual desires and had spent much time accompanying him on his travels. There may not have been anything too extraordinary about the incident, but the grieving Hadrian ordered a city to be built in the young man's honor, at the site where the drowning occurred, and called it Antinoopolis, bestowing upon it special privileges. Antinous was placed among the gods, and statues and busts of the beautiful youth, who was often compared to the Greek god Apollo, appeared throughout the Roman world as a cult developed and Greek culture was strengthened in Egypt.

In Palestine, however, Hadrian was less successful in his city-building enterprise. For all his learning and knowledge of his Empire and its peoples, he failed to

Hadrian's tomb reflected in the waters of the Tiber River. Later known as the Castel Sant'Angelo, it got its name in the 6th century when Pope Gregory the Great, praying for an end to the plague as he was crossing the bridge, saw the vision of an angel.

The massive walls of the enormous complex of Hadrian's villa have withstood the test of centuries. Inside the hall of the Philosophers, a young thinker marvels at the intricate stonework.

understand the sensitivity of the Jews when he ordered the building of a new city on the site of Jerusalem, to be a colony peopled with gentile Romans. Palestine exploded in a rebellion which raged from A.D. 132 to 135, resulting in particularly savage repression and casualties of catastrophic import. It was estimated that half a million men were slaughtered and in Judea, the southern portion of ancient Palestine, the population was almost completely exterminated. It was a black page in Hadrian's book and an act that once more saw Rome in serious conflict with a civilization that could not be reconciled with its own.

Hadrian's visible legacy, however, has been the buildings throughout the Empire, made possible in great part through the creative use of otherwise idle legions. Rome was not neglected and was to be forever enriched by some truly incredible buildings, which provide further proof of this emperor's creative genius and wide interests. The pantheon that still stands almost undamaged was the work of Hadrian, built on the site of a temple founded by Agrippa in the time of Augustus. So also was his mausoleum on the Tiber, known as the Castel Sant'Angelo, which later became a prison and eventually was connected to the Vatican by an underground tunnel, providing an escape route for popes and a place of refuge.

Finally, there was the magnificent villa at Tivoli, near Rome, the present-day ruins of which are among the most beautiful ones left on Italian soil and attest to its former extent and the creative genius of Hadrian. Along with the Roman architect Apollonius, he designed the villa, incorporating much of what he had seen around the Empire. More like a city than a dwelling, the villa was a complex of buildings that included pools, lakes, canals, avenues of cypress trees, fountains, statues, and even theaters. The massive red brick walls still rise majestically into the sky as figures of Venus are reflected in the pools.

The end of Hadrian's life was sad and lonely, and he was increasingly ill. He spent his last four years mostly in or near Rome, out of favor and desiring to put an end to his suffering, which he was not allowed to do. Hadrian was sixty-two when in July A.D. 138 he died at Baia, on the beautiful Bay of Naples. It may be said that Hadrian, more than any of his predecessors, epitomized the greatness and diversity of the Empire and was in many respects a precursor of the Renaissance man by the scope of his knowledge and interests. He was a good soldier, but a scholarly man nonetheless, who was a lover of literature, poetry, mathematics, and architecture. Though not, of course, a Christian, he shared the growing religious sensitivity of his age and dabbled in astronomy. Emperor Hadrian was a homosexual and left no offspring to continue his line. His immortality is ensured, however, by the great monuments in stone that he left behind on his death.

Antoninus Pius

Hadrian chose to succeed him as emperor a man known simply as Antoninus Pius, although his real name was Titus Aurelius Fulvus Boionius Arrius Antoninus, which included the names of relatives who boasted distinguished public careers. This was his impressive pedigree. The name Pius that was bestowed on him, meaning "virtuous" or "God-fearing," proved to be appropriate.

Antoninus, whose family actually came from Nimes, France, had been in charge of the judicial administration of Italy during the rule of Hadrian, and he had governed the province of Asia, an area now the western portion of Turkey. He had also been a close advisor of Hadrian, knew the burdens of office, and had proved himself to be a good public servant. In contrast to his predecessor, however, Antoninus was a stay-at-home emperor, although there was still much to be concerned about on the frontiers. Hadrian's Wall had not held back the troublesome tribes of northern Britain; and later on there were disturbances in Mauretania, Egypt, Germany, and, as to be expected, Dacia, the bubble across the Danube. The frontiers were maintained by the Roman legions, whose soldiers were recruited increasing from the local populations. Romanization through colonization continued and the Pax Romana had not been broken.

In A.D. 140 Antoninus's wife, Faustina, died, and a growing awareness of the plight of the poor is suggested by the fact that an institution for bringing up the daughters of poor citizens was founded in her memory. They were called "puellae Faustinanae," the Daughters of Faustina. The Emperor himself had been generous with the poor and just in his legislation. He was seventy-five years of age when he died on March 7, A.D. 161. It is said that the password he gave the tribune of the watch for the day he died was *aequanimitas,* meaning "peace of mind," a fitting word to punctuate the end of a good life and twenty-three years as emperor.

Marcus Aurelius: The Philosopher Emperor

Marcus Aurelius Antoninus became emperor in A.D. 161 on the death of his adoptive father, Emperor Antoninus Pius, whom he loved and admired. Marcus expressed the degree of indebtedness to Antoninus, who had held fast to the old Roman values of virtue in an age of increasing moral confusion, in these lines from his celebrated *Meditations,* which were actually written in Greek: *"There is only one fruit of this earthly life, a pious disposition and social acts. Do everything as a disciple of Antoninus. Remember his constancy is rational behavior, his even temper in all things, his piety, and the serenity of his countenance, his sweetness, his disregard of empty fame, and his effort to understand things."* Marcus also considered himself lucky when he wrote, *"To the gods I am indebted for having good grand-fathers, good parents, a good sister, good teachers, good associates, good kinsmen and friends, nearly everything good. . . . I thank the gods for giving me a brother. . . ."*

The brother he mentions is his brother by adoption, Lucius Verus, and in a departure from tradition Marcus had the Senate proclaim him as co-emperor. This was the first time since the Empire had replaced the Republic that two men ruled with equal rights. It was reminiscent of the old system of having two consul-commanders, but the major difference was that whereas the term of the consul was for one year, the emperor ruled for life. There is no record of conflict between the two men, although Marcus seems to have been the stronger leader and is given credit for much of what occurred during the dual emperorship. The family relationship had been made even closer by Marcus's marriage to Annia Galeria Faustina, daughter of Antoninus and Faustina, generally referred to as Faustina II to avoid confusion.

Marcus Aurelius was by nature a man of peace, but fate ordained that he spend a lot of his time with the legions defending the frontiers of empire. The Parthians invaded Syria during the first year of the new rule, and the wars that followed lasted for four years. Verus, his co-emperor, was nominally in charge of that campaign, the aftermath of which had devastating consequences on account of the pestilence that was brought back by the returning soldiers. There are no accurate eyewitness accounts or figures, but it is known that the legions suffered heavy losses. The disease, which may have been smallpox, hit Rome around A.D. 166, and spread throughout the Empire. Fields remained uncultivated as the population in the rural areas as well as urban centers dropped dramatically.

More trouble was brewing on the northern frontiers, where the tribes were continually pushing down and threatening the Romanized regions of the Danube. In A.D. 167, Marcus and Verus rode north on a punitive expedition across the Danube, and at the same time German hordes crossed the river behind them and moved down into Italy in great numbers. It was only thanks to the many legions that had been garrisoned along the Danube line that the Romans prevailed. It was at this time that Verus died at the age of thirty-nine, leaving Marcus alone in the midst of it all. Some years passed before peace could finally be restored in the area.

But there was to be no peace for poor Marcus, who stoically accepted his duties as protector of the Empire and in A.D. 175 made his way to Egypt to settle matters there. Further tragedy awaited him as his beloved empress, Faustina, died on the journey. She had accompanied her husband in the Danube wars and was given the title of "Mother of the Army." The loss for the Emperor must have been devastating— he cherished and admired the wife who had been his close and constant companion in very difficult times.

The following year, Marcus proclaimed his son Commodus joint emperor, although he was just a boy of sixteen, and soon thereafter he was back again on the northern frontier where the Danube wars resumed. The philosopher-emperor died suddenly at the camp of Vindobona (Vienna) on March 17, A.D. 180, just before reaching the age of fifty-nine.

Marcus Aurelius spent much of his time as emperor on the battlefield, and we know him as the soldier-emperor astride his horse, immortalized in the equestrian statue that stands in the Piazza del Campidoglio in Rome. However, he survives through his *Meditations,* many portions of which were written during his difficult years in the Danube campaigns. They were apparently written to help him bear the heavy burdens he believed were his destiny. However, they also provide a sort of code of living for the reader and have the tone of a thinker whose advice might be expected from a priest or counselor.

All of this goodness notwithstanding, it was during the rule of Marcus that the Christians suffered severe persecution; it was an age of martyrs. Christianity was spreading rapidly throughout the Empire; Gaul, in particular, had many adherents to the faith who were often in conflict with the authority of Rome. Christians at Lyons, a major city at this time, suffered terrible persecutions in A.D. 177. Although Marcus Aurelius apparently did not actually order such cruel and excessive methods of repression, there is no record that he did anything to prevent them. Indeed, he does not appear to have been moved by the martyrdom of people who were considered fanatics, and he continued to see his role as the protector of the Empire, to which he himself was totally and perhaps fanatically dedicated.

Marcus Aurelius did not live to see his work completed, however, and it must have been a sad man that died on that March day in a camp on the Danube line. Perhaps some lines from his own *Meditations* provide the most fitting epitaph:

> *Man, you have been a citizen in this great state. . . . Where is the hardship then, if no tyrant nor yet an unjust judge sends you away from the state, but nature who brought you into it? The same as if a praetor who has employed an actor dismisses him from the stage. "But I have not finished the five acts, but only three of them." Good, but in life the three acts are the whole drama. For what shall constitute a*

complete drama is determined by him who first caused its Composition, and now its dissolution: but you are the cause of neither. Depart then serenely, for he who releases you is also serene. (XII, 36)

Marcus Aurelius had barely played those three acts when he died, passing the script to his son who would take over his role and give the part of emperor quite a different character. Writing half a century later, the historian Dio Cassius said that with the passing of Marcus Aurelius, "the age of gold turned to rusty iron."

The equestrian statue of Marcus Aurelius still graces the Piazza del Campidoglio in Rome. Created in bronze in the year 173 A.D., the original is now housed inside for protection.

CHAPTER EIGHT

The Empire Under Threat

Dark Days Ahead

As the second century drew to a close, it became apparent that the rust had indeed set in and was but a prelude to the upheaval that would follow. On the death of Marcus Aurelius in A.D. 180, the burden of empire had been suddenly and prematurely placed on the shoulders of the young Commodus, who displayed none of the qualities of his meditative father. Perhaps he was just a typical rebellious teenager, an orphan cut loose from all parental ties and free to follow his worst wild instincts.

His first act was to make peace with the Germans, with whom Rome had been fighting for thirteen years. The boy had grown up with this war, and now he chose to put an end to it. It was probably the right move for the wrong reasons, for Commodus wanted to get back to Rome, where there was circus and all kinds of entertainment. Not merely a spectator, he wanted to be part of it all and even took to the arena to show off his skills in archery, much to the delight of the mob and the embarrassment of the Senate.

As the young emperor played, the Empire seemed to be falling apart. There was rebellion in Britain, deserters along the Danube following the end of the war, and in Gaul a peasant force had taken control of some of the towns. At home, there had been a reign of terror, following an assassination attempt on the young emperor early in his rule, in which many of the Latin aristocracy were executed.

Commodus survived for thirteen years, meeting his end on the night of December 31, A.D. 192, when he was strangled to death by a group of plotters in collusion with his mistress. His flair for exhibitionism had reached the absurd, and the dignity of office was ridiculed. He had planned to make himself the ultimate public spectacle by leading a New Year's Day procession from the gladiators' barracks dressed as Hercules.

With the death of the gladiator-emperor at the age of thirty-one, a dangerous vacuum had been created because there was no provision for a successor. This was the prelude to a long series of succession problems that rocked the Empire, and it turned into a large arena where provinces and commanders became the contestants. First to be proclaimed emperor was Pertinax, son of a freedman from northern Italy, who was assassinated by disgruntled soldiers after just eighty-seven days. He was followed by four more contenders. The soldiers wanted money, and the seat was up for sale to the highest bidder, who happened to be the wealthy Didius Julianus. Outraged, the legions at the frontiers took matters into their own hands and a four-year civil war ensued. The Empire might have been a sick beast, but the parts were

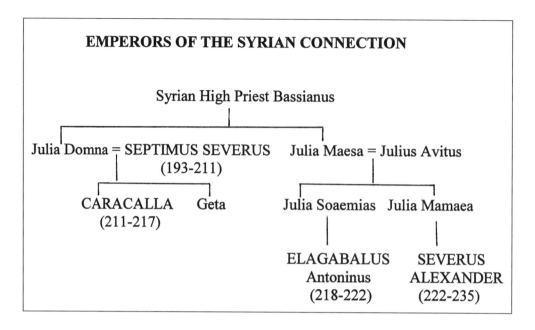

EMPERORS OF THE SYRIAN CONNECTION

Syrian High Priest Bassianus

Julia Domna = SEPTIMUS SEVERUS   Julia Maesa = Julius Avitus
(193-211)

CARACALLA   Geta   Julia Soaemias   Julia Mamaea
(211-217)

ELAGABALUS   SEVERUS
Antoninus   ALEXANDER
(218-222)   (222-235)

very much alive and kicking. In Syria, the troops had their own champion in C. Pescennius Niger, and in Britain they chose D. Clodius Albinus. The fourth contestant for the seat was Septimus Severus, declared "first man" by the legions of the Danube. And now the legions from the far-flung corners of the Empire were on the move again, converging on Rome. Severus had the advantage of being the closest and was soon on his way.

A historian of the day described the situation in Rome as this rival approached the gates:

> The city during these days became nothing more nor less than a camp, in the enemy's country, as it were. Great was the turmoil on the part of the various forces that were encamped and drilling, — men, horses, and elephants, — and great also was the fear inspired in the rest of the population by the armed troops, because the latter hated them.

Julianus offered Severus half of the Empire, but the army was behind Severus and the Senate found it expedient to declare him emperor instead. Julianus, who had paid such a high price for the coveted imperial seat, had also purchased his own death, for he was slain in his palace where he had been a tenant for just sixty-six troubled days. Severus made a triumphant entry into Rome, dismounting from his horse outside the city and walking the rest of the way accompanied by his troops. The spectacle was brilliant, with garlands of flowers and the citizens in white robes shouting good omens.

Not resting on his laurels, however, Severus lost no time in going after his rivals. He first captured and killed Pescennius Niger in Syria, where severe punishment was meted out to the inhabitants. Antioch, a city that was third in importance in the Roman world, was sacked, and its position as capital of Syria taken away. Byzantium (now Istanbul) fared even worse. A city built on one of seven hills and founded even before Rome by the Greeks, it was besieged and taken in A.D. 196 and virtually destroyed. Its famous walls were demolished, and many of its citizens put to the sword. It would rise like a splendid phoenix just over a century later as capital of the Eastern Roman Empire, and it would be named Constantinople.

Severus next made his way northwest to confront Albinus. Although he had previously proclaimed this man his Caesar, he apparently had no intention of keeping his promise. Albinus was on his way with his legions from Britain to claim his share of glory, but was intercepted by the troops of Severus near Lugdunum (Lyons) in France, where he was eventually defeated in an extremely bloody battle. Albinus wisely took his own life rather than fall into the hands of the victor. Indeed, Severus spared no mercy on the city, which had been the birthplace of his oldest son, the terrible Caracalla, and the city was ruthlessly ravaged and burned.

The struggle had lasted four years and now in A.D. 197 the reins were fully in the hands of a man who was truly a citizen of the Empire. Septimus Severus had been born in Leptis Magna, North Africa, a splendid city possessing the attributes worthy of the great Roman Empire. He had also served in North Africa, as well as Spain, Syria, Gaul, Sicily, and finally the Danube region, where he had commanded the largest army, which had given wings to his ambitions.

Now Emperor, Severus had at his side a worthy Empress, Julia Domna, an intelligent and lively Syrian lady of priestly stock. With her help and desire to reconcile opposing ideas, he had dreams of a return to a Golden Age. To secure the succession, he made his oldest son joint emperor in A.D. 198. He had been proclaimed a Caesar the previous year and was given the auspicious name of Marcus Aurelius Antoninus. We know him by his nickname, Caracalla, a word that described a kind of duffel coat, a garment native to Gaul and the Rhineland, which he was always seen wearing.

One of the problems that plagued Severus and his empress was the ongoing feud between Caracalla and his brother Geta, born in Milan and three years his junior, who was also made a Caesar. Though merely titles at the time—the boys had not yet reached their teens—the rivalry between the two, encouraged and exploited by their respective supporters, was lethal and occupied much of the Emperor's time. But when things apparently settled down he set out to fulfill his dream of conquering the whole of Britain, which Hadrian had divided by his wall. Severus took his armies beyond Loch Lomond and as far north as Aberdeenshire. But the poor Roman soldiers were no match for the hardy inhabitants of those inhospitable regions, who knew the deadly bogs, the dark forests, and craggy hiding places from which they could harass the enemy with guerrilla tactics. Severus was forced to withdraw. He was sixty-seven years old now and was in the city of York, in northern England, when he died on a gloomy February day of A.D. 211, a far cry from his birthplace in sunny North Africa.

Two young eagles now occupied the imperial nest and, as in nature, the stronger often destroys the weaker one. So Caracalla planned to get rid of his younger brother. This was not such an easy task, as Geta was always under the protection of bodyguards and soldiers. The wicked and wily Caracalla contrived to have his mother invite him and his brother alone to her chambers, ostensibly for the purpose of reconciliation. The chilling account of the event is told by the historian Dio Cassius, a senator at that time, and his words echo in their stark simplicity what was to be the climate of the times and a prelude to the horrors that would follow:

> *Thus Geta was persuaded, and went in with him; but when they were inside some centurions, previously instructed by Antoninus [Caracalla], rushed in in a*

body and struck down Geta, who at sight of them had run to his mother, hung about her neck and clung to her bosom and breasts, lamenting and crying: "Mother that didst bear me, mother that didst bear me, help. I am being murdered." And so she, tricked in this way, saw her son perishing in most impious fashion in her arms, and received him at his death into the very womb, as it were, whence he had been born; for she was all covered with his blood so that she took no note of the wound she had received on her hand. But she was not permitted to mourn or weep for her son, though he had met so miserable an end before his time [he was twenty-two years and nine months old], but on the contrary she was compelled to rejoice and laugh as though at some great good fortune. . . . Thus she alone, the Augusta, wife of the emperor and mother of the emperors, was not permitted to shed tears even in private over so great a sorrow. (283)

This murder was followed by the outright massacre of brother Geta's supporters, soldiers and freedmen, men and women alike. As Caracalla's ruthless acts put terror into the Italian hearts, it was evident that resentment against the "foreigners" was beginning to manifest itself, as he was accused of inheriting all the vices of the three races to which he belonged, but none of their virtues at all. These vices included the fickleness, cowardice, and recklessness of Gaul, where he was born; the harshness and cruelty of Africa, his father's homeland; and from his mother's side the craftiness of Syria. It should be mentioned, however, that Julia Domna displayed the most laudable virtues of her race, rather than the vices attributed to it by the Romans.

It was evident, however, that Italians were beginning to find themselves pushed aside. Severus, in particular, had been accused of ruining the youth of Italy, forced into brigandage as the army recruited from the provinces, evidenced by the motley collection of soldiers seen in Rome as being "savage in appearance" and "most terrifying in speech." Caracalla spent much of his time engaged in wars, and to read the accounts of the incredible atrocities committed against humanity is to make a trip through hell. The figure of Nero seems to pale in comparison to the bloodthirsty nature of this new monster. He did not kill his mother, however, but used her astutely to take care of his interests at home while he engaged in battle. It was fitting, therefore, that he should die at the hands of his own soldiers. His end came at Carrhae, in Mesopotamia, on April 8, A.D. 217, before he had reached the age of thirty. His decomposing body was secretly brought back to Rome at night, and his reign of terror was over.

Caracalla is mainly known to posterity as the builder of the great Roman baths, the ruins of which now form an impressive backdrop to the summer opera performances. Built in brick, they could accommodate up to 1,600 bathers at a time. The immense complex consisted of a central building, surrounded by gardens, shops, and apparently sideshows. This he did for the living, and the ruins we see confirm his most significant gift to Rome, but it might also serve as a monument to the dead.

The Syrian Connection and Boy Emperors

The Italians might have rejoiced at the passing of the monster Caracalla, but A.D. 217 could hardly be called a lucky year because the succession problem was still with them and the Senate was still at the mercy of the legions. An emperor had to have the legions behind him. Caracalla summed it up when asked by his mother how he would hold this power: He is said to have pointed to his sword and replied, "With this, Mother." He pampered his soldiers and had their support, but the old discipline was lacking, and they easily became mutinous.

It was Marcus Opellius Macrinus, a man born in North Africa, that the legions proclaimed emperor. He was the one who apparently engineered Caracalla's murder, but he was shortly murdered himself as the legions in the east transferred their allegiance to a member of the Syrian line, Caracalla's mother, Julia Domna. There is mystery surrounding the fate of this lady who died shortly after her son was murdered. Some accounts said she starved herself to death, while others believed Macrinus forced her to take her life because her supporters in Rome must have been a threat to his power. Julia Domna had a sister in Rome, Julia Maesa, who had married a senator, Julius Avitus (probably a Gaul). Perhaps it was through her machinations that the legions in Syria killed Macrinus and transferred their allegiance to her grandson, Elagabalus, proclaiming him emperor. This was the nearest male, because Julia Maesa had only daughters and a generation had to be skipped.

The practice of choosing the "best man" was now a lost cause, for the Empire did not even get the "best boy." Elagabalus had a little problem that came out of the closet in the most outrageous fashion after he became emperor. He was just a boy of fourteen years, in his puberty so to speak, when he began to display his homosexual tendencies and his flagrant effeminate practices, as well as disgusting goings-on at the palace involving his "ladies." He had also imposed on the Romans the worship of the eastern god Baal, actions that could no longer be tolerated by the people. Grandmother Julia Maesa saw the new Syrian dynasty at risk and forced Elagabalus to adopt his young cousin, Alexander Severus, as heir and colleague. Later, Elagabalus wanted to change his mind and was thereupon slain by the guards, along with his mother, Julia Soaemias, who clung to her eighteen-year-old emperor son in a last display of maternal protection. The anger and outrage of the populace was clearly manifested as their heads were severed and their naked bodies dragged through the streets, then cast aside without burial.

Alexander became emperor with the support of the Syrian legions; like his dead cousin, he was only fourteen years of age at the time. Strong Syrian women continued to play an important role, however, as Alexander's mother, Julia Mamaea, was made regent of her young son under the control of a council of sixteen senators, with the surviving grandmother, Julia Maesa, also exerting her influence until her death in A.D. 226. The following years were characterized by profound unrest on the part of the populace as well as the army. The dislike of government had become intense as lawlessness increased. There were uprisings and street battles in Rome; the chief minister of state was murdered at the palace in the very presence of the young Emperor and his mother; while deserters, runaways, slaves, and outright criminal elements took refuge in the provinces.

Danger now loomed large from the East, where a Persian called Artaxeres had emerged with a mission to restore the former Persian Empire. He made war against Parthia, killing their king and laying claim to Asia Minor. The fear of losing the eastern part of the Empire was expressed by Dio Cassius, the senator historian of the day, in the following words:

> He accordingly became a source of fear to us; for he was encamped with a large army so as to threaten not only Mesopotamia but also Syria, and he boasted that he would win back everything that the ancient Persians had once held, as far as the Grecian Sea, claiming that all this was his rightful inheritance from his forefathers.

In the years A.D. 231–232, Rome was at war in the East. The young emperor, now only twenty-three years old, was in command of the legions along with his ever-present mother, who accompanied him on the campaign. After staggering losses, there was no clear victory for either side, and Alexander withdrew to Antioch, where he pampered his remaining forces. Later he was accused of cowardice for not pushing forward at all cost.

The campaign in the East was immediately followed by trouble in the Rhineland in A.D. 233. Alexander apparently bought off the Germans, which enraged the legions there. Early in A.D. 235 he was murdered along with his mother. He had lived just twenty-seven years and had borne the burden of emperor for thirteen. In that confusing world of cultures and religions in collision, where Christianity was taking hold, Alexander is said to have wanted Christ included with the Roman gods.

Victims of destiny, the boy emperors both died with their mothers who had, nevertheless, sought to promote a gentler rule at home amid the growing internal turmoil. On this tragic note the short Syrian dynasty had come to an untimely end.

A Period of Crisis

For the next fifty years, some twenty-two emperors came on stage, but the roles of many of these consisted only of a few lines, symbolic of as many days in the spotlight. The actual administrative network of empire remained intact, however, in spite of the confusion at the top. The emperors represented a variety of men and boys from all over the Roman Empire and from different backgrounds of learning and race. Some would warm the seat of emperor for a brief period of time, and others failed to sit there at all.

The man who succeeded the young Alexander was Maximinus, who hailed from the remote mountains in the Balkan peninsula, born to a half-barbarian peasant couple. Of exceptional strength and size when he grew to manhood, this uneducated youth had risen through the ranks of the military with alarming speed. Maximinus was in command of the Rhineland legions when the unfortunate Alexander and his mother met their end at the hands of the very troops who declared Maximinus their emperor. Always close to her young son, Julia Mamaea had been a powerful regent and, according to the contemporary Syrian historian Herodian, these rough men resented a woman's authority.

The Senate, out of fear, confirmed the appointment of Maximinus, but must have found it embarrassing to confer the purple robe of emperor on this rough-hewn giant who spoke very little Latin. Fortunately, perhaps, Maximinus was an absentee emperor, for he never came to Rome during the three years of his rule. He considered his first task the defense of the northern frontiers that were constantly under attack.

While Maximinus was busy in the north, another drama was being played out in Africa where, following troubles in A.D. 238 the governor, Gordian, along with his son of the same name, had also been declared emperors. The Senate seized on the opportunity to depose Maximinus and give their blessing to the Gordians, but the young Gordian was killed in battle with the neighboring Numidia (although the body was apparently never found), and the grieving father hanged himself. Their rule, if it may be called such, lasted just twenty-two days, between March and April A.D. 238.

The Senate's double-cross had backfired, and two respected senators were declared emperors to replace the Gordians. At this juncture, an enraged Maximinus, who had been campaigning along the Danube frontier, marched on Italy with his troops. He got as far as Aquileia, just northwest of present-day Trieste, and was treacherously slain by his own men, along with his son, as he took an afternoon siesta. The Roman force that had been sent to intercept him found their work had already been completed, but it is more than likely that Roman money had paid the assassins.

It is hard not to feel some sympathy for this emperor, who had known nothing but war. Poor Maximinus never did make a triumphant entry into Rome. Instead, just his head was taken there under cavalry escort, a grizzly end to one who had dedicated his life to protecting the frontiers of empire.

Back in Rome, the people and the guards expressed their outrage against the Senate, going after the two senators that had been foisted on them. The helpless men were seized by the mob and dragged through the streets of Rome, and their bodies defiled by the angry crowds.

Who would be next to occupy this very dangerous seat? There was another Gordian, the grandson of the old man who had hanged himself, and the choice of the people fell on this boy of thirteen years of age. Propped up as the figurehead with his mother by his side, he grew almost to manhood during the six years of his reign. At the age of nineteen he was killed during a campaign against the Persians when his troops mutinied.

The Millennium: Philip the Arabian

As time approached for Rome to celebrate her millennium, just four years away, the seat of the emperor was once again vacant. It was as though a knight in armor had come galloping to the rescue of a lady in distress when Philip, son of an Arab chieftain of distinguished equestrian lineage, symbolically took the reins from the hands of the dead Gordian. Philip (Marcus Julius Philippus) ended the war with Persia, then proceeded to take care of matters along the Danube.

The man with the Roman name to be known as "Philip the Arabian," was the first of his race to sit on the imperial throne. It was he, not a Roman or even an Italian, who returned from his long campaigns to be in Rome in A.D. 248 to celebrate the 1,000th anniversary of the founding of the city. This was indeed a landmark year of some significance, and, whatever the situation might have been on the frontiers, Philip saw to it that the event was celebrated with all the pomp and extravagance that the occasion warranted.

New coins were issued, there were the traditional religious ceremonies, and games unending in the Circus Maximus. To judge from the coinage, all kinds of wild and exotic beasts had been arrayed for the occasion, and the people of Rome were given bonuses. The mood was one of optimism and the citizens were encouraged by the adoption of the elephant to symbolize Rome's continued longevity.

Philip seems to have envisioned a new dynasty. He proclaimed his son a Caesar and granted the title of Augusta to his wife (Otacilia Severa), whose profile appeared with his own on the new coinage. An insight into Philip's beliefs, as well as the corrupt practices of the period that he endeavored to correct, may be seen in some of his edicts concerning civil rights, later to become part of the Justinian Codex. He also passed laws to make illegal the practice of castration and homosexual behavior, which was rampant at the time.

Philip was a gentle and clement man who was regarded as a protector of the Christians, if not a Christian himself, by writers of a later century. The times in which he ruled, however, were violent, and the situation was increasingly volatile as the threat to the Roman Empire grew. His place as emperor was challenged as usurpers popped up like mushrooms.

In the autumn of A.D. 249, Philip the Arabian met his death at Verona in a battle to defend his imperial seat. Slain along with his father was the young Caesar who could have been the next link in a new dynasty. Philip had ruled for just five years, and the Empire he had saved was once more at risk.

Barbarians at Italy's Backdoor

The celebration of Rome's millennium in A.D. 248 may have been the high point of the century, but the twenty agonizing years that followed saw the Roman Empire fight for its very survival as even the Italian peninsula came under threat. The floodgates were opened on all fronts. The Goths had poured across the borders and were met by the next emperor, Decius, who was unfortunately killed in battle. Hordes crossed the Danube and invaded Italy from the northeast; behind them others continued to pour down the rivers of Russia. They crossed the Black Sea, overran Bythnia (Turkey), and savagely sacked its cities. In the west the Franks crossed the Rhine and marched southward, creating terror in Gaul, the most Romanized of the provinces, killing and pillaging as they made their way to Spain.

Commanders and usurpers came and went in the various regions with alarming rapidity, but Valerian had somehow prevailed, becoming emperor in A.D. 253. Emperors during these times were fighting men; Valerian, although an old man, was soon on his way east to meet the Persian threat. It was a serious blow to Roman morale and military pride when he was captured by the enemy. No one came to his rescue—not even his son Gallienus, whom he had made his co-emperor and left to take care of the western half of the Empire.

Gallienus had his own problems and left his son, Saloninus, in the western region of the Rhine while he took off for the Danube to take care of matters there. What might have been a mere incident became a major event when a dispute arose between two commanders concerning the award of booty, and the troops took the side of the one called Postumus, even declaring him their emperor. Saloninus, on the wrong side of the argument, was killed by the troops. Postumus became the ruler of the breakaway western half of the Empire, which included Britain, Gaul, and Spain, and a new capital was set up at a site which is now the town of Trier in northern France.

Gallienus had no choice but to recognize Postumus, and he set about the task of defending the peninsula. He chose as his military base the city of Mediolanum (Milan), which was just about halfway between Rome and the northern frontiers and linked to other cities in northern Italy. Milan grew in importance as a stronghold, protecting the middle and southern half of Italy. Gallienus made another innovative change by putting his armored men on horseback, establishing a cavalry strike or defense force. This élite corps was celebrated for its attributes of speed and loyalty.

Rome enjoyed five years of relative peace between A.D. 262 and 267, during which period Gallienus took a break from being a soldier and played the role of Emperor. He sponsored a renaissance in literature and the arts that was taking place, and it was during this period that the brilliant philosopher Plotinus founded the Neoplatonist school. Danger was always lurking in the north, however, as hordes of Goths, as well as newly arrived Heruli, massed in terrifying numbers along the Black Sea. In the path they took through Greece and Asia Minor they created devastation of the most terrible nature, but the invaders were eventually intercepted by Gallienus in the

Balkans in A.D. 268. Naissus became the ultimate killing fields in what would be known as the battle of the century, but the invaders were stopped.

Gallienus had won a great victory, but he hardly had time to bask in its glory, for another usurper had appeared on the scene. The commander of the so-called loyal élite cavalry in Milan had revolted, and Gallienus was obliged to rush back to Italy with his troops. There he lay siege to the very military stronghold he had created. Italy's savior would never again enter Milan, for in A.D. 268, after fifteen years as emperor, Gallienus was assassinated outside the city he had made great.

The usurper was suppressed, and a new commander of the cavalry, Claudius II Gothicus, took the reins with the approval of the Senate and protected the Empire for the next two years. He died in A.D. 270, a victim of the plague while preparing a campaign against the dreaded Vandals. His brother succeeded him as "first man" for a few months, but before he got to Rome yet another Danubian from the élite Milan-based unit was proclaimed emperor. We know him simply as AURELIAN.

Aurelian: Savior of the Empire

The men who came from the Danube regions knew better than anyone the dangers that lurked to the north. The next emperor expressed his worst fears in a great wall around the city of Rome. Lucius Domitius Aurelianus, known as Aurelian, was fifty-six years old when he came to power in A.D. 270. Born to a peasant family in the eastern Danube region, like so many others he had worked his way up through the ranks of the Roman army. His first task was to repel the German invaders that had broken through the Brenner Pass and entered northern Italy. With this accomplished he made his way to Rome, but there was no great fanfare, and his stay was brief. It was a mark of the times that the emperor should be with the troops that created him, and so he was northward-bound again to stave off attacks from the Vandals, followed by invasions of other German tribes that scattered in bands in the north. Invaders were pushed back beyond the Danube, and it was decided to abandon the lands beyond this natural barrier. The Roman province of Dacia (Rumania), the bubble that was the last addition to the Empire, had become too difficult to defend. Dacia had been Romanized, and many inhabitants of the region chose to remain Roman citizens rather than submit to the barbarians. Their bubble had burst, and they became refugees.

Aurelian next turned his attention to Rome. It seemed far enough away, but it would be vulnerable to attack if the invaders breached the defenses in the north. Though a Danubian by birth, Aurelian was a Roman in spirit, and Rome had to be made safe. Like a massive sea wall against a rising flood, the Aurelian wall went up around the city by his order. It was twelve miles in circumference, far longer than the previous one built by the sixth king of Rome more than eight long centuries ago when the city was much smaller. This great wall, twelve feet thick and twenty feet high, had eighteen gates and towers to accommodate heavy artillery. Because the soldiers were needed to protect the frontiers, it was built by civilian labor and provided work for the many men who swelled the welfare ranks and spent their days in idleness. These walls contained the city right up to the twentieth century when the population grew, spewing outside these limits and fanning out into suburbs, though the skyline remained low and the vistas from the Roman hills are still incomparable.

With the wall under construction, Aurelian now had to deal with a woman, the widow Zenobia, who played no small role in the history of the Roman Empire. For some ten years, Syria had been ruled by princes who did not recognize the authority of Rome, and on the death of her husband, Zenobia had established a little empire of her own, controlling not only Syria but also Egypt, the main source of the grain supply. She has been compared to Cleopatra, and the Romans probably feared her power just as much. Aurelian took off to confront Zenobia and her son, who had proclaimed themselves Augusta and Augustus. Pushing into Asia Minor, Aurelian met with little or no resistance, and Egypt came back into the Roman fold by surrendering to the Roman general Probus (later to become emperor himself). Zenobia was the next target; after defeating her forces Aurelian pursued her to Palmyra, an ancient city in the desert of modern Syria, where she was captured. Zenobia was a survivor, and perhaps she, like Cleopatra, had used her charm to persuade her captor that it was really her chief advisor who was to blame. At all events, Palmyra surrendered, the advisor paid with his life, and Zenobia was spared.

Soon thereafter, however, a revolt against the newly appointed Roman governor-general brought Aurelian galloping back full speed to Palmyra. This time, a severe Roman lesson was administered as the city was captured and sacked. Zenobia, the queen who had for a while basked in the sunlight of empire, found herself in the spotlight in the triumphal procession through Rome in A.D. 274. Whether by astute diplomatic maneuver or a return of the old Roman virtue of clemency, Zenobia was married off to a Roman senator and lived the life of a Roman matron at Tivoli.

Aurelian had much to celebrate in that triumphal procession for Spain, Gaul, and Britain, declared a separate empire in A.D. 259 by Postumus, had been recovered. With the eastern and western parts back together again, the Roman Empire had been miraculously salvaged. As a thinking man, Aurelian also sought to bring it together spiritually in some symbolic way, and he introduced religious innovations to unite the various religions of the Empire.

To the pantheon of Roman gods had been added more monotheistic ideas, including sun worship. Elagabalus had brought this religious rite to Rome during his reign, though without success. Palmyra, in the important province of Syria, was a center of solar theology. Aurelian tried to bring all the religions under an established and subsidized cult of Sol Invictus (the Unconquerable Sun), and a splendid temple was built in the capital. Aurelian did not try to eliminate any religions, but sought to unite East and West in a kind of universal faith where the Sun was the head of the pantheon. The birthday of the Sun was to be celebrated on December 25, believed to be the date of the winter solstice. Christianity later replaced this pagan festival with a new celebration to honor the "sun of righteousness," Jesus Christ. This date established by Aurelian has remained a pivotal one over the centuries.

Emperor Aurelian had dedicated himself to recovery of a broken empire and to protecting it from outside threats. It was during a mission to the East that he came to an inglorious end, cut down by his own troops through the treachery of a few in the autumn of A.D. 275, just as the sun was beginning to shine again over a reunited Roman Empire.

CHAPTER NINE

Carving Up the Empire

Emperor Diocletian and a New Order

Human waves of Vandals, Burgundians, and various Germanic hordes swept westward following the death of Aurelian, spilling across the northern borders of the Empire. One after another, soldier-emperors jumped into the breach to stem the tide, and they in turn were often engulfed by the half-barbarian soldiers who created them. The one who survived the longest was Probus, a man of Balkan stock whose life was spent on the frontiers of the Empire in continual warfare. He ruled as emperor for six tumultuous years, fighting what must have seemed like a losing battle against invaders.

Ten years after Aurelian's death an emperor with bold and innovative ideas appeared on the scene and survived long enough to bring about a new order. This was Aurelius Valerius Diocletianus (DIOCLETIAN), who became emperor in A.D. 285 after being proclaimed "first man" by his troops the previous year. Like many of his predecessors, he came from the periphery of the Empire, born to a peasant family in Dalmatia.

Diocletian realized the enormity of the task of ruling such a large empire all alone, and in A.D. 286 he took as his co-emperor a loyal colleague called Maximian, a rough-hewn, uneducated man from the Danube region. Diocletian began to put into practice his scheme to solve the problems that plagued the great empire, which had not only become too large but also was extremely complex by reason of its diversity. He divided the Empire into East and West, taking the eastern half for himself and delegating to Maximian the western part, which included Italy, Spain, Gaul, Britain, and Africa. In A.D. 293 he created what was know as the "Tetrarchy," whereby the two emperors (Augusti) would each have a subordinate (Caesar). The Caesars were also men from the Danube region, Galerius and Constantius Chlorus.

There were four emperors for all practical purposes, because each had his area of responsibility and his own capital, to be adorned with beautiful buildings befitting an imperial city. Diocletian first chose Nicomedia in Turkey as his capital, but then moved it to Antioch in Syria, where elaborate ceremonials more in the style of the Persian court replaced the simpler Roman practices. The Eastern Caesar was put in charge of Illyricum and the Balkans with his capital at Thessalonica, a strategic point on the Roman road linking Italy and Asia Minor. Closest to Rome was Maximian, who had his capital at Mediolanum (Milan). The city continued to grow in importance with the addition of imperial buildings, the ruins of which are now buried under the modern city, and it remained an important political and military center for a long time. Maximian's Caesar, Constantius Chlorus, was in charge of

Gaul and Britain with his very sumptuous capital at Trier, capital of the previous secessionist territory under Postumus.

And what about Rome? No longer the great heart of the Roman Empire or the one focal point from which all emanated and everything converged upon, it was instead protected by the canopy of new capitals. The Aurelian walls that enclosed it materially seemed to have metaphorically entombed this great imperial giant. Diocletian strengthened the legions by doubling the number of soldiers and reorganizing the structure of the army, which fanned out like a protective shield. The burden of maintaining the legions, as well as the creation of fine new capital cities, fell on the backs of the ordinary citizens through heavier taxes, and tighter controls were also exerted over the provinces.

Rome had ceased to be the residence of emperors, but it was still the imperial city and the one link that symbolically held everything else together. Diocletian saw to it that coinage was appropriately minted to do Rome credit, and a major building project in that city bore his name. This was the enormous Baths of Diocletian, the remnants of which may be seen near Rome's central railway station, Stazione Termini. Don't look for the baths, however. What was the frigidarium (cold room) is now the church of Santa Maria degli Angeli, and certain other parts that remain house a museum. Actually, it was co-emperor Maximian who initiated the building of the Baths on his first visit to Rome in A.D. 298.

As for Diocletian, he was the absentee emperor *par excellence,* for it seems he did not visit the city until A.D. 303, and the occasion was the commemoration of his twentieth anniversary as emperor. Both emperors were present for the festivities, which lasted one month and were presided over by Maximian, the Emperor of the West. Rome was once more, for a brief time, the centerpiece of empire, the neutral meeting ground of the two emperors, who then returned to their respective capitals.

In accordance with Diocletian's plan, both emperors abdicated two years later, when Maximian had also ruled for twenty years, and coinage was minted for the occasion with the interesting inscription: THE MOST HAPPY SENIOR EMPERORS. Maximian was apparently less "happy" about retirement than Diocletian, who was quite ready to relinquish power to the Caesars as he took up residence in his retirement home, an extravagant palace at Split. The old part of present-day Split was actually built inside the seven-feet-thick walls of what was once an enormous palatial complex.

One last act of Diocletian, however, seems to be as puzzling as it was uncharacteristic. In A.D. 304, the year before his abdication, he issued an edict of persecution of the Christians. The orders were carried out most savagely, and chilling accounts of martyrdom in the eastern half of the Empire are given by Eusebius Pamphili, Bishop of Caesarea in Palestine, who lived at the time and documented persecutions that raged for seven years. The atrocities perpetrated in the Roman arenas seem to pale before the graphic accounts recorded in Eusebius's *Book of Martyrs.* In light of subsequent events, it is thought that perhaps the aging Diocletian had been persuaded to issue such an edict by his Caesar, Galerius, and it was known that an attempt had been made to purge the army of Christian soldiers who were considered a threat to the Empire.

It was Galerius, who seven years later, issued the edict that canceled the persecution of the Christians. This occurred on April 30, A.D. 311, as he lay on his deathbed in Nicomedia, where he had been suddenly stricken with a fatal disease.

Here is the picture of this man's death as painted by the words of a contemporary — words written seventeen centuries ago by Eusebius:

> *Hence he was visited by some divine judgment sent from God, which beginning in his flesh proceeded to his very soul. For a sudden tumor appeared about the middle of the body, then a spongy fistula in these parts which continued to extend and penetrate with ulcerations to the inmost parts of the bowels. Hence sprung an immense multitude of worms, hence also an insufferable death-like effluvia exhaled, as his whole body before his disease, by reason of his gluttony, had been changed into an excessive mass of fat, which then becoming putrid, exhibited a dreadful and intolerable spectacle to those that drew near.*

We are not only brought most graphically into the presence of this dying emperor, but the strong words of the Christian writer also suggest the culpability of the man and makes clear the religious struggle that was taking place. The pagan gods, it seems, had forsaken Rome and her Empire. The final act of this desperate emperor, who died the day after issuing the edict that would presumably save his soul, ushered in a new religious era.

The Edict of Diocletian, whether or not he was the instigator, had set in motion a terrible struggle with hideous martyrdom, but eventually resulted in a triumph for Christianity.

Constantine the Great

Flavius Valerius Constantinus would eventually emerge as sole emperor, and he is known as Constantine the Great. He has gone down in history as the champion of Christianity, but not before some bitter struggles for power among the players on the scene and to whom, according to Diocletian's great plan, the power was to be peacefully transferred when he and Maximian retired in A.D. 305. What ensued was a spider's web of intrigues within the boundaries of the Empire, with the final battles fought on Rome's doorstep as the action moved southward.

When the old emperors retired, Constantine had been in the service of Galerius in the East, virtually a hostage, but now his father, the Western Emperor Constantius I Chlorus, asked that he be returned to help in the defense of Britain where the Picts were making trouble. Galerius was reluctant, but Constantine was finally able to join his father, and the two set out for England. Constantius died in Britain in the summer of A.D. 306 at the fortified Roman town of York, and Constantine was proclaimed emperor by the troops.

The ambitious Galerius wanted his own men in power, and he appointed his friend Severus as the Western Emperor, conceding to Constantine the lower title of Caesar. Maxentius, son of the old retired Emperor Maximian, was completely cut out of the picture. Trouble was soon on the way as the disgruntled Maxentius staged a *coup* in Rome where he had the support he needed, and he was established as emperor. He even recalled his father from his forced retirement, and this not-so-happy senior was delighted to be back on the scene to take up a fight against Severus, who was promptly defeated. Father and son were soon at odds, however, which was not surprising, as Maximian has been described as "thoroughly coarse, savage, brutal, impatient and impossible to get along with." Maximian turned against his son and decided instead to support Constantine, to whom he had given his daughter Fausta in marriage.

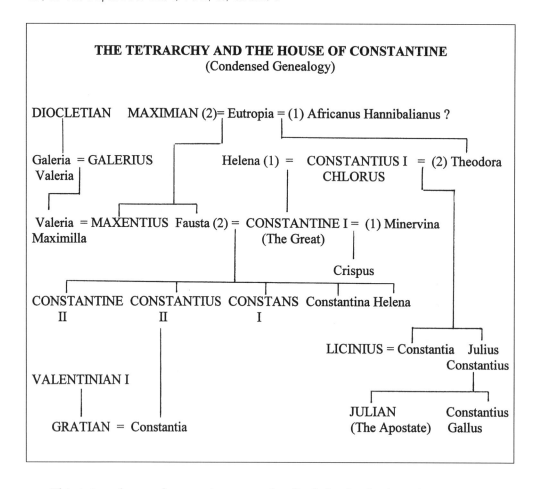

THE TETRARCHY AND THE HOUSE OF CONSTANTINE
(Condensed Genealogy)

This internal war of succession was a family fight that had tragic consequences, for it was not long before Maximian double-crossed his daughter and son-in-law Constantine, staging a revolt at Arles in southern Gaul. Constantine lost no time in returning from the Rhine where he was campaigning and promptly defeated his father-in-law, who was forced to commit suicide. Maximian had returned from his retirement to gain power and had treacherously betrayed both his son and his daughter. Now he was dead. This was Constantine's first family victim.

When Galerius, the Eastern Emperor, died the following year—in circumstances already described—Constantine made the move against the Emperor of the West, brother-in-law Maxentius, and invaded Italy. Soon, his victorious army was at the gates of Rome. Maxentius made the mistake of leaving the safety of the impregnable Aurelian walls and led his army to meet his enemy outside the city across the Tiber. Caught between the hills and the river, Maxentius's army was defeated. In the confusion thousands drowned when a bridge of boats collapsed. Maxentius was killed in the rout that occurred following the famous battle of the Milvian Bridge in A.D. 312.

The battle of the Milvian Bridge was more than a military victory for Constantine. It is of significance as a turning point in Christian history as it was also considered a victory for Christianity. The story is told that Constantine dreamed he would win the battle if he painted the monogram of Christ on his soldiers' shields, which was done, and he attributed his victory to this divine intervention. Constantine entered Rome as the victor. No blood having been spilled within the city, he was welcomed by the Senate and immediately recognized as emperor. However, he had become emperor over the dead body of his wife's brother, Maxentius, the second family victim.

The Emperor of the East was now Licinius, who had supported Constantine's cause. It was all in the family because the two emperors were brothers-in-law, Lucinius being married to Constantine's sister Constantia. Each emperor ruled his own half of the empire for thirteen years (311–324), but the arrangement was not always harmonious, and incidents beginning in A.D. 316 culminated in a major battle at Chrysopolis on the Bosporos. Licinius was defeated and took flight to Nicomedia with some 30,000 of his troops. There was no escape for him, however, as he was captured by Constantine. Licinius's wife, Constantia, pleaded with her brother for Licinius's life to be spared. He was imprisoned briefly at Thessalonica, but was later accused of plotting a comeback with the help of the Goths. An order for his execution was issued by Constantine, and one more relative was added to his list of victims.

Constantine was hailed as a liberator by his eloquent biographer and historian, Bishop Eusebius, and the victory is recorded in the following words: *To him, therefore, the Supreme God granted from heaven above the fruits of his piety, the trophies of victory over the wicked, and that nefarious tyrant, with all his counselors and adherents, be cast prostrate at the feet of Constantine.* The Christian writers of the period did not dwell on the more gruesome aspects of the emperor who later accepted baptism. Moreover, this was not the end of the killings—there was worse to come.

In A.D. 324 Constantine became the sole emperor, ruling over both East and West. But this emperor, who came to be known as Constantine the Great, did not make his capital at Rome, although the city lost none of its constitutional privileges. Instead, he made the ancient Greek city of Byzantium, sitting strategically on the Bosporos Strait between Europe and Asia, the new capital of the Empire. It would be a Christian city without the pagan influences of Rome. He named it Constantinople, a monument to his name that was far greater and more lasting than a triumphal arch, a temple, or public baths. It soon eclipsed Rome and, formally dedicated in May A.D. 330, it heralded the beginning of a Christian empire.

Constantine's contributions and defense of the Empire are far overshadowed by his conversion to and promotion of Christianity, the impact of which on the western world cannot be overstated. The first act of major import for Christians was the Edict of Milan, promulgated in A.D. 313, coming one year after the victory at the Milvian Bridge and ten years after the terrible persecutions ordered by Diocletian. This agreement was also incorporated into one issued in the East and was a pronouncement of tolerance toward the Christians.

Constantine became increasingly involved in religious matters during the years that followed, and he was troubled by the disputes between the bishops, particularly the conflict with Arius, whose views had created a schism. A landmark event in the history of Christianity was the conference called by Constantine at Nicaea in A.D. 325 and attended by some 220 bishops from throughout the Empire. Out of this conference came an agreement known as the Nicene Creed, in which it was declared that the Son (Jesus) was "of one substance" with God the Father. The theological matter, for the time being, was settled.

After his victory over Licinius, Constantine issued an edict urging his subjects to convert to Christianity, then he embarked on one of the most remarkable building programs in history as churches went up throughout the Empire to the glory of God. In Rome he built the first church of San Pietro on the spot where the saint was martyred. This survived until the sixteenth century, when it was replaced by the present Basilica of San Pietro.

Constantine's legacy to the western world was staggering, but the man himself was something of an enigma. The glowing account of the Emperor afforded us by Bishop Eusebius, his chief biographer, seems to ignore the darker side of Constantine's character. Indeed, the Emperor's lavish support of Christian churches may have been his desperate attempt to expiate his sins, of which there were many. The most tragic acts of his life surely involved his favorite son, Crispus, and his second wife, Fausta. Constantine had this son by a first marriage put to death for allegedly assaulting Fausta. It seems that he later found out that Fausta wanted Crispus out of the way so that there would be no rivals to her own sons. On discovering that his son, who had been considered most pious, had been falsely accused and put to death, Constantine had Fausta put to death shortly thereafter. Now the two people closest to him had been added to his list of victims.

Constantine died on May 22, A.D. 337, after a rule of a quarter of a century. He accepted baptism from Bishop Eusebius just one day before his death. Some assumed, at the time, that baptismal cleansing should cover as many prior sins as possible. In spite of the delay, this act marked him as the first Christian emperor, with enormous consequences for western civilization. Significant also was the church's endorsement of "empire," eloquently stated by Eusebius in the following passage:

> But the mighty and victorious Constantine, adorned with every virtue of religion . . . recovered the east as his own, and thus restored the Roman empire to its ancient state of one united body; extending their peaceful sway around the world, from the rising sun to the opposite regions, to the north and the south, even to the last borders of the declining day. (Ecclesiastical History, book 10)

One can only wonder how another biographer might have worded an epitaph to this man who came to be the first Christian emperor.

A House Divided

Constantine had worked hard to create an empire with the help of the Christian god and on his death had handed over its trusteeship to his three surviving sons and two nephews. The three sons were proclaimed Augusti and they soon set about purging their family ranks of rivals. A bloodbath ensued in which the two unfortunate nephews, along with many other relatives and their supporters, met their death. These young brothers, the oldest of which was only twenty, divided the Empire between them, and then fought with each other.

In the final partition, Constantine II got the West, Constantius II got the East with Constantinople, and the youngest brother, the teenager Constans I, got the Middle with Italy, Africa, and Illyricum.

It seems that young Constans did not pay due respect to the more senior Augustus, brother Constantine II, who in A.D. 340 decided to march on Italy. He got as far as Aquileia in the north when he was ambushed and killed by his brother's forces. Constans now took control of the western half of the Empire as well the middle. He ended up with the lion's share, yet the two surviving brothers were divided less by the question of frontiers than by their allegiances to the two branches of Christianity that had emerged. Constans supported the Western Catholic orthodoxy based on the Nicene Creed, whereas Constantius II subscribed to the eastern branch. This dispute between brothers on matters of religion was symptomatic of the confusion that prevailed at the time and was a departure from the old Roman days when more was better, the pantheon had room for all, and religious tolerance was the rule.

Constans successfully defended his realm against invaders, but he was not a popular emperor and the thirteenth year of his reign proved to be unlucky. It was not his brother who engineered his downfall, however, but a former slave of his father, Flavius Magnus Magnentius, now an officer of his own élite legions, which proclaimed him emperor in January A.D. 350. Constans was only twenty-seven years of age when he was overthrown in Gaul by Magnentius, who had him killed.

Magnentius assumed the purple and ruled the West for three years in place of Constans. Italy came under this pagan who was more like the rough soldiers he commanded than one for the imperial seat. Magnentius, whose coins bore the words "Restorer of Liberty"—although liberty from whom or what is not clear—was recognized by the whole western part of the Empire, including Africa, but not of course by Constantius in the East.

A clash between East and West became inevitable as the usurper and Constantius failed to reach a compromise. After all, it was hardly likely that Constantius could accept his brother's murderer as a fellow emperor. Battles were fought in various arenas, and the dispute culminated in the most bloody battle of the century when the opposing imperial armies came face to face on September 28, A.D. 351, at a place called Mursa (Osijek in Yugoslavia), far from Rome. That day in September witnessed the worst scenes of hell as metal and flesh clashed, and men and horses were massacred by the thousands. An empire was at war with itself and it is believed that some 50,000 men perished.

The following summer, Emperor Constantius II invaded Italy, and Magnentius fled to Gaul. After three years of turmoil to hold on to the bone he had claimed, fortune had now abandoned this bold usurper, who committed suicide at Lugdunum (Lyons). Constantius II, the only surviving son of Constantine the Great, became the sole and undisputed emperor of East and West.

Constantinople, capital of the eastern half, became the capital of the reunited Roman Empire, but in A.D. 357 Rome was honored by a visit from the shadowy Constantius II, now a man of forty years. The Romans greeted him with great cheering and pomp, at which they were very good, and seemed to have lost none of their zeal when it came to a good celebration. The Emperor responded to the fanfare with the utmost self-control, exhibiting no emotion in the face of Roman exuberance. To quote an eyewitness, he was "like a dummy, gazing straight before him as if his head were in a vice and turning neither to right nor left." These were the words of Ammianus Marcellinus, the last Roman historian who, admittedly no great admirer of the Emperor, describes him as a dull-witted, frugal, temperate, and extremely chaste man. Accustomed as he was to the rigors of war on the one hand and a strict Christian environment on the other, he must have been awestruck by what he saw in this ancient city that his father Constantine had considered unbefitting to the new faith.

Ammianus through his words has given us a chance to sneak back into Rome and follow him as he describes in satirical form the goings-on in that city. He mentioned the disorderly frivolity of the rich, the ostentatious style of dress, and the abandonment of learning. Not bearing in mind where they were born—by which he meant they were expected to set an example to the rest of the world—they behaved "as if they were licensed to indulge in vice and debauchery." He describes the way they galloped their horses through the paved streets of the city and how the womenfolk raced about in litters, followed by a retinue of servants and hangers-on, creating a wonderful picture of life and foolish abandon. These were the rich ones, but Ammianus also painted us a picture of the poor, and these are his own words:

> Of the lowest and poorest class, some spend the night in bars, others shelter under the awnings of the theatres, . . . They hold quarrelsome gambling sessions, at which they make ugly noises by breathing loudly through the nose; or else—and this is their prime passion—they wear themselves out from dawn to dusk, wet or fine, in detailed discussion of the merits and demerits of horses and their drivers. It is most extraordinary to see a horde of people hanging in burning excitement on the outcome of a chariot race. Things like this prevent anything worthy of serious mention happening at Rome.

In the eyes of Ammianus, the city of Rome had come full cycle, and he used the metaphor of the human life span to describe its growth through infancy to old age. Yet the mystique still survived and the "old man" might yet command respect for what he had been, but the real power was in Constantinople where the Emperor had his residence.

Constantius lived four more years after his historic visit to Rome. He died in A.D. 361 after a rule of a quarter of a century. The succession had been taken care of by the appointment of a Caesar during his lifetime, a cousin and husband of his sister Helena, Flavius Claudius Julianus, but we know him by another name.

Julian the Apostate

Julian was a survivor of the house of Constantine, and compared with some of his predecessors he was an old man at the age of thirty when he found himself sole ruler of the united Roman Empire. Julian was an orphan from an early age. His mother died soon after his birth, and his father was killed along with most of his relatives of the bloodied House of Constantine. His life had been spared, but he had been relegated to a remote place in the rugged region of Cappadocia (Turkey), where he received a strict Christian education. His later experiences included residence in Athens, where he grew to admire the Hellenic culture. He eventually abandoned Christianity and espoused paganism. Julian wanted the pagans to be organized as well as the Christians, and he tried to rebuild the Temple at Jerusalem. Fate—or God—took a hand in that because the work was destroyed by an earthquake.

Inspired by the feats of Alexander the Great centuries before, Julian also craved military glory. With an army of some 65,000 men he invaded the Persian Empire and crossed the Tigris River. Victory eluded him, and in the face of strong resistance he was forced to undertake a long retreat. Julian was killed in a skirmish on June 26, A.D. 363, though it was widely believed he died at the hands of one of his Christian soldiers.

Julian's rule was a temporary setback for Christianity, but the tidal wave could not be stopped. This Emperor, whose short life was so full of personal tragedies, pathos, and glorious dreams, left many works of great literary merit that revealed his love of the Greek culture, but he left no lasting mark in the pages of Italy's history. With his death, the House of Constantine came to a sad end.

THE HOUSE OF VALENTINIAN
(Condensed Genealogy)

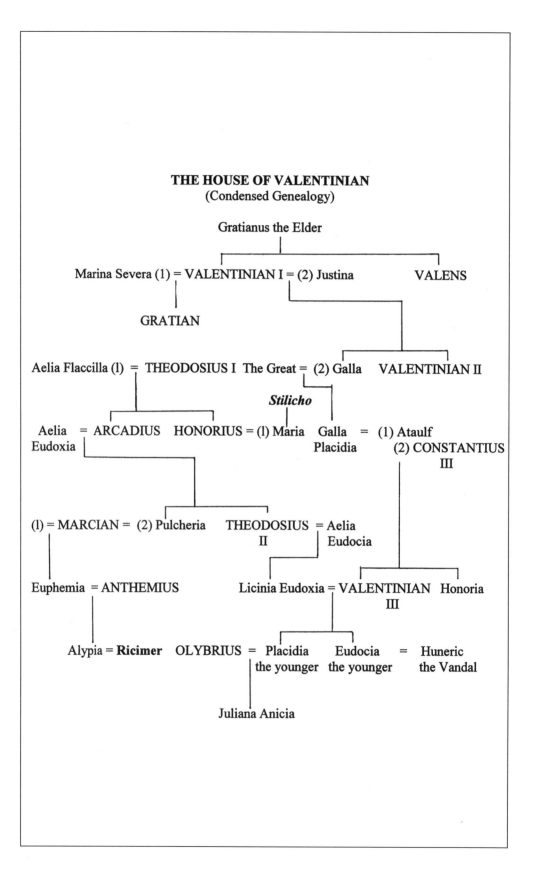

CHAPTER TEN

A New Dynasty and Barbarian Invasions

The House of Valentinian

Valentinian I came to power when he was proclaimed emperor by the legions at Ancyra (Ankara) on the death of Julian in 363. It was the beginning of a new dynasty that would control the destiny of the Roman Empire almost up to its collapse a hundred years later.

Faced with the task confronting him, Valentinian took his brother Valens as co-emperor, giving him the East, while he chose the West with his imperial seat at Mediolanum (Milan), establishing headquarters at Lutetia (Paris) and also Treviri (Trier), where he spent seven years campaigning against the invading tribes and building fortifications along the Rhine.

During his rule, Valentinian walked a tightrope between Christianity and the pagan practices that had been revived by Julian the Apostate. He had agreed with his brother on a policy of universal tolerance, although that tolerance did not extend to the barbarians, for he forbade on pain of death any intermarriage between their people and Romans, meaning all citizens of the Roman Empire. As a soldier he defended the Empire, under threat from outside, and as an administrator he sought to address the ills of society and protect the poor and underprivileged by appointing defenders of the people to help the less fortunate.

In November of 375, Valentinian died after falling ill as he was about his business in the Danube provinces, and he was succeeded by his sixteen-year-old son, Gratian, previously made his co-emperor.

Boy Emperors

A few days after Gratian came to power his four-year-old half-brother, Valentinian II, was proclaimed Augustus by supporters in Budapest. With the consent of his uncle, the Eastern Emperor Valens, young Gratian allotted to Valentinian II the territories of Africa, Italy, and western Illyricum, later a bone of contention between East and West. Because of the tender age of the brothers, the government was in the hands of advisors, one of the most influential being their tutor, the Latin poet Ausonius. In effect, Italy had no imperial presence, for although Gratian visited Rome the year after his father's death, his place of residence was Treviri (Trier) and for some time Mediolanum (Milan), where he came under the influence of the powerful Bishop Ambrose.

Shortly after the young brothers had come to power, Valens was killed while fighting the Visigoths at the Battle of Adrianople. In a rather extraordinary and historic decision, Gratian called on Theodosius, the son of a supreme cavalry commander who had been executed for treason, to replace his uncle as Emperor of the East. An elegant man with blond hair and an aquiline nose, he was born in northwest Spain where he might have lived as a grandee for the rest of his life, but destiny had other plans for him. He was a major player in the events that followed.

Like all his predecessors, Theodosius was dedicated to the business of protecting the Empire. He had his work cut out for him in the east, where he solved the problem with the Visigoths by eventually allowing them to stay as "immigrants." They were inside the gates, refugees fleeing from the Huns who were constantly pushing at their backs, and they were supposed to keep the gates closed behind them. In 382 they became a federation within the borders of the Empire, governing themselves and supplying much-needed soldiers and labor.

While all this was taking place in the east, the Italians basked in the sun of "retirement" as Gratian was defending the realm from a usurper from Britain, the notorious Magnus Maximus and Gratian met his death at Lugdunum (Lyons), treacherously assassinated by one of his men after much of his army had deserted to the usurper.

Now the little half-brother Valentinian II, who had barely reached puberty, was alone with his mother. Emperor Theodosius made an agreement with the usurper, allowing him to remain as rival emperor in the West and leaving young Valentinian with Italy, which was probably the safest place to be at the time, but not for long. The big bad wolf, Magnus Maximus, was soon knocking on the backdoor with his armies massed on Italian territory at Aquileia and even threatening the Eastern Empire of Theodosius, a far greater prize than Italy. One can only imagine the anxiety that the Italians must have felt on learning that their young Emperor had fled with his mother, Justina, and sister, Galla, to seek Theodosius's protection. Of the mother's encounter with Theodosius, the pagan historian Zosimus wrote:

> Justina, however, was neither inexperienced in practical affairs nor at a loss for hitting upon clever solutions, knowing Theodosius' erotic proclivities set before him her extremely good-looking daughter Galla, grasped him by the knees, and besought him not to let go unavenged the death of Gratian, who had bestowed upon him his Empire, nor to leave the two of them lying there abject and devoid of any hope. Theodosius as he listened was smitten at the sight of the girl's beauty.

The meeting, if indeed it did take place as Zosimus described, was a historic event because Theodosius, whose wife had died, asked for Galla's hand in marriage, to which the mother agreed on condition that the death of her stepson, Gratian, would be avenged and the young Valentinian would have his empire restored to him. Justina was certainly no fool—she knew that her own life as well as that of her young son would be in jeopardy without the protection of this powerful emperor. Justina, her emperor son, and Galla (who was soon to become empress) were given an escort and set sail on their return to Italy, making their way to the relative safety of Rome. Meanwhile the fastest ships of the usurper Magnus Maximus put to sea and scoured the Ionian waters in a fruitless endeavor to catch the elusive little emperor and his family.

As for Magnus, he was later defeated in battles against Theodosius, whose troops he had tried to win over to his side. Magnus was captured and "led stripped of his royal clothing into the presence of Theodosius," who showed no mercy. Magnus, the usurper, was executed on August 28, 388.

Theodosius stayed in Italy for a while, and the recalcitrant Gaul was entrusted to Valentinian. He was later murdered there, barely on the threshold of manhood at twenty-one years of age, as yet another usurper, Eugenius, came on stage. Theodosius defeated the usurper two years later and ruled as sole emperor for a fleeting five months. For this brief period, the sun shone for the last time on a united Roman Empire.

Theodosius proceeded to Rome with his youngest son, Honorius, and he designated to him the western regions of Italy, Spain, Gaul, and all Africa, and then departed for Constantinople. On his way back he was stricken with a disease and died in January 395 in Milan, a dreary place in winter when a cold fog hangs over the plains obscuring the massive Alps that form a distant backdrop of snowy peaks.

Theodosius had sat on the imperial throne for fifteen years, and he was succeeded by the orphan brothers Arcadius and Honorius, his sons by his first wife from Spain, Aelia Faccilla. Arcadius at age eighteen got the East and the twelve-year-old Honorius got the West.

Theodosius left behind another orphan. He had indeed married the lovely Galla, as previously arranged, but she had died in childbirth along with an infant son. However, she had previously given Theodosius a daughter, Galla Placidia, whose life was even more eventful than her mother's. We will soon meet this orphan girl again down the road of history in some most unusual circumstances.

Alaric the Visigoth: Hero or Villain?

Although East and West were nominally ruled by the brothers Arcadius and Honorius, behind the two were two powerful advisors who held the power. In the East was the notorious eunuch Eutropius, and in the West it was Stilicho, half-Vandal and half-Roman, a most trustworthy man whom Theodosius had made his Master of Soldiers.

Now at a time when the Empire was vulnerable, the hearts and minds of the two supposed "defenders" — or their seconds, as the case may be — were focused on the disputed territory of Illyricum and the presence of a Visigoth named Alaric. He had become a thorn in the side of both East and West.

Son of a chieftain, a nobleman by birth and an Arian Christian, Alaric had come into the Empire with his people from Rumania in 376 and became the chief of his tribe in 395, the year of Theodosius's death. It seems that the new emperor did not honor the agreements made by his predecessor to pay certain subsidies so, Alaric marched on Constantinople, the first of many acts against his host that included sacking several cities over the years. Together the two Emperors could have crushed the troublesome Visigoth, but he always got away and was used by both.

Alaric first appeared in Italy in 401, supposedly at the urgings of the East. He laid siege to the strategic northern city of Aquileia, pushed into Piedmont, and was defeated on Easter Sunday in 402 when his camp at Pollentia (Pollenzo) was raided by the Romans. Alaric's wife and children were taken hostage, but he was allowed to leave Italy. That was a mistake, for the following year he was back again, this time to threaten Verona. Once more he was defeated, and once again he was allowed to escape.

Clearly, Mediolanum (Milan) was no longer a safe place, and in 404 it was decided to move the imperial capital to Ravenna. This city on the Adriatic coast was protected by marshes, and if the need should arise, an escape could be made by sea.

So Ravenna, not Rome, became the last imperial capital of the Western Roman Empire. It turned out to be a prudent move.

The following year, coming like a tidal wave, the Ostrogoths rushed through the territory of the Middle Danube and across the Hungarian plain, pushing the Roman population there ahead of them. Like a flood they came into the Italian peninsula and moved south to Fiesole (Florence), where they were eventually defeated in the fall of 406 by the capable defender Stilicho. In the end, there was no stopping the invading hordes, massing from all directions. A few months later, in December of 406, the frozen Rhine River, no longer an impediment for people without boats, offered them a stepping stone into the Empire.

Taking advantage of this situation in the west, Alaric was back at the northeast door, bribed by Emperor Honorius with gold, but the short-sighted Senate accused Stilicho of conspiracy with the enemy, and in August of 408 he was put to death. The tide of reaction against the Germans he had commanded quickly followed as a sentiment of mistrust of these legions was fueled by the Senate's actions. The Germans, in turn, deprived of their leader and fearful for their own families, deserted to Alaric. Rome was defenseless.

Alaric invaded Italy again, this time reaching the walls of Rome and cutting off the food supply. It was now the Senate that used bribes and promises to deal with Alaric, who departed with promises that were not fulfilled. The following year, with Honorius remaining intransigent and safe from harm in his capital of Ravenna, Alaric was back again with a greater force to lay siege to Rome. This time he set up a rival

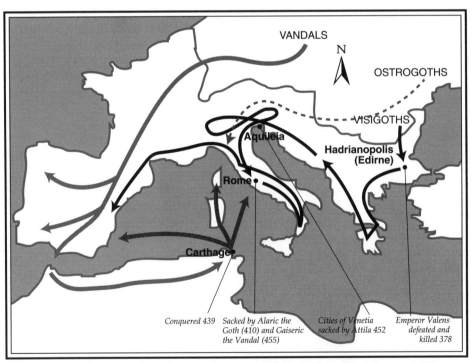

VANDALS

N

OSTROGOTHS

VISIGOTHS

Aquileia

Hadrianopolis
(Edirne)

Rome

Carthage

Conquered 439 · Sacked by Alaric the Goth (410) and Gaiseric the Vandal (455) · Cities of Venetia sacked by Attila 452 · Emperor Valens defeated and killed 378

The Barbarian Invasions of the Fifth Century A.D.

emperor, but Honorius refused to be bullied, and the puppet emperor was soon deposed.

The die was cast. In 410 Rome was besieged for the third time. Alaric followed the voices he had heard in a grove after his defeat in 402 that told him, "Thou shalt penetrate into the city," which he understood to be Rome. Now he could live up to his name, Ala-Reiks in the Gothic tongue, which meant "Master of All." The unthinkable would become the inevitable. Rome, the Eternal City, which had not been invaded by a foreigner for 800 years, would be raped by a man who, for all his noble origins, learning, and Christian beliefs, had been rejected as a "barbarian." Why would the Romans not accept him as they had the Spaniard Theodosius or the half-Vandal Stilicho?

On August 24, the city gates were treacherously opened to Alaric, who indeed "penetrated the city," but he did not stay long. His soldiers took some loot and burned some buildings, but he had instructed them to respect life and not touch the churches. The Christian historian Paulus Orosius described one incident as follows:

> While the barbarians were rushing hither and thither through the City, one of the Goths, a powerful person and a Christian, by chance found in a church building a virgin, advanced in years, dedicated to God, and when he asked her respectfully for gold and silver, she, with faithful firmness, replied that she had a great deal in her possession and would presently bring it forth, and she did so, and when she perceived that the barbarian was astonished by the riches that were displayed, the quantity, weight, and beauty, although he did not know their nature, the virgin of Christ said to the barbarian: "These are the sacred vessels of the Apostle Peter. Presume if you dare; you will answer for the deed."

The matter was reported to Alaric, who ordered that the objects be returned to the basilica.

Alaric had humiliated Rome, but he did not destroy it. He had his sights set on Africa and the grain supply that was Italy's lifeline. So after just three days he gathered his men together and made his way south. As his share of the booty he took with him as a hostage none other than the Emperor's half-sister, Galla Placidia, now a ripe twenty years of age. Alaric, by this act, was at least ensured safe passage to the south and, at the same time, he could avenge the capture of his own family by the Romans.

In spite of his grandiose plans and his belief in his destiny, the curtain would soon rise on Alaric's tragic final act. He reached Reggio di Calabria, at the very toe of Italy, but the ships he had assembled to take him to the shores of Africa were wrecked in a storm. The attempt was abandoned, and he decided to return northward, but he was taken ill and died at Cosenza in that same fateful year of 410. The Visigoths buried their revered chief, along with many treasures deep in the bed of the Busento River so that his body could not be found and desecrated.

Alaric's place was taken by his brother-in-law, Ataulf, who continued northward with the precious hostage along the western coast of Italy and into southern Gaul. Ataulf had a dream not only to find a resting place for his people but also to fuse the Romans and the Visigoths into one people. To achieve this goal, he married his hostage princess, Galla Placidia, in 414 at Narbonne, near the Spanish border. This did not give him legitimacy, however, as Emperor Honorius refused his consent and recognition. A year later, Ataulf was driven out of Gaul into Spain and assassinated at Barcelona.

The new Visigoth chief, Wallia, had a much better idea, trading the widowed Galla Placidia for permission to settle in southern Gaul. The wanderings of the Visigoths displaced from the abandoned Roman province of Dacia (Rumania), now ended on the other side of the Alps, where they later became a federation with their capital at Toulouse. The saga of Alaric, the Moses for his people, was finally over.

Galla Placidia: The Dynastic Link

Back in Ravenna, Galla Placidia, the childless young widow of the Visigoth Ataulf next became the pawn in the imperial game. This lady, whose life story reads more like fiction, played no small part in maintaining the thread that symbolically held the Eastern and Western parts of the Empire together, although both followed separate destinies.

Emperor Honorius, meanwhile, had his own plans for his unfortunate half-sister. She was invited, coaxed, and finally coerced into a marriage with Constantius III, a man who had been his trustworthy Master of Soldiers since 411 and the real power in the West following the death of Stilicho. Galla Placidia and Constantius III were duly married on January 1, 417; four years later he was made joint emperor of the West and Placidia was given the title of Augusta. Carried on the waves of fate from hostage to empress, she seemed to be riding the crest of fortune. The arrangement was short-lived, however, as Constantius died in September of the same year. Placidia was thus widowed for the second time, but now she had two children, a son who would one day be emperor as Valentinian III, and a daughter, Honoria.

Emperor Honorius died in 423, just two years after his co-emperor, but before his death he had fallen out with his widowed half-sister. It seems his interest in her had been more than brotherly, but she repulsed his amorous attentions, and the split between the two also divided the imperial court into two factions. Fate dealt Placidia another blow when she was banished from Ravenna after Honorius's death. She fled to Constantinople and took refuge with Theodosius II, the Eastern Emperor and relative. She played the role of exile there for the next two years while Johannes, a man of Gothic origin, was proclaimed emperor in the West.

An invading force was sent from the Eastern Empire and after setbacks—in which no small part was played by the fickle Adriatic Sea—and a series of adventures, Johannes was finally dragged from his marshy lair of Ravenna and taken into the presence of Placidia, now back on Italian soil at Aquileia. With barbaric savagery, the poor Johannes had his right hand severed, was exhibited in the circus on a donkey for all to see, and then put to death. One might detect certain antireligious overtones in the despicable and needlessly savage treatment of this man who, according to the historian Procopius, had been a wise and gentle ruler.

The six-year-old Valentinian III was proclaimed emperor and Placidia, by this strange reversal of fortune, was now his regent, a function she held for twelve years, until her son had reached the age of eighteen.

Valentinian III sat on the imperial throne for thirty years as the Empire continued to crumble around him. He did not shine as an emperor. Another man was caught in the footlights instead.

Attila and the Huns

The period of Valentinian's rule was characterized by the rise of new leaders, intent on making inroads into the Empire. A formidable figure had appeared on the northern horizon whose very name struck terror at its mention — Attila.

Attila, the fearful leader of the Huns, gained supremacy on the murder of his brother and then proceeded to rally around him an army that included not only the Huns but also Vandals, Ostrogoths, and Franks. His people had ravaged the Eastern Empire and exacted large amounts of gold from the Emperor, but in 450 Attila turned his attention to the west, moving north across the German plains and threatening Gaul.

Fate seemed to be on Attila's side when Honoria, sister of Valentinian III, called on him to rescue her from her brother, who had plans to marry her off to a Roman whom she detested. Attila took this as an offer of marriage, since Honoria had sent him her ring, and he boldly requested half the Empire as dowry. Valentinian might have sacrificed his sister to remove the threat of the terrible Attila, but he was certainly not willing to give up half his empire into the bargain. It seems that history was repeating itself as the Visigoth Ataulf had married Honoria's mother, Galla Placidia, with the same goal in mind. It is hard to imagine, however, that young Honoria had intended to give herself to the Hun warrior, described by one who had visited his camp as a short, stocky man with a flat nose and whose deep-set eyes peered out of a large head.

The frustrated Attila next resorted to force and, poised as he was across the Rhine River that was the frontier of the Empire, he launched an attack on Gaul, besieging and occupying the strategic Roman city of Aurelianum, known later as the French city of Orleans. The Roman general Aetius went forth with an army that was pitifully inadequate as, to quote Gibbon, "the youth of Italy trembled at the sound of the trumpet." They had relied for too long on the people they had conquered to protect their Empire, and few now became warriors.

A great battle took place on the northern plain southeast of Paris, described by surviving Gothic warriors to the historian Cassiodorus as "a conflict, fierce, various, obstinate and bloody, such as could not be paralleled either in the present or in the past ages." Attila had been caught in a trap and finally lost the day, forced to retreat back the way he had come with what was left of his tattered hordes.

Attila had not given up the idea of getting Honoria as his bride — along with the coveted dowry — and again made his demands known to her brother, who remained adamant.

Attila was ready to inflict a punishment on Italy that would never be forgotten. He had meanwhile moved behind the great barrier of the Alps to make his entry into Italy from the northeast, laying siege to the rich, populous, and fortified city of Aquileia, a crossroads between East and West so frequently in the spotlight. This strategic city was surrounded by walls and defended by the crème de la crème of the Roman army. For three months the city held out while Attila's troops grew increasingly restless and disgruntled. Attila made ready to lift the siege and depart when the course of history was suddenly changed by the appearance of a flock of long-necked white birds. The storks that had built their nests in the city had taken flight, and Attila read this as an omen that they were deserting a doomed city. With renewed hope he exhorted his soldiers to attack, and the city was penetrated. Aquileia, the city whose name means "north wind," was destroyed by the Hunnish hordes that had grown more ruthless by the long wait and those not slaughtered fled to the islands on which would later rise the city of VENICE.

Moving swiftly west on their quick horses across the Po valley, the Huns proceeded to ravage the plains of northern Italy, reducing some cities to ashes and stone and literally erasing them from the map. Vicenza, Verona, and Bergamo suffered dreadful cruelties inflicted by the savage Huns, who met little resistance and finally entered the former imperial capital of Mediolanum itself. Attila spared Mediolanum and took possession of the imperial palace where the emperor Theodosius had expired almost half a century earlier. Italy was defenseless; General Aetius could do no more than harass the enemy with his handful of Romans, no help coming from the Visigoths in Gaul or the Eastern Empire.

In desperation it was decided to negotiate with Attila and the safety of Italy was to be bought with dowry and the Emperor's sister Honoria. In 452 a delegation, which included none other than Pope Leo I, was sent to Attila's encampment on the Mincio River. A treaty was made, and Attila was persuaded to depart with promises that his bride would be delivered to him. With the persuasive urging of the powerful Pope, symbolic of the future role of the church, the pestilence that had weakened the ranks of his army, and the fear that the Eastern Emperor would send help, Attila left Italian soil and returned to his home beyond the Danube, presumably to await the arrival of his bride. He threatened that worse would follow if the promises were not honored.

Back beyond the Danube the impatient Attila, in a surprising display of pomp and rejoicing that should have been reserved for his promised Honoria, added yet one more wife to his already long list of ladies in the person of a beautiful young maiden called Ildico. This wedding night was to be his last. After much feasting and revelry, he retired to the nuptial bed, where he fell sleep, never to awake again. Attila's attendants found him the next morning dead in his bed, the terrified bride trembling with fear beside him. An artery had burst in the night, and the blood had flowed into the lungs and stomach as he lay on his back, suffocating him in his sleep.

Attila's earthly remains were enclosed in three coffins, one gold, one silver, and one iron, and he was buried under the cloak of night with much treasure. The poor captives who dug his grave were slaughtered so the place would forever remain a secret, reminiscent of the burial accorded Alaric deep below the course of the Busento River.

The famous Dirge of Attila, recorded by historians, sums up the life of this dreaded warrior who played no small role in the history of Italy.

> Here lies Attila the great king of the Huns,
> the son of Mundzucus,
> the ruler of the most courageous tribes;
> enjoying such power as had been unheard of before him,
> he possessed the Scythian and Germanic kingdoms alone
> and also terrorized both empires of the Roman world
> after conquering their cities, and
> placated by their entreaties
> that the rest may not be laid open to plunder
> he accepted an annual tribute.
> After he had achieved all this with great success
> he died, not of any enemy's wound, not betrayed by friends,
> in the midst of his unscathed people,

happy and gay,
without any feeling of pain.
Who therefore would think that this was death
which nobody considers to demand revenge?

(from *The World of the Huns,* J. Otto Maenchen-Helfen)

Attila had made his final exit, and when the curtain came down his cast scattered like shepherdless sheep. The Hunnish threat had died with him.

Portrait of the Huns

The people of the Huns, who are mentioned only cursorily in ancient writers and who dwell beyond the Sea of Azov (Palus Maeotis) near the frozen ocean, are quite abnormally savage. From the moment of birth they make deep gashes in their children's cheeks, so that when in due course hair appears its growth is checked by the wrinkled scars; as they grow older this gives them the unlovely appearance of beardless eunuchs. They have squat bodies, strong limbs, and thick necks, and are so prodigiously ugly and bent that they might be two-legged animals, or the figures crudely carved from stumps which are seen on the parapets of bridges. Still, their shape, however, disagreeable, is human; but their way of life is so rough that they have no use for fire or seasoned food, but live on the roots of wild plants and the half-raw flesh of any sort of animal, which they warm a little by placing it between their thighs and the backs of their horses.

✳ ✳ ✳

They wear garments of linen or the skins of field-mice stitched together, and there is no difference between their clothing whether they are at home or abroad. Once they have put their necks into some dingy shirt they never take it off or change it till it rots and falls to pieces from incessant wear. They have round caps of fur on their heads, and protect their hairy legs with goatskins. Their shapeless shoes are not made on a last and make it hard to walk easily. In consequence they are ill-fitted to fight on foot, and remain glued to their horses, hardy but ugly beasts, on which they sometimes sit like women to perform their every day business. Buying or selling, eating or drinking, are all done by day or night on horseback, and they even bow forward over their beasts' narrow necks to enjoy a deep and dreamy sleep.

✳ ✳ ✳

They are totally ignorant of the distinction between right and wrong, their speech is shifty and obscure, and they are under no restraint from religion or superstition.

(Ammianus Marcellinus, Book 31, extract from section, "The Nature of the Huns and the Alans")

Murder and Chaos

As threats against the Empire continued from outside, a deadly poison was doing its work within the walls of Rome. Who could have imagined that the Emperor would bloody his hands with the murder of his loyal general, Aetius, whose enemies wanted him out of the way and persuaded the Emperor that his life was in danger? Attila was gone, but in that same fateful year of 453, Emperor Valentinian struck and mortally wounded the unsuspecting Aetius as he was making a report on finances, while two of the Emperor's henchmen stood by and allowed the murder to take place. As one outspoken person had supposedly remarked at the time, the Emperor had "cut off his right hand with his left," for the man he killed had been his faithful defender for twenty years.

One of the instigators of the despicable act was Petronius Maximus, whose hopes of stepping into the dead man's shoes were thwarted. His resentment and anger simmered for two years, exacerbated by the belief that the Emperor had seduced his wife, then he made his move. To do his dirty work he engaged as avengers two men who had been under the command of Aetius to assassinate Valentinian. Valentinian was struck down and killed on March 16, 455, by two assassins who had emerged from the crowd as the Emperor, accompanied by his party for an event at the Field of Mars, dismounted from his horse. It was an act reminiscent of the more familiar Ides of March some 500 years earlier when Brutus murdered Julius Caesar to save Rome, for the assassins of Valentinian proudly claimed credit for their actions.

Valentinian was only thirty-six, and he had been emperor for thirty of those years. His times had been fraught with danger, but he had been surrounded by capable men who held the reins of the empire while he pranced on his pleasure horse. Perhaps his own contributions were negligible, but he did put Rome back into the picture, however, as in his later years he chose to reside there rather than in the austere Ravenna. He did one more thing for Rome, for by his decree promulgated in 444, an important element of which made Pope Leo I, the Great, supreme head over the provincial churches, Rome became the spiritual capital and seat of Catholicism.

An Invitation to the Vandals

Valentinian III had no male heir, and the villain, Petronius Maximus, who had waited two years in the wings, now claimed the seat of emperor. Petronius wasted no time in establishing his position, and his first act was to marry the Emperor's widow, Licinia Eudoxia, even forbidding her to mourn her husband whose body was barely cold. At the same time, he betrothed his son to one of Eudoxia's daughters, thus securing his position by placing an egg in the imperial nest.

Once again, a lady in distress would appeal to the enemy to rescue her. The desperate Eudoxia, caught in the net of marriage, called on the Vandal king, Gaiseric, who now controlled much of North Africa, just as her sister-in-law Honoria had appealed to Attila.

Gaiseric had been establishing his awesome power and nibbling away at the fringes of the Western Empire, which had been engaged with Attila to the north. Now the danger came from the south, blowing like a fast, hot wind from the deserts of North Africa. A Germanic people, the Vandals had followed a trail of migration westward, breaking through the Roman defenses along the Rhine in 406, finally crossing the Pyrenees Mountains and moving down into Spain where they remained. Then in May of 429 the new leader, Gaiseric, styled as "King of the Vandals and the Alans," crossed over the Strait of Gibraltar and set foot in North Africa with the remnants of his tribe.

The Vandals, who had converted to Arian Christianity during the great migration, earned much of their reputation during their conquest of the territories they now entered where their actions against the Catholic Christians were especially brutal. In 435, they were recognized as "federates" by the Romans, who allowed them to retain Mauretania and part of Numidia. As a pledge of good behavior, Gaiseric's son, Huneric, was sent to Rome as a hostage to live under the tutelage of the imperial family, where he could be fashioned into a good Roman and ally. It is not known how many years Huneric remained a hostage, but in 439 the bold Gaiseric attacked and captured Carthage, the second most important city of the Western Empire, and declared independence. With the loss of that province, control of much of Italy's grain supply was lost.

The Mediterranean Sea was no barrier for Gaiseric, who had built up a fleet and harassed the coasts of Sicily. This was the man that Eudoxia had called on to save her, and Gaiseric lost no time in going to her rescue. He would not take a back route as Hannibal had done centuries before him, but entered by the front door — Rome itself. At the news of this threat, many Romans gathered their possessions and fled the city. As for Petronius Maximus, he was to blame, and now he was abandoned by all as he tried to make his escape on May 31 in 455. Like a beast tracked down by the hunters, he was recognized and stoned by a mob as he attempted to flee on horseback. Once unhorsed he was at the mercy of the angry crowd, which tore him to pieces and then cast his dreadfully mutilated body into the Tiber River, whose waters carried away yet another victim. His reign has lasted barely two and a half months.

A letter written to a friend by Sidonius Apollinaris, a Romano-Gallic noble and literary figure of the time, contains some revealing insights into popular sentiment:

> [Petronius's] supremacy over that court, as emperor, was characterized by extreme violence, amid risings of the soldiers and the citizens, and the federate peoples. And all this was revealed also by his end, which was strange and swift and terrible: after Fortune had long flattered him, her last treacherous act bathed him in blood, for like a scorpion she struck him down with her tail. (Quoted from Grant, *The Roman Emperors*, p. 309)

Two days after the hated Petronius's death, the Vandal Gaiseric entered the city of Rome and what he did there made Alaric's previous sack look more like a friendly visit. For two terrible weeks Rome was systematically looted and devastated. The wanton destruction perpetrated by these people have made their name synonymous with such acts. They survive in the word *vandalism*.

Gaiseric then set sail for home with his spoils. He also took with him the now twice-widowed Eudoxia — if one could call Petronius of the short-lived marriage a husband. Along with Eudoxia were her two young daughters, Placidia the Younger and Eudocia the Younger, as well as a large number of Roman citizens taken as captives.

The tragic year of 455 had seen the death of two emperors, the humiliating sack of Rome, and the abduction (or was it rescue?) of the Empress herself.

Gaiseric, the King of the Vandals, was riding high now as he gave his son, Huneric, to the princess Eudocia the Younger in marriage. Obviously, they had been previously acquainted with each other when Huneric was a hostage at the imperial palace. Gaiseric returned to North Africa more powerful than before and pursued his grandiose schemes to control the Empire. The Romans desperately needed a champion that could match him, but for now the imperial throne of the West was vacant. In the years that followed, Gaiseric continued to gain supremacy over the vast waters of the Mediterranean while he watched as one emperor after another floundered and drowned in the fickle waters of imperial politics.

CHAPTER ELEVEN

The Last Years of the Roman Empire of the West

The King-Maker and his Puppet Emperors

During the next twenty years, no less than eight emperors made their entrances and exits, but the two characters who played the principal roles were Gaiseric, the Vandal king whom we have already met, and a barbarian, Flavius Ricimer, whose mother was the daughter of the former Visigoth king, Wallia.

The next emperor, Avitus, was responsible for bringing Ricimer on stage. Faced with the ever-present threat of the Vandals, Avitus needed a strongman, so he appointed Ricimer as his Master of Soldiers. This appointment proved to be the beginning of this man's extraordinary rise to power, for he soon became not just an actor in the unfolding drama but the director as well. He came to be known in history as the "king-maker."

In the beginning, Ricimer set about the task of defending the Empire, and he immediately proceeded to Sicily to deal with the Vandals at Agrigentum on the south side of the island. This encounter was followed by a naval battle off Corsica that took place in 456. Things seemed to be going well, but there was a problem that had been created by the clever Gaiseric who, holding the trump card, had cut off the grain supplies to Rome. When bellies began to growl and unrest increased, Emperor Avitus tried to ease the food shortage by decreasing the number of mouths to be fed and he dismissed the Gallic and German troops, paying them off by selling some of Rome's treasures. His popularity had waned and the powerful Ricimer, in his act as "king-maker," like a wicked king cobra turned to strike down the very man who had appointed him to the position of trust, forcing him to abdicate.

For six months there was no emperor of the West, nominally under control of the Emperor of the East who, in February of the following year, with the approval of Ricimer, proclaimed as emperor Majorian (Julius Valerius Maiorianus). Born of a distinguished military family, he was actually an old friend of Ricimer.

Meanwhile, the Vandals had lost no time and by now virtually controlled the Mediterranean waters and threatened the Italian mainland. It was decided to wage all-out war against Gaiseric and the Vandal menace. Plans went ahead to assemble an army on the plains of northern Italy, and a fleet of some 300 ships was built at lightning speed to recapture the sea-power that had been lost. The Army and Navy were to converge on Cartagena (New Carthage) in Spain, where they would engage the enemy. Led by the Emperor, the troops took the land route, followed by Hannibal some six centuries earlier in the opposite direction.

Roman forces met up as planned, but none could have foreseen the impending disaster. Helped by secret intelligence, Gaiseric made a surprise attack on the Roman fleet as it lay at anchor. Soon the bay was ablaze with burning ships, and three years' worth of preparations were destroyed in a single day. Majorian was forced to conclude an unfavorable agreement with Gaiseric and had to retreat with his troops by the way he had come. It was a humiliating defeat and a tragedy for the Emperor. On reaching northern Italy, a mutiny broke out among the troops, presumably instigated by Ricimer who on August 2, 461, captured Majorian and forced him to abdicate. He died five days later at Tortona, apparently put to death by order of his old friend Ricimer.

As for the Vandal King Gaiseric, he emerged stronger than ever, still happily splashing around in the Mediterranean and now also master of Corsica, Sardinia, and the Balearic Islands. He wanted yet another piece of the Empire as a dowry for Eudocia the Younger, wife of his son, Huneric and he came up with the perfect plan. To gain the support of the East he suggested that the nobleman Olybrius be proclaimed emperor. Olybrius had escaped to Constantinople when Gaiseric and his Vandals sacked Rome and "rescued" Empress Eudoxia, and he was now the husband of Placidia the Younger, sister of Gaiseric's daughter-in-law Eudocia. Gaiseric was quite a diplomat for he had treated his royal hostages as his "protégés" and had sent Eudoxia and her daughter Placidia the Younger to the court of Constantinople. However, the Emperor of the East paid no heed to Gaiseric's request as the West remained without an emperor while Ricimer held the reins.

Three months later a man from southwestern Italy, Libius Severus, was chosen successor, ostensibly as Ricimer's puppet, but although he is credited with four years as Emperor of the West he was never acknowledged by the East. He died on campaign in Sicily in November of 465, though it was widely believed that Ricimer had a hand also in this most "convenient" death. For the next two years there was no emperor in the West, and Ricimer remained in control.

The Vandal king was beginning to lose patience, and in 467 he carried out a raid against the uncooperative East. The Eastern Emperor decided that a man must be appointed for the West and he proclaimed as emperor his son-in-law Anthemius. The new emperor realized he needed the blessing and support of strongman Ricimer, and this he secured by giving him in marriage his daughter Alypia.

East and West now combined forces in an expedition against Gaiseric, but the imperial fleets came to grief, partly because of discord and treachery and partly because they fell victims to the unpredictable elements of the Mediterranean. The shrewd Gaiseric had played for time and waited for a change in the wind, which became his ally.

Ricimer took defeat badly and immediately looked for a scapegoat, pointing an accusing finger at his Emperor. As would be expected, relations between the two rapidly deteriorated as insults between father-in-law and son-in-law were openly exchanged, Ricimer calling his Emperor a "Greekling," and Anthemius retorting with the slur of "barbarian."

Italy was now divided into two opposing camps with the Emperor in Rome and Ricimer in Mediolanum. Poor Alypia was caught between her barbarian husband on the one hand and her Greekling father on the other. Anthemius soon realized that the marriage alliance was to no avail and was quoted as saying: *"I have not spared my own flesh and blood, but have given my daughter to this skin-clothed Goth, an alliance which I cannot think upon without shame for myself, my family, and my kingship. But the more I have distinguished him with my gifts, the more bitterly he has become mine enemy."*

Relations between the two had reached an impasse when the powerful Ricimer, who had already brought his next puppet to Italy, decided to remove the Emperor by force and marched his armies on Rome itself. After a siege of several months, a rescue force arrived from Gaul to give assistance to the Emperor and his faithful Visigoth defenders but their brave leader was killed in battle against Ricimer's forces near the bridge leading to Hadrian's mausoleum, known later as the Castel Sant'Angelo. It was at this point that Ricimer's men created a breach in the walls and poured into the Eternal City.

The defenseless Emperor Anthemius was now at the mercy of his ruthless son-in-law, and what followed was a real-life drama played out on the Roman stage as he disguised himself and mingled with the beggars, taking refuge in a basilica across the Tiber in Trastevere. He was soon discovered, however, and on that fateful day of July 11, 472, the curtain came down on one more tragic scene in Rome's imperial history as Anthemius was beheaded by Gundobad, a nephew of his own son-in-law.

The dreams of the Vandal king Gaiseric finally came true in April of 472, when he saw his daughter-in-law's sister, Placidia the Younger, become Empress of the West. The time for her husband, Olybrius (Ancinius), to play his role had arrived. It was a windfall for Gaiseric, who had been waiting for this moment for seven years. Now Olybrius was finally pushed on stage as his predecessor was dragged out.

It was apparently not the intention of the Eastern Emperor for Olybrius to take the place of the murdered Anthemius. He had been sent to Italy ostensibly to mediate the differences between Ricimer and the Emperor. However, Ricimer obviously saw in this ailing man the stuff of a puppet and proclaimed him emperor. It was a brief moment of glory, however, as on November 2 of the same year Olybrius died of dropsy. His was a natural death, at least, and he had outlived Ricimer—the "king-maker" who had wielded such incredible power for so many years had died in August.

With the death of Emperor Olybrius, the saga of a dynasty had finally come to an end. Olybrius and Placidia had a daughter, Juliana Anicia, but she played no role in Italy's history. As for Gaiseric, her most famous relative, he died an undefeated man in 477, one year following the date carved on the tombstone of the Roman Empire of the West.

The Death of an Empire: Appearance of the Last Eagle

The tempo of history had speeded up as emperors came and went like shadowy figures across a screen. Events were crammed into months, not years. Gundobad had become the strongman following the death of his uncle Ricimer and he, too, had created his puppet, Glycerius, only to leave him in the lurch to be become the King of Burgundy on the death of his brothers beyond the Alps.

Presiding over the imminent death of the Empire was Julius Nepos, sent by the Eastern Emperor, who sailed into the harbor of Ostia and made his way to Rome for a bloodless takeover. During his reign Gaul was finally lost, a calamity elegantly stated as follows: *"The only memorable events in the fourteen months' reign of Julius Nepos are those which relate to the affairs of Gaul, that country which gave her first province to the Republic, and whose allegiance was the last jewel hacked from the fingers of the dying Empire."* (Thomas Hodgkin, *Italy and Her Invaders*)

Julius Nepos appointed as his Master of Soldiers none other than a man who had once been secretary to Attila the Hun. His name was Orestes, and he takes his place in history as the father of the last emperor. Orestes soon decided to depose his emperor in favor of his own young son, Romulus. Taking his forces from Rome, he marched on Ravenna, where the Emperor had his residence. Not trusting to the safety provided by the surrounding marshes and city walls, Nepos escaped by sea to Dalmatia as the last eagle took his place.

Dominus Noster Romulus Augustulus Pius Felix Augustus was the name on the coins minted for the last Roman Emperor of the West. Although Orestes had the support of the Roman army, which by now was almost completely composed of German troops, he placed his son Romulus on the imperial throne instead of claiming it for himself. If there could be any magic in a name, then it would seem that no element was lacking. For one year, from October 475 to September 476 Orestes ruled in his son's name. But like vultures fighting for their share in the kill, the German soldiers demanded that Italy itself be parceled out to them, as had been done in other parts of the Empire where soldiers were rewarded with land.

Orestes was a full-blooded Roman provincial, not born on Italian soil, but a Roman nevertheless and he could not accede to the demands of his soldiers, believing that Italian soil, the heart of the great Roman Empire, should at least remain whole. He might have known that his men would abandon him, but as a man of honor he clearly could not associate himself with such an act. His soldiers found a new leader in Odoacer (Odovacar), a German whose father had served Attila and who had joined the army of the Emperor Anthemius. Just as Orestes had marched on Ravenna and deposed Julius Nepos, Odoacer in turn marched on the walled city of Ticinum (Pavia), twenty-two miles south of Milan, where Orestes had taken refuge. Odoacer placed the city under siege as the terrified citizens recalled the sacking of the city by Attila in 452. Again it was stormed and pillaged, this time by the terrible troops of Odoacer. Orestes tried to escape, but was captured at Placentia on August 28, 476, and executed by the sword.

Odoacer could now turn his attention to Ravenna, within whose walls the young Romulus, thought to be around fourteen years of age at the time, was residing. It is said that Odoacer was moved by the beautiful face of the young boy who had not tried to escape but threw himself on the mercy of his captor. Odoacer spared his life, for he was confident in the power he now held. Romulus was sent to live in Campania and was given the splendid palace built centuries before by the Roman general Lucius Lucullus, whose extravagant living style has given our language the word *Lucullan*, meaning "luxurious." Romulus lived there with the members of his family and a generous allowance for the rest of his life. What became of him later remains a mystery, as there is no further mention of his activities or his death. He just disappeared from the pages of history in circumstances as obscure as his namesake, the first Romulus, who had emerged from the mists of legend twelve centuries earlier.

The Roman Empire of the East would continue for almost ten more centuries, ending with the capture of Constantinople by Mahomet II in 1453, but for the West it was all over. Rome's greatness had begun and ended with a Romulus, the first one the legendary nursling of a she-wolf and the last a boy-emperor.

Omens and oracles had played a role in the reading of events, and the eagle had symbolized and sanctified the role of the emperor. The omen of the twelve vultures seen by the Etruscan augur on the Palatine Hill when the city of Rome was founded, interpreted by the ancients to mean twelve centuries, had been much on the minds of the Romans during this last century of struggle and disaster. Whether they believed in this as their inevitable destiny or not, they passively submitted to the German who was now their king. It was the end of an era of greatness and the dawn of a new day for Italy.

Chronological List of Roman Emperors

B.C.	A.D.	
27	14	Augustus
	14-37	Tiberius
	37-41	Caligula (Gaius)
	41-54	Claudius
	54-68	Nero
	68-69	Galba
	69	Otho
	69	Vitellius
	69-79	Vespasian
	79-81	Titus
	81-96	Domitian
	96-98	Nerva
	98-117	Trajan
	117-138	Hadrian
	138-161	Antoninus Pius
	161-180	Marcus Aurelius with Lucius Verus 161-169 and Commodus from 177
	193	Pertinax then Didius Julianus
	193-211	Septimus Severus with Caracalla from 198 and Geta from 209
	211-217	Caracalla with Geta (211-212)
	217-218	Macrinus with Diadumenianus in 218
	218-222	Elagabalus
	222-235	Severus Alexander
	235-238	Maximinus Thrax
	238	Gordian I, Gordian II, Pupienus (Maximus) and Balbinus
	238-244	Gordian III
	244-249	Philip the Arab with his son Philip 247-249
	249-251	Decius
	251-253	Trebonianus Gallus and Volusianus
	253-260	Valerian with Gallienus
	260-268	Gallienus
	268-270	Claudius II Gothicus

270-275	Aurelian
275-276	Tacitus (and Florianus 276)
276-282	Probus
282-283	Carus
283-284	Carinus and Numerian
284-305	Diocletian
286-305	Maximian
305-311	Galerius (over various periods with Constantius I Chlorus, Severus II, Licinius, Constantine I, and Maximinus Daza)
311-324	Constantine I and Licinius
324-337	Constantine
337-340	Constantine II, Constantius II, and Constans
340-350	Constantius II and Constans
350-361	Constantius II
361-363	Julian
363-364	Jovian
364-375	Valentinian I and Valens with Gratian from 367
375-378	Valens, Gratian and Valentinian II
378-395	Theodosius I (The Great) with Gratian and Valentinian II (378-383) with Valentinian II and Arcadius (383-392) with Arcadius and Honorius (392-395)
395	Partition of the Empire into West and East. The following Emperors reigned only in the West.
395-423	Honorius
425-455	Valentinian III
455	Petronius Maximus
455-456	Avitus
457-461	Majorian
461-465	Libius Severus
467-472	Anthemius
472	Olybrius
473-474	Glycerius
474-475	Julius Nepos
475-476	Romulus Augustulus (deposed)
	This was the end of the Roman Empire in the West

PART TWO

The Medieval World

CHAPTER ONE

The Gothic Kings of Italy

The First Gothic King of Italy

What is known as the Medieval Era began in 476 and was a dramatic turning point in the history of Italy. The last emperor of the Western Roman Empire had been deposed, and in his place was a king, Odoacer, the first Gothic king to wear the crown of the Kingdom of Italy. Yet for all his barbarian origins and the title of "king," which was still distasteful to the Romans, he would not prove to be like the Tarquin tyrants of ancient times. Along with his Germanic followers, Odoacer became the protector of Italy and had the support of the Roman Senate, with whom he governed the land. It was an unlikely partnership that worked.

The story of Odoacer reads more like legend than reality. He did not inherit power, but came up through the ranks of the Roman army. As a ragged ruffian he was among the many Goths who streamed across the Danube river after the confusing times following the demise of Attila. It was in the shattered province of Noricum, a mountainous region between Venice and the Danube, that a party of these Arian Christian men, on their way to enlist in the Roman army, went to visit a holy man known for his good works in those parts. According to the chroniclers, this was none other than Saint Severinus who, when he set eyes on Odoacer, a tall, raggedly clad young man with a yellow mustache, recognized in him a leader destined to greatness. The story goes that the Saint, in response to the Goth's *"Farewell," blessed him in the following terms: "Fare forward into Italy; thou who art now covered with a mean raiment of skins, but who shalt soon bestow on many men the costliest gifts."* (Hodgkin, *Italy and Her Invaders,* p. 533)

The prophecy expressed in the blessing came to pass. Odoacer would go into Italy, described at that time as being peopled only by slaves and despots, and he brought with him a barbarian sense of virtue and equality to rejuvenate the land.

King Odoacer began his rule with the approval of the Eastern Emperor, Zeno, whose authority he recognized, but he was beset by many problems, especially in the Danube regions that had been part of the Roman Empire. He eventually brought the Roman provincials who lived there into Italy under his protection. The outer limits of the former Empire had become the lairs of enemies who threatened the coveted peninsula. The Vandals, lurking in southern France, were kept beyond the borders at the natural barrier of the Liguarian Alps, whereas Sicily was recovered from Vandal control by treaty.

The Italian peninsula was kept safe under Odoacer's rule, the structure of government and administration was left unchanged, and as an Arian Christian, Odoacer was tolerant of both Catholics and Jews.

Odoacer's last years as Italian king were fraught with problems from outside as the Eastern Emperor Zeno, having problems of his own, began pulling the strings of destiny. Under threat from the Ostrogoths, led by Theodoric, what better way than to steer him in the direction of Italy and claim that land from the one that Emperor Zeno now referred to as a "tyrant"?

Theodoric followed the Emperor's suggestion, and he set out not just with his soldiers but the whole Gothic tribe of women and children. Having no boats, he had to take the long land route, entering the peninsula by the northeast door and clashing with Odoacer's troops as the area around Verona became the battleground. Odoacer was forced to retreat to Ravenna, protected by the surrounding marshes, where he held out for two more years. He must have thought back to the time when he had stormed that city years before and found the little Romulus there at his mercy.

Theodoric finally entered Ravenna on March 5, 493. They purportedly reached some kind of understanding whereby the two antagonists would rule Italy jointly. Was this a ruse that was to cost Odoacer his life, or was it Odoacer who was plotting to overthrow Theodoric as the latter is reputed to have claimed? The story recorded for posterity is that Theodoric invited Odoacer to a banquet, at which he treacherously killed him with his own hands.

The day on which the first barbarian King of Italy met his death was, by uncanny coincidence, on the 15th day of March in 493, recalling another fateful "Ides of March" recorded in the annals of history.

Theodoric the Great (493–526)

Theodoric, the Ostrogoth, would rule as King of the Italians and the Goths for thirty-three prosperous years. He chose as his capital the city of Ravenna and left Rome to the Romans. Theodoric was the restorer of peace in the peninsula and proved to be a compassionate and just ruler, in spite of the grisly deed attributed to him that had brought him to power. Perhaps Odoacer's death was the result of a dispute settled between champions in barbarian style through honorable hand-to-hand combat rather than treacherous murder.

Theodoric was born in North Pannonia (the Danube region) when it was a federate of the Romans, but following a dispute between their leaders and the Eastern Emperor, he ended up as a hostage in the court of Constantinople at the tender age of seven. There he remained for the next ten years, where he was given a Roman upbringing as well as an insight into the world of kings and emperors. At seventeen he returned home and followed the career of a warrior, becoming the leader of his people on the death of his father. He later helped Emperor Zeno recover the power he had temporarily lost to a rival. The former hostage was now the favored ally of the Eastern Emperor, who not only made him his Master of Soldiers but also adopted him as a son. When this "son" became a threat to his adoptive father, he was steered toward Italy with imperial blessings.

We have already followed Theodoric to Ravenna where he is the undisputed ruler of Italy. His reign is one of the best documented, thanks to the pen of the historian Cassiodorus who lived though these times at his side. Because of his learning, eloquence, and the position of his father before him, Cassiodorus, a Roman of noble birth, became at an early age the mouthpiece of Theodoric and the equivalent of prime minister. It was an incredible alliance, wherein Cassiodorus held the pen and Theodoric the sword. It was said, in fact, that like the great Emperor Charlemagne,

Theodoric never learned to write in spite of his Roman upbringing. The responsibilities in the kingdom were divided along the same lines, with the Goths and the Romans doing what they did best. The army was completely Gothic by now, and no Italians were called to military service, while Italians kept control of the administration and no Goths sat in the Roman Senate. Goths and Romans lived side by side, but they remained separate, and a 100-year-old law promulgated by Valentinian I that forbade marriage between Romans and barbarians "on pain of death" was apparently still in force, if not enforced. In religious matters, the Goths kept their Arian Christian faith and in turn respected the Roman Catholics.

Theodoric proved to be a true champion of the Italian people, and this is evidenced by the letters written by Cassiodorus in his name and later published. They cover a wide range of matters involving public welfare, justice, preservation of buildings, water supplies, and the like. All of these documents, though written in the flowery manner of Cassiodorus, convey the spirit of Theodoric's rule, where he played the role of father in the everyday workings of government and maintenance of order. The following short extracts are given as examples of letters written by Cassiodorus in the name of King Theodoric.

12. To the one in charge of Customs Officers.

Italy ought to enjoy her own products, and it is monstrous that anything which she produces should be wanting to her own children. Therefore let no lard be exported to foreign parts. . . .

25. An Edict concerning evasion of taxes by the rich.

The King detests the oppression of the unfortunate, and encourages them to make their complaints to him. He has heard that the powerful houses are failing to pay their share of the taxes, and that a larger sum is being exacted from the tenues.

27. To all Jews living in Genoa.

The Jews are permitted to roof in the old walls of their synagogue, but they are not to enlarge it beyond its old borders.

The word *civilitas* recurs frequently in his letters and one addressed to the Jews of Genoa confirming privileges includes the following assurance: "*The true mark of civilitas is the observance of law. It is this which makes life in communities possible, and which separates man from the brutes.*"

Matters outside the borders of Theodoric's Italian kingdom always posed a threat as the lands that had been part of the Western Empire were constantly disputed. Theodoric chose the path of diplomacy when possible in dealing with his restless neighbors, and this included marriage alliances with the leading families and not only with the Visigoths but also the Franks, the Burgundians, and the Vandals. Unfortunately, these alliances were not always respected as Theodoric's own kin became helpless victims. He learned of the death of a grandson, Segeric, ordered by none other than the child's father, the Catholic King of Burgundy. His sister, Amalafrida, whose husband (the King of the Vandals) had died, had been shut up in a prison by his successor, the Catholic Hilderic.

Theodoric, with proverbial tolerance, had worked for harmony between Romans and Goths, but inevitable differences arose between the two religious groups and caused him to become mired in a bog of intrigues, accusations, persecutions, conspiracies, and fear. This troubled period of his last years found him dragged along by events and led to the execution of the philosopher-senator Boethius, along with others wrongfully accused of treason. These acts cast a black shadow over the last years of Theodoric's great rule.

Troubled by visions of the wrongfully executed Boethius, weakened by dysentery and shivering under his covers in the final days of his life, Theodoric conveyed these feelings of remorse to his attending physician, Elpidius. Before breathing his last, he recommended to the Goths that the Kingdom of Italy should pass to his grandson, Athalaric, child of his daughter Amalasuntha. Around him were the Gothic chiefs and Italian magistrates who pledged their loyalty to the eight-year-old boy and his mother.

Theodoric died on August 30, 526. His mortal remains would rest in the soil that he had claimed for his Gothic people to share and that he protected for the Italians. On a prominent site in Ravenna, looking out over the city and the harbor, is a mausoleum covered by a thirty-six-foot monolithic dome and crudely decorated in barbaric style with the twelve apostles. Meanwhile, the peace that the peninsula had enjoyed under the second barbarian king seems to have been interred with him.

In Ravenna there still stands the church that Theodoric had built and dedicated to Saint Martin. Now known as Sant'Apollinare Nuovo, the interior of this glorious sixth-century church is resplendent with mosaics in vibrant colors, freezing in time processions of martyrs and virgins bearing gifts for Christ and the Virgin. But outside, the devil was at work.

A Gothic Lady in Charge

Although Athalaric was the king in name, his widowed mother, Amalasuntha, ruled as regent with the ever-faithful Cassiodorus in her service. An educated and intelligent woman, she wanted her son to be a true Roman, schooled in letters. This led to disagreement with Gothic nobles who objected to the upbringing of their new leader, so he was removed from the tutorship of old men and given the company of boys more his own age—young Goths, of course. The dispute over the boy's education was just the beginning of a series of events that proved disastrous for Italy. Amalasuntha, a good and capable woman who had the welfare of the Romans as well as her Gothic people at heart, soon lost control of her son who spent his teenage years in bad company, drinking and womanizing. Powerless to save him, she watched his approaching death and her own safety at stake.

Athalaric died on October 2, 534, before reaching maturity, and Amalasuntha's stormy eight-year regency came to an end. In an effort to hold the reins of power, she looked around for a male heir with whom to "share" the throne and called on her only male cousin, Theodahad, offspring of Theodoric's ill-fated sister Amalafrida. Hatred and mistrust between the two combined to create a dangerous situation that Justinian, now the Eastern Emperor, soon capitalized on for his own ends.

Neither Goths nor Italians liked or trusted Theodahad, who was reputed to be too cowardly to be a Goth and not honorable enough to be a Roman. But Amalasuntha also had her enemies, for she had exiled and then ordered the execution of three Gothic nobles whom she believed had conspired against her and her son. It was not long before the wily Theodahad saw the opportunity to rid himself of his cousin and, joining ranks with her enemies, contrived to have her imprisoned.

Amalasuntha was taken to a tiny island in Lake Bolsena in Tuscany, and there in the spring of 535 she was murdered as she bathed. She was mourned by Goths and Italians alike for her father had been a great king and she herself had been a kind and virtuous regent.

Cassiodorus continued to scribble flowery letters for the court of Italy, but his pen was in the service of Theodahad who, since he had not been chosen as leader by the Goths, was in trouble right from the beginning. The greatest threat, however, came from Emperor Justinian, whose aim was to bring the Western half of the Empire back under his control, and on hearing of Amalasuntha's death he made plans to recover Italy. That task he assigned to his loyal general, Belisarius, who now entered the realm of Italian history where he would remain for the next chaotic years.

Holy Wars Against the Goths in Italy

Emperor Justinian takes his place among the great men of history, in particular for his legal work in organizing and codifying the mass of Roman laws into a Codex on which our own laws are largely based. However, the result of the wars waged on his behalf against the Goths in Italy were devastating for Goths and Italians alike.

In 535, the year of Amalasuntha's death, trouble came from the south as Belisarius, the brilliant Byzantine general who had just won back the Vandal kingdom of North Africa, sailed with his troops to Sicily and quickly took over most of the island, defeating the Gothic protectors who fought bravely. Belisarius led his victorious army across the Strait of Messina and advanced rapidly to Naples. The people of the peaceful south immediately surrendered to the advancing army, which marched northward through Calabria and Campania.

Naples was fortified and defended by a large Gothic garrison. Belisarius first negotiated with the Neapolitans, asking them to surrender, but many were unwilling to betray their Gothic protectors whose families they believed would be slaughtered by the imperial forces. Finally, after much discussion, the Jews having given assurance of provisions and the Goths their protection, the Neapolitans sent word to Belisarius that they would not surrender. Belisarius then lay siege to the city, and a cry for help was sent out to Theodahad. He never answered the call. In the meantime, one of Belisarius's scouts discovered a way of entering the impenetrable city by an aqueduct. The Neapolitan spokesman was called once more and Belisarius, keeping his secret, again asked for surrender, saying: *"I have often seen cities captured and know well what happens in those times. They kill all the men from boys up, and the women . . . are dragged to disgrace and suffer dreadfully and pitiably."* These ominous words were recorded by the Byzantine historian Procopius, Belisarius's advisor and right-hand man who accompanied him on this first campaign. As an eyewitness, he reported the wars in great detail and with compassion and is the chief source for what happened during these tragic and eventful years.

In spite of threats, the unsuspecting Neapolitans refused to submit. So it was that, like stealthy cats in the darkness of night, the enemy crawled though the aqueduct and opened the doors of hell. The siege that had lasted twenty days was ended the next day when the soldiers rushed through the gates and stormed the city, inflicting unimaginable brutalities on its helpless inhabitants. These savage invaders did not even respect the churches and ruthlessly slaughtered anyone taking refuge there.

Belisarius was ready to move on Rome. The Goths and Romans had meanwhile heard the dreadful news of what had happened in Naples, and Theodahad's suspicious behavior cast doubt on his true intentions. The Goths assembled on the plains outside Rome and there, while their horses fed on the rich pasture, they chose a new leader for themselves. His name was Vitigis, a man who had distinguished himself under the beloved King Theodoric. Theodahad's treachery had been established, and he was soon tracked down and killed. His reign had been short, for he died in the year following Amalasuntha's death.

The Roman Cassiodorus, who had written in the name of all the Gothic leaders Theodoric, Athalaric, Amalasuntha, and Theodahad now put his pen to the service of Vitigis, who addressed one of the first letters to his fellow Goths and presented himself as their chosen leader saying, "not in the corner of a presence-chamber, but in the wide-spreading plains I have been chosen king" (letter 31 p. 444) He went on to exhort his kinsmen to follow the example set by Theodoric to respect the welfare of the whole people.

The newly proclaimed King Vitigis entered into the city of Rome, where he left a garrison, then proceeded to Ravenna with the rest of his army and some senators. To consolidate his position he married Matesuentha, daughter of the murdered Amalasuntha, albeit much against the will of this young virgin who was destined to become a pawn on the chessboard of history as we shall see later.

Meanwhile, Belisarius was making his way north to Rome, accompanied by our good reporter Procopius who, awestruck by the skill of the ancient Romans in road building, describes for his readers the great Appian Way, built some 900 years earlier and on which the Byzantine army was moving.

Belisarius entered Rome with his army December 9, 536, through the gate called the Asinarian (the donkey driver), while the small Gothic garrison, unable to confront such a formidable force and given leave by the Romans to depart, left by a northern gate, and, taking the Flaminian Way, made its way to Ravenna.

The die had been cast. The Eastern Empire was at war with the Goths, and as other cities in the south quickly surrendered, King Vitigis prepared his army while he made overtures for peace. He reminded the Emperor of the fact that the treacherous Theodahad had been killed, and he introduced himself as an ally.

Entreaties were to no avail, for the Emperor wanted the Goths destroyed, so in 537 Vitigis and his Gothic soldiers returned to regain Rome and began a siege that lasted for the next year. Meanwhile, Belisarius received reinforcements consisting of a cavalry force some 1,600 men, which included large numbers of the dreaded Huns. Bloody battles took place between the Imperial forces and the Goths outside the walls of Rome. Once more, the Goths sought to end the conflict, pleading with Belisarius not to prolong the misery of the Romans whom Theodoric had protected and kept in freedom, but their pleas were in vain.

By the spring of 538, both sides had been weakened by hunger and sickness. So after one year the Goths, under threat of more reinforcements arriving from the East, began to lift the siege and return to their stronghold of Ravenna. The war continued, however, as other cities suffered sieges or changed hands. Belisarius never had enough forces to put an end to the war or even to secure his conquests with adequate garrisons.

Suddenly the spotlight turned on Pavia. All this time the Franks had been sitting on the fence of neutrality, but like jackals, they saw their chance for a share in the prey. They crossed the Alps into Liguria, and the Goths, thinking they had come to help them, allowed them to cross the Ticino River and enter Pavia. Much to their dismay, the treacherous Franks whom they had received as allies seized the Gothic women and children they found at the garrison, slaughtered them, and threw their bodies into the fast-moving waters of the river.

Finally, by 539 Belisarius had regained enough territory to give him the advantage, and he laid siege to Ravenna. Emperor Justinian invited King Vitigis to make peace in exchange for land north of the Po River for himself and his Goths. He could use the Goths as a buffer against the Franks as well as against the Lombards lurking at his door.

The Goths insisted on a document that Belisarius promised to produce once in Ravenna. The trusting Goths were even led to believe that he would be prepared to abandon his Emperor once in that city and resolved to proclaim him Emperor of the West, for they had grown to admire their enemy, this blond Dalmatian of peasant stock. Thus the Gothic garrison allowed the Imperial army to enter Ravenna, but to their surprise Belisarius refused their offer and chose to remain loyal to his Emperor. The Goths found themselves trapped in his net in their own capital.

So in the spring of 540 the devastating war against the Goths had come to an end. The Goths were given leave to return to their homes, but the captured King Vitigis was kept under guard. Belisarius was soon called back to Constantinople by his Emperor, and he took with him as hostages King Vitigis and his wife, Matesuentha. Italy was now under Byzantine rule.

King Totila: A New Champion for the Goths

King Vitigis was a prisoner in Constantinople, and the Goths chose Ildibald to be their leader. He did not last long enough to prove his mettle, for he was soon murdered as a result of some grievance. In his place they elected a man who proved a match for Emperor Justinian and his generals for the next several years.

Totila came on the scene like a whirlwind in 541, sweeping up and carrying along with him his Gothic followers, who over the next five years succeeded in regaining many of the cities and territories that had been lost, even recovering Corsica and Sardinia.

In many ways, Totila had fate on his side, for in 542 a devastating bubonic plague struck Constantinople. Belisarius and Procopius found themselves in this stricken city, where it was estimated that as many as 300,000 people died. Not even Emperor Justinian escaped the disease, although he was lucky enough to survive, weakened and discouraged. Famine followed the plague, but when all of this was over, Emperor Justinian was ready to give his attention once more to Italy, where the terrible Totila had fast regained control of much of the land.

Belisarius was sent back to Italy in 544, and the peninsula was once again a battleground for the Emperor's holy war against the Goths. Rome had been guarded by Imperial troops since 538, and Totila had carefully avoided sieges, which would involve casualties. But in 545, a hard-pressed Totila did besiege the city and captured it in 546, burning many of the buildings. The following year it was recaptured for the Imperials by Belisarius. The poor Romans could hardly have had time to get used to the new masters when in 549 back came Totila to "free" them; the following year the Goths were once more in control.

Totila had often sent peace envoys to the Emperor, and the Goths had agreed to pay tribute and be his subjects, but their words fell on deaf ears for as Procopius wrote, "*the Emperor paid no attention to what they said and dismissed them, bitterly hostile to the name of Goth and determined to drive it out of the Roman Empire completely.*"

Meanwhile, Belisarius had been once more recalled to Constantinople, but Emperor Justinian had not abandoned his holy war, which was about to enter a new phase. His cousin, Germanus, was to lead a new force to Italy. King Vitigis was dead, and the astute Justinian had married Germanus off to his widow, Matesuentha, believing that the Goths would not fight against the granddaughter of their revered Theodoric. Unfortunately, Germanus died of malaria on the way and the command was given to Narses, a eunuch who had been an official of the imperial household. Narses set out with the entire Imperial army to make war against the formidable Totila. This army, which at the time was referred to as "the Roman army," was composed of everything but Romans, or, for that matter, even men from the Italian peninsula. It was a collection of mostly mercenaries, including Eruls, Huns, Persian deserters, Gepids, criminals released from prisons for the venture, and, most significantly for the future of Italy, over half a million Lombards under their king, Audaun, who got his first glimpse of this fair land south of the Alps.

The eunuch and the king, Narses and Totila, faced each other with their armies for the final showdown in a wide valley of the mountainous regions of central Italy near Gubbio. When negotiations failed for the last time, they set a date for the contest. Our reporter, Procopius, takes us to the site of the impending battle, where Totila, the proud Goth, deliberately showing the adversary his identity and bedecked in all his regal splendor of gold and purple, rode out in front of the enemy formations and put on the performance of his life.

> *He rode a horse of immense size on which he gave a most skillful performance of the war dance there in no-man's land. He wheeled his horse around in a circle and turned it about with another circling movement. From his horse, he flung his spear to the breezes and caught it again as it spun, and he passed it from hand to hand many times, transferring it with expertise. In this performance he took a great pride leaning back and moving his seat and bending to either side, as if he had been well taught in dancing from his childhood.*

This marvelous show was intended to gain time so other troops could join him, but Narses realized that Totila was just stalling.

In the battle that followed, Totila's soldiers were being slaughtered, and soon the remnants took flight. Totila, too, was killed as he fled, perhaps slain in the darkness by a soldier who did not even know his identity. The Goths had lost an important battle, but worst of all they had lost the king who had led them so well through the past eleven years. They did not give in to defeat, however. Across the Po River they regrouped near the city of Pavia, where they chose a new leader in the person of Teias. Narses was soon back to retake Rome, which the small Gothic garrison could not defend. Castel Sant'Angelo again became the silent witness of confusion and slaughter as soldiers, citizens, and senators fell to the sword. Once more the helpless Romans had changed masters as the keys of their city were sent to the Emperor in Constantinople.

The Goths still held many cities, and Narses pursued them as the campaign moved southward. An important battle was fought in the shadow of Mount Vesuvius, quiet now after another eruption that took place during the reign of Theodoric in 512, but death lurked in the shadows below as the adversaries faced each other for two months on opposite sides of a narrow river. In the desperate struggle that eventually took place there, the last Gothic leader, Teias, put up the fight of his life, but it was his last battle. Narses displayed the head of his fallen enemy on a pike, but the Goths continued to fight until dark. Dawn came and with it the realization that they were defeated. They now asked that they be allowed to retreat in peace and the last remnants straggled northward to join their brothers beyond the Po River.

The year 552 marked the end of seventeen years of devastating campaigns and the end of three quarters of a century of Gothic power in the peninsula. Without their former protectors, the Italians were now at the mercy of their new masters.

In the Shadow of Constantinople: Narses, the Eunuch-General

Instead of a brave Gothic king to protect them, the Italians now had to submit to a seventy-five-year-old Byzantine general named Narses who exercised civil and military power in the service of a far-off emperor in Constantinople. This was indeed a dark age for Italy as her inhabitants picked up the pieces and went about the daily business of their lives in their shattered country. A silence seems to have settled over the land as the educated went off in seclusion or shut themselves up in monasteries, the only safe haven left to them. Even the busy Cassiodorus, who had wielded such power alongside his Gothic masters, took himself off into seclusion, became a monk, and put his pen to the task of interpreting the scriptures.

The aged Narses, like an imperial shadow darkening the skies, remained in Italy as the oppressive representative of the Emperor for the next fifteen years. Finally, in 567 when he was fully in his dotage at age eighty-nine, he was recalled to Constantinople by Justin II, who had become Emperor two years earlier. A disgruntled old man, Narses spent his last years in Italy and died in Rome at the ripe old age of ninety-five.

It is widely believed that Narses, who had lost favor with Justin II, may have invited the Lombards to come into Italy to spite his Emperor. One can only speculate on the role this eunuch-general may have played in shaping Italy's destiny, which took a new turn with the arrival of the Lombard invaders.

CHAPTER TWO

The Lombards—568-774 A.D.

The First Lombards

It was in the year 568 that the Lombards, a relatively small tribe, came into Italy through a narrow mountain pass on the eastern side of the Alps and quickly spread out over the Po valley, which would bear the name of their tribe: LOMBARDY.

Who were the Lombards? Our chief source of information is Paulus Diaconus (Paul the Deacon), an educated Lombard of noble birth who compiled a history of his people, much of the early part of which may be based partly on legend. Born in 720, Paulus lived through part of the times about which he wrote and was close to the court during the later years of Lombard rule, witnessing the fall of the Lombard Kingdom in 774.

The Lombards were a Germanic people, just one of the many tribes that disputed territories north of the Alps and beyond the Danube. The sagas place these people in ancient times in Scandinavia, but they had long since moved down the Elbe River and into the middle Danube region. They came to be known as the Longobardi (long beards) from which came "Lombardi." They spoke a low German and they were not only unlettered but also reputed to be among the fiercest of the Germanic tribes at the time of their entry into Italy.

Distinctive in appearance, it was said that they cut the hair of their heads and "they made bare the neck, shaving it up to the back of the head, having their hair let down from the face as far as the mouth and parting it on either side from the forehead" (Quoted from Hodgkin. *Italy and Her Invaders*). This hairstyle, along with the striped linen clothes they wore, gave them the appearance of some hairy-faced beasts. The chroniclers of the time referred to them as the "unspeakable" Lombards. Yet these are the people whose legacy to Italy included the blood of their own strong race, for, unlike the Visigoths, Huns, and Vandals, their arrival in the peninsula, like that of the Ostrogoths (who had since been largely eliminated) represented not just an invasion but the mass immigration of a whole tribe. They established a kingdom in Italy that lasted for two centuries.

Paulus writes that on April 2, 568, which was the day after Easter Sunday, the Lombards, led by their king, Alboin, set out on their journey into Italy, along with a motley horde of tribal elements that included Gepids, Bulgarians, people from the Ukraine, and even some Saxons.

The long column of invaders came though the Predil Pass and, virtually unopposed, moved quickly through the province of Venetia, then proceeded to Vicenza and Verona. Alboin did not want anyone else to follow him to this promised land, and he blocked the way behind him by settling his noblest Lombards in Friuli.

The dialect there still retains distinct elements of a language that disappeared with the adoption of vernacular Latin of the time. Alboin was probably aided by the calamitous pestilence, which had raged toward the end of Narses's rule, and which the Lombard historian Paulus later describes as a most dismal scene . . .

> *of flocks deserted in the pastures, of farm-houses, once teeming with peasant life, abandoned to silence or only tenanted by troops of dogs; of parents left unburied by their children, and children by their parents . . . The harvest in vain expected the reaper's sickle: the purple clusters hung on the vine till winter drew nigh. An awful silence brooded over the fields where the shepherd's whistle and the sportsman's eager tread were alike unheard. And yet more dreadful than the silence were the sounds of a ghostly trumpet, the mysterious tramp of unseen multitudes which were their doom.* (As paraphrased by Hodgkin from descriptions of Paulus Diaconus, p. 167)

Milan opened her gates on September 3 of that year, along with many other cities in the north, and Alboin took the title of "Lord of Italy," dating his reign from that day. Pavia held out for three years, but eventually became the capital of the Lombard monarchy. At the same time, Alboin's followers crossed the Apennines, pushing through central Italy and subjugating most of the southern half of the peninsula. The Byzantine Empire could only retain a foothold on the seaports and coastal areas.

Within a few short years, Italy had been overrun by the Lombards, except for the heel and the toe and a band about her girth, wide at the levels of Rome and Ravenna and narrowing to a tenuous buckle in the Apennines at Perugia, an ancient Etruscan stronghold and an essential link between east and west. The great Flaminian Way, built almost eight centuries before during the fledgling Roman Republic to move troops quickly to the front, was now the umbilical cord that kept Ravenna and the Imperial Governor, Longinus, in touch with mother Rome and her Catholic Pope, whose authority had become increasingly secular.

King Alboin seemed to be unstoppable, but his end came as swiftly as his successes. In the spring of 572 his wife, Rosamund, had him murdered. The circumstances afford a glimpse into the world of this rude, warlike race that now ruled over much of Italy. Full of wine during a banquet, Alboin had forced Rosamund, a Gepid lady, to drink from an ornamented goblet fashioned from the skull of her father, King Cunimund, slain in a war with his tribe. In revenge for being forced into such a dreadful act, she had her husband murdered and was then forced to flee along with her co-conspirator, Helmechis. They took refuge in Ravenna, where the wily Imperial Governor became enchanted with the savage beauty, who then decided that Helmechis was in the way. The scene of her next act is the frigidarium of the Roman baths in Ravenna where she comes to offer Helmechis a goblet of "healthful" drink, but having consumed half, he realizes that it is poison. Saving the other half for Rosamund, he forces her at sword point to drink the rest. For the second time she is made to drink from a goblet against her will, but this one contains her own death.

Meanwhile, the Lombard warriors gathered at Pavia and chose Cleph as their king, but when he was slain two years later the chief nobles decided to go kingless. There were thirty-six of them, and they came to be known as "The Lombard Dukes." The most important six controlled the cities of Milan, Bergamo, Brescia, and Trento, the backdoor at Friuli, and the highest in rank Pavia, which became the capital of a kind of confederation. So these men from the mountains and forests beyond the Alps had moved into the cities as lords, made a jigsaw puzzle of the Italian peninsula, and set the stage for the city-states that made up medieval Italy. This period of the Dukes, which is referred to as the "Interregnum," lasted ten years. During this time, Rome was besieged, but not taken, but in 579 the Lombard Duke of Spoleto occupied and pillaged the seaport of Ravenna, the escape route to the East. Communication between Rome and Ravenna was dangerous and difficult at best, and there were times when the two cities were completely out of touch with each other.

The Dukes had their own territories, which they guarded like dogs, but did not combine forces to conquer the whole peninsula. It was perhaps their need to unite against the common foe in the north, the Franks, that induced these thirty-six despots to come together in April 584 and choose a king. By consensus the crown was given to Authari, son of the short-lived Cleph. He had grown into manhood, most likely in Bergamo.

King Authari took the title of Flavius, in deference to the Romans, it was thought, and the Italians looked forward to a better world under one who had been raised on Italian soil. His praises have been sung in sagas, for he ruled his kingdom with wisdom and sought to protect it from the ever-troublesome Franks, whose incursions were frequent and devastating.

When the trumpets of war were finally silent, Authari was ready to take a wife, at the same time forming an alliance with a neighbor. He had heard of the beautiful and accomplished princess Theodolinda, daughter of the Bavarian king. Authari obtained permission from Theodolinda's father, but before the marriage took place he wanted to meet his bride. He traveled incognito to Bavaria to meet the comely princess without her knowing his true identity, but as he left with his envoys they knew that the tall young man of regal bearing and waves of golden hair must indeed be the king himself. The enchanted Authari returned to Italy to prepare for the wedding, but meanwhile the King of Bavaria had been overthrown. News came that Theodolinda had escaped and, accompanied by her brother Gundwald, was on her way to Italy, a refugee princess coming to meet her king. She was met with great ceremony on the shores of Lake Garda, and the marriage was celebrated in May of 589 in the city of Verona.

The romantic union was destined to be short. The year 589 was quiet, but the peace did not last, for the following year the Franks would be back with assurance of help from the Byzantine Emperor. Some battles were fought, and the Lombards retreated to their fortified places while King Authari sent peace envoys from his stronghold of Pavia to the King of the Franks.

Tragedy struck the Lombards in 590 when on September 5 Authari died in Pavia, not knowing the results of his peace overtures. He had been married to the beautiful Theodolinda for just one year and four months, and he left no heir, but in that time Theodolinda had captured the hearts of her Lombard subjects. It is a tribute to this lady, of a noble Lombard mother but half Bavarian and a Catholic, that the Arian Christian Lombards wished to keep her as their queen with whomever of the dukes she should chose as her king. Her choice was Agilulf, Duke of Turin, "well fitted by manly beauty, as well as by courage, to grasp the helm of the kingdom" (Hodgkin, vol. 5, p. 281). It was the beginning of a dynasty destined to last for over a century.

Left: The cathedral at Monza, founded by the Lombard Queen Theodolinda, was rebuilt at the end of the 14th century in Lombard Gothic style. The striking façade is of alternating white, black and green marble. The chapel contains 44 frescoes depicting the life of the pious queen who is buried behind the altar. Also kept in the cathedral, among other treasures, is the famous "Iron Crown" of the Lombards.

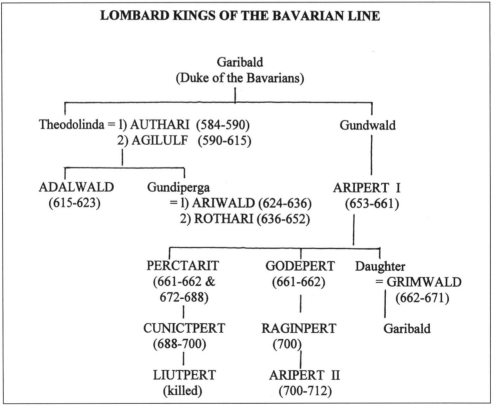

LOMBARD KINGS OF THE BAVARIAN LINE

Garibald
(Duke of the Bavarians)

Theodolinda = 1) AUTHARI (584-590)
2) AGILULF (590-615)

Gundwald

ADALWALD
(615-623)

Gundiperga
= 1) ARIWALD (624-636)
2) ROTHARI (636-652)

ARIPERT I
(653-661)

PERCTARIT
(661-662 &
672-688)

GODEPERT
(661-662)

Daughter
= GRIMWALD
(662-671)

CUNICTPERT
(688-700)

RAGINPERT
(700)

Garibald

LIUTPERT
(killed)

ARIPERT II
(700-712)

The Three Worlds of the Peninsula

King Agilulf came to power when about three quarters of the Italian peninsula was safely under Lombard control, but it was a time of turmoil in which three forces were in conflict—the Arian Lombard king, the Byzantine governor in Ravenna, and the Pope in Rome.

The Franks were gone from the north and with them the threat that kept the Lombard dukes together. Not all of these independent Lombard nobles were thrilled to have a king, in spite of their love and respect for Queen Theodolinda, who, with their blessing, had chosen a husband from among them to be their chief. One with an attitude problem was Gaidulf, the powerful duke of Bergamo, who had his eye on the crown, but was not Theodolinda's chosen one. King Agilulf had twice pardoned this duke in exchange for a promise of loyalty.

Recalcitrant dukes were not the only ones that disturbed the peace. The middle section of the peninsula continued to be nominally part of the Byzantine Empire, with power held by an imperial governor, the Exarch in Ravenna. In Rome the Pope became increasingly independent as the road connecting the Holy City and Ravenna was often only a tenuous line of communication frequently cut by the Lombards. But just as this line had held the two parts together, so was the Lombard Kingdom of the north separated from the dukedoms of the south, which became more and more powerful, representing a threat to the Lombard King as well as to the Exarch in Ravenna and the Pope.

The year 590 brought a new cast of players when Agilulf became king and Gregory the Great was called on to be the next pope. Rome was practically surrounded by the Lombards, who were closing in on her, occupying the towns of Viterbo and Terni. No help came from the Emperor in Constantinople and the Exarch in Ravenna was of no help either as he had his own problems. Pope Gregory's first task was to protect his Christian flock and their remaining territory from the Lombards. The threat had first come from the Duke of Spoleto, who tightened the net around Rome. Gregory sought peace with the rascal duke, and a separate truce made with the "unspeakable" Lombard spurred the complacent Exarch into action. He marched to Rome, recovering from the Lombards many towns that had been lost, including the ancient Etruscan city of Perugia, strategically located as an essential link in the line of communication. This brought an immediate response from King Agilulf, who in 593 sprang into action by retaking Perugia, a strategic link also for the Lombards, and making his way to Rome. For Pope Gregory, it must have seemed that the end of the world was near as he saw citizens returning to Rome, their hands chopped off by the "unspeakable" Lombards. In a desperate letter that he addressed to the Emperor, Gregory wrote these words: *"A heavier stroke after this was the arrival of Agilulf, when, with my own eyes, I saw Romans coupled together like dogs, with ropes round their necks, being led away to be sold in France."*

King Agilulf with his army was finally at the gates of Rome. Pope Gregory met him at the steps of the Basilica of Saint Peter, where, as if by miracle, the Lombard king was stopped by the presence of the Pope and his words, just as Attila had been subdued by Pope Leo I over two centuries before. Peace finally came about in 599 when all sides agreed to a treaty. Pope Gregory wrote a letter to King Agilulf and a separate one to Queen Theodolinda, praising her efforts to bring about peace and for "staying the effusion of blood on both sides." Clearly, this Catholic lady had interceded with her Arian husband and saved Rome.

But there was bloodshed in the Lombard ranks, for with this new peace the dukes of Verona and Pavia, as well as the incorrigible Gaidulf of Bergamo, rebelled against their king, who had them all slain. King Agilulf was also under threat from another quarter. As the peace treaty terms were about to expire, the Exarch of Ravenna, then a man named Callinicus, did a really stupid thing. He had his soldiers abduct Agilulf's daughter and her husband from their home in Parma and take them off to captivity in Ravenna. (This was Agilulf's child by a first wife, not a daughter of Queen Theodolinda.) Agilulf chose not to storm Ravenna to rescue the pair, but took action by forming an alliance with the dreadful Avars and threatening Constantinople, while back in Italy he took revenge by capturing Padua, which was burned to the

The shaded areas were under the control of the Byzantines, but borders changed with later Lombard conquests. The much disputed Perugia was on the road connecting Rome to the eastern coast and was at times held by the Lombards.

Lombard Italy Around 600 A.D.

ground. It was the second time the city had been destroyed — the first was by Attila in 452.

King Agilulf was riding high on his successes in Italy, and there was more joy when Theodolinda gave birth to a son in the palace she had built at Monza, a town about ten miles north of Milan and known today especially for its auto racing track. The joy of this royal birth was even greater because Theodolinda had waited eleven years before her firstborn child finally arrived. She named him Adalwald, and he was baptized by Catholic rite with the permission of his as yet Arian father.

The Lombards had nibbled away at the remnants of the Byzantine Empire in Italy and finally, in April of 605, a peace treaty was agreed on between all the parties involved. Pope Gregory did not live to see the fruits of his tireless diplomatic efforts, for he died on March 11, 604, after being one of the most powerful figures in the peninsula for fourteen eventful years. He was the founder of the Medieval Papacy and had reinforced Rome as the seat of the Catholic Church.

A newly appointed Exarch in Ravenna returned Agilulf's daughter and her husband to Parma after two and a half years of captivity. Sadly, however, the princess died in childbirth shortly after regaining her freedom.

As for the Lombards, their control of most of the Italian peninsula was not just a fact, but had been legalized by the treaty. The "unspeakable" Lombards had come to stay and had changed the map of the peninsula.

Theodolinda's Successors

The century had begun on a peaceful note as far as Italy was concerned. Within the Lombard Kingdom, the new rulers lived alongside the Italians, following their own laws and separated by their two different persuasions of Christianity, Arianism, and Catholicism. The Lombards were now "insiders" and were gradually being absorbed by the superior Roman civilization, taking from it the learning, for they came with none, and also the Latin language that was the vehicle of such learning.

King Agilulf died in 615 after a reign of twenty-five years. On his death the eleven-year-old Adalwald became king with his devout Catholic mother, Theodolinda, at his side. Little is known of this period, but the Lombards believed that he fell under the bad influences of the Romans and lost his mind. He supposedly died by poisoning in 624 at around the age of twenty. Taking his place was Ariwald, a staunch Arian and the husband of the dead king's sister, Gundiperga, Theodolinda's daughter. Ariwald reigned over the Lombard Kingdom for twelve years. When he died in 636 his widow was instructed to take another husband in his place to continue the rule, just as Theodolinda had been asked to do. Gundiperga's choice fell on Rothari, another one "stained by the infidelity of the Arian heresy," according to the historian Paul the Deacon.

Rothari's personal life was questionable, but as a king he left his mark in Lombard history. He collected all the laws of the Lombards and in 643 had them written down in what was called the Edict. This was an important event because the Lombards could not write when they arrived in Italy, and their laws, based on customs and memory, were recorded here for the first time. They had learned much from the Romans, whose administrative qualities they admired, and their laws now contained some elements of the Roman law by which the Italians lived. The prologue to the Edict, which contained 388 chapters, begins as follows: *"In the name of our Lord Jesus Christ begins the Edict which with God's help the most excellent man Rothari, king of the Lombards, hath renewed with the nobles who are his judges. In the name of Almighty God, I, Rothari, most excellent man and king . . ."*

What follows is an incredible document, one interesting element of which is the list of compensation to be paid for injury, right down to the "cutting off of the fifth toe." The motive of this aspect of the law is explained as being a way of curbing the blood feuds and savage practices of the ancestors. The document stipulated that on payment of compensation "let the cause be finished between the parties, and friendship remain." (Hodgkin, p. 184–85).

Rothari died in 652 after a successful reign of some sixteen years, and he was succeeded by his son, who reigned just five months. His rule and his life were cut short by a Lombard whose wife he had seduced. It is indeed ironic that Rothari's laws, which were designed to prevent blood feuds, could not protect the life of his own son and heir. They were still, according to the Romans, those "unspeakable" Lombards.

The line of Theodolinda had come to an end. The death of her daughter Gundiperga is not recorded, but is believed to have occurred around the same time as Rothari's. There were some uncanny similarities between the lives of mother and daughter:—both were Catholic, both were married twice to Arian Lombard kings, both had sons who became kings, and both sons died young.

The next wearer of the Iron Crown of the Lombards was Aripert I, son of Queen Theodolinda's brother, Gundwald, her companion when sixty-five years earlier she had fled across the Alps as a refugee princess to marry a Lombard king.

The World of Aripert I: Religions in Collision

Aripert I acceded to the Lombard throne in the year 653, the same year that a Catholic pope was imprisoned by a Byzantine emperor. It was a barbarous age when tribes disputed the remnants of Empire and great religions were in collision, coming together like immovable rocks and crushing those that were caught in between.

The Lombards were consolidating their power at a time when the Eastern Empire was plagued by turmoil within and threats from without. Emperor Constans II ruled after having had his brother murdered, while Rome and Constantinople were enmeshed in a dispute that was centered on a point of doctrine. Pope Gregory had differed with the Bishop of Constantinople, whom he even perceived as an anti-Christ. Tired of the religious wrangling, Emperor Constans created a document known as "the Type," designed to end the war of words. These internal problems were soon overshadowed by a new movement that would threaten kingdoms and empires alike.

In the year 570, in the town of Mecca, far beyond the boundaries of what was once the Roman Empire and in the middle of the hot sands of Arabia, a boy was born who would begin a new chapter in the history of the world. His name was Mohammed. He came on the scene like a whirlwind with the message, "There is no God but God, and Mohammed is his apostle." A new religion was born that would be known as Islam (meaning "confident submission"), which rapidly gained adherents and spread like wildfire far beyond Arabia. The Christian world would refer to these followers of Islam as "Saracens," or "infidels."

By this time, the clergy had become very powerful and resented the fact that the Emperor should meddle with matters of theology, which was their domain. While many bishops in the East kept silent under protest, Pope Martin of Rome convened a

Above: The old Lombard town of Pavia boasts the most beautiful churches in Lombard Romanesque style. The oldest one is San Michele, built in yellow sandstone from the neighboring hills. Already existing in 661 A.D., it was rebuilt in 1155 following an earthquake. It is the richest in sculptural decorations.

Right: Details of the portals, on the post and arch-doors, of various decorations and strange animal sculptures which include monsters, snake-tailed fish and griffons.

council of 202 Italian bishops and defied the Imperial decree. Constans responded by ordering his Exarch in Ravenna to arrest the rebellious Pope and bring him to Constantinople, but the Exarch found the Roman flock solidly behind their Pope and gave up the attempt.

Pope Martin apparently came to some kind of agreement with the Exarch, whose failure to carry out his Emperor's orders was conveniently camouflaged by his being called to Sicily to combat a Saracen invasion. That imperial mission was also doomed to failure, for the unfortunate Exarch died of pestilence on the campaign, along with the greater part of his army.

Emperor Constans had not given up on his quest to destroy the powerful Pope Martin and soon resumed his attack, maintaining that he had been irregularly elected and guilty of a variety of crimes. These included insufficient reverence to the Virgin Mary and, worst of all, being in contact with the dreaded Saracens.

Pope Martin was captured in June of 653 and banished to the island of Naxos, where he was kept for one year. Being sickly and suffering, his captors hoped he would soon die, but he failed to oblige, and his spirit was unwavering. His martyrdom continued when he was taken to Constantinople, where he was imprisoned in a dungeon for ninety-three days, brought to trial, found guilty, and sentenced to death. Loaded with irons, this Catholic pope was dragged through the streets to be jeered at by the populace. His death sentence was commuted, and he was taken on a ship to be set ashore in the Crimea, where he died on September 17, 655.

The religious controversy that pitted an emperor against a pope provided the backdrop when Aripert I became King of the Lombards. He reigned for eight years, and his death in 661 was the beginning of a deadly power struggle in the Lombard ranks. The Lombard kingdom was inherited by Aripert's two sons, Perctarit in Milan and Godepert in Pavia. Their squabbles for supremacy ended the following year with the death of Godepert and the exile of Perctarit to the land of the Franks. Through treachery and bloodshed, the Iron Crown came to be placed on the head of a usurper, Grimwald, who made his son, Romwald, the Duke of Beneventum. The realm was solidly in the hands of father and son, but the Lombards were about to come under attack from the Byzantine Empire.

Grimwald the Usurper and Emperor Constans

Emperor Constans II decided it was time to recover that large part of fair Italy held by the Lombards. In 663 he set sail from Greece and landed at Tarentum—just as Pyrrhus had done almost 1,000 years before—and like Pyrrhus he sought the counsel of one who could predict the future, an old hermit. Constans asked the question: "Shall I vanquish and hold down the nation of the Lombards which dwell in Italy?" The answer was unfavorable, but he pressed forward nevertheless and invaded the Duchy of Beneventum.

The Lombards were unprepared to meet the invaders, who advanced rapidly and placed the city of Beneventum under siege. Duke Romwald sent an urgent cry for help to his father who was soon on his way southward with a formidable army. Emperor Constans did not wait for them to arrive and was quickly persuaded that he had best retreat with all speed, but before doing so he made a truce with the Duke, who handed over his sister Gisa as a hostage. What valuable bargaining chips women had become during these times! Constans proceeded to Naples, still part of the Empire, but there were battles along the way between his Imperial forces and the

Beneventum Lombards who dogged their steps. The disparity between the Lombards and the Greeks is illustrated in the story of a brawny Lombard called Amalong. He is said to have struck a Greek soldier with his spear and with both hands hoisted the little man into the air, pierced through and writhing in the throes of death. Confronted with such frightening Goliaths the Imperial soldiers took flight.

Emperor Constans decided to proceed to Rome, which, although part of the Empire, had not been paid a visit by a man calling himself "emperor" for nearly two centuries. It was a great event to be sure, but one could hardly expect the Romans to be overjoyed in view of what had happened to Pope Martin just eight years earlier on orders of the same imperial visitor. It was probably a nervous Pope Vitalian who made his way along the Appian Way with members of his clergy to greet the Emperor six miles outside the gates of Rome and escort him into the city. This emperor really had nothing that the Romans could admire as, in addition to the religious persecutions which had been a hallmark of his reign, he was himself a foreigner, Greek by language and education.

It was July 5, 663, when Constans entered Rome and went to the great Basilica of Saint Peter. He remained in Rome for twelve days, visiting churches and attending mass, but he also took away some of the adornments of the holy places, including the copper tiles that had covered the dome of the Pantheon. In short, he prayed and then helped himself, for he was in dire need of money to finance his campaign. It was not a sacking like that of past invaders, but the Romans had been fleeced by their so-called Emperor. Great was their relief when he departed with his troops and made his way south to Sicily, taking with him his Lombard hostage and all his treasures.

Emperor Constans set up his headquarters in Syracuse, where he remained for the next five years. During this time, he tried to regain North Africa from the Saracens with little success. His dream of reuniting the Empire was costly, and citizens bore the brunt of his taxation. To pay the Imperial tax collectors, slaves had to be sold, and family members were often separated. Churches in Sicily, as well as the islands of Sardinia and Corsica, were stripped of adornments to replenish the Imperial treasury.

Finally, on the Ides of September in 668, Constans's long and unwelcome visit came to an end in his bath at Syracuse. It is recorded that he was killed by his valet, Andreas, who struck his master on the head with a heavy soapbox while he was scrubbing himself with his Gallic soap. Andreas was nowhere to be found when the attendants, after waiting outside for a long time, entered and found the Emperor lying dead on the floor with the bloodstained weapon nearby. Few mourned his passing—least of all the Italians—but he may have halted the advance of the Saracens for a little while longer.

This was the Italy of Grimwald, a battlefield where Lombards and Imperial forces vied for control and the Saracens threatened from the south. The Lombard Kingdom remained united, but it was not without conflict, for the Avars had been called in to put down the rebellious Duke of Friuli, and Grimwald had meted out severe punishment to the Romans at Opitergium (Oderzo) who were responsible for the death of two of his brothers years before. He had the city literally wiped from the face of the earth in revenge. But perhaps the most sacrilegious act attributed to this usurper was the attack on the town of Forlimpopoli, whose inhabitants were accused of harassing his messengers between Beneventum and the north. According to the Lombard historian Paulus, he rushed upon the city on the holy Sabbath of Easter when baptism was taking place, and slaughtered even deacons baptizing little babes.

Grimwald died three years after Emperor Constans. The two bitter enemies whose rules overlapped had one thing in common, for they both killed for power: Grimwald had slain Godepert (whose sister he then married), and Constans had his own blood brother murdered. Grimwald's disregard for religion was matched by Constans's efforts to stamp out differences, even if it meant sacrificing a pope.

The circumstances of the deaths of both Grimwald and Constans were bizarre and questionable. Grimwald met his end in 671 at home while recovering from an ailment for which his surgeons had bled him and he died, so it was recorded for history, when a vein in his arm ruptured. A more colorful and symbolic version describes the King on the ninth day of convalescing in his palace. He sees a dove and, taking his bow, he raises his arm to shoot the little bird, but he ruptures a vein and dies.

Grimwald's young son Garibald, fruit of his marriage with the sister of the man he had slain for a kingdom, was proclaimed king, but the reign of this little eaglet was cut short by the return of the exiled Perctarit.

Usurpers, Mutilations, and Exiles

When news of Grimwald's death reached the exiled Perctarit, he returned to Italy, where he was once again king with the approval of the Lombards. Soon he was reunited with his wife and their son, Cuninctpert, who had been held hostage at Beneventum. Perctarit ruled for sixteen years, the last eight with his son who, on his father's death ruled for another twelve years until he died in 700. These Catholic Lombards had been fair and just, and they had faithfully protected their Italian subjects.

Cunictpert's young son, Liutpert, now became king under the guardianship of Ansprand, a noble Milanese Lombard, but he soon became a victim of the restless dukes, who were jostling for power. He was imprisoned and then killed by rival claimants. Ansprand, who was powerless to save his ward, managed to escape to Bavaria, but his family had been captured, and following the hideous custom of mutilation, more common to the Byzantines of that time, his oldest son was blinded and his wife and daughter had their noses and ears cut off. Destiny had a role for Ansprand's youngest son, Liutprand, who was somehow spared these atrocities and was later allowed to join his father in Bavaria.

Twelve years later, Ansprand invaded Italy with an army provided by the Duke of Bavaria. A battle was fought on the plains near Pavia and the usurper, Aripert, took refuge inside the walls of the city. He drowned while trying to escape by swimming across the Ticino River, his body laden with gold that conspired with the fast eddies of that treacherous river to drag him down to a watery death.

Liutprand: The Greatest of the Lombard Kings

Ansprand's long exile had ended, and the Lombards acclaimed him as their king. It was as if this man of Milanese origin had waited for the chance to die in his native land, for he lived just three months after his return. His joy must have been immense, however, when he learned on his deathbed that his son, Liutprand, had been chosen by the Lombards to succeed him. Destined to be spared the atrocities perpetrated against his family—his older brother blinded and the faces of his mother and sister mutilated by the usurper King Aripert—Liutprand had grown up in a foreign court with his exiled father and married a Bavarian princess, Guntrut, who was now his queen.

Liutprand was just a young man when in 712 he was given the Iron Crown of the Lombards, which he wore for the next thirty-two years. His long reign brought continuity to Lombard Italy at a time when much of the world outside seemed to be crashing around the peninsula. The Saracens continued their conquests, while in Constantinople emperors came and went, their exits and entrances often accompanied by bloodshed. Byzantine control over the remaining portions of Italy diminished as papal power grew stronger.

Liutprand, like his predecessors, had to deal with rebellious dukes, but the early years of his rule were relatively uneventful as he took control of the Kingdom and occupied himself with its administration. A devout Catholic, he believed that he governed by divine right as an instrument of God, and the laws he added each year for the better governance of his people were by the "will and inspiration of God." Like Solomon, Liutprand sat in judgment in some difficult cases, many of which showed a concern for social relationships as well as a greater value for human life. We see also that Lombard Italy lived by two sets of laws, Roman and Lombard, but if, for example, a Lombard woman married a Roman, she and her offspring lived by Roman law.

Liutprand, like Rothari before him, sought to end the cycle of bloodshed:

> *Law CXXXV – Insult to a Woman. – It has been reported to us that a certain perverse man, while a woman was bathing in a river, took away all the clothes which she had for the covering of her body; wherefore, as she could not remain in the river forever, she was obliged to walk home naked.*

The man was ordered to pay his whole *guidrigild* (blood money) because the family of the lady would have sought revenge with resulting breach of the peace or *scandalum,* and someone might get killed. Better that the wrongdoer live and pay the price of a life. The laws that address the question of accidental death and compensation were also very specific in addressing the problem of responsibility:

> *Law CXXXVII – Death of a Child from a Horse's Kick – It has also been reported to us that a certain man lent his mare to another man to draw his wagon, but the mare had an unbroken colt which followed his mother along the road. While they were thus journeying, it chanced that some infants were standing in a certain village, and the colt struck one of them with its hoof and killed it.*

The compensation for this death was to be borne two thirds by the owner and one third by the borrower because both were guilty of negligence.

Reading of Liutprand's laws gives glimpses into the world of his day, but it was the events of the time and the role he played in the political-international arena that had a bearing on the future fate of Italy, for better or for worse.

The map of the peninsula remained largely unchanged, but Rome and Ravenna were sometimes at odds with each other, and Liutprand used one or the other to his own advantage. In 730 he even formed a league with the Exarch in Ravenna to deal with his rebellious southern dukes of Spoleto and Beneventum, who had sided with Rome against their Lombard king. Over the next years, however, Liutprand sought to expand the Lombard Kingdom as he nibbled away at what was left of the Byzantine lands of the Exarchate and moved closer to Rome. In 739, the frightened pope, then Gregory III, sent a cry for help to the Franks, but they were busy stemming the tide of Saracens and, with the support of the Lombards, pushing them back beyond the Pyrenees into Spain. Moreover, Liutprand was a kinsman of the Franks, his sister-in-law being married to Charles Martel, the powerful Mayor of the Palace who virtually ruled as a king and whose role in Italy's history will soon be apparent.

The year 742 marked the zenith for Lombard Italy, and it seemed that unification of the peninsula was only a matter of time. But the papal hold on the middle of the peninsula, both spiritual and secular, was still strong, and the Lombards never controlled Rome. Zacharias, who had just become pope, was a mediator willing to try diplomacy instead of calling on foreigners. Ravenna had sent out a call for help against the Lombards who wanted to chase out the Byzantines, and Zacharias, at great risk to his person, traveled to Terni where a meeting between the "unspeakable" Lombard and the Catholic man of God took place. There king and pope ate together in an atmosphere of cordiality. Liutprand, by the Treaty of Terni, agreed to relinquish four cities previously captured from the Exarchate.

Liutprand's respect for the Pope prevailed, but the same feeling did not extend to the Exarchate. Refugees streamed into Ravenna from towns of the Adriatic coast taken by the Lombards who resumed their attacks and, once more, Pope Zacharias was called on to intervene. This time, embassies to the King having failed, the Pope set out on a perilous journey through the "war zone," calling on the Exarch and proceeding to the Lombard capital of Pavia. The chronicler records that on June 28, 743, he came to a place where the Via Emilia crosses the Po River, near Piacenza, and from here he was conducted to Pavia by Lombard nobles who came to meet him. Was it astute timing that brought Zacharias to a church outside the walls of the city one day before it celebrated the martyrdom of Saints Peter and Paul? The next day pope and king met, and after attending mass they entered Pavia together. Liutprand agreed to restore most of the territories won from the Exarchate, and he accompanied his Catholic guest as far as the Po River where he bid him farewell.

This last meeting with Pope Zacharias was a landmark for the future of Italy. Lombard conquest of the peninsula had been stopped by the intercession of Zacharias and the Catholic sympathies of the Lombard King, whose devotion and reverence had already been demonstrated. It was Liutprand, the Lombard King, who at great cost redeemed the body of Saint Augustine, whose resting place in Sardinia had been profaned by the Saracen invaders, and brought it to Pavia. The church of San Pietro in Cielo d'Oro contains the magnificent marble tomb of the saint dating from 1362.

Liutprand died in January, 744, one year after his historic meeting with the pope. To close this chapter on Lombard Italy's greatest king, perhaps the words of Paulus Diaconus provide the most appropriate epitaph:

> He was indeed a man of much wisdom, very religious and a lover of peace, shrewd in counsel, powerful in war, merciful to offenders, chaste, modest, prayerful in night-watches, generous in charities, ignorant of letters indeed, yet worthy to be likened to philosophers, a supporter of his people, an increaser of the law.

Enter the Franks

On Liutprand's death, his nephew Hildebrand became king. For the previous eight years, Hildebrand had been co-ruler with his uncle, but now the Lombards rejected him, and he was dethroned after half a year.

Ratchis, the courageous and respected Duke of Friuli, was chosen king, and his first act was to conclude a truce with Pope Zacharias, guaranteeing the peace that had prevailed between Romans and Lombards. What a shock it must have been when just five years later King Ratchis suddenly abdicated to become a monk, entering the Benedictine monastery at Monte Cassino. Ratchis's brother, the ambitious Aistulf, was proclaimed king by the Lombards. During his reign the tenuous balance of alliances was upset.

Beyond the Alps in the Kingdom of the Franks events had occurred that would eventually prove to be a watershed in time, dramatically changing the course of Italian history. With the death in 741 of Charles Martel, the brother-in-law of Liutprand, the kingdom was divided between his two sons, Pepin and Carloman. Five years later, sickened by the wars and killing that he himself had been a part of, Carloman abdicated, leaving his share of the realm to Pepin. The following year he crossed into Italy, where he eventually entered the famous Benedictine monastery of Monte Cassino, introducing himself with these words: "I am a Frank, and I have quitted my country on account of my crimes."

Far from the sounds of war and the cries of death, Carloman met King Ratchis. What strange destiny had brought together two kings, one Frank and one Lombard, who had exchanged crowns for a monk's garb to share the chapel and the refractory of this sanctuary in the Pope's territory! And what a strange parallel was in the fact that both had abdicated of free will, and their brothers were ruling in their places! Here for the moment we will leave the two royal monks with their prayers and their peace, but we shall meet them again in perhaps even stranger circumstances when they return to their respective homelands to fulfill their destinies.

Two years after assuming power, King Aistulf (749–756) took up arms against the Exarchate, determined to remove the last vestiges of Byzantine control. On July 4, 751, Ravenna fell to the Lombards. It seemed that they would soon eliminate the last imperial foothold that was like a thorn in the side on the eastern shore of their kingdom.

At the end of March 752, the peacemaker Pope Zacharias died. The new pope, Stephen III, proved to be less friendly toward the Lombards, for he realized that with the territories of the Exarchate under their control they were getting far too powerful and becoming a threat to Rome. The following year he made overtures to Pepin for help, but the Franks were not easily persuaded to move against their friendly Lombard neighbors. When there was no progress, the Pope decided to negotiate with the Lombards in an effort to persuade them to return the captured lands to the Byzantine Empire, and on October 13, 753, set out for Pavia with imperial envoys to talk to the Lombard King Aistulf in person. An angry Aistulf refused the request, but made the fatal mistake of allowing the papal party safe passage to Frank-land. Losing no time, the Pope and his party quickly proceeded to the Great Saint Bernard pass and out of the reach of Aistulf, who soon regretted his folly. It was Christmas when Pepin, who had celebrated the day at his villa in Champagne, sent his son Charles 100 miles east to meet the Pontiff. Who could have imagined that this fourteen-year-old youth was the one destined to become the Emperor Charlemagne of history and legend? The historic meeting of Pepin and the Pope took place on January 6, 754, the feast of Epiphany. It was not a king who came bearing gifts, but a pope who came begging for the gift of support against the Lombards.

In July of that year, the Pope anointed Pepin and his two sons, thereby showing his spiritual authority over kings. Pepin agreed to help the Pope, but his nobles were unwilling to fight his battles across the Alps. While this was going on, he received an extraordinary and unexpected visit. Appearing before his eyes was his brother, Carloman, barefoot, with tonsured head, and clad in the rough raiment of a Benedictine monk. Carloman begged his brother not to wage war against the Lombards, but his words fell on deaf ears. His journey had been in vain, and he died shortly thereafter.

The Franks eventually invaded northern Italy, sweeping away the Lombard defenders as remnants of their army fled to the safety of Pavia, but the Franks were soon at the gates of the city. No match for Pepin's battle-hardened forces, King Aistulf agreed to restore the conquered territories to the Byzantine Empire, and a treaty was drawn up.

That treaty appears to have been nothing more than a scrap of paper in the eyes of the "unspeakable" Lombard king. Not only did he fail to restore the territories as promised, but on New Year's Day of 756 he besieged Rome with the help of the Lombards of Beneventum. Aistulf was quoted as saying, "Open to me this Salarian Gate and let me enter the City and I will deal gently with you." The gate was not opened, but Aistulf chose to wait patiently rather than commit the sacrilegious act of storming the holy city.

Now in dire straits, the desperate Pope again called on Pepin for help, this time warning him that God would harden his heart against him if he failed to come to the aid of the Church. Faced with such a divine threat, Pepin sent a second army to Italy. Presumably at this time, Aistulf raised the siege on Rome, much to the relief of the Romans. The Lombard king returned with his men to Pavia, where under threat of the Franks, he was forced to make good on his promises. A written document was drawn up that stipulated that the Lombards would not only surrender the territories conquered but also would pay a yearly tribute to the King of the Franks. The keys of the cities in question were duly procured by Pepin's emissaries, but instead of being handed over to the Byzantine Emperor as the Lombards had agreed, they were given to the Pope in what came to be known as the *Donation of Pepin*. The bone that was Ravenna had been snatched from the mouths of the Lombards and tossed to the Papacy.

The lands under papal control now formed a wide strip, stretching from the west across the mountains to the east coast, and would divide Italy in two for the next millennium.

Desiderius: The Last Lombard King

King Aistulf met his death in that eventful year of 756, not in battle with the Franks, but from injuries suffered when he was thrown from his horse while hunting. The Lombards spoke of him kindly, but the Pope, quite understandably, gleefully recorded the fact with such epitaphs as "follower of the devil," "devourer of the blood of Christians," and "destroyer."

Desiderius, the Lombard Duke of Tuscany, was most highly regarded by the dead king and favored by the Lombards to wear the Iron Crown, but a *coup de théâtre* occurred when opposition came from an unexpected source. Meditating in his monk's cell for the past seven and a half years was the deceased king's brother, Ratchis. On hearing the news, like a quick-change artist he slipped away from his monastery and hastened to Pavia to claim the crown for himself. What a dilemma this must have been for the Lombard dukes when this monk, once their king, suddenly appeared on the scene! Ratchis did, in fact, regain the crown, but there was opposition from the Franks and even the Pope who, for whatever reason, favored Desiderius over the monk. Three months into his reign, Ratchis abdicated for the second time and returned to the monastery of Monte Cassino.

Pope Stephen had lived only long enough to recommend Desiderius, for he died on April 26, 757. He was succeeded by his brother, Paul, who shared his philosophy and wisdom. For the next decade, Pope Paul, Pepin the Frank, and the Lombard King Desiderius kept the peace, but this was shattered with the deaths of the Pope in 767 and Pepin the following year.

There was a dramatic change in cast as the realm of the Franks was divided between Pepin's two sons, Charles, now twenty-six years of age, and the teenage Carloman. Rome was a war zone as there was a savage struggle for the seat of the pontiff, which had now become more like a king's throne coveted by seekers of power, complicated by the fact that Lombards, Franks, and Byzantines sought to have "their" personal choices installed. It was Stephen III who finally emerged one year later. He appeared on the scene like a cuttlefish, blackening the political waters in his resolve to put a wedge between the Franks and the Lombards.

A lady now takes center stage in the person of Pepin's widow, the strong-willed Berta who would defy a pope. Taking matters into her own hands, in 770 she set out for Italy with the intention of reestablishing friendly relations with the Lombards through marriage alliances. As a match-making mother she arranged for her son, Charles, to marry Desiderata, daughter of the Lombard King Desiderius. For good measure, she also offered her little daughter, the twelve-year-old Gisila, to the Lombard king's son, Adelchis, although this wedding never came about. At this time Berta also paid a visit to the Pope in Rome before returning home, taking with her the Lombard princess. Charles already had a lady at his palace to whom he was probably married, but she was simply "removed" out of political necessity.

The alliance between Frank and Lombard was restored, and the Pope, obviously not made privy to the deal by the visiting queen, was beside himself with rage when he learned of the alliance. He wrote to the young Frankish kings expressing his anger and racial prejudice in the following terms:

> Now a thing has been brought to our hearing which we cannot even speak of without great pain in our heart, namely, that Desiderius, king of the Lombards, is seeking to persuade your Excellencies that one of your brotherhood should be joined in marriage to his daughter. Certainly if that be true it is a veritable suggestion of the devil, and not a marriage but rather a most wickedly imagined concubinage. How many men, as we learn from the Holy Scripture, through unsanctified union with a woman of another nation, have departed from the commandments of God, and fallen into grievous sin! But what indescribable folly is this, . . . the most royal line of yours, should be polluted by union with the perfidious and fouly stinking race of the Lombards, which is never reckoned in the number of nations, and from which it is certain that the tribe of lepers hath sprung!

The long letter, containing invectives and admonitions, did not frighten the staunch dowager queen-mother or Charles, and Desiderata was proclaimed Queen of the Franks. The marriage was short-lived, however, for the following year Desiderata was sent home to her father, presumably for personal rather than political reasons.

The alliance of friendship so carefully engineered by Berta was irrevocably broken, and we come to another bend in the road of history.

The failure of Charles's marriage with the Lombard princess caused a major shift in alliances, and this was followed by yet another shock. Charles's brother, King Carloman, died on December 4 of that same year, on the threshold of manhood at the tender age of twenty. Big Charles, supported by his nobles and churchmen, moved rapidly to take over the dead brother's part of the Frankish kingdom. A few weeks later, he celebrated Christmas as the sole ruler of the entire realm.

Charles's actions would have been perfectly normal had his brother Carolman been without heirs, but in his short life he had sired two sons who should have inherited his part of the kingdom. Carloman's young widow, Gerberga, fearing for her safety in this hostile environment and distrustful of her brother-in-law, fled with her infant boys across the Alps into Italy, seeking asylum at the court of the Lombard King. A strange twist of fate brought these two women to the court of Pavia, both ex-queens of the Franks and sisters-in-law, one a dispossessed widow and the other a rejected wife.

If ever a man had reason to hate the Franks, Desiderius did, but he thought he held the aces with Gerberga's two sons, the rightful heirs to their dead father's kingdom. In addition, the legitimacy of Charles was in question when it was rumored he may have been born out of wedlock. What was needed now, however, was the Pope's recognition of the two boys as rightful heirs of their father's part of the kingdom, but the new pontiff, Adrian I (772–795) was no more sympathetic to the Lombards than was his predecessor.

Peace was shattered as a frustrated and angry Desiderius chose the military route, and papal cities and possessions were put to fire and sword. City after city fell to the Lombards, and in early 773 Charles received a messenger from the Pope, who was now screaming for help. Desiderius was marching on Rome with his armies, taking with him the widow of Carloman and her innocent babes that they might be justly anointed as kings of the Franks. Rome prepared for the worst, securing the gates of the city against the Lombards. Once more the Pope's words, no doubt with the threat of eternal damnation, prevailed over the sword of the Lombards, and Desiderius returned to Pavia "with great reverence and full of confusion."

Meanwhile, Charles had answered the Pope's call for help, and the Franks were massed on the other side of the Alps, ready to stream down through the mountain passes into Northern Italy. For a while history teetered on the brink of uncertainty as negotiations took place. Finally, panic struck the army of Desiderius as his soldiers took flight, retreating to Pavia. For eight months the Franks lay siege to the city, during which time Gerberga fled with her sons to Verona; when that city was later captured, they fell into the hands of the Franks. What became of the two little princes? There is no record of their fate, but it is believed that uncle Charles was clement enough to spare their lives. The Lombard king's son, Adelchis, who had fled Pavia with the royal party, managed to escape from Verona and eventually made his way to the Byzantine court in Constantinople. He would later turn up to do mischief.

Charles proceeded on his victorious route to Rome, and the religious reception he received as he finally entered the city was like that accorded in centuries past to a visiting emperor. Charles descended from his horse and walked with his nobles the last short stretch of the journey to the Basilica of Saint Peter where King and Pope met and embraced. Pope Adrian I, a true Roman of noble lineage with the bearing of an emperor, and the young Frankish warrior-king of thirty-two years of age came together on that day, Holy Saturday, April 2, 774.

Following this historic visit to the holy city, Charles returned to finish off the business at the besieged city of Pavia, where hardship and disease were taking a toll. It was the end of June when Pavia surrendered, and Charles took prisoner the Lombard King Desiderius, his former father-in-law, along with his queen. They apparently ended their days in a monastery in Picardy, France.

The last Lombard king had tried to stop Charles from robbing his little nephews of their own share of a kingdom and had ended up losing his own. After two centuries, the Lombard Kingdom had come to an end and the Iron Crown would be placed on the head of foreigner.

A young warrior of yet another barbarian race to enter Italy had changed the course of history and set the stage for the next centuries to come. The young Charles came to be known as CHARLEMAGNE, a giant of history and legend.

The Lombard Kingdom, with its capital at Pavia, came to an end in 774, but it was during the 8th century that the Duchy of Benevento reached the height of its extent and power. The marble map displayed on a wall in the old city is a constant reminder of Benevento's historic importance.

CHAPTER THREE

Charlemagne and his Legacy
774-875 A.D.

Charlemagne

A new and dramatic chapter in the history of Italy began as Charlemagne assumed the title of "King of the Franks and the Lombards."

The man that history and legend have depicted as the champion of Christianity spent much of his life at war, often against Saxon pagans or followers of Islam. His battles to keep the invading Saracens confined to Spain on the other side of the Pyrenees Mountains gave rise to his legendary figure as a Christian soldier riding out against the "infidel," and eulogized in the epic French poem, "La Chanson de Roland." This was not the Charlemagne of Italian history, however, where he became the strong arm of the Papacy. Charlemagne was duty-bound to defend Rome and the tomb of the Apostle Peter as a place of pilgrimage to be revered and protected for the whole Christian world, a role that pitted him against not only the "infidels" but also the Lombards. This pact between Pope and Charlemagne constituted the embryonic beginnings of what would later become the Holy Roman Empire.

The peninsula had been liberated from Lombard rule, much to the relief of the Papacy, but not from the Lombards who merely transferred their allegiance, such as it was, from the deposed Lombard King Desiderius to the Frank who had assumed his title. Even the laws and administration were left largely in Lombard hands, and no attempt was made to impose the system of the Franks. It is likely that for the average citizens little had changed because the new monarch, like the Byzantine Emperor, kept his court in a distant land and his visits were infrequent.

Although Charlemagne did show his face in northern Italy in the spring of 776 to quell a revolt in Friuli, his second historic visit to Rome did not take place until 781 when he came with his young children and his queen, Hildegard, a beautiful young Swabian girl whom he had married after rejecting the Lombard Desiderata. The purpose of this visit was to present their young son, Carloman, to the Pope, but it gave the Italians a chance to see the mighty King who had remained such a shadowy figure. He had set out in 780, and his first stop was the Lombard capital of Pavia, where he celebrated Christmas in the usual stately manner, finally arriving in Rome on Easter Day.

It had been seven years since Charlemagne last visited the eternal city and because this was a friendly visit he was received with great pomp and ceremony as Romans must have crowded the streets, craning their necks to get a glimpse of the imposing Frank, his beautiful wife, and their children looking for all the world like fair angels. The main event during this visit was the baptism of Carloman by Pope Adrian. The boy went in as "Carloman," but came out as "Pepin," symbolically replacing the hunchback half-brother Pepin of Charlemagne's union with Himiltrud (legitimate or illegitimate). This little fellow and his baby brother, Louis, were next crowned by the Pope to denote their status as kings, Louis of Aquitaine and the reborn Pepin, King of Italy.

An interesting event in international diplomacy also took place when ambassadors arrived from Constantinople to conclude a treaty of marriage between the eleven-year-old Emperor Constantine, who ruled with his recently widowed mother, Empress Irene, and Charlemagne's eldest daughter, Hrotrud, still a child of only nine years. With the Pope in the middle of it all, the worlds of the Franks and the Byzantines, each having a stake on the Italian peninsula, came together to seal a treaty of friendship by the union of children. The Byzantine court meant business, for a tutor (the eunuch Elisha) had also been dispatched to instruct the little Frankish princess in the Greek language and the customs of the Byzantine court.

Charlemagne left Rome and returned to the north, visiting cities along the way, and now Milan received attention. In this important city Charlemagne chose to have the baptismal ceremony of his youngest daughter, Gisila. Finally, in August, Charlemagne and his party returned across the Alps, the Italian affairs apparently settled and in the hands of a Frankish regent and governors of the newly crowned King Pepin, a four-year-old boy.

In the next five years things began to fall apart. Charlemagne's beloved wife died in 783 at the young age of twenty-six years, after bearing nine children, the last of whom bore her name and died that same year. One more tragedy was visited on Charlemagne that year with the death of his beloved and powerful mother, Berta. Meanwhile, the diplomatic horizon had become cloudy, and the marriage treaty with Hrotrud was in jeopardy.

Back in Rome, a nervous Pope Adrian, increasingly under threat from the Lombards of Beneventum (who were suspected of conspiring against Rome and the Franks), kept up a desperate correspondence with Charlemagne, imploring his immediate intervention. Finally, in 786 Charlemagne crossed the Alps again and proceeded to Florence where he celebrated Christmas, clearly timing his visits to coincide with important days of the Christian calendar. Charlemagne was alone this time; when he arrived in Rome, summoned by the Pope, the Beneventans knew that this was no friendly visit. They greatly feared the wrath of the Frank. Arichis, the Lombard Duke of Beneventum, sent his son Romwald to Charlemagne with gifts and a promise of obedience. Charlemagne was inclined to accept the promise, but not Pope Adrian who wanted war against the Lombards, whom he saw as a constant threat to his own safety. Not part of the Kingdom of Italy to the north, the southern Lombard dukes were too arrogant, too independent, and too close for comfort. Indeed, the wife of Arichis was none other than the daughter of the deposed Lombard King Desiderius, and her brother, Adelchis, was at the court of the Byzantines, with whom relations had soured.

In a desperate move to avoid war, Duke Arichis next offered Charlemagne thirteen nobles as hostages and two of his own children, his son Grimwald and daughter Adelgisa. Charlemagne knew the love of a father for his children and the sacrifice of Duke Arichis, so he took only Grimwald. By this noble act of personal sacrifice, the Lombards of Beneventum were spared great suffering and the ravages of certain war.

Charlemagne spent Easter in Rome and then, to the great relief of all, made his way across the mountains to Ravenna (taken from the Lombards and handed to the Pope as the "Donation of Pepin" in 757), finally disappearing once again beyond the Alps and taking with him as precious hostages the Lombard nobles and young Grimwald.

While Grimwald was being held hostage in the faraway court of Charlemagne, tragedy struck his princely family back in Beneventum. His older brother, Romwald, had died in his twenty-sixth year and his fifty-three-year-old father, Duke Arichis, died one month later. The widowed Adelperga did all in her power to obtain the return of her son, Grimwald, but Pope Adrian continually advised Charlemagne not to release his precious hostage, for he feared the power of the "unspeakable" Lombards as much as ever.

Our Lombard historian, Paulus Diaconus, lived during this period and was a participant in the history. He had once been a guest at the court of Charlemagne and a close companion during his leisure hours. He may well have been working in the interest of Grimwald and his widowed mother, for he had pleaded for the release of his own brother, apparently taken prisoner in 776 during the Lombard revolt in Friuli. Here are a few lines of his long poem to Charlemagne which tells a story of one family's grief:

> Hear, great king, my complaint and in mercy receive my petition;
> Scarce in the whole round world will be found such a sorry story as mine
> Six long years have passed since my brother's doom overtook him,
> Now it is the seventh that he, a captive, in exile must pine.
> Lingers at home his wife, to roam through the streets of her city
> Begging for morsels of food, knocking at door after door
> Only in shameful guise like this can she nourish the children
> Four little half-clothed babes, whom she in her wretchedness bore.
> There is a sister of mine, a Christ-vowed virgin of sorrows . . .

Whether or not Paulus had also used his powers of persuasion in the case of Grimwald we do not learn. However, the young Lombard hostage was allowed to return to Beneventum in 788. He remained true to his oath of allegiance to Charlemagne, even taking his side against his own uncle Adelchis who had sought asylum in Constantinople and later joined the Byzantines in an unsuccessful invasion of Italy.

As the century drew to a close, a power struggle was taking place in Constantinople between Empress Irene and her son, Constantine, the co-emperor. Constantine fell victim to the unspeakable savagery of his own mother, who ordered him arrested and blinded so she could rule alone. This was the fate of the boy born to be emperor and once promised to Charlemagne's daughter Hrotrud.

In Rome, Pope Adrian had died on Christmas Day of 795. His pontificate had lasted almost a quarter of a century and he had given Charlemagne, the defender of the faith, quite a lot of trouble during those years. Two days after his death, a new pope took his place as Leo III. He was not a popular man among the powerful Roman nobles, and his life was often threatened. A crisis occurred when, four years into his pontificate, he was actually attacked by his enemies who wanted to blind him and cut out his tongue. The Pope had been injured in the savage attack on his person, but luckily the threat of mutilation was not carried out. Nevertheless, he sent an urgent cry for help to Charlemagne, and once more the Frank crossed the Alps and made his

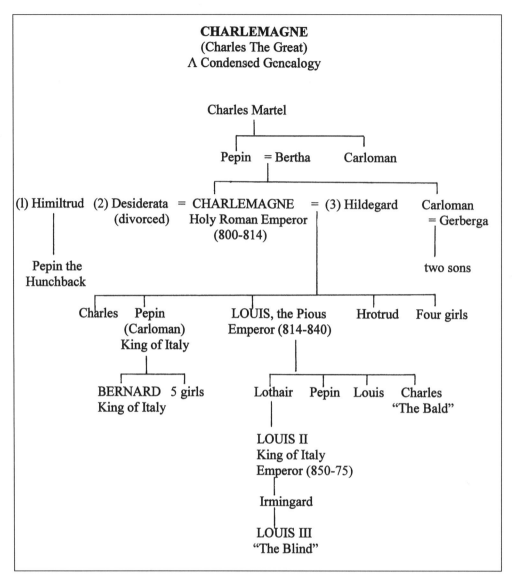

CHARLEMAGNE
(Charles The Great)
A Condensed Genealogy

Charles Martel

Pepin = Bertha   Carloman

(1) Himiltrud   (2) Desiderata = CHARLEMAGNE = (3) Hildegard   Carloman
                     (divorced)   Holy Roman Emperor   = Gerberga
                                      (800-814)

Pepin the   two sons
Hunchback

Charles   Pepin   LOUIS, the Pious   Hrotrud   Four girls
           (Carloman)   Emperor (814-840)
           King of Italy

           BERNARD 5 girls   Lothair   Pepin   Louis   Charles
           King of Italy   "The Bald"

                                 LOUIS II
                                 King of Italy
                                 Emperor (850-75)

                                 Irmingard

                                 LOUIS III
                                 "The Blind"

way to Rome. This time it was to save a pope not from the Lombards but from the Romans themselves. Of this visit his advisor Alcuin wrote:

> But Rome, which has been once touched by the discord of brethren still keeps the poison which had been instilled into her veins, and thus compels your venerable Dignity to hasten from your sweet abodes in Germany in order to repress the fury of this pestilence.

Charlemagne visited Rome for the fourth and last time in December 800. He came as a mediator for a papacy in disarray, to preside over a court where a Catholic Pope, Leo III, was the accused. Leo was cleared of all allegations against him; his pontificate, restored to him through the intercession of Charlemagne, lasted for fourteen more years. What happened as a result of that outcome, however, was an event that significantly changed the course of Italian history.

A New Empire

On Christmas Day of 800, Charlemagne, in the company of his Frankish nobles, made his way to the Basilica of Saint Peter, appropriately attired in Roman garb instead of his customary dress of a Teutonic chieftain, and there, at the tomb of the apostle, Pope Leo III placed on his graying-golden head the brighter golden crown of Emperor. This symbolic act marked the beginning of a new partnership and a milestone in the history of Italy.

This aging hero of Christianity took his task seriously and immediately set about strengthening the administration of his vast realm through his officials, the *missi dominici,* who were promptly dispatched to the chief cities of every province of his Empire. They were usually men of the cloth and included archbishops and abbots, all specially selected and schooled in the court of Charlemagne. Part of their function was to protect the interests of ordinary citizens and ensure justice.

In case there should be any misunderstanding as to who was the supreme head, these same *missi dominici* were to administer a new oath of allegiance to all imperial subjects. Here in part is what it said:

> I order that every man in my whole kingdom, whether ecclesiastic or layman, each one according to his prayer and his purpose, who may have before promised fidelity to me in the king's name, shall now repeat that promise to me in my name as Caesar. And those who may not yet have made that promise shall now all do so, from twelve years old and upwards. And let this be done in public, . . . et cetera.
> (Hodgkin, *Italy and Her Invaders,* p. 8:207)

Of course, the peninsula remained fragmented as the Lombard dukedoms of the south remained outside of Charlemagne's empire, not to mention areas still in the clutches of the Byzantines.

Charlemagne took his crown and returned to his court in the north, leaving in his shadow his son Pepin, the King of Italy. Poor Pepin had his work cut out for him, for he had to deal with the rebellious Lombards of Beneventum. One case in point was Grimwald, whose sworn allegiance to Charlemagne did not extend to Pepin. He is recorded as having given the saucy answer to the younger Frank with these words: *"Free was I born and noble my forebears on either side. So by the help of God, free will I ever abide."*

Grimwald resented the Franks who had been made dukes in Lombard territories, and there was conflict between the appointed Frankish Duke of Spoleto and the Beneventans, resulting in destruction and death on both sides and ending with the death of Grimwald in 806. King Pepin next turned his attention to Venetia, which he invaded and briefly wrested from the Byzantine Empire. It was his last battle, for he died soon afterward on July 8, 810. Pepin was buried in Milan, and there lay forgotten over the centuries. It was not until 1874 that a slab of white marble was discovered in the church of Saint Ambrogio. It bears the Latin inscription: *"Hic Pipinus rex quiescit in pace qui in hac regnavit provincia ann."*

Pepin was only thirty-two years of age when he died, but he left five daughters and a son, Bernard, who two years later became King of Italy at the age of fifteen. His reign was short, for an unimaginable fate awaited him.

Emperor Charlemagne's last years were relatively uneventful, but saddened by personal tragedies. His beloved daughter Hrotrud, who might have sat on the throne of Constantinople, died in 810, the same year as Pepin, and Charles, the eldest son who played no part in Italian history, died in December of the following year, unmarried and leaving no heirs.

Charlemagne was at this point a sick old man with white hair, weighed down with grief and more closely resembling the figure of legend in the epic poem "La Chanson de Roland," riding out to conquer the heathen. The real Charlemagne was a warrior and champion of Christianity who had protected the Catholic Church and her popes, giving Rome a vital role in the order of things as the popes henceforth assumed to symbolic power to crown emperors.

Charlemagne died in 814. He was sincerely mourned by his subjects and these words, written by a monk of Bobbio in an ode to the deceased Emperor, were forebodings of what was in store for Italy:

> Woe to thee Italy, fair land and wide,
> And woe to all the cities of thy pride!

✳ ✳ ✳

Louis the Pious succeeded his father Charlemagne and ruled as Emperor until 840. He was not a visible figure in Italian history, as he had his own problems trying to keep the imperial crown on his royal head. His quarrelsome sons fought for their share of the realm, and the ambitious Lothair even managed to have his father deposed for a time. It was after the power struggle and rebellions in 818 that Italy lost her king. The young Bernard was one of those accused of conspiracy. He was blinded by order of his not-so-pious uncle Louis, and he died shortly after this terrible mutilation, a young man in his early twenties. The kingdom of Italy was administered by the Imperial *missi dominici*.

Wars of succession followed the death of Louis the Pious in 840, culminating in the famous Treaty of Verdun in 843. Lothair, who had once been co-emperor with his father, got the Middle Realm, sandwiched between his brother and half-brother, a strip running from the North Sea to just south of Rome and cut in half by the great Alps. Although Lothair's share included the Kingdom of Italy, he was more at home north of the mountains. Indeed, he had no love for Italy, a place where his father sent him for punishment, and he soon unloaded that portion of his realm onto the shoulders of his eldest son, Louis II, on whose head the Pope, according to tradition, placed the Iron Crown of the Lombards on June 15, 844.

Ten years later, in 855, there was a surprising turn of events when Lothair abdicated and entered a monastery, where he died soon thereafter as a penitent monk. His realm was divided between his sons, but Louis II became the next emperor and he chose to remain in Italy.

Emperor Louis: Crusade Against the Infidels

The dream of Louis II was to reunite the peninsula under his Empire. His efforts to bring the south into the imperial orbit and his quest to conquer the "infidels" brought the south back into the spotlight, revealing the cancer that was spreading there.

Before we follow the pious Louis on his quest, we must step back in time and get acquainted with the world that he was about to enter. The southern part of the Italian peninsula, long separated from the northern half by the Papal States, was the domain of Lombard dukes and the neglected remnants of the Byzantine Empire. Unhampered by a central rule, cities and duchies had grown strong and independent, but the region was a hotbed of intrigues, little wars, petty squabbles, and changing alliances.

The island of Sicily, far from the influence of the Franks and a long sea voyage from Constantinople, had long since followed a separate destiny. The Sicilians had been on friendly terms with the Saracens, their trading partners, and when in 827 they decided to throw off the yoke of the Byzantine Empire, they called on the Saracens for help. The Saracens came, but instead of leaving when they were no longer needed they decided to stay on. The conquest of the island by the Saracens, the "infidels," had begun.

Palermo was the first city to fall under Saracen control, and it became a base for further conquests over the next half a century. The invaders were not confined to Sicily, however, but had spilled into the mainland, where Naples recruited them as mercenaries against the encroaching Beneventans and the latter in turn used their services against Naples. But it was Bari, in the heel of the peninsula, that became the base of operations on the mainland. Eventually no longer just a springboard for incursions in the south, it was an established Emirate that lasted for a quarter of a century.

Louis's first involvement with the south came in 848 when he interceded to put down a civil war between Lombard princes. This ended when one year later the Duchy of Beneventum was split into two parts with a line drawn through the territory between Capua and Benevento. The two adversaries pledged not to use Saracen mercenaries, but formed a united front against them. Nevertheless, a Muslim emir still controlled the former Beneventan city of Bari and the surrounding territories. From this base, the Saracens continually carried out raids, pillaging and plundering villages and cities. Louis was called back by the Dukes in 852, this time to deal with the Saracens. He achieved nothing, for it seemed after all that the petty Lombard princes and lords preferred to pay tribute to the Muslim Emir rather than put themselves under the Christian Emperor. Louis returned northward with his troops and stayed away from the chaotic South for the next eight years.

In 857 a most extraordinary man became the third Emir of Bari and the chief antagonist of the next dramatic act. His name was Sawdan. Emir Sawdan soon made his unwelcome presence felt and began by invading the Beneventan territory of Duke Adelchis, taking rich booty and making off with prisoners to be sold as slaves. Small groups of Franks sent to help him achieved nothing, and the powerless duke decided to make a deal with the Emir, agreeing to pay tribute and hand over hostages in exchange for peace. It was perhaps at this time that he handed over a daughter of his, found in the custody of Sawdan some years later. With the Duke of Beneventum thus neutralized, the clever Sawdan looked with glee on the quarrelsome Christians, who easily became his targets because their energies were used up fighting each other. His raids of pillage and plunder continued and, in addition to the treasures that were lost and the crops destroyed, captives were taken away and sold as slaves in a booming new trade of humans with the East.

Finally, Beneventans and Capuans alike called on Emperor Louis to help them put down the marauding Saracens. From past experience, however, Louis knew that he needed a force capable of keeping these southern princes in line because they could not be trusted. In a bold new move, he ordered a general conscription to mobilize all those within his realm of Italy for a war of independence. With imperial efficiency and speed, recruitment centers organized by the *missi* were set up throughout the Kingdom. All would outfit themselves for war and supply provisions to last until the next harvest.

The mighty armies raised converged on the South. In the spring of 866, Louis II, accompanied by his empress, paid a visit to the monastery of Monte Cassino. Meanwhile, the southern princes became suspicious of Louis's true motives, and Louis in turn suspected that the Capuans were planning a double-cross. Mistrust was mutual; the nervous Louis, taking no chances, captured Capua after a brief siege and put it under the control of the Duke of Spoleto, who was a Frank, a move that made the Lombards even more suspicious. A frightened Naples quickly negotiated with Louis and gave a pledge of allegiance and fidelity, avoiding the risk of being overwhelmed by the northern army. Louis put his campaign against the Saracens on hold as he proceeded to subdue his so-called allies of the south, including Salerno, Amalfi, Pozzuoli, and Sassola.

In December Emperor Louis finally reached Beneventum, where he was received by Duke Adelchis, a villain in disguise as it later became apparent. Having thus flexed his imperial muscles and shown his mettle as a warrior, he prepared to winter in Beneventum with his formidable army. The following spring, Louis was ready to continue his quest and take on the main target of his expedition, the Muslim Emirate of Bari. The outlying towns were taken, communications were cut off, and crops were destroyed as the siege began. Here Louis's luck ran out when the Frankish reinforcements sent to booster the Italians and Lombards were stricken with dysentery and were overcome by the unaccustomed heat. Many deserted and returned to France. Louis then abandoned the siege and returned to Beneventum.

Matters took a new turn when the forceful new Eastern Emperor, Basil, became interested in reasserting his claim on the southern Italian cities with the excuse of joining Louis against the Saracens. Basil with his naval forces and Louis with his ground forces could easily take the city of Bari, but who would get the prize? The two Emperors were still rivals, and they were after the same prey. Negotiations on this point had reached an impasse when the resourceful Basil proposed a marriage between his son and Louis's only daughter, Irmingard. Diplomatic relations, broken off since 853 when Louis himself had been engaged to a Byzantine princess, could be conveniently renewed.

Louis had, of course, planned to take Bari all by himself, but now with Basil butting in he had no choice but to accept the proposal of collaboration. Basil took him at his word and finally, in September of 869, a fleet of 400 ships appeared off Bari. The commander, Niceta Orifa, had orders to assist Louis and also take on board his daughter Irmingard, promised in marriage to Basil's son. However, on his arrival he discovered that the forces promised had not turned up, and Louis was nowhere to be found. He seemed to have evaporated along with his beloved daughter, whom he probably had no intention of sending to the alien court of Constantinople. Commander Orifa, in disgust, simply set sail with his fleet back across the Adriatic, leaving behind a few ships and cutting Bari off from support from the sea. Emperor Louis was on his own now. It was getting late in the season for war games, so he planned to winter once more in Beneventum, but as he was making his way there with his army he was taken by surprise. The Byzantine fleet had sailed away and the Franks were on the move when, like a jack-in-the-box, out popped the incredible

Sawdan with his Saracens. Following the rear guard of Louis's retreating troops, they stole over 2,000 of their horses, then adding insult to injury took off to attack the Sanctuary of San Michele on Mount Gargano, returning to Bari with rich booty.

An indecisive Louis, encouraged by his brother, finally resumed his campaign against the terrible Emir. A final assault on the walls of Bari took place on February 3, 871, and the victorious Frankish and Lombard troops entered the city.

A dramatic scene follows. Louis and Duke Adelchis together enter Bari to capture Sawdan. Their quarry had no escape, but he has retreated to the safety of a tower of the palace. From there he shouts down to Adelchis, asking him to spare his life. He argues that he has kept safe and unharmed the daughter that Adelchis had entrusted to him as a hostage. Adelchis manages to persuade Louis to spare the life of their enemy, and Sawdan is taken away unharmed as their prisoner.

Louis's clemency would turn out to be a mistake, but now he is riding high on his success as he recovers from the Saracens most of Apulia and Calabria. Taranto resists. He needs the help of the Byzantine fleet to achieve his goal and negotiations with Emperor Basil are reopened.

Meanwhile, Louis returns to Beneventum to wait on events as his troops disperse in towns and castles to enjoy some rest. He has with him his still unmarried daughter Irmingard. It is believed that Louis is scheming to depose Duke Adelchis, while the latter would like to get rid of Louis who is becoming a source of embarrassment. As mistrust between the two grows, Adelchis steals away to seek the advice of his noble prisoner, Sawdan. The wise and knowledgeable Emir had given valuable counsel in the past and noble Lombards had even consulted him on such matters as medicine and the care of horses. Now Sawdan comes up with a dangerous plan of treachery against the Franks with Adelchis as his accomplice, but he warns that action must be taken before word of the plot gets abroad.

In a lightning attack, the scattered Franks are soon captured and imprisoned. Louis is caught by surprise in the ducal palace of Beneventum where he was residing.

Now in an almost comical reversal of fate, it is the Emperor's turn to take refuge in the tower of a palace, just as Sawdan had done before. For three days he holds out, but eventually the great Frankish Emperor must give himself up and become the prisoner of Duke Adelchis, the stealthy Lombard whom ironically he had committed to save from the Saracens.

For forty days, from August 13 to September 17, Adelchis holds his imperial captive as news of this outrage spreads like wildfire throughout the Christian world and soon reaches uncle Charles, King of the Franks, who believes Louis is dead and prepares to claim Italy for himself.

Meanwhile, Adelchis has a real problem. He cannot hold two such important prisoners as Emir Sawdan and Emperor Louis without dire consequences. He also learns that the Saracens have landed some 20,000 strong in Calabria and Taranto. Saracen reaction to the capture of Bari, now back under the Beneventans, had been swift and decisive. They had returned to reclaim southern Italy and strengthen their hold on Sicily.

Adelchis releases Emperor Louis, making him swear that he will never again show his face in Beneventum or take revenge on the Lombards. Thus Louis regained his freedom, but his dream of unification had long since evaporated. A brief victory over the Saracens near Capua in 872 was his last gasp in the fight against the infidels.

He then withdrew to northern Italy, leaving the south once more a battleground of warring princes and Saracen invaders.

Emperor Louis II closed his eyes for the last time near Brescia on August 12, 875. He was buried in the church of Sant'Ambrogio in Milan, the city that he had made his imperial capital.

CHAPTER FOUR

A World in Turmoil
875-1014 A.D.

Popes and Emperors: The Deadly Struggle for Power

Compared to what would take place in Rome following the death of the Emperor, the three protagonists of the past act, Adelchis, Louis II, and Sawdan, look like gentlemen engaged in a game of playing foxes and rabbits. None of the three were killed, blinded, or even suffered bodily harm.

A situation had arisen that was really a legacy of the relationship between Pope and Emperor that began with the crowning of Charlemagne almost a century earlier. The Pope had given legitimacy to the imperial title, which had entailed obligations for protection of Rome, but no power over the city and its surrounding territories, which the Pope now ruled like a monarch. With such a scenario it is easy to understand why the Catholic Church was infiltrated by the rich and powerful nobility of Rome who coveted the seat of the Vicar of Christ.

As to who would be the emperor-protector, the pendulum of papal preference swung back and forth between Germany and France as claimants to the imperial crown came and went, their Italian supporters dragged along with them.

Louis II, before his death, designated his uncle, Louis the German, as his successor, but Pope John VIII favored Charles the Bald from the French side and crowned him Emperor on Christmas Day of 875. He was also crowned King of Italy at Pavia the following year. When he died two years later in the fall of 877, his son inherited his useless title of King of Italy, but he did not become emperor, for the papal pendulum now swung over to the German side and Charles the Fat was crowned emperor in 881. In spite of several expeditions into Italy, Charles was unable to help the Pope against the Saracens. This listless, epileptic emperor died in 888, and his death marked the disintegration of Charlemagne's empire.

In this confused situation the title of King of Italy was up for grabs, and the Italians looked for an able leader of their own. Two strong men entered the arena as contestants. In the north was Berengar, the Marquis of Friuli, related to Charlemagne on his mother's side. In the center was Guido (Guy), the Duke of Spoleto, unacceptable to the Romans because of his Lombard connections, his wife being a daughter of Duke Adelchis, who had imprisoned Emperor Louis II.

Berengar in the north was first proclaimed King of Italy by his Italian supporters. However, the situation became complicated when in 891 the Pope placed the imperial crown on the head of Guido of Spoleto, a reward for having saved Rome from the Saracens.

The next pope, Formosus, confirmed papal support of Emperor Guido, but then changed his mind and invited the German Arnulf to come and depose him. The reward would be the crown of emperor. Northern Italy was destined to become a battleground. Arnulf crossed the Alps with his Germans and began his conquest of the north. The brave defenders of Bergamo were overcome and butchered, and the Count of Bergamo, still dressed in all his finery, was hanged in front of the city gates. The terrified people of Milan and Pavia sent embassies with their submission, Guido fled south to Spoleto, and Arnulf marched to Rome in late 895. Arnulf was no welcome guest of the Roman citizens, who defended their walls against the Germans, but he finally entered the city by force and received the imperial crown from the hands of Pope Formosus in February of 896. Now there were two emperors.

Emperor Arnulf was ready to go after his rival in Spoleto when he was suddenly and mysteriously stricken with paralysis. There was a change of role as Emperor Guido came out of hiding and pursued the soldiers of the incapacitated Arnulf, now the quarry, as they fled northward carrying their helpless leader with them. They fought their way home as cities rose up in rebellion against Arnulf and his party. This was the inglorious exit of Arnulf, harried by the people that a pope had made his subjects, as they made their way by Hannibal's old route over the Great Saint Bernard pass.

Destiny had delivered a cruel blow to Arnulf, but his pursuer, Emperor Guido himself, never lived to enjoy the fruits of his victory. The time and circumstances of his death are disputed, but it seems that he died in pursuit of his enemy.

With the two emperors removed, one dead and the other incapacitated beyond the Alps, back on the attack sprung Berengar, the Duke of Friuli, who quickly took Pavia by force. Lambert, son of the deceased Emperor Guido, was soon on the scene to claim the crown that he should rightfully have inherited from his father. He shrewdly made a pact with his rival to partition Italy. Meanwhile, back in Rome the treacherous Pope Formosus has died and the new pontiff, Stephen VI, crowned Lambert King of Italy and Emperor.

At this juncture a most dreadful and macabre event occurred in Rome. Pope Stephen, pressured by Lambert, put Pope Formosus on trial to discredit him and annul his acts, especially the crowning of Arnulf, who was still alive. The fact that Pope Formosus had been dead for eight months seemed to be no impediment. They simply disinterred his rotting remains, which were brought to the court and propped up in a chair as though he were alive. A deacon, seated beside the putrid corpse, served as the mouthpiece. The charade ended with Pope Formosus being properly condemned and his decaying body, stripped of all papal raiment, was cast into the Tiber.

The Romans were outraged by this sacrilegious treatment of one of God's representatives. They seized Pope Stephen, who was in turn condemned, imprisoned in a monastery, and eventually strangled to death in August 897.

Two popes were dead, but the men they had crowned, Arnulf and Lambert, were still alive, although their days were also numbered. The young and accomplished Lambert made good his promise to the Marquis of Friuli, leaving him in Verona with part of the kingdom.

Lambert's reign as king and emperor was fraught with problems as dukes and counts rebelled against his harsh rule. His young life came to an end in 898 as he was engaged in the kingly pastime of hunting wild boar. The official version was that he fell from his horse and broke his neck, but others believed that it was no accident, and that he was murdered on that fatal day.

Lambert did not live long enough to play a significant role in Italian history, but as the historian Liutprand of Cremona regretfully wrote: *"He evidently gave more glory to the state than the state gave to him. If swift death had not snatched him away, he was one who might have followed the path of the Roman Empire and subdued the whole world to his forceful sway."*

The following year, Emperor Arnulf died an agonizing death in Germany. The two rival emperors had been carried off stage and, as the curtain was about to come down on the ninth century, one who had been waiting in the wings was ready to make his appearance. Enter Berengar, the Marquis of Friuli.

Berengar was soon proclaimed sole king by his supporters. His first challenge was to stem the tide of the invading Magyars (Hungarians) who appeared at Italy's northeastern frontier that same year. These ruthless raiders laid waste the land, pillaging and burning as they went and killing men, women, and children. Feared like the Huns centuries before, they were described as small in stature, with sunken eyes and long tresses that sprouted from shaven heads. It was said that these primitive people ate human flesh and drank the blood of their enemies. They were expert archers, and the very sight of them struck terror in every heart as they appeared like lightning, glued to their fast horses.

Berengar and his army were unable to stem the tide of invaders, a mighty force that swept through Aquileia and Verona to arrive unchecked at Pavia, the capital city. There was much slaughter, but it seemed that the Hungarians had been defeated when they made a last desperate stand on the banks of the Brenta River. Instead, the Italians were caught by surprise when the Hungarians rushed on them in their camp, chasing away their horses and slaughtering them even as they ate.

Berengar was defeated and forced to reach a settlement with the Hungarians and concede territory, but this did not end his troubles. Up popped a claimant from the French side in the person of Louis of Provence, the son of Irmingard, daughter of the late Emperor Louis II, invited by the Italian nobles who wanted Berengar out of the way. No time was lost, and Louis was soon across the border to be crowned King of the Lombards at Pavia in 900. The following year he received the imperial crown at Rome from yet another pope—Benedict IV. Berengar was soon on Louis's imperial tail and in 902 succeeded in driving him out of Italy and back into France. He would have been wise to have kept his useless crown and stayed away, but three years later he was back across the border to attack Pavia and Verona. On July 21, 905, Louis was surprised at Verona by his opponent. He was taken prisoner, ruthlessly blinded on Berengar's orders, and then sent back to France. He lived for another twenty-three years and came to be known as Louis the Blind.

The next event of consequence occurred some ten years later. A strong new pope, John X, had appeared on the scene, supported by a powerful Italian family whose acquaintance we will make later. With a disunited southern peninsula, the Saracens had made progress and were threatening Rome. Pope John, with the skill of a seasoned statesman, enlisted the support of Berengar and rallied the various factions, as well as the Byzantines, the Neapolitans, and Duke Alberic of Spoleto. The formation of the Italian League at this juncture was a historic event. Surrounded by forces on both land and sea, the Saracens are caught north of Naples at the mouth of the Garigliano River and soundly defeated. Berengar got much of the credit for this victory and for his support received the imperial crown from Pope John X in 915.

Berengar was now the Emperor, but it did not help him to control the various elements in his kingdom. It became a real liability when in 922 disgruntled Italian factions invited Rudolf of Burgundy to depose Berengar and accept the crown of the King of Italy. The desperate Berengar made the mistake of enlisting the support of the Hungarians, whose savage intervention was disastrous. Rudolf was forced to retreat, but Pavia was put to the torch by the Hungarian soldiers. The terrible conflagration, which began at nine o'clock in the morning of March 12, 924, is remembered in Liutprand's eloquent memorial in verse, the last line of which read, "Our fair Pavia in fire has passed away."

Berengar took refuge in Verona, but on April 7, 924, he was murdered by a Judas within his own camp who came upon him as he prayed in the church. We owe the following description of Berengar's death to the historian Liutprand who told this portion of history in verse: *"The stone before the church door with its blood marks is plain evidence to all who pass by. However much they are washed and scrubbed, those stains can never be wiped away."*

Berengar was dead, and his rival, Louis the Blind, who had received the imperial crown from a different pope, followed him in death four years later.

For half a century men had fought for the lethal imperial crown. Thirty-seven years passed before it was placed on another head.

Sex and Scandal in the Holy City

The power struggles of the early tenth century were many and fierce, yet nowhere were the battles more lethal than in the Holy City. Rome was a different kind of arena where ambitious families fought not with swords but the more covert (but no less deadly) weapons of politics, intrigue, and even murder. They were the puppeteers who pulled the strings in the dark, creating and destroying popes whose hands placed crowns on selected heads.

To appreciate what had been happening in the Kingdom of Italy in the previous chapter, we must go back in time and acquaint ourselves with the goings on in Rome. Women also play an important role on the Roman chessboard. One in particular stands above all the rest. She may well have begun as a pawn, but she ended up as a queen. Her name was Marouzia.

Marouzia's father, a senator and senior member of the noble Roman Theophylact (Teofilatto) family, held the reins of power with the help of his women, celebrated for their exceptional beauty—his wife, Theodora, and daughters Theodora and Marouzia. It was presumably with the support of the Theophylacts that Pope Sergius III took office in 904, after two opponents had been killed, but what is most significant is the fact that this man was the lover of the beautiful young Marouzia. Far from being a secret affair, this was common knowledge and the talk of Rome. Marouzia's lover-pope died in his bed in April 911, but from this scandalous relationship a son was born who would one day also be made pope.

Following two more popes of little consequence (presumably puppets of the Theophylact family), there came one who remained in office for fourteen years. This was John X, who had been appointed bishop of Ravenna and was brought by the Theophylacts to take office in 914. The rumor in Rome at the time was that he was the lover of Theodora (the elder, not the daughter). The historian Liutprand, writing later on the basis of such gossip, said that the lady had a passion for this handsome man and when the papal seat became vacant,

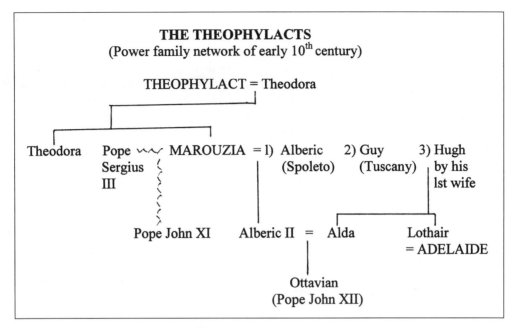

THE THEOPHYLACTS
(Power family network of early 10th century)

THEOPHYLACT = Theodora

Theodora   Pope ∿∿ MAROUZIA = 1) Alberic   2) Guy   3) Hugh
            Sergius   (Spoleto)   (Tuscany) by his
            III   1st wife

            Pope John XI   Alberic II = Alda   Lothair
                                                      = ADELAIDE

                            Ottavian
                            (Pope John XII)

> *Thereupon Theodora, with a harlot's wanton naughtiness, fearing that she would have few opportunities of going to bed with her sweetling if he were separated from her by the two hundred miles that lie between Ravenna and Rome, forced him to abandon his archbishopric at Ravenna, and take for himself— O monstrous crime! — the papacy of Rome.*

Whatever the circumstances, honorable or dishonorable, by which John X had been made pope, he proved to be the man for the times. He was the one who had successfully formed the Italian League and saved Rome from the Saracens.

After Pope John X took office, the notorious "harlot" Marouzia married Alberic, Marquis of Spoleto and an ally in the Italian League, and when Theophylact and Theodora died soon thereafter, it was Marouzia and Alberic who inherited the family power. Pope John X did not enjoy the same support from Marouzia as he had from her mother, but he had the protection of Berengar, on whose head he had placed the imperial crown in 915. Emperor Berengar's death in 924 had left Pope John X defenseless against the scheming Roman nobles, and he looked outside of the peninsula for help, inviting the Frenchman Hugh (Ugo), Count of Provence and Arles, to claim the crown of Italy, which he received in Pavia in 926.

Pope John's action in crowning Hugh merely aroused the ire of the Theophylacts, and the formidable Marouzia was soon on the warpath. Having lost her husband Alberic about the time of Berengar's death, she had married Guy (Guido) of Tuscany, a powerful rival of Pope John X. Marouzia and Guy assembled all the factions opposed to King Hugh and the Pope and staged a *coup*. One day the supporters of Guy and Marouzia stormed the Lateran Palace where Pope John and his brother Peter were visiting with friends. In the bloody scene that followed, Pope John saw his brother slain before his very eyes. The assassins spared the life of the Pope, but he was taken away and imprisoned in Castel Sant'Angelo, where he died in May 928, murdered by suffocation with a pillow, some said.

Two popes followed briefly, propped up by the unstoppable and unscrupulous Marouzia; then, in a most unbelievable move she connived to have her young son, the bastard of Pope Sergius III, proclaimed pope. He took the name of John XI, another helpless puppet at the service of his ambitious mother.

Marouzia was widowed for the second time on the death of Guy of Tuscany. Was it by pure coincidence that Hugh, now the crowned King of Italy, became a widower at around the same time? At all events, Marouzia saw her chance and lost no time in making advances to her former rival to whom she unabashedly offered herself in marriage. Marouzia, of course, got her way, and the two were duly married with the approval of the Pope, her illegitimate son. Marouzia was now Queen of Italy. It would only be a short step to the title of Empress of the Holy Roman Empire with her son to place the imperial crowns on the heads of his mother and her third husband.

At this point, in 932 or 933, Marouzia's luck finally ran out. Alberic, the son by her first husband, now a young man of eighteen, appeared on the scene. He hated his stepfather and saw him and his mother as a threat to his own future. Alberic had no difficulty in gaining the support of the Romans against King Hugh and his mother Marouzia. Back in the picture was Castel Sant'Angelo, where the royals had taken up residence, now surrounded by their enemies. Once more Liutprand's voice echoes from the past with these words: *The king, indeed, was so alarmed that he let himself down by a rope on the side where the fort touched the city wall, and deserting his lady made his escape back to his own men.*

Marouzia was taken prisoner and at this point disappears from history. Her fate is unknown, and there is no record of how this beauty who had wielded such terrible power for so many years ended her life.

Marouzia was gone from the scene, but she lived on in her two sons who now held the power, one the spiritual and one the temporal. The victorious Alberic, out of respect for the clergy, allowed his half-brother Pope John XI to complete his pontificate, but kept him under very close scrutiny until his early death in 935. Young Alberic was now the master of Rome, and *he* chose the next popes.

King Hugh

King Hugh ruled his kingdom from his capital of Pavia, but keeping the slippery crown on his head was not always easy. Whether marquis, count, or duke, those who were the lords of cities and territories resented the presence of a king. As for Hugh, he was determined to eliminate the young Alberic and become master of Rome as well, a struggle that would be a central theme of the period.

Alberic proved to be a worthy opponent in spite of his youth, for he was a real statesman. He took no chances with his enemy and saw to the protection of his realm, organizing his army into twelve units that were headed by nobles. The citizens of Rome rallied to his support because they valued their independence and accepted Alberic as the rightful heir of Theophylact power in Rome which he ruled as a lord, recognizing neither the King of Italy nor the Empires of East or West.

King Hugh's attempts to take Rome by force were fruitless, and he finally decided to try the diplomatic route. Through the intermediary of a well-respected monk, he negotiated the marriage with the young Alberic of his only legitimate daughter, Alda, his child by the wife he lost before becoming embroiled with Marouzia. By this arrangement Hugh hoped to gain control of Rome and eventually win the imperial crown, while Alberic expected to neutralize the ambitious Hugh by taking his daughter for wife. Both parties were disappointed when nothing changed, and in 941 Hugh was back with an army to storm the walls of Rome, making war against his own daughter. It had been Alberic, the stepson, who had chased him out before, and now it was Alberic, the son-in-law, who frustrated his efforts.

Fortunately for Alberic, troubles called Hugh to the north where the Marquis of Ivrea, Berengar II, was plotting to overthrow him. Hugh went after him, intent on putting out his eyes, but to quote Liutprand:

> His little son, Lothair, who was still unaware of his own best interests, got knowledge of this design and being but a child incapable of concealment sent a messenger to Berengar to acquaint him of his father's intention.

Berengar beat a hasty retreat over the Alps and took refuge at the court of the German king, Otto. King Hugh's quarry had escaped, and now he offered money to buy his enemy. Otto, to his credit, refused such a deal.

Hugh had failed yet again, and by 945 the slippery Berengar was back in Italy with King Otto's blessing. Hugh's power began to erode as Berengar gained adherents by promises of rich rewards and high offices. King Hugh could now see the writing on the wall, his dream of Rome had faded, and he decided to abdicate.

> He sent his son Lothair to present himself to Berengar and the whole nation, asking them, as they were getting rid of him as not being to their taste to welcome his innocent son for the love of God and make him compliant with their wishes. (Liutprand)

Hugh was then asked to stay, along with his son, but he eventually returned to Provence, where he died in 950, leaving Lothair as king under the wing of Berengar. Lothair should have been safe with the man whose life he had so innocently saved through his warning, but he did not long survive his father, and it was said that he had been poisoned.

At this juncture, Berengar II climbed onto the empty throne and had himself proclaimed King of Italy, along with his son Adalbert, thus ensuring the succession of the latter. He also decided to take out insurance by having his son marry the dead King Lothair's widow, Adelaide, then in about her twentieth year. The problem was that Adalbert was just a boy and the grieving Adelaide adamantly refused to agree to such a ridiculous alliance, even though she knew her own life was in jeopardy. Berengar had the stubborn Adelaide spirited across the waters of Lake Como to an island prison. The lady was later helped to make an escape, and she fled to the German court of King Otto.

Berengar had not only lost his prize but also alienated Otto by his actions. It was the reason, or excuse, for the first German expedition to Italy the following year (951), which concluded with Otto assuming the title of King of Italy and taking in marriage none other than the beautiful Adelaide, now queen again with a different husband. There followed a compromise with Berengar whereby he was "entrusted" with the Kingdom of Italy. However, he had to recognize the superiority of the German king by paying tribute, thereby reducing the Kingdom of Italy to a vassal of the Germans.

An Emperor Is Crowned: More Scandal in the Holy City

While Berengar and Otto had been fighting for the crown of King of Italy, under the enlightened rule of Alberic II the Romans prospered in a spirit of independence and a return to the glory of ancient times. The separation of church and state inaugurated in 931 had prevailed even after the death of Alberic's half-brother four years later, and it was Alberic who chose the next popes.

Alberic's death in 954, three years after Otto's first expedition to Italy, would change the course of events and bring the spotlight once more on Rome. The legacy Alberic left to the Romans proved catastrophic. He had extracted from the nobles a promise that on his death his son Ottavian would succeed him, not only as the temporal prince but also the spiritual head when that seat became vacant, although this was contrary to what he had advocated throughout his own rule. Ottavian was only sixteen years old when the ruling pope, Agapetus, died one year later, yet the Romans kept their promise to Alberic and accepted this teenager as their pope. In this capacity he took the name of John XII.

The indecorous lifestyle and decadent ways of this young man eventually caused him to be stripped of his temporal power, but not before he had undone all that his wise father had accomplished for Rome. Thinking to regain the power he had lost he decided to look beyond the Alps for help and called on Otto. Seizing the moment, Otto gathered his men, crossed the Alps again, and made his way to Rome right through the Kingdom of Italy, his so-called vassal state. The arrogant and rebellious Berengar, who had not remained true to his pledge to Otto, fled with his son as German armies approached.

Otto was received in Rome with pomp and ceremony and on February 2, 962, in the sacred Basilica of Saint Peter in Rome, the crown of emperor was placed on the head of the powerful King Otto by a pope in his early twenties. Otto's queen now became Empress Adelaide.

Otto proclaimed the temporal power returned to the young pope, who now had to swear fealty to the German. As soon as the Emperor's back was turned, however, the young pope began to regret his actions. No doubt prompted by his relatives, the still powerful Theophylacts, he now looked around for someone to protect him from the emperor he had just created and sent envoys to the exiled Adalbert, to Constantinople, and even to the dreaded Hungarians. Even though news traveled slowly at the speed of the horse, Otto soon became aware of these schemings, and the following year he was back in all his strength. The terrified young pope fled to Tivoli, along with Adalbert, who had meanwhile joined him.

When the Emperor arrived in Rome a synod was held in Saint Peter's. The list of bishops, deacons, representatives, and princes was impressive. Liutprand, an eyewitness to these events, wrote in his history: *"When all had taken their seats and complete silence was established, the holy emperor began thus: 'How fitting it would have been for the lord pope John to be present at this glorious holy synod.'"*

Testimony was then given on the unfitness of Pope John XII in discharging the duties of his office. He had not followed the rituals, and more serious allegations had to do with the young pope's dissolute lifestyle, including adultery.

Otto listened to the charges brought against the young pope who had anointed and crowned him and gave his reply. He spoke in his native Saxon tongue, and his words were translated into Latin through an interpreter, none other than our historian Liutprand, the Bishop of Cremona. Otto pleaded for leniency in view of the Pope's tender age, but members of the synod were outraged. The final outcome was to give him a chance to reform his ways. When one year later there was no sign of changed behavior, Emperor Otto was persuaded that another man should be made pope and on December 4, 963, the incorrigible rascal was duly deposed. This time it was the synod that chose one who took office under the name of Leo VIII.

Matters did not end here. Just outside of Rome in Tivoli, the deposed John was still very much alive and kicking and had the support of many of the Roman citizens, including his loose ladies of high birth. Together they plotted to do away with both the Emperor and his new Pope. What happened then must have had the Romans sitting on the edge of their seats. They were not mere spectators, however, in the front row of a theater, but part of the real stage of life where Roman and Saxon blood flowed and the dead did not rise to their feet when the curtain came down.

A revolt took place on January 3, 964, when Pope John's supporters descended on Rome, but the bridge over the Tiber was barricaded with wagons and defended by Otto's soldiers, who "leaped forward among the foe like hawks falling on a flock of birds, and drove them off in panic without resistance" (Liutprand). Many died fleeing, as lethal wounds to the back confirmed, and others were taken hostage. Castel Sant'Angelo was yet again silent witness to a Roman tragedy.

Having put down the revolt, Otto then made haste to Spoleto in pursuit of Adalbert, who was said to be hiding there. Here we leave poor Adalbert to his fate, chased by one who was wearing the crown that should have been his and who was married to the lady Adelaide who would have been his wife had she not refused him before he had time to grow into a man.

Back in Rome, Pope John was still on the loose and the women with whom "he was accustomed to carry on his voluptuous sports, being many in numbers and noble in rank, stirred up the Romans to overthrow Leo," but Leo escaped and fled to Otto for protection. Otto hastily made plans to march back to Rome, but he was robbed of the satisfaction of laying hands on the incorrigible John, who was meanwhile called to his maker. The story goes that he was stricken while visiting the bed of some man's wife, an end in keeping with his reputation as recorded, no doubt, by hostile chroniclers. The historical fact remains that on a fateful day in May 964, the darling of the Roman ladies met his death, probably murdered by one of his enemies. He had survived his father by ten years, and what a mess he had managed to create during that eventful decade!

At least one of Otto's problems was solved. Perhaps one can say that the Roman Catholic Church had finally been delivered from the greedy, grabbing hands of the power-seeking Theophylacts.

The actions and destinies of a few colorful characters had brought the German presence to Italy and changed the whole course of her history. The Holy Roman Empire created by Charlemagne, defunct for the past forty years, had been re-inaugurated. A large part of the Italian peninsula would remain under its shadow for the next several centuries.

The Holy Roman Empire of the Ottos

The troubles of Otto I did not end with the death of the young rascal Pope John XII. The office of pope remained a bone of contention as both Romans and Emperor fought for the right to choose the man who would occupy this powerful seat. In 965 an emperor foisted a new pope on the Christian world, but the Roman nobles rebelled. Otto hastened back to Italy to defend him and remained there for the next six years. The Holy Roman Empire was strengthened, but was not recognized by the rival Emperor of Constantinople, Nicephorus II Phocas, who considered Otto a usurper and sought to reassert his claims in southern Italy.

Otto chose to exercise diplomacy, and what better way than by a marriage alliance. Off went his messenger, the able Bishop of Cremona, to negotiate for the hand of a Byzantine princess for Otto's son, but the mission was a failure. Fortunately for Otto, the unfriendly Eastern Emperor was assassinated in his bedroom during a palace revolt in 969. His successor wanted peace and even recognized the legitimacy of the Holy Roman Empire. Otto junior got his bride, the lovely Greek princess Theophano, and they were married on an April day in 972. Otto I had achieved his goal to unite the two empires just in time—he died the following spring.

Otto II was only eighteen when he succeeded his dead father at the Saxon court. Far beyond the Alps, the young man seemed to pose no threat to the Romans, who immediately took advantage to reassert their power. They rose up and killed the imperially proclaimed pope, replacing him with one of their own choice, Boniface, who after barely one month was forced by a rival group to make a dramatic escape to Constantinople. Benedict VII became the imperial choice, but six years later (980), Boniface and his supporters staged a *coup* and Benedict was forced to flee for his life in this deadly game of papal musical chairs.

Disputes over the papacy brought the German emperor across the Alps in 981 to reinstate his pope and at this time he established himself in Italy. The south was under attack from the Muslims, who had invaded Calabria from their stronghold of Sicily. Otto now became the crusader, waging war against the infidels. A devastating defeat the following year was a personal disgrace for his imperial majesty, obliged to save his own skin by taking to the waters and swimming to the safety of a Greek vessel.

Otto II had planned to return and confront the invaders, but he died in December 983 at the age of twenty-eight. He had done his best, but his life was too short to leave a personal seal on the pages of Italy's history. However, he had sired the next emperor, another Otto, then a little boy of three.

Otto III inherited the German throne under the regency of his Greek mother, Theophano, the widow-empress, and following her death he was under the wing of grandmother Adelaide, the lady who had lived through so many changes of fortune. Beyond the Alps, as the little boy was growing up and being groomed to become the next emperor, the Roman nobles struggled for the powerful seat of the pope. In the lethal feuds that raged in the Holy City, there was murder and mayhem as angry crowds took matters into their own hands.

Otto III was only in his fifteenth year when he was declared of age to take the reins from grandmother Adelaide. Shortly thereafter he was called across the Alps by the ruling pope, John XV, who wanted help against the Crescenti family, but when he arrived in Pavia at Easter in 996 he learned that the Pope had died.

Otto III chose as the next pope his German cousin, the twenty-four-year-old Bruno, consecrated as Gregory V to become the first German pope. The Western Empire was now in the hands of a German youth as the imperial crown was placed on the head of Otto III by his young cousin on May 21, 996, in the Basilica of Saint Peter. Otto was now emperor at sixteen years of age.

The Romans resented having a pope of German origin and proclaimed another of their choosing. Otto was soon back in Italy to settle matters; in the events that followed the rival pope was captured, horribly mutilated, paraded around the city on the back of a donkey, then thrown into a monastery where he died two years later. Giovanni, the head of the Crescenti family, was decapitated on the battlements of Castel Sant'Angelo by order of Otto III.

Pope Gregory's papacy lasted only three years, for he died in 999. The Bishop of Ravenna was appointed in his place, taking the name of Sylvester II. He was a Frenchman and the first of this race also to hold the office. A brilliant man versed in science, music, mathematics, and literature, he is said to have dazzled his contemporaries with his superior intellect.

Meanwhile, Otto III had visions of making Rome the capital of the Holy Roman Empire. He signed his name as "Romanus, Saxonicus et Italicus, apostolorum servus, dono dei Romano Orbis Imperator Augustus," thereby stressing the Roman nature of the Empire and calling himself Roman, as well as Saxon and Italian. One of the most important documents of his short reign, No. 389, begins with these words: *"We proclaim Rome capital of the world, we recognize the Roman church as the mother of all the churches,"* and he proceeds to condemn in strong terms the decadence of the papacy. Yet the document also enlarged the territory of the papal state.

Building of a palace was begun on the Aventine hill, and it seemed that Rome once more would become the center of a great empire. But for all his good intentions, poor Otto was not able to win over the hostile Roman nobility. After serious uprisings, he withdrew to Ravenna. He died of malaria at Mount Soracte on January 23, 1002, before reaching twenty-two years of age.

Otto III's plans to reestablish a Greco-Roman empire had included a Grecian princess, like his own mother. That princess was on a vessel sailing toward the Italian shores even as he lay dying. By the time she arrived, her promised husband had already expired, and she became one more tragic victim on the stage of history. The body of the youthful emperor was taken back across the Alps to Aachen to be laid to rest next to Charlemagne, his idol, in accordance with his wishes. It might have seemed at the time that the German presence in Italy disappeared without trace when the body of the dead emperor was carried back across the Alps. The Germans would continue to play a role, but they eventually shared a very different stage with a host of new characters. No one could have imagined the incredible events that were about to take place.

Succeeding Otto III in 1002 on the German throne was his cousin, Henry II of Saxony (1002–1024), a pious man known later as a saint. He was immediately crowned king of Germany, but the Iron Crown of the Lombards had been given to Arduin, the Marquis of Ivrea. This did not prevent Henry from being crowned king in Pavia in 1004, and the coronation was followed by a popular uprising against the German soldiers. Henry did not stay in Italy, and it was not until February of 1014 that he got the imperial crown. Once again, there was an uprising of the populace against the German soldiers, who managed to get the upper hand. Henry returned to Germany with ringleaders of the rebellion as hostages.

Some years passed before Henry made his third and last visit to Italy, reluctantly answering a call for help from his friend, Pope Benedict. In the meantime, the spotlight was on the fast-moving and dramatic action in the southern half of the peninsula where the fermenting mixture of Byzantines, Lombards, and Muslims exploded with the addition of some newcomers, the Normans.

CHAPTER FIVE

Arrival of the Normans in Italy
1016-1059 A.D.

Ferment in the South: Arrival of the Normans

One third of the peninsula had remained outside the Kingdom of Italy and the influence of the Holy Roman Empire. Constantly under threat from the Saracens, ruled partly by the Lombards, and partly still under the heel of the Byzantines, the region was a hotbed of intrigues and changing alliances, with each duke and petty baron seeking to hold on to the power acquired through conquest or birthright. This was the world into which Emperor Louis II had been drawn almost a century and a half earlier with dire consequences and into which Emperor Henry II was reluctant to enter.

Bari would once again be the stage of conflict. Melus, a man of noble Lombard birth, incited the citizens to rise up against the Byzantines who controlled the city. He took as his companion-in-arms his brother-in-law, Dattus, and staged a revolt in Bari, but after some success they were betrayed by a Greek element within the city. Melus managed to escape, but his wife and children were taken hostage and carried off to Constantinople.

More determined than ever to pursue his goal, Melus traveled to the Lombard cities of Salerno, Capua, and Benevento to seek their support, but help came from an unexpected quarter and in a different guise. Whether truth or part legend, the chroniclers of the day told of a chance encounter in the sacred shrine on Monte Gargano, in the eastern spur of the southern boot. The story goes that a party of about forty Normans—descendants of the Viking raiders who settled in northern France at the beginning of the tenth century—were making their way home to Normandy after a pilgrimage to Jerusalem, and they stopped at the shrine to pray. There, they met a man of unassuming countenance and simple garb who was none other than the Lombard Melus. Following this encounter, Melus invited these adventurous pilgrims to return to Italy and join forces with him and his Lombard supporters to drive out the "Greeks" and the "infidels."

At the same time—or were they the same men?—a party of returning pilgrims had also stopped at Salerno. The city was under attack from a band of Saracens because her Lombard prince, Gaimar, had refused to pay them tribute. The Normans zealously took part in the defense of the city against the Saracens and got much of the credit for driving them off. These were not monkish individuals traipsing barefoot across hills and vales, but able-bodied young men who could take up the sword and fight like soldiers. Prince Gaimar, impressed by their valor, sent envoys back with them to Normandy and begged them to return with more of their kind. Laden with gifts of "lemons, almonds, pickled nuts, fine vestments, and iron instruments chased with gold," the Normans were persuaded to come back to the land that flowed with milk and honey and so many beautiful things. To make it worth their trouble, they were promised half the land that would be recovered from the enemy.

Soon the towns of Normandy buzzed with news of the promised land, and there was no shortage of men ready to exchange their green and rainy homeland for the warm waters and sunny hills of Italy. Many of those who answered the call were the younger sons of knights and squires of the very prolific Normans.

The following year, 1017, the first expedition of Normans set out for Italy, captained by a man accompanied by his four brothers. The "Five Fair Brothers," as they came to be known, and their party made their way through Provence and down the coast of Italy to the south. Finally, they reached the Garigliano River, the southern border of the Papal States, and crossed over to Capua to be met by their new patrons. Melus was waiting and lost no time in leading his contingent of men across the mountains to Apulia to take the Byzantines by surprise. By September of the following year, the Lombards and their Norman mercenaries had driven the Byzantines from a vast area that had been under their control. Then disaster struck.

Byzantine forces arrived from Constantinople in such great numbers that Melus and his men were forced to retreat. At Cannae they came face to face with the Byzantines, and the slaughter that took place was reminiscent of the fate the Romans had suffered at the hands of Hannibal over twelve centuries earlier at this place. Ironically, this time Normans were pitted against their own kin, for the Byzantine Emperor had sent his best fighting regiment of Vikings, a force received from a northern prince as a dowry in exchange for his sister.

Melus again managed to save his own skin, making his way northward and across the Alps to the court of his friend, Emperor Henry II. The leader of the Norman expedition had been killed, but his place was taken by his brother Rainulf and the remnants of the force soon found that their services were in great demand as they became the hired swords of princes and dukes and even the Byzantines. Some joined their countrymen with Gaimar in Salerno, while others found a paymaster in Gaimar's brother-in-law and rival, Prince Pandulf of Capua, known as the "Wolf of the Abruzzi," for there was much rivalry between the Lombard princes.

Many of the southern princes now found it expedient to recognize the suzerainty of the Byzantine Emperor. By 1020 Pope Benedict VIII, with the prince of Benevento being his only ally in the south, made the long journey northward to the court of the reluctant Emperor Henry II to beg for his help. Pope and Emperor planned now an expedition. It was decided that Henry would lead a full-scale army into Italy, where he would be joined by papal forces. Henry procrastinated. Melus, who would have been his guide for the expedition, had died after soon after the Pope's arrival in Germany, and all seemed quiet on the southern front. Henry vacillated.

Peace was shattered in June of the following year when the Byzantines attacked the tower at the independent monastery of Monte Cassino, where Melus's brother-in-law Dattus and his Lombard and Norman followers had taken refuge and established their headquarters, having been assured of their safety by the Pope himself. The Norman mercenaries were spared, but the Lombards were slaughtered to a man except one. The unfortunate Dattus was dragged off in chains to Bari where, on the eve of June 21, 1021, he was secured in a sack along with a snake, a monkey, and a cock and cast into the sea.

News of the dreadful death of Dattus finally reached the court of Emperor Henry. It was the catalyst for action. The Roman Catholic Church was under threat, and Henry must honor his pledge of protection.

In December of 1021, the earth trembled as three columns of an imperial army some 60,000 strong moved southward. The goal was to drive out the Byzantines and bring the South under the Holy Roman Empire. During the first part of the campaign, the monastery of Monte Cassino was freed from the clutches of the pro-Byzantine abbot while the Wolf was captured and put in chains. Prince Gaimar of Salerno capitulated after a siege of one month and pledged allegiance to Emperor Henry. The smart Neapolitans did not wait for the frightening troops to arrive at their gates, but sent envoys and hostages with their submission.

The imperial campaign had so far met with success, but on the eastern side one small Byzantine fortress hill-town called Troia kept the great armies at bay in a siege that had lasted for three hot, southern Italian months. The Emperor was in agony with gallstones, and his army was stricken with malaria in this inhospitable region. Nothing had been achieved against the Byzantines in Apulia, and the Emperor returned home, stopping at the monastery of Monte Cassino before proceeding via the capitals of Rome and Pavia.

This was Henry's last visit to Italy, for the saintly emperor died just three years later, in 1024, leaving no heirs.

The Normans Win Their Place in the South

Emperor Henry's successor, his cousin Conrad, made a grave mistake when he released Prince Pandulf of Capua, the Wolf. He was soon on the prowl again and set about recovering Capua, which had been given to an imperial puppet. He enlisted the swords of the Norman Rainulf; in 1026, following a siege of eighteen months, the Wolf was back in power. With Norman swords at his service he next took Naples, whose Duke Sergius fled into hiding.

As the proud and independent Neapolitans fumed under the rule of the Wolf, their exiled Duke Sergius tempted the Norman Rainulf with a prize far greater than a mercenary's wages—he offered land. Rainulf needed little persuasion to switch sides and put his double-edged sword to the service of the man he had so recently dislodged.

It was a historic date for the Normans when in 1030 Duke Sergius, back in Naples and true to his promise, presented Rainulf with the nearby town of Aversa and its territories. For the first time a Norman mercenary had become a feudal lord in the promised land. Rainulf also got a bonus by marrying the sister of Sergius, the recently widowed wife of the Duke of Gaeta.

Just as it seemed that all was calm, fate took a hand with the sudden death of Rainulf's wife through whom he had claim on Gaeta. The Wolf, now seeing an opportunity to coax Rainulf back into his camp, offered the grieving widower his niece, whose father was now the Duke of Amalfi. The mercenary Rainulf, lacking any sense of loyalty to his recent benefactor, switched sides again and was back trotting with the Wolf. Naples was isolated, and poor Sergius, betrayed by the Norman to whom he had given a part of his dukedom and his sister who was now dead, left Naples in grief and entered a monastery, where he soon died.

At this juncture, the ambitious Rainulf requested reinforcements from Normandy.

It was the beginning of yet another chapter in the history of the South when in 1035 three brothers made their way across the Alps and down to join Rainulf in Aversa. They were William, Drogo, and Humprey, sons of the prolific petty baron Tancred de Hauteville of Normandy, who fathered no less than twelve sons and a daughter from two wives. A glance at the family tree of this most extraordinary brood tells what destiny had reserved for them and for southern Italy.

Idle swords needed conflict, and it was not long before the opportunity presented itself. The Wolf had many enemies; his wicked ways, particularly his sacrilegious acts against the monastery of Monte Cassino, were more than legend. But it was the young Prince Gaimar of Salerno who rose up against his uncle, the Wolf. Rainulf once more found it in his interest to switch sides, and for the second time he abandoned the Wolf.

Gaimar called on his neighbors for help and also appealed to the two emperors. Emperor Conrad, at that time in northern Italy, made his way south to deal with the rascal he himself had so unwisely set free. This time the Wolf did not wait to be captured, but slipped out of his lair and made his way to the rival emperor in Constantinople. This was not the last of him, however, for he would be waiting in the wings for his next appearance.

Using his imperial prerogative, Emperor Conrad gave Capua to Gaimar, who was now Prince of Salerno and Capua. Rainulf became his sworn vassal and was given the title of Count, which meant that he was now a member of the imperial nobility. This milestone bore the date of 1038 and was the beginning of the Norman dynasty of Aversa and Capua.

When Emperor Conrad died the following year, the fate of southern Italy was still intrinsically linked to events in Constantinople. It was the very same year that the Byzantines sent an expedition to recover Sicily from the Saracens whose hold over the island had lasted for a century and a half. With the Saracens at the backdoor, Salerno and the south were always under threat, and Gaimar now pledged his help against the "infidels," relieved to have some sword work to occupy the restless and recently idled Norman soldiers. Rainulf, now his vassal, would stay on the mainland, but 300 others got their marching orders for Sicily. Among the contingent were the three Hauteville brothers. This was a campaign made to order.

It was in Sicily that William de Hauteville, later to be known as Iron-Arm, distinguished himself by unhorsing and slaying the Emir of Syracuse outside the walls of the city. The Byzantine campaign was going well, and within two years the eastern half of Sicily was back in the hands of the Byzantines. But there was discord in their ranks, the campaign collapsed, and the Normans who had fought so hard went back to the mainland in disgust.

All attention was suddenly focused on the other side of the peninsula, in Apulia, where two Lombards who had served the Byzantines rose up in revolt. They were Argyrus, son of Melus, the man who had invited the first Normans, and Arduin, who had fought for the Byzantines in Sicily. Arduin had been entrusted with the Byzantine hill-town of Melfi, but like Argyrus, his Lombard blood proved stronger than any sense of loyalty to the Byzantines and he persuaded the inhabitants of Melfi to join the insurrection. Arduin needed swords to carry out his plans, and he secretly slipped back across the mountains to Aversa to enlist the support of the Norman Rainulf who had at his command twelve Norman chiefs, including William and Drogo de Hauteville who captained several hundred knights. In recompense for their help,

Arduin promised them Melfi as their headquarters. The grand plan was for Lombards and Normans to team up and drive out the "Greeks." The contemporary historian, Amatus, records these inspiring words as being those of Arduin:

> *Venez après moi, et je irai devant e vous après; at vous dirai pouquoi je voiz devant, que sachiez que je vous menerai à homes comme fames, liquel demorent en molt ricche et espaciouse terre (II,17)*

> *[Follow me. I will go before you and you will follow. And I will tell you why I go ahead. It is because I will be leading you against men living in this rich and spacious land who are like women.] (Written in Latin, the old French transcription is all that remains)*

Arduin led the revolt. Normans and Lombards tested their mettle against the Greeks at Cannae, once more the killing fields where twenty-three years before the blood of the same people had drenched the earth in fierce combat. Again the Normans were outnumbered, but their general was the indomitable William of the enchanted sword who, though suffering from a high fever, joined the battle and with his men won the day.

This was followed by other victories in Apulia, but disputes then arose as to who would be the supreme leader. It was the Lombard Argyrus, the instigator of the revolt, who was finally chosen at Bari in February of 1042.

Once again, however, what happened in Constantinople sent waves crashing against the Italian shore. A new emperor had been dragged from the throne and his eyes put out in a dreadful public spectacle. What came across the Adriatic in the wake of these events, however, was a tidal wave of terror that the poor inhabitants of Apulia would long remember, if they lived through it. Maniakes, the Greek Goliath who had fought in Sicily, was back like a wounded beast to take revenge on all those who had deserted to the rebel Argyrus. During that summer of 1042, men, women, children, monks, and nuns were brutally massacred.

Just as it seemed that the whole of Apulia would be retaken by the Byzantines, the hot-headed Greek Goliath was declared emperor by his soldiers, whereupon he sailed out of Italian history to go after his rival in Constantinople. Meanwhile, Lombards and Normans continued the struggle and were besieging Trani, the port city that had always remained faithful to Byzantium, when there was an astonishing *coup de théâtre*. Argyrus, no doubt brainwashed while a hostage in the court of Constantinople, bought off by the new emperor Constantine who offered him high rank and riches in return for his allegiance, abandoned his followers and betrayed the revolution he had started. Loyalty, as we have seen, came at a very high price.

The Normans, who had put their swords and their very lives to the service of the Lombards, decided to take matters into their own hands and chose one of their own kinsmen to be their champion. There was one man who had the respect of all—William de Hauteville, the Iron-Arm. In September of 1042 he was proclaimed leader and Count of Apulia by the Normans.

In an era of vassalage one must be part of the feudal chain, so William rode off to seek a suzerain. What more worthy a man than Gaimar, the wise and beautiful young Lombard prince of Salerno whom he had already served so valiantly in Sicily? And so it was that William requested him to be his suzerain lord. Gaimar gladly accepted and at the end of 1042, with Count Rainulf at his side, William rode across the

MELFI, the first capital and headquarters of the Normans. Narrow streets lead up to the imposing Norman castle, built on a high promontory with a precipitous drop to the valley below.

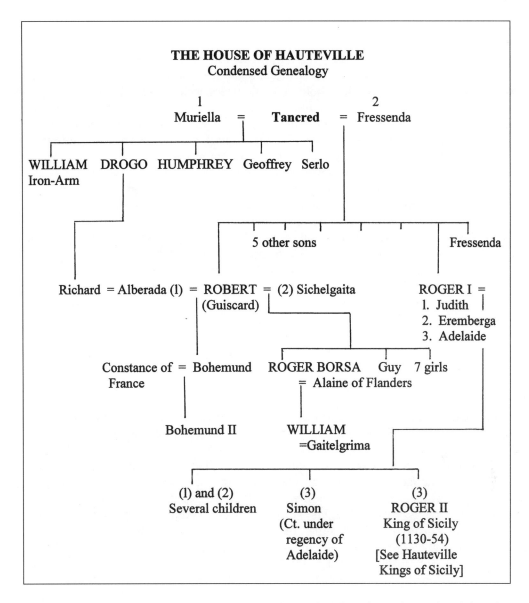

THE HOUSE OF HAUTEVILLE
Condensed Genealogy

Apennines to Melfi, where he was duly acclaimed Duke of Apulia and Calabria by the Normans assembled there.

Melfi, perched 1,742 feet up in the Apennines, became the capital and headquarters of all the Norman chiefs in Apulia and the nest of the brave new eagles.

Growth of Norman Power and War with the Papacy

Melfi became the pot of honey to which new Normans flocked from France. In 1046, three years after the events described above, two young Normans, destined to achieve greatness and each create a dynasty, joined their kinsmen in the South. They were Richard, the son of Rainulf's brother Asclettin, and Robert de Hauteville, sixth son of Tancred and firstborn of his second wife. Robert, the tall young man with flaxen hair and blue eyes that belied his Viking ancestry, would later become the Norman hero known as "the Guiscard," the cunning one.

The two young men arrived in Italy at a time when confusion raged in the feverish foot of the peninsula and the fires of conflict still smoldered. The Byzantines, who maintained their precarious hold in many places, found a useful ally in the Wolf, who had sought asylum at Constantinople, and set him on the tail of his archrival, Prince Gaimar of Salerno. The powerful Lombard/Norman alliance had been further cemented by the marriage of Prince Gaimar's daughter with Drogo de Hauteville, now Count of Apulia following the death of William in 1046.

That same year, the twenty-nine-year-old Holy Roman Emperor, Henry III, had come to Rome to settle disputes over who would be the next pope, and then proceeded south to deal with conflicts there. The following year, 1047, he held a conference with four powerful leaders—two Lombards and two Normans: Prince Gaimar of Salerno; Pandulf, the Wolf of the Abruzzi; Drogo de Hauteville, Count of Apulia; and Rainulf II, Count of Aversa (succeeding deceased uncle Rainulf)

It was thought that Gaimar and his Norman allies were becoming too powerful and needed to be checked, so Capua was taken from Gaimar and restored to the Wolf. Such was the power of the Emperor in that feudal world. The alliance would remain unshaken, however, when that same year, with the death of Rainulf II, newcomer Richard became Count of Aversa. It was the beginning of his role as a leading player in the south, a role that lasted for the next three decades.

The Normans were still in large part mercenaries in the service of the Lombards, but they also gained a reputation as raiders and pillagers as they sought to exert their control over the countryside, especially the Byzantine-held regions. Tensions between the Byzantines and the Normans mounted. When in 1051 Drogo de Hauteville was assassinated by unseen hands as he entered his chapel to pray, suspicion fell on the Byzantines.

The following year there was a *coup* in Salerno when Prince Gaimar was killed by a pro-Byzantine faction and his son was taken hostage. The dead prince's brother, Guy of Sorrento, rode off across the mountains to get help from Humphrey de Hauteville and his Norman knights. The Normans immediately responded to the call to avenge the death of Prince Gaimar, their suzerain lord and, within a few days were at the gates of Salerno. Gaimar's young son was rescued as the conspirators and their supporters were captured and slain by the Normans.

Norman power in the south had grown and although they were in their own manner devout Christians, never allying themselves with the infidels as the Lombards had often done, there was one who believed that they had become a threat to Christendom. This was Emperor Henry's second cousin, who had been ordained as Pope Leo IX. A tall, red-haired Alsatian who had once commanded an imperial army in Italy, this warrior-pope had no qualms about taking up the sword against the Normans to drive them out of the south. To this end he appealed to Emperor Henry, who was unsympathetic. Pope Leo then turned to the Eastern Emperor, represented in Italy by the turncoat Lombard Argyrus, who promised fighting units. What a chance it would be for the Byzantines to strengthen their hold in the peninsula!

For this "crusade" against the already entrenched Normans, Pope Leo recruited an army of his own, and many flocked to his side. Emperor Henry, finding himself in a most embarrassing situation, not to be left out, contributed a unit of 700 tough Swabians.

Lined up against the Pope and his allies, the drastically outnumbered Normans were organized into three units under their outstanding leaders: Humphrey de Hauteville, Richard of Aversa, and Robert de Hauteville (the Guiscard).

The chroniclers of the time tell of the massing of every Norman male adult converging rapidly to one meeting point, where they planned to prevent the papal forces from the north joining up with their Byzantine/Lombard allies from the south. On June 17, 1053, the Normans flooded over the plains of Apulia to block the papal army at the Fortore River, near Civitate.

It must have been a terrible dilemma for the Normans to find themselves confronted in battle with their own Vicar of Christ, for in spite of their naughty ways they were in their own way most devout Christians. Reluctant to make a move against the church, last-minute negotiations were hurriedly carried out without success. The die was cast. Their very survival was in the balance.

The bloody battle that took place at Civitate is immortalized in southern Italian history by the colorful epic poem of an Italian, William of Apulia, in which he glorifies the Norman de Hauteville brothers. Here are some of its dramatic lines:

Then Robert, seeing his brother enmeshed in a furious struggle,
By a desperate foe who would never bow down in surrender,
Called up the troops of his ally Girard, Lord of bright Buonalbergo,
With those who obeyed him alone, his devoted Calabrian cut-throats.
And splendid in courage and strength, he flung himself into the battle.
Some were despatched by his lance; there were others whose heads were sent spinning
With a blow of his sword — while even his hands wrought dire mutilations.
The lance in his left hand, the sword in his right, ambidextrously flashing
Turning aside every blow, confounding all those who attacked him
Dashed three times from his horse, three times he leaped back to the saddle
Inspired by unquenchable fire in his heart, that would lead him to triumph.

The poem continues with the gory details of battle so characteristic of the ancient epics.

Alone on the ramparts from which he had watched the battle of Civitate stood the white-clothed general, Pope Leo, his brave soldiers slaughtered. Why had Agyrus and the Byzantine units never come to help him? And now to his dismay, the inhabitants of Civitate even refused him asylum. Fearing for their own lives, they delivered the holy man, their Pope, into the hands of his enemies—the victorious Normans.

Li pape avait poeur et li clerc trembloient, Et li Norman vinceor lui donnerent sperance et prierent que securement venist lo pape . . .(Amatus Book III, Chapter 41)

[The pope was afraid and the clergy trembled, and the victorious Normans reassured them and gave word that the pope would come to no harm]

The Normans, for all their faults, revered the Pope and now prostrated themselves before him and asked forgiveness. Then for two days they buried the dead.

For eight centuries the battle and the dreadful slaughter remained part history and part legend, kept alive by the epic poem of William of Apulia. It was in 1820 that excavations outside the city walls of Civitate revealed piles of skeletons. It told the tale of men, some over six feet tall, whose bones bore the marks of ghastly wounds and mutilations. Some traces of the ancient ramparts of Civitate remain today like ghosts, marking the spot where so many men had perished.

Pope Leo was lead away to Benevento by his Norman captors, who treated him well and kept him as their "guest" for nine months while they persuaded him to recognize their conquests. He was returned to Rome in the spring of 1054 and died soon after his arrival. He had been defeated in battle, but he would be known as a saint for his reforms of the church, whereas the Normans he had fought as enemies would soon become the defenders of the new Papacy.

A New Alliance: The Papacy and the Normans

Civitate was only a milestone in Italy's history of the South, for the game was not over. The Byzantines still had a foothold and the southern Greeks would not be easy prey for the Norman foxes. Once again, conflict proved to be the best ally of the Normans and it came from an unexpected quarter.

In church matters, 1054 saw the rupture between Rome and Constantinople. Disputes that had long been brewing regarding doctrine and practices reached the boiling point when legates of the just deceased Pope Leo IX brazenly excommunicated the Eastern Church. The Bull of Excommunication was angrily delivered at the High Altar of Santa Sophia in Constantinople at 3 P.M. on Saturday, July 16, 1054. This schism between the Eastern and Western Churches proved permanent.

In Constantinople, demonstrations broke out against the "Latins" and the aging Emperor Constantine IX, the target of much of the anger, looked around for a scapegoat. The blame was laid on the Lombard turncoat Argyrus, his imperial representative in Italy, now caught between the Byzantines and the Normans.

The stage was set for more conquests, and Robert Guiscard lost no time leading his victorious knights back to the heel of Italy, where he soon took several cities including Otranto. Over on the western side, the Normans there nibbled away at the territory around Salerno whose prince they had saved but who had not supported them against the Pope at Civitate. Norman ranks were again strengthened by the arrival in 1056 of Roger, the youngest of the de Hauteville brothers. Destined to greatness and to sire the first king of Sicily, the last of Tancred's sons was perhaps the old man's masterpiece, for he was not only "a youth of great beauty, tall of stature and elegant proportion . . . friendly and cheerful," but he also possessed great strength and courage (Malaterra 1:19).

Robert Guiscard greeted his young brother Roger with open arms as he continued his conquests and brigandage in Calabria. But Roger's destiny lay to the west, where he soon joined his brother William (Tancred had two sons called William, one from each wife), another newcomer who had acquired a foothold around Salerno in the four years since his arrival. The Normans were fast replacing the Lombards on that side of the peninsula where Richard had driven the Wolf's cub and his Capuans into the citadel and taken the title of Prince of Capua. Two centuries of Lombard rule there had come to an end.

Meanwhile, Robert Guiscard's own star had risen when, following the death of his half-brother Humphrey in the spring of 1057, he had been proclaimed Duke of Apulia at Melfi. Robert soon faced problems in Calabria, however, compounded by famine, uprisings, and now-uncooperative Lombard elements that impeded his progress. But he was not called "the Cunning One" for no good reason. He looked around for a diplomatic solution and decided that a marriage alliance was the best way to rekindle a Lombard alliance and neutralize resistance. The only ruling Lombard of prestige was Prince Gisulf, gradually being devoured by the Normans around Salerno. Fortunately, Gisulf had a sister, Sichelgaita. She was an Amazon of a woman for size and strength and might well have scared away other suitors, but not Robert Guiscard. He quickly took her as his legal wife, and it turned out to be a most marvelous match. She gave him two sons and at least seven daughters, but her main qualities were anything but womanly. She fought alongside her husband in battle and, dressed in full armor with her long hair flying out beneath her helmet, this Norman Joan of Arc fearlessly charged into the enemy ranks along with the men, for whom she served as an inspiration.

The Normans were gradually throwing a net over the south when once more fate intervened in their favor to help them pull in their catch. There had been trouble since the death of poor Pope Leo IX and a man with a vision, Hildebrand, had set about the task of reforming the Church. It was time for the members of the clergy to take a stand and elect their own pope without interference from Roman aristocracy or the Holy Roman Emperor. In a bold move, Hildebrand called on the Normans who, just five years before, had defeated the papal army and taken the pope prisoner. The first contingent of soldiers came from Richard of Capua. A rival pope was defeated not by the sword but a synod at the Lateran where Pope Nicholas II, along with 113 bishops, protected from the Romans by a mere 300 Normans, promulgated a decree that substantially regulates how popes are elected to this day. No longer the prerogative of the Holy Roman Emperor to choose the man or the money of Roman aristocracy to purchase the position and place a puppet on the throne of Saint Peter, it would henceforth be the function of the cardinals to select their Vicar.

Now emboldened by his success, in June 1059 Pope Nicholas II, accompanied by Hildebrand and a retinue of clergy, made his way through the mountains to Melfi and there met Robert Guiscard of the other Norman group. The historic treaty of Melfi of August 23, 1059, that came out of this meeting was seen as papal permission and a clear invitation to the Normans to conquer not only the South, but Sicily as well:

> "I, Robert, by the Grace of God and of St. Peter, Duke of Apulia and of Calabria and, if either aid me, future Duke of Sicily, shall be from this time forth faithful to the Roman Church and to you, Pope Nicholas, my lord."

In the remainder of the document, Robert pledges his support and protection of the Pope and the Roman Church and promises support for proper election of future popes. The document ends with, "So help me God and his Holy Gospels."

From lethal adversaries the Normans had been transformed into bright angels in shining armor who would protect the interest of the Church. Even more significant for the Normans was the implicit invitation to wrench Sicily from the clutches of the "infidels." For Pope Nicholas this was the beginning of a crusade, but for the Normans the name of the game was conquest, and it would be achieved by a handful of Normans with the Pope and God on their side.

Enna was a stronghold of the Saracens when the Normans arrived in Sicily.
Perched on a high crag in the very center of the island, Enna commands a
magnificent view of the fertile valleys below and was once the seat of the Cult of
Demeter, the Greek goddess of agriculture.

CHAPTER SIX

Norman Conquests in Southern Italy and Sicily

Two Norman Brothers and the Conquest of Sicily

After the famous meeting at Melfi in 1059, Robert and his young brother Roger rode southward to Calabria. Threading their way through the mountains they reached Aspromonte, where they could look across the Strait of Messina to Sicily. Below them lay Reggio, the last Byzantine capital of Calabria, a rich jewel sparking with marble villas and palaces, a Greek treasure chest. The prize would soon be theirs.

Robert and Roger together placed Reggio under siege, but its fall was mainly brought about by rich bribes offered to the Greek soldiers of the garrison who fled to Constantinople, abandoning the city to its inevitable fate. Calabria was now completely in Norman hands and the way to Sicily was clear.

Across the beautifully colored and changing waters, often referred to as the Rainbow of Italy, was the Sicilian town of Messina. Sometimes seen reflected in the calm waters of dawn, it is called the "mirage of the fairy Morgana." Paradise beckoned, but it would not be easily won—the struggle was to last for the next thirty-one interminable years. Sicily was the exclusive domain of the Saracens, who had controlled the island since 859. Not even the Byzantine emperors had been able to dislodge them.

The first foray by the impatient young Roger across to Messina was unsuccessful, but the following year spies brought word of the perfect scenario, a conflict between two emirs. At this juncture we meet two important players on the Sicilian stage in the persons of Ibn at-Timnah and his rival, Ibn al-Hawas. They had tried to settle their differences when Ibn at-Timnah married the sister of his rival; later on, following an argument with his lady, he had tried to have her killed by ordering his slaves to slit her veins. Saved by her son, she had escaped and joined her brother, Ibn al-Hawas, who took her off to the safety of his eagle's fortress at Enna, the most impregnable stronghold of all Sicily.

What an incredible stroke of luck it was for the Normans when the would-be wife-murderer, Ibn at-Timnah, crossed the Strait of Messina and made his way to Mileto in Calabria where he presented himself to Roger, offering him Sicily if he would conquer his old enemy, Ibn al-Hawas. It was the beginning of a real offensive and now, by a strange turn of events, a Christian Norman had joined ranks with a Saracen, one of those "infidels" he had set out to expel.

Brother Robert supplied the ships, a force of Normans was quickly assembled, and along went the new Saracen ally whose primary objective was to recover his wife and his pride. After some quick success on the part of the Normans, the formidable

Ibn al-Hawas arrived on the scene and turned the tide, routing the Normans and chasing them to the beaches. There they huddled, unable to board their ships because of a storm that raged in the strait, while their Saracen ally evaporated.

Roger survived his mistake, along with most of his men. It was always better to escape with one's life and settle for a mere setback when victory could not be had. The Normans were masters at riding the horse of opportunity, but they also knew how to find the way of escape. Robert, who meanwhile had been fully occupied in Apulia, was soon back in Calabria, this time with a formidable fleet of ships. They were ready for another attack on the coveted island a few months later.

This time God was with the brothers who outmaneuvered and outsmarted the Saracens, and Messina was soon in Norman hands with little blood being spilled. Most of the Muslim population fled inland, leaving behind the mainly Greek Christian element. On Robert's command, a Catholic service of thanksgiving was arranged in the church, and Messina became the Norman bridgehead as walls went up, ramparts were raised, and a contingent of cavalry was installed as a permanent garrison.

Guess who now appears on the scene once more asking for Norman aid? None other than Emir Ibn at-Timnah, who presents himself most obsequiously to Robert with the same incredible offer he had made to Roger. The prize would be SICILY. Now it was the turn of Robert Guiscand to ride off with the wily Saracen at his side.

Ibn al-Hawas was again the target, holed up in Enna. This impregnable mountain stronghold could not be easily stormed, so the enemy would have to be coaxed out. For four days the Normans laid waste the surrounding countryside; on the fifth day the angry Saracens, grossly outnumbering their pesky opponents, came down to fight. They had sadly underestimated their foe, however. By nightfall, after suffering terrible losses, they retreated to the citadel, leaving their dead strewn along the riverbanks. Ibn at-Timnah could only look up and shout curses to the man who still held his wife safe from the cruel clutches of her husband.

The siege of Enna dragged on for two hot Sicilian summer months with no sign of capitulation on the part of the Emir. The Normans decided to waste no more time and rode back down the valley. Robert then returned to Messina to join his darling warrior-wife, Sichelgaita, who had kept herself busy inspecting her husband's new domains. Leaving behind a garrison of men who built the first Norman fortress in Sicily at Alutium, the two made their way back across the strait and over to Apulia where they spent Christmas.

Roger accompanied his brother to his mainland headquarters at Mileto in Calabria, and there the two parted company. Young Roger had no wife with whom to spend Christmas, and he was soon back in Sicily in the company of his knights. But Cupid was on his way—Roger's bachelor days were numbered. The story of a lady in distress and a knight in shining armor is about to be told.

The conquest of Sicily must wait while we introduce Roger's lady. Her name was Judith of Evreux, daughter of a first cousin of the great Duke William of Normandy, later know as William the Conqueror. Following a violent dispute, Judith's half-brother and guardian, abbot of an important Norman monastery, had fled with Judith and a party of faithful monks to southern Italy. The party had been warmly received by Robert, who founded for them the abbey of Sant'Eufemia in Calabria. Roger was overjoyed when he learned of the lovely Judith's arrival in Calabria and he was soon on his way to the little town where she was waiting for her knight. They were married immediately, but the official celebration took place at Mileto in the tradition of the Norman church.

Love did not turn Roger's head, however, for he lost no time in getting back to the business of conquest. Leaving his new bride behind on the mainland, he took off for Sicily, but he later returned to the mainland to settle matters with brother Robert regarding his share of conquests. Campaigns were stalled while the brothers quarreled, but they needed each other and agreements were reached. Robert then went back to Apulia and Roger returned to Sicily, this time taking Judith with him.

Meanwhile, Roger's Saracen ally, Ibn at-Timnah, had been slain by his enemies, and the Norman garrisons established in the hills had fled in fear to Messina. Roger returned to Troina, previously captured from the Saracens and, leaving Judith behind with a new garrison, he confidently rode off with his knights to resume his campaign. What the trusting Roger did not realize was that the Greek population of Troina liked the Normans even less than the Muslim Saracens, who had been less harsh and more civilized in their ways.

When Roger's back was turned they seized his wife and with the help of the surrounding Saracen element took control of the town. Roger was shocked when news reached him of the treacherous act; he galloped back to find a battle raging in the narrow streets of Troina, where his men were grossly outnumbered. Roger ordered his men to retreat to the citadel where, under siege, they spent four months of an uncharacteristically cold Sicilian winter. Some 4,000 feet high in their stronghold, they huddled together to keep warm. Roger was lucky enough to have Judith, whom he had found unharmed. Totally unprepared for siege, the Normans were forced to eat their beautiful horses to stay alive. The Sicilian dream had turned into a long, cold nightmare and paradise a bleak hell.

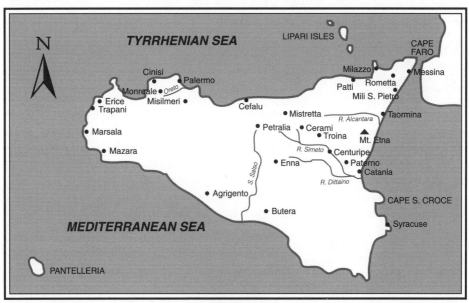

Sicily

Salvation came in the guise of the grape. The Saracens had discovered the properties of the local red wine for keeping the body warm and spirits high. Roger's scouts had been observing with interest the effect that the local beverage, forbidden by Mohammed under normal circumstances, was having on the besiegers and saw their chance to take advantage of the situation. One cold January night as the Saracens slept soundly in the embrace of Bacchus, Roger and his men came down and slipped over the barricades. With the snow as their ally to silence the sound of their footsteps, they surprised the slumbering Saracens and recovered Troina.

While Roger and his Normans had been cooped up in their cold stronghold, two Saracen princes, Ali and Ayub, had been sent from North Africa to help their Muslim brothers in Sicily. When Roger got word that Saracens numbering in the thousands were headed east he decided to go out and meet them, for they were already near Cerami, not far from Troina. It was there that Christians and Muslims locked horns in battle with great loss of life. The Saracens were eventually routed, fleeing to the hills with the Normans on their heels. It was a victory of pivotal importance as the northeastern portion of Sicily was now securely in Norman hands.

Roger and his men took rich booty from the abandoned Saracen camps and sent four fine camels as a gift to the Pope, then Alexander II. The appearance of these exotic animals in the streets of Rome was a powerful visual symbol of victory over the infidels. The Pope's response was to grant absolution to all those who joined Robert and Roger in the conquest of Sicily, a veritable crusade against the Saracens. From their lair in Palermo, their pirates had been a constant threat to the western coast of the peninsula and the trading ships of the rich Pisans in particular.

Robert and Roger, having refused an offer for help from the Pisans (whom they mistrusted), got together in 1064 and decided to leave the craggy strongholds of the Sicilian interior and go for the big prize. They would target the very heart of Saracen control in Sicily, the city of Palermo itself. With 500 more knights brought by Robert from Calabria, the Normans made their way along the northern coast and encamped on the hilltops overlooking the great and prosperous city-port of Palermo. For three months they watched as ships came and went; the Saracens paid little attention to their pesky foes perched in the hills. It was soon clear to the Normans that they could make no move without sea power. For the time being, the brothers parted company; Robert went back to Apulia, leaving Roger in Sicily.

For the next four years, the spotlight moved from the Normans in Sicily and southern Italy to their brethren in Normandy. In 1066 William the Conqueror crossed the English Channel with his Norman knights to claim the throne of England. During those years of activity in the north, Robert and Roger remained in the doldrums, then in 1068 it was as though the winds, fanned by conflict, filled their sails again to carry them to further victories.

Things began to happen in Sicily when the surviving Emir, Ibn al-Hawas, fell out with the two princes who had come to help him. They had fought, the old Emir had been killed, and a jubilant Prince Ayub claimed the succession. His fall was sudden and unexpected, however. On a summer morning in 1068, Norman soldiers, out on their usual forays, came across Prince Ayub's army at Misilmeri, just ten miles from Palermo. A pitched battle took place in which the Saracen force, taken completely by surprise, was practically wiped out. Carrier pigeons captured from the Saracen camp and released by the Normans flew back to Palermo with a sinister message of massacre. Prince Ayub managed to escape with his life and fled back to North Africa with the surviving remnants of his army. His dreams had been turned into a nightmare by one fatal encounter.

Roger was intelligent enough to realize, however, that the fruit was not yet ripe for the picking. He had won a battle, but the big prize, Palermo, was still beyond his grasp. He chose the waiting game, for he needed his brother, the Guiscard, to help him.

Meanwhile, we must leave the Sicilian stage and, during this intermission, see what is happening in another theater, the heel of the Italian peninsula.

As Roger was engaged with the Saracens in Sicily, Robert had his hands full with the other enemy, the Greeks, and was taking advantage of trouble in the Byzantine Empire to expand his dukedom of Apulia. He had laid siege to Bari, the last major Byzantine stronghold on the Italian peninsula, blockading the city by land and by sea. On the promontory that jutted out into the Adriatic, Bari remained tenuously attached to Constantinople by the umbilical cord maintained by the ships that got through the Norman blockade. The siege that had begun on August 5, 1068, dragged on throughout the winter, all through the following year, and the year after that. Robert had bribed the inhabitants and helped the poor within the city, but the commanders refused to capitulate as they waited in vain for a rescue fleet from Constantinople.

The siege of Bari had lasted for two and a half years when in early 1071 Robert Guiscard summoned his brother Roger. It was none too soon, for a Byzantine fleet of reinforcements and relief for the beleaguered Bariots was on the way even as Roger hastened with all speed from Sicily to join Robert.

Byzantine ships appeared on the horizon at night, and Robert's lookouts spotted their lights. This rescue fleet never got to Bari, for the brave Roger had arrived in time to lead his Normans out to meet it, sinking nine of its twenty vessels and capturing the commander. Faced with certain starvation, Bari finally capitulated a few weeks later.

It was a joyous day when on April 16, 1071, the two de Hauteville brothers, Robert and Roger, rode triumphantly through the streets of Bari. Robert showed clemency in victory, and the Bariots lived to pledge their allegiance to the new master, the Duke of Apulia.

With the Byzantines chased out of southern Italy the spotlight was now back on the Saracens of Sicily.

The whole island of Sicily was the next challenge for the Norman brothers. Its conquest, implicitly sanctioned by Pope Nicholas II in 1059, was just a matter of time. Palermo, a pulsating and luxurious city of trade and culture, had remained the heart and soul of Saracen Sicily. It had been seven years since the Normans had looked down on the marvelous city that lay beyond their grasp, but now they were wiser and more prepared. Robert had added more ships to his fleet and built up his land forces, which included Normans, Lombards, Italians, and Greeks recruited from all the lands under his suzerainty. They had one common foe—the Saracens.

The two brothers planned their campaign together. Robert would be in charge of the fleet, and Roger would lead the land forces. Like a tidal wave sweeping away all resistance, Roger's fast-moving army of knights and horses headed for Palermo across the hills and dales of Sicily. It was the middle of August in 1071 when they pitched camp a few miles east of Palermo at a place where the Oreto River empties its waters into the warm Tyrrhenian Sea. Roger and his men found themselves in a real paradise of gardens, orange groves, and palaces where the richer Saracens, centuries ahead of the Normans in their mode of living, enjoyed life to the full. The harsh hilltops of the center were in stark contrast to this Garden of Eden.

Brother Robert arrived with his galleys off shore at the mouth of the Oreto. When all was ready the city was placed under siege from land and sea. There was no repeat of the long siege of Bari this time. As the sun peeked over the eastern horizon on January 5, 1072, Roger's army attacked. The battles that followed—graphically documented by the chroniclers with details of bravery, victories, and defeats—were costly for both sides, but the Palermitans soon realized that the battle would eventually be lost and were willing to discuss terms with Robert de Hauteville, the now legendary Guiscard.

What a beginning for 1072 when five days later, on January 10, the Guiscard and his warrior wife, Sichelgaita, her brother, Gisulf of Salerno, and Roger rode through the streets of Palermo as victors! Then in the Basilica of Santa Maria, which for almost a century and a half had served as a mosque for the followers of Mohammed, there was a joyful celebration of thanksgiving by the Norman brothers and their Christian soldiers.

It was a Christian victory to be sure, but Robert had no intention of destroying the Muslims. There were too many of them, and he needed their superior culture and learning. He simply wanted their allegiance; in return they were given his word of honor that they would be allowed to continue to worship in their own way and live by the laws of Islam. Robert commanded his knights that there be no reprisals, no looting, and the lives and property of the Palermitans be respected regardless of religion, language, or dress.

A Norman administration was put in place alongside the Saracen. Arabic was recognized as an official language equal to Latin, Greek, and Norman French. Call it enlightenment or pragmatism, the Guiscard was no fool when it came to understanding the psychology of man, his sensitivities, his beliefs and his needs both physical and spiritual. A Norman governor was appointed for Palermo, but he was astutely given the title of "Emir." The Muslims had been tolerant masters of the Christian element in their midst, and likewise the Guiscard showed equal tolerance to the Muslims. They kept all the mosques they had built and continued to worship Allah just as before.

This was not a crusade of killing and destruction the likes of which Christians would later visit on the Muslims in Jerusalem, but a takeover by a benevolent leader whose actions were the seeds of a marvelously rich culture that would blossom like a flower in the Mediterranean Sea. That flower was Sicily.

However, complete control of Sicily was not achieved until some fifteen years later when in 1087 the last Saracen emir was coaxed from the impenetrable Enna. He was not run through by Norman swords, but resettled magnificently on the mainland.

The Guiscard took the title of Duke of Sicily and left the island at the end of 1072. Before doing so, he called a meeting with the Saracen nobles. They came with rich gifts of gold and horses and, most important of all, a pledge of allegiance, which some guaranteed by entrusting their sons to the great new leader.

The Guiscard had succeeded in doing what two empires had failed to achieve; he had not only subdued the Saracens but had won their allegiance. His work was complete, and he now left Sicily in the hands of Roger, his faithful vassal, and he

Italy at the end of the 11th century. Map showing the Kingdom of Italy and the Norman controlled south with the peninsula cut in two by the Papal States

never to set foot on the island ever again. His destiny lay not where the sun sets but where it rises — the East.

The World of Robert Guiscard

Ten years passed before the Guiscard took his ships and sailed across the Adriatic to confront the Byzantines in their own backyard. In the meantime, there was much to keep him busy on the mainland, where his vassals easily got out of hand when his back was turned. Much of South Italy was now within the de Hauteville family web, although its members were not always in step with the ambitious Guiscard, whose thirst for conquest set him against popes and emperors and created conflicts with his own kin.

The first victim was the Lombard Prince Gisulf of Salerno, in league with the Pope, who had openly taken sides against his brother-in-law, the Guiscard, who in turn called on his Norman brother-in-law, Richard of Capua, to intervene in this family squabble. In the summer of 1076 they laid siege to Salerno, which capitulated after six months with no blood spilled. Salerno, the glorious city that had been the shining center of a Lombard principality for 200 years, now became the Guiscard's capital. It must have been a bittersweet moment for Sichelgaita, whose husband's triumph meant the demise of her own brother.

Now it was the turn of Richard of Capua, who had his eye on the prosperous and independent Naples, to call on his brother-in-law for a return favor. Together they laid siege to the city, the Guiscard's fleet barring the harbor. It was during this time that the Guiscard launched an unprovoked attack against the papal territory of Benevento; on March 3, 1078, the desperate Pope once again excommunicated the incorrigible Guiscard, already under excommunication, but this time all the Normans were included. Unfortunately under this shadow Richard fell ill and died. His death was a great personal loss to the Guiscard, who for a quarter century had shared the south with this man who had married his only sister, Fressenda. Another blow came when Richard's son, Jordan, not wishing to begin his rule under the shadow of excommunication, hastily lifted the siege on Naples and hurried off to Rome to grovel at the feet of the angry Pope.

Meanwhile, things had not been going well for the new Pope, Gregory VII. He was the reformer, Hildebrand, who along with Pope Nicholas II had been instrumental in changing the way popes were elected. However, the tug-of-war between Emperor and Pope continued as Gregory and emperor-elect Henry IV played games of excommunicating and deposing each other. In 1080 Henry decided to go to Rome with his own appointed pope, Clement III, to place the crown of emperor on his head. The desperate Gregory, now under threat of an imperial army, called on the Guiscard and the Normans for protection. On June 29, 1080, he lifted the excommunication and the Guiscard swore fealty to Pope Gregory, just as he had sworn allegiance to and protection of Pope Nicholas II at Melfi some twenty years earlier.

This new obligation to the Roman Catholic Church was an impediment to the Guiscard's own grand plans which had been on hold for so many years. But since all seemed quiet he was not about to wait around on the chance that Henry would turn up soon. The time was ripe to move against the Byzantines, for there had been a new turn of events in Constantinople and the Guiscard, optimistic and full of vigor at sixty-four years of age, was ready to seize the moment.

Following overtures from Emperor Michael a marriage alliance was agreed between a daughter of Robert Guiscard and the Emperor's young son, Constantine, though he was still just a child. The prospect that a daughter would one day become empress was an offer that the Guiscard found too good to reject, and one of his girls was shipped off to Constantinople to be rebaptized with the name of Helena and tutored in the Greek tradition. Of course, she had to wait until the young boy grew to marriageable age, but before this happened fate had taken a hand and Emperor Michael was deposed. A state of chaos existed when his successor was in turn deposed by a brilliant general, Alexius Comnenus, who had himself crowned on Easter Day in 1081. Helena had not been sent back. Was she a hostage or had she been packed off to the safety of a gloomy monastery or convent? Indeed, was she still alive?

It may not have actually been a campaign to rescue his daughter, but it served as a justification. By the end of May, 1081, the Guiscard was on his way with a fleet of ships carrying some 1,300 Norman knights, along with Saracens, Greeks, and foot soldiers numbering in the thousands, so say the chroniclers. The target was Durazzo, capital and chief port of Illyria. From there the old Roman road, Via Agnatia, led across the Balkan peninsula to the very heart of Constantinople. In spite of setbacks — rough seas that swallowed many of the Norman ships (along with the men and horses they carried) and a naval battle with the Venetians — the Normans finally reached land, established a foothold, and placed Durazzo under a siege that lasted through the summer.

The real test came in October, when Emperor Comnenus himself arrived at the head of an army and a bloody land battle took place. The Norman battle line was drawn up. Guiscard commanded the center. By his side in full armor was none other than his incredible Lombard wife, Sichelgaita, still his most faithful warrior after bearing no fewer than nine children. Beside him also is Bohemund, the beautiful son by his first wife. We will not follow them into battle, but the following lines, written by the daughter of Emperor Comnenus, give credit to Sichelgaita, who inspired her fleeing army to return to the fight and eventual victory:

> Directly Gaita, . . . saw these soldiers running away. She looked fiercely after them and in a very powerful voice called out to them in her own language an equivalent to Homer's words "How far will ye flee? Stand, and quit you like men!" And she saw that they continued to run, she grasped a long spear and at full gallop rushed after the fugitives; and on seeing this they recovered themselves and returned to the fight. (Anna Comnena, The Alexiad, IV, 6 trans. Dawes)

The Emperor and his army were routed and Durazzo fell to the Normans.

Things were going well when the Guiscard received news that Emperor Henry was in Italy. He now had two emperors on his hands, but he chose to put Constantinople on hold and honor his pledge to protect Rome. Placing the campaign under the command of his son, Bohemund, he set sail for Otranto, collected a few troops from son Roger Borsa, and headed for Rome, which in 1082 was under siege by Henry's imperial troops. They tried to storm the city in June 1083 and, as battles raged around the Basilica of Saint Peter, Pope Gregory made his escape and fled to Castel Sant'Angelo, where he barricaded himself in, there to remain for a long, long stay.

Where was the Guiscard? He had taken time out to put down rebellious vassals in his own territories. Brother Roger had been there to help him with reinforcements, but he had been obliged to gallop back to Sicily to protect his own realm. The Guiscard was alone.

Fall came and so did winter, and still the Guiscard had not come to the rescue of his Pope. Meanwhile, the Romans had a change of heart and opened the gates of the city. Henry entered Rome with his wife, and on Easter Day, March 31, 1084, the imperial crowns were placed on their heads by the rival pope, Clement III.

Where was the Guiscard?

He had been busy gathering a great army. According to the historian William of Apulia, 6,000 horses and 30,000 foot soldiers set off for the capital in the early days of May, thundering north up the Via Latina over which Roman soldiers had marched centuries before. The Normans were still three days' march away when Henry grabbed his crown and, with his empress, accompanied by the bulk of his army, took the route in the opposite direction with his pope following in his wake. On May 24 the Guiscard and his men pitched camp outside the walls of Rome. In the light of dawn three days later they stormed the city at the Flaminian Gate across from Castel Sant'Angelo, once again the silent spectator of killing and fire as the Romans, guilty of having let the imperial army enter the city, desperately resisted out of fear.

The Normans prevailed, and Pope Gregory was led from his hiding place back through blackened ruins to the Lateran. The holy city was ruthlessly pillaged by all kinds of races that made up the Guiscard's army: Italians, Greeks, Lombards, and Saracens alike. The angry Romans, blaming their pope for all their suffering, would have lynched him had not the Guiscard taken matters into his own hands. It was like Civitate all over again where thirty-one years before the Normans had rescued Pope Leo from the inhabitants of that frightened city.

The Pope's life had been saved, and he was escorted south to the safety of the Guiscard's capital of Salerno, where he died in exile the following year. He was buried in the new cathedral built by the Guiscard and consecrated by Pope Gregory himself. On the façade one may still read the boastful words: "DUKE ROBERT, GREATEST OF CONQUERORS, WITH HIS OWN MONEY."

The humble words on Gregory's tomb, in sad contrast to those of the legendary Guiscard, read: "I have loved justice and hated iniquity and I die in exile."

The Final Curtain

Leaving the Pope safely at Salerno, the Guiscard returned to the campaign, taking with him his three sons, Roger Borsa, Guy, and Bohemund. There were defeats and victories, winter was behind them, and Constantinople beckoned. The Guiscard was ready to reach out and grab his star when he suddenly became ill. Within a week, on July 17, 1085, he was dead. His faithful Sichelgaita had been by his side. This man's life had been full of adventure and it was not yet over. Sichelgaita and son Roger accompanied the body that had been carefully packed in salt, but the fickle Adriatic sea again played tricks, whipping up a raging fury, and the coffin was swept overboard. Happily, it was recovered, and the remains of the Guiscard were finally laid to rest at Venosa in Apulia, along with his half-brothers and his first wife, Alberada.

So ended the life of the legendary Robert de Hauteville, known as the Guiscard, in his seventieth year. Merciful, optimistic, diplomatic, seemingly joyful throughout his long, eventful life, he was gone. The magic spell had been broken.

The tumultuous and eventful century finally drew to a close and the two most faithful companions of the Guiscard soon joined him in death. Sichelgaita, Italy's own Joan of Arc, the military mother whose astounding career appears to have been largely ignored by historians, died six years after her husband, in 1090. She had used those last years of her life to support her son Roger Borsa, the one in whose veins Lombard and Norman blood mingled and who was destined to stumble his way through the rest of his life in the giant footsteps of his legendary father.

No one man had the stature or the touch of magic needed to replace Robert Guiscard in southern Italy. The inevitable forces of dissent quickly split up a region that had been so tenuously held together largely by the efforts of one incredible man. Unfortunately, the legacy he left was his own flesh and blood in his two sons, half-brothers and rivals. Even as Roger Borsa was returning to Italy with the body of his dead father, Bohemund was at work claiming his share of the dukedom. He was, after

VENOSA: Excavations of baths and amphitheater attest to the importance of the site as a Roman colony. Behind the skeleton of La Trinità, a vast abbey complex in its time, stands an 11th century building which was the burial place of Robert Guiscard, his half-brothers, and his first wife, Alberada. Only her tomb has survived.

all, the oldest son and the most like his father in temperament and physique, the latter eloquently lauded by Anna Comnena in the history of her emperor father before whom the handsome Bohemund was later forced to bow his head.

At this time a call went out to all Christians to join a crusade to save Jerusalem from the infidels. Here was a chance for an ambitious and idle knight to seek adventure and save his soul at the same time. In answering the appeal of Pope Urban in 1095, Bohemund left Italy, but secured his place in history as a crusader and Prince of Antioch, in Syria, a principality created in territory taken from the Muslims. Fortunately for Roger Borsa, Bohemund took along with him many of his restless companions, including several de Hautevilles of the new generation.

Roger of Sicily was the next one to make his exit. He died on June 22, 1101, at his mainland capital of Mileto at the age of seventy. He had remained a faithful vassal of his nephew, Roger Borsa, who became his suzerain lord on the death of the Guiscard. Nonetheless, Roger had always been virtual Lord of Sicily.

Ten years later, the Normans mourned the passing of two more of the de Hauteville clan. In February of 1111, Roger Borsa died. By an uncanny coincidence, just two weeks later Bohemund also passed away. His luck had run out, and he had returned to Apulia a broken and dispirited man. He was laid to rest at the cathedral of Canosa, where one may see his tomb, a domed, Muslim-style cube recalling the principality of Antioch over which he had ruled.

Now the stage belonged to three foreign ladies and their young wards. Bohemund's widow, Constance of Flanders, became regent for young Bohemund II, Prince of Antioch; Alaine of Flanders, widow of Roger Borsa, became regent for William, the young Duke of Apulia; and Adelaide of Savona was still the regent for Roger II, Count of Sicily, now about to reach the age of maturity.

CHAPTER SEVEN

The Kingdom of the Two Sicilies

Roger II

Roger II, Count of Sicily, was a vassal of young William, but he is the chief protagonist of the next acts, four decades of astonishing events that set the stage for centuries to come. Through him the story of Sicily and the south will be told.

The young Count of Sicily was the youngest child of Roger de Hauteville and his third wife, Adelaide. Roger had fathered many children, but he had been particularly unlucky with sons. Jordan, his firstborn, was illegitimate; although he became a worthy knight and fought alongside his father, who loved him dearly, he was never considered a legal heir. He died of a fever in 1091. Roger's legitimate son, Geoffrey, was a leper and had been bundled off to live out his life in a monastery. At sixty years of age, Count Roger had no legal male heir and, hoping to ensure the succession, in 1089 he took a third wife, Adelaide, who four years later presented him with a son, Simon. Two years later, on December 22, 1095, Adelaide was delivered of a second son, known as Roger II.

On the death of her husband in 1101 and with two little boys in her charge, Adelaide had to rely on her ministers, native Sicilians of Greek and Arab blood, Christians and Muslims alike. Simon's untimely death in the fall of 1105 thrust little Roger into the limelight as he became sole heir and Count of Sicily at the tender age of ten.

Roger II, of Norman father and north Italian mother, was brought up Sicilian. His father had always kept the family at his mainland capital of Mileto, but after her husband's death Adelaide chose to make Palermo her place of residence. The dark and handsome Roger had grown up in this beautiful and cultured city set in a Mediterranean paradise where Christians and Muslims lived in harmony and affairs were conducted in three languages: Arabic, Greek, and Norman French. Here in the palace of the emirs in June of 1112, Roger was knighted, having reached the age of maturity at sixteen. He took from both the West and the East and proved to be a capable ruler as the product of the multicultural society that had formed him.

With her son's coming of age, Adelaide's regency came to an end, but she was still young and beautiful. It so happened that the King of Jerusalem, a Christian ruling over a territory recovered from the infidels during the first crusade, was looking for a wife, and he set his sights on the immeasurably wealthy and lovely Adelaide. A marriage was arranged and the following year she sailed east to become the Queen of Jerusalem. The chroniclers painted for posterity a picture of the splendor of Sicily at that time:

> *She had with her two triremes, each with five hundred warriors, and seven ships carrying gold, silver, purple, and great quantities of precious stones and magnificent vestments, to say nothing of weapons, cuirasses, swords, helmets, shields blazing with gold, and all other accoutrements of war such as are employed by mighty princes for the service and defense of their ships. The vessel on which the great lady had elected to travel was ornamented with a mast gilded with the purest gold, which glinted from afar in the sunlight; and the prow and the poop of this vessel, similarly covered with gold and silver and worked by skillful craftsmen, were wonderful to behold.* (Norwich, *The Normans in the South* p. 287)

Unfortunately, the marriage did not last; poor Adelaide, shamed, rejected, and despoiled of her treasures, returned to her beloved Palermo, where she died the following year. As for Roger, far from having any crusading spirit, he developed a hatred of the Kingdom of Jerusalem, which had humiliated his mother, and he hated the people who lived there under the pretext of rescuing the land of Jesus after brutally butchering Jews and Muslims alike in a most savage conquest.

The crusades benefited Sicily and the maritime cities such as Pisa, Naples, Amalfi, and Venice. While princes, paupers, and adventurers joined the religious crusaders from the northern countries of Europe, these cities grew rich on trade with the so-called enemies of Christianity who had long been their trading partners. Roger II was in the right place at the right time, and he could build on the legacy left by his prudent father who, while much of Christian Europe was caught up in the crusader movement in one way or another, had created a climate of enlightened political and religious thinking in which all races, creeds, languages, and cultures were equally encouraged and favored. Greek cities, feudal castles, and Muslim villages shared the island with colonies of Lombards and ethnic groups of Pisans, Genoese, and Amalfitans. Bells of Christian churches harmonized with the voices of the muezzins from the minarets of mosques calling the followers of Mohammed to prayer. The Arab cloak mingled with the Muslim turban, the Norman coat of mail, the long Greek tunic, and the short Italian sagum. Such a phenomenon was not only without parallel in the Middle Ages but also was unusual at any time or place.

Sicily had become the center of the Mediterranean world. Roger II expanded the navy, which his father had wisely built up, and had the good fortune to have great emirs whose functions included the command of the navy. (The Arab word *amir* or *emir* became *amiral* in French and *admiral* in English with the more restrictive meaning.)

Of the vast domain that the Guiscard had left behind, only Sicily flourished as an island of calm in a world of tumult where the vassals of young princes took matters into their own hands and challenged the authority of their liege lords. On the mainland the Duchy of Apulia was being torn to pieces. At Bari, a usurper had seized power, the Archbishop had been killed, and Princess Constance, the mother of Bohemund II, had been imprisoned. On the death of his mother in 1115, the gentle and much loved Duke William of Apulia was at the mercy of the wolves. Things were chaotic when in 1121 a desperate and helpless William appealed to Roger II, his kinsman and vassal, in these words: *"Noble Count, I appeal to you now in the name of our kinship and because of your great riches and power"* (Norwich, p. 306, quoting from Falco of Benevento). He goes on to tell of threats from a neighbor and his inability to defend himself.

Roger II answered the call the following year, but in keeping with his preferred modus operandi it was with his riches that the matter was settled. He simply bought off the troublemakers and purchased William's safety. At this juncture a grateful William named Roger II heir to the title of Duke of Apulia in case of his death without heirs. He had not long to wait—hardly five years later, on July 25, 1127, William died childless at the age of thirty. Gaitelgrima, his loving wife, as a sign of grief cut off her hair to cover the corpse, and Salerno joined her in mourning the death of their gentle duke.

Roger II lost no time in appearing with his fleet of ships off Salerno, the capital city of the Duchy of Apulia, to claim the succession as William had willed. Naturally, there were many contestants for the territories comprising the extensive duchy, but with patience and diplomacy Roger was eventually anointed duke without spilling precious blood, which he seemed to value like gold itself.

The newly acquired and vast power of this Norman whose tolerance of the followers of Islam was frowned on and whose relations with the popes of Rome were ambiguous at best, put fear into the heart of the ruling pope, Honorius II, who even went down to the papal city of Benevento to get a closer look at what was happening. He promptly sent a message to Salerno and, using the only weapon he had at his disposal, threatened to excommunicate Roger if he should dare to assume the title of duke. Roger seems to have turned a deaf ear, toured his new dominions, and then returned confidently to Sicily.

Excommunication may not have worried Roger II one bit, but his vassals were not at all immune to the offer of "indulgences." They were soon persuaded by the Pope to betray their lord, to whom they had so recently pledged allegiance, and join the ranks of his opponents. Flanked by his trusted Emirs, Christodulus and George of Antioch, Roger was soon on the scene with a huge army in May of 1128 to put down a rebellion.

Meanwhile, Pope Honorius had raised an army of his own and came looking for his elusive Sicilian prey. He found him calmly encamped in the hills close to the Brandano River. The Saracen shock troops that formed part of Roger's army must have been an intimidating sight for the Pope's untrained collection of souls encamped on the sunny side of the river, where they sweltered in the July heat for over a month. As his army began to disintegrate, the Pope prudently sought to negotiate with Roger, agreeing to recognize him as Duke of Apulia. So it was that after sunset, in the light of blazing torches and before thousands of spectators, Roger II was invested by the Pope with the lance and gonfalon. Once more he had won a bloodless victory, and now he had received the blessing of Pope Honorius. He was still only thirty-two years old, and it seemed that he had the world at his feet.

Roger's troubles were not yet over, however. Accustomed as they were to unbridled freedom, the great feudal fiefs of Apulia were apparently not very impressed by Roger's investiture and were soon battling with each other once again. By the spring of 1129 Roger was back with an even larger army of knights, infantry, archers, and Saracens, and sixty ships under his trusted Emir, the brilliant George of Antioch, to take care of rebellious Bari. By September his authority was reestablished, and he summoned all the counts of Apulia and Calabria to hold court at Melfi, the first center of Norman power and a fitting place for such a gathering.

A central government in southern Italy was in the making. The vassals assembled at Melfi took a solemn, three-part oath in the presence of their peers, the essence of which was as follows:

- to pledge fealty and obedience to the Duke and each of his two eldest sons, Roger eleven years old and Tancred, a few years younger. Their succession was thus theoretically ensured.

- to observe a ducal edict forbidding private wars.

- to maintain and uphold order and justice and to surrender thieves and robbers to the Duke's Courts; to promise protection of all feudal inferiors, pilgrims, travelers, and merchants.

It was a document conceived by an enlightened leader of this medieval world, and it also gave a glimpse of the kind of social climate that the offspring of those Norman soldiers of fortune had helped create. The right of feud that had caused such chaos was now replaced by the Duke's Peace.

Sicily and most of southern Italy was now under one ruler, Roger II. It seemed that he had everything except a crown. He did not have to fight, and he did not have long to wait. Here is how it all came about. Pope Honorius died the year following Roger's investiture. As to be expected, there was a scramble for the vacant seat as two

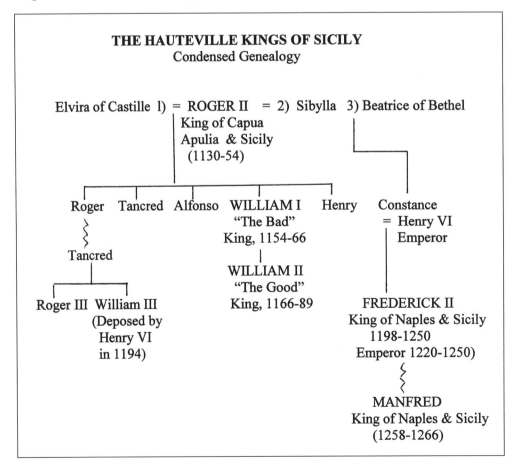

THE HAUTEVILLE KINGS OF SICILY
Condensed Genealogy

Elvira of Castille 1) = ROGER II = 2) Sibylla 3) Beatrice of Bethel
King of Capua
Apulia & Sicily
(1130-54)

Roger Tancred Alfonso WILLIAM I Henry Constance
"The Bad" = Henry VI
Tancred King, 1154-66 Emperor

WILLIAM II
"The Good"
Roger III William III King, 1166-89 FREDERICK II
(Deposed by King of Naples & Sicily
Henry VI 1198-1250
in 1194) Emperor 1220-1250)

MANFRED
King of Naples & Sicily
(1258-1266)

opposing groups in Rome supported different candidates. Even before the body of the old pope was cold — or, as some suspected, even before he was dead — battle lines were drawn to decide who would be the next one to occupy the vacant seat. By noon the next day there were two popes, Innocent and Anacletus II. The latter, having local support, got the seat while his opponent fled beyond the Alps to grovel at the feet of the French and the Germans.

As Innocent's support grew, Anacletus became more nervous, and there was only one place he could turn. He called on the Normans for protection, and it was a simple matter for Roger II to pledge his support in exchange for the crown of a king with the blessing of a pope. A bull was signed on September 27, 1130, whereby Roger was invested with the Kingdom of Sicily, Calabria and Apulia, the principality of Capua, the fief of Naples, and the protectorate over Benevento. In return, Roger recognized the Holy See's suzerainty with payment of tribute.

Palermo would be the capital of the new kingdom, and there would be a coronation the likes of which perhaps no other European capital had ever witnessed. On Christmas Day 1130, the archbishop of Palermo crowned Roger II King of Capua, Apulia, and Sicily. Alexander of Tease, a primary source from that time, described an event of incredible splendor. They came from all corners of the realm to this most cosmopolitan city of the medieval world. In addition to the inhabitants of Palermo and the island of Sicily, there were the vassals from the mainland, Italians, Normans, Greeks, Lombards, Spaniards, and Saracens. The sights and sounds that greeted Roger II as he emerged from the cathedral were those of rejoicing. Bells pealed, crowds cheered, and the clomp of horses hooves mingled with the happy jingle of gold and silver trappings that caught the rays of sunlight of a Sicilian winter's day. Surrounded by a whole city and its visitors, turned out in their finest silks and brocades of dazzling colors, Roger II was escorted to the Palace for a great and sumptuous banquet.

That December 25, 1130, was an historic date for Sicily and the South of Italy, all of which would be pacified and eventually joined into one great kingdom.

Struggles of the New Kingdom

The decade following the coronation of Roger II as King of Sicily was filled with events of historic magnitude, rebellions, cruel wars of repression, and the demise of princes and dynasties as the deadly games of politics and war were played out against a backdrop of religious turmoil. Once more, the problem with the Papacy in Rome spilled over into the south, threatening the very kingdom it had so recently created.

Roger's first problems involved his own jealous relatives and barons. He was king in title, but much of the region had yet to be pacified. Just two years after receiving his crown, he was faced with a rebellion that involved Richard of Capua, Richard of Avellino, and his own brother-in-law, Rainulf of Alife, married to Roger's sister Matilda. Thanks to Roger's capable emirs, the uprisings were put down, and Matilda was taken back to Sicily for a while as a hostage of own brother. Many of the ringleaders fled the kingdom to seek asylum at the imperial courts and other cities, Pisa in particular.

The most serious threat to the fledgling kingdom, however, came from outside it. The rival pope, Innocent II, got the support of emperor-elect Lothair II, who in 1133 entered Rome with an army and had himself duly crowned as Holy Roman Emperor.

Detail of Bari's Norman castle, founded by Roger II and later adapted by Frederick II in the mid thirteenth century. The massive structure, surrounded by a moat, stands guard on the land side of Città Vecchia, an unusual wing now pointing to the modern city.

It was now the turn of Pope Anacletus to scamper over to Castel Sant'Angelo and take refuge.

Both Lothair and Pope Innocent feared Norman power and conspired to crush the Kingdom of Sicily. Their cause was aided by a great personal tragedy that befell King Roger when Elvira, his wife of fifteen years, passed away in February of 1135. Her death was a devastating blow to Roger, who shut himself away in his grief, refusing to receive even his closest friends. His foes took cruel advantage of his absence, and the following year armies of Pope and Emperor agreed to confer on the treacherous Rainulf the title of Duke of Apulia, setting Normans against Normans.

Once more Providence came to Roger's aid when an ailing Lothair left Italy and returned to his fatherland, where he died on December 3, 1137. Pope Innocent was determined to continue his crusade alone. On the death of his rival, Anacletus, in January of 1139, he promptly excommunicated all the dead pope's supporters, King Roger and his sons in particular. Suddenly, Pope Innocent found himself without his chief ally in the south when the treacherous Rainulf whom he had made Duke of Apulia was stricken with fever and died at Troia at the end of April.

King Roger gathered his army together, left Sicily, and marched northward to the papal patrimony of Benevento, where he confronted the papal army. The Pope's army was led into an ambush and defeated in the historic "Rout of Galuccio." It was said that thousands of men were drowned as they fled across the Garigliano River. Three days later, the victorious King Roger with two sons knelt before Pope Innocent to receive absolution and swear allegiance to the Holy See. In return, Roger's right to the Kingdom of Sicily was confirmed by the very pope that had stripped him of his title and set out to destroy him.

The maritime jewel of Naples was soon added to the Kingdom. Prince Sergius, the last of a noble Lombard dynasty, had died. An embassy from the city came to pledge allegiance to King Roger and accept his son as their duke. Roger's entry into Naples in 1140 was a great triumph and was described in magnificent detail by Falco, a historian of the period. He tells how Roger was met and accompanied into the city by processions of rejoicing crowds. King Roger rode in with four noble knights holding the bridle of his horse and four others forming an honor guard. Roger rode alone in kingly solitude; although he had been a widower for five years, he had not taken another wife.

When Roger sailed for his capital of Palermo a few days later, he knew that Providence was on his side. His enemies had been defeated and he had the blessing of the only reigning pope. He set about establishing the boundaries of his kingdom, claiming all that he could justly claim as his, except Benevento, which remained like a papal island in the bosom of the Norman kingdom. A line running across the peninsula from the west coast to the east was a frontier that remained practically unchanged for the next 700 years.

King Roger and the Second Crusade

The Kingdom of Sicily now entered a Golden Age not shared by the two great empires that had sought her demise. In 1142, Archbishop Peter of Cluny, a former enemy, wrote a letter to King Roger with the following flattering words of admiration for a man whose stature was now recognized:

> *Sicily, Apulia, Calabria, before you the refuge and the robber dens of the Saracens, are now through you an abode of peace . . . they are become a magnificent Kingdom, ruled by a second Solomon: would that also poor and unfortunate Tuscany and the lands about it might be joined to your dominion and enter into the peace of your Kingdom!* (Edmund Curtis, *Roger of Sicily*, p. 210)

In northern Europe, the religious movement that had been gathering momentum whipped up a storm, dragging in its wake men of every ilk; poor sinners in search of salvation, as well as noblemen who believed they could purchase a passage to paradise, and kings would lead them on a crusade to the Holy Land. But not King Roger. He was busy expanding his influence beyond his bright kingdom and pushing his frontiers to the coast of Muslim North Africa, but he went not as a Christian crusader against the infidels. Indeed, some of his most loyal subjects and friends were followers of Islam. Roger went instead to reap the fruits of conflict when he responded to an appeal for help against a belligerent neighbor. His brilliant Emir, George of Antioch, was dispatched to the "rescue" with a sizable fleet. Among the prizes of that campaign was Tripoli, one of the chief Muslim cities of the time, which fell to the Sicilians in 1146.

Meanwhile, Christians were frantically preparing for the Second Crusade, spurred on by the loss of Edessa (site of modern Urfa in Turkey) in 1144 to the infidels. By the spring of 1147 the crusaders were headed for the Holy Land, led by King Louis VII of France and King Conrad of Germany and converging on Constantinople. King Louis's arrival coincided with the appearance of the Sicilian armada under George of Antioch. King Roger had plans to persuade King Louis, his unofficial ally, to join him in an attack on Constantinople, but Louis kept his vow and proceeded on his way to Jerusalem while Roger's emir, having already captured the Greek island of Corfu, in a pure act of piracy attacked Corinth and sacked Thebes before returning to Palermo with rich booty. He also brought back as captives some skilled workers who formed a colony and later established a silk industry in Sicily.

It was a wild time in the Eastern Mediterranean as the Venetians joined in the fray to recover Corfu from the Sicilians and George of Antioch was back on the scene to defend it. Sailing home in the midst of this turmoil, King Louis's flotilla was surrounded by unfriendly Greeks, but thanks to the Sicilians he and his queen, Eleanor of Aquitaine, reached the shores of the Kingdom of Sicily in safety. King Roger went to meet Louis at Potenza in the wild region of hill towns, one of which the Italian author Carlo Levi in his book *Christ Stopped at Eboli*, described as "a streak of white at the summit of a bare hill, a sort of imaginary Jerusalem in the solitude of the desert." This was no imaginary Jerusalem, but a safe venue for a friendly meeting between two kings. From there Roger personally escorted his royal guest through the craggy regions of his kingdom to the border of the Papal States at Ceprano, where they parted company.

The year 1149 came quietly to an end, and the seas were once more calm as survivors of the disastrous and costly crusade straggled home to the north, while Roger returned to his beloved Palermo. There he engaged in scientific speculation and indulged his passion for mathematics and geography. He gathered around him men of learning from all parts and formed a commission to collect information about the world. It was headed by the brilliant Arab geographer Edrisi, who said that the world "is a ball floating in the clouds of Heaven like the yolk of an egg," and that the island of Sicily was "a pearl of the world." The massive body of knowledge that resulted was dedicated to the king and came to be known as *The Book of Roger.* It was published in 1154, the year of King Roger's death, only to be lost to the world for four and a half centuries. In the meantime, Columbus would set out to prove that the world was indeed round.

Roger de Hauteville, the Man

History records the deeds of Roger II, the first king of Sicily, but his successes as a great ruler are in stark contrast to the tragedies that marred his personal life. For four decades, like a master puppeteer on the stage of history, he had been pulling the strings of his marionettes. Now at the end of the show, we go behind the scenes and meet the man who held such power for so long. We are left with the image as portrayed in the magnificent mosaics of the Martorana (also called Santa Maria dell'Ammiraglio), a church in Palermo founded by George of Antioch, his Emir.

Roger's last years must have been sad ones since of the five legitimate sons of his beloved wife, Elvira, the only survivor was young William. The princes Tancred and Alfonso died in the flower of youth in 1138 and 1144, respectively, but the greatest blow of all was the untimely death in 1148 of his oldest son, the gallant and soldierly knight who would have worn the crown of the Kingdom as Roger III had he lived. Loved by all, his praises were most eloquently sung by the Arab poets, one of whom wrote that "on the darkness shines his brilliant face, the sun might be envious of him." He was thirty years old and left no legitimate heir. One wild oat later turned up to play a brief and most tragic role in the history of the South, however, as we shall see later.

Soon after the death of his oldest son, King Roger took another wife, Sibylla, but she died two years later, childless. Apparently still hoping for more sons, he took a third wife, Beatrice. She was with child when her king died a natural death at Palermo on February 27, 1154. He might have been disappointed had he lived to greet a little girl, but she was the one who was destined to carry on the de Hauteville bloodline and one day wear the crown of Empress. Her name was Constance.

At Cefalù, against a backdrop of cliffs there stands a cathedral of gold-tinted stone. Roger built it to fulfill a vow he made when once in danger of shipwreck off that coast. It was here that Roger was first laid to rest in the fine raiments of a king, some say the greatest of them all. His final resting place is in the Duomo of Palermo, along with his kin.

The Two Williams

As the great King Roger II passed quietly from history, his surviving son, William, was left alone on the throne he had shared with his father for three years. The transition was peaceful, and there were capable men to guide the kingdom through the next tumultuous decade.

Within the realm, jealous barons rebelled against their king, encouraged by supporters from outside. The Pope, the maritime cities of Pisa and Genoa, the Holy Roman Emperor, and the Byzantines all feared the power of the Kingdom of Sicily. The breakaway Apulia had to be subdued by force of arms, and a fleet was then dispatched against the Byzantine Emperor, who was forced to make peace and recognize William as king.

The greatest threat of all came from the north where Frederick I, the King of Germany, had in 1155 become the Emperor of the Holy Roman Empire. He would come to be known in Italy as "Barbarossa" on account of his red beard. His lifelong ambition was to bring southern Italy into the fold of his empire, but for now the Kingdom was safe thanks to the efforts of King William who, unfortunately, is known as "William the Bad" for his unspeakably cruel punishment of rebel subjects. However, as far as the Kingdom of Sicily was concerned he might have been more aptly called "William the Savior."

King William died at the age of forty-six on May 15, 1166, having reigned twelve of those years as sole monarch of the still most powerful and prosperous kingdom of the Mediterranean. The de Hauteville dynasty continued as he was succeeded by his young son and namesake who, by contrast, was known as "William the Good."

William II was just thirteen years old when his father died, but he was the undisputed heir to the throne. Into the breach came the widowed queen, Margherita, who proved, as did so many women of the Middle Ages, to be an able regent. In the brilliant court of Palermo, the young king was educated by the brightest and most eminent scholars of the civilized world and in 1171, having reached the age of maturity at eighteen, William took the reins of the monarchy. His reign lasted for eighteen splendid years, cut short by his early death at thirty-six and ending what had been a Golden Age for Sicily. Unlike his father, William II was much loved by his subjects, and the peace and prosperity that prevailed within the realm seemed to be in contrast with the rest of the world. William often faltered on the tightrope of international politics, which were an essential element of the times. Early on he found himself dragged into wars against the Muslims of North Africa, yet the more than 100,000 Muslim subjects of his own kingdom continued to enjoy religious freedom and tolerance.

However, the specter of Barbarossa, the Red Beard, was ever present to the north. Was it for this reason that William sought to placate the determined Emperor by bringing him into his own family through a marriage alliance? William was still childless, however, and of the de Hauteville dynasty the only legitimate survivor was his aunt Constance, the daughter of Roger II. An alliance was therefore arranged between Constance and Barbarossa's son, Henry VI. The union did not meet with universal approval, and it terrified the Pope for it strengthened the position of the Holy Roman Emperor, whose power the popes sought to diminish.

Although this union would much later result in an extraordinary birth, it was hardly a match made in heaven. Young Henry was only twenty years old when he took as his bride the beautiful, modest, and pious Constance who was thirty-one years of age at the time. The discrepancy in ages was not an impediment when kingdoms were the dowry, but the Pope refused his blessing for political reasons. The marriage took place in Milan on January 27, 1186, and some of the splendor of Sicily was brought to that Italian city in the throes of a northern winter with the arrival of 150 fine horses carrying gold, silver, and precious materials for the bride's trousseau. Barbarossa came to the city that had been his implacable enemy to witness a ceremony that would soon change the course of history. William the Good died three years later, on November 18, 1189, still without heirs, and was mourned by his subjects of all faiths. He is immortalized by Dante in the "Paradiso" of the *Divina Commedia*, where the souls of six just rulers appear in the eye of an eagle.

El quel che vedi nell'arco declino
Guglielmo fu, cui quella terra plora
che piange Carlo e Federico vivo:
Ora conosce come s'innamora
lo ciel del giusto rege, ed al sembiante
del suo fulgore il fa vedere ancora. (Canto XX, lines 61–66)

[And the one you see in the downward arc
was William, whom that land mourns
and weep because of the living Charles and Frederick:
Now one knows how heaven loves the
just ruler, and in the likeness of its own
radiance shows him still.]

The image of this last legitimate male of the line of the de Hauteville dynasty may be seen in the beautiful mosaics of the cathedral at Monreale, which he himself had founded. In one he is shown offering the cathedral to the Virgin Mary; in another he is seen receiving the crown from Christ. It is a powerful visual epitaph to the king known as "William the Good."

Left: The magnificent cathedral at Monreale, overlooking the Conca d'Oro, is one of the masterpieces of Norman Sicily. Founded by King William II in 1172, it is a blend of Norman and Byzantine expression in art and architecture. The interior is rich with mosaics that depict scenes from the Old Testament, the Teachings of Christ and the Gospels, among others.

The view from the inner court shows the columns, each one uniquely different, that support capitals and Saracen-style arches.

CHAPTER EIGHT

Holy Roman Emperors on the Italian Scene

Emperor Frederick I, "Barbarossa"

The figure of Barbarossa looms large and constant during the latter part of the twelfth century. He may have been a mere specter for the Kingdom of Sicily, but for the north of Italy he was a reality. By the time the reign of William II had come to an end, Barbarossa had been trying to shape history in the north for over a quarter century.

Unlike his predecessors, Barbarossa set out to actually "rule" his empire, but he was in for some surprises. None disputed the fact that by long tradition the German king became the emperor-elect, to claim the symbolic Iron Crown of the Lombards and proceed to Rome where he would be legitimized as Emperor by the Pope. However, he was expected to take his empty titles and retreat beyond the Alps with his soldiers and his retinue. The northern regions of Italy had been part of the Holy Roman Empire since the days of Charlemagne, but the Italian cities had long enjoyed a freedom from central rule, which permitted their development as veritable little states in charge of their own destinies as the great families became dynasties and ruled like princes and kings. Yet because the smaller ones were at the mercy of the larger, especially of the powerful and arrogant Milan, it is easy to understand why some cities favored the intervention of an emperor to protect them against the big brother, enabling Barbarossa to play a key role in Italian history.

Barbarossa was the epitome of the medieval knight; noble, courageous, glorious, charming, much loved and admired, patient, and merciful—he had been described as all of these. He was an eloquent man who grew up German but learned to speak Italian. His home was not a palace, but the back of his horse, where he spent a great deal of his life. That being said, he was not welcome in Italy where his involvement lasted for thirty years, during which time he made six visits to the peninsula.

Barbarossa's first visit was in October 1154, while he was still emperor-elect, when he led an army across the Brenner Pass to be welcomed by Pavia, Cremona, Como, and Lodi among others, who saw him as a protector against the aggressive and powerful Milan. The purpose of this first visit was to impose imperial rule by appointing local officials and collecting taxes. Milan refused to comply, and Barbarossa responded by destroying two of her allies, Asti and Tortona. For the time being, the north had been subdued. Barbarossa then proceeded with his German army to Rome, where Adrian IV (Nicholas Breakspear), the only English pope, was under attack from a certain Bishop Arnold, who was leading a revolution against corrupt papal power. With Barbarossa's help Arnold was captured, tried, summarily condemned, burned to death, and his ashes thrown into the Tiber whose waters carried away any possible relics. The Roman mob turned ugly and Barbarossa, before officially receiving the imperial crown for which he had also come to Rome, was forced to leave the city and camp outside its walls. On a Saturday, June 18, 1155, he quietly slipped back in to be crowned at the Basilica of Saint Peter. An English pope had crowned a German head against the wishes of the angry Roman people.

Barbarossa did not wait around to face the angry mob, but withdrew from the city and made his way home. He and his Germans took a parting shot by looting and burning the unfriendly and rebellious Spoleto, whose inhabitants were mercifully allowed to leave their city and watch its destruction from the surrounding hills. It was hardly a beginning to endear the Emperor to his Italian subjects.

Three years later, Barbarossa was back for the second time with a large army and legal authorities, determined to subdue the Lombard cities where he planned to install German governors. Brescia was subdued and a five-week siege of Milan followed, ending with an agreement. Barbarossa proceeded to spell out his preposterous "rights" as sovereign to:

- levy tolls on public roads, rivers, and ports
- assume ownership of estates without landlords
- confiscate property of persons who had contracted forbidden marriages
- demand horses, ships
- impose war tax
- be declared sole owner of silver mines, salt mines, and fisheries

These were some of the items on an extraordinary list that was totally unacceptable to the Italian cities. Milan rebelled by breaking the truce and attacking an imperial fortress. Barbarossa struck back, attacking Milan's ally, Crema, which was defeated in 1160 after savage fighting. Barbarossa's troops continued to devastate the surrounding territory; Milan, exhausted and half-starved after two years of struggle, finally capitulated on March 1, 1162. Barbarossa was again merciful by medieval standards, for there was no massacre or rape. However, the city was systematically destroyed, building by building, and Milan's Italian enemies took part in her destruction.

Barbarossa's third expedition to Italy came in 1163–64, but he accomplished nothing. In 1166 he returned with a large army for his fourth visit. His adversary was a new pope, Alexander III, an anti-imperial pope who sided with the Lombard cities. For unknown reasons, Barbarossa had himself crowned a second time by an antipope of his choosing. In the eyes of most it was an act of blasphemy that brought on the Emperor the wrath of God, for disaster soon struck the German army. Pestilence broke out in the sweltering heat of that Italian summer, and thousands of soldiers died or fled. The beleaguered Barbarossa left Rome in August 1167; on reaching Pavia in September he learned that many Italian cities had formed an alliance against him to be known as the famous "Lombard League."

Fearing for his life, Barbarossa fled to the city of Susa at the foot of the Alps, only to be stopped by local officials who guarded the frontiers. He was now forced to play a role in a real-life cloak-and-dagger drama as a loyal friend took his place as emperor while the real one somehow managed to get away disguised as a servant. So ended dramatically and under most humiliating circumstances Barbarossa's fourth visit to his Italian realm, where his "subjects" refused to be subjugated.

By now the Italian cities had realized that a powerful Milan was preferable to domination by Barbarossa's corrupt German governors. He might still be their emperor in a symbolic way, but they wanted to rule themselves without his interference. They helped the Milanese rebuild their city, which then assumed the lead against the Emperor. The League now consisted of thirty-six towns.

In 1174 Barbarossa returned to Italy for a fifth visit. It had been six years since he had made his inglorious escape, but his spirit had not been diminished. At fifty-two years of age he was optimistic, having secured the support of the maritime cities of Genoa and Pisa. Barbarossa began by burning Susa to the ground in revenge for the humiliation he had suffered there, then marched to Alessandria, a new fortress city named for his enemy Pope Alexander III (successor of the pope who had crowned him and who had prevailed over no less than four antipopes). It suffered a six-month siege, but held firm. The following year, more troops were called from Germany; the imperial army, which included 2,500 armed horsemen, proceeded to encircle the indomitable Milan. It was the beginning of the final showdown between Italians and Germans.

The Lombards had wasted no time and could boast a cavalry of 4,000 strong, supported by infantry, pikemen, and crossbowmen. They marched out of the city on the historic morning of May 29, 1176, to intercept the forces of the Empire near the village of Legnano. Here, one of the most famous battles of the Middle Ages was fought. Barbarossa rode with his men, driving back the Lombard cavalry and attacking the infantry.

The Italians were united against a common foe, and the tide turned when fresh horsemen arrived from Brescia. In the battle that followed the Emperor was thrown to the ground and his horse killed. The Germans panicked and took flight. Many were slain as they fled, and the Ticino River proved to be the watery grave for others who were dragged down by their heavy armor. This famous battle, in which the Italians were the victors, was the inspiration for Verdi's opera *La Battaglia di Legnano,* later to symbolize Italy's struggle for independence against foreign domination.

The Emperor's body was not found among the dead and wounded. Did the Italians who had him at the point of their spears spare his life and allow him to get away? It may never be known for certain what happened, but he turned up miraculously three days later in the friendly Pavia and it must have been quite a shock for the Emperor to find that the city was mourning his death. Meanwhile, news of the Lombard victory spread like wildfire as Milan sent a dispatch to Bologna, which included the following details:

> We have in our hands the shield, banner, cross and lance of the Emperor and have found in his coffers much gold and silver, while the booty taken from the enemy is of great value; but we do not consider these things ours but the common property of the Pope and the Italians.

From May to July of 1177, Venice was the venue for a peace conference with the Lombard League, Pope Alexander III, and the Emperor. Peace was ensured when a truce was concluded with the powerful Lombard League, and on Sunday, July 24, the Doge of Venice escorted Barbarossa to Saint Mark's Square, where the populace had gathered and the Pope awaited him. After twenty-two years, Barbarossa finally resigned himself to the fact that he was only a symbolic emperor. He stayed for a while to cheerfully present himself to his subjects in the various cities of Italy in this new role before returning home. Peace returned to the north.

Eight years later, in 1185, Barbarossa made his sixth and final visit to Italy. Now he came as a guest to the city of Milan to attend the marriage of his son Henry to

Constance of Sicily, the dazzling event described in the previous chapter, following which he returned beyond the Alps and passed out of Italian history. For thirty years of his life, he had devoted his energies to subjugating the Italian peninsula, but he had failed.

Four years after his last visit to Italy, Barbarossa took up the cross of a crusader, along with the kings of France and England (Philip Augustus and Richard the Lionheart) in what was known as the Third Crusade, to recover Jerusalem from the infidels. He failed once more to reach his goal, for on June 10, 1190, he drowned accidentally while crossing the Saleph River in Cilicia on his way to the Holy City. Another Frederick later took his place in Italian history—his own grandson, Frederick II, who had not yet been born.

Emperor Henry VI: The Struggle for Control of Sicily

The Italian peninsula, seething with anti-German feelings after the reign of Barbarossa, was now at the mercy of the dead emperor's son, Henry VI, who had already been given the crown as King of Italy by his crusading father. It was an ambitious man who now held the reins of power, and the Italians would soon know the extent of his wrath.

By his marriage to Constance, Henry also laid claim to the rich Kingdom of Sicily, which had just lost her beloved King William. A faction of the Norman nobility had looked around for a replacement and brought from the Norman closet the illegitimate son of Constance's eldest brother Roger, the valiant Tancred. In early 1190, they crowned him king in defiance of Henry VI, and amidst the turmoil poor Constance, as wife of the hated Henry, was for a time a prisoner of the rebels in Salerno. The peace of the south had been shattered as supporters rallied either to the side of Constance or Tancred, splitting the kingdom into rival factions. Tancred was faced with rebellions within his kingdom in Apulia and Campania, and Henry laid siege to Naples.

In the midst of the struggle, in February of 1194 Tancred died in Palermo, ending a tumultuous reign of three years. That same year death had claimed his oldest son, Roger III, and now the heavy crown was placed on the head of young William III. Once more a lady was thrust into the limelight of history as Tancred's widow, Sybilla, became regent for her young son.

By the end of that fateful year, the angry Henry VI was back in Italy and made for Palermo, where he seized the young William and his regent mother along with many of their supporters. They were shipped off to Germany, where they suffered the ghastly fate of blinding and mutilation at the hands of the Germans.

On Christmas Day, 1194, Emperor Henry VI had himself crowned kKing of Sicily in Palermo. The day after his coronation, on December 26, Empress Constance, on her way south to join her husband, gave birth to a son at Jesi, just outside Ancona. It was an unusual event, for Constance was now forty years of age and this was her first child. The babe was given the name of Frederick Roger, after his two grandfathers. In June 1195, Henry left Constance as his regent, along with the six-month-old infant, and returned to Germany and the affairs of empire.

Three years later, Henry was in southern Italy where insurrection had broken out against the harsh rule of his officials. He had survived the hatred of the ones he had so cruelly tried to subdue, but on September 28, 1197, at just thirty-two years of age, he fell victim to an unseen enemy when he died of malaria at Messina.

Little Frederick inherited the kingdom of his father with his mother, Constance, as Regent. It seemed, however, that the wheel of fate had come full circle, for she died one year later on November 27, 1198. The little boy-king celebrated his fourth birthday as an orphan, and the future of his kingdom was in jeopardy. Who would now protect him from the wolves?

PART THREE

The Renaissance and
the Rise of City-States

THE HOHENSTAUFEN HOUSE

FREDERICK I
(Emperor "Barbarossa")

HENRY VI = Constance
(Emperor) (Daughter of Roger
de Hauteville

FREDERICK II
(1194-1250)
Emperor, King of Sicily

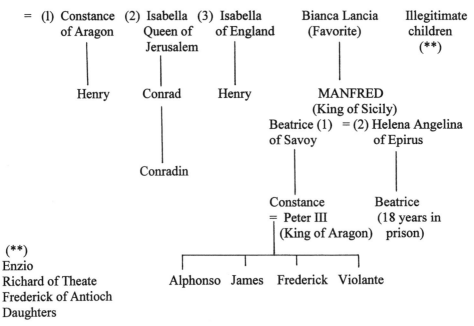

= (1) Constance (2) Isabella (3) Isabella   Bianca Lancia   Illegitimate
of Aragon   Queen of   of England   (Favorite)   children
          Jerusalem   (**)

Henry   Conrad   Henry   MANFRED
                           (King of Sicily)
                      Beatrice (1) = (2) Helena Angelina
                      of Savoy   of Epirus

Conradin

                             Constance   Beatrice
                             = Peter III   (18 years in
                            (King of Aragon) prison)

(**)
Enzio
Richard of Theate   Alphonso James Frederick Violante
Frederick of Antioch
Daughters

CHAPTER ONE

The Empire of Frederick II

Frederick II: Medieval Knight or Renaissance Man?

With the dawn of the thirteenth century, there appeared on the horizon a man who, though born in the medieval world, would emerge as a herald of the Renaissance. The child with the golden-red locks, baptized Frederick Roger after his German and Norman grandfathers, respectively, inherited only the crown of the Two Sicilies, but would one day wear the crown of Emperor as Frederick II.

From the circumstances of his birth, the role that destiny had reserved for him, and his extraordinary intellect, there was nothing ordinary about Frederick. His tutors recognized in him a pupil of awesome intelligence and precocity and called him "Stupor Mundi," the wonder of the world. The rich environment of Palermo provided the soil in which he blossomed early and grew in wisdom, but it was a world without close kin. His mother had cut him off from his Teutonic roots, dismissing the Germans from the palace, and before her untimely death she entrusted her son to the newly elected Pope Innocent III (1198–1216). However, Frederick was not dragged off to Rome to grow up in the shadow of the Vatican, but remained with a pope-appointed regent and his tutors in the Norman palace of Palermo.

The years following the death of his mother were fraught with danger as others claimed their rights to the crowns of Italy, Germany, and Sicily. On the first day of November 1201, Markwald, a powerful German who had been banished by Constance, took over Palermo with the help of the Pisans and the Genoese, and seized the young king. An eyewitness reported that little Frederick, not yet seven years of age, flew into a royal rage, shouting and renting his clothes in protest. Markwald died the following year, but his death brought no relief as he was succeeded by other German adventurers.

The circumstances of Frederick's childhood remain obscure, but if we are to give credence to the chroniclers of the day he lived much of the five years after his removal from the palace free and unfettered, taken care of by the friendly populace, who saw to his needs. The boy had been schooled in the tools of learning, but his early exile gave him the extraordinary chance to learn in the classroom of experience as he roamed through the narrow streets and markets of the half-Arab Palermo, his refuge and his playground, where he learned the vernacular of the common people.

In 1207 Frederick became once more the protégé of a papal appointee, Walter of Palear, but he was mature and wise for his age and Pope Innocent III, quoted as saying that "the manhood of a Caesar sets in before its time," declared his majority on December 26, 208, making the fourteen-year-old Frederick ruler of the Kingdom of the Two Sicilies. The following year, the Pope arranged a marriage with the twenty-four-year-old recently widowed Constance, sister of King Peter II of Aragon. What a strange coincidence that Frederick, like his father, should be married to a woman several years his senior and also named Constance! The teenage Frederick resisted such a match, but it seems that the 500 Spanish knights that the lady would bring as a dowry may have played a role in his acceptance, and they were duly married. Two years later, in 1211, Constance gave birth to her only child, a son whom they named Henry after his paternal grandfather.

In the world of international politics, Frederick soon became an instrument of Pope Innocent's plans. As German princes disputed the title of King of Germany, with the eventual title of emperor-elect, the Pope saw the advantage of having the inexperienced young Frederick under his control as emperor. So it was that in the midst of confusion and dissent in Germany, Frederick was invited, with the complicity and blessing of the Pope, to claim the throne of Germany as rightful heir of his father. He had not yet celebrated his eighteenth birthday when in 1212 he left his kingdom in the care of his wife, Constance, and made his way to Rome, where he apparently set eyes on his protector, the Pope, for the first time.

The young king's adventures had just begun when he left Rome and set sail for Genoa, eluding enemy Pisan ships, and with a small escort made his way through the hostile regions of north Italy and the less-traveled, bleak mountain passes of the Alps. Frederick finally reached the town of Constance (Konstanz), on the lake of the same

Photo by Charlotte A. Masiello-Riome

Castel del Monte. Built in the 13th century by Frederick II, the imposing and enduring castle stands alone on a hill some 25 miles west of Bari. Octagonal in shape and mysterious in concept, the Castel del Monte symbolizes in stone the uniqueness of a great man.

name, which was ceremoniously bedecked in preparation for the imminent arrival of his rival, Kaiser Otto. A bizarre *coup de théâtre* took place when the confused citizens were confronted with the party of Frederick. The Archbishop of Bari, in the papal escort, read the excommunication of Kaiser Otto, and demanded entrance in the name of the Pope. The gates of the city were opened, and Frederick was welcomed in place of the royal visitor expected. When Otto arrived some hours later he found himself locked out. In all probability, the great feast prepared for Otto was consumed instead by Frederick and his party.

Frederick's actions and adventures over the next eight years belong more strictly to German history. On December 9, 1212, he was officially declared King of Germany, and by tradition emperor-elect, but his chief rival, Otto was a force to contend with for the next six years until his death in 1218.

Finally, on November 22, 1220, amidst great ceremony and rejoicing, King Frederick and Queen Constance rode along the coronation route to the Basilica of Saint Peter to receive the crowns of emperor and empress from the hands of Pope Honorius III (1216–1227). The imperial crown came with a price, however. Frederick's power was to be curbed by making his young son, Henry, co-king of Germany, where he was soon shipped off to be brought up with the German princes. In addition, a promise was extracted from Frederick to lead a crusade to the Holy Land.

With the crown of emperor on his head, Frederick returned to the Kingdom of Sicily, much neglected during his long absence. Realizing that he needed educated men to administer his extensive realm, in 1224 he founded the University of Naples, among one of the oldest in Europe, to which he brought the best teachers and most knowledgeable scholars.

One of the first tasks confronting Frederick on his return to the Kingdom was the result of an uprising of his Saracen subjects in Sicily. The crusading fervor of the times was in conflict with the idea of religious tolerance and harmony that Frederick had known during his boyhood. Now the Saracens, though loyal subjects of their king, were being ruthlessly persecuted. They had risen up in armed revolt and many had been forced to flee, taking refuge in the rugged interior of the island. Through a veritable ethnic transplant, Frederick created a new home for the Saracens on the mainland; in 1225 some 10,000 of them left Sicily for the town of Lucera, not far from Foggia, where they were assured religious freedom. The new colony flourished especially as a military center and provided the Emperor with many of his most loyal soldiers.

The long promised crusade could be delayed no longer. Pope Honorius III had died and a new one, the aging Pope Gregory IX (1227–1241), threatened Frederick with excommunication if he did not hold to his promise. In the fall of 1227, a fleet set sail from Brindisi with an army of crusaders. Unfortunately, an epidemic broke out on the ships and the Emperor, also stricken with the sickness, ordered a return to port. Pope Gregory was furious and, stubbornly refusing to listen to any explanations, he promptly carried out his threat to excommunicate the Emperor along with all the subjects in places where he had resided.

The crusade, known as the sixth, finally got under way in the summer of the following year. This was not a crusade in the traditional sense of the word where Christians were expected to fall on the infidels and cut them down with their swords. Frederick was going to claim the throne of Jerusalem and the lands held by the infidels. How could this happen?

Empress Constance had died in 1222; two years later Frederick had taken as his bride the fourteen-year-old Franco-Syrian Isabella of Brienne, titular heiress to the crown of Jerusalem. In April 1228, the young girl had died in her seventeenth year giving birth to a son, Conrad. Now just two months following her death in Apulia, Frederick the widower sailed out of Brindisi bound for the Holy Land to claim a kingdom in the name of his motherless child.

Frederick had made a deal with the "devil," for in July he acquired Jerusalem, Bethlehem, and Nazareth through a treaty with his friend, Sultan Al-Kamil. The following year, on March 17, 1229, Frederick entered Jerusalem, where he crowned himself king.

Frederick had broken all the rules of true crusading. He was in league with the infidels, no blood had been spilled, and he had gone without permission of the Pope by whom he was once more excommunicated. By the time he returned to Brindisi, papal troops had penetrated far into the mainland part of his kingdom, and a campaign was launched to drive them out. The young emperor had locked horns in a deadly battle of wills with the aging pope whose struggle against Frederick, the "Baptized Sultan" as he was referred to, had become a crusade in itself.

With papal invaders expelled, the victorious Frederick set about the task of strengthening the Kingdom of Sicily. In the Constitution of Melfi of 1231, he promulgated a new set of laws, building on the best of Norman rule and integrating much of the Roman. He created state monopolies—including salt, copper, and silk— to fund the treasury. Her also created cities such as Monteleone and l'Aquila (the Eagle) the present capital of the Abruzzi. Doctors and apothecaries became state officials under the control of the Emperor. Prospective doctors had to study logic for three years, followed by a long period of medical studies at Salerno, after which they practiced for a full year alongside a physician before being given an appointment by the Emperor who, incidentally, was very knowledgeable in the field of medicine. The Emperor had a passion for the sport that kept his knights occupied in time of peace, but he understood the cycles of nature and imposed a strict season for game. All aspects of government seem to have been included in this far-reaching Constitution, some items of which remain in force to this day. Salt is still sold by tobacconists, along with postage stamps and other items of state monopoly.

While Frederick had been devoting his energies to the peninsula, the northern part of his empire beyond the Alps had been in revolt. His young son Henry, the King of Germany, in league also with the Lombards, had openly rebelled against his father. In 1235 Frederick marched north and carried out one of the most painful acts of his life—the capture of his firstborn as a traitor of the Empire. He might well have been sacrificed on the altar of justice, but he was still a young man in his mid-twenties, and as the son of an emperor he was spared the death penalty. Instead the young rascal was escorted back to the Kingdom of Sicily as his father's prisoner where he remained until his death in 1242 at thirty-one years of age. It was believed that while being transferred from one prison to another in the craggy hills of Calabria, the young man rode his horse over a precipice to his death. The real truth will never be known.

The son of Frederick's second marriage, the seven-year-old Conrad, made his exit from the Italian scene when he was sent off to replace his dead half-brother, while the Emperor turned his attention to the north of Italy with the aim of reestablishing his rule there. To this end he set out on his First Lombardy Campaign in 1236. He found himself at odds with the Italian cities of the north who quarreled among themselves, but were nevertheless solidly against the interference of the Emperor. A second campaign against the recalcitrant cities followed in 1237 and a third in 1238 as Frederick, like his grandfather Barbarossa, was determined to impose his imperial will.

Frederick had never threatened papal patrimony, but when in 1238 he arranged a marriage for his illegitimate son Enzio with the heiress of the Kingdom of Sardinia, the Pope became alarmed. The lady was also the widow of a Visconti and took to the marriage a vast territory in Tuscany, part of which the Pope claimed as papal domain. This was tantamount to poaching, and the frustrated Pope threatened excommunication. By this time Frederick should have been immune to such threats, but popes can create a lot of political problems and embassies were sent to Rome in the interest of peace. Such overtures were summarily rejected. In fact, the Pope seemed bent on destroying the Emperor, at the time wintering at Padua along with an ungodly retinue of Saracen soldiers, a shocking harem of dancing girls, and a menagerie of exotic animals, which, according to the records, included an elephant and twenty-four camels.

The excommunication was issued in Rome on Palm Sunday while Frederick, oblivious to what had taken place, was in Padua watching the amusements of the people, believing that his embassies to the Pope could avert this action which shattered any hope of reconciliation between pope and emperor. War was inevitable. The terms *Guelph* and *Ghibelline* (supporters of the Papacy and the Empire, respectively) began to take on a new and terrible significance as cities and individuals rallied to one banner or another.

The die had been cast, and both sides prepared for war as the Pope recruited the help of the Venetians and the Genoese, ostensibly to attack Sicily. Cut off from his loyal kingdom to the south by the papal lands that belted the belly of the peninsula, an express sea lane was established between Pisa and Naples so that contact with the well-organized south could be maintained. Papal territories were invaded, and in the spring of 1240 Frederick's imperial troops were at the gates of Rome, only to withdraw in the face of strong resistance.

The Emperor's war was against the old Pope whose one goal was now to depose him. Accordingly, Pope Gregory convened a council of representatives from the Christian world. Genoa gave its ships to bring prelates from France and England to Rome. Then the unexpected happened. When the fleet carrying the would-be conferees approached the Tuscan coast, out popped the long arm of the Emperor in the person of his son, Enzio, now King of Sardinia. The Genoese fleet was attacked in the Tyrrhenian waters near the mountainous little island of Giglio (the Lily) and the precious cargo of prelates, bishops, and archbishops fell into the hands of the very man they had come to depose. Many drowned as their overloaded ships went down, whereas others were taken away as prisoners of the Emperor. The aged pope's plan to put an end to the red-headed renegade ended in disaster. Three months later, in August 1241, the Pope died.

Things did not change for Frederick, however, for although the papal seat remained empty for the next two years, the war between papal and imperial forces continued as cities and individuals took sides. Having seized the papal territories of Spoleto and the March of Ancona, Frederick now had a corridor joining the Kingdom of Sicily with northern Italy. Peace negotiations took place with the newly elected Pope Innocent IV (1243–1254), but in 1244 he took fright and fled to Lyons, where another council was convened, and Emperor Frederick was officially deposed the following year. Never before had a pope deposed an emperor, and there was much confusion as to whether one should obey the pope and risk the wrath of an imperial army or, by remaining loyal to the emperor, risk the punishment of excommunication. What a dilemma!

In this climate of fear and confusion, Emperor Frederick was warned in 1246 of a widespread conspiracy to assassinate him, along with his son Enzio. The instigator of the whole plan was believed to have been the Pope himself, who now saw the Emperor as the anti-Christ to be eliminated along with his breed. Frederick found some of the chief conspirators hidden like a nest of vipers in the very heart of his own kingdom. Their last stronghold was the citadel of Capaccio, near Salerno.

With the conspiracy discovered and the perpetrators brutally eliminated, Frederick emerged more powerful than before. He appointed to important positions throughout the north the many illegitimate children he had fathered, both sons and daughters, who were married off to influential people. Henry, the legitimate nine-year-old son from his third wife, Isabella (sister of King Henry III of England), whom he had married in 1235, was sent to Viterbo, uncomfortably close to Rome.

Frederick now received a cry for help from his young son Conrad, King of Germany. Gathering a huge army, he prepared to march north to settle matters there, and on the way he planned to "call on" Pope Innocent, still holding out in Lyons. Unfortunately, Frederick had to abandon his plans when a political storm broke out in the emotionally charged north where Parma had defected and sided with the Papacy, encouraging others to follow suit. Parma was placed under siege and a town on the model of a real city was built close by and given the name of Victoria. It was intended to replace Parma, which was to be destroyed. However, the inhabitants of Parma caught the imperial forces by surprise, destroying Victoria and capturing the royal treasure.

Where was the Emperor? He had confidently ridden out at dawn to the marshes with his beloved falcons, say the chroniclers. All seemed lost, but Frederick's sons kept up the fight on other fronts. Four months later imperial forces fought and won a battle on the site where Victoria once stood. Neighboring Cremona aided in carrying out imperial punishment of Parma that was seen as the catalyst in the wars between empire and papacy.

Conflicts continued in the north, but there was no battlefront when it came to traitors within the heart of the Empire. In 1249 Frederick believed that he had been betrayed by the one man he most trusted, Piero della Vigna, his right-hand man and eloquent, smooth-talking mouthpiece. The poet Dante believes him to be innocent and has him speak from the Inferno in these terms: "I am he who held both keys to Frederick's heart, locking, unlocking with so deft a touch that scarce another soul had any part in his most secret thoughts. . . . I swear to you, that never in word or spirit did I break faith to my lord and emperor who was so worthy of honor in his merit" (Hell XIII—John Ciardi's translation). Dante placed della Vigna in Hell for the crime against God of having taken his own life.

Guilty of betrayal, however, was Frederick's trusted physician. Someone had warned the Emperor of a plot to poison him and when, shortly thereafter, the doctor came to offer a potion to cure an ailment the wary Frederick said, "Drink to my health and share the draught with me." Caught in his own trap, the terrified physician then spilled the contents of the cup and what remained was given to a criminal who, as suspected, died immediately. How ironic that the man who took such care in the training of doctors almost lost his life at the hands of one of them.

Saddened by the loss of the two men most trusted and close to him, Frederick left Lombardy and returned to his kingdom in the south. Fate dealt yet another blow. Enzio, back in Lombardy, had fallen into the hands of his enemies after a minor skirmish that left him unhorsed, and he was imprisoned in Bologna. All attempts of the Emperor to obtain his release were to no avail. Enzio was destined to spend the rest of his life a prisoner, although it was said he was treated well. Indeed, the Bolognese so loved their royal captive that on his death in 1272 they had his body embalmed and gave him a funeral befitting a king.

Frederick never knew the cruel fate that awaited Enzio before his own death in 1250. He had been on a hunting outing at a favorite place near Foggia, where he enjoyed nature, when he was suddenly stricken with dysentery and fever. He took refuge in Castel Fiorentino, where he died a few days later. It was December 13 just thirteen days before his fifty-sixth birthday. The feared prophecy that he would die *sub flores,* under the sign of the flower, had come to pass, but Frederick always thought this meant he would end his days in Florence and had carefully avoided that city.

At Frederick's deathbed, among others, were his son Manfred and the faithful octogenarian Archbishop of Palermo who, almost four decades earlier, had accompanied the young king on his journey to Germany. The Archbishop administered last rites and gave absolution. Keeping watch over the castello where Frederick died as a Christian emperor were loyal Saracens who had known his infinite tolerance of their religion and his protection. His casket was carried to Taranto and placed on a ship, accompanied by vessels bearing the black eagle, which sailed out to the Ionian Sea and then to Palermo by way of the narrow Strait of Messina. Frederick was laid to rest in a sarcophagus of dark-red porphyry in the Duomo of Palermo next to the tombs of his parents, Constance and Henry VI, his grandfather Roger II, and his first wife, Constance of Aragon.

It has been said that Frederick came on the scene of Italian history like a comet and disappeared like one, having lost nothing of his brilliance. His dream of uniting Italy, however, died with him. It was his struggle to make Italy whole through uniting north and south into one harmonious kingdom that brought him into conflict with the popes. The deadly feud that characterized the middle of the thirteenth century eventually brought the French into Italy with disastrous consequences.

Frederick's legacy came not from his rule, but rather from his intellect and great love of learning. He was a scholar of a wide variety of subjects and a great observer of nature. His scholarly treatise, *The Art of Falconry,* has survived the centuries as a primary source on the subject even today. Frederick had not only a passion for the sciences but he was also a linguist and a poet with an unusual appreciation for language. He himself spoke Latin, Arabic, Provençal French, Greek, Hebrew, and the vernacular of Sicily, an Italian that was emerging from the Latin with Provençal influences, and it was in this medium that he wrote poetry. The poets patronized by Frederick in his court circle came to be known as "The Sicilian School," and the Italian in which they wrote became the vehicle of the greatest Italian poet of all, Dante Alighieri, who just fifteen years later was born in the very place that Frederick had feared most — Florence.

Copies from the richly color-illustrated book, <u>The Art of Falconry</u>.

Photographed from a facsimile and reprinted here with kind permission from the Rare Book Room, Western Michigan University.

King Manfred of Sicily

The death of Emperor Frederick did not end the battle between the papacy and the emperor as persecution of Frederick's German kin, the Hohenstaufens, continued. It was ruthless and in the end complete, ending forever the tradition of a German emperor in tandem with a pope.

Conrad IV, co-king of Germany, as the legitimate son of Frederick II inherited his empire, which included the kingdoms in the north and south of the Italian peninsula. He played but a small role in Italian history, however, because in his will Frederick appointed his natural son Manfred as vicar to his half-brother Conrad. Child of his favorite, Bianca Lancia, Manfred was not only the most loved by his father but also the most like him, for he shared his interest in philosophy and the sciences.

Unfortunately, Manfred inherited the enmity that had dogged the rule of his father. The all-powerful popes could make or break kings and create or bring down dynasties in the wicked world of international politics, and Manfred knew the wrath of more than one: in the fifteen years of his rule there had been four popes.

Conrad IV died in May 1254, and his heir was his young son Conradin. At this point Pope Innocent IV persuaded Manfred to switch allegiance and recognize the Kingdom of Sicily as a vassal of the papacy. The Pope sent an army southward to make his claims known, but his soldiers clashed with Manfred's Saracen troops near Foggia. A battle took place on December 2 and papal forces were routed. Five days later the Pope himself was dead. Manfred must have breathed a sigh of relief on the

BARI—A bar in the Città Vecchia keeps alive the memory of Emperor Frederick II.

death of the man who had approved the use of torture by the Papal Inquisition and made all-out war against his father.

The next pope, Alexander VI (1254–61), promptly excommunicated Manfred and the following year simply invested the son of the English king with the Sicilian kingdom. He even sent a papal army against Manfred, who succeeded in resisting and there ended the matter.

The next turn came following a rumor that little Conradin had died. Manfred, as the papal vassal, was somehow able to have himself crowned King of Sicily in Palermo on August 10, 1258. Manfred followed the policies of his father. He rose in power and popularity, winning supporters among the Ghibellines in Lombardy and controlling much of Italy. He even claimed the crown of Sardinia from his half-brother Enzio, still languishing as a beloved prisoner of the Bolognese in papal territory. In short, Manfred had become a real threat to the papacy, and the crusade against the Hohenstaufens was about to resume more deadly than before when Pope Alexander died in 1261.

The next pope was a man of humble French origins who took the title of Urban IV (1261–64). He declared his predecessor's agreements void, the coronation therefore invalid, and now offered Manfred's kingdom to Charles of Anjou, brother of the ruling King Louis IX of France, inviting him to take up arms against Manfred and claim the crown for himself. Nothing happened for four years.

Pope Urban died in 1264, succeeded the following year by another Frenchman, Clement IV, who confirmed the invitation to Charles to accept the crown of Sicily. Charles arrived in Rome with an army in June of 1265 to a triumphal welcome. King Manfred, for some unexplained reason, failed to stop Charles's advance south. The following year, on a fateful February day, a decisive battle took place at Benevento in which Manfred, just thirty-four years old, was killed along with many of his most valiant soldiers. Just as his father before him, he had suddenly disappeared like a comet, plunging the land into darkness.

Friar Salimbene, who lived at that time and is the chief chronicler of the period, provides this dramatic and moving account:

> And Manfred was buried at a bridge near Benevento on Friday, February 26. And Manfred's wife and two children were captured, along with all his treasure in the city called Manfredonia, which city Manfred himself had built and given his own name.
>
> This city was built near the city of Siponto, which is situated two miles from it. And if the prince had lived a few more years, Manfredonia would have been one of the most beautiful cities in the world. It has a circle of walls four miles around, they say, and it has a splendid harbor. It is situated at the foot of Mount Gargano. Only the main street has been completed and fully settled, although the foundations of all the other buildings have been laid. The city also has very wide streets which add to its beauty. But King Charles hates it exceedingly, so much so that no one is allowed to call it by its rightful name.

The wrathful Pope Clement later ordered the body of Manfred disinterred and cast on a river bank to be washed away by the waters. Such was the hatred toward the Hohenstaufen blood, although Manfred could boast little of it because he was a son of Italy through mother and culture. The waters of the river may have carried away Manfred's mortal remains and the city that bore his name was stopped in its

BENEVENTO: In 1947, across from the old city where the Ponte Vanvitelli spans the river Calore, a monument was erected to the memory of Manfred at a place where his body was found among the dead. The inscription on the column contains a quotation from Dante's <u>Purgatorio</u> that reads:

> . . . I am Manfred
>
> If the pastor of Cosenza, sent by Clement to hunt me down, had properly read God's book, the bones of my body would still be at the head of the bridge near Benevento, under the protection of the heavy mass of stone.
>
> S.P.Q.B.

Here fell, never to rise again if not in the dream of Dante, the foundation of the Holy Roman Empire. Time flees over the ruins, memories flash over the waters that flow by and admonish.

first embryonic stages, but one can imagine that the waves breaking on the shores of the beautiful Gulf of Manfredonia still sing in his memory.

Death of Conradin

Charles of Anjou had crushed his opponent, but in the fall of the following year, 1267, out of the shadows came the excommunicated Conradin, the sixteen-year-old grandson of Frederick II, invited by Italian Ghibellines. He was greeted by Verona, Pavia, Pisa and Siena. Gathering supporters along the way, he marched into Rome on July 24, 1268, to be greeted with the same rejoicing as had been accorded to his rival, Charles of Anjou.

Riding high on the waves of success, the young man took the road south with his army, only to be defeated by the superior cavalry of Charles of Anjou near Tagliacozzo, not far from Rome. Conradin managed to escape and return to Rome, but the friendly city he had known a few weeks earlier had fallen into the hands of the papal Guelphs. Fate had turned cruelly against the young Conradin who was captured, along with others of his party, and handed over to Charles.

No exile or imprisonment was possible. The dreadful crusade against the Hohenstaufen line demanded Conradin's death. On October 29, 1268, he was beheaded in the marketplace of Naples. Charles himself was present along with a host of onlookers who came to witness the merciless decapitation of a sixteen-year-old youth who was born to be king.

The Christian world was shocked by this cruel act, which marked yet another turning point in the history of Italy.

In the deadly game played on the chessboard of Italy, the German influence would be replaced by the French. The cities of the north of Italy, divided by the conflict between popes and emperors, would struggle to find their own destinies amid bitter conflict, while the south would suffer under the yoke of a new ruler. The Hohenstaufen dynasty that had been infused with much Italian blood, as well as a diverse and sophisticated culture, would soon be replaced in the south by a more alien one. Not only had Emperor Frederick's dream of unity been shattered, but by the end of the century the peninsula, cut in half by the papal territories that stretched from west to east, would be more fragmented than ever, and the terms "Guelph" and "Ghibelline" — that we read in guidebooks with little understanding — now begin to take on a whole new meaning.

CHAPTER TWO

French Masters: The House of Anjou

The Sicilian Vespers

Charles of Anjou had come on to the Italian scene on the invitation of the Papacy. A French pope had invested a Frenchman, brother of the French king, with all the lands south of that central belt, which since the arrival of the Lombards some seven centuries before had divided north from south. It was the Papacy's plan to use Charles as a means of protecting those papal lands and the coveted temporal power that the popes enjoyed. The Angevin dynasty that Charles founded would rule the south of Italy for a century and a half, when it was finally replaced by the Spanish.

Pope Clement never lived to see the fruits of his actions, for he died on November 29, 1269, at Viterbo with the blood of Conradin on his hands and the ghost of Manfred perhaps haunting him during his last days. The pope that gave Charles his crown would be followed by no less than nine others over the next fifteen years, while the capable and ambitious Charles took center stage, without hindrance, not just in Italy but also in the Mediterranean world order as his title suggests: Count of Anjou and Provence, King of Sicily, Albania, and Jerusalem.

Charles was never a popular ruler, however, and his harsh measures in the Kingdom of Sicily contrasted sharply with the more benevolent rule of his predecessors as Dante so dramatically recorded in his *Inferno*. Moreover, as his power grew, so did the fear among the Guelph factions; Florence in particular became a hotbed of dissent as the city where the boy Dante lived entered a period of turmoil.

Yet the threat was to come from the one quarter that Charles had neglected as unimportant. He had failed to foresee that the rich island of Sicily with its population of mixed races and religions could ever be a threat. The islanders, unhappy when the court of the Kingdom was transferred to Naples, had been cruelly exploited by corrupt French officials, tentacles of the hated foreign king who policed his subjects from some forty-two castles scattered throughout the island. They had borne the burden of heavy taxes and still greater losses as royal agents confiscated their crops and their animals without due compensation and rounded up horses for their knights. French clergy and friars were also being brought to the island in increasing numbers.

By the year 1282, with pent-up emotions of hatred for the foreign overlords, the island was ready to explode in revolt and the match that started the incredible popular uprising that came to be known as the Sicilian Vespers was struck on Easter Monday, falling that year on March 29. The streets of Palermo were filled with people that day, and the mood was festive. The French soldiery had also been moved by the spirit as they mingled with the crowd to share in the celebrations, but many were filled with another kind of spirit, the wine that makes man carefree and impairs good judgment.

The incident which changed the course of history was triggered when a French sergeant named Drouet grabbed from the crowd a young woman on her way to church with her husband, and tried to force his attentions on her. The husband drew his knife and stabbed Drouet to death. The Frenchman's comrades rallied around to defend him, but they found themselves immediately surrounded by the angry Sicilian crowd armed with swords and daggers. The slaughter of the French that followed was without mercy and left none alive. As the bells of the city began to peal, calling the people to vespers, messengers ran through the city streets giving the signal of uprising. Palermo fell into the hands of the rebels, and before the next day dawned in that city it is estimated that some 2,000 French men and women lay dead.

There were similar scenes of slaughter throughout the island, and neither the French nor their supporters were spared. Sicilian girls married to French soldiers were cut down along with their innocent children. Dominican and Franciscan monasteries were raided, and friars were dragged out so that foreigners could be identified by having them repeat the Sicilian word *ciciri*, which was difficult for the French to pronounce. Those that failed the test of the tongue met the same terrible fate as their secular brothers. It was, in short, a bloodbath from which few escaped to tell the tale, and its savagery bespoke the intensity of Sicilian hatred of the French presence, which they were determined never again to tolerate.

Soon almost the entire island was in the hands of the rebels. Only Messina, which had been the administrative center and protected by the Angevin fleet anchored in its harbor, remained loyal to Charles. The Palermitans appealed to Messina to join their cause, and in April a revolt broke out in the last French stronghold. The French were forced to flee for their lives, although there was less slaughter and some were given safe passage off the island. The fleet was set on fire and destroyed.

The Sicilians appealed to Pope Martin IV (1281–85) to put them under his protection as his vassals, but the Church had given the crown to Charles of Anjou, and the appeal was firmly rejected. Adding injury to insult, on Ascension Day, May 7, the Pope excommunicated the Sicilian rebels and their supporters. For good measure, he also excommunicated the Emperor of Constantinople and the Ghibellines of North Italy because they were in sympathy with the Sicilians.

Charles finally realized the seriousness of the situation and tried to coax the Sicilians back with promises and bribes. When this failed he called his ships from other Italian ports and hired galleys from Venice, Pisa, and Genoa. Sicily was not without help, however, for Ancona and Venice sent galleys to defend her. Even Genoa sent vessels in spite of the fact that some others had been hired by the opponent. All these ships converged on Sicily. Charles had assembled a formidable army, which crossed the Strait, blocking the harbor of Messina and placing her under siege as soldiers took up positions in the surrounding vineyards. Repeated attacks were repulsed as men and women tenaciously defended their city.

Meanwhile, the Sicilians looked around for another champion and found one in the person of King Peter III of Aragon. Even more providential was the fact that his queen was none other than Constance, daughter and heir of the dead Manfred, whose place the hated Charles had taken. King Peter, not in the Pope's favor at that time, was on an expedition in North Africa when a delegation arrived from Sicily to offer him the crown of Sicily in exchange for help. By the end of August, the Aragonese camp on the North African coast was quickly dismantled as men, horses, provisions, and arms were loaded on transports and galleys that set sail for Sicily. In those days news traveled by messengers at the speed of a galley or a fast horse, and Charles did not know that his rival was sailing straight to the northwest tip of the island, reaching Trapani at the end of August.

King Peter lost no time in proceeding to Palermo, arriving there on September 2, as a savior to a most tumultuous welcome. Just two days later the Sicilians proclaimed him their king. With the arrival of King Peter, the incident that occurred on Easter Monday of 1282 had become an international war in which the island of Sicily was the central issue. The conflict between the French and the Spanish was about to begin in earnest.

The incident that took place in Sicily in 1282, splitting the island from the mainland, was the historical basis for Giuseppe Verdi's nineteenth opera, *I Vespri Siciliani*. It seems almost ironic that it should have been commissioned by the Paris Opera and was first performed in French in Paris in June 1855, almost six centuries after the fact, as *Les Vêpres Siciliennes*. Nowadays, it is almost always sung in Italian.

The Duel of the Kings

The Spanish (Aragonese) and the French (Angevin) powers confronted each other on the island of Sicily. King Peter, with the crown now securely on his head and the backing of the islanders, moved quickly eastward with his army and his fleet to meet his rival holding out at Messina.

Negotiations took place between the two kings as embassies went back and forth between the royal camps. Charles decided it would be prudent to withdraw from the island rather than run the risk of being be cut off from the mainland forces, and Peter gallantly allowed him time to get away so that it would look like a strategic move in which his rival would not lose face. Back across the narrow Strait of Messina went the army of Charles, which established camp in Calabria. At the beginning of October, a triumphant Peter entered Messina to be greeted as a savior.

Separated now by water, the navies took on the major role in the conflict between Charles and Peter. Two weeks later the Spanish captured twenty-one galleys as they sailed down from Naples to assist the Angevin garrison. Charles remained adamant in his desire to recover Sicily, and Peter was just as determined to defend his newly acquired kingdom as the two faced each other from opposite shores of the Strait. Neither side wanted to engage in a costly all-out war, the outcome of which depended in large part on the questionable loyalty of the many mercenary soldiers who made up their armies.

An original solution to the stalemate was found. Europe was about to witness a farce played out on the international stage in true theatrical tradition. A friar came with a proposal from King Charles that God should be the final judge, and the two kings should decide the outcome of Sicily's destiny by single armed combat. Peter accepted, but on condition that the war should continue in the meantime. Charles then wanted to change the rules of the game because Peter was fifteen years younger, his youth giving him an unfair advantage. It was finally agreed that each king would take 100 knights of his choosing to fight at his side.

A date was set, and a meeting place for the duel on neutral ground was chosen. The first day of June 1283 was the time, and Bordeaux, then part of the Kingdom of England, was the place.

There was no turning back now, for all Europe knew of the event. It was to be a meeting where one of the kings would most likely meet his death. Both solemnly drew up their wills. King Charles invested his eldest son, Charles, prince of Salerno, with power over his kingdom during his absence. King Peter sent for Queen Constance, who arrived in Sicily on April 16 with their two younger sons, James and Frederick, and their daughter, Violante. Alfonso, the eldest, was left behind in Aragon as he would inherit his father's kingdom. James was given Sicily with his mother Constance as the regent. Three outstanding men were with her, but the one who played the most vital role in the next acts was Roger of Lauria, the Grand Admiral.

The kings with their knights and royal retinues proceeded to the agreed place, although it is unlikely that either one really intended to fight the duel. Nevertheless, there had to be an end to the comedy in which both could save face. The solution arrived at was nothing short of brilliant.

On the appointed day, King Peter arrived in the early morning with his champions and the heralds announced his presence, but since his opponent was not there to meet him he promptly took his men and went back to his camp. Some hours later, Charles arrived with all the pomp and ceremony expected of a king. Similarly, there was no opponent there to meet him. Quite simply, the date and place had been carefully established, but the hour had not been announced. Clearly the kings, or their seconds, had arrived at an understanding.

The charade was over with each king claiming victory and accusing his opponent of cowardice. This was indeed theater on a grand scale where the actors gathered up their props and marched their cast back to prepare for the next act as the fate of Sicily still remained in the balance.

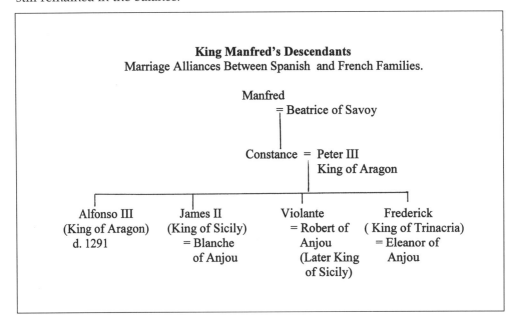

King Manfred's Descendants
Marriage Alliances Between Spanish and French Families.

Manfred
= Beatrice of Savoy

Constance = Peter III
King of Aragon

| Alfonso III (King of Aragon) d. 1291 | James II (King of Sicily) = Blanche of Anjou | Violante = Robert of Anjou (Later King of Sicily) | Frederick (King of Trinacria) = Eleanor of Anjou |

War Between the Aragonese and Angevin Dynasties for the Island of Sicily

The farce was over, and each king had to return and face the many problems at home. King Peter had to prepare against an attack on his own Kingdom of Aragon and Valencia that the Pope planned to give to a "good Catholic," Charles of Valois, the youngest son of the French King Philip. Sicily was left in the hands of Queen Constance and their son James.

There was much activity in the Mediterranean seas where Roger of Lauria, Queen Constance's able Grand Admiral, had gained control. After destroying much of the Angevin fleet, he brought his galleys to the Bay of Naples and captured Capri and Ischia, the islands that stand like sentinels guarding the entrance to the bay. A new fleet was being built in the shipyards of Naples even as Roger used Capri and Ischia as a base for raids along the coast.

The proud Neapolitans were quite understandably infuriated by the blockade of their harbor and blamed the French for their plight. Taking advantage of Charles's absence in France where another fleet was being prepared, they took matters into their own hands and pressured his son and heir, the Prince of Salerno, to disobey his father's orders to remain on the defensive. A new fleet was ready in Naples and on June 5, 1284, just a year after the duel of the kings was supposed to have decided everything, the unsuspecting prince led his galleys out of the harbor and right into the arms of Roger of Lauria's main fleet, which had been assembled to await the arrival of King Charles with his formidable armada from Provence. It was a tragic mistake on the part of the prince, and it cost him dearly. Admiral Roger soon had his rival's galleys surrounded, and most were captured along with their crews. The greatest prize of all, however, was the Prince of Salerno himself. The young eagle had tried his wings, risking his life by leading his men into battle, and had lost not only his navy but also his own freedom.

Roger of Lauria lost no time in using his royal hostage to good advantage. He advised the Princess of Salerno that he would guarantee the safety of his prisoner, her husband, in exchange for the release of one who had languished in Angevin prisons for eighteen years following the death of her father. This was Beatrice, the daughter of Manfred by his second wife, and the half-sister of Queen Constance, who had over the years tried without success to gain her release. With her husband's safety at stake, the Princess of Salerno agreed to hand over the prisoner. Roger took his flagship to pick up Beatrice, then set sail for Sicily with his two royal passengers on board, one to freedom and the other to captivity.

King Charles and his fleet arrived in Naples one day too late, and his first task was to put down the riots that had broken out. It was a "Sicilian Vespers" all over again as many Frenchmen were massacred by the angry mob. Some 150 of the suspected ringleaders of the uprising were ordered hanged, and calm was restored. Naples was the place where the hated King Charles had witnessed, on his own orders, the decapitation of the young Conradin. This must have given him pause as he now contemplated the fate of his own son, the eldest and the only one living, yet he is recorded as having made the following remarks on hearing of his son's capture: "Who loses a fool loses nothing" and "Why is he not dead for disobeying us?"

Charles despised his son, who had limped his way through life following a childhood accident. One thing he did well, however, was produce royal offspring. He had thirteen legitimate children to his credit, eight of whom were boys, so the succession was in no danger. King Charles consoled himself and reassured the Pope with that fact.

Determined to pursue his goal to recover Sicily, Charles left Naples in June with an awesome force, described by the chroniclers as in the tens of thousands, and marched southward as the navy followed closely off shore. In spite of superior numbers, Charles was unable to land on Sicily or dislodge the Aragonese from their foothold on the mainland. He decided to retreat eastward to the peaceful Apulia and winter there, planning for the next campaign. He spent Christmas at Melfi and then proceeded to Foggia, where he died on January 7, 1285. The dying king was said to have uttered these last words as recorded by Friar Salimbene: *"Lord God, as I believe that Thou art my savior, I pray Thee to have mercy on my soul. Thou knowest that I took the Kingdom of Sicily for the sake of the Holy Church and not for my own profit or gain. So Thou wilt pardon my sins."*

Charles was not loved by his subjects, nor were the Frenchmen he brought with him to lord over the Italians whose sentiments were summed up in these words of the friar:

> For the French are extremely proud and foolish people, terrible and accursed, a people who hold all other nations of the world in contempt, especially the English and the Lombards, and by "Lombards" they mean all Italians. . . . For after the French have a few drinks they think they can conquer the whole world with a single blow.

Charles died as his kingdom crumbled around him and with the humiliation of knowing that his heir was a prisoner on the island that had eluded his grasp—Sicily.

A New Cast and Independence for Sicily

The year 1285 was characterized by a series of deaths. The death of Charles I in January was followed by that of Pope Martin IV in March, King Philip III of France in October, and King Peter of Aragon in November. As a teenager of seventeen, Philip IV became King of France. Succeeding his father as King of Aragon was Alfonso, while his younger brother James was crowned King of the island of Sicily in Palermo in February 1286.

It was a young and exciting new cast that now came on the scene, but they were no more successful than their predecessors in making peace. It seemed that every prince and king in Europe was somehow involved, not to mention the opposition of the next popes, who insisted there could be no peace until Sicily was returned to the Angevins to whom it had been given by the papacy. The new pope, Honorius, not only refused to recognize James as King in Sicily but excommunicated him, along with his mother, Constance, and all the people of that rebel island.

Charles II (the Lame), who had succeeded his father as King of Sicily (Naples), began his reign as a powerless prisoner of the Aragonese. He was quite willing to relinquish claims on the island of Sicily in exchange for his freedom, but the Pope adamantly refused to sanction such a deal and planned an invasion of the island instead. Once again the gallant admiral, Roger of Lauria, came to the rescue of the Sicilians; in June of 1287 a great battle took place in the Bay of Naples that was watched from shore by thousands of excited spectators. Roger captured forty-eight galleys and the Pope's crusade to bring Sicily back into the Angevin fold was aborted.

In an attempt to reach a settlement, King Alfonso freed his captive, King Charles II, on condition that he would give up his sons as hostages and *not* take the title of "King of Sicily," which implied the right to both the island as well as the mainland. The Pope forced the title on him in spite of his promise to King Alfonso, whereupon the frustrated Charles, as a man of honor, offered to have himself rearrested. The whole Sicilian affair had the world in turmoil, and Alfonso was ready to abandon the island to its fate—along with brother James and mother Constance as well—when in

February of 1291 he suddenly died of fever at the age of twenty-seven. We reach another turn down the winding road of Italy's history.

Alfonso died as a bachelor king without heirs, so his brother James suddenly inherited the Kingdom of Aragon. He left Sicily in the hands of young Frederick, who acted as his lieutenant. James, like his brother Alfonso, was soon pressured to return Sicily to the Angevins. A solution was sought through a series of marriages: King James agreed to marry King Charles's daughter Blanche, while his sister Violante would marry Charles's son Robert. With these double knots the ties between the two dynasties would be strong, but Frederick would have to be removed from the disputed island of Sicily. This would be achieved by marrying him off to the heiress of Constantinople, but he was saved by her intelligent refusal to marry a dispossessed prince. Still more significant was the fact that the Sicilians, on learning of the arrangement, made it clear once more that they would never again live under any hint of French rule and would not have Blanche either. Instead they asked Frederick to stay on as their king. He was crowned King of Sicily at Palermo on December 11, 1295, in defiance of King James.

The brothers James and Frederick were now at war with each other. Admiral Roger of Lauria had followed James to the court of Aragon, and it was he who had the unpleasant task of destroying the fleet of young rebel-brother Frederick. A solution came in an unexpected way. In accordance with the previous agreement, in 1298 Constance took her daughter Violante to be married to Prince Robert, now heir to the throne of Sicily (Naples) following the death of his older brother.

It was no doubt through Violante's mediation between her new husband, Robert, and brother Frederick that a treaty was eventually reached between the warring parties. On August 31, 1302, in the hills on the western side of the island of Sicily where Angevin troops had been fighting, the historic "Peace of Caltabellotta" was signed. Sicily was given its independence, and Frederick would be king for his lifetime with the title of King of Trinacria, the Three-cornered-Isle. The title "King of Sicily" would remain with the Angevins, but would in the meantime be restricted to mean just the mainland. What was in a name change as long as the island was free?

As part of the treaty, Frederick agreed to marry Eleanora, the thirteenth and last child of King Charles II. The wedding was celebrated with great pomp in May of the following year at Messina. The Aragonese and the Angevin dynasties had now been united by one more marriage knot as three children of Constance and Peter III of Aragon had married children of King Charles II. After an often bitter twenty-year struggle, Sicily was at last free with a new name and her own king. For thirty-five years, until his death in 1337, Frederick ruled as King of the Three-cornered Isle—TRINACRIA.

CHAPTER THREE

The Fourteenth Century: An Age of Turbulence

Dante and His Times

"And thus Fortune turns this world, and shifts its inhabitants with the revolutions of her wheel."

—Leonardo Bruni Aretino

We will now retrace our steps in time and travel northward, leaving behind the world of kings, princes, knights, sea, countryside, castles, churches, and southern cities that dip their feet in the warm waters of the Mediterranean to enter another world. Not of the royal dynasties, our guides will be poets, popes, adventurers, saints, and heroes.

We will first walk with the great poet Dante Alighieri (1265–1321) who lived during the period covered in the previous chapter. The world knows Dante as a poet, but as we travel at his side we will see another man who was so tragically, and perhaps providentially, a part of the history of his time. The conflict between Pope and Emperor had resulted in the emergence of two rival factions in the north, the papalist Guelphs and the imperialist "Ghibellines." Allegiances to these parties set city against city and family against family. This was the world of which Dante was both a unique product and a helpless victim. No wonder we find some of the protagonists of his time suffering the torments of his *Inferno*.

We now enter the urban, land-locked, commercial center that was medieval Florence. This is where Dante was born in 1265, the same year that Charles of Anjou arrived in Rome to take over the south. Florence was a rich and prosperous city that flourished through commerce, the wool trade, and banking on an international scale. Even the popes relied on the Florentine moneylenders to finance their wars. Dante's own father and grandfather were moneylenders, and his family was part of the economic life of the commercial commune. As a city boy, Dante wandered the streets with the rest of the pack; as a young man, although he was a serious student, he found time to enjoy the mundane side of life in the city along with his friends.

Yet for all her wealth and apparent prosperity, Florence was a city in which the Ghibelline and Guelph factions had been engaged in a power struggle that went back to the beginning of the thirteenth century. Florence and Tuscany had always been a close ally of the papacy, but during the reign of Emperor Frederick II the city began to slip away from papal control. In 1239 Guelph leaders were forced to leave town when Frederick of Antioch, a bastard son of the Emperor, was sent there as the *podestà*, an imperial governor. In 1246 and again in 1248, the Guelphs had been chased into exile by German horsemen.

The tide turned again when Charles of Anjou arrived on the scene. Ghibelline domination ended, and Florence was back under the control of the Guelphs as she aggressively expanded her territory, making war against the cities of Pisa and Arezzo, supporters of empire. On June 11, 1289, Arezzo was defeated by the Guelphs. Dante, a young man of twenty-four years, took part in that battle as a patriotic Florentine, mounted and in the first rank according to one of his earliest biographers, none other than Giovanni Boccaccio, better known as the author of the famous *Decameron.*

Nevertheless, trouble was brewing in the now ruling Guelph party. With the rise of the guilds a new middle class had emerged, referred to as *popolani grassi,* "fat commoners." In fact, Dante entered political life as a member of such a guild, the physicians and apothecaries guild because of his studies in philosophy which, thanks to Frederick II, were a required prelude to medicine. After 1295 Dante was an important figure in Florentine politics and in 1300, which turned out to be a fateful year, he became a *priore.* In the spacious and beautiful Piazza della Signoria still stands the imposing Palazzo Vecchio, begun in 1298 and called the Palazzo dei Priori. This was the political stage of Florence where Dante was one of the actors.

The tragic sequence of events which were to unfold began when the papal Guelphs split into two factions: the Blacks (Neri) roughly representing the bankers, merchants, and artisans, and the Whites (Bianchi), which included the nobility. The ambitious, worldly, and powerful Boniface VIII, who became pope in 1294 and whose acquaintance we have already made, played a key role in Florentine politics when the conflict between Blacks and Whites had erupted in outright belligerence. Families took sides and even within some families loyalties were split between the two parties. Fear reigned in the city, which was like a house divided as rival gangs made the streets unsafe. Unable to bring order to the city, the Pope called on Charles of Valois, brother of the ruling king of France, to invade Tuscany. Once more a pope had called on the French to intercede on behalf of the papacy in Italian affairs.

Dante was a patriot rather than a partisan, favoring neither party, but he opposed the solution of Pope Boniface, who had the support of the Blacks, so Dante became a leader of the most resolute element of the Whites. He journeyed to Rome in October 1301 as one of the emissaries to negotiate with the intransigent Pope. Little did the young Dante know that he would never see Florence again. During his absence, Charles of Valois entered the city with French soldiers on November 1, and in his wake the Blacks took power. Vendettas, arson, rape, and plunder followed. Important Whites were exiled or forced to pay fines. Dante was exiled along with countless others and later condemned to death for his political activities. He had lost all his worldly possessions as well as his family. Remaining in Florence were his young children and his wife, Gemma Donati, whose family supported the rival Blacks.

Dante's wanderings took him from city to city over the next years as he sought ways to return home, but he was destined to watch history unfold as an exile. The death of Pope Boniface in 1303 and subsequent transfer of the papal seat to Avignon were of no help to him, nor was the brief appearance of another emperor in the person of Henry VII, who came on the Italian scene in 1310 to get crowned. With Henry's death by fever at a place called Buonconvento, near Siena, in August of 1313, Dante's hopes of returning to Florence faded. He found a last place of refuge in Ravenna, whose lord treated him with respect and kindness. It was here that the Florentine exile completed the greatest work of his life, the *Divina Commedia.* Instead of using the traditional vehicle of the Latin language, Dante wrote in the Florentine vernacular, which he elevated to a literary form, following on the foundations of the "Sicilian School" of poets.

The *Commedia* takes the reader back through history and on a spiritual journey through Hell, Purgatory, and Paradise, but it has its beginnings with an event in real life. In writing to a friend, Dante had said: "All my troubles and hardships had their cause and rise in the disastrous meetings held during my priorate." Compare now the words of the poet as he sets out on the journey of his spiritual life in these powerfully poetic first lines of the poem that describe similar beginnings:

> *Nel mezzo del cammin di nostra vita*
> *mi ritrovai per una selva oscura,*
> *che la diritta via era smarrita.*

> *[In the middle of our life's course*
> *I found myself in a dark forest,*
> *for I had lost the right path.]*

The action of the poem begins on Good Friday in 1300; Dante was thirty-five years old when he lost his way, halfway through the normal seventy-year life span of a man.

Yet it was not in the capacity of a poet that Dante would spend his last days. Once more he was caught up in the nets of history. Aggressive Venice was planning to attack Ravenna, and Dante, the man with the persuasive golden tongue, was sent to mediate with the Doge, an assignment he gladly accepted out of gratitude to his hosts. Dante's words were his only weapon, but the Doge feared his power and refused him audience. Stricken with malaria and burning with fever, Dante began the arduous journey back to Ravenna. He died during the night of September 13, 1321, only a few days after his return.

For all the power of his pen, Dante made no impact on the political history of Italy. It was as though he had been swept from Florence and carried along on the tide of events to be washed up on the eastern shore of the peninsula at Ravenna. However, during his stormy journey through life, Dante produced one of the greatest creative works ever written. In doing so he gave Italy a language that would later be known as Italian and immortality to the name—Dante.

Here is the door to a restored medieval house in Via Dante Alighieri, reputedly the birthplace of the poet. The caption over the door reads: "I was born and raised on the beautiful River Arno in the Great City."

Marco Polo: The Venetian Merchant's Son and His Travels

A contemporary of the great Dante was the Venetian Marco Polo (1255–1324). Marco was born ten years before Dante and outlived him by two or three years. Both men are well known to posterity for the accounts of their travels, but whereas Dante's great journey was one of the imagination through his *Inferno, Purgatorio, and Paradiso,* Marco's journeys took him to the edge of the world. So extraordinary were his experiences that the account of his travels was considered tales of marvels. Dante wrote his *Commedia* while in exile, whereas Marco Polo's incredible account took form in a Genoese prison.

The person of Marco Polo, in spite of the familiarity of his name, remains something of an enigma. His father, Niccolò, and his uncle Matteo were merchants who traded with Constantinople. Caught up in the events of the time when the Mongol hordes were pushing their way to the very gates of Europe, in 1255 the brothers found themselves invited to the court of the great Kublai Khan, where they remained or were detained. After many years of service at the court, they were sent back to Italy on a mission to the Pope with a request from Kublai Khan for preachers and teachers to instruct his subjects in western ways and religion.

The two brothers had been away for fifteen years. Niccolò returned to find that his wife, who was expecting a child when he left on his long journey, had died giving birth to Marco, whom he now set eyes on the for first time. The Polo brothers kept the promise made to Kublai, and when they finally set out on their return voyage to China in the year 1272 they took with them the young Marco, now a bright young man of seventeen, ready for adventure alongside his father and his uncle.

The trio set out from Venice by ship, but their journey continued by the land route, through Persia, across great ranges of mountains, the wild region of the Pamir, and the Gobi desert. Three years later, in 1275, they were finally once more in the presence of the great Khan. Marco was particularly well received. He learned the Mongol language and entered the service of the Khan, who entrusted him with important missions throughout his empire. Seventeen years were spent in the service of the Khan and the Polos were anxious to return home. The opportunity finally came when the Khan received a request for their services to escort a princess to the Persian court. The Khan agreed to let them go, for who else could carry out such a dangerous mission! Plans were made, vessels were prepared, and in 1292 the Polos and their party set out on a long sea journey. After innumerable adventures, difficulties, and sickness that claimed many lives, the three Polos arrived at the Persian court with their precious charge, then continued on their way home.

It must have been an emotional moment when in 1295 they finally caught sight of the city of Venice, from which they had set sail almost twenty-five years earlier, as if emerging magically from the shimmering waters of the lagoon, a magic exquisitely captured on canvas by the great Venetian artist Canaletto some four centuries later.

Marco, now a mature man entering his forties, was back to play his role in Italian history. Venice and Genoa, the great maritime rivals on opposite coasts who could only strike at each other by taking to the sea, were at war again. A Genoese fleet had arrived in the waters of the Adriatic, and a Venetian fleet was sent out to engage it. Marco Polo had been given the command of a Venetian vessel, which sailed to encounter the Genoese off the Dalmatian coast. Unfortunately, the Venetians were defeated in their own waters, and Marco was captured and taken back to Genoa as a prisoner.

It is not known how long Marco was held, but his father and uncle feared that he might have to live out the rest of his life in captivity, such was the climate of animosity between Genoa and Venice, and they used their power to gain his release. Sources suggest his captivity was anywhere between one and four years, but whatever the case may be the time of confinement proved fruitful. He chanced to have as a prison companion a Pisan by the name of Rusticiano, a writer of romantic tales of some note, to whom Marco Polo apparently dictated his story with the help of notes sent to him from Venice. It is believed that this first manuscript was written in a Provençal French, the language Rusticiano used for his romantic writings, and because it was not in Latin may have been considered part fantasy. Rusticiano introduces himself in the prologue, in which he praises Marco for his great knowledge, which deserves to be recorded, and ends with these words:

> And may I tell you that in acquiring this knowledge he spent in those various parts of the World good twenty-six years. Now, being thereafter an inmate of the Prison at Genoa, he caused Messer Rusticiano of Pisa, who was in said prison likewise, to reduce the whole to writing; and this occurred in the year 1298 from the birth of Jesus.

In any event, the account of these travels, written and circulated in the year 1298, would bring immortality to Marco Polo who might otherwise have disappeared from the annals of history along with many others like him.

For the next quarter of a century there is no record of Marco Polo's activities. It is known that he married and fathered daughters, but he had no son to carry on his name. He died in Venice on January 8, 1324, and was buried according to his wish at the church of San Lorenzo. However, Marco Polo's tomb was obliterated when the present church of San Lorenzo was built over the site of the old one. More lasting even than stone, his monument is the book which we know as *The Travels of Marco Polo*, and which for the Italians is simply *Il Milione*.

The Papacy of Avignon (1305–1377)

The death of Pope Boniface VIII marked the dawn of a new era in papal history. The seat of the papacy was moved to Avignon, France, where it remained for the next seventy-two years. How did this come about, and what were the consequences for Italy?

Boniface had become all too powerful and when he issued his famous bull of *Unam Sanctam*, virtually making himself a Caesar, the French king demanded he be tried as a heretic. Before Boniface could respond with excommunication, he was arrested by French emissaries who broke into his palace at Anagni. With the collusion of the rival Colonna family of Rome, Boniface was hauled back to Rome as a prisoner. Although his captivity lasted only a few days before he was rescued by his supporters, the trauma no doubt hastened his death, barely a month later on October 11, 1303.

Boniface's successor, Benedict XI, died within a year, and eleven months passed before the conclave elected the archbishop of Bordeaux (then within the territory of the English) who took the title of Clement V. Clement chose Lyons, France, as the place of coronation in November 1305 and on March 9, 1309, he moved his residence to the safety of Avignon.

In Rome, rival factions continued the struggle for power. No longer the center of the Christian world, the population dwindled as the city was gradually deserted and buildings succumbed to the ravages of time. All the pomp and splendor that came with the papacy was gone. It was in strange contrast to the days of Boniface VIII during whose pontificate the papacy had reached the height of temporal as well as spiritual power. Boniface, described as "less a priest than a king," had held sway over kings and princes. The chroniclers have given us a fleeting image of this man who, following his coronation at Saint Peter's, is said to have proceeded along the route to the Basilica of San Giovanni in Laterano mounted on a white horse led for a stretch of the way by King Charles II of Naples and the King of Hungary.

Dante, who it will be remembered had met Pope Boniface as an emissary on that fateful visit to Rome in 1301, left for posterity a different kind of vision, one of Boniface hanging upside down in hell with flames leaping from his feet. Yet there was another side to this great man of learning who founded the University of Rome as well as the University of Avignon. His philosophy concerning learning was spelled out in the edict establishing the latter university in which he states *"that uncultured man . . . should be trained by science and art, and for this reason divinely granted that the different races of men, speaking various languages, should by means of Latin literature be enabled to hold intercourse with one another."*

Universality and mutual understanding, notwithstanding these lofty ideals, were becoming more and more an impossible dream. In the Italian peninsula, city-states and republics made war against each other and only their hatred of the foreigner gave them common cause, an embryonic sense of nationalism. The popes continued to pull political strings from the safety of Avignon. The Holy Roman Empire, in the last throes of death, would now and then show a glimmer of life when a brave and ambitious German king, following the outdated tradition established by Charlemagne centuries earlier, would dare to cross the Alps, walk carefully through the mire of Italian politics, then run from Milan with the symbolic Iron Crown of the Lombards as his passport to enter Rome and get the final prize—the Crown of Emperor. Those who ventured on such a course during the fourteenth century were few in number and their influence was limited.

Henry VII was crowned Emperor in 1312 and died in Italy in 1313. He is buried in the cathedral at Pisa. Louis IV, of Hohenstaufen lineage, was excommunicated by the pope. He was crowned in Rome by representatives of the citizens in 1327 and was therefore not considered a legitimate emperor. Charles IV was crowned in Rome by a papal legate on April 5, 1355. As promised, he left the next day and returned home to Prague, which he made his imperial capital.

In the absence of popes and emperors, the power vacuum was filled by the strongmen or *Signori* who ruled as despots, giving rise to the sovereign states in northern Italy known as *Signorie*.

Francesco Petrarca and Cola di Rienzo: A Poet Laureate and His Idol

There is a story to be told about two great men who lived during the absence of the popes from Rome. They were Francesco Petrarca (1304–74) and the Roman Cola di Rienzo (1313-54). What these two men had in common was a profound knowledge of antiquity and a dream to make Rome great once more. When their paths met in Avignon, there began an association in which Petrarca was the ultimate inspiration and the younger Cola di Rienzo the instrument which could make his dreams a reality.

Petrarca stands out as one of the few great literary men of the fourteenth century, along with Dante and Boccaccio. Petrarca's father was a victim of Florentine politics, for he had been forced to flee the city at about the same time as Dante and arrived in Avignon in 1311 in search of employment. It was here that Petrarca, though born in Italy, grew up and finally made the family name famous. As a young man he studied law, first in France and then in Italy at the famous University of Bologna, but at age twenty-two he abandoned his legal studies and returned to the court of Avignon. His exceptional talent as a poet soon blossomed and was recognized early in his career. Virgil was his model and studies of ancient civilizations his passion, but a visit to Rome in 1337 provided the emotional experience that awakened in him a strong sense of patriotism. Just three years later, when the cult of poetry that had been dead for 1,000 years was being celebrated, Petrarca received invitations from both Paris and Rome to be crowned poet laureate, but he chose Rome, and there on April 8, 1341, he accepted the laurel wreath, which he placed on the tomb of Saint Peter in a symbolic gesture. At this time Petrarca was writing one of his major works, "Africa," his epic poem of Italy in which his hero was Scipio "Africanus," the general who had conquered Hannibal and freed Italy from the foreigner.

Petrarca was grieved by the condition of Italy, the wars of princes, and the presence of foreigners strutting around the ancient imperial capital, but he was a powerless poet. He was to find his hero in the person of Cola di Rienzo, the young Roman who had been chosen by the Popular Party to lead an embassy to Avignon in 1342, one of whose missions was to entreat the Pope to return to Rome and bring order to the city.

Cola di Rienzo had already come a long way. Son of an innkeeper and a humble washerwoman, he grew up surrounded by the crumbling buildings and monuments that were the pages of Rome's history book, and he asked himself, "Where are these good Romans?" Cola became a notary by profession, but his passion was history and antiquity; Petrarca found in him a kindred spirit who shared his interests and his dreams. The new pope, Clement VI, was equally taken by Cola's learning and eloquence. When this young Roman returned to Italy after a lengthy stay in Avignon, it was as notary of the Roman City Treasury.

Cola's giddy rise to power as a protégé of the absent Pope was phenomenal, much to the surprise and joy of Petrarca, who continually championed his career. Cola became leader of the Popular Party, but was constantly at odds with the powerful baronial families who controlled parts of the city, continually feuded against each other, and neglected the citizens of Rome, a lawless place where there was constant fighting. How could one continue to live in a city where wives were dragged from the beds of their husbands, workers were robbed at the very gates of the city, and the throats of pilgrims were cut by robbers? Cola di Rienzo appealed to the Romans from the steps of the Capitol to take back their city. They made him their leader and on August 1, 1347, he was given full dictatorial powers. He took the title of "Tribune," as in Roman times, and he was so crowned on August 15.

For the time being the nobles had been beaten. Riding high on success, Cola di Rienzo, who had declared all Italians to be Roman citizens, invited the princes and potentates of other cities to come to Rome. With this action he fell from the Pope's grace, for he had become a threat to papal interests. Indeed, the messenger who carried a letter to the Pope announcing Cola's coronation was not received at Avignon. Beaten and bloodied by order of the Pope or his cardinals, his letters torn and scattered, the young man returned to Rome. An outraged Petrarca penned words of indignation and regret to his hero, whose position was now weakened. The nobility was back on the offensive, and a desperate Cola took extreme measures against them. There followed a period of atrocities and killings, and Cola began to lose the support of the people. But his most tragic mistake was his alliance with King Louis of Hungary, whose help he sought against the Italian nobility. For the patriotic Petrarca, Cola's move was a devastating blow. How could his hero appeal to a foreigner when it was foreign influence that they were trying to eliminate?

Before the year was out, Cola's actions had alienated even his supporters, and he was forced to resign. On December 15, 1347, like an actor booed by his audience, he slipped from the Roman stage and took refuge in the wild hills of the Abruzzi. There he remained with the Franciscan friars for the next two years, a fugitive and excommunicate.

During this period, the worst disasters were visited on Italy. Rome was shaken by strong earthquakes, which further damaged or destroyed her already crumbling buildings, and freak floods in the north inundated the fields and brought even more destruction to the cities. Worst of all was the catastrophic plague, later to be known as the Black Death, which in 1348 swept through the cities like a silent killer, leaving in its wake a scene of death and misery beyond imagination. It was at this time that the third great literary man of the century, Giovanni Boccaccio, fled plague-ridden Florence and wrote his famous *Decameron*. For all the humor and naughtiness of the 100 stories contained therein, the Preface to the Ladies contains some chilling descriptions of the Black Death, which is said to have claimed the lives of almost half the population of Italy.

Petrarca, who was in Parma at the time, survived the plague, which claimed most of his friends there. The plague also took his beloved Laura, the lady who inspired his poetry. Cola di Rienzo, somewhere in the hills, was another survivor, and he was about to emerge from hiding. In July 1350 he journeyed to Prague to seek audience with Charles IV, claimant to the imperial throne. The reception he received was most unfriendly, for he was soon clapped into prison as an enemy of the Pope from whom Charles expected to receive the worthless crown.

As for Petrarca, he was back in Avignon and continued to advise the Pope in matters relating to Rome where the baronial families, the Colonna and the Orsini, continued to battle it out with each other and the plebeians, and a papal legate had been forced to flee for his life after being set upon by the populace. One might well ask what an angry mob might have done to a French pope had he set foot in that wild and wanton city?

Meanwhile, the matter of what to do with the languishing Cola came to the surface when the Pope ordered Charles IV to return him to Avignon to stand trial, presumably for heresy, and in July 1352 Cola was taken from his cramped, cold cell in Prague to enjoy the fresh air and the long journey to his new lodgings, a spacious tower in Avignon where he was attached to the vaulted ceiling by a large chain around his foot.

Before the trial took place, Pope Clement VI became ill, and on December 6, 1352, he died. The problem of what to do about Cola was inherited by his successor, Innocent VI. Petrarca, who had not forgotten his unfortunate hero, pondered on how he might save this man whose only crime had been to champion the cause of the Italians; Petrarca had been the most responsible for encouraging him. The Italians should decide his fate or, at the very least, Cola should be given a public trial. Petrarca took up his pen once more and in his inimitable way called upon the Roman People in a very lengthy epistle to "be sure to exact the return of the prisoner, or to demand justice" (Sine Titulo, IV) Cosenza.

The new pope, displaying a high degree of diplomacy, solved the Cola problem most craftily. He not only absolved him but returned him to his people as a senator in his name, and wrote to the Romans on September 16, 1353, asking them to welcome him back joyfully. Cola was released and sent on his way, for the second time in his life returning to Rome from Avignon armed with a papal appointment.

That year had been a violent one in Rome, and the Pope may have thought that he was indeed throwing his prisoner to the wolves. The restless Roman mob had rioted as a result of grain prices. They had even set upon their own appointees, one of whom had been stoned to death. By the end of the year the newly appointed Spanish Cardinal Albornoz had taken possession of the city, all others having fled.

Cola di Rienzo did not arrive in Rome until August 1 of the following year, 1354, the seventh anniversary of his becoming a tribune. However, his moment of glory was even shorter this time. Just sixty-nine days later, October 8, 1354, there was a violent uprising as people stormed the Capitol. When Cola appeared on the steps he was met with a shower of stones. One chronicler reports that he tried to escape, but was dragged back to the steps of the Capitol and there, near the lion statue, he was struck down. His headless body was dragged from the capitol and hung near the church of San Marcello close to the Colonna palace, where it remained for two days. The Colonnas ordered the Jews to burn the body in the Mausoleum of Augustus as a

ROME: Statue of Cola di Rienzo near the steps leading up to the Capitol. This monument to his memory was placed on the spot where he was massacred. The sculptor left the features vague which adds to the mystique.

mockery of Cola's dreams of Rome's former glory. His ashes were then scattered to the wind. He is remembered by the enigmatic statue on the steps of the Capitol and the long Via Cola di Rienzo running from the Tiber River to the Vatican City.

Born five centuries ahead of his time, Cola di Rienzo was an Italian patriot. Petrarca never ceased to consider his hero an instrument of his dreams of peace and unity in Italy, and has immortalized him in his writings. Petrarca, who left Avignon at the same time as Cola, never to set foot on French soil again, lived with the memory of his hero for twenty more years until his death near Padua during the night of July 18-19, 1374. He was found the next morning with his head resting on a manuscript of Virgil. It was a peaceful end and in stark contrast to the violent death of his unfortunate countryman.

CHAPTER FOUR

Anatomy of a Signoria

The Rise of the Visconti

By the middle of the fourteenth century, the northern part of the Italian peninsula had been fragmented into a number of city-states of varying sizes and importance. Some of these were republics, whereas many others were under the control of powerful families, often identified by their names, as a glance at the map will show. The city-state came to be known as a *Signoria* and the lord in power was the *Signore*. Any interference by popes or emperors met with strong resistance, but allegiance to one or the other could be used by a state against a neighbor or by one family against another.

The poet Petrarca had hoped that a growing hatred of the foreigner, French popes, and German emperors would bring all Italians together in the common cause, and his chariot of dreams would be pulled by the patriot Cola di Rienzo. That dream became a nightmare as he watched each *Signoria* proceed to make its own unique and colorful history.

The trend of the times is no better illustrated than by following the fortunes of the Visconti of Milan. Their emblem, depicting a viper devouring an enemy, aptly describes the era of the city-states in the northern part of the Italian peninsula.

Visconti power may be traced back to 1262 when Pope Urban IV appointed Ottone Visconti as archbishop of Milan, a position that brought with it both spiritual and temporal power. He was for a while exiled from the city when a powerful rival family, the della Torre, took over. Ottone later defeated his enemy in battle and returned to power in 1277. Bad blood remained between the two families and divided the city into two camps.

Ottone Visconti transferred his temporal powers to his grandnephew, Matteo I, the founder of the Visconti dynasty, who later became virtual lord of Milan. This was the position he held at the turn of the century when bitter struggles broke out between Guelphs and Ghibellines. At about the time the poet Dante was forced to flee from Florence, the della Torre family again seized power in Milan; Matteo, along with his family, became an exile in the city of Verona.

Matteo Visconti saw his chance to return to Milan when Henry VII came to Italy in October 1310 to claim his crown as Holy Roman Emperor. Matteo wanted to be the first to welcome the emperor-elect when he reached his first stop across the Alps at Asti. Matteo set out at once on the perilous journey from Verona along dangerous roads, for these were days of spies, travelers in disguise, fake friars, fast horses, and city gates that slammed shut at dark. Matteo arrived late at night at Asti and insisted on seeing Henry right away, but he was told, "Go to bed and come back tomorrow."

THE VISCONTI OF MILAN
(Condensed Genealogy)

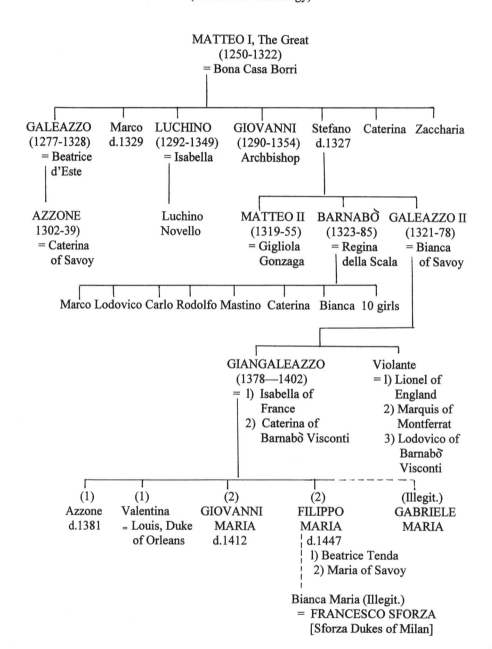

MATTEO I, The Great
(1250-1322)
= Bona Casa Borri

GALEAZZO (1277-1328) = Beatrice d'Este

Marco d.1329

LUCHINO (1292-1349) = Isabella

GIOVANNI (1290-1354) Archbishop

Stefano d.1327

Caterina   Zaccharia

AZZONE 1302-39) = Caterina of Savoy

Luchino Novello

MATTEO II (1319-55) = Gigliola Gonzaga

BARNABÒ (1323-85) = Regina della Scala

GALEAZZO II (1321-78) = Bianca of Savoy

Marco Lodovico Carlo Rodolfo Mastino Caterina Bianca 10 girls

GIANGALEAZZO (1378—1402)
= 1) Isabella of France
  2) Caterina of Barnabò Visconti

Violante
= 1) Lionel of England
  2) Marquis of Montferrat
  3) Lodovico of Barnabò Visconti

(1) Azzone d.1381

(1) Valentina = Louis, Duke of Orleans

(2) GIOVANNI MARIA d.1412

(2) FILIPPO MARIA d.1447
1) Beatrice Tenda
2) Maria of Savoy

(Illegit.) GABRIELE MARIA

Bianca Maria (Illegit.)
= FRANCESCO SFORZA
[Sforza Dukes of Milan]

There were many exiles and Ghibellines who awaited the arrival of the emperor-elect. As head of the noble Milanese families in exile, Matteo was the most useful to the would-be emperor in gaining entry into the hostile city of Milan, which was under the Visconti rival, Guido della Torre. Guido refused to send emissaries to greet the future emperor, let alone agree to open the gates of the city to him.

Henry had come to Italy as a peacemaker, and through negotiations he had tried to reconcile the feuding parties even before he set out on the last stage of his journey, but without success. Finally, with Matteo's help Henry was on his way, escorted by a large force of German cavalry, along with Matteo Visconti and a retinue of exiles. They reached Magenta, some 30 kilometers outside Milan, around sunset on December 22. It was snowing, the sky was dark, and no one dared enter the hostile city of Milan that night, but the next day the clouds had cleared and the city sparkled white in the sunlight. Citizens came to meet the imperial party, and an unwilling Guido della Torre, fearing civil strife, was obliged to open the gates and even make his palace available to the unwanted and uninvited guest.

The unimposing Henry, squint-eyed and slow of speech, had nevertheless quietly imposed his will and ordered the feuding families to be reconciled, prisoners to be freed, and exiles to be readmitted to the city. As the traditional first step in getting the coveted crown of emperor, Henry got the Iron Crown of the Lombards in the church of Sant'Ambrogio in Milan on January 6, 1311, a day that symbolized the giving of gifts and recognition of status. Disturbances then broke out involving the feuding families; Guido della Torre came under suspicion and fled with his followers, and Henry set up a government with his own officials, leaving the city safely under German control.

When Henry set out for Rome he was accompanied by Matteo Visconti, whose help he needed to find his way. Henry's attitude hardened as he came up against the hostile Italian cities. Brescia refused to submit and courageously resisted a siege of four months. Under the walls of this city the now-frustrated and impoverished Henry made a deal with Matteo Visconti. Desperately in need of money to continue his mission, he would appoint Matteo Imperial Vicar of Milan in exchange for 60,000 florins. A resourceful Matteo managed to raise the money and returned to Milan as the *signore.*

Henry proceeded to Rome, but it was not until June 29, 1312, that he finally got the imperial crown from cardinals nominated for this purpose by the Pope in Avignon.

Rome, where Cola di Rienzo was born a year later, was a city in turmoil. Robert of Naples was in control of Saint Peter's, so the coronation took place at Saint John Lateran. From there Henry left to deal with a hostile Florence; unsuccessful, he retreated to Pisa to await a large German force. Henry was to pay a high price for the hollow imperial crown, however, for in August of 1313 he fell victim to an Italian killer fever. He was buried in the beautiful marble cathedral of Pisa and with him also Dante's hope of returning to Florence.

Matteo Visconti was back in control in Milan and, with the help of his sons, he began to expand his territory through the wars that characterize his rule and brought upon his family the wrath of the Pope. The city of Piacenza, which had been considered papal domain, came under the control of the Visconti and Matteo's eldest son, Galeazzo, ruled there as its lord. As the Visconti pushed westward, a frightened Genoa invited King Robert of Naples to be their lord and protector, bringing yet another party into the widening conflict. In an attempt to gain a port for their expanding but landlocked realm, Visconti forces placed Genoa under siege in March 1317, but they withdrew one year later.

Matteo Visconti's eventful life ended January 24, 1322. His death must have been received with joy by the French Pope, who had excommunicated him. Matteo's sons kept his death a secret for several days and buried him in a secret place for fear that papal representatives would disinter his body. Little wonder that when Galeazzo traveled back to Milan from Piacenza to take his father's place he disguised himself as a Germany mercenary to avoid being caught by the Pope's spies. The real war between the Pope and the Visconti was yet to be waged in all its fury.

The Pope's Crusade Against the Visconti

Galeazzo was officially proclaimed *signore* of Milan on December 29, 1322, almost a year after his father's death. Another chapter in Milan's history now began when the Pope launched all-out war against the Visconti family, promising absolution to any who would join the crusade. Visconti gains, beginning with Piacenza, were lost as a motley papal army moved toward Milan and established a base of operations at Monza, just outside the city.

Galeazzo's brothers, Marco and Luchino, headed the Visconti forces, but the German mercenary elements, who had not been paid, rose in mutiny and seized their paymaster, Signor Galeazzo, as hostage. They then threatened to hand Milan over to the della Torre family, whose members were lurking on the outskirts of the city with the Pope's army. Brother Giovanni, who was negotiating with Louis of Bavaria, the next claimant of the imperial crown, was able to come to the rescue and resolve the situation. Papal forces, whose members were lacking any crusading convictions, were finally routed in 1324 and the Visconti's archenemy, Simone della Torre, drowned as he tried to flee across the Adda River. The crusade against the Visconti had failed.

A New Emperor is Crowned

Another chapter in Galeazzo's life and Milan's history is about to begin. For the past fourteen years, since the death of Henry, there had been no Holy Roman Emperor to worry about as a result of succession disputes in Germany, but that was about to change. Louis of Bavaria had emerged as claimant to the imperial crown in spite of the Pope's opposition. In fact, the Pope had excommunicated him; Louis, in turn, had done the unspeakable by accusing the Pope of heresy and declaring him deposed.

In January 1327, a determined and ambitious Louis marched down to Italy. On May 16, he entered Monza with 4,000 cavalry, and the next day a solemn procession came through the gates of Milan. Two weeks later, on May 31, 1327, the excommunicated Louis received the Iron Crown of the Lombards from the hands of an excommunicated bishop. Galeazzo Visconti, the *signore* of Milan, was proclaimed imperial vicar and his brother Giovanni was made archbishop.

Amid the excitement and confusion of an imperial visit, tragedy struck the Visconti family. On July 3 the youngest Visconti brother, Stefano, suddenly died. The cause of his death remains a mystery. Some say he became ill after tasting food that was to be served to Louis. It was later rumored that Stefano's widow, Valentina, accused his brothers of his murder in her will. In those days of rivalry and treachery, poison was usually thought to be the cause of unexplained deaths, and an accusing finger was immediately pointed at a possible suspect.

The day after Stefano's death, Louis ordered the arrest of the newly elevated Galeazzo, along with his brothers Luchino and Giovanni and Galeazzo's son Azzone, on suspicion of conspiracy with the papacy. This was apparently based on a nervous Louis's knowledge of a letter that had been exchanged between the Visconti and the Pope. Here was a real *coup de théâtre* that left the city in a state of shock. Of Matteo's five sons, suddenly three are imprisoned, one is dead, and Marco, the least trustworthy of them all, is running free.

In August Louis set out for Rome, leaving Milan in the hands of a government organized with his German officials. But the Milan incident loomed like a dark shadow as news of the Visconti downfall shook Italy and shocked Europe. Only the Pope in Avignon could chuckle with glee as he witnessed one enemy devouring another, but it soon became evident that the German would have a hard time killing the Visconti viper. Nor could the imperialist supporters understand how Louis could strike down his most ardent defenders on such flimsy grounds of betrayal, and they feared for themselves as many others had diplomatic relations with the Pope. A council of lords of other cities resulted in the release of the Visconti with the exception of Galeazzo, but a very high ransom had to be paid for their freedom.

Louis, like Henry before him, was soon to find out that getting to Rome was no easy task, and he needed more than his German troops to find his way through the maze of intrigues and unfriendly cities. His greatest support came from the lord of Lucca, Castruccio Castracani, later to be a model for Machiavelli's *Il Principe*. Castruccio was a close ally of Milan, and it was he who obtained the release of Galeazzo Visconti. In a reversal of fate, the Visconti, along with Castruccio, were again part of the imperial party that made its way to Rome. Louis was declared Emperor by a Roman People's Parliament on January 17, 1328, and he appointed his own pope, who performed the coronation on May 12 of that year.

Castruccio was soon forced to abandon Emperor Louis to his fate, for his own territory of Lucca had meanwhile come under attack. Galeazzo, accompanied by his son Azzone, went to his aid, but was forced to leave the field of battle with a fever and died on August 6. Just one month later, on September 3, 1328, the same deadly fever, so prevalent in the region, claimed the life of his good friend Castruccio, whose death left the newly crowned Emperor Louis without his right arm.

Emperor Louis's Italian campaign was doomed to failure. In January 1329, we find him in Pisa in dire straits with his mercenary soldiers unpaid. The Visconti are still with him, however, and the astute young Azzone persuades him that he will get the money to pay the troops in exchange for the title of Imperial Vicar of Milan, replacing his deceased father. Azzone got his title, and his uncle Giovanni was made a cardinal. On February 10, Azzone and his two uncles returned to Milan proudly carrying the emblem of the Visconti viper. The party was greeted by a jubilant throng, happy to see the end of a government of German officials, as bells rang out and there was rejoicing and singing in the streets.

The young Azzone, barely twenty-seven years old, had risen above the pack, and a new chapter was about to begin. By the following year, the helpless Emperor had retreated back beyond the Alps. His legacy was the abandoned army of unpaid mercenaries who pillaged the countryside until the next lord needed swords for hire. They would not have long to wait.

Azzone's Signoria

Azzone inherited the position of his father as *signore* of Milan with no threat from his uncles, Luchino and Giovanni, with whom he was on excellent terms. The black sheep of the family seems to have been the impetuous uncle Marco, who arrived in Milan in the middle of August, survivor of his adventures in Tuscany where he had been captain of the Emperor's mercenaries. There were rumors that he had conspired to overthrow Azzone. Whether this was true or not, Marco was invited to a banquet with all the Visconti relatives, following which he was strangled and tossed from a window. A veil of secrecy shrouded the circumstances of his death, as was the case with the demise of brother Stefano. If there had been strife within the Visconti family it had been removed, intentionally or accidentally, and peace brought prosperity.

Azzone consolidated his *Signoria,* improved the conditions of the citizens, drained the fertile lands of the Po valley (which became a rich agricultural region), and brought industry and commerce to Milan. The threat to his power would come from outside.

During Azzone's time the Visconti alliance with the neighboring *Signoria* of Verona, sealed by marriage, turned sour, when in 1329 Mastino della Scala succeeded his father, Cangrande, at one time a patron of Dante. Verona was the setting for Shakespeare's *Romeo and Juliet,* but the first lines of the Prologue that opens the play might well apply to many others, for this was the backdrop of countless dramas of the time.

> *Two households, both alike in dignity,*
> *In fair Verona, where we lay our scene,*
> *From ancient grudge break to new mutiny,*
> *Where civil blood makes civil hands unclean.*

In an era of shifting boundaries and changing alliances, Mastino had swallowed up Treviso, Feltre, Belluno, Brescia, and Parma, and then cast his greedy eyes about for his next victim. He became a threat to the Republics of Venice to the east and Florence to the south, and the two formed a league against the tyrant, joined by smaller neighbors and also the Visconti.

Many of the idle mercenary soldiers were back in the field again as war between Verona and the League broke out, ending with the eventual defeat of Mastino della Scala and the Peace of Venice in January 1339, Verona having lost much of her territory. The wily Mastino had signed a peace treaty, but he found a way of taking revenge against the Visconti by using one of their own. Lodrisio, a disgruntled Visconti cousin, had clashed with Azzone some three years earlier and had fled to Verona. Mastino decided to use him now against his enemy. Mercenaries were rapidly rehired and organized in what came to be known as the famous "Società di San Giorgio."

Milan was shocked when the large force rumbled its way through the regions of Brescia and Bergamo, and was soon across the Adda River. The exiled Lodrisio and his soldiers, no doubt paid by Mastino, were soon on the outskirts of Milan. Like wolves they camped in the snows of this harsh winter and lay in wait for three days. This was Lodrisio's terrain and true hunting ground, for he had owned land here. He, too, carried the emblem of the Visconti viper, and he would soon strike like one. With heavy snow covering his movements, he fell on the Milanese forces before dawn as they slept in their camp outside the city. In the battle that took place in the fields of

The viper swallowing its enemy is a constant reminder of former Visconti power. Here it is part of the logo of the School of Industrial Art which occupies a wing of the Castello Sforzesco in Milan.

Parabiago, the Milanese forces were taken by surprise and were soon overcome by Lodrisio's German mercenaries.

Luchino Visconti was thrown from his horse, grabbed by his enemies, and tied to a tree. As if by miracle, with a thunder of hooves and a cloud of white snow, there appeared on the scene some 300 Savoy cavalry, sent by Milan's ally Turin, who routed the enemy and freed Luchino, whose fate was in the balance. Now that the tide had turned, the German mercenaries took flight and abandoned Lodrisio, who was captured and taken prisoner along with two of his sons. Lodrisio had lost not only the battle but also his freedom.

The battle fought on the snowy fields of Parabiago ended the political-military crisis of Lombardy. Under Azzone, the Visconti *Signoria* was firmly established, but he did not live to enjoy the fruits of this victory. Already ailing at the time of the battle, he died on August 16 of the same year at the age of thirty-six. He left no heir to the Visconti *Signoria* as his wife, Caterina of Savoy, was childless. Milan's destiny was now in the hands of the two uncles that had supported him, Luchino the soldier and Giovanni the archbishop.

The Soldier and the Archbishop

Prosperity had come to Milan under the Visconti and the *Signoria,* like a miniature monarchy, continued to loom large on the colorful canvas of northern Italy. The Visconti had ruled successfully for three generations and on Azzone's death the Council General of Milan elected his two uncles, Luchino and Giovanni, as joint rulers. Luchino assumed the administrative duties while Giovanni continued in his role as spiritual head.

Luchino's position was challenged early on when a conspiracy by the ministers of his young nephews, the sons of deceased brother Stefano, was brought to light. The alleged ringleader of the conspirators was caught and beheaded, along with his wife and their sons. It was a harsh lesson to discourage others who might disturb internal peace. Stefano's children were allowed to live in Milan, where they grew up under the protection of uncle Giovanni, but eight years later, when they reached adulthood, Luchino had them banished.

In addition to a bastard son, Bruzio, who was made Lord of Lodi, Luchino had a son, Luchino Novello, by his lovely young third wife, but her behavior on a trip to Venice with her ladies in waiting created such a scandal that doubts were cast on the paternity of little Luchino Novello. At all events, when Luchino suddenly died in October 1349, it was widely suspected that his wife had arranged to have him poisoned out of fear for her own safety.

Notwithstanding Luchino's troubled private life, Milan had prospered. It was now a bustling manufacturing city, producing fine cloths of silk and wool and even rich materials of gold and silk. Fine armor and coats of mail were prized by all of Europe, and their sale swelled the coffers of Milan, where church and state came together. Great estates produced corn, rye, oats, barley, oil, and wine. Canals were built that connected Milan to the great Po and other rivers of the realm. Irrigation created grassy meadows where fine horses grazed, a great source of riches at a time when the world moved by horsepower. Luchino exempted the commoners from serving in the military so that they were free to work the land and make goods for industry. The plague that had decimated and devastated Florence in 1348 had left Milan relatively unharmed, probably due to Azzone's exceptional hygiene measures. Luchino's last endeavor had been to try to acquire a port for the impressive agricultural-industrial complex that had emerged, but he died before this could be accomplished.

On Luchino's death, Archbishop Giovanni took full power. He followed his brother's policy of expansion, but his methods were very different. Peace treaties were sought with many of the states against whom Luchino had made war in an effort to extend the Visconti domain. Having no heirs, the Archbishop immediately called back his banished nephews and used them to enter into alliances with neighboring states. Two marriages were celebrated in Milan in 1350 when Galeazzo was married to Bianca, sister of the ruling prince of Savoy, and Barnabò to Regina della Scala, of Verona.

Giovanni next sought to extend the boundaries of his *Signoria* even further, but not by wars. His way was more subtle. In 1350 he saw the chance to acquire the coveted Bologna, which he literally bought for an enormous sum from a banker who ruled the city as its lord and tyrant. Bologna had been considered a papal fief, and the Pope immediately sent a legate to protest its purchase by the Visconti vipers, but Giovanni was said to have sent him packing with the message that he, Giovanni, ruled the spiritual domain with a cross in one hand and the temporal with a sword in the other.

It was now time to turn attention to Genoa. Constantly having to defend itself from one foe or the other, the city was under siege by the Aragonese fleet when in 1353 the starving citizens had appealed to Milan for help. Giovanni cleverly refused, whereupon the desperate city agreed to place itself under his rule. Food poured into a hungry Genoa, which now became virtually a part of the Visconti *Signoria*.

Giovanni's long and brilliant career suddenly came to an end with his death on October 5, 1354, after an operation to remove a growth that had appeared above his eyebrow. He had been a power in Milan for a quarter of a century, first alongside his nephew Azzone and then in tandem with his brother Luchino. The unusual and lengthy epitaph inscribed on his tomb lists the cities under his control at his death and also includes these words: "with the right hand I held the staff of the pastor, with the left I held up the sword as a happy lord."

It was in Rome on October 8, 1354, just three days after Archbishop Giovanni's death, that Cola di Rienzo, the poet Petrarca's hero, was killed by the mob. It is here that we meet up in time with events of two separate worlds, Rome and Milan. Petrarca has meanwhile put himself in the service of the Visconti, and we will remain in Milan for the next act, "The Three Vipers."

The Three Vipers

On the death of Giovanni Visconti his three nephews, Matteo II, Galeazzo II, and Barnabò, were confirmed in their roles as *signori*. Now there were three in the driver's seat of the Visconti chariot. The territory, as well as the actual city of Milan, was divided between the three brothers, each controlling two of the city gates giving access to his part of the realm. The enemies of the Visconti were delighted by such an arrangement, which they believed would weaken the power of the *Signoria* of Milan.

The first task of the brothers was to play host to yet another emperor. Charles IV finally fulfilled his threat, or promise, to come down to Italy for his crowns. Indeed, before the body of the Visconti archbishop was cold, Charles had crossed the Alps and with his retinue of German knights was on his way to Milan. As the host city, Milan spared no expense. The Visconti agreed to pay the cost of the coronation—50,000 gold florins—and purchase the imperial vicariat for the price of 150,000. (Compare with the 200,000 previously paid for the city of Bologna.) The coronation took place in Sant'Ambrogio on January 6, 1355. Six days later the newly crowned "King of the Lombards," his pockets full of gold, must have been relieved to get out of Milan, where the gates had been shut both day and night and armored cavalry filled the squares in a show of Visconti strength. As one Italian historian remarked, it was "the Eagle under the control of the Viper."

Charles IV proceeded to the dilapidated Rome and at Easter got his imperial crown. As previously agreed with the Pope, still in Avignon, he immediately left the city to return home. Unfortunately, at Pisa he became involved in the dispute between the Pisans and the Luccans and the place where he was staying with his Empress and retinue was put to flames. Escaping with his life, he fled back through Lombardy where all doors were slammed in his face. As for the Visconti, the real kings of the north, they had already taken leave of their guest and were back to the business of defending their own interests.

In September of that year, the Visconti rule was simplified by the sudden and unexplained death of the oldest brother, Matteo. Since he left no heir, his domain was divided equally between the surviving brothers, Galeazzo getting the western half and Barnabò the eastern part. Although the two brothers ruled as separate lords of their respective areas, they loyally supported each other against threats from the outside. It was a partnership that lasted for a quarter of a century.

The brothers divided Milan into two spheres of influence, but Galeazzo had his mind set on bringing Pavia back into the Visconti orbit. The struggle to recover this city and hold it lasted for most of his lifetime. His archenemy was the Marquis of Montferrat, who had been made imperial vicar of the city by Emperor Charles. Through a series of dramatic events—which included siege, proposed marriage alliances, and wars—Galeazzo finally gained control of the city on November 13, 1359, and took up residence there, leaving Milan to Barnabò. In Pavia he ruled without hindrance as a compassionate gentleman and the city flourished as a capital. The Ticino River was bridged and construction began on a beautiful castle surrounded by high walls, which may still be seen today. In 1361 the famous University of Pavia was founded, giving western Lombardy its own seat of learning.

The Marquis of Montferrat was the cloud on the horizon that was never far away. In 1362 he saw the chance to make his move. Hope had appeared wearing a white cloak when the notorious English soldier of fortune, Sir John Hawkwood with his "White Company," made his fateful entry into Italy at the head of 3,500 cavalry and 2,000 foot soldiers. The English mercenaries, hardened on the battlefields of the Hundred-Year War between England and France, were savage beasts compared to the Italians, who fought according to the rules of chivalry. Sir John was soon on the payroll of the Marquis of Montferrat, and as he advanced on Pavia, leaving a path of devastation in his wake, many were those who joined forces with Montferrat out of fear. Once more Visconti wealth came to the rescue. Galeazzo knew that soldiers of fortune could be bought, and he offered Sir John a handsome reward to simply go away, steering him in the direction of Pisa and Florence, where he would be sure to find yet another paymaster.

Galeazzo brought Pavia into the limelight, but perhaps among his most noteworthy accomplishments were the marriages of his two children into the royal houses of England and France. Once again, the Visconti's wealth was a major factor. As a young boy of twelve, Gian Galeazzo was married off to Isabella, daughter of the impoverished King John II of France, who was desperately in need of money. The young husband was only fifteen when in 1362 Isabella presented him with a baby girl, Valentina. Little could one suspect that she would one day be the excuse for French claims in Italy.

The most spectacular event of the century occurred six years later, when Galeazzo's daughter Violante was married to Lionel, the second son of the English king, Edward III. The wedding, which took place in Milan in June 1368, was the talk of Europe and was recorded in great detail by chroniclers of the day, giving us a glimpse into a world of dazzling extravagance. Violante's dowry, in addition to gold florins, included castles and the town of Alba, some forty miles from Turin. Uncle Barnabò took leave from his war to give the bride away, and the poet Petrarca, whose acquaintance we have already made, was a guest at this wedding of the century. As for the eighteen-course banquet, a glance at the list of dishes served tells much about the culinary art of the "court" of Milan. The feast that was set before the son of the English king included the following:

- whole suckling pigs with flames coming from their mouths
- grilled trout
- sturgeon
- lampreys
- roast calf
- quail and partridges
- ducks and heron
- chicken with lemon sauce
- fat capons with garlic sauce
- beef and eel pasties
- roast kid
- leverets and fawns
- venison and beef galantine
- pullets with red and green sauces
- salted tongues
- rabbits
- peacocks with vegetables
- cheese and fruits

Gifts were brought in with each course and included greyhounds and bloodhounds with beautiful collars and leashes of velvet and silk; hawks and falcons with bells of silver gilt; Milan's famous products such as suits of armor, rolls of gold brocade, and silk from the city's looms; horses bred on the surrounding pastures with gilded leather saddles; lances and shields; chargers with gold bridles and fancy harness; horses for tourneys; and seventy-six steeds for the English barons and gentlemen.

It was with dismay and horror that one learned of the tragic and untimely death of the new groom just a few weeks later. He had died of a fever at Alba, the town his wife had brought as a dowry. Lionel's men treacherously abandoned Galeazzo, who had so lavishly welcomed them, and joined ranks with his old enemy, the Marquis of Montferrat. It must have been a devastating blow for Galeazzo to see his daughter so soon widowed and the money he had spent now turned against him by the barbarians from England.

Four years later, in 1372, still plagued by Montferrat, an ailing Galeazzo was further saddened by the death in childbirth of his daughter-in-law, Isabella. Both his children had now lost their royal spouses.

Galeazzo died at the age of fifty-six in 1378. Gian Galeazzo, his only male heir, now took his father's place alongside a man best known to posterity for his cruel nature—his uncle Barnabò Visconti.

Gian Galeazzo and Uncle Barnabò

The widowed Gian Galeazzo now shared the Visconti *Signoria* with his uncle Barnabò, a man who had gained a reputation as a cruel monster even by medieval standards. Barnabò was a hard worker, and he had no pity for bums and beggars, but wrongdoers were treated ruthlessly, and atrocities committed in the name of order were no secret. Nevertheless, citizens enjoyed prosperity and could walk the streets at night without fear.

Barnabò's rule is characterized by his constant struggle against the papacy, which he hated with a passion, declaring himself pope in his own realm. The conflict went back to 1358 when he took steps to recover Bologna, where the rebellious Giovanni di Oleggio had previously declared himself the *signore*. Hard-pressed, he then sold the city to the papacy, and it was immediately occupied by Church forces. Barnabò laid siege, but Cardinal Albornoz, the papal legate who played such a vital role during the years that followed, built up a large army with Hungarian mercenaries and in 1361 engaged in all-out war. During the years that followed there were endless warfare, changing alliances, leagues formed and broken, and the ever-present problem of foreign mercenaries. It was the threat from the mercenaries that briefly brought together all parties, including the Visconti, in a league against them. But even the Church used their services when they were needed. In 1367 that notorious English soldier of fortune, Sir John Hawkwood, turned up in the service of Barnabò, but five years later we find the rascal on the Pope's payroll. Fearing that a strong papacy would be a threat to her own dominance in Tuscany, Florence entered into an alliance with the Visconti against the volatile Sir John and in 1375 Florence and Milan together "bought" Sir John from the Pope. Loyalty could not be bought, however, and no one knew that better than the astute Barnabò, who sought ties of a different nature. He took out insurance by arranging a marriage between Sir John and his daughter Donnina, an illegitimate child of a favorite mistress.

For the papacy, Barnabò Visconti appeared to be the devil incarnate, and there could be no lasting truce between the two. But in addition to being the target of the papacy, Barnabò was for most of his rule outnumbered and boxed in by the pesky little city-states on his borders, which prevented territorial expansion. These domestic problems did not prevent him from playing his hand at the table of international politics, where the stakes were even higher than the price of a city. It was this broader vision which set the Visconti above their neighbors.

In his personal life, Barnabò was fortunate to have at his side a loyal and extremely fertile wife, Beatrice della Scala, appropriately known as Regina. He had no less than sixteen children by her and claimed another twenty illegitimate offspring. An important part of Barnabò's foreign policy, like that of his brother, was to seek powerful alliances through the marriages of his children, and he cast his line in international waters for the bigger fish. The family became an integral part of his foreign policy as many of his children were married into the powerful families of south Germany.

In contrast to his formidable uncle Barnabò, Gian Galeazzo was alone with the motherless Valentina, his widowed mother, Bianca of Savoy, and his luckless sister Violante for a second time widowed, sacrificed to the Marquis of Montferrat to whom she was married in 1377 and who was killed the following year. Uncle Barnabò had been keeping an eye on happenings in his own backyard and successfully thwarted his nephew's plans to marry Maria of Sicily. He had a plan of his own—what better way of securing control of the western part of the realm than by marrying off one of his daughters to Gian Galeazzo? One of his numerous brood was available and in 1380 the cousins, Gian Galeazzo and Caterina were duly married. No doubt thinking that two knots would be better than one, the following year the widowed Violante was married off to her cousin, Barnabò's son Lodovico.

Now with the Visconti world tied together with matrimonial bonds, attention was once more turned to the outside. The French connections of Gian Galeazzo had been severed with the death of his first wife, Isabella, but Barnabò planned to renew them to his own advantage, using another of his daughters for the purpose. At this juncture Barnabò's real intentions became suspect, and Gian Galeazzo was warned against his uncle by friends and his mother Bianca, who said he should stay away from Milan, where his life may be in danger. Treacherous plans were clearly being hatched and Gian Galeazzo decided to take the initiative in this silent war and go out to meet the danger head on with courage. Taking the bull by the horns, he wrote to Barnabò that he would be passing near Milan on May 5 on his way to visit a shrine and wanted to pay him his respects. Barnabò agreed to meet the timid, priestly nephew whom he despised, and in accordance with his plan Gian Galeazzo rode out of Pavia with an escort of 500 lancers under his capable captain Giacomo dal Verme. The historic event which took place is best described by a chronicler of the time:

> Two miles outside Milan, two sons of Barnabò, Lodovico and Roldolfo, were waiting for their cousin. When they arrived at Porta Ticinese, Giangaleazzo turned outside the walls toward the castle of Porta Giovia that was his by right. At Sant'Ambrogio Barnabò rode up on a mule: he appeared to have no escort. Things happened fast. Barnabò and his sons were surrounded by the Count's officials as previously planned. Giacomo dal Verme grabbed Barnabò and said: "You are a prisoner!" Barnabò exclaimed: "Would you be so bold?" The other retorted: "My lord has so ordered me." Barnabò then turned to his nephew and said: "Do not betray your blood!" Giangaleazzo remained unmoved: Ottone di Mandello seized the reins of the mule, some others took Barnabò's staff of command, some his sword; still others did likewise with Rodolfo and Lodovico, then without delay they proceeded to the castle at Porta Giovia where the three captives were imprisoned and put under strict guard. (Translated from Storia d'Italia)

In that short span of time an important event in history had taken place. Gian Galeazzo rode into Milan as a prince who had come to liberate the people from a cruel tyrant, and they could expect to look forward to better days.

No one came to the aid of the helpless captives, who were imprisoned for life. Barnabò's wife had died the previous year, but his mistress, Donnina Porri, was also imprisoned. Where was Sir John that he did not come to the rescue of his mother-in-law? Neither did help come from the powerful relatives north of the Alps. Barnabò died on December 19 of 1385, after six harsh months of captivity, apparently given poison in a bowl of beans. His two sons, less fortunate perhaps, lived as captives for the rest of their lives. It is believed that poor Violante never again set eyes on her husband, Lodovico, although he lived for another twenty years. He died still a prisoner in 1404.

The blackest deed in Gian Galeazzo's life was undoubtedly the imprisonment of his father-in-law and his brother-in-law. Yet this treacherous and bloodless coup ushered in a still greater era of Visconti power.

Gian Galeazzo: The Greatest Visconti Prince

Gian Galeazzo proved to be the greatest of all the Visconti. During the seventeen years that he ruled alone the *Signoria* of Milan reached its zenith, gaining the new title of duchy. He was the only one of his century who came close to uniting northern Italy against the foreigner. He symbolized a growing sentiment of nationalism against

German emperors, French popes, and the barbarian mercenaries that both parties brought into the peninsula.

Gian Galeazzo was an educated and enlightened man with modern ideas for a modern state. Petrarca saw in him the embodiment of Italian patriotism that he had first so admired in the unfortunate Cola di Rienzo. There is a story that as a boy Gian Galeazzo was asked by his father to point out the wisest man in the court, whereupon he went over and took Petrarca's hand. There may be no truth to the story, and Petrarca didn't live to see this quiet little boy with golden locks become the wisest and most revered prince of Italy, but it associates two great Italians of the century in a symbolic way.

Gian Galeazzo had seized power not by force of arms but by a clever ruse, and he held that power by using his wits, for his well-conceived plan included a small technicality. He had taken care to have himself reconfirmed as imperial vicar and the old Visconti trick of using the emperors when it suited them was still a good tactic. Uncle Barnabò had made the serious and fatal mistake of allowing his term to expire, either by oversight or arrogance, and as a result neither he nor his sons had any legal claim to power under the Holy Roman Emperor. Not taking any chances, however, Gian Galeazzo saw to it that the dangerous male heirs remained in prison, but the young Mastino was exiled to Venice with a handsome pension. That left the girls, who had no right of inheritance and many of whom were already married off to powerful husbands. The unmarried ones, who were at the same time both Gian Galeazzo's first cousins and sisters-in-law by his marriage to Caterina, became part of his household. To his credit, he found suitable husbands for them and gave generous dowries.

Gian Galeazzo's problems with his relatives were not over, however, for another little viper had cropped up in the person of Barnabò's granddaughter, Isabella of Bavaria. In 1385 she was married to the feeble-minded French king, Charles VI. This "she-wolf," as she came to be known, would rob Gian Galeazzo of the French support he enjoyed while his own wife was still alive, but now he used his daughter Valentina to renew those ties for political reasons. A marriage contract was secured with the French king's brother, Louis, and in July of 1389 Valentina left Italy for the French court, her dowry being the Italian town of Asti. This well-educated young Italian beauty with black eyes framed by chestnut hair duly exercised her charm at court, and the King especially liked her company. She failed to be of great value to her father, however, for the King suffered long periods of madness and the Queen, her unfriendly and jealous relative, finally contrived to have her exiled to Blois in the Loire Valley.

Meanwhile, without his daughter's help Gian Galeazzo had to walk a tightrope of foreign diplomacy over a quagmire of dangers, which involved French and Italian popes, German emperors, and the problem of mercenary soldiers left behind by retreating foreign armies. Three invasions occurred during his rule, two French and one German, where Gian Galeazzo almost alone fought off the threats from outside.

The *condottieri* were now mainly of Italian birth and Gian Galeazzo was fortunate to have at his side the loyal Giacomo dal Verme, joined later by Facino Cane, both of whom were more like generals than soldiers of fortune. The notorious Sir John Hawkwood, known as Giovanni Acuto in Italy, where he was a presence for thirty years, had ended up being a loyal supporter of Florence, the longtime enemy of the Visconti and most responsible for inviting foreign armies into Italy. As Gian Galeazzo

Above: Façade of the
Duomo of Milan.

Right: Detail
showing some of
the 135 pinnacles
and 200 white
marble statues
which adorn the
roof.

Photo by Elizabeth Omar

had said in a speech to the Venetians, it was Florence that "had brought into Italy the French and the Germans, strange and barbarous nations, enemies of the Italian name, and would have set over Italians those whom Nature, by the barrier of the Alps, has excluded from Italy" (Dorothy Muir, *A History of Milan Under the Visconti*, p. 104).

In spite of Florence's anti-Visconti policy, Gian Galeazzo had chased the foreigners out and by the end of his rule had won control of Verona, Vicenza, and Padua, and others came under the protective Visconti umbrella of their own accord. Such was the case with Siena, Perugia, Spoleto, Nocera, Assisi, Lucca, and Pisa, Florence's deadly enemy, which now provided the much-needed seaport for Milan after Genoa had broken away.

Gian Galeazzo might well have won a king's crown had he lived a little longer. He was riding the crest of the wave when he was suddenly stricken with a fever and died on Sunday, September 3, 1402, at the age of fifty. Without Gian Galeazzo, the brilliant duchy was like a ship without a captain setting out into the troubled waters of intrigue and politics.

Gian Galeazzo's kingdom of the north may have been washed away like sandcastles on a seashore, but two great monuments dedicated to Christianity were built of stone and marble and remain for posterity. In Pavia, the city he loved best of all, is the Certosa, a Carthusian monastery founded by Gian Galeazzo in 1396, which became the final resting place of the Visconti. In Milan, the magnificent Duomo still sparkles like a white jewel in the very heart of the city, the figure of the Madonna, which the Milanese lovingly refer to as the "Madonnina," still towering over a sea of rooftops. Gian Galeazzo ordered the construction of this great cathedral in 1386 and dedicated it to the Virgin Mary, to whom he prayed for male children.

He had been unfortunate with his male offspring from his first wife, Isabella. The babe given the name of Gian Galeazzo had died at birth, and the mother had died giving birth to the last one, Carlo, who also died. Azzone had been the only male to survive, but he died in 1381, leaving Gian Galeazzo with his firstborn, daughter Valentina. Gian Galeazzo vowed that if his prayers were answered for male heirs from his second wife, they would be given the name "Maria" in honor of the Virgin. He kept his vow and his two legitimate sons by his cousin, Caterina, were named Giovanni Maria and Filippo Maria, and a bastard child was named Gabriele Maria.

The fate of the Duchy of Milan for the next forty-five years was now in the hands of these three Marias.

The Three Marias

The brilliant Visconti duchy was soon to lose a large part of its realm, reduced to the city of Milan and some surrounding territory. The events of the next ten years contain all the pathos of Greek tragedy as a mother is murdered by order of an insane son who, in turn, ends his days at the hands of assassins, and the last boy called Maria rules from the seclusion of a castle stronghold.

In his will Gian Galeazzo left the Duchy in the hands of his eldest and least able son, Giovanni Maria, a teenager of fourteen years who ruled with the Council of Ten and the widowed Caterina as regent. The younger Filippo Maria, a ten-year-old, was given Pavia and the western territories, which he held as a fief of his brother. Gabriele Maria, the bastard and the brightest, was made the *signore* of Pisa, which he also held as a fief and later sold to Florence.

Cities gradually declared independence from Visconti domination as their lords reasserted their power. Milan itself was torn by factionalism as survivors of the dispossessed members of Barnabò's family, including his illegitimate children, found their way back to reap the spoils. Chaos reigned in the city as the mentally unbalanced Giovanni came of age and took matters into his own hands. With his supporters he rose up against his own mother, Caterina, and even had her put in prison, where she died. It was believed that Giovanni ordered her murder; to clear his name he accused the prison warden of the crime. The poor man was literally thrown to the bloodhounds to be torn to sheds. Caterina had suffered a fate similar to that of her own father at the hands of one of his kin, but hers was all the more tragic because the perpetrator was her first born son. With his mother out of the way, Giovanni Maria was free to give expression to his cruel nature. A decade of terror came to a sudden end when on May 16, 1412, he was assassinated by unknown hands.

In all the confusion of those years, the *condottiere* Facino Cane had managed to save the Duchy of Milan but had also become very powerful, having been rewarded with territories of his own. His sudden death, on the very same day as that of Giovanni Maria, seemed to be the last straw for Milan, whose Council of Ten immediately confirmed Filippo Maria as the next duke.

The young Filippo Maria had the support of the Milanese as he began his rule and in an extraordinary political move he took as his first wife the *condottiere* Facino Cane's widow, Beatrice Tenda, although the lady was fully twenty years his senior. Her influence was considerable, for she brought to the marriage a sizable fortune and, what was an even greater asset, her deceased husband's army, which remained loyal. Milan prospered in the hands of Filippo Maria, who dominated Italian affairs during much of his rule and regained much of the territory that had been lost.

As a person, Filippo was a strange and suspicious individual. He was as ugly as his father was handsome. Awkward and stocky in body with a thick neck and a mop of black hair (uncharacteristic for a Visconti), he shunned the public gaze and ran the government from the seclusion of his castle at Porta Giovia, safe within its red walls and towers and surrounded by trusted attendants. Although preferring the gloomy darkness of his castle, he nevertheless sought the spiritual light through his continued patronage of the Duomo. The masons and stonecutters, ceaselessly at work on the great cathedral, created a symphony with stone and white marble throughout the thirty-five years of Filippo's rule. His death occurred, by uncanny coincidence, on August 14, 1447, eve of the Assumption of the Virgin Mary for whom he was named.

Filippo Maria was the last of the Visconti dynasty, for he left no legitimate heirs. Neither Beatrice Tenda nor his second wife, Maria of Savoy, bore him any children. There were many claimants, but his only bastard daughter, Bianca Maria, was destined to become the mother of the next dynasty, that of the Sforzas.

The Sforza Dynasty

Three years after Filippo Maria's death, in 1450 Francesco Sforza triumphantly entered Milan and overthrew the unstable republic that had been proclaimed. Francesco was a *condottiere* like his father, Muzio Attendolo, who had earned the nickname "Sforza" on account of his exceptional strength, and by this name the dynasty was styled. Also like his father, as a hired sword Francesco had served several masters, but it was his sometimes stormy association with Filippo Maria Visconti that eventually proved to be the most fortuitous.

Francesco had not only fought for Milan but also managed to get himself betrothed to Filippo Maria's illegitimate daughter Bianca Maria (not to be confused with the other Bianca Maria, the bastard child of Barnabò who married the English soldier of fortune Sir John Hawkwood). Francesco Sforza and Bianca Maria had been engaged for eight years when they were finally allowed to marry in 1441. The bride came with the generous dowry of the cities of Pontremoli and Cremona, a prize worth waiting for.

Francesco Sforza ruled as Duke of Milan for sixteen years, the first of a dynasty that survived for close to a century, ending with another Francesco in 1535. But we must take leave of him and travel back in time to see what has been playing on other stages of the Italian peninsula. Our journey will take us back to the succession struggles that provided such lucrative opportunities for the soldiers of fortune and to the battlefields of Naples where Muzio Attendolo "Sforza" lost his life.

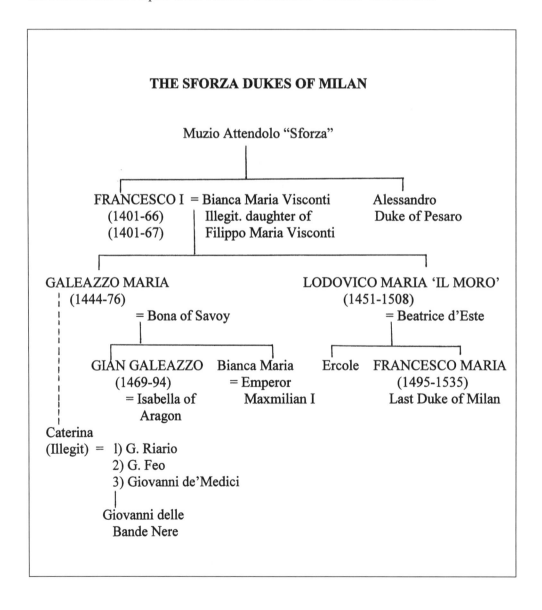

THE SFORZA DUKES OF MILAN

Muzio Attendolo "Sforza"

FRANCESCO I = Bianca Maria Visconti
(1401-66)   Illegit. daughter of
(1401-67)   Filippo Maria Visconti

Alessandro
Duke of Pesaro

GALEAZZO MARIA
(1444-76)
        = Bona of Savoy

LODOVICO MARIA 'IL MORO'
(1451-1508)
        = Beatrice d'Este

GIAN GALEAZZO   Bianca Maria
(1469-94)   = Emperor
= Isabella of   Maxmilian I
Aragon

Ercole   FRANCESCO MARIA
(1495-1535)
Last Duke of Milan

Caterina
(Illegit) = 1) G. Riario
             2) G. Feo
             3) Giovanni de'Medici

Giovanni delle
Bande Nere

CHAPTER FIVE

The Kingdom of Naples

Good King Robert of Naples

We left the kingdoms of Sicily (Naples) and Trinacria after the signing of the Peace of Caltabellotta in August of 1302, a treaty that joined the Spanish house of Aragon to the French house of Anjou through marriage alliances.

We have taken roads north and become acquainted with some of the myriad city-states and republics, despots, murderers, and soldiers of fortune, and watched borders move back and forth or be washed away by the Visconti wave. In the south, by contrast, the borderline that marked the limits of the Kingdom of Naples remained unchanged even as violent storms and deadly undercurrents were raging below it. The Kingdom of Naples followed its own separate destiny, inevitably becoming enmeshed in the affairs of the north and most significantly as the supporter of the French popes, constant enemies of the Visconti.

Just as the *Signoria* of Milan was the saga of a family, the fortunes of families shaped the history of the Kingdom of Naples. The enormous number of children, often used to good advantage as political pawns and spread out into various countries, would be the cause of claims later on and eventually give rise to succession problems. The family tree dramatically illustrates the problems that might arise with so many siblings where divine right of inheritance dictated who would be the next ruler. The seeds of catastrophe were sown when on the death of King Charles II (the Lame) in 1309 his third son, Robert, was the choice of pope and people. The choice was right for the times as the rightful heirs, sons of his deceased oldest brother who had become King of Hungary, had grown up as Hungarians and inherited the throne of their father. Robert was not the next in line, but he was born, grew up, and lived in Naples. He was one of their own.

Robert was one of thirteen children. It will be remembered that his father had been imprisoned, and young Robert had also been held hostage at the Spanish court of Aragon. He was married off to Violante of the House of Aragon as part of the peace treaty of Caltabellotta, but by the time he became king in 1309 she had already died. He ruled for thirty-four years with a second wife as his queen, the devout Sancia of Aragon.

Robert was a faithful champion of the papacy, which had confirmed him in power, and as its guardian he was inevitably dragged into the arena on the side of the papacy when conflicts arose. Robert's forces were engaged to stop the expansion of the anti-papal Visconti who in 1317–18 laid siege to Genoa. The Genoese called on King Robert for help and even proclaimed him their *signore* for ten years.

In his own realm Robert was a popular king, revered by his subjects, and came to be referred to as "Good King Robert." As the capital of the kingdom Naples grew in importance as this wise king attracted to his court scholars, poets, and artists from near and far. Boccaccio spent some twenty years in the court of Naples; Giotto and Simone Montini painted masterpieces there; and the poet Francesco Petrarca was also a welcome guest.

Robert died on January 16, 1343, and his tomb may be seen in the Church of Saint Clara, erected by his pious Queen Sancia. The peace that the Kingdom of Naples had enjoyed seems to have been laid to rest along with the king, for the most bloody events followed. Unlike his father, Robert had only one son, Carlo, who had died fifteen years earlier leaving two daughters, Giovanna and Maria. Before his death, King Robert willed his kingdom to his oldest granddaughter, the lovely young Giovanna, and made the French Pope in Avignon her guardian. It was the beginning of a painful chapter in the history of the South when Giovanna, a girl of seventeen, began a reign that lasted for forty troubled years.

Giovanna I, Queen of Naples

The poet Petrarca, well acquainted with the court of Naples in his capacity as a papal representative, had said that Queen Giovanna was surrounded by "a pack of wolves." Her reign was a dramatic struggle not only for her crown but also for her very life. The disputes over succession, Hungarian invasions, and rebellions within all contributed to weaken the Kingdom and visit suffering on her subjects.

Queen Giovanna's character has been sullied by chroniclers of her enemies with the result that she has been cast most often in a negative light. Her reign was a troubled one and her incredible life story affords a glimpse into the world of her time.

King Robert anticipated the problems that might come from the Hungarian side of the family. As a move to pacify the children of his dead brother, legal heirs to the kingdom who came to make their claims later, he arranged to wed his granddaughter Giovanna to Andreas, brother of King Louis of Hungary, when both were little children. The marriage took place when they were seven and six, respectively, and the young Andreas was brought to the court of Naples to be groomed for his adult role as prince consort, for in the Kingdom of Naples a woman could inherit the throne. With him came a retinue of Hungarians, whom the Neapolitans despised, finding them most coarse and unrefined. Giovanna watched her little husband grow up into an unattractive, squint-eyed, clumsy youth.

The coronation had not yet taken place when the members of the court left Naples to spend some autumn days at the royal retreat in nearby Aversa. On the night of September 18, 1345, Andreas was summoned half-dressed from his bedchamber as he was preparing to retire, leaving the six months' pregnant Giovanna in bed. Andreas was then gagged, a rope was placed around his neck, and he was thrown over the balcony to hang. We will spare the reader the gruesome details told of the unprofessional job done by unskilled hands. His still-warm body was later found in the garden below by one of his attendants who had come looking for him and gave the alarm, but the perpetrators had already fled. Were they Hungarian-hating rebels, pranksters on the prowl for adventure, or paid assassins? Their identity remains one of the most tantalizing and unsolved mysteries of history and one that opened the floodgates of hatred from the Hungarian court.

When news of the deed reached the court of Hungary, the dead Andreas's brother, the twenty-year-old King Louis, and the redoubtable dowager queen mother swore vengeance. An army was mustered, and two years later a punitive expedition was announced to seek out and punish the guilty, Giovanna and her relatives being the accused. Meanwhile, Giovanna gave birth to a son, Charles Martel. Needing a husband to protect her, in August 1347 she married her cousin Luigi, Prince of Taranto. News of this new alliance and the forthcoming coronation sparked the anger of the Hungarians. Their king, with a dreadful horde of his soldiers and German mercenaries, marched on the Kingdom of Naples. Prince Luigi took command of the defending forces, but the Hungarians met little opposition as the helpless and terrified citizens simply opened their gates to these foreign hordes.

The year 1348 ushered in tragedy and disaster. Giovanna had wished to spare her people bloodshed and implored them to offer no resistance. On January 16, accompanied by her weeping subjects, she went down to the harbor to embark on her state galley that would take her to the safety of the Pope in Provence. Her little son was wrenched from her arms to be carried off to the court of Hungary and disappear from history. On that tragic day, as white sails offshore billowed in a winter breeze, bearing a weeping queen to yet another ordeal, her archenemy and persecutor, brother-in-law King Louis, arrived at nearby Aversa. Prince Luigi had made a desperate last stand, challenging King Louis to mortal combat in a duel of swords, but Louis refused to accept the invitation. Prince Luigi realized that his situation was hopeless and chose to follow his queen to Avignon.

King Louis had already made contact with those of his Italian relatives who had everything to gain by removing Queen Giovanna. He was joined, among others, by none other than Robert and Philip of Taranto, the new brothers-in-law of Queen Giovanna, and Charles of Durazzo, husband of the Queen's sister Maria, and his brothers. On January 22, the party was royally entertained by King Louis who, like a crafty fox who had entered the coop, had his chickens taken prisoner. He had planned to make a meal of his chief suspect, the ambitious husband of Queen Giovanna's sister Maria, Charles of Durazzo. Guilty or not, he would pay for the crime and at the same time be removed from the line of succession.

King Louis asked to be shown the site where his brother had been so savagely murdered, and there had the unsuspecting Charles of Durazzo decapitated with the sword. His body was then thrown from the same balcony to remain in the garden below, a garden that received the dead bodies of two men, the husband of Queen Giovanna and now the husband of her sister Maria. Maria, disguised as a friar, escaped the country with her two daughters to follow a destiny hardly less dramatic than Giovanna's. In her womb she carried the unborn Margaret, future queen of Naples.

The following day, King Louis made his entry into Naples and prepared to take over the Kingdom. His progress was halted, however, for the excesses of the hated Hungarians incited the Neapolitans to resistance and rebellion. The Pope, who had previously forbidden King Louis to enter Naples, now proclaimed Giovanna innocent of complicity in the crime for she had been put on trial in Avignon and absolved. Last but not least, the Black Death struck Naples at this time, and King Louis deemed it prudent to return to Hungary to escape the pestilence. This was the end of his quest for vengeance, which had become one for the crown of Naples.

Queen Giovanna, meanwhile, finding herself in dire straits, had been forced to sell Avignon, a city in the middle of her own territory in southern France. The sale recorded on June 9, 1348, for a bargain price of 80,000 florins, saw the transfer of the beautiful city from the counts of Provence to the papacy, hitherto a tenant.

It was a great day for the Neapolitans when on August 17 of that same year their queen and her consort returned to Naples. The task of recovering the kingdom was not an easy one as King Louis had left garrisons in command of many towns and castles, for he planned to return. He came back with new troops for a second expedition against the Kingdom of Naples and laid siege to Aversa, but the Pope insisted that Robert's will should be respected, and a peace treaty was made through his mediation.

There was nothing now in the way of the coronation of Giovanna and Luigi, which was celebrated on the day of Pentecost in May 1352 with much pomp and joy. One is shocked to learn that such a wondrous day ended in tragedy. On returning to the Castello, the King and Queen were greeted by a household weeping the death of little three-year-old daughter, Francesca. She is a nebulous and faceless child whose story remains untold.

Over the next decade, Giovanna worked at putting together the fragmented pieces of her kingdom with the help of Luigi and able ministers, the greatest and most trusted of whom was Niccolò Acciajuoli. She now devoted herself to improving the lot of her people, a task begun by King Robert.

Tragedy struck once more when on the night of May 25, 1362, Luigi suddenly died of a fever in Naples at the age of forty-two. Giovanna was alone again, but her faithful jewel of a minister, Niccolò Acciajuoli, was there to guide her. She now gave her attention to the succession and, obviously not thinking of marriage again, adopted Carlo of the Durazzo branch of the family, a young man of seventeen, with the plan that he should marry the previously adopted Margaret, daughter of her sister Maria. The two would then jointly inherit the throne of Naples.

Queen Giovanna, still a young and beautiful woman at thirty-six when widowed, was persuaded to take another husband. James, the titular king of Majorca, became Giovanna's third husband in 1364. Following the loss of his kingdom to a greedy relative in the war between Aragon and Majorca, he had made a daring escape from his prison in 1362 after several years of captivity. James failed to protect his queen's realm, spending much of his time trying to recover the kingdom he had lost. He died of sickness at war in Spain in 1375, ending a marriage that had been a disaster.

Giovanna was approaching her fiftieth year when she was widowed for the third time. Misfortune that had dogged her throughout her life was once more lying in wait, but none could have foreseen what destiny had in store for her and indeed for Italy in the following years.

Queen Giovanna and the Popes

In March of 1376, the people of Naples celebrated the fourth marriage of their queen, this time to Otto of Brunswick, who proved to be a most excellent soldier and faithful consort. During this time the papacy finally moved back to Rome after an absence of seventy-five years, and occurrences in the peninsula formed a bloody backdrop to this last union, approved by Pope Gregory XI, the last of the legitimate Avignon popes and the last French pope. Queen Giovanna was very much a part of the history of this period, but instead of being the protagonist she became the most tragic victim.

The fourteenth century, as we have seen, was characterized by wars fought by *condottieri* and mercenary soldiers. Now it was hoped that the return of the papacy to Rome would bring peace to the peninsula. One of the strongest advocates was Catherine of Siena, a sister of the Dominican order, a mystic who possessed uncanny vision and championed Italian unity. Five centuries after her death, she became the patron saint of Italy.

The Pope returned to Italy on January 17, 1377, but his presence was not welcome in many cities that had sought independence from popes who pulled strings like puppeteers offstage in Avignon and put down rebellious subjects. In Faenza an estimated 4,000 men, women, and children were savagely butchered by mercenaries under the command of the notorious soldier of fortune Sir John Hawkwood, then in the employ of the Pope. Shortly after the Pope's return to Italy, there was another victim when a horde of Breton and English mercenaries exterminated the entire population of little Cesena on mere suspicion of rebellion. This time the troops were under the command of none other than Cardinal Robert of Geneva, a man soon to become antipope as Clement VII.

Pope Gregory's return to Rome did not bring peace to the peninsula, and the situation became so desperate that he called on the most powerful man of the north, Barnabò Visconti, to mediate a peace. Who could have imagined that the previously excommunicated Visconti would be invited to open a historic Congress where cardinals would sit down to make a deal with the devil himself? That Congress was attended by representatives of every corner of the peninsula, and representing the Kingdom of Naples for his queen was Duke Otto.

On March 27, 1378, in the midst of this Congress, news was received of Pope Gregory's death. Left at the mercy of the hostile Romans (who clamored for an Italian pope) were the cardinals, most of whom were French; in the conclave that followed they voted for the cardinal of Bari, a subject of Queen Giovanna, who took the name of Urban VI. Soon after, the election was declared invalid by a group of cardinals who got together and chose the above-mentioned Robert of Geneva, who took the name of Clement VII. As these two popes fought for the coveted seat in Rome the Italians were caught in the crossfire. The Italian eventually won over the predominantly mercenary army of his opponent who fled to Avignon. It had become an Italian/French war in which Catherine of Siena gave her support to the Italian pope and entreated Queen Giovanna to do likewise. It was her adamant refusal to follow this advice that precipitated her downfall.

Queen Giovanna's loyalties remained with the French. As a result the Italian pope declared her deposed and called on Carlo of Durazzo to claim the throne of Naples. Having no children of her own, Giovanna had previously adopted Margaret, her sister's child, as well as Margaret's husband, Carlo of Durazzo, and made them heirs to her kingdom on her death. But she was not dead, and the Italian pope's action to "speed things up" forced her to take equally desperate action as she faced her own demise. Betrayed by the two people she loved most dearly, she changed her will and in March 1380 adopted Louis of Anjou, brother of the French king, as her successor. One month later Catherine of Siena died at the age of thirty-three to take her place as a heroine of her country while Queen Giovanna, the one whom she had tried to save, rushed headlong to her doom.

On June 1, 1381, Carlo of Durazzo was crowned king and was coming to claim his throne. As the desperate queen waited for Louis of Anjou to come to her rescue, Carlo moved on Naples with his army and laid siege to Castel Nuovo, where Giovenna had taken refuge with her court. Meanwhile, her own forces under her husband, Duke Otto, had been outsmarted and forced to retreat to the marshes outside Naples and then to Aversa, where they lay in wait. Also waiting for her chosen heir to come to her rescue was Queen Giovanna, but no ships appeared on the horizon. As the end of August approached, now desperately short of provisions, she sent her minister to King Carlo to negotiate her capitulation. The heartless man who had betrayed her and taken her throne gave her five days to accept his harsh terms. Duke Otto, in a last attempt to rescue his queen and wife, launched a courageous attack, but his troops were routed and he was taken prisoner in a desperate last charge.

On September 1, an embassy arrived from the king of France to rescue the beleaguered Giovanna, but she refused to leave. Instead, she was taken prisoner by Carlo's men and carried off to the desolate Castello of Muro in the mountains not far from Venosa. Here the unfortunate queen met her death at the hands of unknown assassins. The version most widely accepted was recorded by the secretary of Pope Urban, according to which four Hungarians entered the sacred place as she prayed, put a cord around her neck, and strangled her. It seems that vengeance had come full cycle; she had, at the hands of the Hungarians, died a death similar to that of her first husband, Andreas, at the hands of the Italians.

It was a tragic end for a woman who had ruled as queen for forty years to be excommunicated by an Italian pope, abandoned by the ones she loved, separated from her husband, and given no public funeral. No one knows for sure where she was finally laid to rest, but it is believed that the Nuns of Saint Clair interred her mortal remains. Reviled in the pages of history with epithets of "cruel," "notorious," "amorous," and "inept," she has been crucified in death. Six centuries later another Saint Clair, the English author St. Clair Baddeley, would come to her defense in the book published in 1893 and entitled *Queen Joanna I*, written as he says to serve as a memorial and "to clear away a little the nightshade and bramble" and allow the reader to judge the character of Queen Giovanna of Naples.

The Last of the Angevin Dynasty

The succession struggles that began when Queen Giovanna named Louis of Anjou as her heir haunted the south for the next half century as one Louis after another—father, son, and grandson—sought to take possession of the Kingdom of Naples.

The reign of Carlo of Durazzo was short and troubled, and the ill-begotten crown weighed heavily on his brow. Louis of Anjou was soon on the scene to claim his rights but he died on campaign in the south in the fall of 1384. It was not the last of Carlo's troubles, however, for he soon locked horns with the Pope, who considered the Kingdom of Naples a mere vassal of the Church. When Carlo did not comply with his wishes, the Pope declared him deposed. Carlo was then called by a certain faction to claim the throne of Hungary, but he was assassinated in Buda on February 27, 1386, and the throne of Naples passed to his nine-year-old son, Ladislao, putting another woman at the helm with the regency of Queen Margaret.

Ladislao's chances of survival looked bleak indeed, for another claimant was on the scene, Louis II of Anjou. With the support of popes, kings, and princes, this Louis had taken up residence in Naples. Margaret took her little king, along with his sister Joanna, to the safety of Gaeta where, four years later, in 1390, he was crowned King of Naples by a new pope, Boniface IX. In spite of his Hungarian name, Ladislao was a fifth-generation of Angevins and born in Naples, so he was more acceptable than any French newcomer. What is more, he had the support of Gian Galeazzo Visconti, among others, who wanted the French out of the peninsula. As Ladislao grew into manhood he proved to be a worthy knight. He was in his early 20s when Louis II was defeated in battle and withdrew to Provence in 1399.

Ladislao's star rose rapidly on the southern horizon just as to the north that of the Visconti was losing its brilliance. King Ladislao had ridden into the fifteenth century as the most promising defender of the Italians and protector of the Church, but the death of Boniface IX on October 1, 1404, ushered in a period of chaos as the papal schism entered a new phase.

In Rome, the two great Roman families that had been kept in check, the Colonna and the Orsini, now rose against each other as barricades went up in Rome and fighting broke out. The Colonna called on Ladislao to intercede and prevent civil war. With his southern troops near at hand, the conclave elected a subject of Ladislao who took the name of Innocent VII. Two days later, the young king entered Rome as a keeper of the peace amid great rejoicing. The schism continued, however, and Roman elements forced the Pope to flee to nearby Viterbo; once again King Ladislao came to the rescue, bringing him back to the Vatican and restoring peace.

With greater confidence, Ladislao proceeded to control the recalcitrant elements of his own kingdom, but in the heel of Italy Maria of Enghein, the countess of Lecce and widow of his most formidable opponent who had died a rebel, could not herself be brought to heel. In 1407, Ladislao solved the situation by making her his queen.

Pope Innocent VII died on November 6, 1406, and in December a new pope was elected, a Venetian who took the name of Gregory XII. There were still two popes, however, and under great pressure the two agreed to meet, but an agreement meant that one or the other would have to give up power. King Ladislao did not really think it such a good idea as he imagined Louis II riding back in on the agreement. Ladislao arrived at the gates of Rome in 1408, and on April 25 he entered the city with 12,000 knights and numerous infantry to be acclaimed as saviors against any possible French tricks.

Meanwhile, as the two popes continued to haggle about the venue of a meeting, the cardinals got together and deposed both as schismatics and heretics. In 1409 they elected the Cardinal of Milan, who took the name of Alexander V, whereupon the Avignon pope fled to Spain and Gregory scuttled off to the court of Ladislao. Now there were three popes, two of whom were in exile. Pope Alexander made ready to enter the Vatican City when he died suddenly on May 3, 1410. Three weeks later another pope was elected taking the name of Giovanni (John) XXIII.

The tide now turned for Ladislao as Louis II, with papal support, was soon back to claim the Kingdom of Naples. This time Ladislao was taken by surprise and defeated on the plain of Roccasecca, halfway between Naples and Rome, on May 19, 1411. As the overconfident and puffed-up Louis rested on his laurels, Ladislao prepared his counterattack. He made peace with Florence and won the support of the *condottiere* Muzio Attendolo Sforza (father of the one who later founded the Sforza dynasty of Milan). Louis was eventually driven out of Italy and retreated to Provence. Ladislao continued to play a major role in the peninsula and gained control of much of central Italy. He had the best *condottieri* at his command and with both the Genoese and the Venetians on his side he worked to keep out French pretenders and German emperors. In 1414 he was at the height of his power when, while campaigning in central Italy, he suddenly fell ill. He was carried on a stretcher to the coast and put on a ship that took him back to Naples, where he died a few days later, on August 6, at the age of thirty-seven, leaving no heir.

Ladislao had emerged from the darkness like a light that shone brightly for a brief period and then went out. He began with a kingdom in pieces, put it back together, and added to it, but what he accomplished during his life crumbled like a pack of cards. We have followed him into the world of the popes as we have turned the pages of history in which he himself has left no real mark, his achievements being washed away like sandcastles by the tide of events.

The burden of the kingdom now fell on the shoulders of his forty-three-year-old widowed sister, who became Giovanna II and ruled for the next chaotic twenty years. Giovanna II was a frail woman whose personal life was complicated by lovers and husbands, scandals and intrigues, imprisonments and assassinations, and the ever-present problem of finding a successor, for she also remained childless. In adopting an heir she wavered between Louis III of France and Alfonso V of Aragon, who was also King of Sicily. These two vied for the crown of Naples and when Louis died at Cosenza on campaign in November of 1434, his claims were taken up by his brother René. Giovanna never knew which of the two would wear the crown, for she died one year later on February 2, 1435, the question of succession still unresolved and the kingdom in a state of turmoil.

The Triumph of Alfonso

Queen Giovanna II was dead, and the fight between the French René of Anjou and the Spanish Alfonso V for the empty throne intensified. Alfonso's Kingdom of Aragon also included Sardinia and Sicily, but more than anything else he wanted the Kingdom of Naples as the rightful heir.

Alfonso was alone in his quest for the coveted crown, for it seemed that all forces were against him. In the north the powerful Filippo Maria Visconti enlisted the support of the Genoese, whose ships engaged in battle against Alfonso and his fleet off the island of Ponza. In early August 1435, Alfonso was defeated and fell into the hands of Filippo Maria. With a silver tongue and good reasoning Alfonso charmed his captor who, in an extraordinary change of heart, betrayed Genoa and joined forces with Alfonso. Filippo Maria was persuaded that he would rather see Alfonso than that Frenchman René of Anjou on the throne of Naples.

Thanks to Visconti help, Alfonso got his wish—Naples fell to him in 1442. The coronation that took place in Naples on February 26, 1443, was a magnificent event. Alfonso, riding a gilded carriage drawn by four white horses through streets strewn with flowers, was acclaimed by a triumphant procession of the people. His entry into Naples is depicted on the triumphal arch erected in his honor and that forms the entrance to Castel Nuovo.

Alfonso made Naples his capital and site of his permanent court, much to the displeasure of his Aragonese subjects, and the city experienced a renaissance not unlike that of Florence. King Alfonso V of Aragon and I of Naples ruled for fifteen years and brought prosperity to a region that had known 100 years of anarchy. Loved by his Neapolitan subjects, he came to be known as "the Magnanimous."

Sicily was back with the mainland again, and the map of the region had been redrawn and simplified, but the expanded realm Alfonso had brought about did not survive his death in 1458. Alfonso had no legitimate heirs, and his brother Louis became King of Aragon and Sicily. The Kingdom of Naples, however, was given to Alfonso's bastard son, Ferdinand, also known in Italy as Don Ferrante. As Ferdinand I he ruled as King of Naples for thirty-six years. His reign was despotic, as the times dictated, but he protected the kingdom against the Turks, who had occupied Otranto in 1480, his own rebellious barons, and the persistent French pretender, René of Anjou. Eight years after Ferdinand's death in 1494 Sicily was reunited with the mainland under the Spanish crown.

We now leave the southern half of the peninsula on the threshold of the sixteenth century and retrace our steps to follow the incredible developments that took place in another world — FLORENCE.

NAPLES—Castel Nuovo, an Angevin fortress built for Charles of Anjou in 1279-82 and used as a royal residence. The triumphal arch of the main entrance was incorporated some two centuries later and commemorated Alfonso of Aragon's entry into Naples in 1443.

The East door of the Baptistry of the Duomo in Florence, known as the Porta del Paradiso, was created by Lorenzo Ghiberti over a period of some 27 years. The masterpiece consists of ten panels representing scenes from the Old testament. New perspectives give the bas relief, covered with a patina of gold, an extraordinary sense of depth. This is further heightened by the sunlight which plays on the various figures of the tenth panel, showing Solomon meeting the Queen of Sheba.

CHAPTER SIX

Florence of the Medici

The Rise of the Medici

In 1401, a competition was held in which sculptors and goldsmiths participated for the honor to design a pair of doors for the baptistry in front of the Cathedral of Santa Maria del Fiore. Among the competitors were some who became famous: Brunelleschi, Donatello, Jacopo della Quercia, and Lorenzo Ghiberti. The latter came out the winner, and his masterpiece was the door which came to be known as the Gate to Paradise, symbolically opening the door to the splendid era of the Renaissance.

Florence has long since become synonymous with the Renaissance that characterized the fifteenth century. It was not the only city where the arts flourished, but it outshone all the others in richness and brilliance. In Florence the pots of gold of the merchants and bankers were transformed by the skilled hands of her artisans, artists, architects, and craftsmen into treasures that gave them immortality. Florence, above all, possessed all the elements required to make her the queen of the Renaissance.

Florence had no standing army, for she had money to pay the best *condottieri* when protection was needed. Her citizens, instead of soldiering, therefore carried on the business of trade and the affluent could luxuriate in the finer pleasures of life. A city of great activity, it boasted hundreds of workshops where skills were passed on from generation to generation. The various trades and activities were recognized in the twenty-one guilds, whose members had a voice in the government. Significantly, the guilds were called *Arti* (arts) and included crafts or trades, and likewise the Bankers' Guild was *L'Arte del Cambio* (the Exchange Guild). Popes labeled moneylenders as "usurers," but nevertheless used their services when it suited their needs.

The banking family of the Medici emerged in the fifteenth century as the great patrons of the arts and were instrumental in making their city the art center of the world, where some of the greatest artists and architects lived and worked. Although the city remained a Republic and the Medici did not actually hold public office, preferring to "stay out of the public eye," they became a formidable controlling force in both city affairs and foreign policy, particularly in dealings with the city-states of Milan, Venice, and Genoa, as well as the Kingdom of Naples.

One did not have to hold office to be powerful, and it was often the ones who held the purse strings who came to be esteemed by heads of states. The Medici had long since earned that reputation, and along with it the enmity of the powerful Albizzi family, who also had followers and had enriched Florence by gaining possession of

Arezzo, capturing Pisa and its port, and actually "buying" Livorno (Leghorn) from the Genoese.

Cosimo de'Medici was a formidable rival. Reputed to be one of the richest men of the world, he headed one of the greatest commercial enterprises that had ever existed, a forerunner of our present international companies. It was one September morning in 1433 that this quiet, unassuming man was summoned to the Palazzo della Signoria on urgent business. Expecting to be led to the Council Chamber for advice, what must have been his dismay when he was taken up to the bell tower and unceremoniously pushed into a small cell, known as the "Little Inn," and the door locked behind him!

Here was the most powerful man of Florence confined high above his city, which he could barely see through a slit in the wall that was the only window. Charges were brought against him of conspiracy against the Republic, and he was summarily condemned to death. Opposition to such drastic action and fear of rebellion in the city resulted in the sentence being commuted to ten years of exile. Cosimo was spirited out of the city under cover of night. His exile was short and painless and with the help of friends and contacts outside of Florence he gained his freedom the following year. The tide had turned and now it was the Albizzi who were to be sent off into exile.

Cosimo remained the most powerful man in Florence for the next thirty years, taking on political and diplomatic missions assigned to him and protecting the interests of the Republic so well that he came to be known as the *pater patria*, "father of the country," deciding peace and war and controlling the laws. It was said of him that he was "King in everything but name." The Medici were the friends of the little people; as such Cosimo avoided ostentatious show so as not to incite envy. He rode a mule instead of a fine horse and enriched the city by his generous support of churches and patronage of the arts. Some of the most talented painters and sculptors of the time were indebted to him, and Donatello may never have created his magnificent "David" had not Cosimo understood, if not condoned, the homosexual lifestyle of that gifted sculptor who drew inspiration from the classical Greek.

Cosimo de'Medici strove to achieve a balance of power in the peninsula, and the traditional rivalry with Milan ended when an alliance was made with Francesco Sforza, the *condottiere* who had married the last Visconti's illegitimate daughter, Bianca Maria, and become Duke of Milan. The turmoil of the previous century was past.

Cosimo was a tired man approaching his seventy-fifth birthday when he died on August 1, 1464, leaving his business as well as his responsibilities of state in the hands of his eldest son, Piero. Known as "the Gouty," Piero had suffered all of his life from arthritis, a Medici weakness, but in spite of his infirmities he was gentle, good-natured, and cultured. He successfully followed in the footsteps of his father for the next six years and through diplomacy kept the borders safe through a treaty with both Milan and Naples in 1468, checking an aggressive Venice.

Like his father, Piero had to contend with enemies at home — for him it was the wealthy Pitti family, whose palace is now a museum. An argument arose over the alliance with Milan. They had rallied their supporters and with Venetian involvement plotted a coup against the Medici. It was the young Lorenzo, Piero's eldest son, who happened upon some of the conspirators as he was galloping back to the city and promptly gave the alarm. Piero could well be proud of his son, Lorenzo, and he was also blessed with a wonderful wife, Lucrezia Tornabuoni, who was gifted and respected. She gave him three daughters and two sons, but it was Lorenzo who would outshine both father and grandfather and earn the title "the Magnificent."

Lorenzo the Magnificent

Lorenzo was the epitome of what came to be understood as a Renaissance man. Not endowed with physical beauty, for which the Medici were not known, his uncomely appearance belied his true qualities. He had a long nose, flattened and askew on his face; his lower lip protruded in a monkey-like fashion; and his deep-set black eyes were surmounted by a deep, uneven brow. All of this was framed by a mop of thick black hair, which he wore at shoulder length. Not even his voice was pleasant, being described as high-pitched and nasal, yet when all of these elements were put into motion he was uniquely attractive and compelling.

At an early age, Lorenzo had shown signs of exceptional talent and maturity. By the age of fifteen he had already carried out important assignments for his ailing father. When, at the age of twenty, he was called on at the father's death to shoulder full responsibility as head of the family and carry the Medici banner for Florence, he was equal to the task.

Lorenzo was tremendously energetic, had an enormous zest for life and a joyful nature and, though not neglecting his duties, he found time for fun, playing football, hunting and hawking, and generally making merry with his young friends. One can easily imagine him speeding his horse through the streets of Florence, his black hair flying out behind him and a bunch of young men in his wake. Yet he had a quiet side to his personality, and in addition to his deep appreciation of art, he loved music, composed songs, and wrote verse. At nineteen he was married off to a "foreigner," a Roman lady named Clarice Orsini.

Much of the Medici banking business came from Rome, and Clarice's family owned large estates in the Kingdom of Naples, as well as north of Rome. Although from a different environment, not to say culture, and lacking the refinement of Florentine ladies, Clarice made a good wife. The wedding was celebrated without the presence of the bride on February 7, 1469, and was really a party for the city. The event was recorded in a famous poem by Luigi Pulci called "La Giostra di Lorenzo de'Medici." The actual wedding ceremony followed four months later in June and the feasting and dancing lasted three days. Florence was a joyful place in those days, especially characterized by amusements of every kind of tournaments, parades, music festivals, and dances in which everyone took part. There was time for fun, as the statutes of the various guilds prescribed a maximum of 275 working days in a year.

Like his predecessors, the young Lorenzo avoided holding public office, but was assigned duties as a representative of the Republic. He was acquainted personally with influential families of other states in the peninsula and abroad, serving as a mouthpiece, and he kept on good terms with Milan where Duke Galeazzo Maria Sforza had succeeded his father. The Duke's state visit to Florence in 1471 could not have failed to impress his hosts:

> he arrived with an enormous retinue of advisers, attendants, servants and soldiers, including five hundred infantry, a hundred knights and fifty grooms in liveries of cloth of silver, each leading a war-horse saddled in gold brocade and with golden stirrups and bridles embroidered with silk. The Duke also brought with him

his trumpeters and drummers, his huntsmen and falconers, his falcons and his hounds. His wife and daughters and their ladies were carried into the city in twelve gold-brocaded litters. (Quoted from Hibbert, *The House of Medici.*)

Duke Sforza comported himself in the regal manner of monarchs whereas the somber-clad Lorenzo claimed to be no more than a citizen of the Republic, but the Duke shared Lorenzo's taste for learning and similarly patronized the arts.

Relations between Lorenzo and Duke Sforza remained cordial. Frontiers were respected, and there was nothing to fear from Milan. Troubles came to cloud the horizon from an unexpected source and had their origins in the world of banking. Pope Sixtus IV, elected in the same year as Duke Sforza's visit to Florence, was an uncouth man bent on taking care of his numerous and equally uncouth relatives. Six of his nephews were made cardinals. Another one, thought to be his own son, Girolamo Riario, had his eye on the small town of Imola, between Forlì and Bologna, as well as the illegitimate daughter of the Duke of Milan, Caterina Sforza, who was just twelve years old when he married her in 1472.

The Pope approached his bankers, the Medici, for a sizable loan to purchase Imola, but Lorenzo did not want this strategic base to fall into the hands of the papacy and found an excuse not to grant it. A disgruntled pope immediately went knocking on the door of rival bankers, the Pazzi, who were only too eager to oblige. The Pope got Imola for Girolamo, and the Pazzi got a profitable new client in the papacy.

Lorenzo now had dangerous enemies in Rome, and the situation on the peninsula was complicated when his ally, Galeazzo Maria Sforza, was treacherously murdered by three citizens of Milan the day after Christmas in 1476. By 1477, a conspiracy to eliminate the Medici power was being hatched in Rome. Here were the conspirators:

- Girolamo Riario, now lord of Imola
- Francesco Salviati, archbishop designate for Pisa, who had his eye on Florence
- Francesco de'Pazzi, manager of the Pazzi bank in Rome

Together the three plotted a coup and took their plan to Jacopo de'Pazzi, the elder. Although they were his competitors, old Jacopo was on good terms with the Medici family and vehemently opposed such action, but the conspirators were undaunted and persuaded a reluctant *condottiere*, Montesecco, to aid them. They even went as far as getting the Pope's blessing, although he insisted that "there be no killing," just a change of government.

Assurances notwithstanding, the conspirators resolved to assassinate Lorenzo and his brother, Giuliano, and it was finally agreed that the two should be dispatched together during mass in the cathedral. Francesco de'Pazzi would stab Giuliano and Montesecco could take care of Lorenzo. Montesecco had met and liked Lorenzo and, although a mercenary, had no stomach for such a sacrilegious deed, especially in the house of God, but two embittered priests had no such scruples and needed little persuasion. The signal to strike was the sound of the sanctuary bell at the elevation of the Host when eyes would be downcast.

On that bloody Sunday of April 26, 1478, as the two unsuspecting brothers were at mass, surrounded by members of the congregation, the assassins fell on their praying victims. Lorenzo had felt the cold blade of a dagger at his neck, and with blood flowing, instinctively leaped back, drawing his sword and striking out at the priests, who were beaten back. He took refuge in the sacristy, but his thoughts and fears were with his brother as he kept asking, "Giuliano? Is he safe?"

Meanwhile, the defenseless Giuliano had been felled by savage blows from Francesco de'Pazzi and an assistant assassin. His bloodied body, slashed by 119 wounds, lay on the floor amidst a scene of general chaos as the assassins made their escape. Archbishop Salviati, the third conspirator, had taken his men to the Palazzo della Signoria with his Perugian mercenaries, disguised as his followers, but they were all trapped inside to be slaughtered like the beasts they were and their heads taken out on the end of lances and swords. The Piazza filled with citizens shouting support for one party or the other, and during the melee that ensued, the archbishop was thrown from a window with a rope around his neck, as was Francesco de' Pazzi, caught and stripped naked. Before it was all over, the angry mob had attacked supporters and would-be conspirators, killing, mutilating, and dragging the bodies through the streets. The squares of Florence, which had been the site of such joyful celebrations, were transformed into the stage for the worst scenes from hell.

The other conspirators were tracked down and killed, including old Jacopo de'Pazzi whose body was defiled and later cast in the Arno River. The two priests were ferreted out, dragged from their hiding places, brutally castrated, and hung. But the most important witness was the unwilling *condottiere,* Montesecco, who was later captured and under torture gave details of the plot, revealing the treacherous involvement of the Pope.

Discredited for all time, the names and coat of arms of the Pazzi were suppressed by public decree and their symbol, the gentle dolphin, was blotted out.

Lorenzo grieved the loss of his only brother, whom he dearly loved. Giuliano was unmarried at twenty-five, but he had an illegitimate child, Giulio, whom Lorenzo adopted and brought into his family as one of his own. Following the disaster, Lorenzo sent his family away from Florence to spend some time at Pistoia while he remained in the city to attend to his affairs. He never wavered in his selfless efforts to serve the Republic of Florence until his own death fourteen years later.

Lorenzo the Magnificent: A Renaissance Man

Posterity appreciates Lorenzo less for his diplomatic and political contribution in keeping the peace in Italy than as a key figure of the Renaissance. Much of his time, and indeed his fortune as well, went to promoting learning and the arts. He brought Greek scholars to Florence, sought out ancient manuscripts of Greek and Latin, and had these priceless finds copied by countless scribes and illustrators as the classical cultures were studied and appreciated. It opened doors that had been closed by the austere teachings of medieval Christianity and the individual found new freedom in thought and expression.

An art lover, Lorenzo founded a school for talented young artists and sculptors to which he brought boys of promise both rich and poor. Such a boy was the seven-year-old Michelangelo Buonarroti, whose early genius so impressed Lorenzo that he took him into his home, where he became a member of the household. These boys were schooled in philosophy and the classics, not to be mere craftsmen but to express ideas. Many may be surprised to learn that Michelangelo, famous for his sculptures and paintings, was also a poet who wrote marvelous lines, much appreciated in his day.

Many were the artists and sculptors who lived and worked at that time in Florence and benefited in some way from the patronage of Lorenzo. Some went with Lorenzo's blessing to help to enrich other cities with their talents. Michelangelo, of course, spent much of his life in Rome, and his works need no introduction. All part of the incredible art scene of the time were such famous artists as Sandro Botticelli, Leonardo da Vinci, Pico della Mirandola, Verrocchio, Donatello, Filippino Lippi, Antonio Pollaiuolo, Giuliano da Maiano, and Domenico Ghirlandaio, to mention only a few.

Lorenzo shared his table with philosophers, artists, musicians, writers, and poets. One of his closest friends among them was the most brilliant humanist of Renaissance

For three centuries the Medici name, symbolized by the famous balls, was linked to the history of Florence and Tuscany. Here they are seen in a marble panel along with the lion, symbol of the people.

THE HOUSE OF MEDICI
(Condensed Genealogy showing descendants of Cosimo)

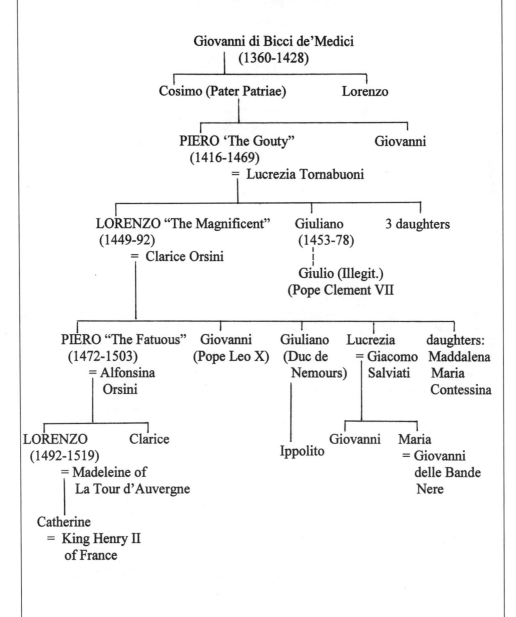

Giovanni di Bicci de'Medici
(1360-1428)

Cosimo (Pater Patriae)   Lorenzo

PIERO 'The Gouty"   Giovanni
(1416-1469)
= Lucrezia Tornabuoni

LORENZO "The Magnificent"   Giuliano   3 daughters
(1449-92)   (1453-78)
= Clarice Orsini

Giulio (Illegit.)
(Pope Clement VII

PIERO "The Fatuous"   Giovanni   Giuliano   Lucrezia   daughters:
(1472-1503)   (Pope Leo X) (Duc de   = Giacomo   Maddalena
= Alfonsina   Nemours)   Salviati   Maria
Orsini   Contessina

LORENZO   Clarice   Giovanni   Maria
(1492-1519)   Ippolito   = Giovanni
= Madeleine of   delle Bande
La Tour d'Auvergne   Nere

Catherine
= King Henry II
of France

Florence, the poet Angelo Poliziano, who had served as a tutor to his children and was with him on his deathbed. Lorenzo, too, was a poet who wrote on a wide variety of subjects. Scorning the traditional medium of serious writers of the day, he wrote in the Tuscan vernacular, as did Dante. He explained his reasons by saying that although it would perhaps seem reprehensible to write in the mother tongue, he wanted to reach the people whom he loved. Had he not been such a renowned statesman, he might well have earned fame as a poet. His long philosophical poem, "The Supreme Good," of some 208 lines, though drawing on classical ideas was written in the Tuscan dialect. The opening lines alone tell us something about the man:

> Lured on, escorted by the sweetest thoughts
> I fled the bitter storms of civic life
> to lead my soul back to a calmer port,
> and so my heart was carried from that life
> to this one — free, serene, untroubled — which
> retains the little good the world still knows
> To free my feeble nature from the load
> that wearies it and stops its flight, I left
> the pretty circle of my native walls.

(Lorenzo de'Medici, *Selected Poems and Prose*, trans. Jon Thiem)

Lorenzo's short life, which had begun so joyously, ended on a sad note. He had lost a daughter two years before the death of his wife in 1487. Accursed by the Medici affliction of arthritis, he frequented the spas where he found temporary relief from pain, but by the beginning of 1492, although he was only forty-three, his health was fast declining. By the spring it was clear that he was dying, and nothing that the doctors could do was of help. A Lombardy doctor in a last attempt to save his life prepared concoctions of pulverized pearls and precious stones, the chemotherapy of the times comparable to the gold salts used today in treating some arthritic conditions. There was no magic cure. Lorenzo, "the Magnificent," lapsed into a coma and passed away on April 9, 1492. He was interred next to his brother, Giuliano, in the old sacristy of the church of San Lorenzo.

Some four months after Lorenzo's death, another great journey began when, before sunrise on August 3, 1492, Christopher Columbus set sail from a Spanish port on a voyage that would change the world forever. Yet the legacy of Lorenzo de'Medici remains a gift to the New World as well as to the Old.

CHAPTER SEVEN

The World of Machiavelli

Il Moro and the Coming of the French

The Gate to Paradise, which symbolically opened the fifteenth century, was now closing. Nowhere was this more apparent than in Florence, where the gloomy Dominican friar Savonarola preached doom and foretold the wrath of God on those fun-loving people who had drawn inspiration from the pagan world of ancient Greece. The dark cloud that fell over Florence after the death of Lorenzo was only a harbinger of what was in store for Italy as other powers of Europe set their sights on the beautiful land dotted with cities that sparkled like rich jewels.

The Italian historian, Francesco Guicciardini, who witnessed the demise of the Italians, begins his *Storia d'Italia* with the ominous words which might well introduce the sixteenth century: "I have determined to write about those events which have occurred in Italy within our memory, ever since French troops, summoned by our own princes, began to stir up great dissension here; a most memorable subject . . . full of the most terrible happenings."

Here are some of the main characters who occupied the stage after the death of Lorenzo de'Medici in 1492:

- King Ferdinand I (Don Ferrante) on the throne of Naples.
- Piero de'Medici in Florence with Savonarola lurking behind him like a shadow.
- Rodrigo Borgia, now the infamous Pope Alexander VI, in Rome.
- Lodovico Maria Sforza in Milan.
- Off-stage, behind the Alps, Charles VIII, the twenty-two-year-old King of France.

Of all of these fascinating characters, the one accused of setting the wheel of misfortune into motion was Lodovico Sforza, known as "Il Moro," a nickname earned early in life for his dark complexion and often used to describe his character. Ambitious, wily and deceitful, few trusted him. Having spent many years as regent of his young nephew, Gian Galeazzo Sforza, he did not step aside when the inept and not too bright young duke came of age. Il Moro was duke in all but name; being wise and capable he served the interests of the Duchy of Milan very well. He maintained a fine court and engaged the best talents that money could buy. The brilliant and versatile Leonardo da Vinci planned fine banquets, designed weapons, and was put in charge of rivers and waterways as chief engineer, improving canals and the irrigation system to mention only a few of his activities.

The threat to Il Moro's power did not come from Milan, but from outside. He knew that sooner or later his young nephew would claim his place as duke. Rumblings came from the Kingdom of Naples as Gian Galeazzo Sforza was married to Isabella, a grand-daughter of King Ferdinand, who called on her royal relatives to help her gain her rightful place as the Lady of Milan. She bitterly resented being pushed aside by her rival, Beatrice d'Este, the beautiful wife of Il Moro.

Il Moro did not wait for trouble, but conceived the plan to provoke the young King of France to claim as his right the Kingdom of Naples as a descendant of the House of Anjou. Like a Satan sitting on the shoulder of the young king, Il Moro sowed the seeds of greed and ambition in his mind and invited him to Italy. The King needed little persuasion. The die was cast, and preparations for the invasion began as frightened Italian princes dispatched their ambassadors hither and thither in a flurry of diplomatic activity while a delighted Savonarola saw the French King as the "arm of God."

A formidable army was assembled to attack the Kingdom of Naples from land and sea, then on January 24, 1494, as French forces were posed to set out, King Ferdinand suddenly died of pneumonia, leaving the task of stopping the French to his son, Alfonso.

The Tyrrhenian Sea came alive with galleys, and the earth rumbled as cavalry and infantry headed north to intercept the invaders. Il Moro began to regret inviting the French when he realized that a land attack would mean that his dukedom would be the first through which the foreign hordes would march. King Charles entered Asti on September 9, 1494 and his incursion introduced much disorder into Italian ways of governing and maintaining harmony. The Italian historian Francesco Guicciardini wrote:

> We have never since been able to re-establish order, thus opening the possibility to other foreign nations and barbarous armies to trample upon our institutions and miserably oppress us. And what is more we cannot mitigate our shame because of the valor of the victor, since he whose coming caused so many misfortunes was, although well endowed in wealth and fortune, almost completely devoid of any natural mental gifts.

He goes on to talk of the French king's unhealthy constitution and his short stature, ill-proportioned limbs, and plain ugliness that made him look more like a monster than a man.

Il Moro greeted his guest at Asti with great pomp hoping that he would move on, but the puny King Charles was stricken with smallpox and lay ill for a whole month before departing with his diabolical force of heavy artillery and cannon, the likes of which had never been seen in Italy. Having recovered sufficiently from his illness, Charles moved on to Pavia, where, still in the company of Il Moro, he paid a friendly visit to Gian Galeazzo, the real Duke of Milan. They were first cousins because their mothers were daughters of the Duke of Savoy. Charles had left his own sickbed to find cousin Gian lying very seriously ill and his wife, Isabella, in a deplorable state for she was not only watching her husband fight for his life but also had to worry about her father, King Alfonso, whose kingdom was under threat. Throwing herself at Charles's feet and weeping bitterly, Isabella begged that her father and the House of Aragon would not be harmed. For Charles there was no turning back, however sorry he may have felt for his young cousin Gian, whom he had left on his deathbed. In fact, shortly after leaving Pavia he received news that Gian Galeazzo had died. It was widely rumored that Il Moro had caused him to be poisoned.

King Charles's move south was swift for he met with little resistance from the terrified Italians, who realized the futility of putting up a fight, unprepared as they were for war. Naples quickly fell to the invaders as did most of the Kingdom.

Il Moro realized very soon that his greatest enemy was now the French, who would next lay claims to the Duchy of Milan and other Italian city-states. They formed a League that was joined by Spain, Pope Alexander VI, the hitherto neutral Venice, and Emperor Maximillian (married to Bianca Maria, the niece of Il Moro and sister of the deceased Gian Galeazzo).

With this new turn of events, the French king decided that it would be prudent to return home and began his departure, leaving his officials behind in charge of his newly won kingdom. His return was not as easy as his arrival, for the army of the League was ready to block his passage and wipe out his army. He was therefore forced to fight his way home through hostile territory.

The invasion had been like a flood; behind them in the south, as the water began to recede, the Neapolitans began to reclaim their land and bring back their own rulers. In the north, however, Il Moro had to bargain to recover some of the territory claimed by the invaders, but he nevertheless took credit for getting rid of the French. He seemed to be riding the crest of a wave, but his joy was short-lived. The first blow came in 1497 with the death of his beloved illegitimate daughter Bianca. Beatrice, too, mourned her young stepdaughter, whom she loved as one of her own. It was ironic that just six weeks later Beatrice herself would be the one mourned, and with her untimely death the court of Milan was plunged into darkness. Leonardo da Vinci was working on "The Last Supper" in the refectory of Santa Maria delle Grazie at the time and took time off from that masterpiece to paint the figures of Il Moro and Beatrice on the opposite wall.

✳ ✳ ✳

Back in France, the sickly Charles VIII died on April 8, 1498, following an accident. This was no consolation to Il Moro, for he was succeeded by a still more bitter enemy in the person of Louis XII, who made clear his intentions when, in addition to the title King of the Two Sicilies, he brazenly assumed the title of Duke of Milan, claiming the Visconti inheritance as a grandson of Valentina Visconti. In his grief on the death of his wife, perhaps Il Moro had neglected to see the danger until it was too late. Unable to get support from outside to defend his Duchy and beset by enemies from within, he knew his was a lost cause. He would seek refuge with his friend Emperor Maximillian and made preparations to flee Milan, sending his two sons, Maximillian and Francesco, ahead with his brother, Cardinal Ascanio. On September 2, 1499, French troops entered Milan through one gate as Il Moro made his escape through another, leaving his massive and impregnable Castello, well stocked with ammunition and supplies, in the hands of Bernadino da Corte, who was to hold out until help could be brought. Without a fight, Bernadino was bought off by the French on September 13. On hearing of such treachery, Il Moro is quoted as saying, "From the time of Judas until today there has been no greater traitor than Bernadino da Corte," and indeed he had earned the contempt of both the French and the Italians. On October 6, 1499, the French King made his triumphal entry into Milan, passing

By the end of the 15th century, one third of Italy had come under the Spanish crown and was ruled by viceroys.

The peninsula was still cut in two by the Papal States, while in the north republics and duchies remained as separate states, often ruled by great families that kept armies and maintained brilliant courts in their respective capitals.

End of 15th Century

through streets decorated with the fleur-de-lis to the great Duomo, and then to move into the fine castle of the Sforzas.

Meanwhile Il Moro had reached Germany, where he proceeded to form an army, while the Milanese who had welcomed the French soon realized their mistake as they suffered the billeting of soldiers in their private homes and foreigners lording it over their city. They wanted Il Moro back; by January 30, 1500, the city was in full revolt. A few days later the scene of the previous autumn was reversed as the French fled through one gate as Sforza forces reentered from another as the city echoed to the shouts of "Moro, Moro!" Their own Duke who now made his way to the great Duomo was after all preferable to the French.

Leaving brother Ascanio to retake the Castello, Il Moro went after the fleeing French, catching up with them at Novara. It was here on April 8, 1500, that the fate of Il Moro was sealed. He made the mistake of refusing permission for his unpaid troops to sack the city. Furthermore, the Swiss elements of his army refused to fight against their Swiss brethren in the service of the French. They asked for safe conducts so they could return home and were allowed to leave. As the flood of deserters filed past the French encampment, Il Moro realized the hopelessness of his position and tried to make his escape with them disguised as a Swiss pikeman. Another Judas had betrayed him for a sum of money, and he was soon spotted by the French. It was all over now.

Il Moro was taken back to France as a prisoner, but he was so weak and ill that he had to be carried part of the way on a litter. He would never know freedom again, although he was treated with the respect due a prince of his stature. His imprisonment lasted eight years, the last four at Loches in the Loire Valley. Not even Emperor Maximilian could obtain his release. In the spring of 1508, Il Moro made a desperate attempt to escape by bribing one of his guards, who allowed him to slip out through the castle gates hidden in a cartload of straw. Unfortunately, he lost his way in the woods around the castle, only to be captured and brought back to stricter captivity. His companion in prison, *La Divina Commedia* had been taken away; now he wrote verses and made designs on the walls of his dungeon. In all his misfortune and suffering, he still showed himself to be a man of Renaissance Italy, a lover of art and beauty and the patron of Leonardo da Vinci.

Il Moro died on May 17, 1508, just a few weeks after being recaptured. He was in his fifty-seventh year. No one knows where he was buried, but perhaps his earthly remains were eventually taken back to Milan and placed in the tomb made for him on the death of his beloved Beatrice.

The Borgias

As Il Moro languished in French prisons, Italy continued to be a battlefield. The whole peninsula was a stage where the action took place, but much of the plot was decided in the wings. The French Cock was determined to crow over the Duchy of Milan as well as the Kingdom of Naples; King Ferdinand of Spain, not content with the lands he had already claimed for himself beyond the Ocean Sea, eventually wanted all the Kingdom of Naples under his control. The German Eagle, wearing the crown of the Holy Roman Emperor, was always ready to swoop down from across the Alps with his armies and meddle in the affairs of the peninsula. Then there was the Republic of Venice to worry about, straddling the Adriatic like a powerful monster, draped across the Dalmatian coast, and now always moving out of its swampy marsh with its long tentacles reaching overland to Milan and down the Adriatic coast for cities that were once papal domain. Added to this was the increasingly temporal role played by the popes to bring back under control of the Holy See those cities in Romagna that were held by princes and tyrants. This was the scenario as we enter the sixteenth century, the world as Niccolò Machiavelli knew it.

If the name of Machiavelli has a certain sinister ring it is because it has found its way into the dictionary as an adjective to mean cold-blooded, cunning in political management, and crafty. Perhaps to some degree Machiavelli's physical appearance gave this definition a human face. He was a thin man of medium height. He had black hair and piercing black eyes set in a bony face. Yet the adjectives did not describe the man, but rather the times that shaped his political philosophy and his ultimate model, Cesare Borgia.

Machiavelli was born in 1469 in Florence where his father was the poorest member of one of the principal Florentine families. Although he was a doctor of laws, he had been barred from his profession as an insolvent debtor and lived frugally with his family outside the city. With little money for tutors, Machiavelli studied a great deal on his own, yet from these obscure beginnings he was recognized for his abilities and entered public service in Florence, a city that had become a house divided shortly after the death of Lorenzo the Magnificent. Piero the Fatuous had fled into exile, the Medici palace was sacked by a mob, and the French had briefly occupied the city.

Machiavelli was twenty-nine years old when he became head of the second chancery, and his first mission was to the French court where in 1500 he spent five months. That was the year Lodovico Il Moro was taken prisoner, the French King Louis II now claiming the title of Duke of Milan. It was also in the same fateful year that the French and the Spanish, by the Treaty of Granada, resolved to join forces to conquer and divide between them the Kingdom of Naples.

When Machiavelli returned to Florence the city was under threat from the sinister Cesare Borgia, son of the Spanish-born Rodrigo Borgia, who became Pope Alexander VI in 1492. Never had such an immoral and cruel man slithered into the papal seat to hold the title of Vicar of Christ.

Machiavelli soon found himself testing the political waters of the day, muddied by the murky dealings of the Borgias, whom Machiavelli came to know well. The ambitious Pope had plans for the children he had by his Roman mistress. Cesare had been relegated to a religious career and made a cardinal, whereas the Pope had plans to turn over the temporal power to the older brother, Giovanni. All that changed when Giovanni was mysteriously murdered one night as he rode alone through the city. It was widely suspected that Cesare was somehow implicated in his death, for it was no secret that he was jealous of his brother. To add to the scandal, according to rumor the two brothers loved and lusted after their sister, Lucrezia Borgia, but such false rumors were often circulated by one's enemies.

With his brother now out of the way, Cesare had no difficulty persuading his father, the Pope, to let him discard the hat of the cardinal in exchange for the sword of the soldier. As the instrument of his father's ambitions, Cesare rose like a comet, first trading his title of Cardinal of Valencia for that of Duke Valentino conferred on him by the French King Louis XII, now allied with the Pope in a mutually advantageous deal. The King had tired of his wife and wanted an annulment that only a pope could grant. The two reached an agreement whereby Louis, after regaining the Duchy of Milan, which he had lost, would help the Pope recover the cities of Romagna which had broken away from papal control and were ruled by potentates. They included Faenza, Forlì, Imola, Rimini, and Pesaro.

Pesaro was held by the Pope's former son-in-law, Giovanni Sforza, once the husband of Lucrezia Borgia, who was her father's political pawn. It was a scandalous affair in which Giovanni had alleged that Lucrezia had incestuous relations with her father, who in turn declared that his son-in-law was impotent and in 1497 the marriage was annulled on account of "non-consummation." Next came a political match with an illegitimate son of Alfonso II of Naples, later assassinated. Once more the accusing finger was pointed at Cesare Borgia.

Lucrezia did not remain a widow for long. She was hastily married off to yet another prince, this time Alfonso d'Este, brother-in-law of Il Moro, who in 1505 became Duke of Ferrara, a city that was a center for humanists, writers, poets and

Ferrara, rich capital of a former city-state and realm of the powerful D'Este family, is the resting place of the much maligned Lucrezia Borgia, who became Duchess of Ferrara.

The magnificent and well-preserved castle with its moat, fed by the waters of canals, has served as fortress and palace for its lords.

painters, including the great Titian. The much-maligned Lucrezia lived peacefully as the Duchess of Ferrara, had several children, and died in the arms of her loving husband ten days after delivering a stillborn child.

Meanwhile, Cesare Borgia was building his own empire through conquest. He met with little opposition, but at the end of the century, 1499, he crossed paths with the "vicar" of Imola, the legendary and courageous Caterina Sforza. The city of Imola had surrendered to the combined forces of Cesare and his French allies, but Caterina did not give up. With her children safely packed off to Florence, she retreated to the Citadel with a few faithful supporters, holding out until the last. When the Citadel fell in January 1500, Cesare supposedly raped his beautiful captive and then dispatched her to Rome for "safe-keeping" in the impregnable Castel Sant'Angelo.

Cesare continued his military activities in Central Italy, capturing Urbino and threatening Florence where Niccolò Machiavelli had become the Secretary of Defense. Machiavelli was sent twice as envoy to Cesare Borgia and in 1502 was with him as without mercy he put down rebellions in the territories he had conquered. For five months, Machiavelli and Cesare were together almost constantly, each spying on the other, and Machiavelli came to be fascinated by this ruthless man whom he saw as the new prince who could conquer Italy, the sick body that needed harsh medicine.

Cesare Borgia had reached the height of his power and was feared throughout Italy when his luck finally ran out. On a sultry hot August day in 1503, Cesare and his father, the Pope, went to dine in the cool of a vineyard not far from the Vatican. This was their last meeting, for the Pope died suddenly after drinking wine that was later thought to have contained poison. Cesare, too, was stricken in the same way, but the powerful antidotes that he was given saved his life, although he remained seriously ill for a long time.

The black and swollen body of the Pope was carried back to the city. Here are the harsh words the contemporary historian, Guicciardini, used to record the event for posterity:

> All Rome thronged with incredible rejoicing to see the dead body of Alexander in St. Peter's, unable to satiate their eyes enough with seeing spent that serpent who in his boundless ambition and pestiferous perfidy, and with all his examples of horrible cruelty and monstrous sensuality and unheard-of avarice . . . had envenomed the whole world.

Cesare's life was now in danger as popular uprisings spread, and many of the cities previously captured were recovered by their former lords. In addition, in 1503 the ambitious Spanish king conquered Naples and the Treaty of Granada became a useless piece of paper as Cesare's French allies went down to defeat.

In Rome turmoil accompanied the election of a new pope. They chose the ailing Cardinal of Siena, Pius III, whose pontificate lasted only twenty-six days. At this time, Cesare was under attack and was forced to flee to the safety of Castel Sant'Angelo, where his former prisoner, Caterina Sforza, had recently been confined.

The next pope to be elected was Giulio della Rovere, who took the name of Julius II. He tried to persuade Cesare to concede to the papacy the fortresses and cities that had remained faithful to him, holding him prisoner at Ostia under the guard of the Spanish. After much negotiation, he was released in April of 1504, and allowed to go to Naples under safe conduct. There he was treacherously arrested by the Viceroy, on orders from King Ferdinand, and put on a galley bound for Spain where he remained in captivity for two years.

The infamous Cesare Borgia passed out of Italian history, but later escaped to die in a battle while commanding forces of the King of Navarre. Borgia power was broken forever, and Machiavelli lost his hero, the prince who might have created a new empire in the peninsula.

Instead it was King Ferdinand who expanded his realm, bringing under the crown of Spain both Sicily and the Kingdom of Naples. The Spanish kings ruled through viceroys with the participation of native representatives, and Naples continued to be the seat of government. The legacy of King Ferdinand lasted for two centuries, but all that remained of the Borgias was the infamous reputation they had earned. Their memory is kept alive by the portraits that look down from the walls of the Borgia apartments of the Vatican. We will now return there to get better acquainted with the next tenant, the warrior-pope.

Art and War

Machiavelli's world had changed little, for the Borgia pope had been replaced by one who was equally ambitious. Pope Julius II occupied center stage during the next period of Italian history as he resolved to increase the power and prestige of the Church by bringing back under the Holy See the cities that had been lost to "tyrants" as well as the expanding Venetian Republic. In contrast to the battles that raged during the pontificate of Julius, this was also a period of great artistic achievement. Under the patronage of this warlike pope, the magnificent Basilica of Saint Peter took shape as artists, sculptors, and architects flocked to Rome.

In the year 1506, as the cornerstone was being laid for the great basilica, replacing the older building, the warrior-pope, as he came to be known, took up the sword and at the head of 500 men at arms marched off to regain Perugia from the despot Giampaolo Baglioni. Three years later, the belligerent Pope excommunicated the Venetians, in possession of several port cities considered papal domain, and went to war to regain cities in the Romagna. In a single battle in May of 1509, papal forces, with the help of the French, defeated the Venetians and broke their power.

As Venetian power declined, it was the French who became a threat, and the Pope readily betrayed his so-called allies to realign himself with their enemies. The new war cry was now "Fuori i barbari" [Out with the barbarians]. As the Pope established his headquarters in Bologna and took up the sword again, it was said that he "had cast the keys of St. Peter into the Tiber." It was during this period, however, that Michelangelo, high on his perch in the Sistine Chapel, was working on the magnificent frescoes of "The Creation." An important event was the creation of the Holy League in 1511 which isolated the French, their only ally being the fiercely independent city-state of Ferrara, where Duke Alfonso d'Este held the power with his wife, Lucrezia Borgia. Florence, the traditional ally of France, refused to join the League and maintained a neutral position. Machiavelli, fearing that his city would be dragged into such a conflict, had done his best to persuade the French King to make peace with Julius II, but war was inevitable. The stage was set for the Battle of Ravenna.

On Easter Sunday, April 11, 1512, the curtain rose on a scene outside of Ravenna with a cast of thousands. On one side were the French and the Ferrarese, and facing them were the papal forces and the Spanish troops. In reality it was a battle between the French and the Spanish for control of Italy. The Spanish Viceroy of Naples was there in person at the head of his forces. With the papal contingent was also Cardinal Giovanni de'Medici, son of Lorenzo the Magnificent, destined to be the next pope. This weak-sighted and gentle-mannered man wore no battle dress. Facing them with their own Cardinal were the forces of Ferrara, with their military leader, the Duke himself; leading the French troops was the brilliant young Frenchman Gaston de Foix, encouraging his men with promises of untold rewards when they reached Rome.

The site of the battle became the killing fields for both sides as young men were mowed down by artillery fire, the highly destructive weapons unknown in the previous century, as well as by hand-to-hand combat. It was believed that each side lost some 10,000 men, not to mention the beautiful horses of the cavalry. The French came out the victors, but their own courageous and beloved commander, Gaston de Foix, had been knocked from his horse and slain by Spanish infantry. For the Italians, the aftermath of the battle must have been worse than the battle itself as the angry victors avenged their dead companions through pillage and unspeakable cruelties.

The tide was soon to turn. A month later, Swiss soldiers, members of the Holy League, poured across the Alps into Italy. The French army abandoned Romagna and returned to defend Lombardy, but from there were called back to France to defend

Navarre, which was under attack from Spain. (It was here that the escapee, Cesare Borgia, met his end.) The Swiss drove the French out of Lombardy, and the Sforzas were returned to power. Massimiliano, first born of Il Moro, having grown up in exile and now a young man of twenty-one, took his place as Duke of Milan.

Changes were also in store for Florence as Spanish forces, in the name of the victorious Holy League, were soon on their way to that rebellious city, which continued to support the French. Machiavelli had been busy forming a local militia, and the proud Florentines made preparations to resist. On August 29, the town of Prato (just twelve miles outside Florence) was taken and mercilessly sacked. Machiavelli's militia had failed to put up a fight, choosing to lay down arms and take flight, giving the Italians the name of "cowards." What followed was described by Machiavelli as "an appalling spectacle of horrors," as fleeing men were cut down by the Spanish troops and women were savagely raped. If the weak-eyed Cardinal de'Medici could not see too well, he could certainly hear the screams of terror of his own countrymen on that day.

Meanwhile, in nearby Florence, Medici supporters were already on the way to the Palazzo della Signoria to demand the resignation of the *gonfoloniere* Soderini, their head of state. Machiavelli was the messenger who requested for him a safe passage to leave the city; three days later, on September 1, 1512, Soderini was on his way to exile faraway in Dalmatia.

The Medici were returned to power with the support of Spanish troops. On the day that Soderini left the city, the gentle and unassuming Giuliano de'Medici (Duc de Nemours and third son of Lorenzo the Magnificent), now thirty-three years old, was the first to return home. He walked unescorted through the streets he had known as a boy, ending years of exile. His brother, Cardinal Giovanni, followed later with an escort of 1,500 Spanish troops and entered his former palace like a returning ruler. Along with the two brothers there was cousin Giulio, bastard son of their uncle Giuliano, who had been assassinated years before, and the young nephew, Lorenzo, son of older brother Piero, who drowned in the waters of the Garigliano while fighting with the French nine years earlier. They had known tragedy, but now they were back together in their beloved native city.

Machiavelli loved his city just as much and would gladly have continued to serve under the Medici, but he had lost his position and was forced to leave along with the Medici enemies. His troubles were not yet over, however, as six months later he was accused of conspiracy. Imprisoned and even tortured, he continued to plead innocence and was eventually released. The public life he had enjoyed was over, and he was forced to watch events from the sidelines. Cynical and embittered, he withdrew to his property in the country where he would produce the work with which his name is best associated, a handbook for the "new prince" who would save Italy entitled *Il Principe*.

The Medici Popes

Pope Julius II died in the night of February 20 in 1513, six months after the Medici were returned to power in Florence. Cardinal Giovanni journeyed to Rome on learning that his benefactor was dying, but he was delayed by his own illness with an ulcer. He arrived after the Pope's death and missed the opening ceremonies of the conclave. As Senior Deacon he was required to count the votes taken from the urn, and on March 11 he had the extraordinary task of announcing *himself* as the next pope. He took the name of Leo X. Florence went wild with joy to have one of their own elected, and four days of celebrations followed as bells rang out, fireworks were set off, and cannon fire echoed from the surrounding hills.

The coronation in Rome was a magnificent event. The Pope, who rode sidesaddle on a white Arabian horse, loved pageantry; so did the Romans, who thronged the streets of the procession. In the solemn ceremonies, the standard of the Church was borne by Alfonso d'Este (Lucrezia Borgia's husband), seeking reconciliation with the papacy he had so recently fought against alongside the French. This particular day was all the more extraordinary for the new Pope who, just one year earlier on that very same day, had been miserably taken prisoner at the Battle of Ravenna.

As Giovanni de'Medici took up his papal duties as Leo X, Florence was left in the hands of the Medici heir, his nephew, twenty-one-year-old Lorenzo, inexperienced and headstrong. Machiavelli again tried to get into the good graces of the Medici, dedicating *Il Principe,* his handbook for rulers, to Lorenzo:

Niccolò Machiavelli
al Magnifico Lorenzo de'Medici

The dedication is followed by a letter in which he tells the young duke that his gift to him is his "knowledge of the conduct of great men." Machiavelli now places his hopes for a "new prince" and liberator on Lorenzo, and this is made clear in the last lines of *Il Principe:*

> *This foreign domination has a bad smell for everyone. May your illustrious House take up this mission with the spirit and hope with which one faces just causes, so that under your banner this country may gain dignity and under your auspices the words of Petrarch will come true:*

> > *Virtu contro a furore*
> > *prenderà l'arme; e fia el combatter corto:*
> > *che l'antico valore*
> > *nelli italici cor non e ancor morto.*

> > *[Virtue will take up arms against violence;*
> > *and the fight will be short, for the ancient*
> > *courage in Italian hearts is not yet dead.]*

These were Petrarch's words to the Italians in his *Italia Mia,* and by this time *Italians* means anyone south of the Alps.

This failed to get Machiavelli back into the good graces of the Medici family. Moreover, the arrogant and inexperienced Lorenzo of pitifully puny physique was equally unendowed in intelligence and unable to live up to his illustrious name. He had come on the scene at a crucial time and was but a small figure in the wings of the Italian arena where the great powers of France and Spain with a new cast of characters continued to fight their battles.

Francis I had acceded to the French throne and, without wasting time, invaded Italy in 1515 and occupied Milan. On the death of King Ferdinand the following year, the Spanish throne was occupied by his grandson, Charles I. Born in 1500, he had been raised in The Netherlands, speaking French, and his knowledge of Spanish was poor. Just sixteen years old, he was already so mature it was said of him that he had never been young. Of all the kings and princes in Europe, he was the one to watch. When his grandfather Maximillian, the Holy Roman Emperor, died three years later, the young Charles succeeded him as German King. He had inherited an empire consisting of Spain, the Two Sicilies, and The Netherlands and was now the Grand Duke of Austria. In 1519, even before he had celebrated his twentieth birthday, he was elected Holy Roman Emperor as well. What could any prince do against such a man who already controlled half of Italy by right of inheritance?

Meanwhile, in 1518 the young Lorenzo de'Medici had been sent to France to marry Madeleine de la Tour d'Auvergne, a cousin of the French King. This was a political match arranged by his uncle, the Pope. On April 13 of the following year, Madeleine gave birth to a baby girl. The young mother died at the end of the month; a few days later Lorenzo followed her in death, the cause given as tuberculosis and syphilis. This orphan babe, who was christened Caterina, was destined to one day be Queen of France.

Cardinal Giulio rushed back to Florence to take care of interests there. It was a lucky break for Machiavelli, as Giulio asked for his counsel in reforming the government and also engaged him to write the history of Florence. Giulio's stay in Florence was cut short, however, by the sudden death of the Pope at midnight of December 1-2, 1521, and he hastened to Rome for the conclave, leaving in the care of a regent the Medici heirs — a half-French orphan baby and two despicable young bastards, the frizzy-haired Alessandro, supposedly the natural son of Cardinal Giulio himself, and Ippolito, love child of the late Giuliano (Duc de Nemours).

Giulio was destined to become pope and in 1523, after the brief pontificate of an obscure monk from The Netherlands, the forty-five-year-old Medici was duly elected after a lengthy conclave and took the name of Clement VII.

Now caught in the limelight, the new pope soon found himself enmeshed in the conflicts of kings who continued to fight their battles on Italian soil. The Spanish-French feud again heated up when the French once more made an attempt to regain Milan. Undeterred by winter weather, French troops crossed into Lombardy and met up with the Imperial army at Pavia. A battle took place on February 24, 1525. It was the Emperor's twenty-fifth birthday, and his greatest gift was victory. The French were routed with tremendous loss of life, but a still greater prize was the capture of the French King himself. He was taken by five soldiers who had no idea they had laid hands on a king until the Spanish Viceroy rode up and recognized his Highness, kissed his hand, and led him away in the name of the Emperor to be taken back to Spain as prisoner.

The young Emperor was now in control of much of Europe. The French were in check, the balance of power had been upset, and the Pope, finding himself walking a political tightrope, now called on Machiavelli.

War Between Pope and Emperor

After spending some months in Spain as an unwilling guest of Emperor Charles, the French King gained his freedom partly through the intercession of the Pope. In January 1526, he put his signature to the Treaty of Madrid, whereby he solemnly renounced all claims to that coveted land of Italy. However, Emperor Charles soon regretted having put his trust in the French King, who shortly after his release joined an anti-imperialist league, the League of Cognac, engineered by the Medici Pope, it not only included Florence but also the powerful Venetians. The Pope thus proved to be less worthy of trust than the ambitious Frenchman, as he had turned against the very ally that had reinstated his family in Florence.

Half way across the Ponte Vecchio in Florence is a statue honoring one of the city's famous sons, the goldsmith and sculptor B E N V E N U T O CELLINI.

Italy soon became once more the battlefield for the conflict between the two young rivals when the French invaded the north. Bloody battles took place, but imperialists gained the upper hand against the mostly Italian defenders, and there was great loss of life. One casualty was the already legendary Giovanni delle Bande Nere, son of the indomitable Caterina Sforza. His death on November 30, robbed the Italians of one of their most courageous and revered young men. Remember this hero whose heirs later became the Grand Dukes of Tuscany.

Following successes in Lombardy, the imperial sword was out of its scabbard and pointed at Rome herself, where the Pope needed to be "taught a lesson." Two formidable armies, the Germans and the Spanish, joined forces in the north. Like a human tidal wave, some 30,000 soldiers moved rapidly southward, creating havoc in their wake. In charge of papal forces was Guicciardini, the principal historian of the period, and with him at the behest of the Pope was none other than Machiavelli.

On the May 5, 1527, imperial forces led by the Duke of Bourbon, a Frenchman who had turned against his king and joined the Emperor, were on the outskirts of Rome. Under cover of a thick morning fog he moved his troops up to the walls of the city, where the battle took place. Leading the soldiers at the first assault on the walls was the Duke of Bourbon himself, but he was killed in this action by a shot from an arquebus fired from the walls of the impregnable Castel Sant'Angelo. The celebrated goldsmith-sculptor Benvenuto Cellini, known for talents of another kind, took credit for firing that fatal shot. One might wonder what the artist was doing there on the battlements, but he had taken it upon himself as a member of the papal household to man the guns set up to defend the Castello, where the terrified Pope had taken refuge by way of the corridor that linked it to the Vatican palace.

Rome was unprepared for the onslaught. It was a ragtag multitude that attempted to defend the city, as many had fled southward and others sought refuge in the Castello. The majority of those left behind were at the mercy of the attackers, who swarmed into the city pillaging, killing, raping, ransacking churches, and even destroying sacred objects. Among the army were many Protestants, followers of new religious leader Martin Luther, who were not inclined to respect the Roman Church they had come to hate. If Michelangelo needed inspiration for his "Last Judgment," he found it in this holy city, a living hell where swarms of rough foreign soldiers continued their cruel rampaging like demons from the worst hell. It was said that on that first day some 8,000 people were slaughtered. Guicciardini gives a chilling account of the atrocities committed against the Roman people. He tells of the loss of life and the destruction of priceless works of art, treasures that were carried off by the soldiers as booty, and the fear that gripped the whole city in the terrible months that followed.

Machiavelli had lived through it all. Not even Florence was calm, for the Medici were once more cast out as their enemies smashed images of the Medici popes, the living one as well as the dead Leo, and tore down insignia of the family. In Rome, Pope Clement VII, guarded by German and Spanish soldiers, was now a prisoner in Castel Sant'Angelo, which had previously been his refuge. He waited in vain for his allies to come and rescue him.

This was the Italy Machiavelli left on his death on June 21, 1527.

A Medici Pope Crowns the Last Emperor

If Machiavelli had lived he would have witnessed the reconciliation between Pope and Emperor and the resumption of a partnership that was established in the days of Charlemagne. It was on Christmas Day in the year 800 that the crown of emperor had been placed on the head of Charlemagne, who would be known as the Defender of the Faith and now, some 730 years later, another Charles would be the last to receive the crown from the hands of a pope in Italy.

The Pope's imprisonment was an embarrassment for the Emperor and became a dilemma for the Christian princes of Europe, who saw their spiritual leader in such straits at a time when the new religion of Martin Luther was quickly gaining adherents. The Pope had been obliged to sign a humiliating treaty and guarantee payment of enormous sums of money, but even that was not enough to buy his freedom. Meanwhile, in a city held hostage by the disorderly hordes of foreign soldiers, his safety was in jeopardy. His escape was therefore urged and "arranged." Disguised as a merchant, he was taken in secret from the Castello and handed over to an imperial soldier, who escorted him to the hill town of Orvieto to be smuggled in under cover of darkness. Far from Rome, Pope Clement quietly endeavored to steer a neutral course as the two great kings of Christendom continued their battles.

The French controlled the Tyrrhenian Sea, with their fleet under the command of the brilliant Genoese admiral Andrea Doria, and were making progress in the south of Italy. Then typhus and lack of provisions struck a providential blow against the French invaders, and the pendulum swung back in favor of the Spanish. But the real catalyst now came when the young French King made the serious mistake of quarreling with his admiral. Andrea Doria simply transferred his loyalties to the other side, joining the imperials. He did not go alone, but took all his galleys and men along with him, liberating the city of Genoa, which had been under French control. It was an incredible stoke of luck for Emperor Charles.

Pope Clement was an astute man. Seeing the writing on the wall, he began to move from his neutral position and lean toward the Emperor, who now clearly held the advantage. The historic Treaty of Cambrei of June 29, 1529, spelled out details of an agreement between Pope and Emperor as they agreed to settle their differences and bring peace to Italy. Of course, being a Medici, the Pope saw to it that Florence was part of the pact. The Medici family would be reinstated in Florence with the Pope's bastard son, Alessandro de'Medici, holding the temporal power. The final seal to this pact would be a marriage alliance between the young Alessandro and a daughter of the Emperor, who came up with the perfect match in the person of his bastard daughter Margaret. Alessandro was seventeen, but Margaret was only eight years old at the time of the agreement.

For very good reasons the Emperor was now committed to having a recalcitrant Florence returned to the Medici, but the Florentines, accustomed to their freedom from dukes, chose to resist and set about working on fortifications. It may be surprising to learn that the great Michelangelo left Rome and returned to Florence to help defend the city against the Medici Pope, who had been his patron. In view of his extraordinary genius, Michelangelo was given the task of supervising the defenses.

And so history takes us back again to Florence, once more the center of attention in that early autumn of 1529, as imperial forces under the command of the Prince of Orange, took up positions in the hills around the city. The sacking of Rome was fresh in everyone's memory, but the Prince chose to starve the Florentines into surrender rather than assault and destroy the city of such priceless treasures. After a ten-month siege, the plague-ridden and starving citizens were forced to capitulate to imperial forces as their only means of survival and accept the teenage Alessandro de'Medici as their duke.

It was during the siege of Florence, in 1530, that the crown of emperor was placed on the head of Charles V by the Medici Pope Clement VII. The ceremony took place in Bologna on Saint Matthew's Day, February 24. The date was propitious, for it was also his thirtieth birthday—and the day that he had made the French King his prisoner.

It seemed that peace had finally come to Italy as Pope and Emperor agreed to unite against two formidable enemies—Martin Luther and the dreaded Turks.

CHAPTER EIGHT

The Spanish Period

The Peace Treaty of Cateau-Cambresis

Italy entered a period of relative peace after the dreadful years of the first part of the sixteenth century. France and Spain continued their wars, but Italy was no longer the constant battlefield.

Religious fires that burned out of control appeared almost to have been checked by the waters of the Mediterranean as the Italian peninsula, for a time, largely escaped the terror that was occurring elsewhere. The Spanish Inquisition established during the reign of Ferdinand and Isabella intensified as heretics were tried and burned at the stake; the struggle against Islam continued; and Jews were systematically persecuted, especially in the fervently Catholic Spain. Many would find safe haven in the more enlightened Tuscany under the protection of the restored Medici.

It was a different world in which Italy ceased to play such an important role in European affairs as Spain became the dominant power. Christopher Columbus had discovered the new world for Spain, which had reached out across the Atlantic to claim those lands as her own and eventually force the Catholic religion on the native inhabitants. Even before Rome had suffered her worst nightmare with the sacking of the city, the Spaniard Hernán Cortés had conquered Mexico in the name of Emperor Charles, Montezuma had been killed, and the Aztec empire was destroyed. In England, King Henry VIII defied the authority of Rome, divorcing two wives and beheading two others before his death in 1547. France, where the young Caterina de'Medici was destined to exert her influence for thirty years, first as queen and then as queen mother, was becoming the cultural center of Europe.

In Italy, the sagas of the great families would continue, however, for Charles V had the burdens of a large empire on his shoulders and saw the advantage of controlling the peninsula through native dukes and princes. The city-states survived with their own individual forms of rule, separate entities pledging allegiance to the young Emperor, who was the ultimate arbiter in Italian affairs.

The Kingdoms of Naples and Sicily and the island of Sardinia were now under Spain and ruled by her viceroys. Milan, too, would come directly under Spain on the death of Francesco Sforza II, her last duke. This son of the unfortunate Lodovico, Il Moro, left no heirs, and the coveted Lombardy was once more the target of French claims and warfare. In 1540 the question was settled when Emperor Charles invested his son, the future King Philip II of Spain, with the Duchy of Milan.

Venice remained independent and intact to follow its own course and prospered in spite of the constant threat from the Turks. The Papal States continued to constitute a solid band dividing the south from a still fragmented north. The independent maritime Republic of Genoa, a coastal crescent stretching from Monaco on the west to the Republic of Lucca to the east, now included the mountainous island of Corsica, which had been snatched from the French. The Medici were no longer confined to Florence, and their hereditary rule extended over an area known as the Grand Duchy of Tuscany. The duchies of Parma, Mantua, Ferrara, and Modena continued to be associated with the names of great families who ruled as virtual kings and maintained their separate and splendid courts.

Not to be forgotten was the tiny Duchy of Savoy, perched astride the Alps at a point where the borders of France, Italy, and Switzerland now converge. With its commitment to neutrality, it was the buffer between the French north of the Alps and the Spanish who controlled the peninsula. This was the one to watch, for it would be the key player in later events.

In 1556 the ailing Emperor Charles V withdrew to a monastery in Spain and divided his empire. Philip II was assigned Spain, her colonies, and the Italian possessions. The historic Peace Treaty of Cateau-Cambresis, signed by Philip II of Spain and Henry II of France on April 3, 1559, saw the end of French claims in Italy and set political boundaries that remained substantially unchanged for the next 100 years.

The Grand Duchy of Tuscany

The history of Italy at this point is still a combination of the sagas of many ducal families. So we will follow the one that we have come to know a little better for its role as a leader in Renaissance Italy.

We left Florence in the hands of Alessandro de'Medici, the bastard son of Pope Clement VII, married to the fourteen-year-old Margaret, daughter of the Emperor. When this unpopular young man was assassinated in 1537, there was a scrabble to find a successor in the Medici bloodline. The choice fell on an eighteen-year-old relative of another branch of the family, the chestnut-haired Cosimo de'Medici, son of the revered *condottiere* Giovanni delle Bande Nere, who died fighting the French.

Cosimo had been born in Florence, and he bore the name of a most distinguished ancestor, but orphaned at the age of seven and having lived in Bologna, Genoa, and Naples, he was somewhat of an unknown quantity. Young Cosimo, in spite of his youth, was worldly and wise, and he took the reins, determined to drive the chariot himself, much to the dismay of those who would have used him as their puppet. His first move was to seek the hand in marriage of Alessandro's pretty young widow, Margaret, but the Emperor had other plans for his bastard daughter and refused his permission. Cosimo ended up marrying Eleonora de Toledo, daughter of the wealthy Spanish Viceroy of Naples. It was a good political decision, but it also turned out to be a happy one because he really loved his wife. Cosimo's next goal was to get rid of the Spanish troops garrisoned in his territory, and this he was eventually able to do. Over the years he gradually gained control of the smaller villages and towns around Florence and by the end of 1557 even Siena became part of the duchy. The rich and proud Lucca might have been gobbled up along with the rest, but kept her independence thanks to the protection of the Spanish and remained like a bite out of the geographical apple of Tuscany.

With the Medici realm now bordering the Tyrrhenian Sea, Cosimo saw the need for sea power as pirates and Turks became an increasing threat to safety. He built a navy and established a naval base on the island of Elba. Livorno (Leghorn), now home of the Naval Academy of Italy, took on importance as a port along with Pisa.

Ruthless with his enemies, Cosimo always feared the assassin's sword. Whenever he went out on foot he wore a coat of mail under his outer garb and was accompanied by a Swiss bodyguard. He had enemies among the Florentines, who feared his repressive measures. Yet his accomplishments cannot be denied. Drainage and irrigation projects were carried out in Tuscany, canals were built, olive plantations were created, and the School of Botany was founded at the University of Pisa. Cosimo was also responsible for introducing medicinal plants from America and farm crops from the Orient.

In the tradition of the Medici, Cosimo was the patron of artists such as Giorgio Vasari, the architect who designed the Uffizi, now a museum, but originally the offices [uffizi] of the Medici administration. He was also a patient patron of the brilliant sculptor Benevenuto Cellini, the boastful defender of the Castello during the sack of Rome, whose comments years before on hearing of Cosimo's election turned out to be prophetic: *"They have mounted a young man on a splendid horse – then told him you must not ride beyond certain boundaries. Now tell me who is going to restrain him when he wants to ride beyond them? You can't impose laws on a man who is your master."*

Cosimo was indeed the master, and in the thirty-seven years he held the reins he rode far beyond the established boundaries. By his ambition and efforts he had expanded the Grand Duchy of Tuscany and ruled like a king over a region that had not been united under one rule since the days of the Roman Empire.

Cosimo had been fortunate in his endeavors, but his later years were marred by personal tragedies, which the Medici could never escape. Eleonora had given him nine children, but within a span of two years he lost four of them. In 1561, fever had claimed the lives of his two daughters, Maria and Lucrezia, both in their teens. Worse was yet to come. The following year, an epidemic of the killer malaria was raging in Tuscany, and Cosimo's wife and two of his sons fell ill. Giovanni died at the age of nineteen on November 20, followed by his fifteen-year-old brother on December 12. Six days later the sick and heartbroken Eleonora, his wife and companion of twenty-three years, died in his arms. Dukes and princes shared the fate of paupers as plagues and epidemics claimed their victims and decimated populations.

Cosimo died on April 21, 1574, at the age of fifty-five with the exalted title of Grand Duke of Tuscany. Unlike his legendary father, Giovanni delle Bande Nere, who died a hero fighting the French, Cosimo seemed to fade away; half paralyzed by stroke, he was but a shadow of his former self. It was said that Florence did not weep on the passing of the man who had been their lord and master for thirty-seven years, perhaps because he had already ceased to be a presence among them. It was not the last of the Medici, however, but just a new beginning—he was succeeded by two of his sons, and four more generations. The dynasty ended 163 years later with the death of the disreputable Gian Gastone de'Medici in 1737. In the meantime, each Grand Duke would bring his own style and personality to Florence and Tuscany as the peninsula, like a big boat with all its passengers, seemed to float in calmer seas with a Spanish captain at the helm.

Battles Without Swords

It might have seemed that during the Spanish period the peninsula was anchored in the doldrums, safe from the storms that still rocked other ships of states, and although the frontiers remained intact, they could not stem the tide of religious storms that raged within her boundaries. The Italian spirit, already restrained by the austere and tight reins of Spain, was further fettered by the papacy's battle to fetter man's mind.

The specter of the Inquisition appeared in Italy in 1542 under Pope Paul III. Born Alessandro Farnese, he might have been a true prince of the Renaissance in the Medici tradition, a patron of the arts and champion of learning, but the times required that he be a patron of reform to eliminate existing evils and abuses and fight against the new religion of Martin Luther that had become a threat to the Catholic Church. Pope Paul III ushered in a period of repression of intellectuals who were persecuted for ideas that were in conflict with Church dogma. It was he who established censorship in 1543 whereby printing was controlled throughout Italy, and in 1559 the notorious "Index of prohibited books" was published.

It was into such a world that one of the most renowned scientists of the century was born: Galileo Galilei (1564–1642). Galileo was a man whose brilliant mind could not be controlled by Catholic dogma. Born in Pisa on February 15, 1564, to a Florentine cloth merchant, he was taken to Florence to be tutored. A true Renaissance man, his father was mathematician, musician, and even composer. Galileo inherited his traits and talents, became a master of the lute, and had a natural flair for drawing, but he wanted to be a math professor. His father was opposed to having his brilliant son end up as a poorly paid teacher and urged him to study medicine, a profession that was much more lucrative with all the diseases that were so prevalent. Galileo enrolled at the University of Pisa, where he soon became a professor's worst nightmare, quickly earning a reputation as troublemaker in the classroom. Medicine was not for Galileo, and he eventually followed his calling, obtaining at the young age of twenty-five a chair of mathematics at Pisa. Legend has left us with a picture of Galileo dropping objects from the leaning Tower of Pisa to study the specific gravity of solids. However, his most serious work was done at the University of Padua, at that time part of the Republic of Venice, where he occupied the chair of mathematics for eighteen years. In 1610 he was coaxed away by the young Cosimo II, Grand Duke of Tuscany. And so we are once more drawn back to Florence.

Galileo eventually ran into trouble with the Church on account of his support of the Copernican view of the solar system, contradicting the theory then held and taught by the Church that the earth was fixed and everything revolved around it. He was called to Rome to stand trial for heresy and was forced to recant. His famous words of defiance—"But it does move"—are said to have been whispered at that time. He got off lightly, his prison sentence being commuted to house arrest, which remained in effect until his death. He lived the last eight years of his life near Florence under Medici protection, where with his telescopes he could continue stargazing. When he died on January 8, 1642, the Church forbade the erection of a monument in his memory. His patron, Grand Duke Cosimo II, had preceded him in death, but the son, Ferdinando II, took his mortal remains to the church of Santa Croce to rest along with other greats such as Ghiberti, Michelangelo, and Machiavelli.

Galileo died exactly 100 years following the introduction into Italy of the terrible Inquisition, which almost destroyed his genius.

The Age of the Baroque

As if in defiance of the censorship imposed by the Papacy, artists, architects, and sculptors alike created works that often expressed exuberance, restlessness, and passion. The style came to be known as the Baroque.

During the seventeenth century, ruling princes presided over their courts, cultivated the arts, and embellished their cities with fine buildings. It was during this period that the baroque Rome we now know largely emerged, taking shape under the many great architects and sculptors of that time, one of whom was Giovanni Bernini (1598–1680). Outstanding architect, dramatist, stage designer, and painter, Bernini was born in Naples, son of a Florentine sculptor and a Neapolitan mother, but he spent most of his life in Rome. He began sculpting at the tender age of eight and continued to display his genius in stonework during his long life of eighty-two years. Stone and water were brought together in the many fountains that grace the squares of Rome. Follow the playful sound of water and you will find him looming large in Piazza Barberini with his Triton Fountain; in Piazza di Spagna with his boat-shaped fountain, the Barcaccia; and in the oblong Piazza Navona graced by the magnificent Four Rivers Fountain, representing the rivers of four continents. Most imposing of all his achievements may be seen in the colonnades in Piazza San Pietro, which encircle and define the space in front of the basilica where the faithful gathered to receive papal blessing.

Turin also was mostly shaped during the Baroque period, in particular by the architects Guarino Guarini of Modena and Filippo Juvara of Sicily. This beautiful city, with its wide, straight avenues lined with arcades, was the pride of the dukes of Savoy with whom we will become better acquainted in the next century. Turin was the city destined to shine for a brief period (1861–1865) as capital of the Kingdom of Italy.

A Fisherman from Naples

Although the lazy fountains of Rome may symbolize peace in the Italian peninsula, there were nonetheless strong undercurrents of discontent in the south where the ordinary masses, kept in check by the Spanish viceroys with the help of the baronial class, struggled under the heavy burden of taxation. Naples, one of the largest cities in the Christian world—bigger than Rome or Milan and second only to Paris—had a population of some 400,000 souls and was a powder keg ready to explode. True revolutionary movements were rare in Italy, and the revolts that did occur were soon put down, but the volcano of pent-up anger of the Neapolitans, aggravated by the discomfort of a hot summer day in a crowded city, finally erupted.

The trouble began on July 7, 1647, when some fruit vendors rioted in protest against a newly imposed tax on fruit. It was a Sunday, and the streets of the city were thronged with citizens in an ugly mood because the fresh fruit supply that day was held up over a dispute as to who would pay the new tax. Luscious figs from Pozzuoli began to fly through the air as the protesters used their produce as missiles. They then took out their anger against the tax collectors, burning their booths and forcing them to flee for their lives. Amid the general mayhem, a young fisherman jumped up on a box and took control of the crowd with these words: *"Long live God, long live the Virgin of Carmel, long live the Pope, long live the King of Spain, long live plenty, death to bad government, out with the tax."*

It was the beginning of a tumultuous nine days that catapulted into the pages of history the twenty-seven-year-old Tommaso Aniello (known as Masaniello) whose name came to be associated with the revolution of the century. Born in the poorest quarter of Naples, he was described by his contemporaries as a man of unimposing physique with melancholy black eyes and light hair, but he had a persuasive tongue and a bold spirit. He lived with his wife in Market Square, occupying a humble dwelling on whose walls could still be seen the faded paint depicting the coat of arms of the Emperor, Charles V, who over a century earlier had granted the city of Naples special privileges, which had been ignored by the Spanish viceroys and were now invoked.

Events moved at a giddy pace as the mob took over the streets, burning the tax booths around the city and forcing the Viceroy, Rodrigo Ponce de Leon, Duke of Arcos, to take refuge in the fortress of Castel Nuovo, where he was joined by justly jittery members of the baronial class. The people chose Masaniello as their supreme captain, and a popular government was quickly formed with two of his shady friends appointed as lieutenants. Days of terror followed as the wealthy became the first targets of popular wrath, and treasures were lost as the mob burned and destroyed homes and possessions. Significantly, however, pictures of the King of Spain were spared out of respect, and it was made clear that they were not rebels against Spain at that time. The battle cry became, "Long live the King. Death to bad government."

The Viceroy realized he was powerless to put down such a popular uprising and invited the new leader and his officials to the Palace for negotiations. The Viceroy had observed the nearly magical power that Masaniello exercised over the unruly mob and gave in to all his demands—abolition of taxation and a return to former privileges. Masaniello had come to meet the Viceroy dressed in silver and astride a fine horse, and he rode away with a newly conferred title of "Duke of Saint George." He was the knight, but the proverbial dragon turned out to be himself.

Masaniello's actions of the following days carried him crashing against the rocks of destruction. A conspiracy against the new regime involving one of his closest and trusted men nearly cost him his life. This betrayal was the beginning of one of the darkest periods in the history of the city. Masaniello reacted with all the ferocity of a wounded beast and with despotic power gave his orders accompanied with the threat "Under pain of death." Suspects were sought out and summarily decapitated, their heads displayed on pikes around the market square. The gruesome scene was recorded for posterity by the contemporary Neapolitan painter Salvator Rosa. Mad rage had taken over, and the revolution had turned against the very ones it was intended to benefit. On that Friday, July 12, the sixth day of the revolution, the sun set on a city where jubilation and euphoria had given way to fear and where the stench of mutilated and rotting bodies pervaded the air after night had covered the dreadful sight with her black cloak. No one was safe from the hero turned demented monster.

Saturday, July 13, was the day appointed for the solemn ceremony to officially inaugurate Masaniello as supreme captain, the events of the past days notwithstanding. The city was transformed that day, adorned with all the trappings of festive ceremony. Eyewitnesses described a marvelous procession that left the Palace at 2 P.M. and proceeded to the Church of Carmel, the ceremonial carriage of the Viceroy being preceded by some 100 beautiful Spanish horses. The sounds of drums and trumpets were accompanied by shouts of "Long live the King of Spain," and "Long live the Duke of Arcos," to which the Viceroy, sticking his head out of his carriage window, replied, "Long live the faithful Neapolitan people." Masaniello, along with his officials, was a part of it all, and it seemed that the people and the Viceroy had reached a harmonious agreement and nothing could spoil the day.

During the ceremony in the church the first shock came. The Viceroy had spoken, and now Masaniello addressed the people with his eloquent tongue. As if seized by demons, he became disoriented, abusive, and irrational, tearing off his luxurious silver vestments in the House of God in a fit of madness, much to the consternation of those present and the stunned Viceroy. The newly recognized leader of the people then dashed from the church, jumped on his horse, and galloped away like one possessed.

A nervous calm pervaded the city the following day, Sunday, July 14. The revolution had produced the desired results, the Viceroy had given his promise, and Masaniello's mission was completed. The people wanted peace restored and no more of the dictator who was worse than the ones they had revolted against. Masaniello had continued to send his death squads to seek out his enemies and even had some of his faithful followers beheaded; others, including his own brother-in-law, escaped to safety.

On Monday a demented Masaniello was taken forcibly from the pulpit of the Church of Carmel as he raved and ranted about the ingratitude of the people. They took him back to his house, where he spent the night as a virtual prisoner, but early the next morning he evaded his guards and returned to the church. It was there the next morning, the day of the Virgin of Carmel, that the archbishop found him hiding in the sacristy. The fallen hero threw himself at the archbishop's feet, imploring his help, and later made an eloquent public confession of his wrongdoings to the crowd assembled in the sanctuary of the church, but once more the dementia returned, and he became obscene and disorderly. Forcibly taken from the pulpit, he was locked in a monk's cell where he collapsed and fell asleep. Perhaps he awoke to the sounds of footsteps and the clatter of arms outside his cell, which looked out on the beautiful Bay of Naples. They did not herald the arrival of his supporters coming to free him. Masaniello's life came to a sudden end as four shots were heard to echo through the cloisters. A butcher among the conspirators severed his head and displayed it to people still in the church, then took it to Market Square, through the streets of the city, and then to the Viceroy. His body was delivered to the crowd to be savagely defiled and mutilated. This was the tragic end of the man whom they had made their hero. He had appeared like a bright star, only to disappear on the ninth day, the day of the Virgin of Carmel from whom he believed his power had derived.

The following day many people had a change of heart when it was apparent that the Viceroy was back in control. They sought out Masaniello's scattered mortal remains, which they brought together and his body, whole once more, was perfumed and dressed in fine vestments ready for burial. The people took to the streets again, this time for the funeral procession and they scrambled to see their dead hero and touch his vestments. His body was taken to the Church of Carmel; at dawn the next day the funeral service took place as bells tolled throughout the whole city of Naples.

Masaniello was dead, but his spirit had indeed risen again as the fires of unrest blazed anew. The rebellion had spread to the provinces, and what started as an uprising against bad government became a revolution against Spanish rule. It was not until August of the following year that the Spanish regained control of Naples and finally put down the rebellion. Feudal repression was back, and Spanish domination was to last yet another half a century.

The Medici still ruled in Tuscany, but Spanish vessels in ports of the Tuscan coast and the islands known as the Presidii were constant reminders of Spanish domination. In Milan, the strong Spanish military presence stifled that city and drained its resources. The Spanish domination of Lombardy in the seventeenth century was dramatized in the following century by the Milanese writer Alessandro Manzoni (1785–1873) in his monumental historical novel *I Promessi Sposi* [The Betrothed], one of the great masterpieces of Italian literature. It tells the story of two peasants against a backdrop of tyranny, insurrection, famine, and plague.

By the time the century drew to a close, however, Spain was but a shadow of her former self as a European power. The sickly Charles II, destined to sit on the Spanish throne for thirty-five of his thirty-nine years (ten years under the regency of his mother), was in failing health. His frail body seemed to symbolize the diminishing power of Spain, which had passed her zenith and was entering the twilight. Already the claimants from France and Austria were at her door like vultures waiting for death to occur.

Charles had no heirs, and this fact changed the course of history, for he was the last of the Spanish branch of the Habsburg dynasty. All the prayers of the three Marys in his life—his mother, Maria Anna of Austria, his first wife, Marie Louise d'Orleans, and his second wife, Maria Anna of Neuberg—remained unanswered. Charles died in Madrid on the first day of November 1700, exactly 200 years after the birth of his great-great-grandfather who had first brought Spanish domination to Italy. His death ushered in the wars of the Spanish succession and opened a new chapter in the saga of Italy.

CHAPTER NINE

The Troubled Eighteenth Century

The Wars of the Spanish Succession

The map of the Italian peninsula was rearranged not by popular revolutions but by the accidents of births and deaths in the dynastic families of Europe. Italy was doomed to become the arena as battles were fought for the right to inherit the possessions of a dead king, the territories in Italy.

The curtain rose on the first scene of the century with two protagonists who remained rivals for the rest of their lives—a French Bourbon and an Austrian Habsburg. The Bourbon was Philip V (1683–1746), born in the splendid palace of Versailles and related to both the French King Louis XIV and the now-extinct Spanish line of the Habsburgs. The childless King Charles II had willed all his worldly possessions to the seventeen-year-old Philip, who would inherit Spain, Spanish America, the Spanish Netherlands and, of course, the extensive Spanish dominions in Italy. These were contested by Archduke Charles (1685–1740), the fifteen-year-old second son of Austrian Emperor Leopold I.

The battles fought by these two teenage bucks for the Italian prize were known as the Wars of the Spanish Succession. They were fought on five fronts as well as at sea and lasted for thirteen years. The main arena of the military conflict in Italy was the north. The sound of armies on the march once more echoed across the plains of Lombardy as French soldiers and cavalry crossed into Italy and entered Milan on April 6, 1701.

Caught in a vise between the two royal powers at opposite ends of the great Alps, Vittorio Amedeo II, Duke of Savoy, proved to be the wild card that played a diplomatic double game, first favoring one side, then the other. The Duke held a strong hand with a strategic position and a loyal military force, and one of the cards he held was his daughter, Maria Luisa Gabriela. First he promised her to Archduke Charles, but, finding it more expedient to side with the French, he gave her to the rival, King Philip of Spain. With the developments in European politics and the appearance of the English on the side of the Austrians, the Duke abandoned his French ally in 1703 and joined the Austrian cause. King Louis of France was furious, and his response was swift as French troops invaded the Duke's territory in Piedmont. Fortunately for him, the French were kept occupied on another front where they were being trounced by the British. From the eastern wing, the Austrians entered on the chessboard of Lombardy with their troops under the command of Prince Eugene of Savoy, a cousin of the Duke of Savoy, recapturing the besieged city of Turin in 1706. In the following year, the Austrians also occupied Naples.

However, the fate of Italy was in the hands of the European powers to be decided around a conference table in the distant city of Utrecht in The Netherlands. Hostilities ended with the Treaty of Utrecht in 1713, confirming the Austrians as masters of Milan, the Kingdom of Naples, Mantua, and Sardinia. Sicily was snatched from the mother mainland to be given like an orphan to the distant Duke of Savoy to add to his domain in Piedmont in recognition for his help. Not only that, but this man of the mountain dukedom was made King of Sicily, a title he held for seven years. In 1720 he was forced to exchange Sicily for the larger and wilder island of Sardinia, with the title of King of Sardinia. The rulers of the House of Savoy would hold that title for the next 140 years, until they became the first kings of a united Italy in 1861.

The last will and testament of a king, Charles II of Spain, had been overridden by the need to balance power in Europe. Two hundred years of Spanish domination had come to an end, only to be replaced by Austrian power. The game was not over, however, for the Spanish and Austrian interests clashed again in the heart of the Italian peninsula in a most bizarre succession contest.

The Duchy of Parma and the Farnese Dynasty

The Treaty of Utrecht in 1713 was the end of just one conflict in a succession of crises that characterized the first half of the eighteenth century and involved Italy. The death of the Spanish Queen, Maria Luisa Gabriela (of Savoy), that same year set in motion a whole series of events that culminated in one of the most bizarre succession squabbles in history. The Duchy of Parma was brought into the limelight as the Farnese dynasty, reaching back two centuries through the male line, was threatened with extinction.

The Duchy of Parma, located in the pathway between the opposing forces of France and Austria during the Wars of the Spanish Succession, was in the precarious position of having to steer a course between the two rivals. In such a situation there emerged on the scene a young man of humble origin, Giulio Alberoni, who rose to become a cardinal and a statesman in the service of Francesco Farnese, the Duke of Parma; through his efforts, a Farnese princess took her place in history.

We will catch up with Alberoni in Spain where, as emissary of the Duke of Parma, he had by astute and crafty maneuvers, cloaked in his "cheese and salami" diplomacy for which he became known, managed to arrange a marriage between the recently bereaved, thirty-two-year-old King Philip V of Spain and Elisabetta Farnese, sole heir of the Farnese dynasty. (She was both niece and stepdaughter of the Duke of Parma, who married his own brother's widow.) Described as pale and pox-faced, Elisabetta was no beauty, and perhaps that is why the wedding that took place in Parma on September 16, 1714, was by proxy. Be that as it may, when Elisabetta arrived in Spain she met her husband for the first time at Guadalajara, and it was soon clear that the lonely Philip was well pleased to have another Italian wife at his side. The young queen quickly learned the ways of the Spanish court with her countryman Alberoni as prime minister and tutor.

Elisabetta and Philip had two sons, but Philip's two sons by his first wife were heirs to the Spanish throne. Now with the death of Duke Francesco of Parma in 1728 with no heirs, the male line of the Farnese was about to become extinct, so Elisabetta set her sights on the Duchy for her own children. But Francesco's surviving brother, Don Antonio, an abbot already in his fifties, inherited the title of Duke. Don Antonio received the news of his brother's death while he was at a banquet, and it not only

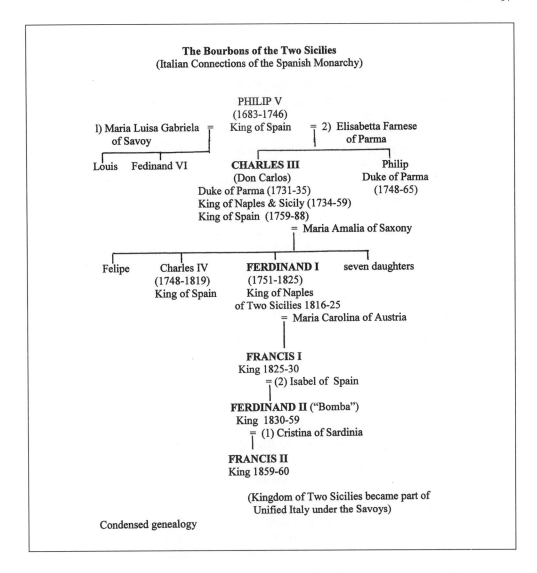

The Bourbons of the Two Sicilies
(Italian Connections of the Spanish Monarchy)

PHILIP V
(1683-1746)
King of Spain

1) Maria Luisa Gabriela = PHILIP V = 2) Elisabetta Farnese
of Savoy   of Parma

Louis   Fedinand VI   **CHARLES III**   Philip
(Don Carlos)   Duke of Parma
Duke of Parma (1731-35)   (1748-65)
King of Naples & Sicily (1734-59)
King of Spain (1759-88)
= Maria Amalia of Saxony

Felipe   Charles IV   **FERDINAND I**   seven daughters
(1748-1819)   (1751-1825)
King of Spain   King of Naples
of Two Sicilies 1816-25
= Maria Carolina of Austria

FRANCIS I
King 1825-30
= (2) Isabel of Spain

FERDINAND II ("Bomba")
King 1830-59
= (1) Cristina of Sardinia

FRANCIS II
King 1859-60

(Kingdom of Two Sicilies became part of
Unified Italy under the Savoys)

Condensed genealogy

ruined his quail pie but also put an end to his carefree life. Even worse, he was prevailed upon by everyone, including the Pope, to make the ultimate sacrifice for the sake of Parma and the dynasty and take a wife.

Abbot Don Antonio was duly married off to the young Enrichetta d'Este for the sole purpose of producing the required male heir, but by 1731 hopes began to fade when nothing happened. The potions of doctors and quacks had produced no results except perhaps to make the young girl ill with symptoms resembling pregnancy. At this juncture Don Antonio died, following the appearance of a boil on his ear supposedly caused by the hot wigs he wore. Four days after his death, Austrian troops entered the Duchy even as Spanish soldiers were about to arrive as the rivalry between Philip and Charles flared up once again on Italian soil. Parma was after all a vassal of Austria; now the astute Elisabetta, by claiming it for her sons, was determined to bring it into the orbit of the Spanish.

The most outlandish event in the succession squabbles was about to begin. Don Antonio had prepared a bombshell before his death, leaving the Duchy of Parma in his will to the fetus in his wife's womb—it would have to be a boy, of course. Enrichetta had a medical problem but few believed that she was actually with child. Was she or wasn't she? That was the question on everyone's mind as the fate of the Duchy was at stake. Whatever the outcome, Parma was disputed territory, and the forces of both sides were poised once more for war.

Poor Enrichetta became the focus of attention as Europe waited with baited breath and the weeks passed. In the meantime, disbelievers insisted on a gynecological inspection in the presence of witnesses to establish her true condition once and for all. Among the witnesses to the embarrassing examination to which Enrichetta was subjected were Spanish ministers, matrons, gentlemen of the Regency, doctors, and midwives. But the Austrians were said to have bribed the witnesses, and a document was issued that stated "according to all the known symptoms" the duchess was seven months pregnant. Whatever it was inside her did not grow any bigger. People began to bet on the odds, and there was mounting speculation that a simulated birth would be staged and another woman's baby presented as the Farnese heir. It was decided that the birth had to be witnessed to make sure there was no trickery. Eventually, poor Enrichetta could prevail no longer, and the pregnancy was "called off." The farce was over.

The way was now clear for Elisabetta's fifteen-year-old son, Don Carlos, to claim the Dukedom of Parma. On October 27, 1731, he arrived on the Italian mainland with 6,000 Spaniards chosen for the garrisons. Sired by the Spanish King and born in Spain, Don Carlos was nonetheless the son of a Farnese princess and the people would welcome him as one of their own. Who could have imagined that he was destined just four years later to exchange his dukedom for the crown of a king?

A King's Crown for Don Carlos

A war broke out in 1733 involving the European powers and created a ground swell that would carry the young Don Carlos to a king's throne. Known as the War of the Polish Succession, it was triggered by a dispute between rivals for the elective monarchy of Poland, but it also offered a pretext for aggression and state-craft where the territories of the Italian peninsula became the bargaining chips.

There were three important players in this new game on the Italian chessboard: France was nervous over the fact that the Austrian heiress, Maria Theresa, was to marry Francis Stephen of Lorraine, who would take that French possession into the Austrian orbit; the ambitious King of Sardinia-Savoy had hopes of expanding his domain by annexing Milan; and the ambitious Spaniards wanted to regain the south of Italy from the Austrians.

Queen Elisabetta was the driving force on the Spanish side, for she saw the opportunity to strike a blow against Austria and win a kingdom for her son. Spain and France came to an agreement to join forces and move against the Austrians, pledging to respect each other's territories, France in the North and Spain in the South. The die was cast, and the wheel was set in motion. Some 40,000 French troops crossed the Alps, to be joined by the Savoyards, and proceeded to the conquest of Austrian-held Lombardy. The Spaniards, approaching from the sea, landed with a force of 30,000 on the Italian mainland at Livorno to begin the conquest of the South.

Joining up with the Spanish forces was Don Carlos, the Duke of Parma who, on celebrating his eighteenth birthday on January 20, 1734, declared himself of age and assumed titular command. He was spurred on by his ambitious Italian mother, who wrote him a letter practically commanding him to go and conquer the Two Sicilies "which elevated into a free kingdom, will be yours. Go forth and win: the most beautiful crown in Italy awaits you."

It all seemed easy, but it must be remembered that although the South had thrown off two centuries of Spanish domination, the Austrians who had replaced the Spaniards turned out to be even harsher taskmasters. The Spanish monarchs had most cleverly paved the way for their arrival as "liberators" by a proclamation issued on March 17, 1734, which assured dispensations, free pardons, and abolition of taxes imposed by the Austrians. No wonder the Neapolitans were ready to accept and even welcome this young prince who rode southward to their rescue with his soldiers, his bodyguards, and his courtiers.

Even before Don Carlos and his army reached Naples, the Spanish fleet had appeared on the scene and seized the islands of Ischia and Procida, which guard the approaches to the Bay. The Austrians were in no position to put up much resistance and withdrew to the city strongholds of Castel Nuovo and Sant'Elmo. The besieged Austrians appeared to be more like men under house arrest as the chivalrous Spaniards supplied their needs and met their requests while they waited for the inevitable surrender. The few rounds of ammunition fired seemed more for the excitement of the curious citizens who came to get a closer look at the siege. A Florentine agent, Intieri, described how both sides gave warning before firing so that the populace could withdraw. When the besieged Austrian garrisons finally surrendered, the Castello was illuminated with torches and lanterns and people thronged the square as music and dancing continued for three nights. It was more a spectacle than a bloody conquest, as only three casualties were reported.

On May 15, even before the rest of the South and Sicily had been conquered, King Philip V of Spain issued a proclamation whereby he ceded the Kingdoms of Naples and Sicily to his son, Don Carlos, who was crowned king in the cathedral of Palermo on July 3, 1734. Naples and Sicily were reunited, free from the Austrians, and they had their own king, who was at least half Italian.

The young Don Carlos left his unmistakable mark on the city of Naples, which he chose as his capital. A lasting accomplishment was the inauguration of the San Carlo Opera House, named for the king who ordered its construction in March 1737 and which was opened to the public on November 4, the King's saint's day. It was a fitting centerpiece for Naples, then the most important city of eighteenth-century Italy, which was considered to be "the land of music." Proof of this was the fact that the French philosopher Jean Jacques Rousseau advised the serious musician to go to Naples, and the French composer Lalande wrote:

> Music is the triumph of the Neapolitans. It seems that in this country the fibers of the ear are more sensitive, more harmonic, more sonorous than in the rest of Europe; the whole nation sings; gestures, the inflection of the voice, the cadence of the syllables, conversation — everything there expresses and exhales music. Naples in the principal source of music.

Don Carlos was himself no lover of opera, but he understood that music to the Neapolitans was like circus had been to the Romans.

The young king, whose chaste ways must have puzzled his new subjects, was married to Maria Amalia of Saxony, and the two became inseparable as had been his own parents, a rarity in an age where mistresses were powerful politicians and bastards were often a threat to the true heirs. They had thirteen children and their blood line survived right down to the last King of Spain, Juan Carlos (1938–). After twenty-five years, Don Carlos inherited the throne of Spain, at which time he ceded the Kingdom of Naples and Sicily to his nine-year-old third son, Ferdinand, whose dynasty prevailed until the arrival of Garibaldi and unification of the peninsula in 1861.

The Final Settlement

We have followed Don Carlos and must now return north to see what happened elsewhere. The Wars of the Polish Succession petered out, and the final peace treaty, putting the seal on what had already come to pass, was signed November 18, 1738. There were winners and losers in this international game of musical chairs in which the Italians were helpless spectators. Don Carlos had been allowed to keep his Kingdom of Naples, but he lost proud Parma to the Austrians. The French were gone from the north of Italy, and the Austrians were once more masters of Milan. They remained there for another 100 years, except for a brief Napoleonic interlude. A sorry loser in the games of war was the King of Sardinia-Savoy, who could only look with jaundiced eye as Milan eluded his grasp and he got only Tortona and Novara to add to his domain. Little could he have imagined that his heirs were destined to become one century later the kings of Italy.

Finally, another important change resulting from the Polish Succession crisis involved Stanislaw Leszczynski, who had lost the Kingdom of Poland. What could be done about this relative of French royalty? They found the solution in Lorraine-Bar. This was the domain of Francis Stephen of Lorraine, who had recently married the Austrian Emperor's daughter, Maria Theresa, the young and beautiful heiress. This marriage brought the Austrians to France's back door and the threat had to be removed. Italy was to provide the solution. The "powers" therefore decreed that Francis Stephen should renounce all claims to Lorraine and he would be rewarded with the Grand Duchy of Tuscany on the death, believed imminent, of the ailing Gian Gastone, the last surviving Medici male. Already in January of 1737, 6,000 Austrian troops had crossed the borders to wait like hordes of vultures for the death of Gian Gastone. They had not long to wait, for he died in July of that same year, a sad end to such a brilliant dynasty.

Surviving Gian Gastone was an aged spinster sister, Anna Maria, whom the Austrians allowed to stay in Florence. The Florentines were witness to the end of an era as they saw a devout old lady, clothed in black, leave the Medici palace and retreat across the Arno River to the Pitti Palace. It was there that she lived out the rest of her days as a recluse, surrounded by priceless Medici treasures and silver furniture.

Meanwhile, down from the buildings came the familiar Medici coat of arms, and abolished were all feasts associated with the Medici rule. It was not just the death of a dynasty but the end of an era that had left for posterity one of the richest collections of art in the world. Anna Maria bequeathed to the new Grand Duke all the Medici fortune, with the stipulation that nothing be removed from Florence. The brilliant jewel of Italy was now an appendage of Austria. The native princes had been replaced by two very young foreigners, propped up by the Emperor in Vienna and an Austrian garrison. They did not make Tuscany their home, however, but preferred Vienna. The Tuscans, under a council of regency, remained a neglected child until the arrival of a truly caring Grand Duke some twenty-five years later.

The War of the Austrian Succession

During the cold, wet October of 1740, the Austrian Emperor went on a hunting expedition that would not only be his last, but the consequences would open up the flood gates of yet another European war. Having caught cold in the chilling rains, he was hurried back to Vienna, where he died just nine days later at the age of fifty-five.

The Emperor's unexpected and untimely death marked the beginning of what was known as the War of the Austrian Succession. At stake were not only the empty seat of the Holy Roman Emperor but also the Habsburg inheritance of the twenty-three-year-old Maria Theresa. The young heiress and her husband, Francis Stephen (now Duke of Tuscany it will be remembered), were catapulted into the limelight. The desperate fight for survival tested the mettle of the blue-eyed flaxen-haired young girl who took up the reins of her dead father and proved her worth against all odds.

Surrounded on all sides by enemies intent on despoiling the young heiress of her rights, Maria Theresa first had to defend her own kingdom, which was immediately attacked by the greedy Frederick of Prussia. As for Austrian interests in the Italian peninsula, it seemed that all would soon be lost. Once more, Spain, with the persistent Queen Elisabetta, saw the opportunity to gain ground, but the British, now masters of the Mediterranean waters, came in on the side of the Austrians against the French and Spanish. Their intervention prevented the Spanish from landing on the Italian mainland.

Once again, one of the key players in the game was the King of Sardinia-Savoy. He, too, continued to contemplate with an eagle eye the fertile plains of Lombardy, but he eventually joined forces with the Austrians rather than risk being "gobbled up" by the French. French soldiers poured through the Alpine passes, and the north again became the arena of battle with the helpless Italians caught in the middle.

The War of the Austrian Succession lasted for seven years with armies on the move on a variety of fronts. Peace was finally restored with the signing of the Treaty of Aix-la-Chapelle on October 18, 1748. Maria Theresa was confirmed in the Austrian succession, having lost a chunk of her territories to Frederick of Prussia. Her husband, Francis Stephen, was recognized as Holy Roman Emperor, and she was now the Empress.

In Italy, as part of the settlement the Duchy of Parma was back with the Farnese when Philip, Elisabetta Farnese's second son by the King of Spain, was made its Duke. However, the Austrians kept control of Milan.

The Private and Public World of Maria Theresa

Maria Theresa governed at a time when the world was in turmoil as France and England fought their wars in the colonies, while in France the seeds of revolution were being sowed. A new and independent nation in the New World was established with the United States of America. Fortunately, Italy would enjoy a half century of peace characterized by enlightened rule and much-needed reforms.

Maria Theresa was the real power in the Habsburg-Lorraine House until her death in 1780, and she used her power wisely. Austrian control of Italy extended to more than her own possessions and was achieved in part through a network of family alliances. She herself may have spent a lonely childhood, but she made an early start to fill her palace with her own offspring. She gave birth to a total of thirteen children; although she lost several in infancy, there were enough survivors to fan out across Italy, some through Catholic marriage into powerful families.

The Duchy of Parma was secured first by the marriage of Maria Theresa's son Joseph to Duke Philip's daughter Isabella, who died young, and then by her daughter Maria Amalia's marriage to the Duke's son Ferdinand. Maria Theresa's son, another Ferdinand, was married of to Marie Beatrix d'Este, of the House of Modena. The bright young Maria Carolina was married off to Ferdinando, the third son of King Carlos of Naples, and she became the powerful queen of that important kingdom in 1759. Tuscany belonged to Maria Theresa and Francis Stephen already, and their son Leopold eventually became its Grand Duke. Italy remained, nevertheless, a kaleidoscope of separate units; even the duchies under Austria retained their own forms of government, composed largely of brilliant and well-chosen Italians.

It had been twenty-five years since the young Maria Theresa had begun her ascent in the world of power and politics with the sudden death of her father. She lost her beloved husband, Francis Stephen, just as suddenly. The tragedy was even greater because it occurred during the grand ceremonies of the marriage at Innsbruck of her son Leopold, Grand Duke of Tuscany, to the Infanta of Spain, Maria Luisa. Leopold himself had taken a chill while crossing the Brenner Pass to meet his bride. He barely got through the marriage ceremony and had to take to his bed, missing some of the activities while he lay critically ill. His father, the Emperor, had kept things together and been "the life and soul" of the party during those worrying days, but the strain of entertaining royal visitors during the week-long festivities must have been too much for him. On August 18, 1765, he suffered a stroke and within hours, he was dead. Albert of Saxony (the future husband of Francis Stephen's daughter Maria Christina), who was present at the wedding, gave a powerful eyewitness account of the tragedy in these brief words which he wrote to his mother:

> Never shall I forget that evening. Imagine it. The Emperor dead, the Empress supported to her apartments by my brother and sister-in-law, who were almost as overcome as she herself; the Archduke ill in bed; the Archduchesses prostrate with grief; and guests all the time arriving for supper and bursting into tears until the whole palace seemed to echo with weeping and wailing.

Fortunately for Tuscany, Leopold recovered and was its Grand Duke for the next twenty-five years. An unpromising schoolboy whose reports from all his tutors would have distressed any parents, he turned out to be the best of all of Maria Theresa's children for his enlightened views and his concern for the welfare of his Tuscan subjects. In keeping with the trend of the times, he was influenced by the views of Cesare Beccaria, a Milanese nobleman and criminologist who wrote a small masterpiece entitled *Of Crimes and Punishments,* which advocated prevention and rehabilitation of criminals. Grand Duke Leopold revised the penal code and even abolished the death sentence in Tuscany, a legacy that, it was argued, dated back to Roman times and was deemed unworthy of a gentler society.

Italy Under the Enlightened Despots

The latter half of the eighteenth century was known as a period of reform. On the death of Maria Theresa in 1780, her son Emperor Joseph continued with even greater vigor the movement that had begun with his mother.

Under the protective umbrella of the Austrian family system, Italy was no backwater, left behind by the currents of change, but was very much alive. The cultural heritage had not been lost, and Italy continued to produce its share of philosophers, scientists, and musicians as the great centers of learning flourished under the "enlightened despots."

There were many bright stars in the Italian firmament. In Bologna, Luigi Galvani (1737–1798), professor of anatomy, advanced the study of the muscles. In Pavia, Alessandro Volta (1745–1827) invented the electric battery and gave his name to our word *volt*. The Neapolitan Genovesi held the first chair of Economics and Trade in Italy and wrote on the subjects of commerce and agriculture. In Naples was the brilliant Tuscan statesman Bernardo Tanucci, who was minister to Don Carlos and kept the kingdom together during the regency of the young King Ferdinando.

In Milan, Pietro Verri worked in cooperation with the Austrians on reforms and wrote the *Storia di Milano*. He also founded a journal crammed with information and ideas to enlighten and wake up its readers. It was appropriately called *Il Caffè*. In Milan, where public patronage and the arts formed a harmonious relationship, the famous Teatro alla Scala was inaugurated in 1778, in the very shadow of the dazzling Duomo of white marble begun in the fourteenth century by order of Gian Galeazzo Visconti. So different in structure and function, these buildings seem to symbolize the dialogue that was taking place in the eighteenth century between the advocates of secular enlightenment and religious dogma and privilege.

The brilliant Antonio Salieri (1750–1825) born at Legnano just outside of Milan, was whisked away to Vienna to place his musical talents at the disposal of the imperial court for fifty years. This Italian may have shone with a more dazzling light had he not lived in the shadow of the brilliant young Wolfgang Amadeus Mozart.

Turin boasted one of the great dramatists and writers of the times—Vittorio Alfieri, a man of noble birth and military training who fought the French with a sharp pen and appealed to the idea of Italian unity against foreign domination.

By the time the century drew to a close, the discontent that had been growing in France had erupted into the Revolution, and Maria Theresa's youngest daughter, Marie Antoinette, lost her head under the blade of the guillotine. On the European stage, dramatic changes were about to occur when a little man, born in the wings, made his appearance to become the protagonist in the next act. His name was Napoleone Buonaparte. Before this incredible character comes onto the stage of history, we will step back in time a bit and take a look at the past century through the eyes of a Venetian and visit the city that was changed forever during the century that followed.

Venice: A City of Merriment

In 1173 the Pope gave the Doge of Venice a ring to symbolize his rule of the sea in gratitude for help against Emperor Barbarossa. From that time until 1797, every year on Ascension Day, a grand ceremony took place in which the Doge boarded *Bucentaur,* the gilded state galley, and sailed out to throw a ring into the waters

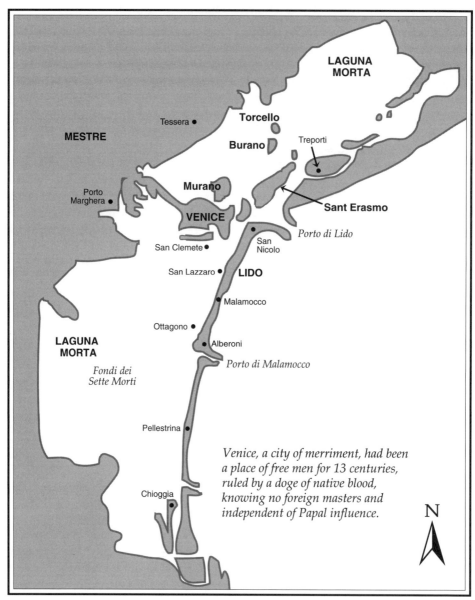

Venice: The Lagoon

saying: "We wed thee, Sea, in token of our perpetual rule." (In 1797 Napoleon ordered the burning of the symbolic *Bucentaur*, saying, "I shall be an Attila for Venice.")

Venice had been a land of free men for thirteen centuries, ruled by a *doge* of native blood, knowing no foreign masters and independent of papal influence. At the end of the eighteenth century Venice was in decline and the waters she once ruled threatened to engulf her, yet nothing could equal the splendor and luxury of her swan song. The Venetians were a joyous people, and if they were now to sink into the silvery waters of her lagoons it seemed that they would go down laughing. The city is still there for us to enjoy today, in part thanks to the unending fight against the waters and the massive walls that were built during the last years of the century to check the flood waters of the nearby rivers and divert their fury. The canvasses of Canaletto, which captured the magical atmosphere of the declining city, now grace the walls of galleries throughout the world, transporting us with transparent colors of light to the city of lagoons and canals that he loved. Eighteenth-century Venice was above all a city of merriment. While merchants and bourgeois gentlemen still counted their golden pieces behind the richly ornamented façades of their palaces, the people danced. Venice was renowned for its masked balls and carnivals, which lasted almost from Christmas until Lent, and where the people were not mere spectators but protagonists. Music and theater were part of life in Venice. It was the birthplace of Tomaso Albinoni, as well as the better-known Antonio Vivaldi, a man who took holy orders, but was a violinist and composer, called in his day the *prete rosso* (the "red priest") on account of his auburn hair. Much of his instrumental music was composed for the young students of the Ospedale della Pietà, a home for orphaned and abandoned girls where he conducted an orchestra, and the joyful exuberance of his music is in sharp contrast to the symphonies of war that echoed across the north of Italy during the Wars of Succession.

Venice was above all, famous for its many theaters. Two Venetians left their marks in history for two very different reasons. Who has not heard of Casanova? No fictitious character, Giacomo Girolamo Casanova was born in Venice to a family of actors and — following an extraordinary life of travel, debauchery, and conquests — came to be known as the Italian prince of adventures. In our day, his name is synonymous with "philanderer," yet he was an accomplished violinist and also a writer of some talent. Among other things he wrote a story about the adventures of two young people in the center of the earth, but his own memoirs read as much like fiction with the graphic account of life in the capitals of Europe and of duels, not to mention a dramatic escape from a Venetian prison that was supposed to put an end to his magic.

Carlo Goldoni: Venetian Dramatist

Spanning the century was a man who became the master of Italian theater as a dramatist. He was Carlo Goldoni whose name remains virtually unknown outside of Italy. Casanova, his contemporary, may have been the prince of adventurers, but Goldoni earned the title of King of Comedy. His statue, which stands in a sunny square not far from the Rialto bridge, is of an eighteenth-century Venetian gentleman with a smile on his round, friendly face.

Born in Venice in 1707, Carlo Goldoni entered the world during the War of the Spanish Succession as the Austrians made their appearance in Lombardy. Goldoni's father seemed to have been a bit of a Casanova himself, for early in life he squandered his fortune through riotous living. Leaving behind his wife and two children, he set out for Rome to study medicine, then settled to practice in Perugia where Carlo was placed in a Jesuit school. The father encouraged his son's very early interest in the theater and actually directed a school play in which young Carlo took a female role, Perugia being within the Papal States which barred actresses from the stage.

The fourteen-year-old Carlo was next placed in a school in Rimini, where he was to prepare for a career in medicine. Neglecting his studies after a bout with smallpox, he met a troupe of strolling Venetian actors and actresses, boarded a boat as a stowaway, and sailed with them up the coast of Chioggia. It was an exciting experience for a teenage boy who seemed to be in his element, and his memoirs tell of the fun times he had on this boat where the food seemed to rival that of a twentieth-century cruise vessel: *"Macaroni! . . . Beef à la mode, cold mutton, a loin of veal, a dessert, and a first-rate wine, oh, what a good dinner"* (Chatfield-Taylor, *Goldoni; A Biography*, p. 19).

The young truant was dragged back to Venice, this time by his mother, and he was placed in his uncle's law office, but he could at least enjoy the summer theater of that lively city. From there he was sent to Pavia to study law. Tonsured and gowned and still only sixteen he began his studies, but his heart was always in the theater, and there was fun to be had outside the walls of learning in that city of "town and gown." Carlo was soon in trouble, falling in with the wrong crowd of playful companions who persuaded him to settle problems by force. He acquired two pistols, but on a tip to the police he was caught and charged with carrying concealed weapons. Now his fellows said, "You are a poet. The stroke of a pen opportunely discharged is a bomb that crushes the chief offender." They brought him compromising anecdotes from town, and he satirized some prominent citizens in leaflets which his "good" friends were only too happy to circulate. The plan backfired, Carlo was summarily expelled from school, and he was forced to return home penniless as a prodigal son at the age of eighteen. Goldoni himself wrote, "after having been seduced and deceived I needed to be loved." His forgiving parents next took him to Modena, where his mother had useful connections, to study with a famous lawyer. Here the impressionable young man came under the influence of the clergy and even thought of becoming a monk. Father came to the rescue and took him to Venice for a "cure," knowing that the theater of that joyful city would get rid of Carlo's religious gloom.

We catch up with Carlo at the age of twenty-five. He earned a degree in law from the University of Padua and returned home where he was admitted to the Venetian Bar. He practiced law and held diplomatic appointments while engaging in theatrical activities, but three years later he was in Milan, where he was attached to the staff of the Venetian minister there.

Goldoni was in Milan when 15,000 Savoyards, cavalry and foot soldiers, took possession of Milan, pouring into the great square in front of the Duomo. It was the beginning of the War of the Polish Succession, when the Bourbon Don Carlos led an army against the Austrian Habsburgs. The Venetians retreated to the frontier town of Crema, and Goldoni was sent as an observer to the allied camp during the siege of Pizzighettone. The war moved southward and Goldoni with less diplomatic pressure decided to visit his mother, who was then in Modena, but he ran into the war. At Parma he witnessed the battle between allies and Austrians on June 29, 1734, the horrors of which are graphically described in his memoirs. Even more disgusting to him was the spectacle on the following day when he saw thousands of bodies, stripped of their clothes, lying naked in heaps.

The road to Modena was alive with military highwaymen, stragglers from both armies. Goldoni was robbed of his money and watch (among other things) while his coachman whipped up his horses, leaving him behind. Goldoni fled on foot and, avoiding the highways, managed to make his way to Brescia and from there to Verona, where he spent the summer of 1734. It was providential that he should there meet the manager of a troupe playing in the Roman amphitheater. He wrote

PART THREE / 307

"interludes" for the troupe to keep himself alive; this marked the beginning of his career as a professional playwright. In the fall Goldoni was back in Venice, where he wrote successfully for the theater and traveled to many places with the touring troupe of Imer, in Genoa meeting with the lady who would be his life's companion. He was writing for the theater as well as acting as Genoese consul in Venice when in 1744 he decided to pull up stakes, and he set out for Pisa to practice law. Goldoni was no more suited to law than he was to medicine, but in Tuscany he studied the pure Italian language so that he could write for the theater in "Italian," not just in the dialect of the Venetians.

It will be remembered that in 1748 the peace treaty was signed marking the end of the War of the Austrian Succession and ushering in a long period of peace. It was also the beginning of Goldoni's rise as the first truly Italian dramatist. Gone were the masks behind which players often spouted obscenities and cavorted across the stage with rude gestures. The improvised theater of the *Commedia dell'Arte* was gradually giving way to a theater in which players learned their lines and the stereotypes were replaced by real people—merchants, bankers, the bourgeoisie, craftsmen, and people from all walks of society. It was a theater for everyone to enjoy, and one that also carried a subtle moral message. For fourteen years Goldoni wrote comedies that amused and entertained the audiences whose thirst for theater seemed insatiable.

In 1762, a tired man of fifty-five, Goldoni was lured away to Paris to write for the *Comédie Italienne,* but after a short time he ended up teaching Italian to royal princesses at the Palace of Versailles. This incredible man learned French and wrote dramas in that language.

Goldoni never returned to Venice, although he wrote:

> From Venice I'm two thousand miles away;
> Yet to my mind are summoned every day
> Her speech, the merry habits of her folk,
> And her sweet name, her memories to evoke.

While peace had finally reigned in Italy, France had moved headlong into the revolution and Goldoni's employers, French royalty, had gone from masters to prisoners. Goldoni died in Paris February 6, 1793, at the age of eighty-six. He lived just sixteen days following the execution of the French King as drums rolled and victims were carried off to the guillotine, like the very sheep for which the terrible device was first conceived.

Four years after Goldoni's death, Venice fell victim to the revolutionary zeal and ambition of Napoleon Bonaparte, the little Corsican who, like Goldoni, had been born in a place bathed by the waters of the Mediterranean and started out speaking Italian, but had ended up in Paris speaking French.

PART FOUR

The Risorgimento and Unification
of the Italian Peninsula

CHAPTER ONE

The Napoleonic Era

The Man from Corsica

Napoleon Bonaparte towers over all others in this next interlude in Italian history. Like a comet, he rose to unimaginable heights, taking in his train relatives and friends, before crashing to earth in his final demise at Waterloo. His passage across Italy would leave the inevitable trail of death and destruction, but it would also scatter the seeds of unity, which was just a half century away.

Who was this man, the loser in love and the winner of wars whose life story reads more like fantasy that fact? This man of unimposing stature, whose mother tongue was Italian and who was ridiculed by his French classmates for his funny accent, was destined for greatness, rising like a phoenix from the fires of the French Revolution. Not King for a Day, but as Emperor for a Decade he created kingdoms for his own kin.

The fascinating story of Napoleon takes us from army camps and battlefields to the salons of Paris and the courts of capitals, from the hot sands of Africa to the snowy plains of a Russian winter. We will stay with him, however, in the beautiful Italian peninsula, which he will eventually catch in his net. Only two little fish get away— Sicily and Sardinia.

Napoleon was born in Ajaccio, a port city on the west coast of Corsica, the most mountainous island in the Mediterranean. Although his parents originated from mainland Italy and his father boasted noble Tuscan origin, they were Corsicans, but Napoleon came into the world as a French baby. Corsica had most recently been a part of the Republic of Genoa, but this troublesome little island was sold like a slave, kicking and screaming, to the French in 1768. One year later, at 11:30 A.M. on August 15, Ascension Day, Napoleon Bonaparte came into the world. It is said that the young mother had felt the pains of labor as she prayed in the church and rushed home, arriving barely in time to give birth to the babe on the carpet. If this is true it surely proved to be a magic one.

After years of hardships, study in French military school, service against a backdrop of revolutionary France, and the vicissitudes of fortune, we find Napoleon at just twenty-six years of age as a general in the French army. On March 7, 1796, he is appointed Commander-in-Chief of the Army of Italy. France was at war with Austria and would attack her on the underbelly, her Italian possessions in Lombardy.

Two days before his departure for the Italian campaign, Napoleon was married at night in a nonreligious ceremony to Josephine, a beautiful Creole lady born in Martinique and widow of General de Beauharnais, a nobleman who had lost his head under the guillotine. Josephine was six years older than Napoleon and she brought to the marriage a son, Eugene, and a daughter, Hortense, both of whom would have roles to play in Italian history.

With a motley collection of ragtag individuals under his command, Napoleon first made his appearance on the Italian horizon of the north. His famous dispatch, an exhortation to his soldiers and a graphic picture of this invading force, read as follows:

> Soldiers, you are ill-clad, ill-nourished; the Government owes you much but has nothing to give you. The patience and courage which you have shown amidst these rocks are admirable, but bring you no glory; no light shines upon you. I want to lead you to the most fertile plains of the world. Rich provinces, great cities will be at your mercy; you will find honor, glory, riches. Would you be lacking in courage and constancy, soldiers of Italy?

NAPOLEON BONAPARTE—March 26, 1796

Napoleon's success was phenomenal, and by the following month he was in Turin, having defeated the Piedmontese and Austrian armies. The next target was the capital of Austria's Italian possessions, the rich and elegant city of Milan.

Napoleon and his soldiers entered Milan on May 15 and were showered with flowers as the Milanese joyfully and naively welcomed them as liberators. The Austrians were gone, but the high expectations for better days were soon dampened by the excesses of Napoleon's soldiers. Had they not been told that great cities would be at their mercy? Unrest and disillusionment soon gripped the Milanese as rebellions broke out elsewhere, only to be ruthlessly quelled. A Proclamation to the inhabitants of Lombardy, issued from Milan on May 25, ended with these words: "Take warning by the terrible example of Binasco! Such will be the fate of every town and village that persists in the revolt." The peasants that had put up a defense had been massacred and their village burned to the ground. Pavia, where the citizens had overwhelmed the French garrison and taken prisoners, was the next victim. A few extracts from Napoleon's own report to the Executive Directory tells a chilling story of carnage and revenge:

> The gates were broken down and the mob scattered in all directions, taking refuge in the cellars or on the roofs, and trying in vain, by throwing down tiles, to prevent our entry into the streets.

The French prisoners managed to break out and Napoleon continued:

> I called over the names and there was not a man missing. If the blood of a single Frenchman had been shed I should have set up on the ruins of the place a column with the inscription: HERE STOOD THE TOWN OF PAVIA.

The town council was shot, and "two hundred" people were sent to France as hostages. Pavia's walls could not save her from the inevitable rape and pillage that followed. As Napoleon himself wrote, "I have no doubt that this lesson will be an example to the people of Italy."

We see the most brutal side of a new husband who, during this campaign, continued to write passionate and desperate letters to his Josephine, letters that went unanswered as his love was clearly unrequited. If Josephine's indifference caused anxiety, it did not dampen the warrior spirit of the general who proceeded to create a republican regime in Lombardy called the Cispadane Republic. It even included the papal cities of Bologna and Ferrara which had been occupied by the French.

Meanwhile, the French repulsed the Austrians, who came across the Alps to recover the much-disputed city of Mantua.

The death of Venice was imminent. She had just one more year to live. The fun-loving Venetians had maintained their neutrality, but they had also angered the French by granting asylum to a brother of the king they had recently guillotined. This one had managed to escape with his Italian wife, Louise Marie Josephine of Savoy, and was living under the assumed name of the "Comte de Lille." Napoleon needed no excuses, however, and war was declared against Venice on May 1, 1797. The Constitution of the Republic was destroyed by the "Venetian Council of Ten" in an attempt to save their city from Napoleon's wrath as he raged, "I shall be an Attila for Venice," but it was to no avail. Their symbolic vessel, *Bucentaur,* was put to flames.

In October of that same year a peace treaty was made with the Austrians. As part of the deal, what had been the independent and proud Venetian Republic was traded like a mere pawn for Austria's Belgian provinces. Venetia was now annexed to Austria.

The first campaign of the north had ended in victory for Napoleon. Leaving his conquests safely in French hands, he then left for the Egyptian expedition, sailing out from Toulon in hot pursuit of the British fleet, captained by the legendary and battle-seasoned Horatio Nelson, the man with one arm and one good eye. Napoleon's early successes were followed by defeat, and he returned from Egypt in October 1799. One month later, however, his luck changed and as a result of a coup d'état he became First Consul and virtual dictator of France.

Much had happened in just three years. The Jacobins, Italians who had espoused the ideals of the French Revolution, with the encouragement of the French were the dissidents who provoked incidents as an excuse for French invasion.

In the north, King Charles Emmanuel had been forced to retire to Sardinia while the French annexed Piedmont. In Rome, Napoleon's brother Joseph, appointed French ambassador there, had helped stir up a hornet's nest against papal power and an incident resulted in intervention by French forces who occupied Rome, deposed the papal government, and in February 1798 established a puppet Roman republic. The eighty-year-old Pope Pius VI, whom the French called "Citizen Pope," had been deposed, chased from Rome, then dragged back to France and imprisoned in Valence. Born on Christmas Day in 1717, this Vicar of Christ was to suffer at the hands of his flock and died in captivity on August 29, 1799.

Feeble-minded King Ferdinando of Naples and his energetic Queen, Maria Carolina, had taken up arms against the French and, backed up by Nelson and his British fleet fresh from victory in the Battle of the Nile, marched on Rome, which was briefly occupied. The French drove the Neapolitans back and as savage fighting broke out in the streets of Naples, on December 21, 1798, the royal court escaped to Sicily. One month later, on January 23, 1799, the Parthenopean Republic was proclaimed. But by July of that same year King Ferdinando was back in Naples, and another kind of terror took place as traitors were tracked down and executed.

Tuscany, like Venice, had declared neutrality, but French troops had occupied the Duchy in 1799 and the Grand Duke had fled to Austria. France was still at war with the British, and now the Austrians and their Russian allies had moved into northern Italy to regain their possessions there. Napoleon, who had brought order to France when everything seemed to be falling apart, now turned his attention to Italy and spent the winter of 1799 and the spring of 1800 preparing the Italian campaign.

Napoleon led his armies across the Alps through the Great Saint Bernard Pass before the snow had melted and marched straight on Milan, entering the city on June 2 and then appearing behind the Austrians, who were busy laying siege to Genoa. Once more northern Italy became the killing fields as two foreign armies clashed in a life-and-death struggle. The great battle that took place near Alessandria on June 14, 1800, is known as the Battle of Marengo. Napoleon had gambled against overwhelming odds and won. By nightfall the remnants of the Austrian army were in full rout. In one day of total hell some 4,000 Frenchmen and 9,500 Austrians lost their lives. The death of each soldier was compounded by the tragedy it brought to his family, multiplied thousands of times beyond the Alps in France and in Austria. Two days later, on June 16, seeking an end to the war, Napoleon wrote a persuasive letter to the Austrian Emperor, which included these descriptive lines:

> On the battlefield of Marengo, surrounded by sufferers, and in the midst of 15,000 dead bodies, I implore Your Majesty to hear the cry of humanity, and not to allow the offspring of two brave and powerful nations to slaughter one another for the sake of interests of which they know nothing.

The Peace Treaty of Luneville, signed February 9 the following year, put an end to hostilities and Napoleon proceeded to consolidate his power in the Italian

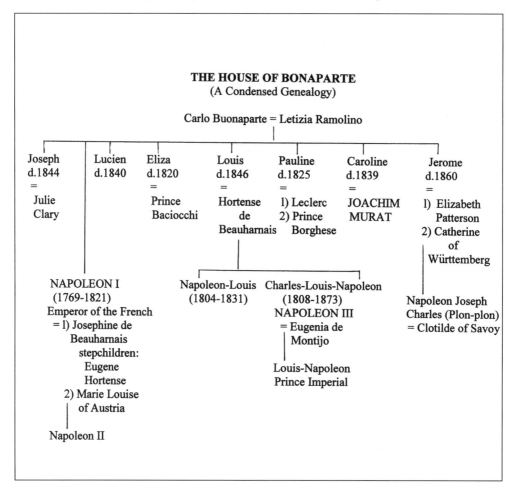

THE HOUSE OF BONAPARTE
(A Condensed Genealogy)

Carlo Buonaparte = Letizia Ramolino

Joseph d.1844	Lucien d.1840	Eliza d.1820	Louis d.1846	Pauline d.1825	Caroline d.1839	Jerome d.1860
=	=	=	=	=	=	=
Julie Clary		Prince Baciocchi	Hortense de Beauharnais	1) Leclerc 2) Prince Borghese	JOACHIM MURAT	1) Elizabeth Patterson 2) Catherine of Württemberg

NAPOLEON I
(1769-1821)
Emperor of the French
= 1) Josephine de
Beauharnais
stepchildren:
Eugene
Hortense
2) Marie Louise
of Austria

Napoleon II

Napoleon-Louis
(1804-1831)

Charles-Louis-Napoleon
(1808-1873)
NAPOLEON III
= Eugenia de
Montijo

Louis-Napoleon
Prince Imperial

Napoleon Joseph
Charles (Plon-plon)
= Clotilde of Savoy

peninsula. By 1810 the map of Italy had been redrawn, Napoleon had become an Emperor, kingdoms had been established, and Napoleon's family members had become the new royalty.

New Royalty for Italy

Many members of Napoleon's family have a place in Italian history. Josephine, whom he loved with a passion and continued to cherish later as his "old wife" and companion, gave him no children, but he accepted hers from her first marriage as his own. Josephine's son, Eugene de Beauharnais, was particularly dear to Napoleon. The young man was with him on his first campaign to Italy, sailed with him to Egypt, and took part in the bloody Battle of Marengo. The bonds between the families were further strengthened by the marriage of Josephine's daughter, Hortense, to Napoleon's brother Louis. Their son, who later became Napoleon III, also played a role in Italian unification.

Napoleon had also been a father to his own brothers and sisters, supervising their education and deciding on their careers. He clearly regarded them as diplomatic assets and sought to arrange their marriages in the best interest of his empire. Not all of Napoleon's seven siblings were cooperative, however, and some of them proved to be troublesome liabilities. The young rascal Jerome had deserted the navy in America and taken as his wife a lady named Elizabeth Patterson from Baltimore, whom he was subsequently forced to give up for a diplomatic arrangement that would make him King of Westphalia. Brother Lucien adamantly refused to marry the Infanta of Spain, widow of the Grand Duke of Tuscany who had been given the more imposing title of King of Etruria.

Pauline, the most beautiful of Mother Letizia's brood, was as difficult to handle as an untrained filly. Her first husband had died of yellow fever in San Domingo, and she took as her second husband the noble Italian, Prince Borghese, although she tired of him after two years of marriage and abandoned him in Rome. Napoleon gave her the little principality of Guastalla, which she then sold to the Kingdom of Italy for 4.6 million lire, just as one would sell a house. Pauline returned to the livelier city of Paris for a scandalous good time, crossed swords with sister-in-law Josephine, and was eventually banished from court by Napoleon. Pauline died of cancer in Florence, but she lives on in the Borghese Gallery in Rome in the beautiful statue created by the renowned Venetian sculptor Antonio Canova, who depicted her as Venus reclining on a sofa. (Canova was later appointed by the Pope as head of a commission to recover art treasures looted by Napoleon and bring them back to their owners in Italy.)

Brother Louis was another headache. He was proclaimed King of Holland in 1806, but abdicated four years later. His wanderings took him to the capitals of Europe, but he later settled in Italy to engage in literary pursuits. He died at Livorno in July 1846. One of Louis's problems with Napoleon was the suspicion, fired by rumors spread abroad, that the latter's affection for Louis's wife, Hortense, was something more than stepfatherly. Louis could never be sure that his firstborn was really his own.

The quagmire of battles, negotiations, treaties, and political maneuvers of all kinds makes it difficult to separate those events that have a direct bearing on the Italy that Napoleon controlled from happenings beyond the Alps. However, one of his first tasks that directly involved the peninsula after driving out the Austrians was reestablishment of the Cisalpine Republic, renamed the "Italian Republic," suggesting the emergence of national identity.

Napoleon ruled through a local administration presided over by a Lombard patriot, but when he was proclaimed Emperor on May 18, 1804, he was offered the Iron Crown of the Lombards, with which he was symbolically crowned in Milan the following year, on May 26, 1805. Instead of complete independence as a kingdom within an empire, however, they got the twenty-three-year-old Eugene de Beauharnais as Viceroy. Napoleon's letters to the young man contain advice that would have benefited any diplomat, but they also reveal his opinions of the Italians, whom he clearly does not trust. Here are a few of his comments:

> *Our Italian subjects are more deceitful by nature than the citizens of France. – The aim of your administration is the happiness of my Italian peoples; and the first sacrifice that you will have to make will be to fall in with their customs which you detest. – In any position but that of Viceroy of Italy you may boast of being a Frenchman. – Nothing is so advisable as to treat Italians well, and to get to know all their names and families. – Cultivate the young Italians, rather than the old: the latter are good for nothing . . .*

Intelligent and of fine bearing, Eugene won the love and respect of his Italian subjects and was approved by the aristocracy in the palaces of Monza and Milan. With the help of Italian ministers, he introduced the French legal system and built new roads. Venice was brought back into the Italian fold by treaty and was incorporated into the Kingdom of Italy, and young Eugene was given the title of Prince of Venice.

There were other changes that took place in the peninsula. Napoleon's sister Elise, married to a Corsican nobleman, was given the tiny principality of Piombino and then Lucca; the proud Duchy of Parma was simply annexed to the Empire; and another boundary disappeared as independent Genoa was incorporated into the Empire.

The Kingdom of Naples was next. Although a treaty of neutrality had been signed between Napoleon and King Ferdinando in September 1805, it was learned that his queen, Maria Carolina, had engaged in secret negotiations with the Austrians and wanted war against the "Corsican bastard." Napoleon exploded on hearing this, and he is quoted as having responded characteristically with the words: "I will send her and her children begging throughout Europe for a piece of bread." He had already decided to make his brother Joseph the King of Naples and dispatched him with French troops to claim the throne and drive out King Ferdinando and his court. The presence of the French brought hope to the revolutionary elements in Italy in their struggle against feudal lords and secret police, and it was this climate and background that provided the setting for the opera *Tosca* with its tragic finale on the battlements of Castel Sant'Angelo. Joseph entered Naples on February 15, 1806. Under the protection of the British, King Ferdinando and his court fled by ship for the safety of Palermo and a much longer stay this time.

Two years later, in a game of royal musical chairs, Joseph was made King of Spain, and the throne he vacated was then occupied by sister Caroline and her husband, Joachim Murat, the brilliant French cavalry leader to whom she had been given in marriage in 1800. The new king had more than proved himself in battle, but as the son of a lowly innkeeper he had even less pedigree than the Bonapartes when it came to royal titles. Nevertheless, the "new royalty" did much to improve conditions while reorganizing the administrative systems and introducing the French civil code. While Caroline helped to maintain a splendid court, Joachim entertained the Neapolitans with magnificent processions in which, still the skilled cavalryman, he thrilled his subjects with his incredible horsemanship.

Napoleon had brought the peninsula under his control in one way or another, but there was one thorn in his side—Pope Pius VII. The tug-of-war between Napoleon and the Vicar of Christ was of long standing. Instead of going to Rome, Napoleon had invited the Pope to come to Paris, where he took the imperial crown from the Pontiff's hands and put it on his own head in a bold gesture of his superiority. Revolutionary France was anticlerical and papal control of the French Church was a constant bone of contention.

In the peninsula, part of papal territory had already been incorporated into the Kingdom of Italy and in 1806 Napoleon had unsuccessfully ordered the Pope to join his Italian confederacy. Relations deteriorated as Napoleon lost patience with the "irascible old man." In 1808 French troops entered Rome, and the following year the Papal States were annexed to the French Empire. The Pope responded with the only weapon at his disposal by excommunicating the invaders, while Napoleon reacted with characteristic speed by having him arrested.

On July 6, the Pope was taken from the Holy City and spent the next five years as a virtual prisoner of the French. Detained for some time in Italy, he was later moved

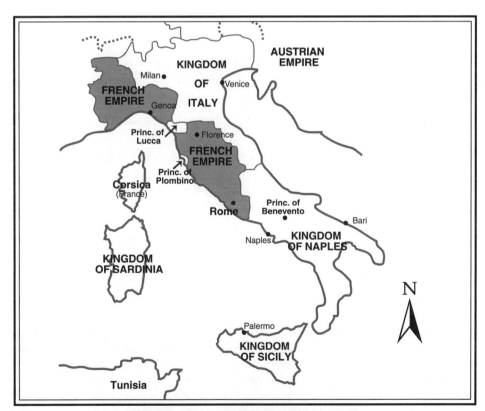

The Italian Peninsula in 1810

to France because Napoleon was afraid that the pesky English would abduct him. He ordered this move while he was on his Russian campaign, and the following quote is from his letter to his brother-in-law, Prince Borghese, then in charge of Piedmont and Genoa.

Dresden, May 21

> *. . . have just heard that there are English vessels off Savona, and I think that the Pope must be put in a safe place. You are therefore to order the prefect and the officer in command of the "gendarmerie" to send the Pope and his people away in two good carriages. The Pope will have his doctor in the carriage with him. Make sure that he passes through Turin by night . . . and that he is taken in this way to Fontainbleau, where orders have been given for his reception.* (Napoleon's Letters, trans. J. M. Thompson)

The other conflict which Napoleon had with the Pope was the latter's refusal to grant divorces. There was the problem of brother Jerome's misalliance with Miss Patterson, but much more serious was Napoleon's decision to divorce Josephine and marry a woman who could produce an heir. He considered this a political necessity and had even gone as far as "experimenting" with another woman to see if he was capable of producing offspring before taking such drastic action. Napoleon and Josephine had been hastily and properly married in a religious ceremony before the coronation, but an Emperor can always find ways to overcome such impediments without chopping off heads, as Henry VIII had done. The choice of a new wife fell on the nineteen-year-old Archduchess Marie-Louise and in 1810 two great empires, the French and the Austrian, were united.

Napoleon remained friends with his "old wife" and took delight in the new one who, the following year, gave birth to a son, Napoleon II. Marie-Louise had brought Napoleon the heir he desired, but with her his luck had changed.

Joachim Murat, King of Naples

Joachim Murat replaced Joseph Bonaparte on the throne of Naples in 1808. Tall and handsome in his gold-braided uniform and a hat with plumes, he had entered Naples to be acclaimed as a monarch by a friendly and enthusiastic populace. A week later, the French ambassador in reporting to the Foreign Office in Paris wrote:

> *the King has already conquered all his new subjects of every class. His affability and his grace have seduced them in less than no time. When he shows himself in the streets and promenades the lazzaroni run in a crowd after him to applaud him, he salutes them and they return enchanted. . . . He is a brave man, they say, he can go alone where he wishes and nothing will happen to him.* (Joan Bear, *Caroline Murat*, p. 102).

Joachim assumed his royal duties with all the enthusiasm of a new monarch, yet he was not truly king as long as he was bound to take commands from the Emperor, who constantly wrote letters disapproving of the measures he took to solve the problems of his new realm. Joachim Murat, the cavalry leader, had faithfully followed his captain, but as King of Naples he eventually abandoned and rebelled against the Emperor who had placed him in such an exalted position. Ironically, the last most significant act of this Frenchman, which cost him his life, was his attempt to unite the peninsula and free the Italians from foreign rule. In this he enters Italian history as a "patriot" and French history as a "traitor." How did this come about?

King Joachim wanted to govern his realm in the best interest of his subjects, but there had been a falling out between him and his brother-in-law, the Emperor, over the place of that kingdom in the greater order of things. It was no secret that Joachim did not like the "continental system," which required him to furnish Italian contingents to his Emperor in case of a continental war. Napoleon saw things differently and was quoted as saying: "I did not put a French King at Naples, so that the Neapolitans should be less French than they were under the Queen [Marie Caroline] and it is the King himself who must have inspired the sentiments which they now have." (*Caroline Murat,* p. 172). Joachim was known to have encouraged "Italic" secret societies, a further threat to Napoleon, who grumbled: "The King wishes to persuade the Italians that that land won't have any existence or future unless the whole of Italy is united under the same scepter."

The ill-fated Russian campaign, which began in the spring of 1812, was the Continental War that brought together almost half a million men from every corner of the Empire and satellite countries to form the *Grande Armée*. The Italians were there, too. Prince Eugene, Viceroy of the Kingdom of Italy, was there with his Lombards, and King Joachim was there to lead the cavalry as no other man could.

Napoleon's army rushed headlong to the heart of Russia as their enemy evaporated ahead of them. The great armies finally clashed in bloody battle at Borodino, just seventy miles from Moscow. In the battle line-up, Prince Eugene was on the left where he and his Lombards distinguished themselves by capturing advanced posts of Borodino. King Joachim and the cavalry supported the French units on the right wing, establishing positions outside the city. The battle began at 6 A.M. on September 7, and raged for twelve hours, leaving 45,000 Russians and 30,000 Imperial troops dead, not to mention the beautiful horses left behind dead or dying on the killing-fields.

The Russians withdrew to the south of Moscow to observe their enemy, and Moscow was abandoned. It was Joachim, King of Naples, who led the first contingent into the deserted and ghostlike city just before midnight one week later. The following day fire broke out and the beautiful city of Moscow was almost completely destroyed. A frustrated Napoleon found no one to fight and no one with whom to negotiate an armistice as the clever Czar, like a wary wolf, lurked in wait at a distance. But a more formidable enemy soon made its appearance. Napoleon and his *Grande Armée* were caught in the deadly trap of an early Russian winter.

Napoleon's disastrous retreat is legend. The Emperor rushed back to Paris, leaving Joachim the task of leading the remnants of the once proud *Grande Armée* back across the desolate white plains as deep snow impeded progress, and men and horses perished along the way, claimed by hunger and cold. King Joachim was not insensitive to the suffering of the Italians in particular, unaccustomed to such a harsh climate.

King Joachim led the straggling remnants of the army back to Koenigsberg from where, on December 22, he wrote to his Queen, whom he had left as regent in Naples. Maintaining that he had performed his duties as promised by installing the troops in winter quarters, though still without word from the Emperor giving him permission to leave, he set out for Naples in mid-January, handing over his command to Prince Eugene. Napoleon did not see things in quite the same light, however, and he considered this action tantamount to desertion. He wrote to Joachim on January 26, "I am not going to tell you how displeased I am with your conduct, which has been diametrically opposed to your duties." He went on to scold and criticize him and ended the short letter with the words: "The title of King has turned your head; if you want to keep it, behave yourself, and be careful what you say" (Letter 253 — Letters of Napoleon, ed. J. M. Thompson).

Back in Naples, Joachim's first concern was to keep his crown, and he saw fit to enter into secret negotiations with England, Napoleon's archenemy, splashing gleefully around the Mediterranean unhindered and protecting the exiled royals Ferdinando and Marie Caroline on the island of Sicily.

As for Napoleon, he had not yet learned his lesson in Russia and, angered by the behavior of the Austrians, was preparing to make war against his own father-in-law, the Austrian Emperor. He again ordered contingents from Naples and Joachim, notwithstanding secret arrangements also with the Austrians, chose to play a dangerous double game and joined forces with Napoleon's newly reconstituted *Grande Armée* in Saxony. Once again the Italians from both north and south were dragged into a continental war.

The culmination of this campaign was the Battle of Leipzig, also called the Battle of the Nations, which took place October 16 through 18, 1813. This time, Napoleon's army, outnumbered by the allied forces of Austria, Prussia, Russia, and Sweden, was torn to shreds. Still a stubborn Napoleon refused to concede defeat, ignoring the advice of his generals. King Joachim favored a separate agreement with Austria, but Prince Eugene would not betray his Emperor, and the two quarreled.

Joachim returned to Naples, and one month later took matters into his own hands, joining forces with the winning side and signing alliances with Austria and the British. In this he was supported by his Queen, who was by now equally fearful of the mad schemes of brother Napoleon. Encouraged by the Italian patriots, Joachim envisioned a United Italy with himself as its king. He moved troops into Tuscany and also went beyond the borders of his kingdom into the Papal States.

Meanwhile, the tide of events in Europe turned rapidly as French power was crushed. On April 6, 1814, Napoleon Bonaparte was forced to abdicate and was exiled to the tiny island of Elba, where he arrived in May. Meanwhile, his Empress, Marie-Louise, along with their son who bore the exalted title of King of Rome, fled to Vienna and the protection of her father, the Austrian Emperor. Prince Eugene retired to Bavaria with his princess following a treaty of May 30, 1814, by which lands in Italy were incorporated into the Austrian fold as the Kingdom of Lombardy-Venetia. The French were gone and the Austrians were back in the north.

Not a year had passed when Napoleon, the unguarded exile, shattered the uneasy peace of Europe by his return to France on March 1, 1815, creating shock waves from the shores of England and eastward to Austria, where news arrived as Vienna danced.

During this period, known as the One Hundred Days, King Joachim lost no time and pressed his plans in Italy, openly declaring war against a stunned Austria with a view to driving her out of the Italian peninsula. On March 30, 1815 he issued his famous proclamation, calling on all Italians to unite and free themselves from the foreigners. He led his army of Neapolitan soldiers northward and met the Austrians in battle at Tolentino, not far from Ancona, on May 3. It was a crushing defeat for

King Joachim, who had too much confidence in soldiers who did not share his ideals. He had gambled all and lost his kingdom.

King Joachim hurriedly returned to Naples and took leave of the Queen, advising her to make the best terms she could for her return to France. At 9 o'clock on the evening of May 18 he went down to waiting boats, never to see his wife or children again, and set sail for France, where he hoped to join up with Napoleon. Joachim reached the south of France, where he waited as events unfolded in the north. Meanwhile, Napoleon had mustered an army and marched into Belgium to fight his last battle on the soggy plains south of Brussels, the Battle of Waterloo, June 15 through 18, 1815, where he was defeated by the British under Wellington with the support of the Prussians. Like his old cavalry commander, Napoleon had reached too high and lost everything.

As we leave Napoleon to his well-known fate, let us return to the south of France where Joachim, with a price on his head, was forced into hiding. He escaped on a fishing vessel to the clan-divided Corsica, where he rallied around him a few hundred enthusiastic partisans willing to join him in his quest to regain his kingdom.

Meanwhile, a bizarre event was taking place in the waters off Naples where the ship carrying the fleeing ex-Queen, Caroline, fired its guns in salute to another British ship that was bringing the true royals, Ferdinando and Maria-Carolina, back from almost ten years of comfortable exile in Palermo. Caroline was escorted around the boot of Italy to Trieste, where she was placed under the protection of the Austrians. On the other side of the peninsula, far from the land that had been her kingdom, she assumed the title of Countess Lipona, an anagram for Napoli. She arranged for a passport for her husband under the name of Count Lipona, but Joachim, always the fearless adventurer who had faced death thousands of times, could never face the thought of exile or captivity and rejected the offer of Austrian asylum as dishonorable.

Joachim had not given up hope of regaining his kingdom. He set sail from Corsica with a mere 298 men, but stormy seas separated the ships of his small fleet, reducing his force to a handful of men by the time they reached the Bay of Naples.

Joachim finally saw the futility of his plans and asked his captain to go to Trieste, where he would join his family, but the ship was not strong enough for the rough, unpredictable waters of the Adriatic at that time of year and they had no provisions.

On reaching the Gulf of Saint Eufemia on the western coast of Calabria, the captain suggested landing at the little town of Pizzo, identified from the sea by a castle built on a promontory by the Spaniards. In a last, desperate bid for recognition, Joachim changed into full dress uniform before going ashore. One can only imagine the dismay of the crowd, gathered in the square for market day, to see such an apparition in their midst! Some recognized Joachim as their former king, but the true monarchs were now in control and they became afraid. Two men came to warn Joachim that he was surrounded by enemies, but before he and his party could escape they were set upon by an angry mob that tore their uniforms with shouts of "tyrant!"

Joachim was taken into custody and imprisoned in the castle while a commission was hastily called together. After five hours of deliberation, the ex-king was condemned to death under a penal code that decreed death to anyone trying to change the government or order of succession to the throne. Ironically, he himself had drawn up the code that now became his death sentence.

When Joachim knew he was going to die he sat down and wrote a touching letter to his family, enclosing a lock of his beautiful black curls. Here is what he said:

> *My last hour has come, in a few moments I shall have ceased to live. My life was not stained by any act of injustice. Farewell, my Achille; farewell, my Laetitia; farewell, my Lucien; farewell, my Louise; show the world that you are worthy of me. I leave you without a kingdom and without means, in the midst of my numerous enemies. Show yourself superior to misfortune; think of what you are and of what you have been. God will bless you. Do not curse my memory. I declare that my greatest*

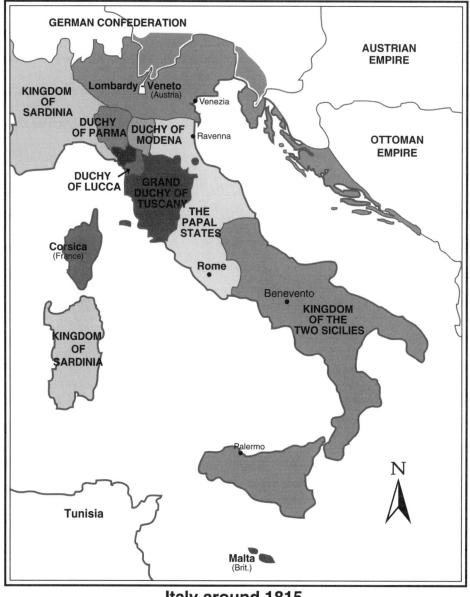

Italy around 1815

grief in the last moments of my life is to die far away from my children.

As a twelve-man firing squad appeared, Joachim is said to have bared his chest and uttered these words: "Soldiers, do your duty, fire at the heart but spare my face."

The shots that rang out in a little Calabrian town on that October 13, 1815, put an end to the life of Joachim Murat and his plan for a unified and free peninsula. The mortal remains of this Frenchman who had a dream for Italy were buried in Italian soil in an unmarked grave. Half a century would pass before that dream would be fulfilled.

Survivors of the Storm

With the final defeat of Napoleon, the relatives that he had taken up with him now followed him into obscurity, stripped of the extraordinary powers they enjoyed, and

Joachim Murat. Gérard. From the Murat collection

relegated to the sidelines to watch as events unfolded. Like survivors of a shipwreck, they found themselves washed back on Italian shores, for there was no place for them on the soil of France that had taken back its Bourbon monarchy.

Josephine had ended her days in France, where she died May 29, 1814, just one month after Napoleon's exile to Elba, but most of Napoleon's brothers and sisters died in Italy before it became a free nation. Eliza Baciocchi died at Sant'Andrea near Trieste in August 1820. The beautiful Pauline Borghese died of cancer in Florence in June 1825. Caroline Murat, following exile, eventually went to live in Florence, where she died in May 1839, and the following year brother Lucien died in Viterbo in the Papal States. The third one to end his days in Florence, always a haven for exiles, was the eldest brother, Joseph, who died in July 1844. Two years later, Louis, the literary man of the family and disenchanted husband of Josephine's daughter Hortense de Beauharnais, died in Livorno in July 1846. The last surviving sibling of Napoleon was brother Jerome, who died in France June 24, 1860, one year before the birth of Italy.

Napoleon's wife Marie-Louise was awarded the Italian duchies of Parma, Piacenza, and Guastalla. Their son was separated from his mother and left in Vienna to be brought up Austrian. Often referred to as *L'Aiglon* ("the eaglet"), the unfortunate youth died of pulmonary tuberculosis at twenty-one years of age, before he had a chance to try his wings.

Of all the survivors, it was the sons of Louis and Hortense who left their mark in Italian history, championing the cause of unification, and the youngest, Charles-Louis Napoleon, was destined to take the seat of his legendary uncle as Napoleon III, Emperor of France, from 1852–1870. Before that time, he had a role to play on the stage of Italian history.

CHAPTER
TWO

The First Phase of
The Risorgimento

The Austrians Are Back

The period that followed the return of the former exiled rulers brought peace to the peninsula, and its young men were no longer taken away to die on battlefields in a foreign country. Battles of a different kind, however, were fermenting.

The map of the peninsula had changed again; gone forever were the maritime Republics of Venice and Genoa. Venice was now part of the Austrian-controlled Lombardy, and Genoa was added to Piedmont as part of the Kingdom of Sardinia with Turin as its capital. Sicily was back with the mainland to form the Kingdom of the Two Sicilies with its capital in Naples. Tuscany was returned to the benevolent despotism of Ferdinand III—brother of Austrian Emperor Francis I—back after twelve years in exile to resume his place as Grand Duke for another ten years. Mere satellites of the Austrians were the Duchies of Parma and Modena. These were the separate and diverse pieces of the Italian puzzle following Napoleon's demise.

The old leaders were back, but things would never be the same again. The seeds of rebellion had been sown. Men of action and ideas took up the pen instead of the sword and fought in their own ways to bring about unification and freedom from foreign rule. Even Napoleon had recognized the inevitability of such when he wrote these prophetic words from exile on the remote island of Saint Helena:

> Italy is a single Nation: the uniformity of customs, language, literature, in the not too distant future, must bring together all its inhabitants under a single government. Roma is without doubt the city which the Italians will one day chose as their capital. . . . It is necessary for the well being of Europe that Italy form a single State. (Translated from Niccolò Rodolico's high school text for Italian schools, 1937)

It had been the French-hating Turinese Vittorio Alfieri (1749–1803) who had coined the word *Risorgimento* (from *risorgere*, to rise again) which would become the battle cry for the new movement. Alfieri was a celebrated playwright of his time, a contemporary of the Venetian Carlo Goldoni, but his writings did more than just entertain, for they had a potent political sting that inspired the romantic patriots who came after him. In a poem entitled "The Free Man," he appealed to the Italians to resist tyranny, although by non-violent means.

Austria had replaced France in its control of the Italian peninsula, however, and was now the foreign power to be dealt with. Secret societies, at first most active in the south and referred to as the *Carbonari* [charcoal burners], became a threat to the rulers as the people demanded reforms that would improve their lives and give them greater freedoms.

Revolution first broke out on July 9, 1820, when rebellious troops commanded by General Gugliermo Pepe and allied with the Carbonari entered Naples. A reluctant King Ferdinand was forced to grant a constitution that stripped him of absolute powers, reducing his role to that of a constitutional monarch, and a new government was formed. Eyewitnesses to the event were Francesco Florimo (1800–1888) and his good Sicilian friend Vincenzo Bellini, whose name is known to us through his beautiful music. The two young men were students in Naples at the time, and in his biography Florimo described the euphoria of being part of the liberation movement. Partly urged on by friends and partly "to swim with the current," they joined the ranks of the Carbonari like so many others.

In addition to troubles on the mainland, the situation was further complicated by the separatist movement of Sicily, unwilling to lose the independent status it had enjoyed under British protection. The desperate King Ferdinand decided to call on the Austrians for help. Troops arrived in March of the following year, the fledgling government of Naples was dissolved, Sicily was eventually brought to heel, and Ferdinand was king again. In the crackdown on revolutionaries that followed, the names of Florimo and Bellini appeared on the blacklist. Fortunately for the world of music, the Rector of the Collegio di Musica took a fatherly interest in the young men, as Florimo later told us in his own words:

> One evening – I remember it as though it were yesterday – it was May 29, 1821 – he summoned us to his rooms and gave us a solemn, paternal talking to, concluding in a gruff way: "You are carbonari and don't deny it, as I have learned from a reliable source – and therefore you are enemies of God and of our august King! I'm going to give you advice for your own good; and I want you to listen to me, because if you don't I don't know where you are going to end up. Tomorrow is the saint's day of the King, our legitimate ruler; in the evening you will go to the San Carlo to celebrate his festa, and will applaud loudly whenever the audience applauds, and will keep on shouting at the tops of your voices: 'Long live our King Ferdinand, consecrated by God and by Right!' And make certain that you force the audience to notice you because of your shouting. In that way I will have cards in my hands to save you when facing the Minister of Police – who is a close friend of mine."
> (Herbert Weinstock, *Vincenzo Bellini*, p. 19)

The advice came from one who had been a prisoner of the French with irons on his feet. The young men, scared out of their wits, took it seriously. At all events, here ended Bellini's political life and, fortunately for posterity, he dedicated himself to writing operas. The Sicilian genius who had left parents and friends to study in the musical capital of Naples during those turbulent years ended his days prematurely in Paris, where he died in September 1835, at the age of thirty-three.

As for the Austrians, they remained in occupation until 1827. A period of repression continued with the notorious police chief Prince Canosa. Spies were everywhere, and one could trust no one. All those suspected of revolutionary thought or subversive ideas were the unfortunate targets, especially those in a position to sway people's minds. Priests were prevented from preaching, teachers from teaching, and strict censorship was applied to writers and playwrights, as well as composers whose music could easily whip up a frenzy.

The next trouble spot was in the north, where the seeds of Carbonist ideas found fertile soil. Turin had long been a center of radical ideas and just across the border in Switzerland were Italian exiles hatching up their schemes. One of the old guard was Filippo Buonarroti, a direct descendant of Michelangelo. A young group of writers in Milan formed a newspaper, *Il Conciliatore,* which came under scrutiny of the Austrians and was suppressed in 1819. Its editor, Silvio Pellico, was arrested and imprisoned and although a playwright of some merit he is best known for his book *Le Mie Prigioni,* which opens with the ominous lines: *"Friday, October 13, 1820, I was arrested in Milan and taken to Santa Margherita. It was three o'clock in the afternoon. They interrogated me all of that day and still others. But I won't say anything about that."* Pellico was lucky enough to have a death sentence commuted to imprisonment. Ten years later he gained his freedom and told his story.

In 1821 there were serious troubles in Piedmont, where an uprising took place against the repressive monarchy. Vittorio Emanuele I abdicated in favor of his brother Carlo Felice, who happened to be in Modena at the time. The revolutionaries, meanwhile, persuaded young Carlo Alberto of another branch of the family to keep the throne warm in the absence of Carlo Felice and meanwhile grant a constitution. When the new king arrived ten days later, Carlo Alberto decided it was time to leave, but more radical revolutionaries who supported him continued their struggle outside Turin. An Austrian army was soon on the scene, and the rebels were defeated miserably at Novara, following which a series of arrests took place and the ringleaders were sentenced to death or imprisoned.

As movements were put down in the north, trouble was fermenting in central Italy with uprisings in Bologna as well as the duchies of Modena and Parma, only to be crushed by Austrian intervention. Uprisings directed against papal tyranny in Umbria were supported by none other than the young Charles-Louis-Napoleon who saw the opportunity of overthrowing the extremely oppressive secular power of the popes and establishing a Kingdom of Italy, taking up the cause for which his uncle Joachim Murat had died. His plan was to bring back his cousin, Napoleon's only son, as king with himself as regent. The plot was discovered and Charles-Louis-Napoleon, the future Emperor of the French, had to get out of the Holy City with all possible speed, taking refuge first in Florence, still the haven of Italian liberals.

Destiny soon took a hand in Charles-Louis's life. With the death of his older brother in 1831 and cousin Napoleon the following year, he became the legitimate heir to the Empire of France and set out to claim his rights. It was as Emperor that years later he returned to play a role in Italian history once again.

The Austrians had managed to put out the brush fires, but discontent smoldered and new men came to fan the flames. One such man was Giuseppe Mazzini (1805–1872) and with him another phase of the Risorgimento began to take shape.

Giuseppe Mazzini

To walk through the streets of an Italian city is to take a walk through history as the names of great men appear with every corner that one turns. Now to be added to such street names as Corso Dante or Via Cristoforo Colombo, come those of Italian patriots: Via Alfieri, Corso Giacomo Matteotti, Corso Massimo d'Azeglio, Piazza Cavour, Corso Garibaldi, Via Giuseppe Verdi, and Via Giuseppe Mazzini. These were not just heroes of a city or region but Italian heroes.

One of the great names of the Risorgimento was Giuseppe Mazzini, whose life spanned the first struggles for independence and the birth of the Italian nation in 1861. Mazzini's sole mission in life was the unification of the peninsula, and for this cause he spent most of his sixty-seven years in exile. Although he died on Italian soil at Pisa on March 10, 1872, he spent his last days disguised as a Dr. Brown and a fugitive in the very country he spent his whole life to create.

Mazzini was born in Genoa, which was at that time under French rule. His father was a doctor, but the great influence in his life came from his fiercely democratic mother, who believed that her son was a genius destined to change the world. Mazzini was a very sickly child who from an early age lived with his books. He studied at the University of Genoa, graduating as a Doctor of Law at the age of twenty-one, and as was the custom at the time did his apprenticeship without pay as an advocate for the poor.

Eloquent and enthusiastic, "the little advocate" as he came to be known was much in demand, but his interest was in literature and politics. After expressing his ideas in journals first in Genoa and then in Livorno, both of which were suppressed as subversive, Mazzini joined the secret society of the *Carbonari*.

Mazzini's writings had already attracted the attention of the authorities and in November 1830, he was arrested and condemned to several months of solitary confinement. Fortunately, he had a room with a view, for his prison cell with its grated window, high on the rock fortress of the gloomy seaport of Savona, looked out on the waters of the Mediterranean. With three books for his companions — a Bible, Byron, and Tacitus — the ideas that were the terror of tyrants matured in his solitude. "It was during these months of imprisonment," he wrote, "that I conceived the plan for *'La Giovine Italia'* [Young Italy], and meditated deeply upon the principles on which to base its organization and the aim and purpose of its labors, which I intended should be publicly declared." Mazzini was released early the following year and went into exile in Marseilles, France, where he founded *La Giovine Italia*.

When the tyrannical and intransigent Carlo Felice, King of Sardinia/Piedmont, died on April 27, 1831, Mazzini believed that his successor, Carlo Alberto, would bring about change. Encouraged by the fact that some ten years earlier Carlo had supported the liberals, Mazzini published an open letter to the newly crowned king, urging him to lead Italy to independence. This bold letter suggested that the king was threatened by Austria, France, and the frenzy for Freedom, and contained such phrases as: *"SIRE! . . . Place yourself at the head of the nation and write on your flag: UNIONE, LIBERTA, INDIPENDENZA! Be the Napoleon of Italian liberty!"* (Geneva G. Mayer, 1831, quoted from *Storia d'Italia*).

The letter backfired. The new king, fearing that his royal boat was being rocked, gave orders for the writer to be tracked down and arrested. Mazzini soon found himself expelled from France on the urgings of Piedmont and took refuge in Switzerland along with other exiles. In 1833 he made mischief by organizing a mutiny in the Piedmontese army. Arrests followed, and Mazzini's closest friend, Jacopo Ruffmi, was captured. He committed suicide in prison rather than run the risk of revealing other names under torture.

At this time Mazzini made the acquaintance of another Giuseppe whose life closely paralleled his own. He was Giuseppe Garibaldi (1807–1882), born in Nice when it was part of France, but borders had since changed and Nice, like Genoa, was now part of the Kingdom of Sardinia/Piedmont. Garibaldi joined Mazzini's organization of *La Giovine Italia.* The plot that the two hatched to provoke a popular revolution in Piedmont was daring. Still from his exile in Switzerland, the resourceful Mazzini, determined that his beloved friend should not have died in vain, recruited members in the Piedmontese army, while Garibaldi, who was enlisted in the Sardinian navy, was to provide naval support. The plot was discovered, and this time the two troublesome Giuseppes were sentenced to death.

Garibaldi fled to South America, where he became a pirate and mercenary serving one revolutionary government or another. Brazil, Uruguay, and Argentina were the far-flung regions of his adventures in war — and romance, too. The story of Garibaldi and Anita might well take its place as one of the great romances of history. From the deck of his ship off the coast of Brazil he spotted in the sights of his telescope as he scanned the shore a lovely young girl who became his wife and companion in wars. We meet this extraordinary woman later as she plays her own tragic role in the unification of Italy. Notwithstanding his life as an exile and adventurer, Garibaldi remained faithful to his ideals as a patriotic Italian, keeping in touch with Mazzini, and in far away South America he helped to form an Italian legion, the first "Redshirts."

In sharp contrast to Garibaldi's life, Mazzini spent much of his time as an exile within the confines of four walls, often under assumed names. He kept in close touch with his mother and concealed his identity by writing to her as "Dear Aunt" and signing himself "Niece." He finally left Switzerland and arrived in London in January 1837 to continue the struggle.

For ten years, Mazzini recruited supporters among the Italian exiles and mounted a formidable propaganda machine to keep the ideals of *La Giovine Italia* alive in the peninsula and elsewhere. Among the names to be listed with heroes of the Risorgimento were many writers, such as Vincenzo Gioberti, Count Cesare Balbo, and Massimo d'Azeglio. All wanted the expulsion of the foreign power and the unification of Italy. Some espoused the idea of a kind of federalism, whereas Massimo envisioned Piedmont as the leader with its King as King of Italy, and it was his vision that became a reality.

How could unification be achieved? The solution was still in the future, but despite all the uncertainties and confusion Italy was still singing. Opera came of age in its most glorious form during this romantic phase of the Risorgimento, and music provided Italy with another great patriot, a third Giuseppe — Giuseppe Verdi.

Opera: Italy's Gift to the World of Music

It had been said that wine was Italian sunshine turned fluid and that opera put it into sound. It was not a new form, but one that had matured over two centuries of operatic civilization and reached new heights during the first half of the nineteenth century. It was also the perfect vehicle through which the soul of Italy found expression.

During the period of *Il Risorgimento,* Italy was blessed with great singers and great composers, and their audiences were drawn from a whole population for whom music was part of life. The creative output of these composers needed to satisfy the thirst of the public for more operas was nothing short of staggering, and the pressure was intense. In the first ten years of the Verdi era, more than 500 new operas were written and performed. La Scala of Milan, San Carlo of Naples, and La Fenice of Venice, as well as the theaters of every other notable Italian city wanted new operas for their festivals. Added to this was the growing appreciation of opera in the capital cities of Europe, who "raided" the peninsula for Italian genius.

During the period in question, Italy boasted four great masters of the opera who came from different parts of the Italian peninsula. From Sicily came Vincenzo Bellini (1801–1835), whom we have already met. Gioacchino Rossini (1792–1868) was from the east coast town of Pesaro; Gaetano Donizetti (1797–1848) had his roots in the northern city of Bergamo. Giuseppe Verdi (1813–1901), the one of most humble origin, was born in the small village of Le Roncole in the Duchy of Parma.

Vincenzo Bellini died in far-off Paris in September 1835, and the world lost a genius who during his short life produced such operas as *Norma*, considered his masterpiece, and *I Puritani*.

It was Giacchino Rossini who took care of all the funeral arrangements of Bellini, his friend and colleague. Tragically, however, although Rossini was still in his mid-forties his musical genius had already dried up. The biographer of his most productive years, the French writer Stendhal had introduced him with these words: "Napoleon is dead; but a new conqueror has already shown himself to the world, and from Moscow to Naples, from London to Vienna, from Paris to Calcutta, his name is on every tongue." This was in September 1823, and at the time Rossini was not quite thirty-two years old. Just six years later, in August 1829, he returned to Italy, physically and mentally exhausted. He had written thirty-nine operas in nineteen years and was in need of a rest, but unfortunately for the world of music, the rest lasted until his death on November 13, 1868, some thirty-nine years later.

Rossini's contribution to the cause of Italian freedom was nonetheless unmistakable, and the manner in which he got around the strict Austrian censorship of his day was inspired. Who could have imagined that the subject of a harem of a fifteenth-century sultan would have aroused in the audiences not just hilarious enjoyment but at the same time whip them into a frenzy of patriotic reaction. *L'Italiana in Algeri* is about a beautiful Veronese slave, Isabella, who uses her wits to outsmart her powerful oppressor. The opera comes to a triumphant end as along with other enslaved Italian compatriots she sails off to freedom. The fun-loving Venetians lapped up the entertainment, but the few short lines of the *finale,* according to Rossini himself inspired by the idea of Italian unification, were not lost on a people now under the heel of Austria. *L'Italiana in Algeri* caught the Austrians by surprise for it was almost like the Trojan Horse of opera. Who could have imagined that an "opera buffa" would be the vehicle to deliver the patriotic punch that Rossini had hidden in his *finale?*

> *Pensa alla patria, e intrepido*
> *Il tuo dovere adempi;*
> *Vedi per tutta Italia*
> *Rinascere gli esempi*
> *D'ardir e di valor.*
>
> *[Think of the fatherland, and with courage*
> *fulfill your duty;*
> *See how in all Italy*
> *examples of daring and courage*
> *are reborn.]*

It should be noted that Rossini was talking about an Italy that at that time only existed in concept.

Rossini's swan song was his masterpiece, *Guillaume Tell,* and with this it might be said that he rode out on the crest of the revolutionary wave. The opera was written for the French stage with French lyrics and was performed in Paris in 1829, out of reach of Austrian censorship. Although set in the thirteenth century, the story of a revolt of the Swiss people against their oppressors readily found its parallel in nineteenth-century Italy under the Austrian Habsburgs. It seems that with this opera Rossini had made his final statement and, having done in music what Italians wanted to do in reality, he put down his pen forever.

Donizetti was the next to leave the scene after a prolific career in the world of opera. His father had plans to make him a church musician, but Donizetti's love of theater took him to Naples, where his merry mood found fertile soil for his thirty-one operas, many of which are now forgotten. The more serious *Anna Bolena* and *Lucrezia Borgia* were performed in Milan. Like Bellini and Rossini, Donizetti capped his career in Paris, where he produced his masterpieces, *Lucia di Lammermoor* and *La Favorita,* the piano arrangement for which was written by the as yet unknown Richard Wagner.

Donizetti's last successful work was the witty opera buffa *Don Pasquale,* produced in 1843, for which he wrote his own libretto. Shortly thereafter he became increasingly melancholy, a condition that degenerated into insanity. In 1847, in reporting to a friend on Donizetti's condition, Giuseppe Verdi wrote: "He looks well except that he always holds his head bent over his chest and his eyes closed," and he ended by saying, "This is Donizetti's real condition. It is dreadful; it is just too dreadful." The lively genius that was Donizetti died in his birthplace of Bergamo on April 18, 1848, oblivious to the disaster and chaos that the year would bring.

Giuseppe Verdi was now the lone survivor. He had already made his name in the opera world, but as the most nationalistic of all he was constantly in trouble with the Austrian censors, not to mention the ruling monarchies and the Church. His music played on the heart strings of the Italians of his day as none other could, and his rousing choruses alone became a threat to the authorities. *Nabucco* (Nebuchadnezzar) was set in a biblical era, but its subject, the captivity of the Jews, expressed the suffering of oppressed people everywhere. It was performed at La Scala, Milan, in 1842; for the Italians of the time it was a protest against tyranny. The words of the stirring chorus, "Va, pensiero, sull'ali dorate" [Go, thoughts, on golden wings] were soon on everyone's lips, and the melody alone was enough to cause the Austrians concern. The rebellious overtones of Verdi's music were unmistakable. A melody struck up spontaneously at his funeral more than half a century later speaks to the power of his music. Next came *I Lombardi,* a saga of the first Crusade. Set in 1099, it seemed to present no problem with the censors, but Verdi ran into trouble with the Archbishop of Milan, and it was his good fortune that the Chief of Police was an opera buff who helped smooth things over. The Austrian authorities, too, were nervous about another Verdi chorus.

A year later, 1844, Verdi's *Ernani* was performed at the Teatro La Fenice, Venice. The theme of the opera was the revolt against the sixteenth-century Holy Roman Emperor, Charles V. For the Venetians, under the Austrian heel, it was a political statement in music that brought out their revolutionary spirit. Finding approval with the censor was always a matter of concern to Verdi and in writing to Count Mocenigo about a possible subject, he said: "One is 'Cola di Rienzi,' a splendid plot, but however carefully it might be treated, the police might not sanction it." (Cola di Rienzi is remembered as the hero of the popular uprising in Rome and for his dreams of unifying Italy.)

Notwithstanding his successes in Italy, Verdi eventually found himself in other European capitals. In 1847 he was in London, where he met Giuseppe Mazzini, who asked him to write music for a poem that was to be a battle hymn. Verdi obliged; the following year when mailing it from Paris he wrote: "May this hymn, amid the music of cannon, soon be sung on the Lombardian plains" (Werfel and Stefan, *Verdi, the Man in His Letters,* p. 142).

In 1848, even as Verdi waged his own war in the world of theater and music — with censors, librettists, managers, and prima donnas — Europe was about to explode in what came to be known as the "year of revolutions."

Garibaldi's Return to Italy

In April 1848 a ship set sail from South America, flying the Montevidean flag, to begin the two-month sea voyage to Italy. It was captained by Giuseppe Garibaldi, who took with him some sixty members of his Italian Legion, the "Redshirts," faithful comrades in past battles on land and sea. A seasoned warrior, he was also now a family man who had sent his wife and three children ahead, but he took on his own ship the remains of a dead daughter, exhumed under cover of darkness, so that she might rest with his ancestors. The ship that entered the harbor of Nice on June 21 was met with an enthusiastic welcome for the exploits that had made Garibaldi a hero in the New World had created a legend in the Old World.

Garibaldi had kept in touch with Mazzini during his absence and had returned at a crucial time — the peninsula had exploded in revolutions from north to south. The revolutions of 1848 enriched the Italian language with the term *fare un quarantotto* [to do a forty-eight], now synonymous with bedlam, chaos, and disorder.

After the years of relative calm, it was the death of despotic Pope Gregory XVI on June 1, 1846, that brought new life to the movement of the Risorgimento. Propped up especially by the Austrians, the Pope had ruled with an iron hand from 1831 until his death, and the fifteen years of papal tyranny and suppression had created an atmosphere of fear and rebellion in the Papal States. Pope Gregory's death brought new hope and when two days later the more liberal Giovanni Maria Mastai Ferretti (1792–1878) was elected, there was general euphoria throughout the peninsula. Taking the name of Pius IX the new pope began a pontificate that lasted thirty-two years, the longest in history.

Rome now took center stage as Pius IX, Italian enough to resent foreign interference, ordered the Austrian garrison to leave Ferrara, which it had recently occupied as a precautionary measure. Meanwhile, political amnesties were granted, prisoners were released, and practical reforms took place. The nationalists saw Pius IX as the new hope, and Mazzini's star was on the rise.

Encouraged by the Pope's actions, revolutionary movements gained strength in other regions. However, the first real troubles of 1848 began in the south, when the Sicilians rose up against King Ferdinand in January and formed their own government. It was a separatist movement, to be sure, but nonetheless one against a tyrant. The unrest soon spread to the mainland where Ferdinand was forced to grant a constitution. Others quickly followed in the wake of Sicily with Florence, Turin, and

Rome taking as their model the French constitution of 1830. These were rebellions against despots, whether dukes, kings, or popes.

Milan and Venice, however, were directly engaged in the task of throwing off the Austrian yoke. On March 18, the Milanese rose up against their foreign masters, and in the famous "five days" of fierce street fighting routed the 14,000-strong Austrian garrison. Four days later, following uprisings in Venice, the Austrian garrison there capitulated, and the old Venetian Republic was restored with a provisional government under Daniele Manin. Most encouraging of all was the fact that Carlo Alberto, seeing that the moment for action had arrived, declared war against Austria on March 24, and Piedmontese troops, flying the tricolor, marched east to meet the enemy. A few days later, they were joined by contingents from Tuscany, Naples, and the Papal States. Italians had united to chase out the Austrians in what was the first real war of independence, but one month later, on April 29, things fell apart when the Pope officially distanced himself from the nationalist movement, refusing to take part in a war against a sovereign nation. Deprived of papal blessing, Tuscany and Naples withdrew their units, leaving Piedmont, Milan, and Venice alone in the struggle.

This was the chaotic situation Garibaldi found on his return to Italy in June 1848. For Garibaldi it was a war made to order, and he first offered his services to his king, Carlo Alberto, who much to his dismay declined to accept. Of his meeting with the King, Garibaldi later had this to say in his autobiography:

> In the interviews I had with him, I perceived a certain diffidence in welcoming me, and deplored the destiny of our poor country, committed to the hesitations and uncertainties of such a man. . . . To unite Italy and save her from the pestilence of foreign dominion, was my aim – as I believe it to have been most men's at that period.

It was clearly an embarrassment to the King to be confronted with this man, a subject of his who had once been under sentence of death, but who was now a legend for the people.

A disappointed Garibaldi took his small party of followers and made his way to Milan, where Mazzini had been busy since April forming a Lombard army. Garibaldi was given command of the volunteers and was soon dispatched to Bergamo to organize the city's defense. Meanwhile, Carlo Alberto, whose army was supposed to defend the north, dilly-dallied while the eighty-two-year-old Austrian fox, the legendary Joseph Radetzky, called in reinforcements. The Austrians won some easy battles; Carlo Alberto, without the consent of his allies, concluded an armistice on August 9 and withdrew from fighting, leaving the poor Milanese in the lurch.

With hopes dashed to the ground, Mazzini knew the cause had been lost and fled to Switzerland. Garibaldi did not give up so easily and, defying orders from his king to demobilize, continued a guerrilla war with his volunteers around Varese and Lake Maggiore. Finally, tracked down by Austrian soldiers on all sides, he made his escape across the border into Switzerland, joining other Italian exiles. Carlo Alberto must have heaved a sigh of relief to know that the two proscribed subjects were now safely out of the way, at least for the time being.

It was a despondent Mazzini who, on October 7, described his mood in a letter he wrote to that champion of downtrodden womanhood, the French authoress George Sand:

> Yes, my friend, life is sad and barren; men are cowardly and egoistical and ungrateful; hope is dead – at least for us; but did we not know this already when I

came to see you in the country? We have dreamed since then; you for France – the revolution of the people, the days of brotherhood; I for Italy the advent of Nationality as it ought to be. . . .

In this long letter, which belies his affection for the lady, he also reveals his plans:

I am now trying to see whether a second insurrection is possible; I have been working at it ever since I came here, and if nothing occurs to frustrate my plans I expect to be on the other side of the frontier in arms towards the end of the month. etc.

We now follow once more in the tracks of Garibaldi, as we catch up with him in his native Nice, where he was allowed to return in September in spite of his disobedience to his king. Here, in the bosom of the family, he hoped to recover from the rigors and disappointments of the past months, but he soon became bored of inaction and, more sick in mind than in body as he himself said, went looking for opportunities in Genoa. There he met a representative of the Sicilian government who invited him to that island. Garibaldi needed no persuasion and with seventy-two faithful comrades boarded a French vessel bound for Sicily. Garibaldi and his men never reached Sicily this time, however, for the vessel put in at Livorno, in Tuscany, where he was persuaded that if he wanted to help Sicily it would be better to recruit a strong unit to march south and go straight to the heart of the trouble – Naples and Ferdinand, King of the Two Sicilies.

Garibaldi made his way to Florence and went straight to the man in charge, Grand Duke Leopold II, the most liberal of all Italy's rulers, who happened to be in the capital at the time. The Grand Duke might have been swayed by Garibaldi's enthusiasm and the suggestion that Florence might be the capital of a united Italy, but the members of the Tuscan government were unwilling to go along with such a madcap scheme. Instead they steered him in the direction of Venice, where his sword might be of assistance against the Austrians.

A new phase in Garibaldi's struggles was about to begin. The official reception in Florence had been cool but the next one would be downright icy. On reaching the frontier of the Papal States, which cut a tortuous path through the Apennines, he found his way barred by Swiss soldiers of the papal army. Here was our hero, caught in the winter snows with his hungry and ill-clad unit at a place called Filigari, unable to turn back and prevented from going forward. Had they crossed oceans to find death by freezing in the land they had come to save?

When word of their plight reached the people of Bologna they were filled with indignation, and the papal government was forced to grant permission for Garibaldi and his party to proceed to Ravenna, from which they were to embark for Venice. The commander of Swiss papal forces wanted the motley crew of vagabonds to embark as soon as possible, but Garibaldi was not to be rushed. The underground movement of *La Giovine Italia* was busy collecting arms and ammunition, and other units were on their way to join him. Garibaldi and his men never did board ship, for as he later wrote: "Things were in this train, when a Roman dagger changed the aspect of our destiny."

The Short-Lived Roman Republic and the Death of Anita Garibaldi

Eyes were now turned on Rome, the capital of the Catholic world, where on November 15, 1848, Pellegrini Rossi, the Pope's minister and right-hand man, had been stabbed to death on the steps of the Palace as he entered on opening day of the

Council of Deputies. Although the Pope had begun his pontificate by bringing about reforms, the people clamored for even more change and were getting out of control. Fearing revolution, he had tried to tighten the reins of the runaway steed through his minister whose zeal in protecting the papacy earned him many enemies and cost him his life.

The day after the stabbing the mob took control, the Swiss Guard was disbanded, and for eight days the Pope was a virtual prisoner. On the night of November 24, with the help of the French ambassador, he fled the city in disguise. The carriage in which he rode with other fugitives, supposedly bound for the coast and France, sped down the Appian Way toward Naples and across the border into the Kingdom of the Two Sicilies. The Pope was given asylum at Gaeta under the protection of King Ferdinand.

On hearing the news Garibaldi left his Redshirts, wintering south of Ancona, and made haste to Rome, arriving on December 12 in that city he had not seen since visiting it with his father some twenty-three years earlier. His visit this time was short as the embryonic government was not yet ready to welcome this colorful hero in their midst, but back east the populace of the city of Macerata had expressed their confidence by electing him as their representative.

Events during the following year moved like a swift current. Encouraged by the coup that had taken place in the Holy City, the Tuscans had chased out their Grand Duke, who joined the Pope in exile at Gaeta, and on February 8, a Tuscan Republic was proclaimed.

The next day, February 9, the new Roman Republic with power vested in a Triumvirate, or Committee of Three, proclaimed the temporal power of the Pope at an end and invited Mazzini to come to Rome. At the end of March he became an important member of a new Triumvirate with extraordinary powers, and his old friend and collaborator, Garibaldi, was back as an elected representative. Along with him came his ragged Redshirts. They were now part of the Roman army, but there was no war to fight now. The restless men, who were beginning to inspire more fear than confidence, were kept outside the city.

While the new leaders went about the business of government in Rome, matters had taken a turn for the worst in the north. Carlo Alberto, pressured by popular opinion and the Milanese he had betrayed, denounced the armistice with Austria and reopened hostilities on March 20, personally leading his troops to Milan in a bid to chase out the Austrians. Just three days later, on March 23, the Piedmontese were defeated at Novara, outwitted by an eighty-two-year-old fox, Colonel Radetzky. To save his own kingdom, Carlo Alberto abdicated in favor of his son, Vittorio Emanuele, the one who later became the first King of Italy.

While events were unfolding in the north, negotiations had been under way to bring the Pope back to Rome solely as the spiritual leader, but he adamantly refused to budge with his papal wings so clipped. Instead, he invoked the help of the Catholics of Austria, Spain, and France.

While negotiations were at an impasse, Charles-Louis-Napoleon Bonaparte came on stage to play another role in Italian history. It will be remembered that some eighteen years earlier he had joined the uprisings against the papal government and championed "Italian liberty," but now he was back to restore a Pope to power, for he was playing with a different hand of cards. The French had meanwhile put an end to their restored monarchy and proclaimed the Second Republic with Charles-Louis as its president. His dream, however, was to become Emperor, and he needed the support of the Pope and the French Catholics.

French troops landed on Italian soil in April, keeping their distance from Rome while political maneuvering and negotiations continued. When all failed, they moved on Rome; now Garibaldi was needed to help defend the eighteen and a half miles of walls surrounding the city. The Roman army consisted of a pitiful 10,000 men, as opposed to a 30,000-strong force of French and Neapolitan soldiers, backed up by artillery. Mazzini was quick to realize the futility of defense, but the fiery Garibaldi, who had quarreled with his old friend and partner, resolved to resist. The most dramatic battle took place on the Janiculum hill, where the Redshirts fought and died to save Rome and the new republic. All was in vain for on July 3, 1849, French troops poured into the Holy City and the keys were delivered to the Pope in Gaeta.

Garibaldi would not be dishonored by laying down arms as long as he could still fight. He withdrew to nearby Tivoli, where he planned to organize his small group of surviving Redshirts and then make his way north to join the Venetians. He later recounted in his memoirs the tragic details of his retreat and these are his words:

> My dear Anita, in spite of my entreaties that she would remain behind, had resolved on accompanying me. In vain I reminded her that she was again about to become a mother, and that I should be exposed to a life of tremendous hardships, privations, and dangers, surrounded by enemies on every side; this consideration seemed only to confirm her resolution. At the first house we came to, having asked a woman to cut off her hair, she put on men's clothes, and mounted a horse. (Chapter 9, Retreat)

Anita, the "Bella Brasiliana," who had joined Garibaldi in Rome in June, was no stranger to danger. Life with her warrior husband had begun under fire of enemy gun-boats when as a girl of eighteen she boarded his ship and fought alongside him. She had been his faithful companion during his most dangerous years in the forests, swamps, and deserts of South America. She would not leave him now in this country that was supposed to be the "promised land."

Garibaldi and his followers left the neighborhood of Rome, dodging French, Austrian, Spanish, and Neapolitan soldiers, but as they moved northward the situation became more desperate with desertions, lack of trustworthy guides, betrayals, shortage of food, and low morale. They finally reached the neutral San Marino, a tiny independent republic, the smallest and most ancient state in the world, perched on a rugged sandstone ridge like a bump on the map of the Papal States. Here Garibaldi and his party were given asylum and from the steps of the church he addressed his men in these terms: "Soldiers, I release you from the obligation of accompanying me. Return to your homes; but remember that Italy must not be left in slavery and shame!"

It was midnight when Garibaldi and his most faithful followers left San Marino to make their way to an Adriatic port. By this time, Anita, in an advanced stage of pregnancy, had also become ill, but still refused to leave her husband. After reaching the port of Cesenatico, some thirteen boats and about 200 men took to the sea and sailed up the Adriatic coast toward Venice, keeping a safe distance from shore to avoid being spotted by the Austrians. Supplies were short, but Garibaldi wrote, "The chief thing wanting was water, and my poor suffering wife was tormented by a feverish thirst."

Left: Anita Garibaldi astride her prancing horse, clutching a child that was never born.

The statue of Anita Garibaldi on the Janiculum Hill in Rome was inaugurated by Mussolini in June of 1932, marking the 50th anniversary of Garibaldi's death, being celebrated with "national solemnity."

Detail from the base of the statue showing Garibaldi with the dying Anita in his arms.

The way to Venice was blocked by the Austrians who, aided by a bright moon, were able to capture most of the thirteen vessels, and later shot to death many of Garibaldi's bravest men. The rest of the party had to put ashore in a swampy area south of the Po River. Garibaldi took his beloved Anita in his arms and carried her off the boat. He knew she was dying, and the only thing he could do was find a place for her to rest. With one remaining Redshirt, the faithful Leggero, Garibaldi struggled along with his heavy burden into the marshes and found shelter at the hut of a brave farmer. It was there as a fugitive that Anita breathed her last.

The Austrians were close at hand. Garibaldi, for the safety of his hosts, had to flee while his dead wife was buried hastily in a hollow, temporary grave. When it was safe, her body was removed to a church cemetery and interred through the offices of a good priest at a secret spot and bore the inscription "unknown woman." Ten years later, Garibaldi returned and carried her mortal remains back to Nice. On the Janiculum hill, outlined against the Roman sky, you can see a magnificent statue that immortalizes the warrior girl astride her prancing horse as she clutches the child that was never born.

For the bereaved Garibaldi, Anita's death symbolized the death of the embryonic Italy, whose resurrection was still in the future. A fugitive from tyranny and laden with grief, he made his way across the Rubicon River and back again over the Apennines, guided by members of secret organizations for forty days and nights, until his arrival at a place on the Tuscan coast.

Garibaldi would soon embark on another adventurous ten years of exile and wanderings that took him to the far corners of the world, then back to a tiny island off the coast of Sardinia, where he found solace and challenge in farming that harsh land. His greatest role in Italian history was still to be played.

CHAPTER
THREE

The Second Phase of
The Risorgimento

Count Cavour: Architect of the Italian Nation

Garibaldi left Italy as the tide of Austrians rushed back in over the land, and under their protection princes and petty dukes reclaimed their rights. When the Grand Duke of Tuscany returned to Florence on July 28, it was unfortunately in the company of some 2,000 Austrian soldiers that "suddenly rained down" as one Florentine witness put it, saying that he "stayed home ashamed and grieved." The Venetians capitulated in August and once more found themselves under foreign domination, while the Papal States were now virtually occupied by Austrian troops.

Finally, on April 12, 1850, the Pope made his return to Rome on his own terms as temporal power was restored to the papacy. But it was an icy populace that received their Pope who, after an absence of well over a year, had come back into their midst accompanied by foreign bayonets. It had been a period of great turmoil, disappointment, and now shame for the Romans. Things would never be the same between the Vicar of Christ and his flock.

The Kingdom of Piedmont-Sardinia, miserably defeated at Novara, was punished by a heavy indemnity imposed by the victors, but was at least free from the Austrian presence and became a haven for some 30,000 exiles from other parts of the peninsula. This kingdom, from which Mazzini and Garibaldi had been proscribed, became increasingly pivotal in bringing about unification, and yet another recalcitrant son of that realm made his appearance on the stage of Italian history to play the leading role. His name was Count Camillo Benso di Cavour.

Count Cavour was born into a rich and noble family in 1810. As a young boy he served for a time in the royal palace of the king. He hated it. Next, as the second son he was destined to the military and was packed off to endure the rigorous discipline of the Academy in Turin. He hated that, too. After some assignments, including frontier stations in the Alps, Cavour decided that a military career was not for him and left the army for good. A career in the government was out of the question by reason of his anticlerical and liberal views, no doubt thanks to the influence of his Swiss mother, whose Calvinist ideas collided head on with those of the conservative government in Turin.

Fortunately for the young Camillo, his father owned vast estates and entrusted him with the management of extensive lands, a task he undertook with considerable success by introducing new agricultural methods, crops, and breeds of animals. While the exiled Garibaldi was becoming a legend in South America, Cavour had divided his time between farming and traveling, especially in France and England where he studied their societies and forms of government. Cavour's political

339

ambitions grew as his ideas for a unified peninsula matured and in 1847, when King Carlo Alberto relaxed the press censorship, the multifaceted Cavour established a newspaper aptly called *Il Risorgimento.*

Cavour's mother tongue was French, so he had to struggle with Italian to write his articles, and he spoke the language hesitantly. This linguistic impediment, combined with his weak voice, made him an abysmal speaker, but nevertheless people listened to what he had to say.

This was the Cavour who made his appearance in politics in the revolutionary years of 1848–49 when Garibaldi was struggling to free Milan from the Austrians and then protect Rome from the French. At the end of that tragic year of 1849, we find these two great patriots traveling in opposite directions: Garibaldi made his exit as a fugitive by way of Tuscany as Cavour began his rise to power in the parliament of Turin. He rose rapidly in the ranks and by October 1850 he was minister of agriculture, commerce, and industry in the government of Massimo d'Azeglio. Two years later, 1852, the forty-year-old Cavour himself was sitting in the seat of prime minister. He dominated Piedmontese politics for the next tumultuous decade and steered the Kingdom toward a role of leadership in the Italian peninsula.

The 1850s were characterized by the struggle between the powers of Europe and the Crimean War (1854–1856) in which 15,000 troops from Piedmont-Sardinia also took part. The Italian question had by now become an international issue and the Risorgimento had entered a diplomatic phase.

First of all, the Austrians must be driven out of northern Italy, and this is where Charles-Louis-Napoleon, now Emperor Napoleon III, came back into the picture, thanks to Cavour's secret negotiations and diplomatic intrigues. Added to Mazzini's continued efforts and Garibaldi's heroic example were the machinations of the clever Cavour, who kept in touch with the Emperor through a variety of pro-Italian individuals who were used to further the cause of Italy. Cavour's private secretary, Costantino Nigra, spent time in Paris. Cavour himself had become friends with Napoleon's personal physician, and then there was the nineteen-year-old Countess Castiglione assigned, so it appeared, to seduce the Emperor with her feminine charms.

But the Italian question was blasted to the top of the Emperor's agenda on January 14, 1858. An Italian exile in England, Felice Orsini arrived in Paris with four accomplices and some very large bombs with a plan to assassinate Napoleon, who was then perceived as the main obstacle to Italian independence.

Orsini takes his place along with many other Italian patriots whose turbulent lives resemble fiction rather than fact. Arrested in 1844 and condemned to the galleys for having participated in conspiracies of *La Giovine Italia,* he was granted amnesty by Pope Pius IX. In 1848 he was a captain in the first Italian War of Independence against Austria and was a member of the Assembly of the Roman Republic of Mazzini the following year. Like Garibaldi, he fled when the Republic fell and took refuge in Nice, from where he continued to serve the Mazzini party. On a mission to Mantua in 1855, he was captured by the Austrians and sentenced to death. Orsini somehow sawed through the bars of his cell and escaped by making a rope of sheets. He found refuge in England where he wrote and lectured on his adventures and furthered the cause of Italy against the Austrians in his book, *Austrian Dungeons of Italy* (1856), which was avidly read by thousands of English readers.

This was the man who on that wintry January eve waited with his accomplices outside the opera house for the arrival of the Emperor and his Empress, Eugénie. Three deadly bombs were thrown at the carriage, and in the tremendous explosions seven people were killed and more than one hundred were injured. By some miracle, the Emperor and Empress got out of the shattered carriage unhurt. Amid the dark confusion of dead and injured bodies, dazed operagoers, dying horses, and splintered wood and glass, the fleeing conspirators were caught and thrown into prison. The news spread quickly throughout a shocked Europe.

In the trial that followed, Orsini won the esteem of many observers for his courage and dignity, and sympathy for such a "noble" cause. In a letter to Napoleon, read at his trial and also published, he recognized his error and pleaded "on the steps of the scaffold" for Italian freedom. Orsini knew his fate; in the cold, gray, early morning of Saturday, March 13, 1858, he mounted the steps that led to his death. Before the guillotine fell he cried out, "Viva l'Italia! Viva la Francia!" It was five past seven and snow had begun to fall.

Six months later, Cavour and Napoleon met at the little spa town of Plombières near the Swiss border and forged an alliance that set things in motion to change the map of Italy.

The Piedmont/French War Against Austria

In July 1858, just six months after Orsini's bombs, Cavour cleverly arranged to turn up at Plombières, where he knew the fatigued Emperor Napoleon was taking the waters. During secret talks, for they needed no interpreters to communicate in either French or Italian, the two conceived a plan to create a kingdom of North Italy that would include Lombardy, Venice, and the central duchies. First the Austrians must be driven out, but a war had to be started whereby Austria would appear to be the aggressor. Cavour's task was to "organize" a conflict that would invite their intervention. There was fast talk, and a deal was struck. What was the price for French help? Napoleon wanted the French-speaking Savoy and also Nice, Garibaldi's birthplace. The pact was to be sealed by a marriage, of course, which would join the Bonapartes to the ancient and prestigious dynasty of Savoy.

King Vittorio Emanuele did not know what his prime minister was up to and he was not happy when he learned that his darling fifteen-year-old daughter, Princess Clotilde, was to be offered for sacrifice on the altar of politics to a man twenty years her senior, the Emperor's unattractive cousin, given the title of Prince Napoleon, but known by the nickname Plon Plon. This was part of the price exacted from Piedmont for a kingdom of North Italy that would stretch from the Ligurian Sea on the west to touch the waters of the Adriatic on the other side of the peninsula.

Meanwhile, Piedmont prepared for war. No time was lost; in August, following Cavour's return from that historic meeting, a messenger from Turin arrived in Caprera to surprise Garibaldi as he was milking his cows. His long exile was about to come to an end, for he was summoned to Turin to take part in the war of liberation as a Major General. His name alone excited the imagination and drew the needed recruits under his banner. The regular army took the finest and the fittest and the rest became part of Garibaldi's army of volunteers, his Redshirts. On March 1, 1859, he issued orders and instructions to his men, the first point of which was: *"When war breaks out between Piedmont and Austria, you will rise to the cry of, Viva Italia and Vittorio Emanuele. Out with the barbarians!"* (G. Garibaldi, *Scritti politici e militari*).

The Kingdom of
Vittorio Emanuele
(as of May, 1860).
At this time his
title was King
of Sardinia.

Things went according to plan. The contrived uprising took place in the region of Massa and Carrara. The Austrians, as it was hoped, took the bait and intervened. Piedmont and France then declared war on Austria.

On April 29, 1859, Napoleon crossed the Alps with a French army some 200,000 strong, joining the Piedmont allies, and the two armies marched on Lombardy. While Garibaldi and his volunteers fought the enemy on other fronts, on June 4, the regular armies were engaged in a most bloody encounter at Magenta, a town just outside Milan. (The brilliant blue-red color derived from coal tar and discovered in that bloody year of 1859 got its name from that battle.) Austrians were defeated, but both sides paid a terrible price. This was the turning point in the fight for freedom, as was another battle that took place four years later on the other side of the Atlantic in the name of another freedom, the Battle of Gettysburg. The Battle of Solferino followed on June 24, with 110,000 French soldiers and 35,000 Piedmontese. Again, the casualties were so high as to make any victory very costly. The wounded and dying piled up on the battlefields with no provisions for help. The tragedy of a staggering 40,000 casualties at the Battle of Solferino prompted Jean Henri Durant, a Swiss philanthropist and an eyewitness at the battle of Solferino, to write a book, *Un Souvenir de Solferino,* and later establish the Red Cross.

Napoleon, appalled by the carnage suffered by his army, sought a separate truce with Austria, abandoning his new allies with a job half done, for Venetia was still in the hands of the Austrians. The Piedmontese were not consulted in the matter, and an irate Cavour, after harsh words with his King, resigned office. Only Lombardy had been liberated from the Austrians but the war had sparked uprisings against the old rulers in the duchies and the rebellious Bologna, where assemblies voted for annexation to Piedmont. By January 1860, with Cavour back in power, negotiations took place with the Emperor who agreed for these regions to come under the umbrella of Vittorio Emanuele, but on condition that Piedmont give up Savoy and Nice.

On April 2, the parliament of the new kingdom, which met in Turin, included Lombards, Tuscans, and Romagnols as the map of Italy was again redrawn. The French had taken a bite out of Piedmont with the acquisition of Nice, as Garibaldi became a foreigner in his own country, while the ancient French-speaking mountain seat of the Savoy dynasty passed peacefully into French hands.

Garibaldi's One Thousand: Sicily and the South

The next phase of unification took an unexpected turn as the new Kingdom of Italy was dragged southward. The agreement that robbed Garibaldi of his birthplace and technically made him a Frenchman also left him with no war to fight. He had been ready to cross the Rubicon River with his army of volunteers and penetrate the papal territories to rescue the people from the tyrannical Pius IX, but he had been halted by his King and left with his enthusiastic followers without direction.

Happily for Garibaldi, other forces were at work. Mazzini had turned his attention to Sicily, where the ground was being prepared for uprisings against the Bourbon King, the next enemy to be chased from the peninsula. Sicily was a hotbed of discontent as the island sought to break away from the repressive regime in Naples. A Sicilian from the region of Agrigento and faithful follower of Mazzini had a leading role to play in preparing the insurrection. His name was Francesco Crispi, an exile who had been living in Piedmont for ten years. In disguise to avoid being caught, he had courageously returned to his island, where he went around agitating for change.

Meanwhile, an impatient Garibaldi had kept his eye on the unstable situation in the peninsula and when Crispi came to ask for his help, he needed little persuasion. He collected arms and ammunition and recruited volunteers for his next and most daring expedition, the liberation of Sicily. The sensible and apprehensive Cavour, with whom Garibaldi had been in violent disagreement over the loss of Nice, tried to stop this foolhardy undertaking. Indeed, the South was to Cavour "terra incognita" and was not part of his plans at that time. The King, on the other hand, disregarding the better judgment of his prime minister, secretly expressed his approval, but would wash his hands of the affair in case of failure.

Genoa became the base of operations where volunteers were recruited and ammunition was assembled. With no help from Piedmont, Garibaldi had to procure his own supplies and ammunition through sympathizers. Some firearms arrived from England, Colonel Colt sent 100 revolvers from the United States, and rusty muskets discarded by the Piedmontese army became part of the arsenal. Those without such weapons would have to rely on their bayonets. As to uniforms, some wore the famous red shirt, but army and navy uniforms mingled with civilian garb, a frock coat, and a priest's habit. The motley collection of soldiers that made up the famous "One Thousand" (actually 1,089) included students trying to avoid exams, Sicilian refugees, poets and writers, seekers of adventure and outright ruffians, but most were idealists ready to follow the legendary hero. Half of them were under twenty years of age, the youngest being a boy of eleven, but the oldest was a veteran who had fought with the first Napoleon. Francesco Crispi turned up with his mistress, the only lady in the party, and the widowed Garibaldi had his son, Menotti, along with him.

On May 5, 1860, two crowded boats set sail from Genoa. In case there should be any misunderstanding of mission, the slogan adopted was "Italia e Vittorio Emanuele." Garibaldi was wearing his traditional red shirt, gray trousers, white poncho, and black felt hat, and he wrote a war song to one of Verdi's tunes. What a scene it must have been when the boats finally left the harbor and headed out for an unknown destiny!

The passage south was not without problems, but the "liberators" eventually arrived off the western tip of Sicily and landed at Marsala. Garibaldi immediately declared himself dictator in the name of the King of Italy and proceeded to move against the Bourbon garrisons. Palermo, caught by surprise, was soon occupied, and most of the island was quickly wrested from Bourbon control. Garibaldi moved into a suite of rooms at the royal palace in Palermo and began the task of governmental reform. He made friends with all ranks, including the downtrodden clergy, and was soon regarded as a hero.

The next goal was the mainland, but garrisons at Messina and the fortress town of Milazzo were still in enemy hands. Garibaldi, whose army had grown in size, decided to take Milazzo, but it was won only after a fierce eight-hour battle and at a cost of 800 valuable lives out of a force of some 6,000 or 7,000. It was after that battle that the French novelist Alexandre Dumas, following events for a French newspaper from the comfort of his luxurious yacht, came ashore in search of excitement and found his hero asleep on the cold floor of a church with his saddle for a pillow.

With Sicily secured and help coming from Piedmont, Garibaldi took his men across the Strait of Messina to the mainland, eluding detection by the Neapolitan fleet. Of his safe arrival he wrote in his memoirs: "Towards the end of August, 1860, and about 3 A.M. on a lovely morning, we landed on the shore at Melito." From that point the army quickly moved up to Reggio, which was taken with little resistance. The Bourbon forces surrendered or fled north and Garibaldi, hot on their heels, took the road to Naples, stopping only long enough to rest his men and horses. On September 7, 1860, a small advance party entered Naples to the enthusiastic welcome of half a million inhabitants, their sheer numbers and support rendering the Bourbon soldiers powerless.

Where was the King of the Two Sicilies? Death had taken Ferdinand II, the terrible "Bomba," on May 22 of the previous year and mercifully spared him the sight of his city being taken over by the ragged army of a popular hero. His son, Francis II, had inherited the unpopularity of his father and knew that he could not count on the loyalty of his subjects. He had not lingered to run the risk of falling into the hands of Garibaldi and his men, but had fled to Capua the day before their arrival. Once more, Garibaldi's own words are the most poignantly descriptive: *"The royal nest, still warm, was occupied by the emancipators of the people, and the rich carpets of the royal palace were trodden by the heavy boots of the plebeian."*

With Garibaldi's successes in the South, Cavour realized that the unification of the peninsula was no longer just a dream, but an imminent possibility. He feared Garibaldi who had become too successful and too popular — but how to deal with this loose cannon? He had to support the movement, but prevent the madcap Garibaldi from marching on Rome. Once more, Cavour's quiet diplomacy was a vital ingredient for the achievement of unification as he persuaded the unhappy Austrian Emperor that the action he was about to take was inevitable for the safety of Rome, where a garrison of French troops protected the Pope. There was no time to lose if the pope-hating Garibaldi was to be stopped and, having given the Emperor assurance that Rome and the surrounding territories would be respected, the Piedmontese forces crossed into the Papal States on the Adriatic coast on September 11, just four days after Garibaldi had entered Naples. One week later, the Piedmontese army defeated the pitifully outnumbered and poorly prepared papal troops at Castelfidardo, and proceeded to take over Umbria and the Marches.

Vittorio Emanuele, as the King of Italy, excommunicated by the Pope along with all others taking part in the expedition, now took over command of the Northern Army and proceeded with all haste to the border of the Two Sicilies, hugging the Adriatic coast and then crossing the Apennines to join up with the Southern Army of Garibaldi on the other side. He was now coming to Garibaldi's aid, for a strong Bourbon army had made a stand beyond the Volturno and on October 1 and 2, fierce battles were fought on the plains of Campania. Garibaldi's men had held their ground and repulsed the enemy, but many of the bravest and most trusted men had given their lives. Garibaldi called this a "fratricidal conflict" because Italians were fighting Italians as the Bourbon army, in spite of many foreign mercenaries, was composed mostly of Italian soldiers.

By the end of the month, the Northern and Southern armies had come together in a pincer movement. Garibaldi and the King met on October 26 at Teano near Capua on the Volturno River as the Southern troops were about to move against the remnants of the Bourbon army. One can only imagine the scene as the two greeted each other. Garibaldi came up on horseback, wearing his unmistakable garb, and supposedly greeted his King by waving his black cap in the air and shouting, "Hail, King of Italy!" to which the King responded, "Hail, best of my friends!" The two then rode along side by side as they talked.

Garibaldi was with the King when he made his triumphal entry into Naples scarcely two weeks later, on November 7, but disappointment soon followed. Garibaldi had wanted to continue to govern with dictatorial powers in the name of the King for the time being, but it was made clear that his services were no longer required as commissioners would be appointed. Garibaldi then thought of his men who had sacrificed so much in the name of Italy and requested that they be taken into the regular army. That, too, was refused. Instead, Garibaldi was offered a ducal title, a castle, and an endowment, all of which he refused. He accepted no favors, and his integrity was untarnished. The man who had won the lands of the Two Sicilies by his extraordinary courage simply handed over his prize to the King in the interests of Italian independence.

Yet the task was not yet completed, for Venetia was still under the Austrian heel and the pope still controlled the Patrimony of Saint Peter. For now Garibaldi had played his part and slipped into the wings as others took the stage. In the dawn hours of November 9, he quietly boarded the *Washington* at Naples. There was no fanfare on his departure, but the foreign ships at anchor in the bay fired their salute as his boat left the harbor.

In the main square of Fiesole, high in the hills overlooking Florence, stands an equestrian statue freezing in time the historic meeting between the Redshirt and his King.

Work of Oreste Calzolai (1852-1920)
Inaugurated on November 20, 1906

Translation: "The meeting at Teano Between Giuseppe Garibaldi and Vittorio Emanuele II on October 26, 1860."

Rocked by the movement of the waters that had been his element for so many years of his life and now safe from the sounds of battle, it was nevertheless a disillusioned Garibaldi who was going back to the peace of his craggy island of Caprera. Here no guns would break the rest of his two battle horses, which were turned out to enjoy their retirement, and Garibaldi could watch events unfold . . . and wait for the next call.

After a meeting with Garibaldi in Naples, where the plight of Venetia was pondered, Mazzini, too, disappeared once more into the shadows.

The Birth of Italy

A new nation was born on March 17, 1861, when the parliament in Turin, which included representatives from all the newly acquired provinces of Umbria, the Marches, and the South, proclaimed Vittorio Emanuele II the King of Italy. The peninsula was almost unified, but there still remained to be won the Papal territory, weighing like a stone in the belly of the new kingdom, and Venetia which was not yet freed from the clutches of Austria.

Count Cavour's task as prime minister was awesome. On the domestic front, the burden of administering the vastly different world of the former monarchy, the Two Sicilies, weighed heavily on his shoulders. Furthermore, the French flag still floated freely over the Eternal City, which was to be the rightful capital of the new Italy, and this was much on Cavour's mind. Averse to war and bloodshed, Cavour favored a diplomatic solution, which he sought through various channels, including negotiations with Pope Pius IX through the intermediary of a certain Father Passaglia. In a letter dated February 21, Cavour wrote to the Pope saying, "I hope that before Easter you will send me an olive branch, symbol of perpetual peace between Church and State, between the Papacy and the Italian people." The negotiations came to naught; Cavour's agents, as well as the well-meaning Father Passaglia, were banished from Rome. The intransigent Pope continued to defend his temporal power and declared, "This corner of the earth is mine; I received it from Christ; to Him alone I will render it again!" Cavour used all argument for a "free Church in a free State" and proclaimed to Parliament that Rome must be the capital. He then enlisted the help of the King's son-in-law, Prince Napoleon, better known as "Plon Plon," in an effort to get French troops removed from the Eternal City.

As Cavour labored under the burden of office on the home front as well as in foreign policy, our popular hero, Garibaldi, about to be nominated deputy by the electors of Naples, suddenly erupted on the scene in Genoa. He had found no rest on Caprera, and his anger against Cavour had been slowly fermenting. The restless Garibaldi craved action and wanted no more shady dealings. He denounced Cavour and his followers as traitors to the country. April 18 was a stormy day in the Parliament building, where questions were raised. Baron Bettino Ricasoli rose to eloquently defend his prime minister, crushing Garibaldi in sharp words that cut like a sword:

> *Who then, after these times just past, who then dares to arrogate to himself the prerogatives of patriotism and of disinterestedness? Who claims to be exalted above all others? One head alone has the right to rule us, that of the King. . . . It is Vittorio Emanuele who made our nation; he is our liberator. Let it be enough for us to march*

behind so noble a leader and to be able to say to ourselves: "In serving him we serve our country well!"

A shaken but grateful Cavour was quoted as saying: "If I die tomorrow, there stands my successor!"

Garibaldi then ascended to the tribune to respond, but confused and ill at ease in his surroundings, his words came forth rough and muddled as he railed against the man who had made him a foreigner in Italy, "the miserable creature who had sold Nice and Savoy to Napoleon." Yet had not the King himself also made a sacrifice of the ancient kingdom of his ancestors when Savoy was ceded to France? A pallid and emotional Cavour responded with these words which have been recorded for posterity:

> *I know that a grief has opened between General Garibaldi and myself. It was a sad duty, the most grievous in my life, to counsel the King to approve the cession of Savoy and of Nice to France. The sadness that filled me then teaches me what General Garibaldi is suffering now, and if he will not forgive me for that necessary act, I shall not reproach him.* (Paléologue, *Cavour*, p. 288)

From that day, Cavour showed signs of extreme fatigue, and Garibaldi's attack on him remained very much on his mind. "I cannot get over that horrible wrangle with Garibaldi," he said. With all the symptoms of the terrible marsh fever that had afflicted him in the past, his condition worsened during May as delirium alternated with lucid moments. On June 5, it was clear that he was dying. Called to his bedside was a Franciscan monk, Father Giacomo, with whom Cavour had in the past made a secret pact to administer the last sacrament, for he was still under excommunication.

The King, too, was for a brief while at the bedside of his dying prime minister, then left him with his brother and friends with whom he shared his concerns about Italy and unrest in the South. Before he died on the following day at the age of fifty, Cavour whispered these last words to Father Giacomo: "Frate, frate, libera Chiesa in libero Stato" [Friar, friar, a free Church in a free State].

Across the ocean where civil war was raging, an article in the *New York Times* of June 18, 1861, began a report with the following tribute:

> *The death of the Minister who in the space of nine years has carried the prostrate monarchy of Piedmont to the rank of a first class European Power, is one of those events which, even in the pressure of our own critical circumstances, commands us to pause and pay our tribute of respect.*

One of the major players in the unification of Italy had left the stage just as the infant nation was taking its first faltering steps in an uncertain world.

Acquired from
Austria in 1866

SAVOY   LOMBARDY

VENETIA

FRANCE

PIEDMONT

Milan •

• Trieste

• Venice

• Ravenna

• Genoa

TUSCANY

Nice •

Corsica

• Rome

Taken from the
Holy See 1870

• Naples

SARDINIA

Palermo •

SICILY

N

*A new nation was born on
March 17, 1861, when the
parliament in Turin, which
included representatives from
all the newly acquired provinces
of Umbria, the Marches and
the South, proclaimed Vittorio
Emanuele II, King of Italy.
A decade would pass before
final unification of the
entire peninsula.*

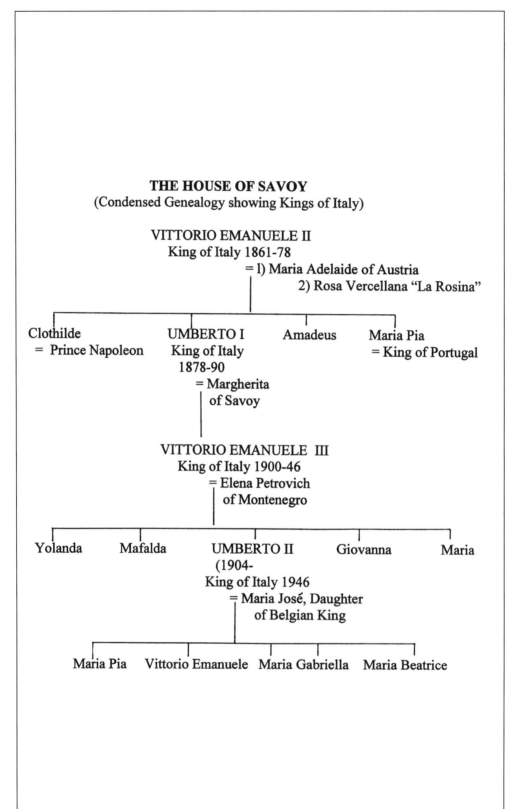

THE HOUSE OF SAVOY
(Condensed Genealogy showing Kings of Italy)

VITTORIO EMANUELE II
King of Italy 1861-78
= 1) Maria Adelaide of Austria
2) Rosa Vercellana "La Rosina"

Clothilde
= Prince Napoleon

UMBERTO I
King of Italy
1878-90
= Margherita
of Savoy

Amadeus

Maria Pia
= King of Portugal

VITTORIO EMANUELE III
King of Italy 1900-46
= Elena Petrovich
of Montenegro

Yolanda   Mafalda   UMBERTO II
(1904-
King of Italy 1946
= Maria José, Daughter
of Belgian King

Giovanna   Maria

Maria Pia   Vittorio Emanuele   Maria Gabriella   Maria Beatrice

CHAPTER FOUR

The House of Savoy

The First King of Italy

The central figure in the unfinished task of unification was Vittorio Emanuele II, the man who on that historic day of March 17, 1861, became Italy's first king. Born in Turin on March 14, 1820, Vittorio Emanuele Maria Alberto Eugenio Fernando Tomaso would wear the crown proudly for the first seventeen years of the new nation's existence. As a descendant of the House of Savoy, the numeral "II" in his title recognized his pedigree, which dated back some nine centuries, making the House of Savoy the oldest ruling family of Europe. The dukes, whose coat of arms appropriately featured the black eagle, had long since come down from their ancestral home high in the Alps and extended their domain to the plains of Piedmont. Savoy, the nest of the Alpine eagles, had now been sacrificed to France for the good of Italy.

Vittorio Emanuele was by bloodline half Austrian, for his mother was Archduchess Theresa of Habsburg, and that family connection was further strengthened when the twenty-two-year-old Vittorio was married off to Maria Adelaide, a princess of the ruling Austrian family. With these family connections it is easy to believe that his father, Carlo Alberto, had waged a half-hearted war against Austria in that disastrous year of 1848, pulling the rug out from under the Milanese by concluding an armistice with the Austrians, only to resume hostilities the following year, to be defeated at the Battle of Novara on March 23, 1849. The outrageously rigorous armistice terms the formidable octogenarian Austrian general, Joseph Radetzky, imposed on the defeated Carlo Alberto included the handing over of his son and heir, Vittorio Emanuele, as a hostage. Carlo Alberto chose to abdicate rather than sign such a shameful agreement and retired to a monastery, where he died shortly thereafter.

Vittorio Emanuele was twenty-nine years old when, in the most dramatic of circumstances, the heavy burden of kingship and the task of peace negotiations fell upon his shoulders. In the dim light of campfires at 9 P.M. on a spring evening and surrounded by soldiers of his defeated army, the young soldier-king received the pledge of allegiance from his officers and court. By the terms of the agreement arrived at, the new king was pushed back within the boundaries of his monarchy of Sardinia/Piedmont while the Austrians regained their hold on a helpless Lombardy.

This is the drama that was being played out in the north even as the short-lived Roman Republic was about to be crushed by the French. The revolutionary fires of 1848–49 had been snuffed out, only to smolder for thirteen years, leading up to the incredible events of 1861.

During this period, Vittorio Emanuele had, with the help of the brilliant Cavour, established himself as a world monarch, esteemed in Europe for his honesty and uprightness. He came to be known as "Il Re Galantuomo," the Gentleman King, and lived up to that reputation in his dealings with other powers. It may seem ironic that the first king of Italy should be a man with such strong family connections with the hated Austrians, but it was also during this period that destiny had taken a hand in partially severing those ties. In January 1855, Vittorio lost his Austrian mother; in March his beautiful and beloved wife, Maria Adelaide, died during her eighth pregnancy at thirty-three years of age. Vittorio had the reputation of being a womanizer, but in addition to his wife he claimed to have truly loved only one other woman, his favorite mistress, Rosina, a woman of humble origin. (He married Rosina in 1869, but she was never queen. Her children by him, born as bastards, had no rights as heirs to the throne.) He had adamantly refused to marry anyone else, notwithstanding the urgings of his ministers. He was a widower king, and Italy boasted no queen.

Now as King of Italy, Vittorio Emanuele's role as a constitutional monarch was difficult as he tried to lead and control his Parliament, made up of elements from the diverse regions of his new kingdom. Prime ministers came and went, but none could measure up to Cavour. Ironically, he also found himself in the strange situation of having to deal delicately with the two heroes of the Risorgimento, Mazzini and Garibaldi, loose cannons in different ways. Mazzini continued to hold republican views and remained unforgiven as his tactics of inciting uprisings were a constant threat now to the monarchy. Garibaldi, on the other hand, accepted Vittorio Emanuele as the true King of Italy, but the actions of this legendary hero were to cause his king no small measure of embarrassment.

Cooped up on his island of Caprera, Garibaldi soon became impatient for action and decided to take matters into his own hands to free the Romans from the Papacy as he had vowed: "Roma o morte." In 1862 he made his move and with a force of volunteers followed the path of his previous triumphs through Sicily and over the Strait of Messina to Calabria. He had received no overt help from the Italian government, but his campaign was no secret, and no one had stopped him. Not until he reached Aspromonte in Calabria was he confronted by Italian troops. Did Garibaldi believe he had the tacit approval of his king to march on Rome? Had he misunderstood the King's wishes? Was it the King who gave orders to stop him? As Garibaldi wrote in his memoirs: *That moment was a terrible one for me, forced as I was to choose whether we should lay down our arms like sheep, or stain ourselves with the blood of our brothers. . . . Can it be that they reckoned on my horror of civil war? . . . I ordered my men not to fire."*

The order was observed except by some "fiery young fellows" under Garibaldi's son Menotti. That fire was returned and Garibaldi was severely wounded in the left hip and the right ankle. Most of his soldiers evaporated into the surrounding forests, but the badly wounded Garibaldi was taken prisoner and loaded on a frigate that took him on an agonizing journey northward and finally back to Caprera. Of course, such a hero could not be allowed to die, but as Garibaldi wrote, "they wanted their prey safe and close at hand." Garibaldi's capture had for the moment spared the King a conflict with the French, who still garrisoned Rome as protectors of the Pope.

Two years later, in September 1864, a convention was signed between Italy and France by which Italy guaranteed the safety of Rome in exchange for withdrawal of the French garrison, and the following year King and Parliament were transferred from Turin to the more central Florence. As to be expected, there were violent protests in Turin, which now lost its status, but this was counterbalanced by great jubilation in Florence. Parliament moved into the historic Palazzo Vecchio and the magnificent Palazzo Pitti became the royal residence.

Meanwhile, the patient King of Italy waited and watched as events unfolded in Europe and he sought an ally that would help him fill in one more vital piece of the peninsular puzzle—Venetia. Rome would have to wait.

Venetia and the Third War of Independence

The Venetians had long waited to be free of their Austrian masters and the foreign troops in their midst. The Austrian Emperor had made concessions, but the undercurrents of unrest permeated Venice like the fingers of the canals and the seemingly innocent graffiti, "Viva Verdi," painted on walls in the dark of night represented a political statement by which *Verdi* became an acronym of Vittorio Emanuele Re d'Italia.

International politics were to play the vital role in the acquisition of Venetia. In early 1866, the Italians signed a treaty of alliance with Bismarck of Prussia, who wanted to wage war against Austria. Napoleon III, who always kept his finger in the political pie, gave his assurance of French neutrality if war were declared, and it was agreed that Italy would get Venetia as a reward for her help. A nervous Austria, fearing the power of the Prussians, attempted to avoid war by offering Venetia to Italy, but the Italian King was a man of his word and chose to stand by his new ally. There was more than Venetia to be gained by a victory over Austria, and that was the southern Tyrol, which geographically belonged to the peninsula. Referred to as the Trentino, this mountainous frontier region of the southern Alps below the Brenner Pass included the rugged and grandiose limestone massif known as the Dolomites.

The legendary Garibaldi soon received a messenger from his King, summoning him to the mainland. He had recovered from his wounds received at Aspromonte and was evidently back in the King's graces. Once more he found himself in northern Italy and again in command of enthusiastic volunteers, proud to wear the proverbial red shirts of Garibaldi's men. Once more Lake Garda, pointing to the cities of Trento and Bolzano beyond, became a backdrop to the events of history as Garibaldi navigated the waters of one of the world's most beautiful lakes and harassed the Austrians on land and water, far from the regular Italian units.

In spite of vastly superior numbers, the Italians suffered costly defeats due to the ineptness of their commanders and gave up too soon, while the Prussians took their battles to within reach of Vienna. The war, known as the Third War of Independence, lasted six weeks. Hostilities ended with a peace treaty, brokered between Prussia and Austria with Napoleon III as mediator. Napoleon, as compensation for his neutrality, was awarded Venetia, which he handed over to Italy, as previously agreed, following the usual plebiscite contrived to make it the people's choice. Italy had gained Venetia not by victory but in defeat by backstage diplomacy. No Italian could be proud of the way in which Venetia became part of Italy, least of all Garibaldi. Furthermore, the coveted Trentino remained under Austria for another half a century, only coming into the fold after World War I. Nevertheless, one more piece had been added to the Kingdom of Italy.

Francesco Crispi stands tall overlooking a square in Palermo. At the base of the monument are these words: "La Monarchia Ci Unisce Crispi" ("The Monarchy Unites Us").

Garibaldi's Last Campaign

Garibaldi, with his troops disbanded, returned in disgust to Caprera. He was sixty years old, prematurely aged with thinning white hair, but his obsession to deliver Rome from the "pestilential" Papacy was as strong as ever. He had planned his campaign seemingly without help or hindrance from his King and in 1867 went forth with a force of volunteers to the papal frontier. It was a short distance from Florence, now the capital, and it was said that troops were given a free ride in a train that ran south to the border. In the dawn hours of a September morning, Garibaldi was arrested by order of the Italian government before he was able to join his units. Once more he had been allowed, if not encouraged, to make a move; once more the way had been unexpectedly barred. Garibaldi soon found himself on a boat bound (of course) for Caprera, guarded by warships as the island was conveniently under quarantine for cholera.

Meanwhile, under the leadership of trusted and seasoned men and his own son Menotti, Garibaldi's units had gone ahead with the campaign. A virtual prisoner in his own home, he learned from newspapers that his sons and friends were on papal soil, and he planned a daring escape, which he justified in these words: "I leave it to be imagined whether I could remain idle while those dear ones, at my own instigation, were fighting for the liberation of Rome, my whole life's ideal." Thanks to the experience acquired in the American rivers with Native American canoes, Garibaldi made a spectacular escape, slipping silently past royal guards and then making his way to join his units in papal territory.

Mazzini's efforts to produce an uprising in Rome were to no avail, and all the sacrifices of Garibaldi's army came to naught at the Battle of Mentana, where papal forces were joined by the French, hurriedly dispatched by Napoleon to prop up the Papacy. On November 4, Garibaldi and his Redshirts laid down their arms and slipped back across the border into Italy, leaving the hills of Mentana "covered with the corpses of the gallant sons of Italy, mingled with those of the foreign mercenaries" (Garibaldi memoirs). It was a sad day indeed. The incorrigible Garibaldi was again taken into custody by the Italian government. This time the King sent Francesco Crispi, now a deputy in Parliament, to escort his troublesome hero back to Florence by train. It seems ironic that the Sicilian companion who had shared Garibaldi's triumphs of the "One Thousand" was the one to talk him into surrender.

Garibaldi had failed to accomplish his goal. Neither was he there when, three years later, Vittorio Emanuele's Italian army entered the city of Rome and filled in the central piece of the puzzle. Garibaldi's colorful life continued as he embarked on yet other adventures, but his part in Italian history was essentially at an end. He died on his island of Caprera on June 2, 1882, at the age of seventy-four, leaving his invaluable memoirs for posterity.

Rome: Capital of the Kingdom of Italy

The year is 1870. Almost a decade had passed since the creation of the Kingdom of Italy, which irascible old Pope Pius IX had even refused to recognize. He continued to refer to Vittorio Emanuele as the "King of Sardinia" and made mischief through his papal puppets to undermine the monarchy. Like a deep thorn in the side of the fledgling kingdom, Pope Pius was the archenemy of unification. For almost a quarter of a century he had ruled as a virtual despot with the swords of his army and the spiritual weapon of excommunication. Nonetheless, his domain had been reduced to Rome and the surrounding area, constituting the Patrimony of Saint Peter, an oblong stretch of land bordering the Tyrrhenian Sea which was his watery lifeline to friendly France. Firmly entrenched with his own papal army and propped up by the French garrisons of Emperor Napoleon III, he remained defiant and kept a tight rein on the Catholic world, convening in Rome in 1869 a landmark Ecumenical Council. Indeed, the important outcome of that Council was the dogma that has become part of the Catholic faith, the "infallibility" of the Pope. Now at a time when his spiritual power had reached its zenith, his temporal power was finally at stake.

Meanwhile, from his new capital of Florence, just a stone's throw from the border of the papal domain, Vittorio Emanuele patiently waited and watched events unfold. Once more the Italian cause was carried forward on the wave of foreign conflict. Northern Europe was in turmoil as the Prussian Bismarck expanded his power; on July 19, 1870, the Franco-Prussian War was declared. A desperate Emperor Napoleon III called home the garrisons that had been protecting the Pope, and the way was open for the Italians to finally claim Rome as their capital.

The Franco-Prussian War was short. An ailing Napoleon had taken command of his troops, but his army was soundly defeated at Sedan, where some 20,000 French soldiers met their death. On September 2 the Emperor surrendered to become a prisoner of the Prussians, and the French Empire came to an end. There was general unrest and uncertainty not just in the north but in Italy also. There had been uprisings in Calabria; Mazzini, the unyielding republican and enemy of both monarchy and papacy, was back on the scene to add fuel to the fires of protest. Grabbed by Vittorio Emanuele's secret police, the indomitable Mazzini was soon carted off to the fortress of Gaeta for a short stay and out of harm's way. It is ironic that the man who had spent his life fighting for Italian unity should end his days as a fugitive in the nation he had helped create. He had spent his whole life dreaming of a "republic" and found himself instead the prisoner of a "monarchy." (Having refused amnesty accorded such a popular hero, he died two years later in Pisa, where he had gone into hiding, posing as an Englishman under the assumed name of Mr. Brown.)

With the French out of the way, the reluctant King was pressured by his ministers to overcome his scruples concerning the Pope and move on Rome. On September 8 in a last attempt to persuade the Pope to see the necessity of his actions, the King sent him a letter, subsequently published by the Italian press and by *The Times* in English translation, in which he wrote:

> *Holy Father. — With the affection of a son, with the faith of a Catholic, with the loyalty of a King, with the sentiment of an Italian, I address myself again, as I have done formerly, to the heart of your Holiness. A storm full of perils threatens Europe. Favored by the war which is desolating the center of the Continent, the party of the cosmopolitan revolution increases in courage and audacity, and is preparing to strike, especially in Italy and the provinces governed by your Holiness, the last blows at Monarchy and the Papacy. I know, Holy Father, that the greatness of your soul would not fall below the gravity of events; but for me, a Catholic King and an Italian King, and as such guardian and surety by the disposition of Divine Providence and by the will of the nation of the destinies of all Italians, I feel the duty of taking, in face of Europe and the Catholic world, the responsibility of maintaining order in the Peninsula, and the security of the Holy See.*

The King's letter went on to advise the Pope to free Italy of the foreign troops that formed part of his army and offer no resistance. Since the letter bore no fruit, some 40,000 royalist troops crossed the border into papal territory and made their way to Rome.

The Times of London kept readers abreast of the situation in Italy, reporting in dramatic and telegraphic form from Florence on September 15:

> *The Italian Head-Quarters were yesterday 14 kilometers from Rome. General Bixio arrived yesterday at Corneto, 20 kilometers from Civita Vecchia. Yesterday the Italian fleet arrived in the Civita Vecchia waters. . . . National demonstrations are being made in several communes, and the troops are everywhere received with acclamation.*

Practically unhindered, Italian troops made their way to the Aurelian Walls of Rome. A breach was made at Porta Pia, and after some skirmishes with little loss of life the white flag was raised. This historic event was summed up in the following telegram received by the Italian Legation in London:

FLORENCE, *September 20, 11* P.M.

> *Today the Royal troops entered Rome, after a short resistance from the foreign soldiery, who desisted from firing by order of the Pope.*

An eyewitness report written by the correspondent of *The Times* has captured some of the excitement of that day.

ROME, *September 20, 6* P.M.

> *I have been witnessing a most memorable and striking event; indeed, I do not believe that as impressive a drama has ever before been performed by more artistic actors, or on a grander scale than that of which I was this day a spectator; but then we must bear in mind that the spectacle was the fall of the temporal power of the Roman Pontiffs, the performers Italians, the theatre Rome.*
>
> *It was a grand and impressive spectacle which now met our eyes. On the one hand, crowds of men and women belonging to the Roman people of all classes and ages, with their classical heads, Grecian profiles, and marble white complexions, were for a moment forgetting their accustomed placid expression, their dignified gait, and majestic bearing, in a frantic burst of enthusiastic applause, clapping their hands, embracing the national flag, surrounding the Italian soldiers who had taken up their position just under those wonderful gigantic Horses of Phidias on Monte Cavallo. On the other, prisoners taken at the gates slowly defiling with their bright dresses,*

spotless and somewhat theatrical uniforms, who formed a striking contrast with the soiled and dusty garments and tanned countenances of our Italians. . . .

The same correspondent reporting at 10 P.M. on the following day described

Italian soldiers, still under arms, bivouacking on all the piazzas, round the monumental fountains, obelisks, and columns in which Rome abounds; and every street, especially, of course, the much-frequented Corso, crowded to excess with people of both sexes and of every age and class. There was not a house to be seen without lamps in almost every window or corner . . . excepting churches and offices of the Papal Government.

Singing, shouting and cheering went on all night as next morning the same reporter found the whole town still full of people and a dense crowd hailed the solemn arrival at 11 A.M. of General Cadorna, followed by four or five regiments of Line troops, Bersaglieri and Lancers, who descended by way of the Quirinale down through Piazza Venezia toward the Corso to the shouts of "Evviva i nostri fratelli!" "Vivano i nostri liberatori!" and "Evviva il Re."

But King Vittorio Emanuele II, whose shining white monument later towered over Piazza Venezia, the geographical center of Rome, did not make his entrance into his new capital until one year later. Missing also on that historic day of September 20 1870, were the three heroes of the Risorgimento, the now-deceased Cavour, the colorful Garibaldi, and the republican Mazzini, but the party was for all the Italians and especially the Romans.

The King and the Pope

The Quirinal Palace, which had been the residence of popes for three centuries, opened its great doors to a new family. Two miles separated the Quirinal hill from the Vatican, where the Pope now shut himself up like a prisoner. Between these two points lay the baroque city of Rome with its sparkling fountains, but beyond the massive Aurelian walls sheep grazed and there were orchards and vineyards. Poor shacks occupied the site of ancient Rome. In short, it was depicted as a pastoral, sleepy place with little vitality.

Neither Rome nor the Quirinal Palace were ready to receive King and Government, but all that was about to change as people began to flock to the new capital. As for the King, he had his own reasons for staying away as long as possible. Meanwhile, he sent his son Umberto with his beautiful wife, Margherita, to test the social waters of Rome and win the hearts of the Romans, divided into two camps, "the blacks" and "the whites," the former owing everything to papal power and nepotism with everything to lose.

It was not until July 2, of the following year that the King made his formal entry into the capital, to be greeted by a jubilant crowd, and took up official residence in the Quirinal Palace. He never liked living in Rome. For one thing, it could never be a real home because his beloved Rosina, whom he had married the previous year, was not accepted as his queen, nor could she share his palatial dwelling. As he had written to daughter Clothilde before the marriage, begging her understanding; "I need therefore to be united with that person who for 17 years was my inseparable companion in all my pain and in all my labors for the fatherland, my companion in all my sufferings." Rosina, wife but not queen, was set up in a residence not far away so that she could be near her king when he needed her.

For the next eight years, the Quirinal and the Vatican might as well have been an ocean apart. During this time the two great rivals, King and Pope, never met and avoided each other's presence. The two who had shared the stage at the time of Italy's formation were destined to make their exits within a month of each other. Pope Pius IX was an ailing octogenarian when King Vittorio and his minister, Francesco Crispi, got together to make arrangements for the impending funeral. It was ironic that no sooner had plans been agreed on than the King himself was stricken with a fever so common in Rome and that took his life. At 2:30 in the afternoon on January 9, 1878, he died in the Quirinal Palace, as he had always feared, for he never forgot the prophecy reputedly made by an old gypsy years earlier that he would die in the Quirinal. Rosina, who lay seriously ill far away in Piedmont at the time, did not long survive him.

There was much disagreement over the final resting place of the King whose untimely death at the age of fifty-eight years had caught everyone by surprise and left the nation in shock. Some believed he should be interred with his ancestors in Piedmont, but others fought to have their first Italian King buried in the capital of Rome. It was the Pantheon, erected 1800 years earlier by the Roman Emperor Hadrian, now a Christian sanctuary consecrated to Saint Mary of the Martyrs, that eventually became his last resting place. A gray January day was appropriate for the mood of the black-clothed mourners, chilled by a north wind as they followed the funeral cortege that wound its way over cobbled streets. The gilded hearse was pulled by eight white horses draped in black, each with a footman in mourning, and up ahead rode another horseman leading the King's famous old Arab war horse with an empty saddle.

Family members, princes, and foreign dignitaries came from far and near as the first Italian King was laid to rest. *The Times* of London wrote: "Victor Emmanuel was the man in whom Italy had the greatest trust. The nation was not unaware of his private errors and did not attribute to him the genius of his great ministers." Vittorio Emanuele had lived and died as the *Re Galantuomo*.

Pope Pius IX died in February, one month after the man whom he had adamantly refused to recognize as the King of Italy. He had been pope for thirty-two years, the longest pontificate in history and the most eventful.

It was the end of an era.

The Reign of King Umberto (1878–1900)

Many were the protagonists who crowded the stage during the next two decades as the young nation was to experience growing pains, coping with squabbles at home, and meeting with threats from beyond her borders. Understandably, it was a nervous man who on that sunny January 19, 1878 was sworn in as King Umberto I. In his acceptance speech, carefully crafted by Francesco Crispi, he expressed his desire to be guided by Parliament and a pledge to uphold the cherished constitution. The thirty-three-year-old Umberto was the symbolic figurehead of united Italy until the close of the century.

"Umberto the Good," as he came to be known, was born in Turin on March 14, 1844, his father's twentieth birthday. As heir to the throne of the Kingdom of Sardinia/Savoy, he had been brought up in the rigid military manner of the Savoyard princes, entering the army as a captain at age fifteen and receiving the baptism of fire one year later at the famous battle of Solferino. Like his father, Umberto was first and foremost a soldier, ungroomed in the manners of the court and alarmingly lacking in cultural education.

At the age of twenty-four, ten years to the month before his ascent to the throne of Italy, Umberto was married in Turin to his first cousin, the beautiful Margherita, who brought to the union the elegance and culture that her prince was lacking. With her charm, she could cut a shine in any of the royal courts of Europe. Along with the royal couple at the Quirinal Palace was their nine-year-old son and heir, born in Naples and given the title of "Il Principe di Napoli," making the Savoyard dynasty more acceptably Italian.

During Umberto's reign some seven premiers held office: Deprentis, Cairoli, Crispi, Giolitti, Pelloux, Sarocco, and Rudini. However, the two men who dominated the political arena were Agostino Deprentis and Francesco Crispi, both of whom had already played a vital role in the creation of a united Italy.

The beginning of Umberto's reign was relatively peaceful as he stepped into his father's shoes. The way had been prepared by Agostino Deprentis, a Piedmontese and a former gun runner for Mazzini and agent of Garibaldi. For almost ten years he held important offices, including that of prime minister, and had managed to corral the members of Parliament, radicals and republicans alike, into his camp through what came to be known as *Trasformismo*. This capable politician weakened the opposition by confusing party lines, partly through bribes and favors, yet he himself remained incorruptible. One deputy had likened him to a toilet that remains clean while all sorts of refuse passes through it.

There was more to being a prime minister, however, than taking care of matters on the home front. Italy was surrounded by European powers jostling for position and expanding their territories. The early 1880s were characterized by the arms race for the build-up of modern armies with destructive weapons of war. Unsure of her place in a world where guns and trains had replaced swords and horses, the fear of war caused Italy to invest vast sums of money in the production of armaments.

It was also the age of imperialism, and Italy could not stand by and see other European powers carve up the rest of the world. Of course, Italians were already all over the place and for forty years her explorers and missionaries had been in North Africa while Genoese shipbuilders prospected for colonies. Close at home was the coast of North Africa, and some wanted to establish a colony in Tunisia, where many Italians already lived, a mere stone's throw from Sicily. Here came a clash of interests—France also had designs on North Africa. In 1881 Tunisia, with the approval of the *bey*, became a protectorate of the French.

Further from home in East Africa, there was an Italian settlement at Assab, on the Red Sea, and in 1882 Deprentis had declared it a Crown colony to be protected. Sea and desert separated the Kingdom of Italy from this colony, but the region had been made accessible by the opening of the Suez Canal in 1869. It was for part of the grandiose celebrations that the great Italian composer and patriot Giuseppe Verdi had been commissioned to write the spectacular opera *Aida*.

The year 1882 was also a milestone for young Italy as it joined the "grown-ups" in signing a treaty of alliance in May with Germany and the old enemy Austria, still occupying that part of the puzzle not yet filled in—"L'Italia irredenta" [unredeemed Italy]. By the treaty of alliance, Italy was no longer alone, but Irredentist claims against Austria were frustrated.

1882 was a milestone year for another reason for one month after the signing of the treaty, Giuseppe Garibaldi, the one who most personified the spirit of the Risorgimento, passed away on his island of Caprera. That spirit has been kept alive, for he is still present all over Italy in the names of places, streets, and squares and in the many statues that adorn the cities. Garibaldi was still a symbol and as such he was interred as an Italian patriot in Rome, not next to his kin in Nice, which was now part of France.

With the death of Deprentis in 1887, political power passed to Garibaldi's companion of the years of struggle, the energetic and ambitious Sicilian, Francesco Crispi. Of all those who took part in the Risorgimento, Crispi was the most enduring. As a deputy in the Parliament of Cavour, when asked what party he belonged to he is said to have replied, "I belong to the party of Crispi! I call myself 'Tomorrow'!" Like a cat with nine lives, before his death in the following century, he had been a lawyer, conspirator, journalist, revolutionist, soldier, administrator, diplomat, minister, and premier.

Crispi needed nine lives for by the time he took the spotlight the Italian dream, with all the euphoria that had accompanied the unification, was beginning to turn into the worst nightmare. The foreign lords were gone, to be sure, but there was little comfort in freedom when bellies were empty and many sought to escape grinding poverty as emigration doubled. Crispi did bring about liberal reforms and abolished the death penalty, but poor Sicily received no favors from their famous son.

Matters went from bad to worse when in 1888 there was an economic break with France, for whom Crispi had no love. It spelled economic disaster for Italy's farmers, who lost a major market for their olives, oil, wines, and even grain, which France began getting from Russia and America. Fair Sicily, which for centuries had been the bread basket of Italy with more to spare, was one of the hardest hit.

Crispi's ministry soon came to an end, to be followed by the short-lived government (1892–93) of Giovanni Giolitti, a man from the north whose time would come later. As general unrest mounted, attention was called to Sicily where groups called *fasci* [sheaves] organized uprisings that were really hunger rebellions. King Umberto called Crispi back to form a government, and we find him once more in the spotlight for another three years (1893–96). Crispi was forced to take stronger action, showing no mercy on the troublemakers in his native Sicily where the peasant movements were suppressed and laws enacted to deal with growing anarchism.

Added to the growing unrest at home, disaster was brewing in East Africa where war had broken out, and in 1896 a massive Ethiopian force defeated the Italians and their African troops in the battle of Adua (Adowa), where some 6,000 men were slaughtered. It was a devastating blow to Italian pride, a severe check to imperialist dreams, and the death knell for Crispi's long and colorful career. Here we will take leave of this brilliant man who ended an incredible life in 1901. Italy did not forget this patriotic son whose death was marked by great pomp and ceremony.

By 1898, as the century drew to a close, the winds of social unrest grew in strength as revolts occurred in Florence, Livorno, Naples, and Milan. Military law was imposed and unrest culminated in what came to be known as the *Fatti di Maggio* [Events of May]. The Marquis di Rudini, heading a coalition government, ordered the army into Milan. There was loss of life and severe sentences were handed down to the ringleaders by military courts.

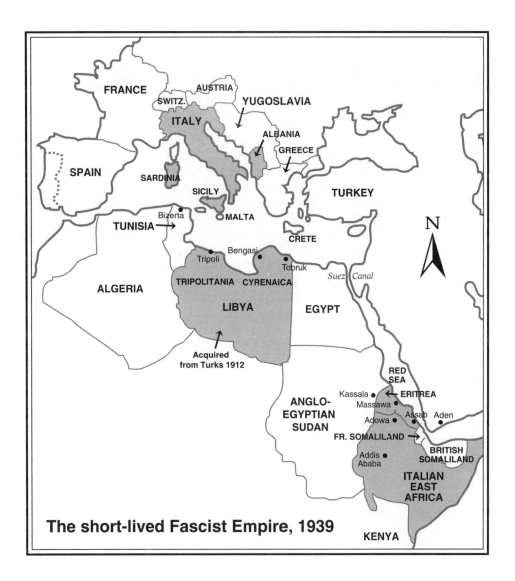

The short-lived Fascist Empire, 1939

Many newspapers were suppressed, but one that survived published a letter of praise that the King had written to the general responsible for quelling the unrest in Milan. That letter found its way into an English-Italian newspaper and was read by a Tuscan emigrant, Gaetano Bresci, an anarchist living in Paterson, New Jersey. Two years later Bresci turned up in Milan, on the trail of the King who, along with Queen Margherita, was on his way to their retreat in the Alps. They stopped at the royal residence in Monza, where on July 29, the King had promised to be present at a sports competition, for he never refused a chance to be with his subjects. What happened next is best dramatically described in the following dispatch, received from Monza the next day in London and published in *The Times*:

> *After presiding at the distribution of prizes, which lasted about an hour, the King left the Palestra, and was just starting in a closed carriage to return to the Royal*

Palace when four revolver shots were suddenly fired by a man standing among the crowd. The King was hit by three bullets, one of which struck his Majesty in the region of the heart. As soon as the bystanders became aware of what had happened they made a rush to seize the assassin, and it was only with great difficulty that the proper authorities rescued him from the hands of the mob and effected his arrest. Meanwhile, the Royal carriage was driven on to the Palace, on arrival at which the King was found to be still living but sinking so fast as practically to be beyond the reach of human aid.

The second King of Italy died during the evening of July 29, 1900, his life snuffed out with a revolver of American manufacture in the hands of an assassin.

Buffeted by the political winds of the time, ministers had come and gone, but the Monarch remained and in spite of the hardships he was for the most part loved by his subjects. He considered himself one of them, the First Citizen. He had ruled during a time of tremendous social upheaval, serious economic problems, and natural disasters. Who could forget the courage he had shown during the floods of Verona in 1882, and the earthquake on Ischia in 1884 where amid gaping fissures and falling houses he himself had helped save lives? His subjects also remembered his visits to the most dangerous spots in Naples during the cholera epidemic that same year when, persuaded to change his plans and attend the festival at Pordenone, he was quoted as saying: *"A Pordenone si ride, a Napoli si muore, vado a Napoli"* [At Pordenone they are laughing, at Naples they are dying, I'm going to Naples].

King Umberto's appointment with death was not at any of the danger spots or on the battlefield, but at Monza where the Iron Crown of the Lombards that had been placed on the heads of emperors still remains in safe custody.

On this tragic note the eventful nineteenth century had come to a dramatic close.

CHAPTER FIVE

The Monarchy in the 20th Century

Vittorio and Elena: The Socialist Monarchy

As news quickly spread around the world and the Italians lamented the loss of their King, Vittorio Emanuele III found himself catapulted into the world of kingly responsibilities. Let us now meet this minuscule man, the third king of united Italy, who wore the crown for almost half a century. It was a period of great social upheaval—Bolshevism, Fascism, Republicanism, and Imperialism were some of the dragons that threatened the Italian monarchy, and two devastating world wars tested the mettle of the young nation. The third Italian king lived through all of this, but he also lived to see the end of the monarchy.

No one in his wildest flight of optimistic fancy could have predicted, or even imagined, that the sickly child born on November 11, 1869, the only offspring of first cousins and whose life after a difficult birth was in the balance, would live to be a man, much less a king. Stunted in growth, with a large chest and spindly legs, the adult man stood only five feet tall. His queenly mother saw to it that he was properly educated, and the boy was soon entrusted to the militaristic rigors of Colonel Osio, a tutor in whose shadow he lived and grew up. Indeed, Vittorio saw little of his royal parents, for whom it seems he had little affection. When the young Prince of Naples reached manhood, the matter of a suitable match for the heir to the throne was of crucial interest, and Vittorio was singularly uncooperative, flatly refusing to even consider the eligible princesses proposed. To make matters worse, the young prince seemed to show little interest in women at all, and at twenty-seven years of age, Europe's most eligible bachelor was unwed and unwilling to take a wife. Then Cupid came to the rescue!

It all happened at the court of the Empress of Russia where the visiting young Vittorio met Elena, a princess of Montenegro, which was then a tiny country protected by Russia as a buffer against the Turks. Elena's father, Nicholas Petrovich, a chieftain rather than a king of his mountain subjects, stood six feet, four inches tall and boasted a brood of similar giants, daughters as well as sons. Vittorio chose as his bride the black-haired, dark-eyed Montenegran princess Elena Petrovich, who fell in love with the Italian prince, (small in stature but comely in appearance), over whom she towered head and shoulders. The two were married in 1896 with the permission of King Umberto, and here is what one eyewitness had to say:

> *Everyone looked with curiosity at Nicholas and the Montenegrin princesses, who were dressed in their national costumes. Nicholas was corpulent and tall, with handsome features and scintillating, very black eyes . . . the entire family was very*

beautiful and of a stature taller than normal. . . . Princess Elena remained kneeling for the entire ceremony, Vittorio Emanuele . . . remained on his feet. (Lumbroso, Elena of Montenegro)

The couple sailed out of the Bay of Naples on their royal yacht and spent the next years exploring the seas that kissed the shores of Europe, from the warm Mediterranean to the frigid zones of the North Atlantic, in a seemingly endless honeymoon. Kingship seemed far in the future because King Umberto was still a man in his mid-fifties. At the time of the assassination, the blissfully happy Vittorio and Elena were somewhere in the Aegean Sea, and it took some thirty-six hours to track them down. A boat flying the tricolor at half-mast was the messenger of the sad news, and the new king was escorted home to find a dead father, a grieving mother, and a country in mourning.

The royal couple moved into a few sparsely furnished rooms of the Quirinal Palace. The King soon dispensed with the ostentatious trappings of court life—the glitter, the balls, the endless receptions and soirées—and the large entourage of servants that had been part of the previous household was drastically reduced. Here was a king of Spartan tastes who seemed to share the hardships of so many of his subjects during the early years of the new century. He did not like living in the Quirinal, which later became his office when he took Elena outside the center of the city to the unimposing Villa Ada located on the ancient Salarian Road, formerly belonging to his grandfather. Surrounded by ten acres of woods and meadows and enclosed by a thick stone wall, the property later became a park for the Romans to enjoy. As for his troublesome mother, he bought her a more elegant residence in keeping with her taste—a red-bricked villa on the fashionable Via Veneto, later occupied by the American Consulate.

At the outset the new king found a government already in place with Prime Minister Saracco at the helm, and he was free to devote himself to domestic affairs. As a monarch, albeit a constitutional one, he was an unknown quantity until a crisis developed when general strikes broke out in Genoa. Minister Saracco and the King disagreed over what action should be taken. Instead of calling in the generals, as his father might have done, Vittorio favored a more lenient approach, allowing the strikers to express their frustrations. Saracco resigned, and Zanardelli was appointed to replace him. It was a turning point when the new prime minister chose the liberal Giovanni Giolitti as his Minister of the Interior, in charge of law and order. Giolitti saw that the world had changed and the popular classes could not be stopped from claiming their share in the government of the country as workers' unions made their voices heard. It was the beginning of a partnership when in 1903 the King appointed Giolitti as his prime minister, placing his implicit trust in this man from the north who was in personality the antithesis of the bombastic and colorful Crispi.

The most influential men in Italian politics had been Cavour, Deprentis, and Crispi before him; now Giolitti's name was added to that list as he became the dominant figure of the decade. His ministry ushered in an era that was referred to as the "socialist monarchy." Giolitti managed somewhat to rein in the bucking socialist bronco, tension was reduced, and there was no threat of war. Leaving matters safely in the hands of his capable and loyal prime minister, it seemed that the King had abdicated his duties and prerogatives, so much so that some felt that there was no need to press for a "republic" with such a laissez-faire monarchy.

During these early years, the King was particularly busy in his private life. After five years of marriage, the royal couple had their first child, a girl born in June 1901 and baptized Yolanda Margherita, followed the next year by another girl, Mafalda, a great disappointment to the queen mother. Finally, in September 1904 the long-awaited prince arrived, born in a centuries-old Piedmontese castle at Racconigi at a time when the country was paralyzed by a nationwide strike that prevented Grandmother Margherita from joining her son. She received the great news in a telegraph that said: "I have had a son. His name will be Umberto." Unlike his puny father, the little prince weighed in at ten pounds. He would be king one day, but in contrast to his father's reign of forty-six years, his only lasted thirty-four days. Two more sisters followed him, and he remained the sole male and everyone's pet.

This period of the reign was the most peaceful, but the world was changing quickly and so was Italy, which was becoming more industrialized. The ranks of the middle class swelled, and more were able to enjoy a higher standard of living, including vacations, sports events, and theater. Puccini's operas portraying bourgeois characters, such as *La Bohème*, were particularly popular. In the more industrially developed north, Italian motorcar manufacturers produced the Fiat, the Maserati, and the Alfa Romeo, cars that could compete with any in the world, and historic Monza became the racing capital of Italy. As the new art of cinematography developed, studios sprung up in Milan, Turin, and Rome.

There were those who believed, however, that Italy had been sleeping and needed a wake-up call. Revolution blossomed in the arts and literary world as writers, journalists, and even artists appealed to the angry "have nots." Filippo Marinetti published his *Futurist Manifesto,* calling for "speed, violence and war." Poetry and war came together in a dangerous combustible mixture with the soldier-poet Gabriele d'Annunzio. However, Italy was soon shaken by a natural disaster of epic magnitude.

The Earthquake

On December 28, 1908, the south of Italy suffered one of the worst earthquakes in history, one that claimed some 150,000 lives. It struck at 5:20 on a Monday morning. Fugitives from the disaster described a prolonged, thunderous noise, followed by a vivid flash of lightning and an interminable series of shocks followed by heavy rain. Messina in Sicily and Reggio di Calabria across the Strait were reduced to ruins along with other coastal towns. The epicenter was thought to have been in the Strait as a report of a steamship's experience suggests:

> *The captain of the steamship "Washington," bound for Messina from Palermo, reported that on entering the straits and near the lighthouse off Messina the ship experienced so severe a shock that he believed for a moment that it had run aground. At the same time, 5:20 on Monday morning, the light of the lighthouse was extinguished and the Calabrian coast disappeared under a dense mist. Other shocks followed.*

During the following days, newspapers in Italy and abroad continued to report on the terrible extent of the damage and the names of ships, cruisers, and frigates in the Mediterranean that were converging on the stricken regions, to convey provisions and render assistance to the victims. For Sicily and the south of Italy the quake had taken a terrible toll, creating thousands upon thousands of personal tragedies and a major catastrophe for Italy.

The Libyan War

It seems almost ironic that two years after the disaster that brought Italy the sympathy and goodwill of so many nations she should be engaged in a war. King Vittorio and his prime minister, Giolitti, were persuaded that a war should be fought to wrest Libya from the Turks. Great Britain had occupied Egypt, once the bread-basket of the Roman Empire, and France had her sights set on Morocco, while Italy was closer to North Africa than either of them.

The year 1911 marked the half-century of the founding of a united Italy and in March of that year the monument to her first king, Vittorio Emanuele II, was inaugurated as part of the celebrations. It was a proud little king who climbed atop the white monster with Queen Elena and from that height promised to make Italy not only the freest and the happiest country, but the most "respected" in the world. There was a new wave of patriotic sentiment that filled the sails of the nationalists and imperialists and emboldened them to take action. The pacifist Giolitti, riding the inevitable wave harnessed its force to his own parliamentary vessel and remained loyal to his king, who, it seemed, had been carried forward by ideas of "bigness."

War was declared on Turkey in 1911, and some Italian bishops even proclaimed a crusade against Islam. It should have been a quick victory, but the Turks put up a good fight and so did the native Arabs and Berbers. It was a savage war in which the Christian Italians were pitted against the followers of Islam. By the time the conflict came to an end in October 1912 Italy had paid a high price for a vast expanse of useless desert—no one knew then that underneath the sands flowed the black gold. Nevertheless, Italy claimed a victory and a colony for the Italians in North Africa.

The End of the Giolittian Era

Times had changed, and so had Vittorio Emanuele, who began to espouse the idea that aggressive nationalism was the best for Italy. He was no longer in step with the loyal Giolitti, who chose the path of neutralism. His fourth ministry, which lasted from 1911 to 1914, had come to an end and so had the period known as the "socialist monarchy."

Although Giolitti returned in his twilight years to serve Italy and her king, the most productive part of his political career was over. During his ministries Italy had moved toward democracy, coming close to universal suffrage. The vote had been given to all literate men of twenty-one years of age and to illiterate males who had completed military service or reached the age of thirty, giving the proletariat a voice in government. A welfare state was beginning to emerge with a Public Health Act, workers' insurance against accidents, limitations on child labor, and old age pensions.

In his quiet and unassuming way, Giovanni Giolitti had in many ways accomplished more than his predecessors for the greater good of the common man. Yet in spite of his efforts to create a better world, poverty for many remained the wolf at the door which would not go away, and the safety nets he had instituted were no substitute for work and wages. Hard-hit Sicily and the South had not enjoyed the new prosperity and progress with the result that the Giolittian era was one of exodus.

The Great Migration

In spite of the progress made during the Giolittian period, during the first decade of the twentieth century the numbers of emigrants grew. Although the early waves of emigrants came mostly from the north, the trend changed later on and those leaving for to the New World were predominantly from the Sicily and the South. By 1913, when the number peaked at almost 1 million, Italy had lost an estimated 7 million people. They abandoned fields and humble homes, crowding into steerage quarters and setting out on a voyage that often took them to more hardships on the other side of the Atlantic. They took with them the dialects and customs of the regions they left behind, pockets of linguistic and cultural diversity in a nation that was still struggling to be "one and indivisible." The third generation of these emigrants with the musical-sounding Italian names can display with pride the old and yellowed photographs of these ancestors of handsome features and elegant bearing that enriched the new continent.

The First Great War

In June 1914, on the eve of the Great War, Italy's new government was faced with uprisings, triggered by riots first in Ancona, which spread like wildfire throughout the Romagna and the Marches. This period came to be known as "Red Week." It was not only a peasant uprising against landowners and an affluent bourgeoisie but also a protest against conscription and the fear that Italy would be dragged into another war even before the wounds of the Libyan experience had healed.

This was the political and social climate in Italy when just two weeks later, on June 28, Austria's heir, Archduke Francis Ferdinand, was assassinated in the Serbian city of Sarajevo. This was the match that set off a concatenation of events beginning with Austria's declaration of war against Serbia one month later. As alliances came into play, Europe was engulfed in a conflict in which the belligerents used the most destructive weapons of war — poison gas as well as firepower.

At the outset, most Italians shared the views of their ex–prime minister Giolitti and were opposed to war. For the first nine months of the conflict, Italy sat on the fence of neutrality, seeking a way around her commitment to the Triple Alliance of which she was a member along with Austria and Germany. It was not in her interest to side with them now. However, Italy was eventually forced to take sides and joined the Allies against the old enemy, Austria.

King Vittorio Emanuele, above all others, saw this as a necessary war and a chance for Italy to take care of some unfinished business, namely to bring into the fold *L'Italia Irredenta,* that last piece needed to complete the puzzle for which Italy had waited half a century. As the Irredentists and the nationalists clamored for intervention in the war, they were helped by the obscure Benito Mussolini, a man who later proved to be the master of turncoats. Abandoning the Socialist Party, he resigned his editorship of its newspaper, the *Avanti,* and founded *Il Popolo d'Italia,* which became a mouthpiece for the warmongers. The socialist Mussolini, who had previously threatened revolution if Italy went to war, now made the same threat if she did not.

Gabriele d'Annunzio: The Soldier-Poet

Mussolini had thrown fuel on the flames with his rhetoric and newspaper articles, but his efforts paled before the contribution made by the revered and celebrated Italian poet and writer Gabriele d'Annunzio. Returning from France where he had been hiding from his creditors, he whipped the Italians into a frenzy. They welcomed him back not as a prodigal son, but as the light to follow at a time of doubt and confusion. He had come from a country at war and when he arrived at Genoa in May 1915, he was greeted by a delirious multitude and shouts of "Viva l'Italia!" The train that took him to Rome was greeted at stations along the route by wildly cheering crowds that showered the poet with flowers when he alighted to give brief but fiery words of encouragement. Not even the King could have expected the welcome he received on arriving in Rome where crowds thronged the Stazione Termini by the thousands and then escorted him to the Regina Hotel in Via Veneto. The following days he made impassioned speeches, stressing Italy's past greatness, condemning the "neutralists," and even accusing the respected Giolitti of high treason.

With the poet on the side of the interventionists, Italy declared war on Austria-Hungary on May 24, 1915; within two months the poet, although fifty-two years old, was on his way to the front as a lieutenant of the Light Horse of Novara. Soon thereafter he was a daredevil pilot flying over the still unredeemed Trieste and dropping Italian flags and messages which said: "From these soaring wings I greet you. Gabriele d'Annunzio."

D'Annunzio's exploits during the war were numerous and varied, from his fighting with the infantry to his daring and dangerous flights over enemy territory, dropping bombs on enemy targets and sinking ships. So formidable was this courageous man that the Austrians offered a reward for him either dead or alive. Throughout the war, d'Annunzio was an inspiration for the Italian soldiers. As a result of a plane crash he lost the sight of one eye and part of the other, but it never kept him from the fight. In spite of impaired vision, he was back in the skies. For a while he had fought as an infantryman alongside countless others, many of whom were poor, illiterate farm boys for whom there was no glory in dying. While the French and British fought and died in the muddy trenches of France, the Italians battled with the enemy in a different terrain, where fast rivers and the craggy ridges of Alpine ranges concealed the opponent and tested the survival skills of both sides.

With the armistice, Italy's boundaries were redrawn as she was awarded the Italian-speaking Trento area with the port of Trieste, and also the largely German-speaking Alto-Adige, which geographically belonged to the peninsula. Italy also got the Istrian peninsula with its Slav minority, but the boundaries with Yugoslavia were still disputed. One bone of contention was the port of Fiume (Rijeka), throughout the centuries tossed between one power and another. In defiance of agreements reached at the peace conference in Paris, claiming that the bulk of the populace was Italian-speaking, d'Annunzio decided to take matters into his own hands. With a few hundred followers he occupied Fiume and declared himself the "commandante." When the Balkan question was finally settled by the separate Treaty of Rapallo on November 12, 1920, Fiume was not awarded to either Croatia that contested it or the Italians that occupied it, but was given independent status. Notwithstanding the agreements, the self-styled d'Annunzio refused to budge, creating an embarrassment for his King and Parliament. Old Giolitti, called back by the King to deal with the postwar problems, may have secretly sympathized with the popular renegade rascal who had once accused him of treason, but d'Annunzio had to go. All coaxing, cajoling, and even threats were to no avail. An ultimatum was issued, and the captain of the Italian battleship *Andrea Doria* received orders to shell the city. It was Christmas Eve when her big guns fired and the first warning shots scattered the happy crowds who scurried to safety leaving the streets deserted. The following day, December 25, 1920, which came to be known as "Bloody Christmas," shells fell on the palace occupied by the defiant warrior-poet who finally conceded that the game was over. A few lives had been lost in that incident, but unharmed and unhampered, d'Annunzio took himself off to beautiful Lake Garda, where he spent the rest of his life writing poetry and living out his fantasies.

The war was over, and Italy's boundaries were secured. It had cost her over 650,000 men lost on the battlefield and 1.3 million wounded. King Vittorio Emanuele got his war and the prize he had expected, but it was not a sweet victory. The social problems had not gone away, and there were those who took matters into their own hands as insubordination became more widespread and the winds of revolution blew stronger.

It seemed that the King had harnessed the revolutionary battle horse for his own purpose, but he soon learned that he had lost control. No one could have foreseen who would be the rider that could tame the runaway beast.

The New Caesar

The little king first met Benito Mussolini in November 1915 during one of his tours of the war zone while the young corporal lay in bed with a fever. Their paths crossed again briefly in 1917 when the King, on a visit to a field hospital, found Mussolini recovering from facial and body injuries sustained when a shell exploded while he and others were learning to operate an artillery weapon, killing five of his comrades. Mussolini got a promotion following these "self-inflicted" wounds, though many might later have wished that he had blown his head off instead. It would surely have changed the course of Italy's history, one way or another.

Mussolini was an unlikely candidate as a savior from Bolshevism. His father had been an active participant in the first Communist movements in Romagna and had served time in prisons for his "subversive" activities. Like father like son — Mussolini was a rebel from an early age and gave his Catholic schoolteacher mother, the devout and long-suffering Rachele, a great deal of grief. But he got his education, and the study of Imperial Rome was his love.

On May 23, 1919, while d'Annunzio was defiantly holed up in Fiume, Mussolini met in a small meeting hall in Milan with some 150 disenchanted followers, and Fascism was born. Called the "Fascio di Combattimento" [sheath of combat], the embryonic organization had no particular purpose, but was born out of a need for action. Fascism, itself lawless and violent, became a deadly tool against disorder and lawlessness. The war against socialism that Mussolini had first espoused and Bolshevist ideas that his father had championed took shape as the action gangs, called *squadristi,* were formed in cities across the country. Many of their members had been at Fiume, and the black shirts they wore then became the uniform of the Fascists. Their task was to break up strikes and go after the Communists. These *squadristi* carried out raids against so-called offenders and in a two-year period some 3,500 individuals in sixty-nine towns were estimated to have been slain.

Did the King know what was going on? Indeed he did, and he even made a note of particular incidents in his personal diary. Yet the situation was desperate as strikes paralyzed the struggling postwar nation in a climate of anarchy. People wanted order restored, and the Parliament, in disarray, was powerless.

Fascism became a political party and on June 30, 1921, Mussolini was elected to Parliament and officially met his King at the Quirinal Palace. Outside of those brief wartime encounters, the two knew little about each other. Mussolini's knowledge came from schoolbooks and newspaper articles. As for the King, he had been keeping his eye on the rising movement, setting his royal sleuths on the tracks of the self-styled vigilante whom he would come to know through police intelligence and secret reports.

Here is part of a government document known as the "Gasti report."

> *Prof. Benito Mussolini, son of Alessandro, born at Predappio (Forlì) 7/29/1883, residing in Milan at 38 Foro Bonaparte, is a socialist revolutionary with a police record, and an elementary school teacher licensed also to teach in secondary school. He was formerly first secretary of the Chamber of Labor at Cesena, Forlì, and Ravenna, and later, from 1912, Director of the newspaper "Avanti!" in whose columns he took violent, suggestive, and intransigent positions,*

> *On December 25, 1915, at Treviglio, he married a woman from his own province, Rachele Guidi, with whom he had already had a child – Edda – procreated at Forlì in 1910. He also had a lover, a Trentinian named Ida Irene Dalser. . . . Miss Dalser worked at the newspaper "Popolo d'Italia" and had intimate relations with Mussolini. A child was born on 11/11/1915, Benito Albino Dalser, and he was later legally acknowledged by Mussolini. (She later died in a mental hospital, as also the son.)*

Even more telling than the bare facts contained in this report of some 7,500 words was the assessment of the man and, above all, how to handle "a man of thought and action, an effective and incisive writer, a persuasive and lively speaker, (who) could become a *condottiere*, a fearsome ringleader" (Katz, *The Fall of the House of Savoy,* pp. 232, 234).

By August 1922, Fascist guns and club-wielding thugs had put down a workers' movement in a particularly savage attack, described by the Fascist writer Italo Balbo in these words:

> *It was a terrifying night. Our passage was signaled with high columns of fire and smoke. The entire Romagnan plain all the way to the hills was subjected to the furious reprisals of the Fascists, who were decided once and for all to put an end to the red terror.* (Quoted by Katz, from Balbo, "Diario," p. 109)

Rumor reached Rome that the Fascists were ready to march on the capital. The key to the success of the undertaking was the King himself. Rome prepared to defend herself as the King sought a solution. He needed a strong prime minister, but there was none. To make matters worse Giolitti, the peacemaker, had left Rome, grieving the loss of his wife. Such are the many personal vicissitudes that alter and trace the course of history!

The King knew that if Mussolini carried out his threat it would mean a bloodbath for Rome and perhaps the end of the House of Savoy. Mussolini knew that the regular army would be loyal to the King. He knew also that he needed the King on his side, for he alone was the symbolic head of unified Italy and he told his followers they must "have the courage to be monarchists."

These were agonizing days with the government in disarray and Fascist forces massed for the imminent march on Rome, October 28, as the fate of Italy and the monarchy lay in the balance. The King, after endless meetings and, one must imagine, sleepless nights, having been given assurance that the monarchy would not be threatened, resolved to summon Mussolini to Rome, not to be part of the government but to form one. The King was later quoted as saying:

> *He is really a man of purpose and I can tell you that he will last some time. There is in him, if I am not mistaken, the will to act and to act well. When I told him to put together an administration on a broad basis and with capable men, I felt that he agreed and was close to my views. I had previously formed quite a different impression of him.* (Katz, p. 250 from Kirkpatrick, *Mussolini*, p. 145)

On October 30, Mussolini arrived from Milan by train at 11 A.M. and dressed in his "black shirt" appeared at the Quirinal Palace to bow his head before his King and receive the royal command to form a government. The next day Vittorio Emanuele III stepped out on the balcony with his new prime minister, Benito Mussolini, to be cheered by a relieved and jubilant crowd. That day marked the beginning of the next twenty years of Italian history, the Fascist era.

Fascist Italy

In the beginning, the little king was well pleased with his prime minister. He placed his trust in the blacksmith's son who presented himself at the Quirinal twice weekly to report and confer with the monarch to whom he displayed the greatest deference. Yet Mussolini, although appearing to walk a few steps behind, was gradually becoming more powerful in the shadow of the King whose power diminished as time passed. What developed was a kind of diarchy where institutions were duplicated; the Army obeyed the King and the Fascist Militia obeyed Mussolini. To the outside world, however, Fascism had brought stability and order to a country that had been paralyzed by chaos, but it came with a price as many who opposed the new order soon learned.

There were fewer opposition members in Parliament, which opened on May 24, 1924. Disturbing incidents had occurred when the dissenting voices had been savagely silenced as deputies had even been beaten up in the streets and their homes ransacked. As for the King, he preferred to appear blind and deaf to what was happening and keep silent.

One who dared to protest the elections was Giacomo Matteotti, a charismatic and rising star in the ranks of the opposition, who had the courage to speak out in the Chamber about coercion and violence, questioning the legality of the elections. Mussolini was overheard to have verbalized his extreme displeasure with his opponent and when Matteotti did not show up in the Chamber two weeks later and failed to return home, foul play was immediately suspected. Indeed, Matteotti had been kidnapped and brutally murdered, stabbed to death in a limousine as it sped out of Rome. The decomposing naked body, hurriedly hidden in a shallow grave, was found and identified three months later. It was not the first time that such crimes had been committed, but this was a respected deputy in the public eye, and news spread fast.

Fingers pointed at Mussolini, who rapidly rounded up the assassins, or "scapegoats," in a effort to clear his name. For awhile, the fate of Mussolini and Fascism seemed to be in the balance as citizens awaited the royal reaction from the Quirinal. Confident that the King would not dismiss him and dissolve Parliament, as was his prerogative, Mussolini metaphorically picked up the big stick and on January 3, 1925, marched into the Chamber, accepted full responsibility for what had taken place, and challenged its members to accuse him as provided by the Constitution. No one in the opposition dared raise his voice as the Fascists shouted "Long live Mussolini." Two days later he ordered his Fascist militia to dissolve "suspicious" organizations, keep a watchful eye on Communists and subversives, and seize all weapons of non-Fascists. Arrests were made and houses were searched. The regime triggered another flood of emigrants, this time political dissidents and intellectuals who became the exiles known as *fuorusciti* in the capitals of Europe. The Constitution was flaunted, and Mussolini held the King in a vise, but the monarchy was safe. It was not Vittorio Emanuele who would rock the boat in such stormy seas. The Fascist state had come into being even over the dead body of Matteotti.

Italy soon became a one-party state and a largely totalitarian one with Mussolini as the dictator. "Fascism was not for export," as he had declared, and it remained a quintessentially Italian phenomenon born of the times. Mussolini, with the power to act and the monarch's pen to put the seal of approval on his decrees, did what in his own mind was for the greater good of Italy. He had managed to bring the masses to heel and put an end to the devastating strikes that had crippled the country. One unique solution to the problem was the idea of the "corporate state" for which representatives were drawn from employers, workers, and professional groups elected to give advice. Parliament, whose members represented regions, became less important and less effective.

In the early years, there was much to be said for what Mussolini had achieved. It was he, son of an atheist anarchist, who regularized relations between the state and the Catholic Church. No pope had recognized the Kingdom of Italy, which had been in existence for seven decades, until the Lateran Pact of 1929 with Pope Pius XI. By this pact the Vatican was recognized as an independent state and the Papacy with temporal power, and Catholicism was recognized as the "sole religion of the state" in Italy.

Many projects were embarked upon. Men were put to work building factories, schools, public buildings, and sports complexes in Rome and other cities throughout the country. One massive undertaking was the draining of the Pontine Marshes, a vast area (290 square miles) southeast of Rome and traversed by the Appian Way. For centuries it had been the breeding grounds of deadly malaria mosquitoes. Various attempts had been made, beginning in 150 b.c., to reclaim the area without success, but now new towns that owe their existence to Mussolini's initiative (Sabaudia, Latina, Pontinia, Aprilia, and Pomezia) cover the area that was once the wasteland inhabited by a few hardy peasants.

Roads were built; in Rome itself the wide Via dei Fori Imperiali replaced the conglomeration of shantytown dwellings, connecting the Colosseum with Piazza Venezia, where Mussolini established his own headquarters in the ancient Palazzo Venezia with its now famous balcony. To Mussolini also goes credit for the appropriately named Viale della Conciliazione, the wide boulevard that runs from Piazza San Pietro to the Tiber River, a major link between the Vatican City and Rome.

Transportation was improved — trains were made to run on time, and electrification of the railways was instituted. The Italian language was officially made compulsory in law courts and schools, and that applied also to the newly incorporated and largely German-speaking Alto-Adige.

Africa

Living as he did with the vestiges of Imperial Rome constantly before his eyes, it seems Mussolini could never forget Julius Caesar, who had been his inspiration. The conquest of North Africa made the Mediterranean once more the Roman *Mare Nostrum*. There was a nucleus of empire with Libya and the two little colonies of Eritrea and Somalia, separated by British and French possessions, and behind that lay the landlocked Ethiopia (also called Abyssinia), whose ill-defined borders gave rise to disputes. In December 1934 an Italian unit was attacked by Ethiopians at a watering hole called Ual Ual. It was well inside Ethiopian boundaries, but the Italians did not expect to be attacked as nearby there were also British "trespassers" in this uncharted territory.

The attack was all the excuse Mussolini needed to take retaliatory action. In October of the following year a massive invasion of Ethiopia took place. Italy was condemned by the League of Nations as an aggressor. An embargo was placed on sales of arms to Italy and there was a boycott of her exports.

The war against the blacks of Ethiopia was also a black page in the history of the Blackshirts, whose appalling and inhuman atrocities perpetrated against the defenseless people were universally condemned. A modern, mechanized Italian army consisting of almost half a million men along with bomber planes and poison gas brought a speedy victory. On May 9, 1936, Mussolini annexed Ethiopia, sticking the title of "Emperor" on the little Italian king, replacing the still more microscopic Emperor Haile Selassie, the "Lion of Judah," who fled to London in exile.

Mussolini's next foreign fling was his involvement in the Spanish Civil War, which broke out in the summer of 1936. Both Germany and Italy provided planes to assist the rebel general, Francisco Franco, against the legitimate Spanish government, which had the support of Russia. Italian military units were sent to Spain, and the Spanish island of Majorca was occupied as an air and naval base as sympathizers of the legitimate government were massacred. Tragically, a fact that would have caused Garibaldi to turn in his grave, Italians found themselves fighting their brothers on Spanish soil, for the *fuorusciti* naturally took the side of the defenders.

Mussolini gained nothing from the Spanish Civil War, but his alignment with the dictators of Europe emboldened him to cast his eyes on Albania, then a monarchy, where he wished to install an Italian garrison. In the face of King Zog's rejection, backed by his navy and air force he invaded the country with impunity on Good Friday in 1939. Another province was added to the empire as Vittorio Emanuele III was proclaimed King of Albania.

Meanwhile, ominous black clouds were forming over Europe, and the storm was not long in coming.

CHAPTER SIX

Italy and World War II

The Axis: A Pact with the Devil

If there were any doubts as to where Mussolini's sympathies lay, these must have been dispelled by the extraordinary reception accorded to Adolf Hitler when he visited Italy in May 1938. It was the backdrop for a contract with the devil himself, a pact that led Italy down the road to doom.

To quote *The Times* of London, the Nazi visitor received "one of the most elaborate and magnificent receptions of which there is record even in the annals of the Eternal City." From the moment the trains carrying the party arrived in Italy via the Brenner Pass, where the station was decorated with German and Italian flags, to the crowds that had been ordered to cheer along the route, and arrival at the new railway station, no detail had been overlooked. Rome was dressed like a bride, as the English newspaper's special correspondent in Rome reports:

> In the decoration of Rome for this occasion the Italian artistic genius has found full scope. Foliage of evergreen oak . . . has been used in graceful garlands to decorate shop fronts. Much woodwork, painted in light tones, has been used in the decorations, and on this the Fasces and the Swastika occur repeatedly as ornamental motifs, picked out in gold. Unpleasing vistas have been masked with hedges of Venetian masts. . . . The illumination is a triumph. In flood-lighting good use has been made of the lovely Roman fountains and also of the trees in the main gardens and avenues.

It was an unwilling King who was forced, by the requirements of royal protocol, to share the stage with a man he despised in festivities that lasted a whole week.

It was evident that Mussolini had fallen under the diabolical influence of Hitler, and proof was soon forthcoming in anti-Semitic legislation introduced that summer. By September foreign Jews were barred from settling in Italy, closing an escape route for many fleeing from Germany. The specific and far-reaching legislation was the beginning of persecution of Jews in Italy, although the Italian citizenry endeavored to circumvent its provisions. Some Jews changed their names, but as the crackdown progressed there was no place to hide. Jews were expelled from academic institutions and barred from teaching in state schools. There were cases where teachers were dragged from their classrooms, before the eyes of their horrified students. A concentration camp was also set up at Trieste.

Where was the King of Italy? Surely he knew what was happening! How could he approve of his Prime Minister now? Although he is recorded as having expressed his sentiments by saying that he felt sorry for the Jews, this did not prevent him from taking his royal pen and signing the damning decrees against a whole race, his subjects who were a vital part of his kingdom. Is it not ironic that his beloved daughter Mafalda should end her days at the notorious Buchenwald! (Princess Mafalda, married to Prince Philip of Hesse, was captured toward the end of the war and sent to Buchenwald to be held in a special compound. She died of wounds received during an Allied bombardment.)

Italy's fate was sealed when an alliance known as "The Pact of Steel" was signed with Germany in May 1939. Mussolini had crossed the Rubicon and from that point there was no turning back. This was stressed by the following words, penned by Count Galeazzo Ciano on December 23, 1943, in a Verona jail, where he awaited death by a firing squad.

> The Italian tragedy, in my opinion, had its beginnings in August 1939, when, having gone to Salzburg on my own initiative, I suddenly found myself face to face with the cynical German determination to provoke the conflict. The alliance had been signed in May. I had always been opposed to it, . . . There was no reason whatever, in my opinion, for us to be bound in life and death to the destiny of Nazi Germany. (*The Ciano Diaries, 1939–1943*, Ed. Hugh Gibson)

Count Ciano, one of the principal protagonists in the last act of the Fascist era, was married to Mussolini's strong-willed daughter Edda, and as Minister of Foreign Affairs he had been his father-in-law's faithful mouthpiece before the latter fell under Hitler's spell. Yet he now shared the King's open hostility toward the belligerent Germans.

When the disastrous Second World War broke out on 3 September 1939, the King encouraged Ciano to work for peace. As the intermediary between the King and Mussolini, Ciano played his part in achieving Italy's short-lived neutrality.

Meanwhile, Hitler's mighty armies had marched across Europe and on June 10, 1940, seeing that France was about to fall, Mussolini declared war on France and Britain. He had appeared like a jackal on the scene of the kill to claim his share.

In the war that was fought on many fronts, from the snows of Russia to the mountains of Greece and the desert sands of Africa, Italy's sons shed their blood as allies of the Germans. Early victories in East Africa, where Italy conquered the coveted British Somaliland and invaded Egypt, were followed in the winter of 1940–41 by defeats as the British chased the Italians out of Egypt and across the Libyan desert. The Germans came to the rescue with Rommel to wage a desert war against the British Eighth Army under General Montgomery.

Maligned as poor fighters by both allies and enemies, the Italians nevertheless distinguished themselves in the air as their daredevil pilots, in the tradition of the legendary soldier-poet Gabriele d'Annunzio, fought courageous if futile battles over the sands of Africa. Another Italian hero, Cesare Balbo, met his death there, unfortunately from friendly fire of the Italian machine guns. This Italian pilot, who had made history by flying the first squadron of planes across the Atlantic to Rio de Janeiro in 1931 and to Chicago and back in 1933 with twenty-five aircraft, deserved a better fate.

On Saturday, January 23, 1943, the Eighth Army marched into Tripoli and hoisted the Union Jack, marking the end of Mussolini's African empire. *The Times* of January 27, while reporting the African victory, gave space to the opening night of Verdi's tragic opera *La Traviata*. The dying heroine might well have symbolized poor Italy, dragged into a war that she did not want by a man she had grown to hate and with an ally that she had never loved.

Meanwhile, the German-occupied Tunisia became a battleground for the Allied and Axis armies as the war moved closer to Italy's back door—SICILY.

THE TIMES SATURDAY FEBRUARY 6 1943

ENEMY BASES BOMBED

TWO TARGETS IN ITALY

LORIENT POUNDED AGAIN

From Our Aeronautical Correspondent

At small cost, the R.A.F. carried out on Thursday night its most widespread bombing operations so far this year. Resuming the offensive against Italy after a lapse of eight weeks, our home-based bombers made their first attack on Mussolini's principal naval base of Spezia, on the Gulf of Genoa, and heavily bombed Turin again. An almost equally powerful force again pounded the U-boat base at

Lorient, and a small number of aircraft dropped bombs in the Ruhr.

For the two major attacks—those against Turin and Lorient—the crews found good visibility. Turin was slowly recovering from the devastating effects of four heavy raids between November 28 and December 11 in which at least 70 industrial plants were damaged, including the extensive Fiat aero-engine and motor transport works.

Lorient experienced its sixth large-scale R.A.F. raid this year. It has also been attacked in daylight by U.S.A.A.F. bombers, and photographic reconnaissances have shown that tremendous damage has been done to the harbour installations, arsenal, and U-boat base

CIANO GOES

DUCE AS FOREIGN MINISTER

GRANDI LOSES HIS MINISTRY

Mussolini has dismissed Count Ciano, the Italian Foreign Minister, and taken over the post himself.

This was officially stated in Rome last night in the following broadcast announcement:—

The Duce has taken over the Ministry of Foreign Affairs. Giuseppe Bastianini remains Under-Secretary for Foreign Affairs.

Count Ciano is appointed member of the Fascist Grand Council for three years.

It was also officially announced that Count Grandi, the former Ambassador in London, loses his post of Minister of Justice, which is taken over by Alfredo De Marsico. Grandi remains President of the Chamber of Fasces and Corporations.

Other changes include:—

MINISTRY OF FINANCE. Baron Giacomo Acerbo, former president of the International Agricultural Institute in Rome, succeeds Thaon di Revel.

MINISTRY OF EDUCATION: Carlo Biggini, rector of the University of Pisa, succeeds Giuseppe Bottai.

PUBLIC WORKS. National Councillor Zenone Benini succeeds Giuseppe Gorla.

MINISTRY OF COMMUNICATIONS. Cini succeeds Host Venturi.

MINISTRY OF CORPORATIONS. Carlo Tiengo succeeds Senator Ricci.

MINISTRY FOR NATIONAL ENLIGHTENMENT. Former Under-Secretary of State Polverelli succeeds Alessandro Pavolini.

MINISTRY FOR FOREIGN CURRENCY. Oreste Bonomi succeeds Riccardi.

The Under Secretariat of State for War Production becomes a Ministry with the former Under-Secretary of State General Favagrossa as Minister. Umberto Elbini becomes Under-Secretary in the Home Ministry in place of Buffarini Guidi.

HILL STORMED NIGHT

BRITISH SUCCESS TUNISIA

STORY OF ACTION

From Our Special Correspondent

TUNISIAN FRONT, FEB 4 (delay)

In the small hours of yesterday troops captured Jebel Mansour, south-east of Bou Arada and overlo the Pont du Fahs-Robaa road.

After a march of several hours a rough and precipitous mountain they climbed the hill at different and took it after a short struggle. darkness and confusion on the h wooded hill they became broken u small parties, and one of these, only 15 strong, attacked an adjoining slightly higher hill, called Alliliga captured this also. However, numbers were insufficient to retain hills, and they later withdrew Alliliga to concentrate on keeping Mansour.

This they still do, though they difficult time yesterday. When day they were subjected to heavy morta machine-gun fire, and had the gr difficulty in getting up ammunition

Cabinet Shuffle and a Royal Coup d'État

CIANO GOES, screamed the headlines which appeared in the *The Times* of London on February 6, 1943. The event was only a prelude to a sequence of events that would tear Italy asunder and set the stage for the political chaos and personal tragedies that were visited on her. Protagonists in these human dramas were the members of two prominent families — the Savoys and the Mussolinis.

Mussolini had dismissed Count Galeazzo Ciano, his loyal Foreign Minister for seven years, and had taken over these functions himself. The shake-up in the cabinet was drastic, but what made Ciano's dismissal somewhat puzzling was the fact that he was Mussolini's own son-in-law.

For Ciano, who had been the faithful intermediary between Italy and the rest of the world, as well as between Mussolini and his King, his sudden dismissal was devastating. Maligned by the British as a man of "shallow talents" and a mere "mouthpiece" of Mussolini, Ciano was no fool but a seasoned diplomat whose missions had taken him not only to the capitals of Europe, where he could "feel the pulse" of the leaders, but also to South America and even China, where he remained for three years. Unlike his Germanophile wife, Edda, who admired the leaders of the Third Reich and found Hitler most charming, the Count never liked or trusted the Germans, and Mussolini was aware of his feelings.

However, the cabinet shuffle came at a time when it appeared that Conspiracy was lurking in the wings and the King no longer shared the views or trusted the judgment of his prime minister.

Ciano accepted his dismissal with good grace and his diary entry of February 8 ends with these words: "Our leave-taking was cordial, for which I am very glad, because I like Mussolini, like him very much, and what I shall miss most will be my contact with him" (Ciano diaries, p. 580). This was his last entry until the final one of December 23 of that year. Count Ciano was made a member of the Fascist Grand Council, a fact that would indirectly cost him his life, and was appointed as ambassador to the Holy See, a comparative place of rest in a neutral enclave.

It was a depressing period for the Italians, who were never very enthusiastic about the war, and by now they had turned against the ones responsible for their plight. Italian cities were suffering ruthless air attacks as war factories were targeted and at the time of the cabinet changes, bombs were raining down on Turin and the naval base of La Spezia.

Leaflets purported to have been dropped by the British over Rome in May of that year as the war closed in around the Italians, contained such messages as: "To the Italian People. You are doomed to destruction as long as the Germans remain in Italy." and "The Planes of the Allies will darken the Sun over Italy."

Sicily was the first to see the waves of British and American forces, which landed on her shores on July 10, 1943, the first battleground on Italian soil between the Allies and the Axis. This was a prelude to all-out war on the mainland, which once more became the arena for conflict between foreign powers.

On July 19, the unthinkable occurred when the first bombs fell on Rome. The targets may have been strategic and military, but nevertheless the air space of the Eternal City had been invaded. It was a wake-up call that did not go unheeded. A few days later, on that fateful July 24, Mussolini agreed to convene the Fascist Grand Council. It was a stormy meeting that dragged on throughout the night, ending with a motion by Dino Grandi condemning the dictatorship and Mussolini's conduct of the war.

The Grandi motion passed with nineteen votes against seven with one abstention. Mussolini would be relieved of some of his powers and the burden would be placed on the shoulders of the King, and Ciano cast a "yes" vote, naively believing that to be the spirit of the motion.

Some decided, however, that Mussolini had to go—he would have to be "arrested." The King would have to give the order and take full responsibility for the consequences. It was agreed that the arrest would take place not at the Quirinal, where he had been handed the reins of government, but in the seclusion of Villa Savoia and away from the public eye. At five o'clock on July 26, an unsuspecting Mussolini arrived at the Villa Savoia for an audience with his King and fell into a royal trap.

The full details of the dialogue that took place behind closed doors would be known only to the King and Mussolini, but a man with his ear pressed against the door collected fragments of that conversation for posterity and recorded the barely audible words. The King quietly explained his actions and his deep regrets and was heard to say, "I like you very much and I have demonstrated it many times, defending you from attack. But this time I must ask you to leave your post and leave me free to entrust the government to others" (Katz). The audience ended with the sound of chairs being moved and the King saying, "I'm sorry, I'm sorry, but there can be no other solution." The two left the room together and shook hands, never to set eyes on each other again. So ended a partnership that had lasted for two decades.

Once outside, Mussolini was ushered to a waiting ambulance and whisked off to a place in the wild Abruzzi mountains where he was told he would be held "for his own protection" and no harm would come to him. While all this was taking place in Rome, his daughter Edda was in a shelter in Livorno that was under Allied bombardment. She learned of her father's loss of power from the newspapers and immediately boarded a train for Rome where she arrived late at night. For Edda, Rome had become a nightmare where angry crowds were soon tearing down Fascist

TORINO
Anno 77   Num. 116

LA STAMPA

GIOVEDI'
9 Settembre 1943
Edizione MATTINO

LA GUERRA E' FINITA

Badoglio annuncia alla Nazione che la richiesta di un armistizio è stata accolta dal gen. Eisenhower

Le forze italiane cessano ovunque da ogni ostilità contro gli anglo-sassoni ma sapranno reagire contro eventuali attacchi da qualsiasi altra provenienza

Resa all'ineluttabile

La decisione imposta dall'impossibilità di continuare l'impari lotta

Il Capo del Governo Maresciallo d'Italia Badoglio ieri sera, alle ore 19,45, ha letto alla radio la seguente comunicazione:

"Il Governo italiano, riconosciuta la impossibilità di continuare l'impari lotta contro la soverchiante potenza avversaria, nell'intento di risparmiare ulteriori e più gravi sciagure alla

Un appello a tutti gli italiani

La notizia alla Casa Bianca

Roosevelt e Churchill hanno avuto un nuovo colloquio - Il Presidente parla di un incontro con Stalin

Party insignia and slashing the photos of Mussolini in a frenzy of frustration. This was merely a prelude to the tragedy that followed.

Italy now had a new Prime Minister in the Fascist Marshal Pietro Badoglio, a hero of the Ethiopian war. Nothing could have prepared him, however, for the role he was to play, caught between the Allies and the Axis in a country that was soon split in two parts.

Meanwhile, a war was being waged in Sicily where the Germans were putting up a desperate fight from west to east. The historic Enna, site of the Norman triumph against the infidels, now formed the backdrop of new battles as the war moved to Catania, the seaport in the shadow of Mount Etna that remained silent as fires raged at her feet. Messina was the last stronghold where German resistance ended on August 17, 1943.

Forty Days in the Wilderness: Between the Allies and the Axis

On September 3, 1943, in the seclusion of a Sicilian orange grove, Italy secretly signed a separate armistice negotiated with the Allies. It was one thing to sign an armistice and quite another to switch sides with the Germans, now the enemies, right in the belly and fighting a war for survival. The "secret" pact was announced to the world on September 8; for the Germans, of course, it was a stab in the back for which the Italians paid dearly.

To fight or not to fight? That was now the question for the Italians for although they had been instructed not to resist the Allies they had received no clear orders to actually fight the Germans who continued their war on Italian soil. Should they let them go unharried and help them escape from their enemies? The Germans did not pack up and run, however, but chose to put up formidable resistance, with or without the Italians. While securing their routes of escape northward, along the roads that the Romans had built for their armies centuries before, they prepared to encircle Rome.

The frightened and confused King did not wait to be caught in a German trap. During the dark hours on the morning of September 9, the day after the official announcement of the armistice, he fled Rome with his family, escorted by Prime Minister Badoglio, who seemed to know which road was not under German control. The convoy headed east toward the Adriatic coast and on reaching the small port of Ortona the royal party boarded the *Baionetta*, whose captain steered southward with no clear destination in mind, casting anchor at the ancient port of Brindisi, where the Appian Way meets the sea. To the relief of the King, the vessel was met by a motorboat flying the Italian flag, and an astounded Italian Admiral Rubartelli on coming aboard learned of the ship's royal cargo. When the King was told that there were no British and no Germans in Brindisi he asked who was in command there, to which the Admiral replied, "I am." It was here that the fleeing King came ashore again to rule a "Kingdom of the South" as twilight descended over the proud Savoy monarchy. It had risen from the Alpine peaks to shine over the whole of Italy and was destined to set symbolically in the south.

Meanwhile, Rome was left undefended and at the mercy of the Germans who poured into the city on the very heels of the fleeing royals. In the confusion of flight, Badoglio had given no instructions to his ministers or generals. A state of chaos prevailed as within a matter of hours the army that should have protected the city simply disintegrated, vanishing without trace as uniforms were quickly discarded for civilian clothes. Only a few units kept vigil at the gates of Rome and vociferously encountered the Germans marching into their city. The last flickering flames of protest had died, but not the spirit of resistance that smoldered unseen by the occupying foreigners.

As the Germans occupied Rome and the King found safety in the heel of Italy, an impressive scene was taking place on the western coast of the beleaguered peninsula. The backbone of the Italian fleet sailed out of La Spezia to surrender to the Allies at Malta, each ship flying a black pennant according to instructions given by the Allies. As an eyewitness described the scene, "The line of ships stretched along the Mediterranean's dark blue surface for a distance of five miles."

The next shock came when on September 12 the Germans staged a daring parachute attack and rescued Mussolini from the hands of Marshal Badoglio's government, ending his "detention" of forty-eight days. The Germans were in control of the north, but they wanted the symbolic figure of the Duce (as Mussolini was known) around which to rally some support from the Italians. The headquarters of the government of what was called "The Italian Social Republic" was set up at Salo, a little port on the western shore of Lake Garda. Just to the north at Gargnano, the Feltrinelli villa became Mussolini's residence, an idyllic setting for the last chapter of his life.

For forty days the Italians found themselves lost in a wilderness of biblical dimensions, the period between the secret signing of the armistice with the Allies on September 3 and Badoglio's actual declaration of war against Germany on October 13. A savage war had meanwhile continued in the south as the Allies blasted their way northward. They had reached Naples on October 1 to find that the resourceful Neapolitans had not waited for the declaration of war but taken matters into their own hands and obtained surrender of the German garrison there.

A line stretching from Pescara to the Tyrrhenian Sea, passing through Monte Cassino, divided Italy into two parts with an ailing Mussolini propped up by his German allies in the north and the failing monarchy, surviving in the shadow of the Allies, in the south.

The real Italy was gradually being reclaimed by the new movement that came to be known as the *Resistenza* with its some 150,000 *partigiani*. In cities and villages, hills and valleys throughout the north, a new Risorgimento was gaining momentum. This vast, underground army was assisted and sheltered by ordinary citizens at great risk to themselves, for the enemy, like a wounded beast, struck out without mercy. German measures against their former allies were brutal. Italians caught with weapons were shot, and villages where the inhabitants had "insulted" German soldiers were razed to the ground. The partisans were not protected under the Geneva Convention as prisoners of war, but were killed in the thousands by the Germans, as explained by the death toll of 35,000 among these latter-day freedom fighters that Garibaldi would have been proud to count among his Redshirts.

On October 13, 1943, the Italians had come out of the wilderness only to find themselves trapped in the worst hell as they secretly confronted the enemy in their midst as the war entered a particularly savage phase. Putting aside their political differences in the common cause, six anti-Fascist parties came together in their resolve to drive out the Germans as Communists and Catholics, monarchists and republicans, merged in a united front, the Comitato di Liberazione Nazionale. (This group was actually formed in Rome on September 9, calling on Italians to regain their fatherland.)

This was the chaotic backdrop for the real-life drama of Edda and Galeazzo Ciano, whose story will serve to symbolize the thousands of others, caught in the crossfire between the Allies and the Axis, and whose personal tragedies would never be recorded in the annals of history.

The Trial of Verona

Edda Ciano, the free-spirited firstborn daughter and favorite of the powerful Mussolini, had lived a charmed life until her father's arrest on July 26, 1943. Suddenly her world came crashing down around her to the noise of anti-Mussolini demonstrations in the streets of Rome. As for her husband, Galeazzo, his troubles had already begun with his dismissal as Foreign Minister, but now his King asked him to resign his ambassadorship to the Vatican, which he did on July 31.

Galeazzo's loss of favor in the eyes of Mussolini should have worked in his favor, but the fact that he was married to the deposed leader's daughter had become an embarrassment. There seemed to be no place for the Cianos in the new order of things with the Badoglio "gang" in power. With no functions to fill their days in the hostile environment of Rome (which they were not permitted to leave), they kept to themselves and lay low as guards were posted outside their residence to check on comings and goings. As their situation became increasingly difficult and with few friends left who dared to keep their company, it was clear to both Edda and Galeazzo that they had not the slightest chance of survival if they remained in Italy. They decided to take their children and flee to Spain, but they found themselves against a brick wall when they tried to obtain the necessary documents. Neither the King nor Prime Minister Badoglio would intervene on their behalf.

Finally, after one month of "house arrest," counting on her connections and friendship with the members of the Third Reich and in spite of Galeazzo's forebodings, Edda approached the German Embassy for help to arrange for a secret flight to Spain. On Friday, August 27, the Cianos separately slipped out of their home and were escorted to Ciampino airport, the gateway to freedom. Euphoria was soon replaced by anxiety when once on board the plane they learned that they were being flown to Munich. Edda was taken to see Hitler, who assured her that arrangements would be made to take the family to Spain, but the promised plane never came. For the Cianos it must have seemed that the door to freedom had been slammed in their face when on September 8 Italy's secret armistice was officially announced to the world. They found themselves under SS guard and realized that they were prisoners, caught in a Nazi trap.

Hope dawned when they learned that Mussolini had been rescued and brought to Munich with his wife, Donna Rachele, and their young children. The members of the Mussolini family were reunited on German soil and Il Duce, for the first time since his arrest, came face to face with the son-in-law whom he believed had betrayed him. Edda went to great pains to justify and explain to her father why Galeazzo voted as he did, apparently without success in view of later events.

Galeazzo read the writing on the wall and knew that his situation was precarious. His main concern now was to recover his notes and diaries, hidden in Italy, which would justify his actions in the eyes of history. Edda became the heroic protagonist of the next chapter. As a virtual prisoner, Galeazzo was powerless, but Edda succeeded in getting permission to leave Germany and on September 27, along with an escort, she boarded a military convoy train for German-controlled Rome. On arrival, she

PART FOUR / 383

embarked on a difficult quest to recover her husband's papers, some secretly stored away in Rome and others buried in his uncle's garden in Lucca. During that eventful month of October, Edda carried out her mission in a part of Italy that was caught like an animal in the clutches of the Germans, battered from the air by the Allies and torn apart from within by a confused population. Edda had to pick her way through a minefield of spies, collaborators, and partisans, not knowing who would help and who would betray her, but she succeeded in finding the papers.

That October her father and her husband were returned to Italy, Mussolini was restored to power in the north, and Galeazzo was imprisoned as a traitor. On October 19, Galeazzo had been flown to Verona under an escort of ten heavily armed SS guards and a beautiful blonde lady spy. He saw the city not as the fair Verona of Romeo and Juliet, but blurred in the fading light of a rainy autumn evening. This was a fitting backdrop for his arrest by men of the new Italian Social Republic's militia who were waiting for him as he stepped from the plane.

Edda was now faced with the greatest challenge of her life—to save her husband from execution. On hearing of Galeazzo's arrest she made straight for Lake Garda, where she was able to visit her father and learned that Galeazzo and others would be tried as traitors. After that meeting she made her way to Verona to see her husband, incarcerated in the Scalzi prison, Cell 27. Her visit, in the presence of a guard, was brief, but she was able to whisper on kissing him good-bye that the papers were safe.

Edda's next task was to get their children from Germany to the safety of neutral Switzerland. Her own mother, Donna Rachele, was a major obstacle, for she was not easily persuaded to release the grandchildren in her care. She believed that her son-in-law was guilty of treason and should be tried and punished. It was Edda's brother Vittorio in Germany, a link between Hitler and Mussolini, who when the legal channels failed took a car and at great risk made a mad dash to the Italian border as Allied planes peppered towns in the north with their bombs.

Finally, on December 12, the children crossed the border into Switzerland. On that same day Edda was allowed to visit her husband, and she gave him the good news. It was their last meeting, for when she came to visit him on Christmas Day she was turned away. Only through the kindness of the blonde guardian, who Edda believed was secretly in love with her husband, was she able to let him know that she had been close by and thinking of him alone in his cell. Not even on that sacred day did his jailers show any mercy for this special inmate, who had been singled out for harsh treatment.

A desperate and angry Edda hastened back to Gargnano to visit her father for one last time the day after Christmas. She had been told by the blonde guardian that the trial was imminent and that Mussolini was not in the mood for clemency. This was confirmed when he let his daughter know that he could do nothing for her husband and that justice must follow its course. The meeting was a stormy one, following which Edda slammed the door on her father, whom she would never set eyes on or speak to again. She would never know whether her father was powerless to save Galeazzo's life or whether he truly believed that he should die as a traitor.

There had been secret schemes for a kidnapping to rescue Galeazzo, all of which had failed, and now there was one desperate attempt to trade his secret papers to the Germans in exchange for his life. The blonde guardian was now the "guardian angel" instrumental in the elaborate plans put in place for a rescue mission. At nine o'clock on the evening of January 7, the prisoner was to be handed over in exchange for the ransom papers at a milestone 10 kilometers out on the Verona-Brescia road. Following some harrowing setbacks and adventures, Edda arrived alone at the spot two hours late. There was no one there. She spent most of the night hiding in a ditch and then, concealing her identity, hitched a ride to Verona, where she learned from the guardian angel that the deal had been called off on Hitler's orders. The lady who had served as a line of communication between Edda and Galeazzo, though a Nazi spy carrying out her duty as warden, proved to be an angel in disguise for she never took the precious papers which she knew Edda had on her person. Instead, she handed Edda a letter that Galeazzo had entrusted to the one who had been his constant warden during the long months of his solitary confinement.

Warned by Galeazzo's warden, later known to be Frau Beetz, that her life was in danger, Edda made her way to Como and the Swiss border. Her escape was now in the hands of faithful friends who took the precious papers into safekeeping, and on a moonlit night, evading German patrols, she walked across an open field into Switzerland and safety. "But in Verona, on that tenth of January, 1944, Galeazzo was fighting his last battle against himself, against anguish. It was to be the last day and the last night of his life" (the words of Edda as quoted from her autobiography, *My Truth*).

On January 10, Count Galeazzo Ciano and four others also accused of treason were read the death sentence. The next day an Italian army vehicle, carrying five condemned men and a priest, left the city for Fort Procolo, the place of execution. There they met their death, bound to chairs with their backs to the firing squad as prescribed for traitors. One man tried to turn around and look back at his executioners as the scene was caught on camera. It was Galeazzo.

CIANO'S WIDOW INTERNED

ILLEGAL ENTRY INTO SWITZERLAND

FROM OUR CORRESPONDENT

GENEVA, Jan. 21

It is officially announced that on Sunday Edda Countess Ciano illegally entered Switzerland and has been provisionally interned with her three children.

The official report also states that the former ambassador, Dino Alfieri, illicitly entered Swiss territory during the night of October 23-24 last, but because of ill-health he went into a nursing home, where he still remains. The Government have decided that Alfieri shall leave the country as soon as he has recovered, but the authorities, in view of the recent death sentence passed on Alfieri, are for the time being postponing his deportation.

My Truth, by Edda Mussolini Ciano, as told to Albert Zarca and published in French as *Temoinage pour un homme*.

(Translated by Eileen Finletter. 1977 New York: William Morrow and Company, Inc.)

This is the tragic story behind the news item which appeared in *The Times* in January of 1944.

Edda Mussolini Ciano and Count Galeazzo Ciano had thus made their tragic exits from Italian history. Thirty years passed before the courageous Edda agreed to relive the horrors of that year and tell her story to the world. It is a poignant document that mirrors Italy's suffering in a war that dragged on for another year and a half and claimed many more innocent victims as families were split asunder by conflicting loyalties and unimaginable circumstances of life or death.

The Monarchy of the South

After the capture of Naples, a savage war had been taking place in the south as the Germans dug themselves in the hilly terrain of the peninsula. Hitler had resolved to make a stand on the Italian front. The battle for Cassino had been bloody, and many more would die on the beaches of Anzio, not far south of Rome, where on January 22, 1944, the Allies launched another front. Hindered by his former allies, terrible reprisals were perpetrated against the Italians. One of the most shocking incidents took place on March 23, when 353 political detainees were taken out of Roman prisons and massacred. Even the sleeping volcano Mount Vesuvius seemed to join the protest that week, belching flames, black smoke, and lava as it came to life in a spectacular eruption.

In the shadow of the smoking volcano, another protest had been smoldering in that spring of 1944. Politics in Italy were alive and well, and the anti-Fascist parties had come together and clamored for the abdication of the King, whom they held ultimately responsible for the mess. They were not alone, for pressure came from another front when four men representing the Allies went to visit the King on April 10 and delivered their apocalyptic ultimatum for his resignation, for they needed a united front in their struggle against the Germans. Two days later Vittorio Emanuele III agreed to transfer the royal powers to his only son and heir, Umberto, prince of Piedmont. However, he stopped short of relinquishing the crown which he had worn painfully for close to half a century. Umberto's new title would be "Lieutenant of the Realm." Furthermore, the King would not step down until the Allies had entered Rome. Had it not been for Winston Churchill, who deferred to the Italian King, the monarchy might have died at that point, for the Americans had no sympathy for such a relic of the past.

Umberto, although in his fortieth year, was an unknown quantity, kept in the background not only by Mussolini but also by his father, whose word was law. Indeed, Umberto had begged his father to let him stay behind in Rome and take his chances, but this was refused. Umberto's coming of age had coincided with the advent of Fascism, and he had been compelled to lie low for twenty years of his adult life. Let us now sit in on an interview which took place in Naples on April 19 with *The Times's* special correspondent and this man, better known on the fashionable ski slopes of Europe than in the political arena:

> *When he comes to Naples the Prince resides in the historic villa overlooking the bay where Nelson first met Lady Hamilton, and it was there that he received your Correspondent to-day. He speaks English easily and with an engaging charm of manner. I told him that the last time I had seen him was in 1939 when, with his father, he attended the inaugural meeting of the Fascist Chamber of Corporations, . .*

. one of the rare occasions when he appeared at a State function. "With the other Royal Princes," he said "I was entitled to a seat in the Senate, but it did not count for anything. My opinion, if ever I expressed it, was ignored even on army matters. I was appointed president of the committee which regulated the promotion of senior officers of the army. I frequently turned down names of officers who were recommended for the rank of general solely because of their zeal as Fascists, but I was invariably overruled by the Minister of War."

"Did you ever come into sharp conflict with Mussolini?" I asked. The Prince made a deprecatory gesture. "That man was very clever in exploiting the feelings of the people," he said. "He knew just how to play on them and to gather credit for everything which went well, and at first he had the full support of the nation. He knew his power, and used it very subtly."

It became clear from the interview that Umberto had much in common with Galeazzo Ciano, who had died on account of his views. Getting to Rome was to cost the Allies dearly in human life, for although the Italians were on their side, the Germans had resolved to make a desperate stand. Ten divisions poured into Italy, which continued, as throughout history, to be the battlefield for foreign armies.

On June 5, 1944, the Allies occupied Rome. With the title of Lieutenant of the Realm, the empowered but crownless Umberto, along with his royal wife, Maria José, occupied the Quirinal Palace, left in a deplorable state by its previous tenants, the Nazis. Unlike his father, Umberto decided that what was needed was a little more magic and majesty in the monarchy, and he eventually brought back some of the royal traditions of his grandmother's days: the horses and carriages and the galas for nobility and people in high places. Maria José could perhaps better put up with a marriage in which the fires had cooled with a husband who found solace in the arms of a mistress. After all, she was in effect the Queen of Italy with royal duties and with their four children, the youngest but a year old, there was little time to fret about her husband's amorous escapades, which caused him to spend, they say, much time in the confessional.

Like an actor suddenly given a new script, Umberto was trying to understand his royal role along with a new cast of characters, the political players. A new government that brought together the anti-Fascist parties was in the making, but Marshal Badoglio resigned for he would not be part of it. On June 8, Umberto received the visit of the respectable and elegant Ivanoe Bonomi, a seasoned septuagenarian statesman who had briefly been prime minister before the Mussolini era. He presented Umberto with a new formula, which he had no choice but to accept. It stipulated:

- once reunited the citizens would be given the choice of institutional reform
- the ritual pledge of fealty to the King by ministers would be limited
- the government would assume legislative power

It diminished the role of the King (or Lieutenant of the Realm) and put the power in the hands of the *Comitato per la Liberazione Nazionale*.

Seven ministers assumed the lion's share of authority as each party got a piece of the power:

- Benedetto Croce for the Liberals
- De Gaspari for the Christian Democrats
- Ruini for the Labour Democrats
- Cianca for the Action Party
- Saragat for the Socialists
- Sforza for the Independents (these were really Republicans who did not want to officially accept the monarchy)
- Palmiro Togliatti for the Communists

It was a truly coalition government, formed in face of wartime emergency and of mainly socialist persuasion, that was seated first at Salerno and transferred to Rome on July 15, 1944. It was a government of the South, but delegates from *the Comitato di Liberazione Nazionale dell'Alta Italia* (the C.L.N.A.I.) would represent the still occupied North.

Umberto was indeed on stage, but rather than play a part he would be obliged to watch the action like a spectator.

The North: Mussolini versus the Resistenza

With the bottom half of the peninsula firmly in the hands of the Italians and the Allies, the northern half was still in the clutches of the Germans and the puppet regime of Mussolini. He was now a suffering and spiritless man who was practically a prisoner of the guards who shadowed him wherever he went. Hitler and the Germans, with the assist of a few hard-line fanatic Fascists, really controlled northern Italy.

The year following the liberation of Rome was a period of great confusion in the north. The Italians, caught in the doldrums as Allied troops were diverted to France where the big offensive was to take place, began to take matters into their own hands. Partisan activity became more organized.

Mussolini's most formidable enemy was not the Allies but the *Resistenza*. Although military exploits continued and many Italian units fought with the Allies, the partisans were the more subtle forces, fighting the war on a different and unseen front against the Germans and organizing the political line-up. The partisans took the war to the workers, calling upon them to prepare for the imminent insurrection of the people to root out *Nazismo* and *Fascismo*. Strikes were called in Milan on March 28 and other centers of the north, followed by Turin in April and insurrections in Genoa. The Eighth Army offensive on the Adriatic front which began on April 9 resulted in the liberation of the hard-won Bologna on April 20 and 21, but by that time Forlì, Ravenna, Modena, and Ferrara were already in the hands of the partisans. The final victory came on April 25 when the partisans entered Milan and the C.L.N.A.I. assumed civil and military powers.

Mussolini had been in Milan in mid-April, only to beat a hasty retreat when partisan formations entered the city. With a German escort and some Fascist followers he headed for the Swiss border at Como, but numbers quickly diminished along the way. He was sick, abandoned, and hunted. When his car was stopped by the Communist partisans who had blocked most of the routes north, the man in crumpled civilian clothes with a hat pulled down over his face was recognized and promptly taken into custody. Mussolini had no family with him, but one person had been following. Claretta Petacci suddenly appeared on the scene, begging his captors for permission to join her beloved Benito. The partisans took her to him, and they spent the night under guard in a humble peasant dwelling, much like the one in which Mussolini had come into the world.

The following day, April 28, 1945, the two were taken to a secluded place outside the village of Dongo, stood against a wall, and summarily shot. Claretta Petacci could have saved herself, but she remained loyal even in the face of death.

The bodies were taken back to Milan, for the partisans wanted the world to know that Mussolini was dead, and along with him Fascism, his brainchild, that had been born there. Piazzale Loreto was suddenly transformed into a Roman arena where crowds gathered to see the bloodied bodies, hanging upside down like animals in a butcher's shop. Some came to leer and jeer, some to spit on the bodies, some to remain in shocked silence, and some to weep at the sight of their fallen hero. So ended Mussolini and the one woman who loved him unconditionally, her shoes still on her feet and her skirt tied up around her legs, dangling beside him.

The philosophy that Mussolini had so eloquently expounded in the famous *Colloqui* at the height of his power had proved to be uncannily prophetic. Here is what he said:

> *Lo scultore non spezza forse talvolta per ira il marmo, perché questo sotto le sue mani non si plasma precisamente secondo la sua prima visione? Qui talora la materia perfino si rivolta contro il suo Formatore. . . . Tutto dipende da ciò, dominare la massa come un artista.*

> [*Doesn't the sculptor sometimes break the marble, because it does not take the exact form that he had first envisioned? In this case the material sometimes turns against its creator. . . . Everything depends on that, dominating the masses like an artist.*]

The great artist was dead, destroyed by the marble that he was trying to fashion into his ideal—Fascismo.

CHAPTER SEVEN

Birth of the Republic of Italy

The End of the War

On May Day 1945, the German Army Corps in Italy surrendered to the Allies. For Italy the war was finally over, and now came the task of healing the wounds, both physical and emotional. Once the euphoria of victory had worn off, Italy was faced with the task of rebuilding a shattered country and facing the reality of her own wounded pride. She had lost her colonies—Libya, Ethiopia, and Albania were gone—as well as her place in the international community.

The most immediate problems involved the northern frontiers, where it was feared territory would be lost. On the eastern side, Marshal Tito had been the first to arrive in the beautiful Adriatic port of Trieste and was planning to hold onto it, along with the hinterland of Venezia-Giulia, claiming it for Yugoslavia. It was a relief for the Italians when in mid-June the Yugoslav flags were lowered at the Town Hall and Prefecture and the Union Jack and Stars and Stripes went up. Springing up like mushrooms around the city could be seen the Italian Tricolor, but the Savoy coat of arms was absent or had been obliterated, sending a clear message to the monarchy. There were also some problems in the northern German-speaking region of Alto-Adige where many of the inhabitants, angered by the harsh program of "Italianization" imposed by Mussolini, wanted to join Austria. On the northwestern side, French troops had occupied the formerly French-speaking regions on the Italian side of the mountains, while an area on the western watershed in the region of Nice was also being disputed. These matters would be settled at the conference table and Italy's borders would eventually be largely restored. However, the much-contested Fiume was given back to the Slavs.

Meanwhile, Prince Umberto had been carrying out his royal duties by touring the newly liberated cities of Bologna, Mantua, Bergamo, and Brescia, where he received an enthusiastic reception from only a fraction of the population. The writing on the wall was that the north, where the partisans had been such a formidable force, seemed to believe that Italy had to be reconstructed from top to bottom as a new nation. On Friday, May 4, as if on the heels of the retreating Germans, Umberto had been in Milan to inspect troops of the regular army, which had taken part in the allied advance. Few had knowledge of his short visit there, but hand grenades were thrown at the villa where it was believed he was staying. Fortunately, he had already left that city where the popular sentiment was clearly antimonarchy, and the news organs of the Socialist and Action parties were demanding the immediate abdication of the useless old king and his Lieutenant of the Realm.

The saga of Italy at this time in history was, however, less about kings and one or two leading protagonists than it was about an extended family whose members, after a long absence and separate lives, find themselves thrown together again to meet the challenge of working out a modus operandi as a single unit—a unified Italy.

The first task was to get the two halves of the country back together again. No time was lost and on May 5, a delegation of five members of the Northern Committee of National Liberation, one for each party, flew to Rome to discuss with Prime Minister Bonomi and his colleagues the delicate process of political fusion. The new government would have to accommodate the interests of the various political parties and also be acceptable to the Allies who now feared the threat of a new political force that had loomed on the Italian horizon—Bolshevism.

It might have been expected that when Fascism receded on an ebb tide, the waters of Socialism would rush in, colored with the red of Communism, which the West most feared. Riding the new wave was Palmiro Togliatti, a name synonymous with Italian Communism. Togliatti had spent seventeen years in exile thanks to Mussolini, but in addition to being anti-Fascist he was capable of bringing the "leftists" together in a coalition as well as reaching out to the Catholics. This seemingly unlikely marriage of two extremes could perhaps happen only in Italy, where survival might depend on the fine art of compromise. This spirit was so aptly captured by the brilliantly witty journalist/novelist Giovanni Guareschi in his delightful stories of the country priest Don Camillo, who uses his pulpit to rail against the "leftists" and the "reds," and the Communist mayor Peppone, who had fought as a partisan with the *Resistenza*. In a comic scene set in the church where Peppone has taken his son to be baptized, Don Camillo refuses to agree to the name Lenin Libero Antonio and Peppone refuses to leave the church until his son is christened as a Catholic. The two come to verbal and physical blows, but in the end the exhausted adversaries reach a compromise and the innocent babe is given the name of Libero Camillo Lenin. As Don Camillo concedes: "Yes, also Lenin; when they have a Camillo next to them, characters like that can't do any harm."

The real world of politics involved many protagonists, thinking men of letters like Benedetto Croce and men who had taken the reins when the Fascists lost power. Who would be the next prime minister of the reunited Italy? Would it be a man like Nenni, representing the "Wind from the North," De Gasperi who espoused "normalcy and order," or the partisan Parri?

The new government would have to observe the conditions of the armistice and not initiate any campaign on the "institutional question." Italy was still a monarchy with the still crownless Umberto surviving in the shadow of the Allies. His government had been in limbo for two months when Signor Bonomi resigned the premiership. Now there was no prime minister, and the parties remained deadlocked while "consultations" took place at the Quirinal Palace and debate continued.

The news that a new government had been formed was greeted with much relief. The first postwar premier of reunited Italy was Signor Ferruccio Parri of the Action Party, a man of unquestioned integrity and with a gift for leadership. He was the one chiefly responsible for organizing the partisan movement of the north and welding together the various units of the *Resistenza*. Parri was acceptable to the Allies, who would not have approved of a Socialist candidate "wrapped" in a new party name. On June 19 *The Times* announced: "Signor Parri's government was eventually formed at 9:30 this evening after a whole day of laborious haggling." The "haggling" was about which political party should be entrusted with which Ministry. The article concluded with these words: "It is regrettable that the good impression created by the emergence of Sgr. Parri as a national leader should have been marred by this final unseemly bout of bargaining, which reveals the basic weakness of the present coalition." The new team included Communist Togliatti as Minister of Justice, while the Christian Democrat De Gasperi became the Minister of Foreign Affairs.

In addressing the foreign press in Rome on July 13, Signor Parri expressed the yearning of the Italian people to be admitted to the ranks of the United Nations and added: "The Italian people submitted to Fascism, but I do not know whether the world realizes how anti-Fascist Italy was." He concluded by saying, "I ask the whole world that Italy be placed in a position to undertake her political and economic reconstruction herself." Cultural reconstruction had already begun. In Rome the return to normal was evidenced on the eve of Parri's remarks by the opening of the summer opera season at the Baths of Caracalla with the spectacular *Aida*. What a treat for Allied troops stationed in the Eternal City!

The Allies, not without some reservations, approved the Parri government, which was officially installed in Rome on July 15, 1945. Misgivings about the strength of Parri's government were confirmed when it became deadlocked just four months after its inception. Parri had been able to reconcile the different parties of the *Resistenza* during the war. Now in peace, caught in an impasse between left and right, he was powerless. On November 24, Signor Parri made his way to the Quirinal and submitted his resignation as prime minister to the still crownless Umberto as the trappings of monarchy prevailed. The flame of the wartime Action Party that had burned so brightly under the leadership of Parri now flickered and the political machinery ground to halt as two weeks of confusion followed.

De Gasperi, the Foreign Minister, emerged as the man to watch as he was called on by Umberto to form a cabinet. Meetings were called at night in apparent secrecy, a fact that troubled and exasperated foreign journalists who were being kept in the dark both literally and figuratively. De Gasperi later came up with his own explanation. Kept awake late into the night by the blaring radio of a woman in the adjoining apartment, De Gasperi decided that it was a good time to hold meetings. Be that as it may, agreements were finally reached at midnight after two weeks of nocturnal bargaining, and the red-eyed representatives of the six parties went home to rest.

The new cabinet, with De Gasperi as Prime Minister, was sworn in at the Quirinal Palace on December 10, 1945. Owing to a power failure, the royal palace was without electricity and the ceremony took place in the dim light of flickering candles against a backdrop of rich tapestry. It was only during the last minutes of the proceedings that the power suddenly returned, flooding the room with light. Could that have been interpreted as an omen for the success of the new government and the demise of the monarchy?

Birth of the Republic of Italy

Italians went about the task of rebuilding their shattered country. Having lost their position of equal status among the nations, they had no place at the Paris conference table, but political activity within the country grew more intense as the date of general elections and the historic referendum approached. On June 2 Italians went to the polls to select the candidates that would decide the political hue of their government, the chameleon that might change color with subsequent elections. The most serious issue was the referendum that would decide the fate of the monarchy and shake the very foundation on which the Italian nation had been built.

On May 9, 1946, perhaps to clarify the situation of the monarchy at this late date, the old king finally, officially, unconditionally, and irrevocably ceded the throne to his son who wore the crown as Umberto II, King of Italy. In the evening of that same day, Vittorio Emanuele and his beloved Elena, bound for exile in Egypt, set sail from the gulf of Naples, the city where as a puny, premature babe he had struggled into the world seventy-seven years earlier. The sun that set over the city that evening was also symbolically setting over the last vestiges of the Savoy monarchy, destined to survive just one more moon.

Rome, May 10. Umberto II broadcast a proclamation to his subjects in which he assured them that nothing had changed as a result of his father's abdication, that he would support constitutional government, and that he would honor the pledge made regarding the upcoming referendum.

Excitement had been building steadily as the day approached for the historic referendum and the general elections. The importance of that day was heightened by the fact that Italians were going to the polls in free voting for the first time in twenty-five years. The electoral registers contained the names of some 28 million people, roughly half of that number representing women who were voting for the first time in Italian history.

Throughout Italy there was a frenzy of activity as the various parties called on the voters for support. In cities and villages men were busy putting up voting instructions bearing all kinds of signs and symbols that appeared on the ballot papers; the Tricolor with stars, hammer and sickle, hooks, crosses, ears of wheat and whatever visual devices were needed to help voters through the election maze. The press, political arms of the various parties, was full of rumors of charges and countercharges, plots and uprisings, and political trickery. Most important of all was the swell of support for either the monarchy or a republic, two opposing forces rising like tidal waves of equal strength that would crash head on.

On May 24, demonstrations occurred in Rome when monarchist supporters staged a march to the Quirinal Palace, cheering for King Umberto. Police road blocks impeded their progress and there were fierce scuffles, but the crowd of tens of thousands could not be held back. The handsome King was called back to the balcony three times by the enthusiastic throng which then surged toward the Ministry of the Interior, blocked by police and tanks.

On the last day of the electoral campaign, just three days before the polls opened, Prime Minister De Gasperi flew to Florence and Milan to champion the cause of the Christian Democrats, while Romans could listen to the leaders of other parties, including the persuasive Communist leader, Palmiro Togliatti. The Communists had prepared the most "irresistible" bill of fare on the Palatine Hill where, in a spectacle reminiscent of the ancient Rome of "bread and circus," they had staged for the mob all kinds of entertainment. There was dancing, boxers for the rougher element, beauty competitions for girls, orchestral concerts, opera singers, and ballet. At the height of it all, Signor Togliatti appeared to the crowd invoking them to vote for the Communist Party and, of course, a REPUBLIC.

Meanwhile, King Umberto had been off on his own campaign for the monarchy. From Turin in the north he traveled to the extreme south, making a tour of the chief cities of Sicily, where crowds gave him an enthusiastic welcome, then sailing across the Strait of Messina to the mainland to be greeted in Reggio di Calabria with a torchlight procession in his honor.

The historic day arrived. By four o'clock in the early morning, even before the first glimmer of dawn on the eastern horizon, people began to line up at the polling booths in Rome. As the day progressed the lines grew longer, slowed by the unfamiliar and complex process of voting. Tempers flared, some women wept, and some fainted as they waited to cast the vote of a lifetime. The only ones not taking part in the elections were the disputed areas whose fate was still in the balance, Alto-Adige and Venezia Giulia with the port city of Trieste.

Even before all the votes had been counted, it became clear that the monarchy had lost in the referendum. The North, with its cities of Bologna, Genoa, and Florence, which had favored the Communists, naturally supported a republic, whereas the South up to and including Rome cast more votes for the monarchy. On June 10, in the Hall of the She-Wolf of Montecitorio, the seat of the Italian Parliament, the results of the referendum were announced:

Republic: 12,672,767 votes

Monarchy: 10,688,905 votes

With a clear majority of nearly 2 million votes, Italy was officially proclaimed a Republic on that day, which, perhaps not quite coincidentally, marked the anniversaries of two of the darkest days of the Fascist regime: the grisly murder of Socialist leader Matteotti and Mussolini's declaration of war on Great Britain and France. Now the monarchy was paying the price for putting the power in the hands of the Fascists. Poor Umberto, notwithstanding the fact that he could not be held responsible for his father's actions, was powerless to turn back the clock of history.

There was something illegal about the timing of the proclamation of the Republic, which the monarchists rightly maintained had been delivered prematurely. Premature or not, the Romans began celebrating that very night, oblivious to the crisis that had developed at the Quirinal Palace where a meeting was taking place between King Umberto and the head of the Allied Commission, Admiral Stone. The King insisted that the Court of Cassation must ascertain that the law governing the referendum be correctly applied. This could not be done until *all* returns were in and counted and claims of alleged irregularities in the conduct of the referendum examined. He had been presented with a "fait accompli" and his refusal to cede his powers placed De Gasperi and the Cabinet in a most embarrassing situation. Admiral Stone urgently summoned De Gasperi to join him and the King at the Quirinal in an effort to find a solution to the dilemma. De Gasperi and his anxious colleagues were in for another sleepless night as the Italian Cabinet met to discuss what action to take, even as Romans were celebrating in the shadow of tanks and amid calls for calm and unity. Not all was calm, however, for that same night shooting broke out in Naples as Monarchists attacked Communist premises. Complicating the situation was the fact that a majority in the north favored a republic while the south wanted to keep the monarchy. Should the new nation be carved in two?

Protests and demonstrations between Republicans and Monarchists grew as the possibility of "civil war" loomed large. Would one end up destroying the other, like Romulus and Remus of ancient legend? Settlement of the impasse was imperative if bloodshed was to be avoided.

Entrance to the Quirinal Palace whose tenants have included popes and kings. It is now the official residence of the President of the Republic. From the beautiful square one can enjoy a fine view of the dome of St. Peter's.

The referendum had split Italy in two along the traditional watershed. Now there were those who clamored for King Umberto to claim the monarchy in the South. That would have meant civil war with more death and destruction visited on a people still suffering from a devastating war and its aftermath. Call it magnanimity, realism, cowardice, or courage, King Umberto's decision saved Italy at that crucial moment in history. He said that it was his family that had brought Italy together, and he would not be the one to tear it asunder.

So it was that on June 13, ending a reign of just thirty-four days, a pale King Umberto took leave of weeping servants and his royal staff. Accompanied by several high officers of his court and two generals, Umberto made his way to the airport, where he boarded a plane for Lisbon to join Marie José and their children, who had sailed out of Naples some days earlier.

The royal standard that had fluttered over the palace since 1870 was hauled down. The night of June 13 the Quirinal was closed, shuttered, and in darkness. The palace on the hill that had been the residence of popes and kings would henceforth be occupied by the future President of the new Italian Republic. It was the end of a long struggle, for although the dukes of Savoy had been called on as the caretakers, the Risorgimento had been the brain child of Gruseppe Mazzini, who had dedicated his whole life to the unification of the peninsula and its islands not as a monarchy but as a republic. The spirit of the man who had been an inspiration for over a century would now rest in peace.

On June 28 Signor Enrico de Nicola, a distinguished elder statesman, was elected as provisional President of the Republic by the Constituent Assembly, a compromise arrived at by Christian Democrats, Socialists, and Communists who represented the majority of the Assembly. The sixty-eight-year-old Neapolitan was wise and persuasively eloquent and in addition to his sense of duty he possessed a grasp of Italy's political situation and reality that was second to none.

The King was gone, Italy remained shaken but united, and it was finally resolved that the date of the referendum, June 2, 1946, would be recorded on the birth certificate of the new REPUBLIC OF ITALY

The Constitution of the Republic of Italy

The Italian constitution is preceded by a statement of basic principles, including "Italy is a democratic republic based on work. Sovereignty belongs to the people, who will exercise it in the forms and within the limits prescribed by the Constitution." Other principles concern the rights of humans and equality of all citizens before the law. One special article concerns the protection of linguistic minorities and refers to German- and Slav-speaking citizens.

Parliament is composed of the Chamber of Deputies and the Senate of the Republic, which have equal powers. It is the constitutional body of greatest significance, since the Italian republic is a parliamentary democracy.

The President of the Republic is the Head of State. The president is elected by Parliament with three deputies from each region also voting. He is elected by secret ballot with a majority of two-thirds of the Assembly. A citizen must be over fifty and enjoy civil and political rights to be elected president. The term of office is seven years. He calls for the election of new parliaments.

The Republic is divided into regions, provinces, and communes. Regions set up in 1948 are autonomous with their own functions and powers. They are Piedmont, Lombardy, Veneto, Liguria, Emilia-Romagna, Tuscany, Umbria, the Marches, Lazio, Abruzzi, Molise, Campania, Puglia, Basilicata, and Calabria. Granted particular forms of autonomy are Sicily, Sardinia, Trentino–Alto-Adige, Friuli-Venetia Giulia, and Val d'Aosta.

TIME LINE

8th century B.C.	Greeks began establishing colonies in Southern Italy and Sicily.
7th to 6th centuries B.C.	Etruscans control vast area known as Etruria.
753 B.C.	Legendary date of founding of Rome.
700	Period of the Kings begins.
509	Last of the Tarquin kings, Tarquinius Superbus. Birth of the Roman Republic.
390	Gauls sack Rome.
343	First war against the Samnite people.
334	Gauls make peace with Rome and return to Po Valley.
312	Appian Way begun by Appius Claudius Caecus
290	End of wars with Samnites.
275	Defeat of King Pyrrhus who came to the aid of citizens of Tarentum.
270	Reggio in Calabria, last Greek city on mainland falls to Romans.
265	Romans subdue last Etruscan city.
264	First Punic War begins.
241	End of First Punic War. Sicily (except Kingdom of Syracuse) becomes first Roman Province.
227	Sardinia becomes second Roman province.
222	Romans conquer Gauls in northern part of the peninsula. All of what is present day Italy now under Romans.
218	Second Punic War begins. Greek city of Saguntum in Spain appeals to Rome for help against Hannibal.
211	Hannibal reaches outskirts of Rome.
202	Battle of Zama, North Africa, between Hannibal and Roman general Scipio.
201	End of Second Punic War.
197	Two new provinces created in southern Spain.
168	Romans become masters of Greece at end of Third Macedonian War.
149	Beginning of Third Punic War.

146	End of Punic War and destruction of Carthage. Province of Africa proclaimed.
135	Beginning of First Servile War, instigated by Syrian slave.
133	Lusitania (Portugal) conquered by Romans. Pergamum becomes Rome's province.
121	Greek colony of Massilia made province of Rome.
103	Revolt of slaves in Sicily known as the Second Servile War.
100	Birth of Julius Caesar on July 12.
91	Italian cities around Rome secede and proclaim a republic called ITALIA.
88	End of war between Rome and secessionist republic. Samnite remants crushed and their Oscan language lost forever.
73	Beginning of Third Servile War instigated by a slave named Spartacus.
64	Pontus, Cilicia and Syria made Roman provinces.
60	Triumvirate established with Crassus, Pompey & Julius Caesar.
49	Caesar crosses the Rubicon river in defiance of Roman Senate.
48	Caesar lone survivor of Triumvirate. Caesar meets Cleopatra in Egypt.
45	Caesar becomes dictator for life. Julian calendar adopted.
44	Murder of Julius Caesar on March 15.
43	Civil war over succession. Territory divided into three zones—East, West and Rome. Second Triumvirate established.
41	Meeting of Mark Antony and Cleopatra.
31	Battle of Actium. Octavius defeats Mark Antony.
30	Death of Antony and Cleopatra. Egypt becomes province of Rome.
27	Title of "Augustus" conferred on Octavius, the first Roman Emperor.
14 A.D.	Death of Augustus on August 19. Tiberius becomes emperor.
32	Pontius Pilate passes death sentence on Jesus.
37	March 16: Death of Tiberius.
43	Invasion of Britain during the rule of Claudius.
54	October 13: Death of Claudius
67	Date attributed to martyrdom of St. Peter and St. Paul.
68	End of Julian house with Death of Nero.
69	New dynasty begins with Vespasian.
72	Building begins on the Colosseum.
79	Eruption of Mt. Vesuvius. Herculaneum and Pompeii entombed.
106	Dacia (Rumania) annexed by Rome.
248	Celebration of Rome's millennium during rule of Philip the Arab.
270	Aurelian Wall built around Rome for protection against invaders.
286	Diocletian divides Empire into East and West and takes Maximian as co-emperor of the West.
304	Edict of Persecution of Christians issued under Diocletian.

312	Constantine defeats rival at Battle of Milvia Bridge, Rome. Considered turning point in Christian history.
313	Edict of Milan guarantees tolerance of Christians.
320	First St. Peter's built in Rome.
324	Constantine becomes sole emperor of East and West.
337	May 22: Death of Constantine, first Christian emperor.
395	Partition of the Empire between the West and the East, each with its own emperor.
401	Alaric, the Visigoth, makes first appearance in Italy.
404	Imperial capital established at Ravenna, last capital of Western Empire.
405	Invasion by the Ostrogoths.
410	Alaric, the Visigoth, enters and sacks Rome.
439	Gaiseric, the Vandal, captures Carthage and declares independence from Rome.
444	Valentinian III decrees Rome spiritual capital and seat of Catholicism.
451	Attila, the Hun, occupies Roman city of Aurelianum (Orleans, France).
453	Death of Attila.
455	Emperor Valentinian assassinated. Rome sacked by Vandal king.
475	Romulus becomes last emperor of the West.
476	Odoacer, the Goth, seizes power from Romulus.

END OF THE ROMAN EMPIRE OF THE WEST

488	Italy invaded by Theodoric, the Ostrogoth.
493	Theodoric the Great begins rule as King of the Italians and the Goths with Ravenna as his capital.
540	Ravenna captured by Byzantines.
552	End of Gothic rule in the peninsula.
568	First Lombards arrive in Italy and soon afterwards establish their capital at Pavia.
589	Lombard king Authari marries Catholic Theodolinda of Bavaria.
595	Lombards control two thirds of the peninsula. Church founded by Queen Theodolinda in Monza.
604	Death of Pope Gregory the Great, founder of Medieval papacy.
663	Byzantine Emperor Constans II begins unsuccessful campaign to regain Italy.
752	Byzantine controlled Ravenna falls to Lombards.
754	Franks invade Italy under Pepin following appeal of Pope Stephen II for help against the Lombards.
770	Charles (Charlemagne) marries Lombard princess, Desiderata.
773	Pope Adrian I appeals to Charlemagne for help against Lombards.
774	Charlemagne visits Rome. Franks defeat Desiderius, the last Lombard king.

800	Charlemagne crowned emperor by Pope Leo III on December 25.
827	Saracens invited by Sicilians to help expel the Byzantines. Beginning of Saracen conquest of Sicily.
844	Louis II crowned King of the Lombards.
867	Louis II's expedition against the Saracen Emirate of Bari.
871	Lombard and Frankish troops take Bari.
878	Syracuse falls to Saracens who now control most of Sicily.
951	First German expedition to Italy. Kingdom of Italy becomes vassal of German King Otto I.
962	Holy Roman Empire reestablished with crowning of King Otto I.
1016	Norman pilgrims returning from Holy Land meet Lombards in southern Italy
1017	First expedition of Normans set out for southern Italy.
1021	Emperor Henry II brings army to Italy for help against the Byzantines.
1035	Norman brothers William, Drogo and Humphrey de Hauteville arrive in southern Italy as mercenaries of Lombards.
1038	Beginning of Norman dynasty of Aversa and Capua.
1042	William de Hauteville proclaimed Count of Apulia. Melfi becomes capital of the Normans.
1046	Arrival in Italy of the Norman, Robert de Hauteville, to be known as "The Guiscard."
1053	Normans clash with Papal army of Pope Leo 1X. Pope captured at Civitate and imprisoned by Normans.
1054	Schism between Eastern (Constantinople) and Western (Rome) Churches.
1059	August 23: Historic Treaty of Melfi between Pope Nicholas II and the Normans.
1066	NORMAN CONQUEST OF ENGLAND.
1071	Normans free Bari from Byzantine control.
1072	Normans enter Palermo as victors. Robert de Hauteville, known as "The Guiscard," becomes Duke of Sicily.
1078	The Guiscard attacks papal territory of Benevento.
1085	Death of The Guiscard.
1087	Last Saracen emir leaves Sicily and Normans control the island.
1095	Pope Urban calls upon Christians to join crusade to Jerusalem.
1130	December 25: The Norman Roger II crowned King of Capua, Apulia and Sicily in Palermo.
1140	Naples becomes part of Kingdom of Roger II.
1147	Beginning of Second Crusade led by King Louis VII of France and King Conrad of Germany.
1155	Frederick I (Barbarossa) King of Germany, crowned Holy Roman Emperor.
1167	Alliance of Italian cities against Barbarossa, known as "The Lombard League."

1177	Peace conference in Venice with Lombard League, Pope, and Barbarossa.
1186	Marriage in Milan of Barbarossa's son Henry to Constance of Sicily.
1189	Death of William "the Good," last male of the de Hauteville dynasty.
1194	Christmas Day, Henry VI crowned king of Sicily. December 26 son, Frederick II, born at Jesi.
1198	Frederick II, crowned in Palermo as King of Sicily at age four.
1201	Seven-year-old Frederick II removed from palace by German Markwald who assumes power.
1204	Conquest of Constantinople by Crusaders
1207	Frederick becomes protégé of papal appointee Walter of Palear.
1208	December 26: Frederick II becomes ruler of the Kingdom of the Two Sicilies.
1220	November 22: Frederick II crowned Holy Roman Emperor in Rome.
1228	Frederick II embarks on crusade and claims crown of Jerusalem.
1231	Constitution of Melfi. Frederick II promulgates new set of laws.
1244	Flight of Pope Innocent IV to Lyons.
1250	Death of Emperor Frederick at Castel Fiorentino in Apulia.
1258	Frederick's illegitimate son Manfred crowned king of Sicily.
1262	Beginning of Visconti power in Milan.
1265	French Charles of Anjou arrives in Rome at invitation of Pope to claim Kingdom of Naples and Sicily.
	Birth of Dante Alighieri.
1266	Charles of Anjou crowned King of Naples and Sicily. King Manfred killed at Benevento.
1282	The Sicilian Vespers, an uprising against the French. Peter III of Aragon proclaimed King of Sicily, separating island from mainland.
1298	Publication of Marco Polo's travels in China.
1302	Peace of Caltabellotta. Sicily given independence as the Kingdom of Trinacria. Treaty joins Spanish house of Aragon to French house of Anjou.
1305	Pope Clement V crowned in Lyons, France.
1309	Papal residence moved to Avignon, France. Rome falls into decline.
1321	Death of Dante.
1339	Peace of Venice ends conflict between warring states in north.
1348	Height of plague known as Black Death.
1355	Charles IV crowned Holy Roman Emperor.
1377	Papacy returns to Rome.
1385	Giangaleazzo Visconti assumes power in Milan, now at its zenith.
1386	Construction begun on the Duomo of Milan.
1402	Death of Giangaleazzo Visconti of Milan.
1434	The Medici come to power in Florence with Cosimo De'Medici.
1442	Alfonso of Aragon takes Naples and is crowned king the following year.

1447	Last of Visconti dynasty in Milan with death of Giangalezzzo's son, Filippo.
1450	Beginning of Sforza dynasty in Milan.
1458	Beginning of war between the houses of Aragon and Anjou over the Kingdom of Naples.
1469	Lorenzo De'Medici, "The Magnificent," comes to power in Florence.
1492	CHRISTOPHER COLUMBUS SETS SAIL FROM SPANISH PORT.
1494	Sicily united with mainland under Spanish crown.
1515	Francis I accedes to Frencb throne, invades Italy and occupies Milan.
1519	King Charles of Spain becomes Emperor Charles V.
1527	Death of Machiavelli. His book *The Prince* is published five years later.
1530	Last Holy Roman Emperor crowned.
1542	Spanish Inquisition reaches Italy under Pope Paul III.
1559	Treaty of Cateau-Cambresis between France and Spain. French renounce claims in Italy but retain Turin.
1600	Palazzo Reale in Naples built for Spanish viceroys.
1642	Death of Galileo.
1647	Revolt in Naples against Spanish taxation.
1669	Major eruption of Mount Etna.
1701	War of Spanish Succession begins.
1713	Treaty of Utrecht. Austrians become masters of Milan, Naples and Sardinia. Piedmont gets Sicily.
1720	Duke of Savoy given title of King of Piedmont and Sardinia. Sicily taken away and given to Austria
1733	War of Polish Succession begins.
1734	Don Carlos crowned King of Naples and Sicily.
1735	Peace of Vienna. Charles III becomes King of Two Sicilies.
1737	End of Medici dynasty in Florence.
1740	War of Austrian Succession begins.
1748	Treaty of Aix-la-Chapelle, ending War of Austrian Succession.
1755	Genoa sells Corsica to France.
1789	FRENCH REVOLUTION
1796	Napoleon appointed to command Army of Italy.
1797	Treaty of Campo Formio. Venice given to Austria.
1800	Napoleon begins campaign to conquer Italy.
1805	Genoa incorporated into French Empire.
1808	Napoleon's brother-in-law, Joachim Murat, made King of Naples.
1814	Napoleon exiled to island of Elba.
1815	Napoleon escaped to France. Murat proclaims himself King of United Italy. Murat captured and shot by Austrians.
1831	Giuseppe Mazzini founds movement called "Giovine Italia."

1848	The year of revolutions throughout Italy.
1849	Republic of Rome established by leaders of the Risorgimento then crushed by intervention of French troops.
1852	Cavour becomes Prime Minister of Piedmont.
1859	War between Piedmont and Austria. Battles of Magenta and Solferino. Piedmont gets Lombardy from Austria.
1860	Tuscany, Modena, Parma and Romagna join Piedmont in new Italian State. Landing of Garibaldi's One Thousand at Marsala, Sicily.
1861	Kingdom of Italy proclaimed with Vittorio Emanuele as King with his capital in Turin.
1866	Third War of Italian Independence. Italy wins Venetia from Austrian control.
1870	Rome falls to royalist troops of Vittorio Emanuele and becomes capital of Kingdom of Italy.
1871	Death of Giuseppe Mazzini.
1878	Death of Vittorio Emanuele. Umberto I becomes King of Italy.
1882	Assab in East Africa declared crown colony of Italy. Death of Garibaldi. Triple Alliance-Germany-Austria-Italy.
1890	Eritrea established as a colony of Italy by royal decree.
1900	Assassination of King Umberto I. Vittorio Emanuele III becomes King of Italy.
1908	Devastating earthquakes in Italy with over 150,000 deaths.
1911	Italy declares war on Turkey.
1912	Libya acquired from the Turks.
1913	Emigration of Italians reached one million by this time.
1915	Italy enters World War I.
1922	Fascists march on Rome. King invites Mussolini to form a government.
1936	Italy annexes Ethiopia (Abyssinia).
1939	Italy takes over Albania. Agreement known as "The Pact of Steel" signed with Germany.
1940	Italy enters World War II on the side of Germany.
1943	January 23: Eighth Army marches into Tripoli—end of Mussolini's empire. July 10: Allies land in Sicily. July 26: Mussolini arrested. September 3: Secret signing of Armistice. September 9: Flight of King and court.
1944	January 11: Verona trial and execution of Ciano, Mussolini's son-in-law. January 22: Allied landing at Anzio. April 12: Vittorio Emanuele transfers powers to son Umberto. June 5: Allies occupy Rome.
1945	April 28: Mussolini shot along with his mistress by partisans in the north. Germans surrender in Europe.
1946	Vittorio Emanuele III cedes throne to son and sails for Egypt. June 2: Referendum and Birth of Republic of Italy.